A Music Lover's Guide to Record Collecting

BY DAVE THOMPSON

Backbeat Books
San Francisco

Published by Backbeat Books
600 Harrison Street, San Francisco, CA 94107
www.backbeatbooks.com
E-mail: books@musicplayer.com

An imprint of the Music Player Group
Publishers of *Guitar Player, Bass Player, Keyboard,* and other magazines
United Entertainment Media, Inc.
A CMP Information company

CMP
United Business Media

Distributed to the book trade in the US and Canada by
Publishers Group West, 1700 Fourth Street, Berkeley, CA 94710

Distributed to the music trade in the US and Canada by
Hal Leonard Publishing, PO Box 13819, Milwaukee, WI 53213

Cover Design by Richard Leeds / bigwigdesign.com
Text Design by Michael Cutter
Page Composition by Interactive Composition Corporation

Library of Congress Cataloging-in-Publication Data

Thompson, Dave, 1960, Jan.3-
    A music lover's guide to record collecting / by Dave Thompson.
       p. cm.
    Includes index.
    ISBN 0-87930-713-7
    1. Sound recordings—Collectors and collecting. I. Title.
    ML111 .5 .T56 2002
    781.49'075—dc21   2002016095

Printed in the United States

02 03 04 05 06   5 4 3 2 1

TABLE OF CONTENTS

PART THREE: A BIOGRAPHICAL DICTIONARY OF COLLECTIBLE RECORD LABELS

ACKNOWLEDGMENTS

Thanks to everybody who helped out on this one—Richard Johnston and Nancy Tabor at Backbeat Books; my agent Sherrill Chidiac; Amy Hanson for suggestions, ideas and "just a thought, but . . ."; and everybody else who brought the beast to life: Jo-Ann Greene, John DeBlaiso, Dave Makin, Gaye and Tim, Miles and Arthur at Holy Cow, the Talbot-Schecklers, Beth and Rick at the Landing, Danny Adler, Anchorite Man, the Bat family (and crab), Blind Pew, Barb East, Ella and Sprocket, Gef the Talking Mongoose, the Gremlins who live in the furnace, K-Mart (not the store), Geoff Monmouth, Nutkin, Snarleyyowl the Cat Fiend, Sonny, Mrs Nips, a lot of Thompsons, Neville Viking and the Walrus Ball.

INTRODUCTION

First things first. This book is not strictly, and merely, dedicated to collecting records, as in the round, black, plastic discs that used to be our primary source of recorded music. A title that encapsulated its full scope, however, would be too unwieldy for words. Cylinders, 78s, 45s, LPs, picture discs, and flexidiscs are all included in here. But so are cassettes, 4- and 8-Tracks, CDs, Pocket Rockers, and a host of other media. "Records" just seems like a sensible umbrella for all of them.

And so it should. Coin collecting has never been limited to simply collecting coins; medallions, tokens, and more are a vital part of the numismatic hobby. Stamp collecting incorporates envelopes, charity labels, and advertising stickers; and baseball card fairs rarely exclude vendors of football, basketball, and soccer images, simply because their subjects aren't wielding sticks. Record collecting, by its very nature, concerns every medium in which music has been made available, a broad-mindedness that this book aims to embody.

It should also be noted that the book was written primarily with the rock and pop collector in mind. Although other publications may attempt to prove otherwise, it is impossible to do justice, in one slim volume, to every musical discipline that can fall under the record-collecting banner. From jazz to classical, from blues to reggae, from spoken word to religious oratory, records have been issued that encapsulate every sound a human has ever made. And that's before we even begin thinking about collections of whale song, birdcalls, and *The Authentic Sounds of the Savannah at Midnight*.

No, rock and pop (with a little soul, funk, and R&B on the side) are more than enough for one book, embracing more than 50 years of musical history, and more sides of vinyl, reels of tape, and slices of aluminum than anybody could ever count, let alone gather up, categorize, and actually listen to.

Because that is what record collecting is really all about—gathering (as in acquiring), categorizing (as in deciding what you like and what you'd like more of), and listening (as in breaking open the airtight vault occasionally, and finding out what the songs sound like). It is for that reason that this book does not address what are, for many would-be record collectors, the most important questions of all—"How do I start?" and "What should I collect?"

It does not address them because you already know the answers. How do you start? You buy some records, you keep them, and you have a collection. And what should you collect? Whatever you want. And that's that, whether you're lining your retirement fund with label varieties of the Beatles first Vee-Jay 45, or simply filling a shoebox with old, ratty 8-Tracks. Collect the music you like to listen to, and the songs you want to play. And don't ever, ever let anybody tell you that you're doing it wrong.

What Is Included in This Book? And What Isn't?

While it would be excellent to be able to answer that question with a confident "everything," clearly that is not the case. To attempt even a general discussion of the thousands of bands and performers who are considered collectible today, from Aardvark (one cool prog album on Deram's Nova subsidiary in 1970) to Zzebra (excellent jazz-rock from 1973), would require a volume many times the size of this one—and besides, that is what specialist publications such as *Goldmine, DISCoveries* and *Record Collector* do in every issue.

Instead, the goal has been to offer a clear and concise summary of the many things that one *could* collect, and attempt to highlight at least some of the more interesting areas you might encounter, in an artist's career, a format's development, a label's history.

The book is divided into three sections. The first is titled Collecting and Collectors, and explores both the history of the hobby and some of its rules—how to grade a record, what to look for, and if you're lucky, where to find it.

Part two, Collections and Collectibles, looks at a few (and, in comparative terms, that really does mean a few) of the individual themes that a collector might choose to pursue, from Christmas records to censored CDs, from magazine flexidiscs to quadraphonic classic rock, and beyond, with each of the alphabetically arranged sections showcasing recordings and releases that are representative of both the individual subject and the field in general.

Part three offers A Biographical Dictionary of Collectible Record Labels, an alphabetical directory of 140 American, British, and European record companies, emphasizing each label's history and pinpointing its most collectible artists and releases.

Throughout the book, too, some 200 Ten Top Collectibles lists are scattered, pinpointing the greatest rarities, variations, and oddities available to collectors of individual labels and musical genres. These include everything from the Holy Grails that collectors go to sleep dreaming about, but which only the fortunate few will ever discover, to the kind of relatively common, but increasingly desirable, one-offs and oddities with which every discography abounds. Each such list, however, offers some indication of the sheer variety of items available to the enterprising collector.

In each of the three sections, the emphasis, of course, is on the best-known and most collectible performers and records: the Beatles, the Rolling Stones, Elvis, the Beach Boys, Queen, U2, Bruce Springsteen, and so on. But the spotlight just as frequently lights upon artists and aspects that may not immediately spring to mind as being a "hot" topic—not out of any attempt at contrariness, but because it is often in record collecting's least frequented corridors that one meets the most interesting people.

At the end of the day, the hope is that whatever your collecting interests are, you'll find something in this book that relates directly to them—and a lot of things that will simply make your collecting even more pleasurable and interesting.

What Is Collectible?

A term that appears again and again on these pages is "collectible."

It is a subjective term, and a somewhat loaded one. Collectible, after all, is one of *the* buzzwords of the modern advertising age, applied to absolutely anything that is sufficiently useless that somebody has to really work hard to persuade you that you need to buy it—"These precious heirloom possum-head egg-cups aren't simply whimsical, they are also very collectible."

In the context of this book, however, "collectible" means what it says. Whether you are shopping in person at a record fair, or in private on an Internet auction site, if a "collectible" item comes up for sale, you'll recognize it immediately. It's the thing that makes your heart skip a beat, as you look around to make sure that no one else is making a grab for it.

It doesn't have to be a particularly hard-to-find item, or an especially rare or valuable one. In fact, the words "collectible" and "valuable" share only a modicum of common ground. Put simply, a collectible item is something that attracts the attention of more than a handful of casual browsers.

It may look unusual—a radically shaped picture disc is always going to draw more glances than a straightforward black-vinyl single; a well-worn '50s Elvis LP sleeve will always receive more admiring comment than a still-sealed copy of the Bee Gees' *Spirits Having Flown;* a U2 single with a German-language picture sleeve will have more people trying to read it than a Spice Girls record in its domestic cover. It's not an inviolate rule, but collectible means something that is sufficiently out of the ordinary that you may prefer to buy now, while it's sitting in front of you, rather than risk losing it to the next person who passes by.

What Is a Rarity?

"Rare" is another word that gets thrown around a lot, and in many ways, it means quite the opposite to collectible, in that some of the rarest records in the world are actually among the dullest looking things you'll ever see.

Drab-labeled 45s from the dawn of the rock 'n' roll era have a shocking tendency to fetch four- or five-figure sums among collectors, yet to look at them you wouldn't think they had the bus fare home.

Other rarities are marked by such infinitesimally tiny details that you wonder how anybody noticed them to begin with. Maybe the catalog number on the label is printed half an inch to the left of center, rather than the quarter inch it normally lies. Maybe the composer credits have been listed back to front, an error that was corrected after just a few hundred pressings.

These records used to simply hang on dealers' walls with their weight-in-gold price tags. Today, you're more likely to find them waiting on the Web, while the bidding rockets into the stratosphere—and isn't it fascinating to watch these events, hitting your browser's refresh button as the auction timer ticks toward zero, imagining the last-minute high bidder poised at his computer, the national debt of a medium-sized European nation entered into the bid box, timing his actions to the very last moment . . . and then getting sniped with 10 seconds to spare, because somebody wants the only known pale-green-label copy of an otherwise unremarkable doo-wop 45 $100 more than he does.

What all true rarities have in common is, there aren't many of them around. Or, at least, not as many as there are collectors who are hunting them.

Rarity is measured by supply and demand. There must be thousands of records whose total sales can be counted on the fingers of one hand, that exist now only in the crazed mind of the unknown hopeful who sank his savings into pressing them, and who was last seen digging a very deep hole in his back garden.

There are discs that were pressed in limited editions of just five copies, and you can't get much rarer than that. But if only two people ever want one, then the market is swamped. Copies might be painfully hard to find, they may be excruciatingly scarce, and anyone who finds a spare might price it in the high thousands of dollars. But they are not considered among the field's great rarities. And why? Because nobody cares.

On the other hand, there are records that may have sold several hundred thousand copies. But when twice that many collectors are chasing them, then you're in the big time.

Am I a Completist?

Completists are collectors for whom, as James Bond's family motto puts it, "the world is not enough." *In extremis,* they seek every variation of every version of every release in a band or artist's catalog, every bootlegged live show and studio outtake, every session appearance and semi-conscious guest spot—and then they deluge Internet chat rooms to ask if there's anything else out there.

In the UK, such fans are also known as "train-spotters," for their avid attention to detail, and "anoraks," after the traditional clothing of real train-spotters. In America, they're just a fact of life and most dealers welcome their attentions. Any knowledgeable fan might point out that your copy of the Konrads' 1964 Decca single "I Didn't Know How Much" is widely believed to be the first-ever record to feature the young David Bowie. But a completist is the only person who'll give you $600 for it, and then ask if you can find him or her the Canadian pressing as well.

Most self-described completists set themselves less lofty aims, though their targets can still be high. Pursuing one copy of every record an artist has released in any given country is a form of completism; so is simply acquiring one copy of every released song, regardless of its original format.

This is the market that many box set compilers bear in mind. The powers behind Cat Stevens' 2001 box set, *On the Road to Find Out,* know that collectors will never find an authentic acetate copy of the 1965 recording "Back to the Good Old Times," so they featured the performance at the start of disc one. Even if a collector has, somehow, acquired every other rarity and outtake included in the package, the presence of that one song will make the box a worthwhile purchase.

So, are you a completist? You tell me.

What Is a Record Actually Worth?

With just a handful (literally) of exceptions, actual values for records are not addressed in this book. Partly, this is because the market itself is constantly changing, rendering out of date any attempt to give a definitive price for an item, before the words have even hit the page. But it's also because the fact that a record is "worth" $200 does not mean that it cannot be found for $2 . . . or vice versa.

The advent of Internet auctions, in particular, have thrown the accepted value of records into utter confusion, sending the perceived value of some long-established rarities into free fall, while at the same time blasting other, hitherto unrecognized, gems into hyper-space.

Even more spectacularly, records and artists that have never previously been paid any heed by the hobby have suddenly exploded into prominence, with more racing to join them all the time. This is especially true of the crop of teenage idols who rose to mega-stardom during the early '70s: from the Partridge Family to the Osmonds and on to the Bay City Rollers, records that once seemed ten-a-penny in the bargain bins are now being avidly sought out, and at a pace that neither brick-and-mortar dealers (that is, non-Internet dealers) nor price guide editors will ever be able to keep up with.

Sometimes the market is easy to predict. REM collectors will always bid high for a picture-sleeve copy of that band's first single; Foreigner fans will do likewise for a clear-vinyl UK pressing of "Cold As Ice."

On other occasions, however, a record will escalate in value for reasons that conform to none of the "rules" by which all hobbies are governed; it will become wildly popular for reasons that cannot be easily quantified.

A generation might "come of age" and suddenly, more or less simultaneously, be stricken by nostalgia for its misspent youth. An artist might unexpectedly break out of a career-long journey through the recesses of underground cultdom, and a vast new audience needs to discover his past. A TV show or commercial may unearth an old record and the entire prime-time viewership cannot live without owning it.

The death of a once-popular icon can also spark an incredible rush for his or her records. It is a matter of historical record, for example, that the day before Elvis Presley died, in August 1977, many record outlets no longer even stocked his back catalog, so low was the demand from customers. Twenty-four hours later, on the other hand, the greatest fleet of delivery trucks on earth would not have been enough to keep up with the demand for fresh stock.

Attempts to predict these shifts are almost unanimously doomed to failure. A number of price guides are available for those collectors who insist on rigidly policing their collections' value, while a quick visit to your local collectors emporium should at least turn up a handful of mortgage-munching treasures.

But the safest rule of thumb when contemplating a record's true worth is, What is it worth to you? Stay within those limits and you will never be ripped off. Oh, and one final point. If a record you own is going to go through the roof, it will only do so after you've sold it. Usually for a dollar.

An Informal History of Record Collecting

I was lucky. I got my start in record collecting in what was a golden age—probably the last one there ever was. Looking back today on the 45s and LPs I carefully plonked down my pocket money for, it seems incredible to believe that such fabulous treasures could be picked up so readily, that the store owner didn't go home every night and kick himself to death for letting another priceless gem slip by for the cost of a can of soda.

You'll forgive me if I don't say exactly when this was, because it really doesn't matter. All who pick up this book and can blissfully recall their own early days in the hobby will know the answer intuitively, because that's when they, too, got involved. A golden age, a time when there was magic in the air and glory in the grooves, and every record that hit the streets was another of the greatest ever made.

Of course it was, because why else would they have started collecting? There were, after all, so many more important things they could have been doing, like improving their grades or cleaning their rooms, or washing behind their ears every day. But no. Instead, selflessly, heroically, they sacrificed the pleasures of a normal, happy childhood to embed themselves in the minutiae of music. And, just as we look back on our school days, convinced that the establishment was at its social, creative, and educational peak during the years in which we attended, so we look back on that other most formative moment in childhood, the discovery of music, with the same sense of wide-eyed wonder. Could things ever be so great again?

It might have been the mid-'50s, when Elvis was on Sun, or the early '60s, when Vee-Jay had the Beatles. It could have been five years later, when every garage was a psychedelic shack, or a decade after that, when new wave ruled the roost. It may have been the early '90s, with the Sub Pop Singles Club blasting classics through the mailbox, or the infant 2000s, with whatever nonsense it is that kids listen to these days, but I'll tell you one thing, it isn't music . . . I'm sorry. I just turned into your parents.

Whenever it was, record collecting is possibly the only (legal) hobby around that offers a shortcut to your soul. Others—excellent schoolwork, tidy rooms, and clean ears among them—may be more aesthetically beautiful or educationally fulfilling. But records, particularly pop (rock, funk and punk, soul and ska, jazz and techno, call it what you will) records, can make you laugh or cry without your ever knowing why, can make you get up and dance or run off to be sick, can force you to experience the entire range of human emotions, and—this is the clincher—can do it so quickly that almost before the moment's begun, and certainly before you can begin to analyze it, it's over. Until the next time you hear the same song.

Sometimes it isn't even the music we connect with. Or rather, it isn't *only* the music. The label itself can have a resonance that mere words can never begin to explain. Perhaps this is why many collectors, desperately searching for a particular song, will nevertheless reject a copy on a foreign, or even domestic, reissue label. For it isn't merely the song they are searching for. It is the artifact itself, the tangible embodiment, if you will, of whichever experience or emotion that dictated their need for the record in the first place.

It could be a classic RCA Victor release, with Nipper the dog and the gramophone horn. Maybe it's an old black British Parlophone or Columbia single, the Beatles or Cliff Richard, the giant silver 45 logo a trademark of quality that has never been matched. The checkerboard of Chess, the wholesome crunchy promise of Apple, the lascivious lips of the Rolling Stones, the bespectacled pig of TMQ. And, if a logo's worth a thousand words, then the slogans are worth many more: "Sounds great in stereo." "If it ain't Stiff, it ain't worth a fuck." "All rights of the producer and of the owner of the record work reserved."

1

Remember when, in the first flush of youth, a new record wasn't simply something you'd spin a few times, and then file away, carefully alphabetically, in an archive-quality protective shrink-wrap jacket? The days when the first thing you did was rip away the shrink-wrapping . . . onto the floor, then into the trash. Out with the record, all fingers and thumbs (you'll wipe away the fingerprints on the front of your sweater tomorrow), onto the turntable, drop down the needle, up with the volume.

Then you'd sit with the sleeve and read every word. More than that, you'd absorb them. Every lyric, every credit, every last iota of information sucked in as if you were the kind of sponge your teachers had despaired of your ever becoming in the classroom—and they were right, because that kind of stuff didn't matter half as much. So what if Wellington won Waterloo? Benny Andersson, Björn Ulvaeus, and Stig Anderson wrote it, and they won the Eurovision Song Contest. In 1974, that was a lot more significant than some dusty old battle.

Old-timers deny it, but it's the same today. No matter that information now zips around the planet at the speed of thought, and that the average eight-year-old knows more about pop idols' lives than his or her parents even cared to imagine. Album jackets are still a mine of arcane information and secret knowledge, the thrill of a new acquisition is still as physical as it is aural, and fingerprints can still be removed with a quick swipe down the front of a sweater.

Maybe some things have changed. No matter how garish and arty they may look, CD labels simply don't have the resonance of the old vinyl counterparts, all the more so since they revolve so fast you can't even try to discover if you can read things in circles.

Remember the old UK Vertigo label? If every record company had selected a mass of black-and-white concentric circles for its logo, the entire psychedelic movement might never have happened. Or, it might never have ended. Comedians Cheech and Chong, during one of their early-'70s routines, referred to playing Black Sabbath at 78 rpm "and seeing God." To American listeners, accustomed to Sabbath releases appearing on staid old Warner Bros., the remark was little more than a throwaway that could have been applied with equal validity to any band in the world.

To British listeners, however, it wasn't a joke. Play one of Sabbath's Vertigo records at 78, keep your eyes firmly focused on the spinning disc before you, and seeing God would be the least of the revelations in store. When Vertigo dropped the design in 1973, urban myth insisted that the government had forced it to, because someone went mad just watching the logo spin.

It probably wasn't true—the story was spread by the same people who claimed the B-side of Napoleon XIV's "They're Coming to Take Me Away Ha-Haaa!," the catchily titled "!Aaah-Ah Yawa Em Ekat Ot Gnimoc Er'yeht," was banned by British radio because someone else went insane trying to decipher the lyrics. The possibility that radio rarely plays records that are simply the A-side spun backward never crossed anybody's mind—not in those naïve days before the evils of "backward masking" were exposed in the media. (And wherefore backward masking today? Surely someone, somewhere, has figured out that if you hold down the CD player's rewind button and listen very carefully, the multimillion rpm gobbledygook has to have something suitably wicked to say?)

It is true, however, that record collecting isn't what it used to be. Turn back the years, to as recently as the mid-'70s, and record collecting as a formal hobby barely even existed. Yes, people did collect records; yes, there was already a thriving network of specialist stores whose sole business was to buy and sell rare music. Even then, records had value; even then, dealers were well aware which would sit gathering dust on the shelves and which would fly out the door the moment they were put on display.

But they gained that information through experience. There were no publications on the subject, or if there were, they were obsessive little discographical creations run off in small-run private editions, barely available and prohibitively priced (by the standards of the day). *Goldmine*, today regarded as the foremost record-collecting publication in the US, was little more than a fanzine, sold at record fairs, swap meets, and via mail-order subscriptions; *Record Collector,* its UK counterpart, was barely a gleam in its creator's eye.

Price guides were nonexistent. The first, Jerry Osborne and Bruce Hamilton's self-published *33⅓ and 45 Extended Play Record Album Price Guide,* appeared in 1977. Grading was an unfathomable mystery (okay, so some things haven't changed), and a book like this would never even have been written, let alone mass-produced, by a major American publishing house.

Things began to change around the end of the 1970s. The *Price Guide* had something to do with that. For the first time, a book was available that not only unlocked the mysteries of a rare record's worth, it also went some way toward explaining why such a record was valuable. But equally important was the music industry itself, and the sudden realization that it wasn't simply marketing music and musicians. It was also marketing a product, and the better that product looked, the more likely it was to be sold.

The concept was road-tested in the UK. British 45s had traditionally been issued in generic paper sleeves since the dawn of recorded history. During 1976–77, an increasing number of limited-edition picture sleeves were the first manifestation of this new mood, and they proved an instant hit. Singles in picture sleeves sold. So more picture sleeves began appearing. Soon they stopped being limited editions. Soon they stopped even attracting attention. By the early '80s, if you wanted to be noticed, you *didn't* have a picture sleeve. People started collecting those records as well.

The advent—again in the UK—of the first commercially available 12-inch single raised the temperature even further. Embarking on another of their frequent raids on the Who's back catalog in fall 1976, but searching for a new way of persuading people to buy it (again), Polydor reissued the Who's 1966 classic "Substitute" on LP-sized vinyl and found itself with the group's first Top Ten hit in five years. A few weeks later, Ariola-Hansa issued the first single by

German disco band Boney M. in the same format. "Daddy Cool" shot to No. 6.

By the turn of the year, and certainly by the following spring, 12-inch singles were pouring out of every label in the land, usually bearing the magic words "limited edition." Some of them even were, but it didn't seem to matter either way. Bands that might never otherwise have had a shot at a UK chart single suddenly found themselves rubbing noses with the richest, most famous hit-makers in the land—New York new wave acts Television, Talking Heads, Blondie, and the Ramones were all promoted early on with the format, while new disco releases were scarcely given a second glance unless they appeared in the large format.

Gimmick followed gimmick. Colored vinyl was next, and this time it was a transatlantic conspiracy. The technology had been around since the days of the 78 and was especially rife in the US during the early '50s. But only a handful of labels had even tried to bring it into the rock age, most recently such enterprising UK independents as Stiff and The Label. Now the majors got to work, utilizing the same limited-edition tactics that had worked so well with the 12-inch, and reaping precisely the same rewards. It didn't even matter that, in many cases, the limited-edition colored vinyl seemed far more common than the regular, boring, black variety. By early 1979, a band without a strangely shaded single was a band without a prayer.

Suddenly record companies were falling over themselves trying to create the next marketing phenomenon. In the US, A&M became one of the first labels to successfully create multicolored records that didn't resemble discarded slabs of chewing gum—the Stranglers' *Something Better Change* EP not only came in fetching pink-and-white marbled vinyl, it also featured liner notes warning that its very label design "may [cause] slight dizziness" if viewed while rotating. It could, indeed. Vertigo revisited!

Experiments were made with odd- and awkward-sized vinyl. In America, A&M, again, was among the first to pioneer a rebirth of the 10-inch LP format, unseen since the 1950s; in Britain, Chiswick went the other way entirely and resurrected the miniaturized "hip-pocket editions" of a decade later.

Picture discs were next. Again, an old 78-era technology found new life after years in the marketing dustbin. In spring 1979, Elektra's UK wing launched the Boston new wave band the Cars with a very fetching picture disc depicting, of course, a car. It sold like hotcakes, and "My Best Friend's Girl" had already stormed to No. 3 when the first disquieting media reports suggested that, whereas other limited editions might have bent the walls of mathematical credulity, Elektra was driving a freight train through them. An acknowledged printing of 5,000 copies had, by some estimates, exceeded that figure ten times over, and the presses were still working.

The ensuing scandal came close to demolishing the entire concept of limited-edition releases in the UK, all the more so since this scandal was very swiftly followed by even more serious allegations of chart hyping (illegally influencing a record's sales to ensure higher chart positions) at other labels. By that time, however, America, Britain, Europe, Asia . . . the whole world, it seemed, was transfixed by an even greater obsession.

The problem with picture discs, colored vinyl, novelty-shaped discs, and all the so-called collectible gimmicks that launched so many sparkling careers, was that they demanded a certain show of confidence on the record buyer's part—not only that the edition truly was limited, but that the record was worth buying in the first place. If every new release was issued with one collectible variant, regardless of whether the record was any good or not, how did you know what to buy? Easy answer—you didn't. So you stopped.

However, what if the same technologies were utilized retroactively, to pretty-up records that you already knew, already loved—and possibly, already owned? This was something that even the US, where niche markets alone had been truly targeted by the inventive marketers of recent years, was unable to resist.

The Beatles' *Sgt. Pepper's Lonely Hearts Club Band*, with a picture of the Lonely Hearts Club Band embedded in the grooves. *The Beatles,* also known as *The White Album,* in pure white wax. The possibilities seemed endless, and so it proved. Entire classic album catalogs were remarketed in exciting new colors, and if, as it very swiftly transpired, these new pressings did not have as high fidelity as they could have, then that simply proved what great investments they were. Unplayed or unplayable—either way, they remained in tip-top condition.

It is difficult to say at what precise point the army of gullible consumers that went into these booms metamorphosed into the army of serious collectors who emerged from the other side. But it happened, and it happened swiftly.

In the mid-'70s, the only people who knew what a rare record was worth were the people who actually determined such things. By the early '80s, the information wasteland of just a few years before had been neatly spruced up and completely paved over. Rare record mega-marts were springing up where once only cultish swap meets had lurked. Price guides grew from obscure private publications—which are now, in some instances, changing hands for as much money as many of the records they list—to sprawling encyclopedias packed with microscopic print. Little old ladies with antique stores on Main Street were adding rows of extra zeros to the price tags on their Beatles LPs, and casual browsers, stunned to discover that a long-forgotten component of their childhood was now worth its weight in gold, suddenly realized that they had to have it.

And just when it seemed that record collecting had gone as far as it could, that every conceivable gimmick had been pulled out of the sack, and every conceivable notion for repackaging the past had been driven into the ground, some bright spark invented the CD, and the whole shebang began again.

Close to 20 years after the first 5-inch aluminum discs began appearing in record stores, claiming to offer superior sound in half the space, and swearing that they were the future of music, it's difficult to remember precisely how much cynicism greeted them. Indeed, even the most optimistic supporter of this exciting new format could never have imagined that, within so brief a period, not only would almost every prized album of the past have been revived, remastered, and remodeled with bonus tracks galore, but that many of the old bands themselves would be back, rejuvenated by the interest stirred up with the reissue of their catalog.

True, there were casualties. Record collections gathered painstakingly together over a course of so many years became . . . not obsolete, for no format (not even 8-Tracks) can ever truly be said to have died out completely . . . but certainly outmoded. New releases no longer appeared on vinyl; older issues were deleted and disappeared.

On the secondary market, in the world of used-record dealers, swap meets, and fairs, the very nature of the business changed overnight. Still a search for hits-you-missed and oldies-but-goodies, the business now needed to expand to assimilate the new format even as it struggled to absorb the vast flood of old material, as entire collections were discarded by owners upgrading to CDs.

In the realm of the rarest records, of course, nothing changed. An Elvis 78 is an Elvis 78, no matter how far technology moves away from wind-up gramophone players. Vinyl that was collectible before CDs, remained collectible after. But no matter how many thousands of records there may be with some kind of inherent value, there are millions more that are simply filler for the dollar bin, or that rot on the street in a box marked "Please take me away." Elvis 78s are the caviar of collecting. *Frampton Comes Alive* is the bread (without butter).

The thing was, a lot of people were now hungry for a few slices. CDs, so perfect for those occasions when you require uninterrupted music for more than 20 minutes at a time, nevertheless seemed cold and sterile in comparison to previous formats. Besides, no matter how much music was now being reissued in the CD format, there was many times more that remained stubbornly unavailable, as the most avid collectors were swift to point out.

RCA reissued Jefferson Airplane's *After Bathing at Baxter's* in stereo, and suddenly it was imperative to pick it up in superior mono. Polygram reissued Roxy Music's *Country Life* with its topless-Fräulein jacket restored, and suddenly, the old American cleaned-up version made a fascinating conversation piece. Old-record collecting skyrocketed in popularity for many different reasons, but new CD reissues had a lot to do with it.

In and of themselves, CDs at first appeared to offer little of interest to the traditional collector, beyond the obvious advantages of previously unissued or rare bonus material, arguably superior sound, and, increasingly as the format aged, an attention to detail and to consumer and collector requirements that vinyl had never taken into consideration. The medium itself was singularly unappealing; the words "cold" and "sterile" again come to mind. As it developed, however, and ironed out the kinks, a whole new discipline came into being.

By the early '90s, CDs were firmly established, both in the marketplace and in the collecting community. Promotional releases, one-track CDs that replaced the DJ 45s of old, assumed at least some of the glamour of their predecessors, while record labels' increasing propensity for samplers heralding forthcoming box sets, hitherto restricted to cassette tapes, took on immeasurably higher value following the switch to CD.

Soon, advance (media) copies of almost every new album were being issued on CD (again, as opposed to the earlier cassette), a handful of which have since ascended to unimaginable heights of desirability and price. The advent later in the 1990s of officially produced promotional CD-Rs appears to have throttled this particular area somewhat, since the gold-colored discs and computer-generated white labels are simply too easy to counterfeit to allow their collectibility to survive. But collectors are adaptable. They'll find a way around that eventually.

It is true that some stalwarts of the old vinyl-collecting world will never be recaptured on CD. But many more have, ranging from inadvertent pressing errors that gift the first few lucky purchasers with alternate versions, mistaken masters, and so on, to limited-edition "secret" tracks. The increasing globalization of the world's record companies has done nothing to stem the flow of exclusive mixes, unavailable B-sides, and unusual sleeves issued all around the world.

And, while the 7-inch single may be dead from a corporate point of view, an entire generation has now grown up for whom the multisong CD single, the mini-album, is all they have ever known, and all they will ever care about.

The European fashion for issuing multiple versions of any given CD single, each bearing its own unique B-sides and mixes, will bedevil completist collectors of many individual artists for years to come, and that's as true for modern stars such as Moby, No Doubt, and Garbage, as it is for crusty old veterans like David Bowie, Paul McCartney, and Bob Dylan. In 1994, the Rolling Stones issued five different versions of their "Out of Tears" single in Britain alone—proof, as if any was needed, that even traditional icons have found a comfortable place in the modern industry.

Today we have music coming out of our ears, almost literally. It can be downloaded from the Internet as MP3 or .wav files, fed into our televisions via the self-styled miracle of DMX, and programmed into the ring tone of our cell phones. It permeates every fiber of modern society. New audio formats harnessing DVD technology promise ever more perfect listening experiences. New methods and standards of manufacturing have seen vinyl make an absolutely unforeseen comeback. Official custom-made CD compilations can now be created and purchased online; unofficial ones can be manufactured by anybody with the necessary toys. One day, we might even have microchips embedded into our skulls, so that all we have to do is think of a song and we will hear it instantaneously.

But through it all, we still collect. People are, seemingly instinctively, acquisitive creatures, and music is what many of us enjoy acquiring. And no matter how it is packaged—on a small spiky cylinder or a flat metal disc, on a scratched-up 45 or an immaculate DAT tape—for as long as people have ears to hear with and eyes to see with, they will continue to collect records. It is the nature of the beast.

How to Grade Records (And CDs and Tapes)

Grading records is like eating spaghetti. Everybody has his or her own way of doing it, and sometimes it can be messy. It is, after all, an extraordinarily subjective topic, largely dependent upon whether one is buying ("That's one helluva gouge across the whole of side one") or selling ("It's only a surface mark; I played it and it's fine"). Attempts to formulate a universal standard founder on so many counts that it isn't even annoying any longer. Accurate grading is, in many ways, the most crucial element in the entire hobby. So why is it so difficult?

The finest grading systems currently in service apply to coin and baseball card collecting, hobbies in which visual appeal and visual perfection are (or, at least, should be) of paramount importance in evaluating an item's value—after all, what else can you do with coins and cards, than stare at them for hours on end? But hobbies in which the collected item actually does something—for example, transmitting music—are equally concerned with making sure that function remains as unimpaired as is possible.

The only way to truly grade a record, tape, or CD is to play it. Eyes can detect any obvious visual flaws; a magnifying glass (some collectors won't leave home without one) will pick up the tiniest ones. But until the music is actually booming out of the speakers, there is no way of detecting the myriad other little pings, dings, and clicks that can send an apparently brand-new disc hurtling down the scale to unlistenable oblivion . . . click . . . oblivion . . . click . . . oblivion.

But you, the listener alone, have the time and inclination to play every piece of music that you purchase, and you alone can tell whether the barely audible pop between tracks two and three is catastrophic enough to merit regrading a disc from Mint to miserable. For the individual you purchased it from, it's enough that the item fulfilled the criteria of whichever grading guide he or she applied to it. The best that you can realistically hope for is that the guide was published on this planet. It's surprising how many seem not to have been.

Remember, too, that grading a record's condition is not the last word in its description. A disc might fulfill every criteria for a particular grade, but still demand further attention: Is it a promotional, DJ, or cutout? Is it mono, stereo, or quadraphonic? Is it autographed? There are dozens of variables that can seriously affect a potential purchaser's decision, and all the more so online, where the item is unavailable for hands-on inspection. When selling, provide as much extra information as you can. When buying, ask before you bid.

Records (45s, LPs, 78s, etc.)

American dealers tend to work from an eight-point scale developed for use in the biweekly magazine *Goldmine* and in the myriad price guides published by its parent company, Krause Publications. In the UK, the seven-point scale formulated by the monthly *Record Collector* is now the accepted system. These scales are applicable to both vinyl and packaging; many sellers will now grade both separately, particularly if there is some disparity between the two—a clean disc and a torn sleeve, for example.

Neither scale is right or wrong. Both function perfectly within those countries' borders. However, problems can arise when transactions cross international boundaries, especially when a record falls outside of the most self-evident of grades.

To begin at the bottom, Poor (P), or in the UK, Bad (B), should leave nobody in any doubt. In a nutshell, the record is wrecked. The sleeve is tattered, if it is even present. The vinyl might be cracked or broken, it might be scratched or warped. It certainly will not play very well, and unless the record represents one of the world's most fabulous rarities—say, a red-vinyl pressing of the Hornets' "I Can't Believe," a $20,000 disc if you care for such things—its value can only be measured in fractions of a cent.

Don't let the seller try to sweet-talk you, either. Every collector, finding a shot-to-hell Shangri-Las LP and asking why it's still $50, has been informed that, "if it weren't for the bullet holes, it'd be in Mint condition." And that's true, especially if the bullet holes are indeed the only imperfection. But if the record

won't play, it's a Frisbee. And some don't even fulfill that function properly.

Mint (M), at the other end of the scale, means that one is purchasing a factory-fresh, unplayed, perhaps even unopened, disc. There will be no creases or ring wear on the cover (picture sleeve for 45s and EPs), no fingerprints on the vinyl, no spindle marks (light silvery lines) around the center hole. Any original extras, ranging from lyric sheets and posters to printed inner sleeves, will be present and pristine. There will be no indication at all that human hands have ever touched the record. And one will notice that very few experienced American dealers or price guides ever advertise their wares in this state, no matter how perfect they appear. Instead, Near Mint is the preferred term, simply because even unplayed, unopened records may well have some undetected defect. Mint, in America, implies "perfect." Near Mint adds "as far as we can tell."

British grading does not make this same distinction. Mint still means exactly the same as it does in the US, but there is no safety net a few points down the grading scale to catch any unforeseen problems. Perhaps the British trust the dealer to make good any serious shortfall in the quality of the disc. Perhaps British customers understand that once they break the seal and spin the record, it is no longer either unopened or unplayed. Or maybe they have simply come to terms with the fact that *Perfect* is just an old John Travolta movie. However they look at it, the system works for them. American buyers may not be so sure.

These are the extremes. On a numerical scale, a Mint record should score 100 (with Near Mint no less than 95); a Poor would barely scrape zero. What, however, of all the numbers in between—for it is there that the majority of used records one finds, whether on the Internet, in a thrift store, or at a record fair, will lie. And it is there that controversy is most likely to rear its head.

There are four basic flaws to which vinyl is commonly prone, most brought about through misuse of some sort—those flaws are warping, dishing, scratching, and breaking. The last of these is self-explanatory. If the record is broken, and that means anything from a minor crack on the edge to a huge chunk torn from the soul of the disc, then that's the end of the story. It's broken. Move along.

Warping, caused by exposure to excessive heat, is the term applied to records that, in the simplest terms, are no longer flat. Sometimes, the warp will gently bow the vinyl, so that when viewed edge-on, it takes on a pronounced wave. In more extreme cases, just one area of the record will be buckled, while the remainder of the disc is unharmed.

Dishing is similar to warping but this time, when viewed edge-on, the record takes on the appearance of, indeed, a dish. Again the effect can be minimal and may not affect the sound quality. But it may.

Scratches are more problematic. Every grade below Near Mint makes some allowance for wear and tear; the question is, how much wear and tear can one expect in any given grade? Some scratches are so light as to barely touch the vinyl—"surface marks," as they are commonly called, can be caused by the record itself coming into contact with absolutely anything, including the stylus that is playing it, or even its own packaging. However, since surface marks lay across the surface of the record and do not cut into the grooves, where the music is stored, they will not affect the sound in the slightest.

The American Very Good Plus (VG+) and British Excellent (Ex) indicate a record that, while showing some signs of use, was also clearly the property of a very careful owner. This is the province of the surface marks and similar light scuffs that do not interfere with the play, but that may be considered unsightly; a barely noticeable warp or dish might also creep into this grade if no other damage is in evidence. Spindle marks will be minimal and the spindle hole will still be tight.

As far as the packaging goes, all original inserts will be present, but will show some signs of handling. There may be some light creasing to the corners of the jacket or a little splitting around the spine. The only permissible "additions" to the original sleeve will be original autographs, items added at source to either point out bonus extras or notable tracks (stickers proclaiming "features the smash hit . . ." or similar), or

devices designating the record as a promotional copy, produced for DJs, journalists, and other members of the media. These can range from "property of" stickers and stamps to "timing sheets" spread across the lower front cover, listing the tracks and their duration—an invaluable service to DJs, of course. Many collectors regard these extras as a defect. However, specialists (and, of course, promo collectors) treat them as an integral part of the packaging and expect the grading to reflect that.

Otherwise pristine LP jackets might also have a punch-hole or indentation in one corner, or might have had about half an inch of corner physically chopped away, branding them as "cutouts"—factory-fresh records whose jackets were thus disfigured by the issuing record company, to indicate that they were made available at a discount price. Because of this damage, no cutout can reasonably be graded higher than VG+/Ex, even if it fulfills all the criteria of a higher grade.

So-called light scratches are those that have cut into the groove and are responsible for occasional, and very brief, sequences of light clicks as a record is playing. Clicking, however, is all that they will do. Medium scratches are those that actively interfere with the music, without actually causing the needle to skip or stick. They can be felt by running a fingertip over the surface of the record (make sure it's a clean tip, though, or you'll just add to the problem). On both sides of the ocean, the grade Very Good (VG) allows these scratches to intrude into the listening experience, together with further deterioration of the packaging, but without significant damage to it.

Another accepted VG ailment is surface noise evident during quiet passages. If the record belonged to somebody who regularly played certain cuts, there may be some minor clicking at the beginning and end of each favored cut, caused by the needle's having been placed less than delicately down on the vinyl. In extreme cases, this can also affect (again, without skipping or sticking) the outro of the preceding cut and/or the intro of the next.

On a VG record, the spindle hole will probably be surrounded by a maze of silver lines; there may be

A promotional LP with timing slip (see page 8).

some wear to the hole itself. The packaging may also be showing both its age and its history. Labels and sleeves alike may have writing, stickers, tape or the like either attached or showing signs of once having been adhered (tape residue will probably outlive cockroaches); tears and creases will be more apparent, and loose extras may well have disappeared.

It is important to note that while a VG record will suffer from some of these faults, it should not suffer from them all. Two or three is more than enough; a record with any more requires a serious reappraisal. Most US price guides regard VG as the lowest grade worth valuing.

On both sides of the Atlantic, the grade Good describes records that have been played a few times too often. Groove wear will be evident in the loss of the shiny black glow that a better-conditioned disc should retain. Label and sleeve alike will be tatty—stained, torn, or defaced. The corner areas of the sleeve, those portions that do not rest against the record itself, may feel soft and droopy, and will prove much more easily creased or folded than they ought.

Upon playing, the record will not sound as sharp as it once did, surface noise will be audible throughout, and the scratches will be louder, too. The record will still be playable without skipping or sticking, but it's a sorry sight to behold, regardless. The wholly unnecessary American grade of Good Plus (G+) is differentiated as not having quite as many defects as a mere Good.

The lowest grade in which a record is actually playable is the American Fair (F), which equates to the British Poor (P). In this state, the deepest scratches come into play, those that not only cut through the grooves but also force the needle to follow them, leading to the dreaded skips and jumps. Or maybe they displace one of the groove walls, shifting it into the path of the needle, thus causing it to become stuck. (Dirt, hair, grease, and a million other foreign bodies can also cause this.) Or maybe they do both and really give you your waste-of-money's worth. The sleeve may still be intact, but it just as likely may not; and if there was a lyric sheet or similar included, it long ago went astray.

Basically, unless we are again discussing some fabulous rarity, records in this condition are as worthless as those graded even more disparagingly, and the only reason they are even offered up for sale is because modern society frowns so fiercely on simply giving rubbish away. One man's meat and all that. Likewise, there are few worthwhile reasons, and even fewer good excuses, for wanting to purchase a record in this state—unless, perhaps, you really hate the song and want to watch it suffer. In which case, are you sure you even need to know about grading?

CDs/Tapes (Reels, 4- and 8-Tracks, Cassettes, etc.)

In these fields, grading is basically a matter of whether or not the product plays perfectly. CDs, while not the indestructible heirlooms that early publicity insisted they were, are nevertheless very difficult to damage in normal use, despite their propensity to hastily accumulate the most unsightly collection of scratches, fingerprints, and dents. In all but the most drastic cases, not only will these problems not affect play, they can often be camouflaged with any one of the many CD cleaning products on the market. Certainly, unless factory freshness is a prerequisite of admission to your collection, a wanted CD should never be rejected simply because the disc looks a little battered.

Cassettes, cartridges (4- and 8-Tracks), and reels are harder to evaluate, though the most common problems—twisted, bunched, and/or broken tape—can often be spotted early on.

In cassettes, defects can be seen either in the open playing area or through the transparent plastic window between the spools; in cartridges, the nature of the format can allow problems to be absorbed back into the case, but more often the tape itself jams, ensuring that the flaw is forever visible in the playing area. Or even hanging limply out of it. Always look at the tape itself to check that it has not twisted; the playing area, facing out, is light brown in color, while the backing, which should not be seen, is shiny black.

On 8-Tracks one often finds large globules of an eternally adhesive black goo in the place where the roller once was. The problem is as common among sealed tapes as it is among those that have been well played. Unless extreme care is exercised upon opening the case and transferring the tape to a new cartridge case, this is a fatal condition; once that goo gets on the tape, you'll never get it off again.

These are the visual checks one should always make. However, tape formats are heir to a number of flaws that remain undetectable until the tape is played. Magnetic tape is prone to deteriorating with age, with the thin cassette tape especially vulnerable; even a factory-sealed cassette can prove unplayable if the circumstances are right. (Or, in this case, wrong.) Tape is also irreversibly damaged by exposure to magnetic sources, and alarmingly, by the irradiation process introduced by the US Postal Service following the fall 2001 anthrax attacks. Paper products (LP sleeves, CD booklets, etc.), too, can be adversely affected by the process, and should the irradiation system become universal, the ramifications for America's musical mail-order industry scarcely bear contemplating.

Both 4- and 8-Tracks, can suffer from the loss of the metallic strips that communicate the conclusion of each program to the playing head of the machine—without them, a player will just loop the same songs over and over, and the most varied album in the world will swiftly start sounding somewhat soporific. Back in the heyday of cartridges, this problem was prevalent enough that several companies actually marketed replacement strips. For obvious reasons, these are less commonly available today.

Reel-to-reel tapes, produced as they generally were for the audiophile market, and uncluttered by rollers and the like, are less susceptible to hidden dangers. However, the very action of preparing to play a reel—looping the tape manually into the second spool—can cause terrible problems, ranging from grease on the playing surface to kinks, twists, and even breakage. When purchasing reels, always check for the presence of a short length of blank (and usually opaque) "run on" tape at the loose end of the reel.

The other key to tape collecting, no less than with LPs and 45s, is to ensure that the packaging is complete and clean.

As far as CDs and cassettes are concerned, this applies only to any appropriate artwork—booklets, liner cases, and so forth. It does not refer to the piece of mass-produced plastic that holds it all together, which is bad news for all those lost souls who complain loudly and bitterly because a mail-order CD arrived in a cracked or otherwise damaged jewel case, and good news for the sellers who know that the case was fine when it was dispatched.

Except in those cases where some kind of customizing incorporates the jewel case into the actual packaging (the personalized "Q" logo on the spine of Queen's *Made in Heaven* CD, for instance), a jewel case (or cassette case) is a jewel case (or cassette case) is a . . . . Damage is regrettable, of course. But it is not the end of the world and it does not irreparably devalue your purchase. Just run down the road and buy a new one.

The World's Most Valuable Records

No book on record collecting would be complete without a list of the world's most valuable records—and no two books on record collecting ever seem to agree on what should actually be included on such a list.

There are those supremely elusive nuggets from the dawn of rock 'n' roll—the first R&B LP of all time, a self-titled release by Billy Ward and the Dominoes (Federal 295-94); the Midnighters' *Greatest Hits* (Federal 295-90); *Johnny Burnette and the Rock 'n' Roll Trio* (Coral CRL 57080); Frank Ballard's *Rhythm-Blues Party* (Phillips International 1985); UK pressings of Ron Harraves' "Latch On" (MGM 956); and Bobby Charles' "See You Later, Alligator" (London HLU 8247).

There are acetates and demonstration discs that one can only dream about: a second copy of the Quarrymen's original 78 rpm acetate of "That'll Be the Day," or one of the 50 replicas that Paul McCart-

ney had manufactured in 1981; Elvis's one-sided "How Do You Think I Feel" test pressing; Queen's five-song Trident Studios demo acetate; or the CD promo for Nirvana's unreleased UK single of "Pennyroyal Tea (Scott Litt Mix)." Dream on.

There are colored-vinyl albums that exist in quantities of just one copy, surreptitiously pressed by a factory worker to take home as a souvenir. There are hopelessly obscure private pressings by now-fashionable British prog and folk bands. There are demo tapes by every band that ever sought a record deal, and a few by groups that got one—even U2, Radiohead, and Slipknot had to start somewhere.

There is so much that could be listed—and so little that anyone will ever actually find. The following, therefore, concentrates on releases that, theoretically, could turn up at any time, any place, mass-produced (more or less) items that might readily pass for just another everyday issue, and that, very occasionally, have done so. All have accepted values in excess of $1,000; all, to be honest, are as likely to turn up in your local thrift store, garage sale, or grandmother's loft as any of the fabled obscurities mentioned above. But the devil, as they say, is in the details, and if you don't know what the details are, then you'll never know when you're holding a little slice of record-collecting heaven in your hand.

The Beatles: *Introducing the Beatles (US Vee-Jay SR 1062, includes "Love Me Do"/"PS I Love You"—1964)*
The Beatles' first American LP was issued in January 1964, at a time when no sane American gave a fig for these longhaired lurkers from Liverpool . . . wherever that was. The album featured 12 songs, including both sides of the band's first UK single, "Love Me Do"/"PS I Love You," plus ten others featured on the band's UK debut album, *Please Please Me*. Planning an issue in both mono and stereo, Vee-Jay ordered 6,000 cover slicks from its printers (Coburn and Co., Chicago), utilizing the same formal band shot that was used on the UK *Beatles Hits* EP (Parlophone GEP 8880); the reverse of the sleeve depicted tiny color photographs of 25 other Vee-Jay album releases, and no track listing.

A revised sleeve, with a full accounting of the record's contents, appeared soon after, leading some researchers to believe that both the ad back and what is now regarded as an intermediate issue, with its back cover absolutely blank, were either an oversight or a subtle subterfuge to postpone the inevitable wrath of Capitol Records, which was now taking a close look at Vee-Jay's right to release the Beatles' music. Ultimately, this led to the production of a revised edition of *Introducing the Beatles*, replacing "Love Me Do"/"PS I Love You" with the hitherto abandoned "Please Please Me"/"Ask Me Why" coupling.

Whatever their origins, the ad-back and blank-back editions of the album are extremely rare in any form, with stereo pressings even harder to find. And then there are stereo versions of the title back, a variation that was not even known to exist prior to 1995.

The Beatles: *Please Please Me (UK Parlophone PCS 3042, gold-on-black label—1963)*

If stereo releases were sporadic and limited in the US, they were even more so in Britain, where the market was limited exclusively to hi-fi freaks. The initial stereo issue of the Beatles' debut album, then, was always going to be tiny, but it was about to get even tinier. The first pressing utilized the gold-on-black label that had served Parlophone LPs for several years, but that was now being phased out in favor of a new yellow-on-black design. And the first pressings of *that* credit the publishing to "Dick James Mus[ic] Co."—later ones (and that's just days later) to the Beatles' own newly formed Northern Songs.

The Beatles: *The Beatles Deluxe Three Pack (Capitol 8X3T 358, 8-Track box set—1969)*

Who says 8-Tracks aren't worth anything? Released in September 1969, the fabled *Deluxe Three Pack* comprised three apparently randomly selected Beatles albums in a unique 12-inch box set. *Meet the Beatles, Yesterday and Today* (with the trunk cover, of course), and *Magical Mystery Tour* were the chosen ones, none of which have especial value in their own right. It is estimated, however, that no more than a dozen copies of the complete box set exist, establishing this as the rarest 8-Track release of all time.

Kate Bush: *"Eat the Music" (UK EMI EM 280—1993)*

Most collectors believe that the greatest Kate Bush rarities relate either to her pre-fame days and the so-called Cathy demos, or to the 1978–87 period when she was at her most active. In fact, the acknowledged rarest Bush record of all was the projected first British single from her 1993 album, *The Red Shoes*, "Eat the Music"/"Big Stripey Lie"—projected, that is, until radio positively refused to bite. Moving fast, EMI scrapped the entire first-print run, and slammed the decidedly jauntier "Rubberband Girl" into its place, while retaining the same catalog number and B-side. Picture-sleeve copies of the abandoned "Eat the Music" escaped regardless, to wreak havoc on the most complete Kate collections—and, doubtless, to raise the hopes of everyone who owns a copy. Good luck. "Eat the Music" was issued as planned in Europe, Australia, and the US, so it's only the British one that's worth a fortune.

Bob Dylan: *"Mixed Up Confusion" (Columbia 42656, orange label—1963)*

Dylan's first-ever single was recorded in November 1962, and released on the heels of a less-than-world-beating debut album, before his second album finally broke Dylan out of the narrow confines of New York's Woody Guthrie–impersonation circuit. Hardly surprisingly, then, "Mixed Up Confusion" sold poorly, and while re-pressings would follow the singer's breakthrough, this original issue is extremely rare.

Bob Dylan: *The Freewheelin' Bob Dylan (US Columbia CS 8786/CL 1986, includes four missing tracks—1963)*

This is one of those rarities whose legend is now so well-known that it is probably more famous than the album that replaced it. When recording his second LP, Bob Dylan included four songs that—for reasons that are still somewhat obscure—were first placed on, and then removed from, the finished product: "Rocks and Gravel," "Let Me Die in My Footsteps," "Gamblin' Willie's Dead Man's Hand," and a pointed piece of anti–right wing politicizing, "Talkin' John Birch Blues" (alternate titles "Talkin' John Birch Society Blues" and " . . . Paranoid Blues" have since appeared on bootleg and official anthologies alike).

The removal of the latter track echoed a decision taken earlier in the year when Dylan appeared on CBS-TV's *The Ed Sullivan Show* and was pointedly refused permission to perform the song. The favorite theory is that Columbia, acknowledging the logic of its broadcasting department, prevailed upon Dylan to drop the song from the record, at which point Dylan decided to revise the entire disc to annoy the label as much as it was annoying him.

The album had already been manufactured at this point, with all four songs included. The entire run was withdrawn and prepared for destruction, while the revised edition went into production. Of course not all the original LPs were lost—a tiny number of stereo pressings are known, though all have (so far) appeared in the "corrected" sleeve. Neither would the re-pressing itself go as planned. An unknown quantity was produced mistakenly using the original mono master, featuring the four deleted tracks, though the correct new label and sleeve were employed. No sleeves listing the four deleted tracks have ever been located. (Interestingly, the precise opposite situation exists in Canada, where no "original" or "mispressed" versions of the LP have yet surfaced, but sleeves have.)

There are American promo editions with the deleted tracks listed on both the timing strip affixed to the front cover and on the label. But none found to date have yet played the banished quartet. No matter: *The Freewheelin' Bob Dylan* is already regarded as the rarest and most valuable record in America. What difference would another variation really make? Have you checked your copy yet?

Jefferson Airplane: *Takes Off (US RCA Victor LSP 3584, with missing/revised tracks—1966)*

The Airplane may have reveled in a world of chemical and sexual stimulation, but their record company certainly didn't. Original mono editions of the group's debut album hit the stores bearing three songs—"Runnin' 'Round This World," "Go to Her," and "Let Me In"—that should probably never have passed the label's internal censorship department. And when they did . . . the album was promptly sent back for a cleanup.

New versions of the latter two tracks were substituted for the original versions. The cleaned-up versions featured politely revised lyrics (the line "as you lay under me," in "Let Me In," was replaced by "as you stay here by me"). "Runnin' Round This World"—which referred to both sex and drugs, and was thus clearly unsalvageable—was dropped altogether, not to be heard again until 1971 brought the *Early Flight* compilation. The other two cuts are still in the vaults today, though alternate uncensored versions appeared on the *Jefferson Airplane Loves You* box set in 1991.

John's Children: *"Midsummer Night's Scene" (UK Track 604 005—1967)*

Alongside the edition of Queen's "Bohemian Rhapsody," listed below, this is the rarest British single of them all. Scheduled for release in June 1967, as the follow-up to the band's mini-hit "Desdemona" (604 003), the creepily psychedelic "Midsummer Night's Scene" was withdrawn from the schedules for reasons that still aren't clear. It was replaced, using the same catalog number and B-side, by "Sara Crazy Child."

Judged a rarity even at the time, the single's value began soaring after John's Children's guitarist, Marc Bolan, emerged at the front of T. Rex, the biggest British band of the early '70s, and still one of the UK's most fanatically collectible artists. Between 25 and 50 copies of this single are rumored to exist today—considerably fewer have actually been accredited.

Paul McCartney: *Ram (US Apple MAS 3375, mono promotional issue—1971)*

By 1970, mono was dead. In just two years, the industry had risen up and squashed it like a bug beneath the shimmering brilliance of stereo sound. A number of radio stations still appreciated it, though, and new singles pressed for DJ use regularly featured a stereo mix of the song on one side, and a mono mix on the other. Mono promos of LPs, too, still appeared on occasion—1971 also saw a limited pressing of the Rolling Stones' *Sticky Fingers*, produced for the delight of DJs everywhere.

It was not, then, notable when Apple pressed up a small quantity of McCartney's second album in marvelous mono; what is eyebrow-raising is the value attached to copies. The mono catalog number and MONAURAL legend on the label are the only visibly distinguishing factors—there were no promo markings, nor was there a custom sleeve. Rather, most copies were delivered sharing a jacket with the regular stereo issue, and many were probably passed by without a second glance. Today, of course, it's a different story. Today, there are even bootlegs of the thing.

The Misfits: *"Horror Business" (Plan 9 PL 1009, black vinyl—1979)*

The New Jersey horror punk band has ascended into the upper realms of collectibility without most "traditional" (read "older") collectors even noticing. The majority of releases on the group's own Blank and Plan 9 labels are extremely rare, but this is the daddy of them all. Conventionally issued on yellow vinyl, 25 copies were produced in exciting black, and if you can find the unreleased picture sleeve too, featuring a group photograph on the reverse, you're really on to a winner.

Elvis Presley: *"Can't Help Falling in Love" (RCA Victor 37-7968 "Compact Single 33⅓," with/without picture sleeve—1961)*

RCA's Compact Single series was launched in 1961, primarily to offer fans an improved audio experience—like the 12-inch 45s of later years, 7-inch 33⅓s allowed more information to be packed into the (wider) grooves, thus leading to better sound. Special picture sleeves were designed for each issue and some 150 releases were made over the course of the next year, none of which are especially common. But three of the five Elvis issues are much sought after—"His Latest Flame" (37-7908), "Good Luck Charm" (37-7992), and "Can't Help Falling in Love" are the rarest of the lot.

Elvis Presley: *Moody Blue (RCA AFL1-2428—1976)*

The world's most valuable picture disc was produced by RCA, apparently as an executive Christmas card, and it depicts, odd as it may sound, Elvis manager Colonel Tom Parker dressed as Santa Claus. That's on one side, anyway; on the other is a photo of an RCA staff Christmas party. Gripping stuff. But apparently no more than a dozen discs were pressed, and even fewer have surfaced on the open market.

Prince: *The Black Album (US Warner Bros. 25677—1987)*

Scheduled for release for Christmas 1987, *The Black Album* was intended as the big pop secret of the year. It was listed on the Warner Bros. schedule as being, simply, by "somebody," and was to be launched into circulation beneath a cloak of impenetrable anonymity. A plain black sleeve (of course) included no artist information and no track details (even the CD long box was plain black), this Stygian vista broken by just two stickers, the requisite barcode and an "Explicit Lyrics—Parental Advisory" warning. Even the Warner Bros. promotions office was instructed to ignore the release altogether: no copies to reviewers, no information to the media, and no advertisements in the press.

Only the club circuit would be served with pre-release copies. Promos, dispatched shortly before the album's street date, were manufactured as two 45-rpm 12-inch discs; stock copies were prepared as conventional 12-inch 33⅓ rpm LPs, and also as CDs. Then, with buyers apparently not gearing up for the release according to plan, Prince abruptly pulled it from the schedules. Suddenly, an album intended to be utterly anonymous was transformed into one of the most famous records of the decade.

Bootleg copies of *The Black Album* began appearing very swiftly; they are convincing, so beware. Authentic vinyl copies are practically nonexistent, while no more than 25–50 genuine examples of *The Black Album* CD are believed to have survived. The first to appear on the collectors market in 1991 sold for a then-record $13,500. An official, albeit limited-edition, release finally arrived in 1994.

Queen: *"Bohemian Rhapsody" (UK EMI 2375, blue vinyl/Queen's Award for Export picture sleeve—1978)*

Currently ranked the rarest UK single ever issued, this blue-vinyl pressing dates from 1978, three years after the song's original release. It was housed in a maroon-and-gold custom sleeve, celebrating EMI's receipt of the prestigious Queen's (the other one) Award to Industry for Export Achievement.

Just 200 copies were pressed, the majority of which were distributed alongside a pair of etched goblets and a commemorative pen, to guests at a three-hour luncheon at London's Selfridges, celebrating the award on July 26, 1978. Check your diary—do you remember where you ate that afternoon?

Rolling Stones: *"I Wanna Be Your Man"* (US London 9641—1964)

The Rolling Stones' debut US single was a proven UK smash, and should have been just as big in America. It was loud, it was brash, and it was custom written for the group by John Lennon and Paul McCartney. Even allowing for the band's unknown status in the US, it should have done something. Instead it sank like a stone, so hard and fast that many of the band's soon-acquired fans weren't even aware that it existed. And by the time they found out, it was too late. There are a lot of DJ copies around, mailed out to people who probably never even played them. But stock copies never seem to turn up.

Rolling Stones: *The Rolling Stones Promotional Album* (US London/UK Decca RSM/RSD 1—1969)

Or, how to turn the mundane into the magnificent. In 1969, the Stones' US and UK labels, London and Decca, respectively, compiled a catalog-spanning promotional album to help publicize the band's latest LP and tour. Just 200 copies were produced in one country, with the catalog number RSM 1; 200 sleeves were printed in the other, with the number RSD 1. The albums were then equally distributed between the two markets—never (or very rarely) to be seen again. It isn't only the album's rarity that attracts attention, either; the album is also the only source for an (admittedly minor) alternate mix of the song "Love in Vain."

Many collectors guides caution their readers not to confuse this issue with a similarly packaged Australian LP, *The Rolling Stones Limited Edition Collectors Item* (which features the "correct" "Love in Vain"). This is indeed sound advice if you're about to drop a couple of grand on a copy. However, since the Aussie release, too, is extraordinarily scarce, it probably wouldn't hurt to lay a copy or two by if you get the chance.

Sex Pistols: *"God Save the Queen"* (UK A&M AMS 7284—1977)

Signed and sacked in the space of one week, the Sex Pistols, and the group's A&M sojourn, is the stuff of which punk rock legends were made—all the more so since production of the group's "God Save the Queen"/"No Feelings" single was already underway.

With rumors swirling that outraged A&M superstars had deluged the office with complaints and disgust, unable to believe such a nice, sedate label had inked a pact with Satan's foulest demons, the company commenced destroying every manufactured copy of the Pistols' record the moment the group was fired. And when "God Save the Queen" did finally appear two months later, it was on a different label (Virgin), with a different B-side ("Did You No Wrong").

The A&M single lived on, however. Up to 300 copies are now believed to have escaped the cull (earlier estimates were considerably more conservative), with the band members apparently owning several apiece. Another dozen were distributed among laid-off A&M executives, following the UK label's closure in 1999.

Tony Sheridan and the Beat Brothers: *"My Bonnie"* (US Decca 31382—1962)

The Beatles by any other name, and this 45 has the honor of being the group's first-ever US release, almost a full year before Swan, Vee-Jay, Tollie, Capitol and all the rest got in on the fun. It sold next to nothing at the time—even in their homeland, the "Beat Brothers" were an unknown quantity, though it was amazing the difference that a couple more years made. In 1964, not only was this single reissued (MGM K13213), an entire album's worth of similar tracks also made it out. In fact, they're still coming out today, so if you're looking for this particular issue, it's unlikely that you want it for its musical content. You probably don't want the bootleg copies, either.

Original pressings feature the then-standard black Decca label with colored bars; original DJ copies feature a pink label with a star beneath the word Decca. Black-label variations on this latter are generally regarded as counterfeits.

Frank Sinatra and Antonio Carlos Jobim: *Sinatra Jobim (Reprise W7 1028, 8-Track—1969)*

Who says 8-Tracks aren't worth anything (part two). *Sinatra Jobim* was scheduled for release in 1969, with production of the 8-Track carried out by the Ampex plant in Illinois. The production—and, indeed, shipping—in that format had already begun when the release was canceled.

Just one LP test pressing is known to have been made; on the other hand, some 3,500 8-Tracks had been produced, and Warner Bros., Reprise's distributors, immediately circulated a memo requesting that all copies be returned for destruction. The company's efforts appear to have succeeded, as no more than half a dozen copies of the 8-Track are known today.

Much of the album (seven of the ten songs) reappeared two years later on the *Sinatra and Company* (Reprise FS 1033) album.

Bruce Springsteen: *"Spirit in the Night" (US Columbia 45864—1973)*

Many artists' rarest releases fall within the earliest days of their careers, and so it is with the Boss. "Spirit in the Night"/"For You" was his second 45, following "Blinded by the Light"/"Angel" (itself a considerable scarcity), issued at a time when Springsteen's future preeminence was already an open secret in the media, but had yet to communicate itself to the general public. DJ copies of this, with a mono/stereo coupling of "Spirit," are relatively common. Stock copies, however, have a nasty penchant for elusiveness.

Thin Lizzy: *"The Farmer" (Eire Parlophone DIP 513—1970)*

A lot of groups debuted under misspelled names. Jethro Tull became Jethro Toe for a now-scarce UK debut 45, and U2 played its first British show under the mistaken name of V2—posters for the show are worth an absolute mint. So Thin Lizzie probably got off fairly lightly—at least it still worked phonetically.

Still, even the band members could never have foreseen just how hard it would be for future collectors to get to hear what their first effort sounded like. Released in Ireland only in July 1970, just 500 copies of "The Farmer" are believed to have been pressed, of which 217 went unsold and were subsequently recycled. Absent from every Lizzy album and collection over the next 15 years, "The Farmer" finally resurfaced in 1986 on EMI's *Supernova* various-artists collection (GAS 101). But this, too, was available only in Ireland, and only for a very brief period.

The song was then exhumed for inclusion (as the opening track) on Universal's *Vagabonds, Kings, Warriors, Angels* four-CD box set in 2000—only for that entire project to be mired down in sufficient difficulties that, for a long time, it looked as though this release, too, was doomed to oblivion. It finally made it out in late 2001 in the UK, but precedent recommends picking up a copy quickly.

Ike and Tina Turner: *River Deep Mountain High (US Philles PHLPS 4011—1966)*

Phil Spector believed that his production of the Turners' "River Deep Mountain High" single was his greatest piece of work yet—though it was translated into his greatest rejection ever, when the 45 crashed and burned at a lowly No. 88. An album cut to similar standards for release in the single's wake was promptly scrapped, even though the records had already been manufactured (though no sleeves had yet been printed). The vast majority were destroyed; a handful, however, drifted onto the marketplace over the years and should not be confused with either the UK issue, which did go ahead as planned (London HAU 8298/SHU 8298), or the eventual US issue released by A&M in 1969 (SP 4178).

The Velvet Underground: *"All Tomorrow's Parties" (US Verve 10427—1966)*

No original Velvet Underground single can be accused of being common, but this, the group's debut, is by far the scarcest of them all. Featuring edited versions of both sides, lucky (and wealthy) collectors have a choice of two equally rare issues: stock copies, and promos in a custom picture sleeve, which is reproduced on the back cover of the Victor Bockris–Gerard Malanga biography *Up-Tight. The Story of the Velvet Underground.*

The World's Most Valuable Sleeves

It might come as a surprise to learn that not all of the world's rarest records are, in fact, records (or tapes, cassettes, CDs, or whatever). Sometimes it's the packaging that attracts the attention and brings in the biggest bucks.

It is important always to distinguish between genuinely rare sleeves, such as those below, and sleeves that have simply gained some form of notoriety—so-called censored jackets for Nirvana's *In Utero* (DGC 24607) album and Jane's Addiction's *Ritual de lo Habitual* (Warner Bros. 25993), for example, are certainly both very collectible, but as yet have attracted no more than modest premiums over their uncensored counterparts, for the simple reason that both versions were readily available in stores, in vast quantities.

Much the same can be said for Lynyrd Skynyrd's *Street Survivors* (MCA 3029), whose original artwork—depicting the group wreathed in flames—was replaced following the plane crash that claimed the lives of three band members, just three days after the album's October 1977 release. Copies can prove elusive, but are by no means rare.

The following, then, lists a selection of sleeves that are known to have made the journey from drawing board to printing press, and sometimes even beyond. But then, on very eve of release, their journey ended. Or did it?

The Beatles: *The Beatles (UK Apple PMC/PCS 7067/8, embossed numbering in lower right of front cover between 00000001-00000020—1968)*
The Beatles' eponymous 1968 double album is popularly known as *The White Album,* because that's what it looks like. The sleeve is plain white, with even the band's name merely embossed on the front, and only an individually printed number in the bottom right-hand corner to break up the view.

It is unclear how high the individual numbering went before the printers stopped counting—one short

of 10 million was the highest figure allowed for by the sleeve. What is certain is that the lower the number, the more someone is likely to pay for a copy—with the first 20 (which essentially means the Beatles' own copies, plus those given away to family, friends, and other associates) fetching the greatest premium.

Several of these have appeared at auction, though the prices realized seem absurdly low today. The copy numbered 00000001 (owned by John, but autographed by Ringo) was sold by Sotheby's, in New York, back in 1985, for the then incredible sum of $715; 00000002 (John's landlord's copy) was auctioned by the Bristol, England, record store Plastic Wax in 1990 and fetched around $750. In 1999, a previously undocumented duplicate copy of 000000001 went under the hammer at Sotheby's for around $15,000; in April 2002, 000000005 was sold by Bonham's for almost $13,000.

The Beatles: *Yesterday and Today (US Capitol ST 2553, "butcher cover"—1966)*
Is this the most over-recited story in record collecting history? For the Beatles' tenth US album, Capitol selected a portrait of the band members clad in butchers' smocks, apparently reveling in the dismemberment of sundry dolls and other meaty items. After 750,000 sleeves were printed, the vinyl was inserted, and copies were distributed to media and radio, the complaints began pouring in.

No matter that the same shot had already decorated the UK press without any ill effect (Robert Whitaker's photograph was used in print ads for the British "Paperback Writer" 45); no matter that the album was scheduled for release just days later. The sleeve could not be allowed to stand.

A new design was hastily obtained—an utterly uncontroversial shot of the band posing around a traveling trunk (ah, but what was in the trunk?), and Capitol staff spent the entire weekend hurriedly gluing this new image over the offending one. And the great thing about glue is, it can sometimes be removed.

Three states of "butcher cover" are universally recognized: "First state" refers to copies that somehow missed the pasting-over process altogether. "Second state" refers to copies on which the "trunk cover" is intact, but the underlying butcher is apparent (look carefully—a black "V" on butcher Ringo's sweater can be discerned halfway up the right-hand side). "Third state" describes a cover from which the trunk has been removed. Different grading points thereafter note how well (or otherwise) the removal was accomplished.

In addition, sleeves intended for stereo pressings of the LP are considerably scarcer than those made for mono.

David Bowie: *Diamond Dogs (US RCA APL1 0576, visible genitals on dog—1974)*

It was, as they say, "the dog's bollocks." Ordinarily, that's an astonishingly wonderful thing—just another of those quaint English expressions that seems quite incomprehensible, even after you know what it means. In the matter of David Bowie's latest album art, however, RCA was not so sure.

The artwork for *Diamond Dogs,* quite sensibly, featured the singer himself in the form of a dog, a vision hatched by the doyen of rock artists, Dutchman Guy Peellaert. But when Bowie told Peellaert to make the representation as realistic as possible, maybe he should have added . . . "but not too real." Flip the familiar album sleeve over, peer between the hound's rear legs . . . and if those generous genitals are jammed in there, then that's the dog's bollocks.

Almost every first-run edition had the offending bagatelles primly airbrushed into oblivion. But a handful—how does one put it?—slipped out. A word of warning, however. The search for the secret scrotum applies only to original RCA LP pressings of *Diamond Dogs.* Reissued in 1990 by Rykodisc, the original artwork was restored in all its original glory.

David Bowie: *"Space Oddity" (UK Philips BF 1801, picture sleeve—1969)*

Quite simple, this one. In 1969, David Bowie released a new UK single called "Space Oddity." It was not issued with a picture sleeve. However, when Philips's Dutch branch was called upon to press up stereo copies for the British market, it appears that somebody there decided to manufacture sleeves to go with them—presumably unaware that Britain, alone

in the industrialized world, had yet to embrace that particular concept. Philips UK took one look at these alien artifacts and probably junked them; either way, no more than a handful are known to exist today; the first wasn't even discovered until 1996.

Bob Dylan: *"Subterranean Homesick Blues" (Columbia 43242, DJ with picture sleeve—1965)*

A picture sleeve was issued only with DJ promo copies. However, DJs are not a breed especially well-known for retaining such things . . . not when there are those nice stiff generic cardboard sleeves to tuck new records into. The sleeves were discarded, the stock copies arrived unadorned—hey, presto, an instant rarity.

Vince Everett: *"Treat Me Nice" (Laurel 41623—1956)*

Vince who? Only confirmed Elvis fans, those who've watched *Jailhouse Rock* enough times to memorize the name of the character he plays, might detect something intriguing about this picture sleeve. It was printed for a record that was never made, by an artist who never existed. Rather, it was a prop used in the movie, and it haunts devoted collectors like no other piece of paper.

Elvis Presley: *Elvis/Jaye P. Morgan (RCA EPA 992/689—1956)*

Reputedly the rarest Elvis Presley release of all, this double-EP package featured Presley's recent *Elvis* offering, the first record in that format ever to sell a million-plus copies, together with an earlier release by Ms. Morgan, accompanied by Hugo Winternalter's orchestra. It was issued as a promotional device only, with the gatefold sleeve reproducing the original EP covers on the front, and an array of sales facts and figures within. The enclosed EPs themselves were no different from regular stock copies.

Elvis Presley: *The International Hotel Presents Elvis 1969/1970 (RCA Victor complimentary box—1969, 1970)*

The King's live reinvention, at the International Hotel in Las Vegas, was a big deal—so big that RCA and the hotel got together to offer guests at the first two shows (July 31 and August 1, 1969) an extra-special souvenir of the event. The gift box included a press release, three photographs, a thank-you note from both Presley and manager Colonel Tom Parker, an RCA label catalog, and two LPs: regular stock copies of the soundtrack to the previous year's NBC-TV special (LPM 4088) and the recent *From Elvis in Memphis* (LSP 4155).

It was a popular gift, so when Elvis returned to the venue in January 1970, a similar package was presented at the show on January 28. This time, the box included a press release, a photograph, a booklet, a dinner menu, the latest RCA catalog, the LP *From Memphis to Vegas/From Vegas to Memphis* (LSP 6020) and the 45 "Kentucky Rain" (47-9791). Find the box, keep the records. They make no difference whatsoever to the value.

Rolling Stones: *"Street Fighting Man" (US London 909, picture sleeve—1969)*

The Stones were no strangers to conceptual controversy. One UK album title, the delightful *Can You Walk on Water,* was done in by Decca for blasphemy, while the original sleeve design for the *Beggars Banquet* album, a graffiti-strewn bathroom, was blocked for indecency. (It was finally restored in 1984.)

Of course the Stones' American label, London, would have to get in on the act at some point, finally pouncing in 1969 when the Stones delivered their chosen image for the "Street Fighting Man" 45, a civil-disturbance scene in which the law, not the rioters, were the street-fighting men. But police brutality has always been a sensitive subject in America. Though the sleeve was printed, London then had second thoughts and the sleeve was hastily withdrawn. It is now considered America's rarest picture sleeve, whether or not there's a record inside.

Neither was that the end to the band's shenanigans. Almost exactly a decade later, in 1978, the Stones' "Beast of Burden" (Rolling Stones 12309) arrived with a possibly saucy shot of a young lady and a lion. The lion is sitting on her, but she doesn't seem to mind. She doesn't seem to be dressed, either. It is all very strange, but the sleeve was withdrawn, just in case. For some reason, the world's loudest prudes always have far filthier minds than the rest of us.

Collecting on the Internet

The Internet has turned the collecting world on its head. From the online presence maintained by brick-and-mortar record stores, which bring a world of new and used releases into your home at the click of a mouse, to the "collection for sale" sites set up by so many individuals, the World Wide Web has revolutionized the way in which we sell, buy, and research music.

No one area has had so profound an impression, however, as the Internet auction sites. The largest and best-known, eBay, originally started life as a forum for an informal circle of Pez collectors. It slowly gathered momentum and scope as the mid-'90s progressed. Even three years ago, if you wanted to shop for rare or unusual records, you attended a record fair, those vast concourses stuffed with dealers and their wares, where Beatles' butcher covers rubbed shoulders with Electric Light Orchestra cutouts; where Presley promos hung alongside Sex Pistols picture discs; and the smell of old vinyl lingered so tantalizingly in the air that you knew that soon, very soon, you'd stumble upon that elusive stock copy of TV Smith's Explorers' *Last Words* debut album.

Of course, there were already mumblings of disquiet. The muttered grumbling of dealers bemoaning the poor attendance, the lack of sales, and the seemingly insatiable need of every customer to come across the greatest bargain in record-collecting history ("Great! *TV Guide Presents Elvis* and it's only 50 cents!"). These experiences were as much a part of record fairs as the apparently endless rows of *Saturday Night Fever* that fill every soundtrack rack and seem to be propping up half the tables as well.

But slowly, around 1998, there were heard the first sounds of an answering grumble, one that—were one to be so gauche as to eavesdrop on other peoples' private conversations—seemed to offer an alternative to all the weary thumbing through endless LPs, the sight-searing scanning of countless CDs, the back-breaking stoop over the $1 singles: "I'm probably not going to be doing fairs anymore. I do much better on eBay."

And back at home, late that night, you'd type the appropriate URL into your browser window, half convinced that it probably wasn't anyplace you'd ever end up visiting again; half repressing the guilty belief that you were somehow betraying all the principles that had sustained your hobby for as long as you remembered. And dimly aware, through all of that, that your collecting life was never going to be the same again.

Let us make one thing clear. Neither eBay nor any other Internet auction site is any alternative whatsoever to attending a fair or entering a store; there is no substitute for interacting with a dealer, and his or her customers and stock. No matter how accurate a cyber-description appears to be, no matter how generous an online seller's return policy is, and no matter how pristine the record looks in the scan, there are still a hundred other issues that you won't have answered until the system finally spits your purchase into your mailbox.

But, for every brick-and-mortar dealer you visit, and for every amazing find (or even passing fancy) you return home with, there are a dozen more occasions when an entire day of sore thumbs, blurred vision, and aching spines turns up nothing more than a couple of 8-Tracks you grabbed on the way out, simply so you wouldn't leave empty-handed, and the nagging certainty that the day could have been somewhat more profitably spent watching paint dry. Or, seated at the computer with a harry in your hand (seasoned Ray Davies fans will understand), scrolling through MUSIC>PRINTED-RECORDED>RECORDS>CLASSIC ROCK> in search of a clean mono copy of the Kinks's *Something Else*. Because you've never managed to find one at any conventional fair you've ever been to.

The Internet auction's capacity for producing some astonishing items has yet to be documented on anything more than a casual level. There is no single source dedicated to tracking and recording the trends that have erupted since the first sites emerged during the late '90s, no place where one can turn to ascertain whether the astonishing $200 bid for a mid-'70s Moody Blues vinyl bootleg in 1999 was a one-off aberration or indicative of a major market surge, whether the paltry $20 received for an unknown Venezuelan pressing of the little-known second Hotlegs *LP Songs* has brought further copies to light, or driven them deeper underground.

Many traditional collectors and dealers choose to regard unusually high auction results as one-offs, with prices driven to extremes either by two equally determined fanatics (or hoaxers), or by the simple thrill of the auction. Poor results, on the other hand, are evidence that the majority of Internet users are mere hoarders who know nothing about the "true worth" of rare records, or even as proof that computers have not penetrated our world as deeply as the cheerleaders reckon. The truth, however, is somewhere in between each of these views.

In fact, a successful Internet auction, for buyers and sellers alike, is dependent on a number of criteria. **Demand:** From a seller's point of view, the most crucial point in any sale, whether conducted online or on Main Street is—does anybody actually want the thing? In the early days of Internet auctions, many people regarded them as a forum in which any piece of household junk could find a willing buyer, and they were often proved correct.

As more people have become sellers, with the corresponding influx of increasingly interesting material, that mentality has faded somewhat, and Internet auctions have instead seen a massive influx of hitherto unknown or rare material appear on the open market. Attics are cleaned, storerooms are emptied, and thrift stores, once the number one repository for untapped treasures of all descriptions, are swept bare of anything that looks even remotely saleable.

With this flood, of course, comes trouble. Not all items considered one-of-a-kind finds by their owners are suddenly revealed as mass-produced trinkets in the cold light of cyber-day. But one of the most frequently heard gripes among professional record dealers involves the hours they spend listing their rarest records at "reasonable," "heavily researched" prices, only to discover that half a dozen know-nothing amateurs have listed the same discs at a fraction of the price. A sale is lost, the market is flooded, and an

LP once cataloged at $100 is frustratingly revealed to be as common as muck.

Before listing any seemingly unusual item, then—or, if you're buying, placing a bid on one—it isn't a bad idea to run a search on the site to see how many (if any) similar items are already on display, and how they are faring. That way, one can also get a good idea of the demand for the item, and figure out if it's even worthwhile trying to compete with other similar listings. Sometimes it can pay to wait until the crowd has dispersed.

Price: This is the area in which most sellers come unglued, be they experienced dealers with a lifetime of buying and selling old records behind them, or impoverished students looking to raise some spare cash for a pizza party.

There are no laws whatsoever. A record can have a catalog value in excess of $100. But if only one person wants to buy it, and that person thinks that $10 is more than a fair offer, then the catalog counts for nothing. Price guides are, as their name should make plain, merely guides to the recommended worth of an item. But they themselves are worthless in a market in which the vast majority of buyers (and many sellers too) have never even heard of such volumes, and probably wouldn't read them if they had. The cold reality is, for sellers, a record is worth the most that they can get; for buyers, it's the minimum they have to pay for it.

The stated opening bid sets the scene. The seller needs to have established a reasonable amount, with the knowledge that, in this forum, "reasonable" does not mean settling for a sum similar to, or in excess of, any catalog or retail value the item might have.

It is an immutable fact of life that the majority of potential purchasers are in search of a bargain, which is why a CD available elsewhere around the country for $15 has more chance of selling in auction for $5, than for $10 plus postage, plus insurance, plus all the other extras that a seller can apply. Indeed, a seller does need to look at these extras too, and either establish a set rate for shipping and handling, or allow the bidder to choose a preferred method. It is surprising how many will opt for a more expensive,

but faster, method of delivery when given an option, yet balk at bidding if confronted with a fait accompli.

If establishing a fair price for an item is a minefield for sellers, it can be just as traumatic for buyers. Again, there are no rules—value is set by demand alone, and if you're going head-to-head with a rival bidder for whom money is no object, there are just two possible outcomes: One of you will win the item for a stratospheric price, and the other will get the (admittedly reprehensible and utterly unsporting) satisfaction of having pushed the winner there. The one who misses this listing can then sit back and wait for another copy to come along on the site. It's surprising how many things do.

The vast majority of Internet auction sales are completed with just one bidder, a statistic further buoyed by the proliferation of "Buy It Now" offers, offers in which an item is listed with both an opening bid price and a firm selling price.

With this provision, however, there are several points worth bearing in mind. First, the temptation can be great to simply purchase an item on the spot, without either the delay of waiting till the auction's end or the fear of losing out to another bidder. Against that, however, one must balance the possibility that there will be no other bidder and that an item one could have purchased for $5 is now going to cost $25.

Nobody can counsel you on this area. Many items do not even receive an opening bid until minutes before the auction is due to an end, as potential purchasers hold fire for fear of igniting some kind of bidding war; many more items that hold a single bid for days will then skyrocket at the end as the "snipers"—last-minute bidders with hair-trigger mousing fingers—move in on their prey. The safest rule of thumb, if you want an item badly enough and feel the stated asking price is reasonable, is to just go for it. You may see other copies at cheaper prices in the future, but by then you'll be looking for something else. A bird in the hand is not a bad thing to have.

The final point to be aware of involves international buying. The Internet is a global marketplace, with prices quoted in what may seem a bewildering variety of currencies. Most sites do utilize software that translates these into local currency, so one always knows precisely how much one is bidding for an item.

Remember, however, to factor in delivery and any applicable customs charges. When purchasing CDs from abroad, it should be no problem for the seller, if requested, to remove the discs and their artwork from the jewel cases (which account for some two-thirds of a CD's total weight, and therefore, its mailing cost). Ask an international seller to wrap your CD in tissue or bubble-wrap before mailing. Vinyl discs, particularly LPs, do not offer this same luxury, however, and can prove extremely expensive to mail. Especially when bidding on bulk lots, always take a moment to visualize how big and how heavy the stack will be. You can e-mail the seller to request a postage estimate before the auction's end; alternately, many foreign postal administrations now offer international rate tables on their Web sites. Either way, make sure you know what you're letting yourself in for.

Customs fees, assessed when a package crosses an international border, are another matter entirely. One person may go an entire lifetime without ever being hit with duty charges; another may be billed every time he or she receives a package from abroad. Like death and taxes, customs charges are a fact of life. Expect the worst and you'll never be disappointed.

Description/Condition: For both seller and buyer, an item's description is crucial, especially if an illustration is either not present or leaves room for doubt on the viewer's part. "Rare Genesis 45 on London" might make for an eye-catching headline, but that is all it is. Titles and catalog numbers are vital; concise, but detailed grading is essential. Are there any visible faults, either to the record or, if applicable, to its packaging? Are there any all-but-invisible ones? Has the record been played? If so, how did it sound the last time it was listened to? "Slightly warped with some scratches but plays great" might satisfy some bidders, but what if the seller's definition of "great" or "slightly" is more lenient than yours?

Nobody is suggesting (although some buyers might expect) that a seller sit down and patiently play through every record, tape, and CD that he or she is listing, noting every audible pop, click, and crackle. However, outside of manufacturing and mastering errors, few audible faults are utterly invisible to the naked eye, and careful grading will identify almost all of them.

Most sellers will happily answer questions about the items they are selling; they will be happier still if both the questions and the subject are clearly delineated in the e-mail. Simply typing "What are the songs?" is *not* acceptable. Many sellers list more than one item at a time; always make sure you name the item you are inquiring about. Similarly, many sellers do conduct personal lives in between waiting expectantly for your life-and-death queries, so always try to keep your requests reasonable.

Asking for a track listing on an LP or CD is straightforward enough and should not inconvenience anybody, though a faster way of procuring that information would be to get the details yourself by visiting one of the multitude of online retailers whose Web sites list track information for albums.

If requesting more specialized information, tailor your question so that it involves the least amount of work and/or time on the seller's part. If there are two pressings of a certain album and you want to ensure you are bidding on the right one, better to ask "Does it contain this song/credit/variation?" than to demand a full accounting of every feature of the disc. And if you have specific concerns about the state of the item, voice them.

Conditions: Many sellers will impose conditions upon their auctions, lengthy lists of do's and don'ts that might weed out any possible time-wasters but can also have the effect of discouraging honest bidders.

A refusal to sell to bidders with fewer than a specified number of "feedbacks" (successfully completed auctions, as detailed on the Web site by other buyers and sellers) might seem a sound way of protecting oneself from newly enrolled idiots who have no intention whatsoever of paying. But don't forget that every single person on the site was, at one point, a beginner without a feedback to his or her name. Yourself included.

Also frowned upon are those sellers who threaten dire retribution if what might otherwise be construed as reasonable terms are not met. Posting negative feedback, for example, should be treated as a last resort in a genuinely problematic case, not an immediate punishment for the mail's arriving late. Remember, most bidders are as anxious to receive their item as you are to bank their payment. Treat them with the same respect you would expect them to extend to you. (For an outline of reasonable terms see **Concluding the Auction** below.)

Locating Items: The next factor to consider is visibility. Although most auction sites do offer subcategories within each subject, into which items can be placed, potential buyers may find it easiest to simply do a general search within the overall category for an artist's name or for the title of a desired song or album, since not every seller will be aware of the precise place in which any given record belongs.

Successfully narrowing searches down within given fields is, unfortunately, an effort in which trial and error alone can assist you. Searching, say, for "the Beatles" will bring up thousands upon thousands of items; you need to specify the kind of Beatles items you require. Searching for "Scott Walker" will present you with far more baseball memorabilia than musical items. Seeking out "10cc" will bring up an awful lot of syringes. Again, you need to specify, either by item or category.

Concluding the Auction: Death, dismemberment, or similar crisis excepted, there is no defense for a high bidder failing to complete an auction. You bid, you win, you pay. It's as simple as that.

The ideal conclusion is equally clear-cut. At the auction's end, the seller should contact the high bidder(s) with clear payment instructions, including postage charges, his or her address, and any other applicable information. Payment should be dispatched with the same immediacy, with the bidder also dropping the seller an e-mail, to reassure the seller that payment is on its way. Many sellers request payment within ten to 14 days, but even if they do not, a conscientious buyer will always attempt to work within that time frame, or at least inform the seller if payment will arrive later.

Similarly, sellers should always dispatch items as soon as possible after receipt of payment. This may (and, indeed, should) include a waiting period while checks clear, but the seller who takes a month to mail out items that have been paid for is as reprehensible as the buyer who takes as long to send in payment—more so, in fact, because the sloppiest sellers are often the ones whose auctions are governed by the most stringent and unfriendly regulations.

All of which, looking back at these pages, seems to involve an awful lot of fuss for what should be a simple and enjoyable transaction between two individuals. And probably, some of the fuss results from being overly cautious. Seasoned Internet auctioneers, bidders, and sellers will develop a set of practices that work for them, and when all is said and done, that's all that really matters. Internet auctions are unique to our age. Enjoy them.

Part Two: Collections and Collectibles

Introduction

There are as many ways to collect as there are collectors to find new ways. Just as nobody can tell you what you should be collecting, nobody can tell you what you shouldn't. This section is devoted to that freedom.

Arranged alphabetically, the bulk of the entries center on the myriad different formats in which we, the consumers, have been offered our music over the years. From 78s to CDs, from uncluttered mono to quadraphonic sound, the music industry has never ceased offering up new and improved ways of hearing and storing the songs we love—and each of those ways has its die-hard adherents.

The stories told, however, are not simply dry dissertations on the history, development, and where appropriate, the quiet discontinuation of these formats. Each entry digs deeply into the collecting lore that surrounds its subject, to unearth the releases that collectors are most commonly searching for, and to find out what makes them so special.

Why is Pink Floyd's *Animals* such an in-demand 8-Track? What is so special about the mono version of *Trini Lopez at PJ's*—or the quadraphonic pressing of Black Sabbath's *Paranoid?* Why is a UK export pressing of the Beatles' *Something New* album worth a hundred times more than an American edition? And what on earth is a Pocket Rocker?

Even if you don't collect, say, Mini-8s, the information within will, hopefully, help you with the formats you do collect.

A Brief History of Recorded Sound

As explained earlier in this book, record collecting has never been restricted to simply collecting records. Cassettes, cartridges, cylinders, reels, CDs, and more are all embraced under that single heading, to become legitimate and popular pursuits in their own right, and to spawn ever more exclusive fields of specialization.

Because this book is primarily concerned with the modern collecting industry—that is, the so-called

rock 'n' roll era that commenced in the mid-'50s, little consideration is given to those formats that were already en route to the Ark when Bill Haley first rocked around the clock. However, with the year 2002 already bookmarked as the 125th anniversary of the invention of Thomas Alva Edison's first phonograph, interest in these earlier formats is rising, with prices escalating likewise. Plus, a quick glimpse at where we came from might help us understand where we're going.

The earliest records, as we would now term them, were metal cylinders, developed from earlier experiments with thin foil and other media, and conducted not only by Edison, but by a host of other sound pioneers—Emile Berliner, Chichester Bell and his cousin Alexander Graham Bell, Charles Sumner Tainter, the Frenchmen Charles Cros and Leon Scott, and others. It was Chichester Bell and Tainter whose patents were sold in 1887 to what became the world's first commercial record manufacturer, the American Graphophone Company, who in turn launched the Columbia Phonograph Company in 1889. Merchandising rights were then leased to the North American Phonograph Company, under whose aegis the first commercial records were produced sometime before 1893 (the year in which the company folded).

The market for these contraptions was understandably limited. A handful of coin-in-the-slot machines, the forerunners of the jukebox, were installed in various public gathering places; most would-be listeners, however, received their first exposure to the medium via traveling showmen, who would charge people five cents to listen to a cylinder via a nest of listening tubes connected to the player. The success of these showmen is an indication of precisely how exciting and novel this newfangled device was.

Refinements and improvements in records, players, and markets continued to be made throughout the 1890s, the most important innovation being Emile Berliner's invention of the flat gramophone disc. Originally pressing his discs on celluloid and rubber-based compounds, Berliner finally switched to shellac in 1894, after noting how the same material had revolutionized telephone manufacturing (phones too were once made from hard rubber).

Revolving at 78 revolutions per minute (rpm), Berliner's earliest discs were seven inches across; by the turn of the century, this had increased to ten and even 12 inches. With very few subsequent improvements, this would become the principal format for recorded sound for the next half century. It would also, even in its infancy, prove astonishingly versatile.

History recalls the first "true" recording to be Edison's experimental reciting of "Mary Had a Little Lamb," then draws a long, thick curtain over the next few decades' proceedings. In fact, one might be surprised at the wide range of recordings that were available as early as 1895—a catalog published by Berliner's United States Gramophone Company that January advertised close to 100 "plates" (as the medium was then called), "with between 25 and 50 New Pieces [expected to] be added every month."

Included were selections of band music ("Dude's March," "The Star-Spangled Banner," Mendelssohn's "Wedding March"); vocal pieces ("When Summer Comes Again," "Old Kentucky Home," "The Maiden and the Lamb," "The Coon That Got the Shake"); opera; light classical pieces; solo instrumentals (cornet, drum and fife, trombone); pieces dubbed "Indian Songs"; Hebrew melodies; and even animal sounds.

Despite the vast strides being made in developing and perfecting the medium, the very notion of the gramophone recording spent much of the early 20th century battling to prove its viability. Broadcasting, in particular, regarded prerecorded music as an absolutely unnecessary addition to an already oversubscribed market; radio, at that time, relied largely on live entertainers for its content and did much to convince its audience that it was simply a waste of money to purchase prerecorded, or "canned" music.

In Britain, the hostility went even further, as the all-powerful Musicians Union introduced the policy of "needle time," by which broadcasters were forced to compensate union members for lost income for every minute devoted to prerecorded music. It was an unpopular regulation, but one that persisted until the early '80s, and it is ironic that rules which were once regarded as the bane of every music lover would ultimately spawn one of the most popular institutions in both British broadcasting and record collecting: live recordings made in radio studios.

To avoid violating needle-time regulations, the BBC (until 1973, the only authorized radio broadcaster in the country) invited popular artists into the studio to record live "session" versions of their hits, to be broadcast instead of their records. The earliest of these sessions dates back to the BBC's very birth, in 1923; however, those recorded from the early '60s on are the most famous, featuring as they do virtually every noteworthy British band of the age.

Many of these sessions have since been released on record or CD, both officially and on bootleg recordings, and they represent some of the most commercially successful archive releases of all time. A collection of the Beatles' 1963–65 broadcasts, *Live at the BBC* (Apple 31796), sold over 4 million copies in the US following its 1994 release. Other BBC session releases from the Kinks, the Yardbirds, the Small Faces, Led Zeppelin, Queen, David Bowie, and dozens more have also proven extremely popular.

All of this was far off in the future, of course, as the gramophone industry entered its fifth decade in the late '20s, still utterly uncertain of its ability to survive.

Broadcasters were not its only foe. The medium itself was still primitive, with the quality of most sound recordings little better than tinny echoes. Attempts to improve the fidelity preoccupied the backroom boys, but even the genius Edison was unable to break through the quality barrier. The early '20s saw him launch a new form of gramophone recording, the Edison disc, which claimed to offer "true representations of vocal and instrumental music as produced by living artists. They are not mere shadows. They are the very substance of the living music, alive with all the emotions of the living artist."

Compared to other discs of the day, Edison records did sound good. But improvement came at a price. Pressed on quarter-inch thick discs, they were both recorded and manufactured to wholly different specifications than were the shellac 78s, and required the use of a special Edison phonograph—attempts to play Edison discs on regular 78 players not only damaged the discs, but could also harm the player.

Record players capable of adapting to both a regular 78 and an Edison disc's special characteristics were manufactured, but—like the records themselves—they were expensive and never took off. The last Edison records were manufactured in 1929, coincidentally the same year that the recording industry received another major blow, this one from opera star Arturo Toscanini. He stated firmly that he would never allow his voice to be captured on a gramophone recording, because the technology was simply incapable of doing justice to his art. It would be 1936 before he finally relented, and his first recordings that same year inevitably became massive sellers. At last, the industry was coming to life.

The so-called jukebox sensation of the post-Depression era provided another powerful tonic. In 1938, more than 13 million records were sold to US jukebox stockists alone, and buoyed by these successes, the industry learned to market itself. The big-band craze of the late '30s, and the bobby-soxer explosion of the early '40s, might have been fired by musicians and live performances, but behind them the record companies were stoking the boilers furiously.

August 1942 brought all activity to a shuddering halt. In that month, with the US now at war, the American Federation of Musicians passed a resolution agreeing to stop recording any music that did not contribute directly to the war effort. In addition, there was a shortage of the very lifeblood of the industry: shellac. For two years, scarcely any new records were manufactured and released in the US.

Normalcy began returning in 1944, and by war's end the following year, it was as though the hiatus had never happened. However, hardly had the dust settled on an international conflagration than the music industry itself was riven by its own bloody battle, as Columbia and RCA Victor, the two mightiest powers in the business, went head-to-head in what has become known as the War of the Speeds.

For years, attempts had been made to increase the amount of playing time available on a record. The standard speed of 78 rpm, however, seemed inviolate, and with it, a maximum playing time of no more than five minutes per side. This was not so terrible for popular songs and dance music. But an hour-long symphony needed to be broken across 12 sides of six separate discs (packaged in bound "albums"), and a three-hour opera required a wheelbarrow simply to transport it.

In 1948, Columbia Records perfected long-playing (LP) 33$\frac{1}{3}$ rpm "microgroove" records, capable of playing up to 20 minutes a side; the company also came up with a new style of record player designed to play the new speed. It was a staggering innovation that the company knew could change the face of the recording industry forever. Yet when it offered the technology to RCA Victor, with the suggestion that the two giants join forces to market it, RCA chief David Sarnoff instead flew into a fury, demanding that his technicians come up with a format that was even better.

The result, unveiled the following spring, was the 45 rpm disc (and its own, correspondingly calibrated, automatic record player). Little better in terms of playing time than the 78, these 45s were superior in that their "unbreakable" vinyl construction allowed them to be stacked on top of one another on the record player, each disc falling into place as the previous one finished. To add further fuel to the coming conflict, neither the Columbia nor the RCA record players were compatible with one another. Anybody purchasing both LPs and 45s required two separate players to listen to them on—and a third, of course, for 78s.

The formats did battle head-to-head, Columbia marketing full-length LPs that allowed the listener uninterrupted listening, and RCA sticking with the old style "album" presentation, trusting automation to keep the listener happy. Of course the LP won, but by that time, RCA had already figured out that 45s were best targeted toward the hit parade. In 1951, RCA and Columbia agreed to accept that each invention had its own unimpeachable place in the market and began manufacturing and marketing both kinds of records. Multispeed record players followed, and with the rest of the industry falling in line behind the two new speeds, the day of the 78 was nearing its end.

The last commercially available 78s were produced in the US during the late '50s, with Britain following suit shortly after; 1958 was the last year in which 78s outsold other formats in the US. By 1963, 78s were no longer in production anywhere in the Western world, though they hung on elsewhere, and the last days of the format did give the modern record-collecting hobby some of its most magnificent—and deliciously anachronistic—collectibles, from EMI's India subsidiary. Beatles singles were still appearing as 78s as late as 1965.

The late '40s also saw magnetic tape recording emerge from the shadows of various laboratories, where its potential had been gathering pace since the late '20s. Germany was in the forefront of the research, with the BASF corporation perfecting tape capable of reproducing the frequency range of gramophone records, as early as 1938.

World War II saw the research come to an end. The technology survived, however, and peace saw it accompany so many other pioneering German inventions (rocket science included) to the US, where the Ampex and 3M (Minnesota Mining and Manufacturing) companies continued its development.

Much as Toscanini had given the traditional recording industry a major shot in the arm when he embraced its technologies in 1936, so Bing Crosby brought magnetic tape to prominence in 1948, when he declared the 3M-Ampex products to be infinitely superior to any of the direct-to-disc methods employed elsewhere. He began recording all his music onto magnetic tape—of course, others followed, and by the early '50s, tape was not only the primary medium for recording, it was also being marketed for reproduction too, in the form of reel-to-reel tapes.

It is impossible to calculate all the advantages that magnetic tape brought to the recording process, but paramount among them is surely the development of stereophonic sound, hitherto an impossible dream. Overnight, tape revolutionized the capabilities of the recording studio. Interestingly, however, although stereo found a ready market among audio enthusiasts, the overall public response was initially so lukewarm that even record companies who did invest in the required equipment continued to release the majority of their records in mono only (stereo mixes from the format's infancy are still being discovered today).

Through the early-to-mid-'60s, stereo grew in importance, aided not only by the sometimes miraculous strides being taken elsewhere in the recording industry—many of the sonic effects we take for granted today were startlingly novel when first heard in the mid-'60s—but also by the development of a new rival to records, the all-American 4-Track and 8-Track cartridge tapes, and—from the European labs of Philips—the cassette.

Introduced just a couple of years apart, the cartridges immediately fell into competition for the lucrative in-car entertainment market, while the cassette ambitiously targeted everything in sight. All three were designed with stereo reproduction firmly in mind. (Half a decade later, when quadraphonic sound first became a reality, it, too, was pioneered by the 8-Track, with the first commercially available Quad-8 cartridges appearing a full year before equivalent LP pressings.)

The cartridge formats offered little in the way of improved audio reproduction. It was their portability that sold them, with the first in-car sound systems appearing as early as 1964. No matter what faults the format was heir to, its ready absorption into the American art of motorvating ensured its immediate success. Cassettes took off more slowly, suffering initially from poor sound and spasmodic performance. But with the arrival of the Dolby Noise Reduction System in 1969, they, too, moved into prominence, not only consigning cartridges to the junk heap, but moving in on vinyl as well. By the late '70s, the two formats were neck and neck in the marketplace.

Their joint reign was to be short. In 1982, the first digital compact discs (CDs) made their debut; by

1987, both LPs and 45s were well en route to being phased out by every major record company in the US and Europe, to be replaced by the CD. Cassettes lingered on in the marketplace, but the advent of DAT (Digital Audio Tape) in 1987 spelled a similar end to magnetic recording tape in the professional sphere. By 1992, some 80 percent of recording studios in the US had converted to DAT recording, and the race was on to draw the public to the format as well.

A decade later, and that battle, at least, seems to have been lost. Sony's Mini Disc (MD) and Philips's Digital Compact Cassettes (DCC) were introduced during 1993–94, both offering digital playback and recording possibilities—DCC even had the advantage of being compatible with cassettes, at least in playback mode. Within a year, however, DCC had fallen by the wayside, to be joined by MD, around the same time as computer technology introduced the first recordable compact discs (CD-Rs), offering all the advantages of MD but without the need for another total upgrade of one's hi-fi system.

At the time of this writing (early 2002), the hottest names on the audio front appear to be Panasonic's DVD-Audio (DVD-A) and Sony/Philips's Super Audio Disc formats, both repeating the old CD mantra of "best possible sound" in yet another attempt to persuade us to rebuild our collections once again.

Time alone will tell whether or not people will accept these new arrivals, though experience somewhat gloatingly points out that the most successful formats in recording history so far—the 78, the long-playing record, the cassette, and the CD—have been those that offer the consumer something more than improved fidelity. Easier storage, longer playing time, nearly weightless portability, uninterrupted listening experiences—these are the points that matter. "Better sound" really doesn't cut it. If it did, we'd all be sitting around listening to quadraphonic Edison records, and making mixtapes on a reel-to-reel.

Acetates—The Rock Star's Rough Draft

Acetates are a relic of the days before cassettes, DAT, and recordable CDs came into widespread use in recording studios. Manufactured from aluminum, and coated in a thin sheet of vinyl, they were produced to allow the concerned parties to hear how a particular version of a recording would sound outside the studio, on their home hi-fi, for example.

Manufactured on very basic disc-cutting machines, most acetates exist in extremely limited quantities—sometimes no more than one or two copies would be produced, and when they are found on the open market, they often bear no identifying marks whatsoever. Most studios utilized a blank label, adorned with the studio's name and address at most; it was up to the disc's recipient whether the artist or song title was then scribbled on by hand.

Neither were acetates "built to last." The vinyl coating is so thin that even three or four plays will cut through it, while the aluminum is susceptible to problems of its own. A pale greenish mold can grow on the playing surface with surprising rapidity.

For these reasons, many of the acetates on the market today are irreparably damaged, and consequently, few collectors give them serious attention. Yet the field also represents one of the most fruitful hunting grounds around, the source of some unimaginable treasures—financial and musical.

Many acetates contain music that is otherwise unavailable in any form. For every band that actually gets a record out, there are many, many more who book a studio under their own steam, record their music, collect the acetates, and are never heard of again. Even among those who do go on to great things, their closets might still overflow with the acetate reminders of long-forgotten sessions, undertaken in their distant youths.

In 1958, a young band from Liverpool, England, named the Quarrymen, recorded two songs, "That'll Be the Day" and "In Spite of All the Danger," at a small studio operated by one Percy "P.F." Philips, from his living room at 38 Kensington, Liverpool, L7. Just one 10-inch 78 rpm acetate was produced—it was all the band members could afford—and, for more than 20 years, it lay all but forgotten in piano player Duff Lowe's personal collection.

In 1981, he rediscovered it and offered it for auction at Sotheby's. Three of his fellow Quarrymen, after all, had indeed gone on to greater things—John Lennon, Paul McCartney, and George Harrison later became three of the Beatles. If nothing else, this scratchy representation of their earliest strivings was a unique conversation piece. The auction never occurred. Shortly before the sale was scheduled, McCartney himself stepped in with a private bid that Lowe accepted. Since that time, both songs the group recorded have been released to the public, on the Beatles' own *Anthology* box set. The acetate itself, however, remains under McCartney's lock and key.

The Quarrymen acetate is certainly the best known acetate in the world today. The question that haunts many acetate collectors, however, is how many similar items are out there that no one knows about?

In 1988, a three-track EMI studios acetate—bearing a standard Emidisc label, with its contents handwritten below the center hole—went on the block at Phillips auction house in London. Who would have known, without the catalog's guidance, that "Soon Forgotten," "Close Together," and "You Can't Judge a Book" represented the first-ever recordings by the embryonic Rolling Stones? So embryonic was the group that it had not even obtained drummer Charlie Watts and bassist Bill Wyman.

Acetates are not confined, however, to a group's first strivings. The Beatles, for example, produced acetates for almost every stage of their album *Sgt. Pepper's Lonely Hearts Club Band*, meaning discs were pressed for every mixdown of every song; the Beatles were not alone in their practice. Many artists, at the end of a recording session, would have an acetate or two pressed up to listen to at home. Some would then return to the studio to try the song again; others would agree that they'd finally got it right.

Either way, acetates represent a key moment in the recording process and are both treasured and valued accordingly. The Beatles and the Stones, of course, are among the select handful of acts whose acetates fetch high prices, no matter what the contents—even discs that offer no variation whatsoever from the released version of a song may fetch three-figure

sums. The Who, Bruce Springsteen, Queen, Bob Dylan, David Bowie, Elvis Presley, and Led Zeppelin rank among the other acts whose collecting profile is high enough to rate similar valuations. However, acetates by lesser-name acts can bring a decent price, and even unknown, or unidentified, acetates should not be passed over if the price is right.

Acetates were not only produced for individual songs. Entire albums would be pressed in this form, to allow listeners to contemplate such issues as running order, and again, these can be highly prized— especially if the album itself was then never released, or more commonly, was released with songs rearranged and/or replaced. (Acetate pressings should not, incidentally, be confused with factory samples, known as test pressings. These are very different items, manufactured under very different circumstances.)

Legendary indeed is the acetate pressing for what became the Rolling Stones' *Get Yer Ya-Ya's Out!* album, in 1970. In its original form, it was envisioned as a double album, with one disc—rejected by the Stones' label of the time, Decca—given over to the support acts, B.B. King and the Ike and Tina Turner Revue; the other disc, while generally adhering to the familiar released version of the LP, offered raw and unedited performances that would be markedly cleaned up for release. Manufactured at the Apple studios, and bearing that company's familiar label (notated *Get Your Yah Yah's Out*), this fabulous item was auctioned in late 1985 at Christie's, in London, where it sold for around $900.

Recording studios are not alone in cutting acetates. One of the most highly prized of all Beatles artifacts is a two-song acetate of "Kansas City" and "Some Other Guy," cut by the Granada TV company from the audio track for the *Look Now* TV special on the Cavern Club in Liverpool, shot in August 1962, before the Beatles even had a record deal.

It was even possible for the general public to cut acetates of their own, from the "Record Your Own Voice" machines that used to lurk around railroad stations, department stores, and record shops across the US and Europe. Both Elvis Presley (at Sun Studios in Memphis) and Cliff Richard (at the HMV Records store in London) made their recorded debuts in this fashion.

So, do you want to devote your life to collecting acetates? Only if you own an endless supply of needles for your record player, and infinite patience for a lot of dreadful music. On more casual hunts, you have little to lose. The chances of stumbling upon a hitherto unrecognized gem are probably good enough; the chances of finding at least a recognizable song or artist aren't too remote either. And someone has to locate the rarities we read about.

A word of warning, however. When purchasing acetates, do not make any attempt to clean the disc, beyond a light swipe with a moist cloth, being careful not to allow moisture to gather on the playing surface. It is also advisable to play an acetate just once, making a tape reference copy as you do so. No matter how clean and well cared for an acetate may look, every listen takes a huge bite out of its playable life, and no matter what a disc's worth may have been the day you found it, it's going to be an awful lot less after a couple more listens.

Bootlegs—Beauties or the Beast?

Take a poll of any sizeable grouping of serious music fans, and few issues raise so many emotions as bootlegging, the art of acquiring unreleased live or studio material by whichever band takes your fancy, and making it available to a fanatical underground of collectors, fans, and anal-retentives.

Legally, morally, and ethically, the subject is unquestionably the most inflammatory issue in the hobby, with even supporters of bootlegging divided over where the advantages end and the problems begin. No less an authority than the *New York Times* once described bootleggers as "cultural heroes," for liberating music that, under normal circumstances, might never have been heard. Today, it is more likely to report on their being sent to prison for the unpardonable crime of copyright infringement.

The fact is, however, that bootlegs exist and they are collected. Whether a person cares to indulge in this forbidden fruit is entirely his or her own decision.

The popular history of bootlegs dates back to the mid-'50s and the advent of the first generally available reel-to-reel tape recorders. Live recordings of blues, jazz, and opera performances were the staples of the field, with both tapes and limited-edition vinyl pressings (often 7-inch 45s) circulating in an underground that was small, but astonishingly fertile.

Even before that, however, privileged enthusiasts were able to make recordings of live events. As far back as 1901, a Mr. Mapleson, the librarian at the Metropolitan Opera in New York, was using a cylinder recorder provided by inventor Thomas Edison to capture snatches of performances on the opera stage. None of the recordings were more than a few minutes in length, but still they offer a unique documentary of their subjects, one that a regular record company would never have deemed worthy of preserving. It is this historical record-keeping that, in many collectors' eyes, justifies the existence of bootlegs.

Bootlegging entered rock and pop music in 1969, with the release of Bob Dylan's *The Great White Wonder*. A two-LP set, it compiled hitherto unreleased material from three basic sources—a tape of home recordings that Dylan made in Minneapolis in 1961; a smattering of studio outtakes which had themselves leaked into the collectors market over the years; and an acetate circulated in 1967 by Dylan's music publishers, soliciting cover versions of material that Dylan himself had apparently abandoned. (Hit versions of "This Wheel's on Fire," "The Mighty Quinn," and so on were developed from this tape.)

Popularly known as *The Basement Tapes* (because they were recorded in one), these recordings were frequently aired on radio and were inevitably recorded by fans and collectors. Less inevitably—simply because, to reiterate the fact, it had never happened before—somebody pressed these recordings on vinyl and marketed the result.

Response was immediate. Private tape (primarily reel-to-reel) collectors had long existed in rock circles, trading among themselves as new material somehow slipped out of record company vaults or concert halls, but rarely making waves beyond their own immediate circle. *The Great White Wonder,* on the other hand, seemed miraculously available to anybody who wanted it. Reviews and features discussing the album appeared as far afield as *Rolling Stone* and the *Wall Street Journal;* radio aired its contents with impunity. The legality of the issue was of no apparent concern—it was the music that mattered.

By the standards of many subsequent bootlegs, *Great White Wonder* was a primitive offering. The discs bore blank labels, the sleeve itself was a plain white gatefold with the title *GWW* hand-stamped on it. No more than 2,000 copies of this original issue made it out; within weeks, however, other enterprising entrepreneurs had stepped in to duplicate it—bootlegging a bootleg—and, though Dylan's record label, Columbia, moved swiftly to stop whichever manufacturers they could locate, the genie was out of the bottle.

A second Dylan bootleg, *Flower* (so named for the hand-drawn picture on each sleeve), brought further *Basement Tapes* into circulation. A third, *Troubled Troubadour,* unveiled even more. It would be as late as 1971 before the entire original *The Basement Tapes* acetate was compiled onto one disc, *Waters of Oblivion;* in the meantime, however, the songs just kept trickling out.

Radio, meanwhile, had moved on to another exclusive clutch of songs. In 1969, while the Beatles argued amongst themselves regarding the final form of their next (and final) LP, *Let It Be,* test-pressing copies of its provisional contents were made by producer George Martin for circulation among sundry interested parties. At least one of these somehow made its way onto American radio, where it was played in its entirety—and appeared on the streets just weeks later as the bootleg *Get Back and 12 Other Songs.*

Produced and sequenced by George Martin in the period before Phil Spector was invited in to sprinkle his magic over the proceedings, *Get Back and 12 Other Songs* would subsequently become one of the highest selling bootlegs of all time, and is certainly one of the best known. Neither did the arrival of the next "real" Beatles album a few months after *Get Back and 12 Other Songs* damage its standing in the slightest. Indeed, if anything, the substantially remixed and rejigged *Let It Be* only increased demand for the original, unbeautified, recordings.

By the end of 1969, bootlegs were firmly established as a serious irritant to the music industry. Bootleggers sometimes used conventional pressing plants that either didn't know or didn't care what they were producing. Sometimes bootleggers reconfigured discarded 78 rpm presses and did the pressing themselves, producing easily identifiable discs, up to twice the thickness of a regular LP.

In late 1969, John Lennon was moved to rush-release a live recording of the first-ever Plastic Ono Band concert, at the Toronto Peace Festival, to quash a bootleg of the same performance. In the new year, both the Rolling Stones (*Get Yer Ya-Ya's Out!*) and the Who (*Live at Leeds*) acted against bootlegs of their own recent tours, the Stones' *LiveR Than You'll Ever Be* and the Who's *Closer to Queen Mary.* Both groups hoped that fans who might otherwise have purchased the bootleg would instead buy the "real thing"—in fact, they probably purchased both. But neither would deny the bootleggers' impact. The Stones sold a million albums and the Who went double platinum with recordings they might never have released without bootlegs to force their hand.

There was a certain pride in being bootlegged, too; admittance into what was—at least in the early days—an exclusive club of superstars whose appeal and audience extended beyond even the most generous record company's boundaries. Bootlegs themselves became legends—when Columbia, in 1974, chose to give an official release to Dylan's *The Basement Tapes,* what better title for the ensuing double album than that which the bootleggers had long since passed into common circulation? And, 25 years later, another fabled Dylan bootleg was not only released under its most commonly employed title, it appeared thus despite the fact that the bootleg's stated source, the Royal Albert Hall concert, was incorrect.

The tape that comprised Dylan's *Live 1966* album had been circulating on bootleg since the early '70s, and immortalized a concert taped in Manchester,

England. The original bootleg, however, relocated the show to London's Royal Albert Hall and the error proved so adhesive that, not only did every subsequent bootleg perpetuate it, but Sony, too, felt obliged to subtitle the official release, *Bootleg Series, Vol. 4: Live 1966*, as *The "Royal Albert Hall Concert"*—*not* to mislead purchasers, but to assure them that they were indeed receiving the same performance they knew and loved from years of bootleg listening. A stronger endorsement of bootlegs and the role they serve in the musical community could scarcely be imagined.

With these examples in mind, it can be argued that, in many ways, bootlegs blackmailed artists and labels into releasing material they might otherwise never have deemed fit for public consumption. Along with the undeniable infringements of copyright and flouting of artistic freedom, this is the most frequently voiced of all cases against bootlegs. However, frequently overlooked in the scramble for ethical sanctuary is the fact that the traffic is not totally one way. Bootleggers profit from bands, but bands profit from bootlegs, and in more important ways than merely financially.

Bootlegs—or, at least, that community of illicit tapers and hoarders who might be described as bootleggers—have unquestionably provided the modern, collector-oriented music industry with any number of now-much-valued recordings, each one effortlessly puncturing the popular record company insistence that bootlegs are low-fidelity, poor quality castoffs that rip off even the most aurally insensitive consumer.

Much of what is now regarded as jazzman Charlie Parker's most important work was only preserved because someone bothered to tape it. Someone who wasn't affiliated with the record company, someone who didn't then blank the tape the moment the next star came along to record.

Many of Hank Williams' classic radio broadcasts were recorded, some might say illegally, and circulated on bootleg long after the original performances were forgotten, and long before anybody decided to seek them out for an official release. By that time, of course, many of the original source tapes had themselves been lost. But bootleg tape and vinyl allowed musical history to be experienced once again.

Elvis Presley's 1961 USS *Missouri* performance is another example of bootlegs' having saved the day. Not including television, this was the only live performance Presley gave between 1957 and 1969, and it exists purely because an onlooker had the presence of mind to record it, illegally, on a reel-to-reel player he brought into the performance.

The recording circulated on bootleg for close to two decades before RCA finally released it officially in 1980, giving Presley buffs a spectacular performance and a milestone event. There is not even room for doubt here; without bootlegs, or at least, bootleggers, this performance would have been lost forever. While RCA could argue that it had no reason whatsoever to record the show (who, after all, could have predicted that Presley would wait so long, and change so dramatically, before his next gig?), that very argument is a justification for the illicit recording of live performances. History is not a matter of hearsay. It needs evidence to back it up. Bootlegs provide that evidence.

There are countless more instances. Jon Astley and Chris Charlesworth, compilers of MCA's universally applauded series of Who remasters, turned on several occasions to the bootleg industry in search of certain rarities, having completely exhausted both official archives and the band members' own collections; and they are not alone.

Purchasers of Van Der Graaf Generator's much-applauded *Boxed* box set in 2000 were treated to early BBC sessions taken from exactly the same less-than-perfect tape source as the *Necromancer* bootleg; while live material from a 1975 show in Rimini, Italy, was lifted directly from a bootleg disc. Again, this is material that, in the first instance, had not survived the passing years in any official archive, and in the second, would never even have existed without somebody undertaking the task illegally.

And perhaps most famously of all, there is the example of the Grateful Dead, who—as documented in the first-ever issue of *Relix* magazine—were once adamantly opposed to people taping their concerts. Today, however, those tapes provide fans with one of the most spectacular (and, via multiple releases overseen by the band itself, profitable) archives in rock history.

Yes, bootleggers do make an unauthorized profit from selling other people's work. But the trade-off is, if they had not recorded that work in the first place (this applies principally to live and occasional on-air performances), or arranged for it to be illicitly borrowed from a record label or radio station vault, it might no longer even exist today.

The 1970s were the golden age of the bootleg. Many of the best-loved boots of all time were produced during this period, together with some of the most successful. The labels Rubber Dubber, Kustom, Phonygraf—and most prominent of all, Trademark of Quality (TMQ or TMOQ) and The Amazing Kornyfone Record Label (TAKRL)—were especially prolific issuers, their wares not only incorporating all the superstars of the era—the Beatles, the Stones, the Doors, Led Zeppelin, Yes, and so forth, but digging deep into the ranks of newcomers, too. And once again, the quality of these releases is borne out by the eventual fate of much of the music contained within.

The Beatles' 1964 and 1965 Los Angeles shows both circulated on illicit vinyl for several years before Capitol finally released them as *At the Hollywood Bowl* in 1977. Deep Purple's *On the Wings of a Russian Foxbat* (TKRWM 1808), featuring the tragically short-lived Tommy Bolin, was reissued wholesale on an authorized disc by the same name. In fact, almost every single release in the official *King Biscuit Flour Hour Live* and *Live at the BBC* series—from the Beatles to Bowie, Led Zeppelin to Julian Cope—existed on bootleg long before the vault was opened to "real" record companies.

Bootlegs also, on occasion, offer a far more authentic view of certain proceedings than official releases ever allow. David Bowie's *His Master's Voice* (TAKRL 1935) featured a recording of a 1974 ABC-TV broadcast of Bowie's final Ziggy Stardust show (recorded the previous year), prior to its remixing for

the movie *Ziggy Stardust: The Motion Picture*. What is especially fascinating about the bootleg is that it includes Bowie's closing "retirement" speech in its entirety, plus an eight-minute "Jean Genie"/"Love Me Do" medley featuring guest guitarist Jeff Beck. Both were absent from the authorized issue.

Genesis's *As Though Emerald City* (TAKRL 1945), excerpted from the 1975 Los Angeles Shrine concert, was released two decades later within the official *Archive 1* box set. Here, again, the bootleg fan receives a more lifelike version of show, via a full and perfectly listenable version of the closing track, "It," which the box set claimed was so damaged that Peter Gabriel's vocal track needed to be re-recorded.

Meanwhile, 10cc's *Going Pink on Purpose* (TAKRL 1958) offered up five live songs excerpted from a King Biscuit broadcast recorded shortly after the group left the UK label for Mercury. What is interesting is that when this same concert was given an official release (by KBFH) two decades later, the entire disc was given over to the UK-era material performed that night. Tracks from the band's Mercury debut, including two of the cuts on the bootleg, were nowhere in sight.

Other classic recordings remain locked in the official archive, but thrive underground regardless. Linda Ronstadt's *Take Two Before Bedtime* (TKRWM 1804) and the Steve Miller Band's *Midnight Toker* (TAKRL 1960) recall sensational live acts whose formidable powers have, perhaps, been overlooked by modern historians; Wings' *Live in Hanover, Germany 1972* (WRMB 500) not only offers an opportunity to experience the deeply underrated early live prowess of Paul McCartney's post-Beatles band, it also serves up a crop of rarely heard and never officially released songs. And Little Feat's Lowell George is widely believed to have mixed the concert tapes that comprised that band's *Electrif Lycanthrope* (TAKRL 1942). Not every bootleg, even from this halcyon age, is actually worth its weight in vinyl. But an awful lot of them are.

During the mid-to-late '70s, when Bruce Springsteen's recording career was tied up by litigation, the singer went out on the road, honing a live

A 1970s-era bootleg collection of the Beatles' BBC sessions.

show that still draws comparisons with the best on the block, and making sure (tacitly if not overtly) that as many people got to hear what he was doing as possible.

Alongside Dylan, Springsteen is the most frequently bootlegged American artist in history (the Beatles and Led Zeppelin take that title among British bands), with the dynamic performance captured on the 1975 *Live at the Bottom Line* (no label or catalog number available) never far from any discussion of the greatest boots of all time. It was also one of the most influential, turning more potential listeners on to his music than any amount of hyperbolic press.

Appreciating this, Springsteen's 1978 American tour saw five entire shows, with over 15 hours of live music, broadcast on American radio with one show famously including the exhortation "Bootleggers, roll your tapes." Another show found the Boss hoping that some distant friends would hear a dedication "through the magic of bootlegging." And when the British *New Musical Express* pinned him down on

the subject, in October 1978, Springsteen's support for bootlegs seemed unequivocal. "Most of the time, they're fans. I've had bootleggers write me saying, 'Listen, we're just fans.' And the kids who buy the bootlegs buy the real records too, so it doesn't really bother me. I think the amount of money made on [bootlegging] isn't very substantial. It's more like a labor of love."

By the end of the decade, he had changed his mind and co-filed a civil suit in a California Federal District Court against two of these "fans," for "infringement of copyrights, unfair competition, unjust enrichment, unauthorized use of name and likeness, and interference with economic advantage." But at least he once understood what drove the bootleg industry on.

Pink Floyd is another band that has at least taken heed of the bootleggers' art. Again, the group's underground catalog features some essential titles: *In Celebration of the Comet: The Coming of Kahoutek*

(TAKRL 1903), preserved the band's 1972 London premiere of the then-unreleased *Dark Side of the Moon. Embryo* (Toasted TRW 1945) featured a stunning 1971 show in San Diego, and most infamous of all, *British Winter Tour 74* (PFL 1701; released in the US as *Raving and Drooling*), arrived so well packaged and recorded that many people thought it really was a new official album from the band. It featured just three tracks: "Raving and Drooling," "Gotta Be Crazy," and "Shine On You Crazy Diamond," all of which were unavailable in any other form—and it sold, according to legend, like the proverbial hotcakes. Indeed, it continued selling even after the third of those tracks turned up a few months later on the Floyd's next studio album, *Wish You Were Here.*

The other two songs, however, were nowhere in sight, and six months later, in an interview with the French *Rock et folk* magazine, Floyd frontman Roger Waters finally bowed to the inevitable. Floyd's bootleg repertoire abounds with the unfulfilled promise of songs in the making, and it would have been very easy for this pair to go the same sad way as "Fingal's Cave," "Oenone," "Baby Blue Shuffle," and "The Embryo." Instead, when asked what he was going to do next, Waters admitted that public demand left him with little choice. "Record 'Gotta Be Crazy' and 'Raving and Drooling,' " he replied. Reworked as "Dogs" and "Sheep," the two songs appeared on the next Floyd album, 1977's *Animals.*

The record companies' take on bootlegs throughout this period was curious. On the one hand, they abhorred the things and worked feverishly to cut the cancer from their midst. The decline in the quantity of bootlegs and operating bootleg manufacturers during the late '70s was, at least partly, the result of increased law enforcement crackdowns. On the other hand, labels were quick to recognize the cachet of outlaw chic that bootlegging could confer upon an artist.

Sony's release of Bob Dylan's *The Basement Tapes* in 1974 is the best-known early example of a bootleg being, effectively, bootlegged by its legal owners (Frank Zappa and Emerson Lake and Palmer later went even further, releasing entire box sets comprising "classic" bootlegs, complete with original cover art and unadorned sound). The mid-'70s, however, saw this process reach magnificent heights, as labels began bootlegging their own artists as well.

Nils Lofgren, Tom Petty, and Graham Parker were all recipients of oxymoronically titled *Official Bootleg* promo releases at the dawn of their careers, as their labels hit upon the admittedly ironic notion of legitimizing an artist by making him appear palatable from an illegitimate angle.

If Nils Lofgren was worth bootlegging, the theory went, he must be worth listening to, and the fact that the limited-edition *Back It Up!! An Authorized Bootleg* (A&M SP 8362) would itself shortly be bootlegged (TAKRL 1999) only proves what an effective idea that was. (The album, one of Lofgren's finest, has since returned to official release schedules as the CD *Bootleg*—Vision VMCD 1007.) Parker's *Live at Marble Arch* (Vertigo GP 1) has likewise since reappeared on several official anthologies, while Petty's one-sided five-track, *Official Live Bootleg* (Shelter 1DJ 24A), has at least leaked out on B-sides and within the *Playback* box set.

History records that the ploy worked from the record companies' point of view—all three artists did indeed succeed. Interestingly, however, none became a star of the bootleg world itself; indeed, with the exceptions of the Sex Pistols, the Cure, Elvis Costello, and Patti Smith, none of the bands thrown up by, or in the chronological vicinity of, the punk and new wave movements ever became stalwarts of the underground industry.

Indeed, by the end of the 1990s, the entire alternative rock era, which history dates back to around 1975, had thrown up a mere handful of acts who could claim entry to the bootlegging hall of fame—Kate Bush, U2, Prince, Stevie Ray Vaughan, Nirvana, Pearl Jam, and Phish, with maybe Radiohead sneaking in under the wire. All of which means that the biggest names in the bootleg world today have remained essentially unchanged since the late 1970s.

That this was so became manifest during the early '90s, when bootleg CDs first began appearing on American streets in serious numbers. This in itself

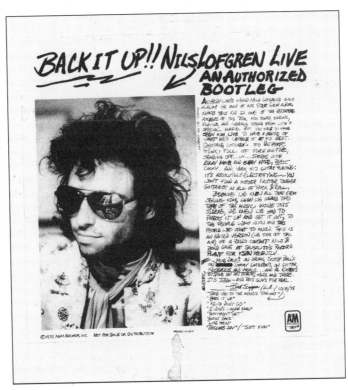

Nils Lofgren's "official" bootleg.

was an unexpected development—as late as 1987, it was a common industry belief that the new format was immune from the scourge of bootlegging, because the manufacturing plants were so tightly controlled. Instead, bootleg CDs were rapidly revealed as even easier to manufacture than vinyl.

Bruce Springsteen was the recipient of the first-ever bootleg CD, the *Castaway* collection of *Born in the USA* outtakes and live cuts, also in 1987. More followed, but the boom really began courtesy of a fascinating loophole in international copyright law. Releases that were deemed strictly illegal in the US suddenly turned out to be perfectly legitimate in a number of leading European and Far Eastern nations, and an industry that had lain moribund for close to a decade suddenly re-emerged with renewed vigor.

The Italian Bulldog label was first out of these newly opened blocks, and by 1993, live CDs featuring virtually every major artist were selling freely across Europe and Asia, and making inroads into the American market as well. Indeed, so confident were these operators of their legal position that the San Marino–based Kiss the Stone label even began taking full-page advertisements in the mainstream American music press, promoting new releases ranging from a broadcast-quality copy of Nirvana's last-ever show in Rome to a string of top-selling Phish titles.

Some fabulous items came to the surface. Long out-of-print vinyl boots were revisited, often via a straightforward transfer from the LP, but sometimes from original source tapes (or from as near the original source as possible). Other discs delved into hitherto uncharted waters, unearthing from who knows where recordings whose existence had never even been suggested. Others still proved that no matter where one stands regarding the commercial and moral rights or wrongs of bootlegging, at the end of the line there sat collectors and enthusiasts who genuinely cared about the music.

Multiple volumes of the Beatles *Ultra Rare Tracks* (Swinging Pig, various catalog numbers) series cut through all the red tape that, even in the aftermath of the official *Anthology* collection, continues to snarl the Fabs' catalog. The series presents an unsurpassed collection of studio, broadcast, and live recordings. Even more specialized studies have, of course, followed, including all but full renderings of every note of music produced during the Beatles' *Get Back/Let It Be* sessions and Dylan's 1966 world tour.

Long lost mono mixes were exhumed, and in the Beatles' and Stones' cases, long-abandoned stereo. Official reissues of both bands' catalogs eschewed the early stereo mixes prepared without the bands' direct supervision; bootlegs restored them to the racks regardless.

Vast sprawling anthologies became commonplace. The Rolling Stones were subject to an eight-CD examination of the sessions for 1967's *Their Satanic Majesties' Request* (Midnight Beat); other classic/legendary albums to be similarly documented (albeit within much smaller packages) include the Beach Boys' unissued *Smile,* Led Zeppelin's *Physical Graffiti,* and Bob Dylan's *Blood on the Tracks.*

The advent of digital recording technology (DAT) allowed for concert recordings to be rendered with unprecedented fidelity—all the more so on those occasions when concerts were simultaneously broadcast either on radio, pay-per-view TV specials, or via an enhanced audio system developed to aid the hard of hearing. The ease with which CDs could be manufactured frequently saw discs of recorded concerts hit the streets within days of the concert. And the most astonishing thing was, it was all completely legal.

Disparate copyright laws have always been with us. Throughout the 19th century and into the first years of the 20th, for instance, American book publishers were under no obligation whatsoever to pay, or even consult, those European authors whose novels were appearing Stateside in such prodigious quantities. So, in the vast majority of cases, they didn't, reducing an entire industry to the level of pirates, and their product—those Victorian and Edwardian-era US editions of Charles Dickens, William Thackeray, and Sir Walter Scott that collectors prize so highly today—to precisely the same status as the Italian CDs of the 1990s.

The same selfish and protectionist policies that ignited that controversy were still at work in the 1980s and 1990s. The difference was, whereas America's refusal to initiate reciprocal copyright agreements with other countries once worked to the Americans' advantage, the boot was now on the other leg. And you could cut the outrage with a tuning fork—or, in this case, a legal brief. Beginning in 1996, the European and Asian loopholes were plugged as tightly as was humanly possible, while a succession of well-publicized busts targeted importers, distributors, and retailers across the US.

Even small-time operators are not exempt. Many record companies today employ staff whose sole purpose, it seems, is to trawl Internet auction sites searching for potentially infringing items, and have the auctions closed, and the sellers threatened with legal action.

No sooner, however, had the imported menace been beaten back, than a new domestic crisis emerged, with the arrival on the marketplace of recordable CDs (CD-Rs). The Head label set the pace for this new explosion, debuting with a staggering launch of 40 titles, in individually numbered editions of 1,000 apiece, and rubbing salt into the industry's chagrin by timing its launch to within a week of a series of March 1997 busts that had the American industry trumpeting the worldwide elimination of bootlegging forever.

The Gold Standard label followed, joining Head in spinning out a dizzying array of what were, at that time, distinctive-looking golden-colored discs. It was, of course, a brief phase; within a couple of years, so many other CD-R labels had emerged to offer both original recordings and straight copies of other labels' bootlegs, that by the end of the century, the market for CD bootlegs was in a state somewhat approaching crisis.

Collectors, and even casual purchasers, wary of the ease with which any potential bootlegger could now spring into action, began differentiating loudly between gold (CD-R) and silver (factory-manufactured) discs—not because there was any discernable difference in quality, but because silver discs were somehow more "real." It is a backlash that has reduced many CD-Rs to the status of the home-made and handwritten cassette bootlegs, which, while once the backbone of many a street market and classified advertisement, are nevertheless of no collectible value whatsoever. But some fascinating dilemmas have already arisen. The Who's official *The Blues to the Bush* Internet-only live album, in 2000, was issued on CD-R; the *Bridge to the Blues* bootleg, documenting the same show, was issued on a conventional silver disc. Which is the *real* real deal?

It is within this climate of self-imposed hostility that bootlegs have again dipped below the radar somewhat. New issues are still pouring out, of course, with many of them readily comparable to the best that official record labels can muster, even at a time when the labels themselves are digging deeper into the vault and expending more time and effort on packaging and presentation than at any time in the past. The result has been some of the best-looking bootleg packages ever seen, rubbing shoulders with some of the most engaging official label products of all time.

Indeed, as the 21st century gets under way, it is easy to believe that the record companies have not only got a handle on why bootlegs are so popular with collectors, they are also, finally, beginning to fight fire with fire.

Throughout the 1980s, Fairport Convention, Richard Thompson, and Peter Hammill were among the first acts to recognize that the true fan's demand for music could never be sated by one new album issued every couple of years, so they began plugging the gaps with limited-edition, fan-club (or similar) albums containing live shows, outtakes, and the like.

Enter the 1990s, and Prince—whose public conflict with Warner Bros. hinged on similar notions of commercial freedom and artistic expression—likewise used the Internet to pioneer new means of making his music available to his audience, openly acknowledging a conflict that previous generations had only tacitly spoken of: that is, a record company's prime concern is to market music that is considered commercially viable; an artist's is simply to make music. Rightly or wrongly, bootlegs at least offered the consumer a middle ground between two so diametrically opposed viewpoints. Today, the Internet serves a similar purpose.

Without ever moving into the murky waters swirling around the late, lamented Napster and similar file-sharing ventures, the Cure, the Beastie Boys, King Crimson, Jimmy Page/Black Crowes, Pete Townshend, and Brian Wilson are among the leading artists to utilize either their own Web sites, or such online retailers as Musicmaker.com, to make available CDs that might never reach conventional retail outlets. Others, most notably David Bowie and They Might Be Giants, have also made rare music available for download.

Pearl Jam, meanwhile, took an even more audacious step—one that fans of every act must surely be wishing was common practice among artists. Well aware of the allure of bootlegs, but well aware, too, that words and threats could never stop people from buying (or manufacturing) them, the Seattle band regularly permitted radio stations to issue limited-edition two-CD albums of select live performances during the 1990s. In 2000, however, the band itself recorded every night of its summer European tour, then made each show available as an individually (and suitably minimally) packaged, budget-priced two-CD set under the umbrella title *The Bootleg Series*.

A total of 25 discs were issued in 2000; the following spring, 47 more appeared, documenting every stop on the band's fall 2000, North American tour. Result? No more Pearl Jam bootlegs (at least from those tours), plus a record-breaking five simultaneous entries onto *Billboard*'s Top 200 LP chart.

Other artists, most notably the Who and the Beatles, as well as the owners of the Marc Bolan, Jimi Hendrix, and Elvis Presley estates, have seen fit to cull the best of their own bootlegged archives for official releases, with rewards that far surpassed any profits made by the bootleggers. Once, collectors were starved for authorized issues of legendary releases. Now, some fans are literally groaning beneath the weight of them all.

Bill Levenson, VP of Artists and Repertory at Universal Music Group, and the man responsible for many of the finest collector-oriented CD box sets of the past decades, acknowledges, "I am always mindful of what bootlegs are floating around on an artist, and I try to assess whether the presence of bootlegs implies that there is a market/music consumer for me to reach."

More specifically, "While working on the Velvet Underground *Bootleg Series Volume One: The Quine Tapes* (a three-CD box of previously unheard live recordings from 1968–69), we collected and reviewed many bootlegs to see: a) what was out there; b) how did they sound; and c) how were they packaged, so that when we moved forward with our ideas, we had an idea on how to improve on what was previously done by 'professional' bootleggers only."

The critical success that met the package indicates that the efforts were successful, all the more so since the greatest plaudits were drawn from a community notorious for its ambivalence toward "official" attempts to anthologize this most sainted of '60s rock legends.

For many collectors, the knowledge that the official record companies are moving in this direction, together with the increasingly regular phenomenon of hitherto bootleg-only material making it onto authorized releases, has seen the market for new bootleg releases decline somewhat.

Bootlegs of earlier periods, however, remain fiercely collectible, with many enthusiasts utilizing what might be perceived as a lull in the present climate to renew their acquaintance with the classics of the vinyl age. Prices for 1970s-era issues by even relatively obscure artists have soared in recent years, particularly those that, making no pretense whatsoever toward professionalism (printed jackets, colored vinyl, etc.), arrive with the simplest of packaging: a plain white-card sleeve, shrink-wrapped around a single-sheet, one-color photocopied "cover," a blank

(or occasionally, preprinted but wholly deceptive) label, a quirky message in the run-off groove.

The sound quality might be bog-awful, the contents mislabeled and misrepresented. The music might be rubbish—the artist might be of no conceivable interest to anybody. But the bootlegs are irresistible for all that, a labor of love in every sense of the word. And isn't that what music should really be all about?

Further Reading: *The Great White Wonders: The Story of Rock Bootlegs,* by Clinton Heylin (Viking, 1994)

Box Sets—All You Ever Needed to Know (Plus a Booklet)

Box sets have traveled a long way from the days when they were, simply, boxes with a handful of LPs in them. Today, even the most unambitious set will pack multiple discs with multiple rarities, while the package itself will hold as many extras as the budget will allow.

Box sets regularly contain booklets the size and thickness of small books (or even big ones: Germany's Bear Family label prides itself on its extravagant publications); most box sets boast discographical exhumations that the artists themselves might sometimes have forgotten about. Even those packages whose main goal is simply to recycle the catalog one more time will throw in an extra disc of rarely heard oddities, or a few bonus tracks, at the end of each album. Today, a box set is a one-stop summary of everything you needed to know—and were probably not quite rich enough to have found out already.

For a number of reasons—size and cost among them—box sets have never truly been accepted as collectibles. Most collectors will own a few releases that dovetail with their own musical interests and that offer a comparatively inexpensive or uncomplicated way of obtaining music that might never come their way in its original format. And, for many serious enthusiasts, that is all that box sets are—substitutes for the "real thing," be it a long deleted B-side, a unique and precious acetate, a lost and forgotten radio broadcast—whatever.

But the idea that a mass-produced CD rendering of the same item might itself hold value as a collectible is entering the equation with increasing speed. Even within the CD age, a number of once apparently ubiquitous box sets have become appallingly hard to find. Track back into the vinyl era and many artists' catalogs will contain at least one scarce item that, though by no means comparable to the box sets of today, was nevertheless packaged in a box and marketed accordingly.

Although boxes have been circulating around the classical, opera, and jazz worlds for years, rock artists were surprisingly slow to make a similar move. Donovan's *A Gift from a Flower to a Garden* (Epic B2N 171) was one of the first rock albums to be marketed as a box set, in 1967. The package contained two LPs, plus a portfolio of lyrics and drawings.

Capitol, constantly on the lookout for new and inventive ways of selling back catalog, moved into the box-set market in late 1967 with a series of *Deluxe Edition* packages, each featuring three albums by a host of popular stars, Dean Martin, Frank Sinatra, and the Beach Boys among them. The series employed both vinyl and 8-Track, with the latter format not only seeing many more releases, but also turning up one of the scarcest Beatles items of all time, a *Deluxe Edition* 8-Track collection.

Capitol also ventured into various-artists boxes, by way of a short series of 1969 releases combining individual LPs by different bands into one package. One popular volume combines the Band, the Steve Miller Band, and the Quicksilver Messenger Service. Meanwhile the Beatles' Apple label, itself distributed by Capitol, was also an early proponent of box sets.

The boxed edition of John and Yoko Lennon's *Wedding Album* (Apple SMAX 3361), released in 1969, featured just one LP, but was weighed down regardless by a photo strip, a postcard, and a poster of wedding photographs, a second poster of lithographs, a booklet, a sleeve, and a photograph of a slice of wedding cake. The following year, early British pressings of the Beatles' *Let It Be* (UK Apple PXS 1/PCS 7096) swan song were boxed, the LP accompanied by a booklet. And, in 1970, Beatle George Harrison's three-LP solo

debut, *All Things Must Pass* (Apple STCH 639), was luxuriously packaged in a custom box, with his *Concert for Bangladesh* (STCX 3385) all-star live album making a similar appearance in 1972.

Crucially, many early box sets were limited editions, either as entities in their own right (none of the Capitol issues remained on sale for long) or, at least, in terms of packaging, with the boxes replaced by more traditional sleeves for later issues. Equally important, from the modern viewpoint, is that the boxes themselves tended to be rather flimsily constructed, easily splitting and tearing unless treated with absolute care. The Donovan and Harrison LPs are extremely common in poor condition; while the John and Yoko set itself is considered rare only if all the inserts are present. Like many other LPs that were originally issued stuffed with ephemera (the Who's *Live at Leeds*—Decca DL 79175—is the best-known example), it is the entire package that attracts attention, not the individual elements.

While one segment of the music industry was marketing box sets as a luxurious cut above the norm, another employed them as a cost-cutting exercise. The early-to-mid-'70s saw a number of budget labels (the TV-advertised Adam VIII label among them) produce a bewildering array of various-artists collections packaged as box sets, to obviate the need for printing individual sleeves for the discs themselves.

Such budget boxes have little value today, either as collectibles or as listening experiences. While rare or unusual stereo mixes may occasionally make their way on board, most discs packed so many songs onto the vinyl that not only did the sound quality plunge to new lows, the songs themselves were frequently presented in re-recorded, edited, and/or prematurely faded form. Much like the budget-CD collections of today, these sets were targeted solely at an audience that wanted the biggest bang for its buck.

Another factor holding box sets back was the sheer paucity of artists whose careers actually merited anything more than a one- or two-disc *Greatest Hits* package. It was as late as 1970 before even Elvis Presley was established worthy of a boxed hits collection, the four-LP *Worldwide Gold Award Hits Volume One* compilation (RCA LPM 6401). A second volume serving up *The Other Sides* (LPM 6402) followed in 1971.

In Europe, Cliff Richard and the Shadows were anthologized across a six-LP package, *The Cliff Richard Story* (World Record Club SMM 255-260), in 1972, an exquisite issue that placed each individual LP into its own custom sleeve, with liner notes and exclusive photographs.

However, the most legendary of early boxes is surely the Beatles' *Alpha-Omega* (Audio Tape ATRBH), a four-LP compilation that tracked the group's entire 1962–70 career (plus a handful of solo recordings), via what its manufacturer perceived as a loophole in a newly instituted copyright law, which permitted them to release the music without being its legal owner.

The first full Beatles compilation ever issued in the US, in 1972, *Alpha-Omega*, was released on both vinyl and 8-Track and was made available via TV advertised mail-order. Unfortunately, the loophole that it exploited turned out to be a dead end. Capitol, the rightful copyright owners of the material, swooped and both *Alpha-Omega* and a projected *Volume Two* follow-up vanished overnight. Today, the common perception of the set is that it is a bootleg; in fact, it not only deserves the same place in the Beatles' catalog as any of the myriad Star Club–era collections issued elsewhere in the group's history, it can also be thanked for inciting the Beatles to finally issue their own compilations, the *1962–66* ("red") and *1967–70* ("blue") anthologies.

Another forerunner of the modern box set was Mike Oldfield's *Boxed* (UK Virgin VBOX 1), comprising quadraphonic mixes of the albums *Tubular Bells, Hergest Ridge,* and *Ommadawn,* plus an exclusive fourth disc, *Collaborations,* featuring Oldfield's work with other artists. A far cry from other limited-edition, and now extremely scarce, packages of the age, *Boxed* became one of the most successful box sets of all time, reaching No. 22 on the UK LP chart in late 1976.

From the same country and era comes *The Electric Muse* (Transatlantic FOLK 1001), a four-LP box set summarizing the story of English folk music as it transformed into folk-rock. Widely acclaimed at the time, and still regarded among the crucial compilations of the genre, the box nevertheless suffered from poor distribution and low sales, and vanished within a year or so of its 1975 release. (A book published to coincide with the album is even rarer.) Neither has a CD reissue taken the edge off the collectors' demand—licensing problems saw several key tracks deleted or replaced.

An Elvis Presley box, 1980's eight-LP *Elvis Aaron Presley 25th Anniversary Limited Edition* (RCA CPL8-3699), is somewhat more common than its original marketing claimed it might be. Still, it remains a magnificent portrayal, littered with unusual material and surrounded by some extraordinary ephemera. A booklet and a set of calendars dated 1963–1980 accompanied original vinyl pressings; the cassette versions of the set featured four tapes, and additionally packed in eight color reproductions of the individual LP sleeves.

Igniting another modern tradition, single-disc samplers for this package also exist—one issued for retail (DJL1 3729), offering excerpts from 37 songs, and one for radio (DJL1-3871), featuring 12 complete tracks. Both samplers are considerably rarer than the actual box.

Other noteworthy vinyl boxes abound. Frank Zappa masterminded several very collectible vinyl box sets. In 1987, three volumes of *Old Masters* (Barking Pumpkin BPR 7777/8888/9999) between them reissued 20 classic Zappa/Mothers of Invention albums, with the first two bolstered by the inclusion of *Mystery Disc* bonus albums featuring outtakes, live recordings, and oddities from Zappa's earliest years as a recording artist. In 1991, *Beat the Boots* (Rykodisc 70537-44) reissued ten equally classic bootlegs dating between 1968–81, with original artwork, and in a wry twist, the original sound quality intact.

Working Backwards 1983–1973 was a nine-LP box set of Brian Eno's work (UK EG EGBS 002), bolstered by the inclusion of one previously unreleased album, *Music for Airports Volume Two,* and a 12-inch EP, *Rarities.* The Rolling Stones were boxed first with a 12-LP recounting of their entire LP catalog, *The Rolling Stones Story* (Germany—Teldec 6 30118 HZ).

The original issue of Bob Dylan's *Biograph* CD box set.

Next came a four-disc roundup of non-album material, *The Rest of the Best of the Rolling Stones* (Teldec 6 30125 FX), the only official source for the Chess Studios outtake "Tell Me Baby How Many Times," and, via a bonus one-sided 7-inch disc, for the legendary "Cocksucker Blues" (Teldec C66 1165601 1).

Bruce Springsteen answered a decade's worth of fan mail with the release of his five-LP *Live 1977–85* (Columbia 40588) package. Queen's *The Complete Works* box (UK EMI QB 1) served up 13 past albums and a still unique 14th LP featuring non-album singles and B-sides, plus two album-sized booklets. Issued, of course, in a gold embossed, leather-bound box, this was one of the last genuinely significant vinyl box sets, before the advent of CDs.

That watershed, of course, introduced a whole new realm to box sets, with Bob Dylan's *Biograph* (Columbia C5X 38830) among the first to take full advantage of the new format, cherry-picking rarities and released highlights alike to show the world how

box sets should really feel. Originally issued in a 12-inch box, the three-CD package has since been repackaged in a far smaller format, a fate that has befallen a number of other early CD boxes, and has conspired to push the value of the original packaging somewhat higher than it ought to be. (A five-LP vinyl pressing of the same collection is, contrarily, genuinely rare and oddly undervalued.)

Original issues of Led Zeppelin's four-CD *Led Zeppelin* (Atlantic 82144) and David Bowie's three-CD *Sound and Vision* (Rykodisc RA 0120/1/2) have also climbed in value, with the latter further distinguished by the inclusion of a bonus fourth disc propagating the then-fashionable (but ultimately doomed) video disc format. These sets, too, were originally accompanied by vinyl versions, comprising six LPs apiece. In the realm of modern box sets, both are highly prized.

Many other early CD box sets have since disappeared, either because they've been deleted altogether, or because they've been completely reconfigured. In the latter category, LP-shaped box sets for the Carpenters, the Monkees, Nick Drake, and Sandy Denny, among many others, have all been shrunken; among the former, Pink Floyd's *Shine On* offered remastered editions of seven Floyd albums, each uniquely packaged in a black case, with the spines lining up to re-create the famous *Dark Side of the Moon* triangle logo, plus a fold-out slipcase for the discs, a package of postcards, a lavish hardbound book, and an additional disc of early rarities. An expensive item at the time of its release, *Shine On* is now very seldom seen today that it might as well never have existed.

Also highly prized is the limited-edition metal box that Rykodisc packaged with reissues of Bowie's *Low, Heroes,* and *Stage* albums. Although it contained just those discs, the box was designed to hold the entire sequence of re-released CDs and was apparently available for just a few weeks at most. The box's value today exceeds that of all its intended contents combined.

The late '80s also saw a number of similarly limited boxes produced around the release of the first Beatles-catalog CDs. These have also escalated in value, but their worth should not be confused with the 1990s phenomenon of speculative limited editions produced not by record companies, but by wholesalers. Custom boxes featuring one (or sometimes more) albums, packaged with T-shirts, key fobs, buttons, and the like, and offered for sale only through collector magazines and mail-order houses, may look attractive—and of course, they are described as being desperately collectible. But as legitimate entries into an artist's discography, they have little more than quasi-official status and little tangible value.

Some box sets were never intended as rarities, but have ascended to that status regardless. Bob Marley's four-CD *Songs of Freedom* box astonished all observers when what was described as a hopelessly optimistic limited edition of 1 million copies worldwide not only sold out, but also created a ferocious secondary market. Originally issued in "bookshelf" form (a hardbound booklet the width of one CD and the height of two), this set, too, was subsequently reissued in a smaller single-CD-sized box, but its renewed availability seems not to have dented the demand for the earlier format.

Other significant releases that have faded from view despite appearing set for long runs as catalog staples include the four-CD *Lennon* box set (Capitol 7243 30614), originally issued in 1990 as a career-spanning roundup of the late Beatle John's solo career; and Elton John's ... *To Be Continued* retrospective, which, having fallen out of print around 1994, was still picking up speed on the collectors market when Universal finally reissued it in 2000. The reissue immediately saw the original's value plunge—but promptly engendered a new collectible, when it was revealed that the new set was itself a numbered, limited-edition release of just 55,000 copies, with a stated availability of a mere six months.

With these examples in mind, it is clear that even modern releases of vintage obscurities cannot be guaranteed to remain available for much longer than the discs they have reissued, with their future desirability only exacerbated by the obvious laws of supply and demand. A rare 45 might appeal to only a handful of fans who are prepared to pay significant sums for a copy. A rare box set might be pursued by everyone who ever cared about the artist—and might well end up costing even more.

Cassettes—Against All Odds

Without doubt, the cassette is the poor relation of the collecting world. Whereas every other format, even such utter obscurities as Pocket Rockers and 4-Track cartridges, has its die-hard adherents, the cassette remains despised and derided.

Part of this undoubtedly is due to the poor quality with which cassettes have traditionally been manufactured. Even in the early '70s, when standards were beefed up to compete with (and eventually overthrow) the 8-Track cartridge, cassettes were markedly inferior to their counterparts in terms of packaging, durability, and sound quality.

They triumphed because they were cheaper (both to produce and to purchase), and because most listeners were simply looking for a format that could be

The liner to the original UK cassette of Genesis' debut album.

easily transported, readily accessed, and that devoured little space. Four cassettes can fit into the storage space required by an 8-Track, and that's a major consideration in such confined quarters as an automobile or a student dorm room.

In addition, cassettes possessed a versatility that the 8-Track would not embrace for several years to come: Cassettes could be utilized for both playing and recording, the first genuinely affordable recording medium in the history of consumer electronics— and they could store more music. The first tapes could hold up to 90 minutes; by the early '70s, capacity had increased to two hours. Weighed against the fact that few potential cassette buyers were numbered among the high-end audio buffs to whom fidelity is of paramount importance, such advantages ensured that the format could not lose.

Cassettes were developed by the Philips and Norelco companies during the early '60s, originally for use in Dictaphones and other business machines. Japan was the first nation to adapt the technology as an alternative to vinyl, with Europe following suit around 1966.

There, cassettes were marketed alongside small, portable, battery-operated players in much the same way that PlayTapes were in the US. The following year, when the first auto manufacturers began offering cassette players as in-dash accessories, the format moved onto the American market as well.

By the end of the 1960s, prerecorded cassette sales were running neck and neck with 8-Tracks (PlayTapes and 4-Tracks had both already given up the ghost); by the mid-'70s, it was a one-horse race. Adjustments to both the quality and reliability of cassettes vastly improved their performance, ridding the format of its early penchant for jamming, twisting, and fluttering. The Dolby Noise Reduction system was perfected to erase the hiss that plagued early tapes, and as the 1970s progressed, further innovations in the composition of the magnetic tape at least gave the format the aura of quality sound reproduction. Reel-to-reels marched on in their own tiny corner of the market, of course, their share of the listening public as unaffected by cassettes as by any earlier tape format. But from here on in, the cassette was unstoppable.

Attempts were continually being made to broaden the cassette's appeal even further. So far, cassettes had simply echoed the contents of their vinyl counterparts. Beginning around 1979, cassette-only bonus tracks came into vogue—one of the best-known early examples is the Kinks's 1980 double live album, *One for the Road* (Arista 8401), issued on tape with the extra song "20th Century Man." Cassettes also began to offer full-length versions of songs that had been edited down for vinyl releases. Cassette copies of Grace Jones' *Warm Leatherette* (UK Island ICT 9592) are prized for their unique inclusion of virtually a second LP's worth of music.

The same record label also introduced a range of releases that featured an entire album on one side of the tape, but left the other side blank, allowing consumers to record their own choice of music onto the back of the album. Yet another innovation, frequently applied to the growing market in cassette singles, duplicated the entire playing program on each side of the tape, thus removing the need to turn the tape over midway through the listening experience.

The advent of the cassette single itself created a boom in the cassette's popularity. Malcolm McLaren, former manager of the Sex Pistols and now overseeing a new band, Bow Wow Wow, is widely regarded as the father of the format, after that latter band issued the *Cassette Pet* single in 1980 (UK EMI 5088). Within a year or two, virtually every new single released in the UK and the US were made available on cassette; some appeared *only* on cassette.

Today, there are numerous cassette singles that command high prices among fans of individual artists, often as a result of some extremely well-designed, limited-edition packaging or the use of exclusive material. Promotional copies of the aforementioned Bow Wow Wow *Cassette Pet* were issued in a mock can of dog food, for example, while several of Frankie Goes to Hollywood's early cassette singles offered otherwise unavailable mixes.

The gradual elimination of vinyl during the mid-'80s only furthered the cassette's domination. Figures published in 1989 claim cassettes outsold both LPs and CDs in the US, and while those figures are

necessarily warped by the fact that LPs and CDs were then engaged in their own, private battle for supremacy, splitting sales as they did so, still it was a remarkable achievement.

Move outside of the rock market and the cassette's penetration is even more impressive. It dominates the music industry in the Third World, both in official, record company–sponsored form, and under the auspices of pirates and bootleggers. It is estimated that pirate cassettes, primarily emanating from Hong Kong, Singapore, Taiwan, and South Korea, have devoured as much as 80 percent of the African market, even forcing the closure of several official record companies.

This specter has long haunted the Western world, hence the periodic vociferous attacks launched by the industry on blank cassettes (today, of course, supplanted as Public Bogeyman No. 1 by recordable CDs). Needless to say, many rock and pop titles are included in the pirates' catalog, both abroad and in the US.

Such misgivings aside, today the cassette is the only mass-market alternative to the CD, continuing to thrive because, first and foremost, it is cheap and cheerful. Attempts to dislodge it as the world's No. 1 tape product with such high-end formats as DAT (digital audio tape) and DCC (digital compact cassettes) have consistently failed for those very reasons: they require new equipment, they demand more outlay, and they require more care. But all the consumer wants is something that will play music any time, any place. The actual quality of that sound is, understandably, secondary to those most pertinent capabilities.

While cassettes have never engaged the general collecting sensibilities, that is not to say they do not have the potential to do so. A huge number of artists opened their recording careers with cassette-only releases, sold at gigs or by mail-order—CD-Rs now fulfill this same function, but during the very late '80s and into the 1990s, Beck, the Smashing Pumpkins, and Marilyn Manson all went this route.

In addition, many conventionally released albums that are scarce, and thus, very high priced on vinyl, can be picked up for a fraction of the price on cassette, and that's a worthwhile consideration for fans who simply want to hear the music and don't care for other considerations. In some—indeed, many—instances, the cassettes might even be scarcer than the LPs. But while all the "serious" collectors are flipping through the vinyl racks, you're cleaning up in the corner with the tapes. Then watch how many of them ask you for a copy.

CDs—The Ultimate Hostile Takeover

Although it has been less than 20 years since the first compact disc was introduced in the US, there is no doubt that the format has become *the* single most popular medium for retailing and collecting music ever developed.

Convenient to use, easy to store, and offering sound quality that (though some folks will disagree) generally outperforms any other media in sight, CDs revitalized the music industry at a time when everybody was predicting its imminent demise, and revolutionized collecting at a time when it, too, was beginning to flag.

Today, an estimated 750 million CDs are sold every year in the US alone—and that figure only reflects sales of new CDs. Add thrift stores and bargain bins, record fairs and the Internet to the tally, and the figure soars. The cry that once went up from "traditional" collectors, that CDs were not and never could be considered "collectible," today sounds too simpleminded for words. Not only are CDs extraordinarily collectible, they are probably favored by more collectors than any other format on earth.

Why bother hunting through rack after rack of dusty 45s in search of that one colossally rare REM B-side, when you can simply pick it up on CD—and at a fraction of the cost that the original would set you back? Why blunt your eyesight on the Internet all night, hoping to find the *1963 Newport Folk Festival* album, when the Bob Dylan track you're looking for is already on a Joan Baez CD? And why break the bank for 50 scratchy freakbeat 45s, when Rhino's *Nuggets II* box set has twice that many, and in pristine condition?

Even ten years ago, the answer to those questions would have been obvious. Because the music is only part of the equation; because the artifact itself is what matters: the vinyl, the sleeve, the physical presence of an original recording. CDs did not have that same presence. Today, however, that mentality has changed. CDs have become accepted as artifacts in their own right, as prone to change and variation as vinyl ever was, and just as valued an item.

True, no CD has yet climbed to the same peaks as did the true giants of the vinyl era. There is no CD equivalent of Bob Dylan's *Freewheelin'* with the four unissued songs, or the Beatles' Vee-Jay album in original stereo. But for most collectors, the very existence of those records was more or less academic. We all hoped that one day we'd find one, but we never did, and what was worse, a lot of the time we never got to hear them either. CDs have made some staggeringly rare music available, so not only can we find out what the fuss is all about, we can also play them to death. A withdrawn pressing of *Freewheelin'* is so valuable you'd be afraid to even look at it.

Neither is it true that no CDs are actually "valuable." Again, there is nothing yet capable of competing with the priceless giants of vinyl, but there are probably 50,000 CDs out there that habitually trade for over $100 apiece, and many times that number which, through deletion, withdrawal, or simply limited availability, are worth far more than they ever retailed at. And that is before one even considers promos, radio shows, and other specialist formats.

Even better, anybody who has been actively buying CDs for more than five years probably already owns a few of the field's medium-rarities—that foldout digipack version of the Foo Fighters' *There Is Nothing Left to Lose*, the Kraftwerk box set on Cleopatra, Alanis Morissette's *Now Is the Time*, Capitol Records' slipcased *Essentials* rarities series, and so on. CDs float in and out of print as regularly as vinyl ever did, and deletion from the catalog still awaits those whose useful life span is nearing its end. Just because CDs themselves are meant to last forever, that doesn't mean they will be available forever as well.

The commercial history of the CD dates back to the early '80s. The story of the format, however, stretches back two decades before that. Dutch electronics giant Philips began working on the concept in the late '60s, when physicist Klass Compan first conceived of utilizing digital technology as a means of recording and storing sound. Neither was the company alone in its researches—as early as 1967, Japan's NHK Technical Research Unit was demonstrating a 12-bit digital audio recorder, with Sony perfecting a 13-bit recorder in 1969. ("Bits" refer to individual pieces of information stored within the disc. The first commercially available CDs were 16-bit; today, 22- and 24-bit discs are the norm, with every increase improving the sound just a little more.)

These earliest experiments utilized videotape as the host for the digital recordings. In 1970, Philips perfected a prototype glass disc that required a laser to read it. It would be another seven years, however, before the first digital audio disc prototypes were unveiled, at the 1977 Tokyo Audio Fair, by Hitachi, Sony, and Mitsubishi. The following year, 35 different manufacturers demonstrated their own prototypes at a specially convened Digital Audio Disc Convention in Tokyo, at which point Philips proposed that a universal standard be set prior to any attempt to launch the system.

By the end of 1978, agreement had been reached regarding such essential topics as diameter (115 mm, modified to 120 mm/5 inches to allow for 74 minutes of data, recorded on a 16-bit disc), the type of laser required to read the disc, and the direction in which the data would be decoded: from the inside out.

Philips also invited Sony, as the leading Japanese researcher, to collaborate in perfecting the system. Each company took credit for different aspects of the CD standard. By the time the partnership was ended, in 1981, the CD was ready for launch.

The first discs and players were introduced in the US in spring 1983, and they made an immediate impression. Some 800,000 discs were sold during the first year, together with 30,000 players. Within three years, those figures had exploded beyond anyone's wildest imaginings—3 million players,

53 million CDs. America's first CD manufacturing plant went on line in 1984; by 1988, there were more than 50 operating worldwide. And suddenly, a bogeyman who had been hanging around the fringes of the record-buyer's imagination for a couple of years began taking his first giant steps forward. The possibility that the industry would begin phasing out vinyl in favor of CDs had been hanging in the air again since the introduction of the first CDs. Now it was official.

Looking back from a distance of almost 20 years, the fears that accompanied that realization now take on the qualities of a really bad dream. They were terrifying at the time, but now we wonder what on earth we were worrying about.

Doomsday predictions that CDs, far from being indestructible, were likely to self-destruct within a few years were raised, then dismissed, when it became apparent that the vast majority were not going to do anything of the sort. Production problems apparently confined to the Philips-Dupont-Optical manufacturing plant did see a number of late-'80s discs issued by the UK Phonogram label turn brown and eventually deteriorate to become unplayable. But other CDs, even those dating from the first days of the format, play as perfectly today as they did in 1983.

Another supposedly significant drawback to the format was its 74-minute time limit—no major concern when reissuing a conventional single LP, but the cause of much concern on occasions when a two-LP set exceeded the time limit by so small a margin that a two-CD set simply didn't seem practical. Early CDs of Joni Mitchell's *Miles of Aisles* (Asylum 202-2), Fleetwood Mac's *Tusk* (Warner Bros. 266 088), the Who's *The Kids Are Alright* (MCA 6899), and Bob Dylan's *Blonde on Blonde* (Columbia CGK 841) were among the major releases that, when squeezed onto a theoretically value-for-money-inclined single disc, were forced to shed several minutes of playing time, or even, in the case of *Tusk*, an entire song.

The gradual pushing forward of the CD's storage capacity would eventually remedy this; so, ultimately, would the discovery that the public was happy to pay extra for the entire experience. It is ironic to discover today, with the full versions of each album readily available, that a sizeable market has developed for these earlier "edited" issues.

Even more ridiculous, in hindsight, were fears that record companies would confine the new format to new releases and past best-sellers. When had they ever done otherwise? Collectors would delve deep into their record cabinets and pull out LPs even they had forgotten about, to hold up and moan, "This'll never be reissued on CD." And fellow collectors would shake their heads in dismay, quite forgetting that it would never be reissued on vinyl either.

In fact, CDs rapidly came to embrace the most unlikely antiquities, and by the early '90s, it was getting difficult to predict what would be coming out next, as the major labels laid bare their archives, and enterprising indies pounced on any crumbs the majors had missed. There are, probably, still several thousand favorite albums that have yet to make it out on CD, but there are many times more that have, and some of them even sold more copies this time than they ever did the first time around. Bad luck for anyone hoping to corner the market in original vinyl pressings of the one and only album by Tickawinda. Good luck for everyone who has finally got to hear the best British folk-rock album of the late '70s in superb digital sound.

Even more excitingly, the bitter taste of needing to replace a lifetime's vinyl collection on CD was expunged first by the realization that many (not all) CDs did sound better than their predecessors, but also by the growing trend of appending old records with new bonus tracks. Soon, it was difficult to even remember a day when a listening session necessitated getting up every 20 or so minutes to turn the record over, and today there's an entire generation of listeners for whom such a chore is as unimaginable as using a mangle to do the laundry, or going to math class without a pocket calculator.

The arrival of the Beatles back catalog on CD, beginning in early 1987, gave further impetus to a format that had, thus far, taken considerable flak for its claim to be the wave of the future, while the

biggest stars of the past had still to endorse the product.

Both Capitol (US) and EMI (UK) were initially criticized for their approach to the subject. Unilaterally, they utilized the original British mixes and sequencing for LPs that appeared in very different form in the US, and they charged the full CD price for discs that barely topped half an hour playing time (similarly brief Beach Boys albums were issued as "two-fers"— two CDs on one disc). They were criticized, too, for issuing the first four albums in band-approved mono, rather than providing the subsequent stereo mixes—and for so much more. But time has softened most collectors' views considerably. Today, the idea that a classic album could be reissued in anything *but* its intended form should be anathema, even to record company executives.

The Beatles, perhaps inevitably, are responsible for one of the earliest CD collectibles, when the *Abbey Road* album was issued in that format by Japan's EMI-Toshiba, some months before the official go-ahead was given, with sound quality several notches below what it was intended to be. Copies were hastily withdrawn, with the estimated 1,500 survivors fetching extraordinarily high prices in the period before an official issue made it out, and still attracting considerable attention today.

A number of other early Beatles discs also merit a second glance. As early as 1985, German Polydor issued the Tony Sheridan–era *Beatles: First* (823 701-2) on disc, though a swift withdrawal saw this set, too, soar in value. Discs translating the Star Club and Decca audition tapes to the new format were quick off the mark, and while all have been superseded (many times over) by issues from Japan's Overseas Records, including *Savage Young Beatles* (30CP 80), *Live at the Star Club in Hamburg, Germany 1962* (38CP-44), *The Silver Beatles* (30CD-45), *Rock 'n' Roll Beatles* (30CP-112), and *1960–62* (38CP-134) all predate the release of EMI's own catalog.

Among the other early signs that CDs were going to develop into a powerful force on the collectors market was the launch, in April 1987, of the CD newsletter *Ice (International CD Exchange)*. Still the leading source for new-release information and gossip today, *Ice* began life as an eight-page, photocopied publication, acting as both a watchdog for the infant industry and an invaluable lexicon of collector-oriented information. "Bruce fans with CD players now have their first *bona fide* collectors item to chase down," reported that debut issue, revealing that the first Japanese CD pressings of Springsteen's *Nebraska* utilized a master tape prepared before the original album underwent its final mix.

It was a neat exclusive, but it was a significant story for other reasons, too, in that it demonstrated that a medium hitherto touted for its perfection was, after all, as prone to error and mistake as any of its predecessors. Indeed, many of the CD age's most treasured rarities are, similarly, errors that somehow passed unnoticed into production.

Some of these are, in themselves, little more than minor snafus, affecting the purchaser's recollections of the original song or LP more than the integrity of the release itself—an unissued stereo mix replacing the expected mono, for example. Occasionally, however, errors creep out that offer something far more precious.

Original CD pressings of Bruce Springsteen's *Nebraska* (Columbia CK 38538) are hotly pursued for the sake of four extra minutes of the song "My Father's House"; collectors identify the disc by its white spine with red lettering, and the absence of the "Now Made in America" notation, which appeared on discs after the opening of the Digital Audio Disc Corporation manufacturing plant in Terre Haute, Ind.

The 1997 reissue of Bob Dylan's 1985 *Biograph* box set (remarkable as the first important box set of the CD age) initially entered the market laden with four unexpected bonuses, in the form of two previously unissued live performances, one hitherto unavailable outtake, and one super-rare single. Even more bizarrely, two of these boo-boos actually corrected mistakes committed on the original 1985 package. Just 5,000 copies of the box had been distributed when the errors were discovered and the package was recalled. In the meantime, just days after the withdrawal, copies were spotted trading for up to $150.

The first widespread collectibles of the CD age were the so-called long box (6-inch by 12-inch) packages, within which the earliest CDs were issued, as an anti-theft measure. It was assumed that the size of this external packaging, which often attractively reproduced the cover art, would deter shoplifters who might be tempted by the otherwise pocket-sized format.

The boxes were never particularly popular and few people ever saved them. So when a phase-out initiative launched by the Rykodisc label promised, among other things, to reduce the cost of a CD by up to $1, few people were sorry to see the long box leave. Label after label followed Rykodisc's lead; store after store turned instead to similarly sized reusable clear plastic cases for their security concerns. And in April 1993, the Recording Industry Association of America, representing most of America's leading record companies, confirmed the permanent withdrawal of the long box. By which time, of course, everybody who'd ever thrown them away were already wishing they hadn't. (The fact that long boxes were beasts to open without tearing them up was conveniently forgotten.) Generally speaking, CDs in their original long boxes are now considered collectible.

Today, the market for CDs—and for new, and ever more ambitious archive projects on CD—remains vibrant. True, not every great LP ever recorded has made it onto disc, but the format has still condensed into 20 years worth of releases, a vinyl library that took almost 100 to create. As a result, CDs—like LPs and 45s before them—offer an enormous vista for collectors that it would be foolish to try to quantify, each one echoing (and, generally, improving upon) specialties that first thrived in the pre-digital days.

One especially challenging area focuses upon one of the first gimmicks of the CD age, the practice of including "hidden" tracks, either as deliberate, or in some cases, accidental, bonuses. Usually secreted at the end of a disc, often following untold acres of silence, these hidden cuts created an awful lot of excitement when originally discovered. Nirvana's *Nevermind* (Geffen DGC 24425) was not the first to employ the device, but certainly became the first CD to truly ignite the craze, all the more so after it was revealed that the bonus cut, "Endless Nameless," appeared only on the first 15,000 copies pressed—by which time sales of the album had topped 600,000.

The list of CDs featuring hidden material is, today, enormous. It includes such stellar names as U2 (1998's *The Best of 1980–90* collection), the Clash (the *Clash on Broadway* box set), and Cracker (whose *Kerosene Hat* album actually indexed 99 tracks, though music and sound appeared on only a handful of them).

An even more unconventional hiding place was developed for such releases as the Adverts's *Crossing the Red Sea with the Adverts* (UK Essential ESMCD 451) and the Astronettes's *People from Bad Homes* (Griffin GCD 424-2) archive projects. The bonus material was secreted at the *beginning* of the disc and could be accessed only by starting the disc playing, then holding down the rewind button. Neither of these discs was intended as a limited edition or a rarity (although the short shelf-life of the latter, a David Bowie production from 1973, has certainly established it as one); the collectibility stems from technology.

As far as other CD innovations are concerned, the miniature CD-3 format was all but stillborn during the late '80s and early '90s, but has nevertheless spun off a number of now-popular collectibles. Video CDs were also short-lived, while enhanced CDs never took off as triumphantly as they deserved to.

The jury is still out, meanwhile, on such sonic successors as Sony's *Mastersound* series of SBM (Super-Bit Mapping) editions, Mobile Fidelity's *Ultradiscs,* Atlantic's *Gold Standard* collectors editions, and other similar audiophile offerings. The smart money reckons that, despite the use of gold discs, the majority of them don't sound that much different than the regularly issued versions. And, of course, it is also highly ironic that, from having once been regarded as the be-all and end-all of sonic excellence, the very use of gold now implies an inferior (as in CD-R) product.

The heart of CD collecting, then, lies in the same place as LPs and 45s before it, in regular issues and rarities, in surprising deletions and unexpected famines. One of the earliest discoveries in this direction was, indeed, the fact that discs that appeared during the first few years of the CD were suddenly disappearing again, with David Bowie among the first major casualties. RCA issued his first CDs as early as 1984. By 1988, however, they had all but disappeared, prior to being reissued in expanded form by Rykodisc, two long, cold-turkey years later.

Overnight, and despite the promised superior packaging and content of the reissues, the RCA discs became highly collectible, reaching a plateau from which they have yet to descend. Ironically, Rykodisc itself did much to further this situation, at least in one instance—the promotion of Bowie's epochal *Rise and Fall of Ziggy Stardust* included the offer to exchange copies of the original RCA disc for a new Rykodisc copy. Whether as a consequence of this generosity or not, *Ziggy Stardust* (RCA PCD1 4702) is now among the scarcest of all Bowie's primary RCA CDs, with only such late-in-the-day compilations as *Golden Years* and *Fame and Fashion* proving harder to locate.

First CD issues of discs are also a popular hunting ground, particularly in the realm of the first-ever CDs. They were, after all, manufactured at a time when the format's future was still uncertain—nobody knew whether the CD was going to take off or simply vanish into obscurity, as the 8-Track had done.

At the dawn of the CD age, even major artists' releases were limited by the fact that there were very few manufacturing plants operating anywhere in the world, with none at all in the United States. American CDs issued prior to 1984 were actually manufactured either in Japan or in Hanover, Germany, while the booklet was printed in America. Spotting these details is the easiest way to identify a first issue; another detail to watch for is the label design—regardless of the issuing record company, the earliest CDs manufactured in Hanover all employed a distinctive row of colored squares across the center of the disc. Even the jewel case can clue collectors in: prior to 1985, the spindle that holds a disc in its tray had eight teeth; later cases had 12.

Other modern rarities include those acts whose careers were flourishing at the dawn of the CD age—and were, therefore, among the first to have their catalogs released—but whose subsequent fall from fame has seen those albums long since deleted. Important (or, at least, once beloved) albums by the likes of the Traveling Wilburys, the Motels, the Eurythmics, and Nu Shooz have long been unavailable, with the reissue market seemingly interested only in producing hits collections. Anybody wanting the original albums must turn instead to the collectors market—and the values there might surprise them.

Maybe the day when a Haircut 100 CD could help put your kids through college is still a long way away. But it is certainly worth more than you ever imagined it might be.

Further Reading: *Collectible Compact Disc Price Guide*, by Gregory Cooper (Collector Books, various editions)

CD-3s—Good Things Don't Always Come in Small Packages

The first collectibles—and the first major casualty of the CD age—were the 3-inch discs that the industry intended to represent the next wave in the revolution, as the replacement for the 7-inch single.

Capable of holding up to 20 minutes of music, 3-inch CDs were launched amid considerable fanfare during the summer of 1987, when the first promotional issues were dispatched to radio. Fleetwood Mac's "Little Lies," Squeeze's "Three from Babylon," and Stevie Wonder's "Skeletons" were among the earliest promo issues. There was just one problem. While the discs' manufacturer, Digital Audio Disc Corporation, of Terre Haute, Ind., launched the discs on schedule, the snap-on plastic adapters necessary to center the discs within the CD player didn't arrive quite so punctually.

The oversight was rectified within weeks, but the damage was already done. Nice format—a shame it can't be played.

From the start, the industry was hopelessly divided over the CD-3. Rykodisc, the newly established CD-only label, was first into the commercial marketplace with Frank Zappa's "Peaches en Regalia" remix. But Philips, pioneer of the CD in the first place, announced that it wanted no part of this latest innovation. For every label that did seem set to jump on board, another seemed equally determined to sabotage the format by continuing to issue all its discs as 5-inchers. And the public, tired of waiting for the businesspeople to make up their minds, did it for them. They rejected the CD-3 outright.

Before that, of course, there was a flurry of releases, and some surprisingly spectacular ones, at that: The jazz and classical specialists at the Delos label issued a number of CD-3s in late 1987. The following year, Rhino launched a series of four-song packages under the overall title *Big Hits Come in Small Packages*, and featuring the Turtles, the Everly Brothers, the Beach Boys, and more. The first Beatles CD-3, Romance Records' repackaging of the pre-fame 1961 Tony Sheridan material, followed.

Atlantic, Dunhill Compact Classics, MCA, Polygram, Virgin (UK), and even Deutsche Gramophone were among the other labels to move into the CD-3 field during 1988–89, while EMI plowed ahead with a CD-3 box set of 12 Queen singles issued in the UK, Germany, and Japan. Criticized at the time for a remarkably eccentric selection of material—the 12 singles seemed to have been plucked at utter random from throughout the band's entire catalog—*The 3" CD Singles* box is now one of the most in-demand CD-3 releases of all time . . . with or without an adapter to play it with.

Public resistance to the CD-3 was not unreasonable. The CD-3 offered no advantages over the CD, in the slightest, particularly when balanced against the tangible inconvenience of needing to attach an adapter to every disc (very few discs were packaged with one of their own) before playing.

Soon, only Sony remained unequivocal in its support for the 3-inch CD, even forging ahead with plans to launch a dedicated 3-inch player on the Japanese market in 1988. However, Sony, too, would run headlong into another of the format's drawbacks that same year, with the long-awaited release of Bruce Springsteen's *Chimes of Freedom* EP.

The original EP ran to 25 minutes, but the format could hold just 20. Cuts were made, fans were outraged. How ironic, then, that when the EP was reissued on a 5-inch disc in 1999, the edited CD-3 master was inadvertently utilized for the first run of pressings! The oversight was corrected for subsequent issues.

Despite the format's unpopularity, it has survived. Several publishers adopted the CD-3 as an inexpensive way of presenting bonus musical material with books (the digital equivalent to the flexidisc [see page 71], perhaps), while occasional new releases at least allow the format an aura of dogged determination. It is not, after all, the disc itself that is outdated, simply its size. With an adapter attached, a CD-3 remains as viable a medium as its 5-inch brethren.

Nevertheless, there are just two primary areas upon which CD-3 collectors concentrate: the optimistic glut of early American issues (with many more existing as promos than as commercial releases), and the often grandiosely packaged Japanese issues that survived into the mid-'90s. These include enduringly popular collections by the Beatles, Madonna, Depeche Mode, Pink Floyd, and Bruce Springsteen (again). Even with the greatest collectibles, however, CD-3 prices have remained comparatively low—testament, perhaps, to the uncertainty that haunted the format almost from the outset.

Further Reading: *Collectible Compact Disc Price Guide,* by Gregory Cooper (Collector Books, various editions)

Christmas—All I Want Is . . . Something Different to Collect

It is a historical fact that more records are sold in the weeks leading up to Christmas than at any other time of year. It is a fact, too, that more "unusual" (read "novelty") songs are released with a shout of success, with seasonal offerings not only paramount on the release sheets, but also on record buyers' minds.

The upshot of this activity is a collecting field that, while scorned by many enthusiasts, nevertheless attracts some of the most dedicated specialists in the hobby, with prices for the most in-demand pieces

at least pursuing the best-known rock 'n' roll rarities into the stratosphere.

In 1998, Tim Neely, one of America's foremost collectors and experts in the field, isolated a lengthy catalog of Christmas releases with current values in excess of $500, including festive offerings by such comparative unknowns as the Moonglows ("Just a Lonely Christmas"—Chance 1150, red vinyl), the Orioles ("What Are You Doing New Year's Eve"—Jubilee 5017), the Five Keys ("It's Christmas Time"—Aladdin 3113) and Georgia Harris ("Let's Exchange Hearts for Christmas"—Hy-Tone 117), alongside such hobby staples as odd variations on Elvis Presley's *Christmas Album* (RCA LOC 1035), the Beatles' annual Christmas flexidiscs, and original (1966) pressings of Booker T. and the MGs' *In the Christmas Spirit* (Stax ST 713).

However, it is also safe to say that even among the most unremarkable Christmas releases, there lurk rarities and obscurities that evade the most completist collector's grasp, even when—as in many instances—the record in question was a sizeable hit. Kate Bush's "December Will Be Magic Again" (UK EMI 5121), Queen's "Thank God It's Christmas" (UK EMI QUEEN 5), and David Bowie's "Peace on Earth"/"Little Drummer Boy" duet with Bing Crosby (UK RCA BOW 12) are classic examples of original 45s that, unreleased in the US and available only for the seasonal period in Britain, disappeared much faster than their Top 30 chart positions might suggest.

Crosby, of course, is probably the artist most responsible for the enduring popularity of Christmas records. His "White Christmas" is reckoned among the best-selling records in world history, having been re-pressed and reissued on countless occasions. Several of these pressings are now as rare as the song itself is popular. For example, finding original 78 and 45 issues from both the US and UK is a challenging proposition for any collector. The sheer popularity of that song, incidentally, is challenged only by "Little Drummer Boy"—a US Top 30 hit for five years running (1958–62) for the Harry Simeone Chorale (20th Century Fox 121), and a staple release for myriad acts every year since then.

The rock 'n' roll Christmas record was launched by Elvis Presley. Accompanied by the EP *Elvis Sings Christmas Songs* (RCA EPA 4108), Elvis's *Christmas Album* was originally issued in 1957, in a deluxe gatefold sleeve with a booklet of photographs. Although the LP itself has remained a catalog staple, that grand, early packaging was already a thing of the past for the 1958 season, rendering the original pressing a highly sought-after item.

In Elvis's wake, a host of artists cut their own Christmas albums—as, indeed, they still do. From Frankie Avalon to the Partridge Family, from the Brady Bunch to the Backstreet Boys, no teen idol's year seems complete without a festive disc, though it is, perhaps, a sorry indictment of the overall quality of these releases (combined with the enormous quantities that are so optimistically manufactured) that precious few have taken on any serious value among collectors.

Christmas singles, on the other hand, exert a fascination that even avowed anti-Christmas listeners find difficult to avoid, and which festive shoppers seem unable to resist. *Billboard* even published a special Christmas chart between 1963–72, and again from 1983–85, since so many Santa songs were invading the regular Top 100. Even today, it is hard to turn one's back on such seasonal delights as Charlie Ace's "Jingle Bells Cha Cha" (Logan 446), Santo and Johnny's "Twistin' Bells" (Canadian American 132—one of an entire subgenre of Christmas records dedicated to the Twist dance sensation), the surfing silliness of the Surfaris' "Santa's Speed Shop" (Decca 31561), or the Paris Sisters' "Man with the Mistletoe Mustache" (Cavalier 828).

Neither is Christmas purely the province of the kitsch and sentimental. Phil Spector weighed in with some of the most sensational Christmas records of all time, collected together on the legendary and oft-reissued *A Christmas Gift to You* (Philles PHLP 4005). It is hard to believe, therefore, that the original album release, in 1963, was an absolute flop. Its release coincided with the assassination of President John F. Kennedy, an event that essentially canceled Christmas across the US, and it would be 1972 before a reissue on the Beatles' Apple label (SW 3400)

brought the record the critical and commercial favor it merited.

In the meantime, however (and, of course, for three decades since then), singles pulled from the LP have become avidly collectible. Look for Darlene Love's "Christmas" (Philles 119), "Xmas Blues" (125), and "Winter Wonderland" (125X); the Ronettes's "I Saw Mommy Kissing Santa Claus," backed by the Crystals' "Rudolph the Red Nosed Reindeer"(Pavilion 03333); and the promo "Phil Spector's Christmas Medley" (Pavilion AE7 1354), issued (like the Ronettes's 45) to coincide with a 1981 re-release of the LP. None will disappoint.

Those other giants of American pop record production, Brian Wilson and Bob Crewe, also masterminded Christmas records. Crewe led the Four Seasons through *The Four Seasons Greetings* (Vee-Jay 1055) in 1962, spinning off the singles "Santa Claus Is Coming to Town" (478) and "I Saw Mommy Kissing Santa Claus" (626). Wilson's *Beach Boys Christmas Album* followed in 1964 (Capitol T2164), again trailing some remarkable 45s, "Little Saint Nick" (Capitol 5096) and "The Man with All the Toys" (Capitol 5312). The latter title, incidentally, is also the source for one of the scarcest of all British Christmas singles, a cover version by the Variations (UK Immediate IM 019); the Beach Boys' own efforts, meanwhile, were subsequently paired with an abandoned second Christmas album, dating from 1977, as 1998's *Ultimate Christmas* CD.

Motown was another reliable source of Christmas material during the 1960s, with suitable (if not necessarily excellent) offerings across the stable. The Temptations' "Rudolph the Red Nosed Reindeer" (Gordy 7082), Stevie Wonder's "Some Day at Christmas" (Tamla 54142), the Supremes' "Children's Christmas Song" (Motown 1085), and as late as 1972, Marvin Gaye's "Christmas in the City" (Tamla 54229) are among this avenue's brightest highlights.

Perhaps the most collectible individual field within the Christmas hobby, predictably, relates to the Beatles. Their own festive flexis notwithstanding, the groups enormous success launched a string of 45s seemingly guaranteed to appeal to lovelorn Beatles fans everywhere, as they waited to see what Santa would bring them. The craze was launched in 1963 by English comedy actress Dora Bryan, who announced "All I Want for Christmas Is a Beatle" (UK Fontana TF 427). It was perpetuated the following year by TV puppet stars Tich and Quackers, who demanded "Santa Bring Me Ringo" (UK Oriole CB 1980).

By far the greatest activity, however, was in America. There, the Beatles' fame had already provoked such spin-offs as Donna Lynn's "My Boyfriend Got a Beatle Haircut" (Capitol 5127), the Four Preps's "A Letter to the Beatles" (Capitol 5143), and Annie and the Orphans' "My Girl's Been Bitten by the Beatle Bug" (Capitol 5144). But as Christmas loomed, the floodgates truly opened.

Becky Lee Beck, Jackie and Jill, and the Fans all strived for success in 1964 with "I Want a Beatle for Christmas" (Challenge 9372, USA 791, and Dot 16688, respectively). Cindy Rella begged "Bring Me a Beatle for Christmas" (Drum Boy 112), while Christine Hunter reiterated Tich and Quacker's demand "Santa Bring Me Ringo" (Roulette 4584). The Beatles drummer was also the subject of Garry Ferrier's "Ringo-Deer" (Canada Capitol 72202).

The Beatles' own contributions to the festivities, meanwhile, remained locked on those aforementioned flexidiscs, until after the band's dissolution. In 1971, however, John Lennon's "Happy Christmas (War Is Over)" (Apple 1842) was issued; George Harrison's "Ding Dong" (Apple 1879) followed in 1974; Paul McCartney weighed in with "Wonderful Christmas Time" (Columbia 11162) in 1979; and Ringo Starr followed with the *I Want to Be Santa Claus* (Mercury 54668) album in 1999. Included among that latter set's highlights, incidentally, was a cover of one of the Beatles' own Christmas flexi performances, "Christmas Time Is Here Again."

None of these solo efforts is especially rare, but there are some neat variations: green-vinyl pressings of the Lennon 45, blue-and-white custom labels for the Harrison issue, and a red-vinyl reissue of McCartney's song.

If the majority of Christmas action took place in the US during the 1960s, the scene shifted to the UK

throughout the early '70s. Chart regulars Mud, Showaddywaddy, Slade, Wizzard, the Wombles, and Gilbert O'Sullivan all scored with seasonal smashes between 1973–75. The festive fancy also struck as far afield as singer-songwriter Chris de Burgh ("A Spaceman Came Traveling"—UK A&M AMS 7627), progressive rocker Greg Lake ("I Believe in Father Christmas"—UK Manticore K13511), folkies Steeleye Span ("Gaudete"—UK Chrysalis CHS 2005), and multi-instrumentalist Mike Oldfield ("In Dulce Jubilo"—UK Virgin VS 131).

Elton John scored a minor British hit with the now remarkably hard-to-find "Step into Christmas" (UK DJM DJS 290), though in terms of fabled rarities, none can touch Marc Bolan and T. Rex. A super-limited fan-club flexidisc, *Christmas in a T. Rex World* (Lyntone), in 1972, was followed by "Christmas Bop" (EMI Hot Wax MARC 12), scheduled for release for Christmas 1975, but pulled before the pressing plant even began production. All that exists today of this release are a couple of sets of paper labels for the A- and B-sides, though the song itself is now readily available on sundry compilations.

The late '70s and thereafter saw no letup in the weight of Christmas records released, though chart placings became considerably scarcer. Although the UK charts continued to turn up at least one monster smash every Christmas, in America the highest-placing festive single of the entire decade was the Eagles' "Please Come Home for Christmas" (Asylum 4555)—which peaked at No. 18. Oddly, this is also the only Eagles single ever issued with a custom picture sleeve.

In the 1980s, glam veteran Gary Glitter, teen idols Wham! (featuring George Michael), and the Kinks all cut very credible Xmas offerings for the UK market, while an American radio promo *Christmas Rarities on CD* compilation, issued in the late '80s, rounded up a number of the most collectible recent issues, including the aforementioned Queen and Kate Bush titles, oddities by REM (including "Ghost Reindeers in the Sky"), and songs by Elvis, the Beach Boys, and many more.

The highest-selling Christmas record of all time, even eclipsing any individual issue of "White

Christmas," also dates from the 1980s. Band Aid's "Do They Know It's Christmas?" was issued in 1984, to raise relief funds for victims of the Ethiopian famine. It drew in performances from across the contemporary British pop and rock spectrum: U2, David Bowie, Paul Weller, Duran Duran, Culture Club, Bananarama, Spandau Ballet, Paul McCartney, and Status Quo are just some of the acts who are featured on the recording.

It is not rare in any format, though two variations are at least of interest. A 12-inch remix contributed by Frankie Goes to Hollywood mastermind Trevor Horn features an otherwise unheard lead vocal from Sting (Columbia 05157); a 1989 Band Aid II remake, produced by Stock-Aitken-Waterman, involves Cliff Richard, Kevin Godley, Wet Wet Wet, and the returning Bananarama, backed by a somewhat less-than-stellar gathering of the producers' own stable of stars (UK FEED 2).

With and without Band Aid, Cliff Richard is also very high among the biggest-selling artists of the Christmas genre. In 1982, "Little Town (Of Bethlehem)" (EMI 5348) became his first-ever religiously themed Top 20 hit; since that time, "Another Christmas Day" (EMI EM 31), "Mistletoe and Wine" (EMI EM 78), "Saviour's Day" (EMI XMAS 90), "We Should Be Together" (EMI XMAS 91), and "The Millennium Prayer" (Papillion PROMISECD 01) have not only helped maintained Richard's record of scoring at least one chart-topper in every decade since his career commenced in 1958, they have also outperformed the expectations of both his fans and his detractors.

"The Millennium Prayer," recorded for Christmas 1999, was rejected by EMI, Richard's record label for the previous 41 years. Richard responded by quitting the company for his manager's own Papillion label, and "The Millennium Prayer" topped the UK chart for three weeks.

These vast successes have not obscured some extremely collectible items within this canon. Despite being a comparative unknown in the US, Richard is avidly collected in the UK and elsewhere, and each of his festive offerings has arrived with its own unique limited edition—a picture disc of "Little Town," an Advent Calendar insert with the 12-inch "Mistletoe and Wine," or a 7-inch double-pack of "We Should Be Together," for example.

Christmas-themed novelties, long a popular field, have also flourished in recent years, with punk-speed carols a period specialty. From the Yobs (aka punk band The Boys), who kicked the field off with 1977's "Run Rudolph Run" (UK NEMS NES 114), to Bad Religion, who contributed a Mach 10 "Silent Night," to an Atlantic label promo, and on to indie favorites Silkworm, Dandy Warhols, the Flaming Lips, and Metal Mike, the alternative rock era has seen a plethora of amusing, wry, or just plain breakneck holiday fare.

Be prepared to search long and hard for most of them, though. Many were issued as limited-edition 45s, others appeared only on now-rare promo collections, and others still were intended merely as Christmas gifts to a band's fan club or friends. Pearl Jam's annual offerings are insanely collectible, though one of the rarest (and greatest) such issues in recent years was British rockabilly heroes Howlin' Wilf's "Bugger My Buttocks for Christmas" (UK NV EP 4). As its title suggests, it is an indelible slab of ribaldry, guaranteed to enliven any festive gathering.

The bootleg boom of the 1980s and 1990s also unearthed a number of quite unexpected Christmas-themed outtakes from some of the giants of '60s rock. A Rolling Stones' *Satanic Majesties'*-era outtake, "Cosmic Christmas," relayed "We Wish You a Merry Christmas" via freaky electronics. Pink Floyd was caught in a riotous mood with the 1969 release "The Merry Xmas Song." Of more contemporary vintage, U2 frontman Bono was captured on bootleg reciting the poem "Driving to Midnight Mass on Christmas Eve," by Irish poet John F. Dean, over his band's "New Year's Day," on an Irish radio broadcast, while Brit-pop heroes Elastica cut a driving version of "Gloria in Excelsis" for the BBC's *John Peel Show*.

Even its adherents admit that collecting Christmas records is neither the most culturally hip, nor the most musically fulfilling, field in which to specialize. Nevertheless, the genre continues to blossom in collectibility, as surely as every Christmas brings another cartload of records to be collected. Jingle bells.

Further Reading: *Goldmine Christmas Record Price Guide,* by Tim Neely (Krause Publications, 1997)

8-Tracks—Clunk, Click, Every Trip

Has any format ever been so cruelly derided as the 8-Track? It was not the first format to be superseded by better technology, nor will it be the last. But it is the only one that is continually held up as the butt of even noncollectors' jokes. Some, including such close relations as 2-Track and 4-Track tapes, have been quietly forgotten. Others—78s and 45s, most notably— are either utterly sanctified, or are constantly on the brink of a major comeback. But 8-Tracks aren't simply remembered, they are remembered with such loathing that the growing band of enthusiasts who actively collect them spend as much time trying to justify their dementia as they do actually buying and playing the things.

The disadvantages of the format are manifold, of course. But so are the advantages, and the 8-Track can also claim to have one of the most fascinating histories in modern recording industry. With the emphasis on the word *modern.*

Several designers can be considered among the fathers of the format, though in reality, each was working toward decidedly different destinations. The basis of the format is the "endless loop," a single band of tape that moves through a hollow body cartridge (affectionately abbreviated to "cart" by modern enthusiasts), and which, when it reaches the end of the recorded program, simply begins again. The advantage of this system is that (barring malfunction, of course) one would never need to touch the tape itself.

A Toledo, Ohio, inventor, Bernard Cousino, was the first off the mark, perfecting a loop tape that he intended marketing toward the retail community for point-of-sale advertising. He visualized, of course, the endless repetition of a slogan or jingle that makes the modern shopping experience such a joyful one. (The in-flight or "black box" recorders utilized by the airline industry also used the endless-loop technology.)

Another pioneer was George Eash, creator of the Fidelipac cartridge favored by radio stations to carry advertisements, spot announcements, and station IDs. A third was Earl Muntz, a former used-car and TV salesman who was now working to create a personal music system for use in automobiles. The fourth innovator was Chicago-based William Powell Lear, Sr., inventor, of course, of the Lear Jet, and a renowned pioneer in the field of instruments and communications devices for use in aircraft; back in the 1930s, he was a leading figure at Motorola, the car radio manufacturer.

What distinguished each of these men's formats was the number of tracks the tape carried; that is, how the music was stored on the tape and how the player read it. The simplest devices, Cousino and Eash's territory, utilized 2-Track technology, and are best visualized as a length of tape that has been divided into two bands, lengthwise, each containing one musical program. When inserted into the player, the machine first reads one band, then when reaching a (usually metallic) marker at the end, switches over to read the other band, and so on, until the tape is removed from the unit.

Muntz's tapes, utilizing the same technology, also contained two tracks, but because they were in stereo, each of those tracks was then divided again—hence the format was called "4-Track." Lear's design, with four stereo tracks, requiring the tape to "turn over" after each one, therefore became the 8-Track.

Although he had been experimenting with endless loops since the 1940s, Lear was inspired to action by Muntz's 4-Tracks, which he began installing in his Lear Jets in 1963. Both the quality of the 4-Track tapes and their restricted length left him somewhat dissatisfied. The optimum length for the tape in any of these formats was no more than 20 minutes. The stereo 4-Track tape was thus limited to a maximum of 40 minutes' playing time; by doubling the number of tracks, the 8-Track doubled the playing time too, with a loss of fidelity that was barely noticeable.

Working in partnership with one of the leading suppliers of tape heads, Nortronics, Lear also succeeded in vanquishing another of the Muntz tape's drawbacks, the need for the tape roller to enter the cartridge from the player's mechanism. The Lear 8-Track's roller was contained within, and while this would cause its own rash of problems should the tape tangle, or (unforeseen at the time) should the roller decompose, it was still an improvement. Within a year, Lear was unveiling his prototype to widespread admiration.

With RCA having leaped aboard the format with a pledge to adapt its entire current catalog to the 8-Track, Lear contracted with the Ford Motor Company to supply the Lear Jet 8-Track as an optional extra in its 1966 models. Chrysler and GM followed suit in 1967. And, while the 8-Track is remembered primarily as an in-car format, as its popularity increased, there was also vast demand for household players.

This was particularly true in the UK and Europe, where an American-style automotive culture has never been more than a minority interest. However, the format never took root, and by the mid-'70s, British manufacture of 8-Tracks had ceased.

Back in the US, meanwhile, even the higher cost of 8-Tracks when compared to LPs could not prevent the format's march forward. All of the advantages that were trotted out to sell CDs in the mid-'80s— from portability and durability to non-deteriorating sound quality—were touted for 8-Tracks, while fears that one's favorite records might not become available in the format (a hurdle that the competing 4-Track was never able to overcome) were allayed by a virtual industry-wide leap onto the bandwagon.

The 8-Track format was not perfect, of course. Among the features that modern-day comedians most enjoy abusing is the metallic "clunk" sound that the player makes as it reaches the end of one program and switches over to the next. If this falls in a logical place—at the end of a song, for example, one swiftly becomes inured to it. However, particularly in the early days of 8-Tracks, logic sadly appears to have been strangely lacking, as record companies simply dubbed an entire album onto the tape, irrespective of where the program ended (and, therefore, where the clunks fell).

The only concession made was to fade the song out a few seconds before the end, then fade it back in once the next program was under way, and it is by no means unusual for a song to begin literally seconds before it needs to be faded, then to pick up again one resounding clunk later. Further problems arise with especially lengthy tracks—"Southern Man" on Crosby, Stills, Nash and Young's *4 Way Street* 8-Track begins on one program, continues across the next, and finally concludes on a third!

Not until the early '70s did record companies make a concerted effort to address this problem. Simply rearranging songs so that each program contained complete performances was a popular and sensible method, though this could create problems of its own. Concept and thematic albums, for example, would emerge utterly jumbled, with Genesis's *The Lamb Lies Down on Broadway* (Atco ATC TP 2-401) just one of those that sheds all semblance to its intended nature via the transference of much of the vinyl's third side to the 8-Track's second program.

Another difficulty lay in trying to even-out the playing time of each of the four programs—an expanse of blank tape at the end of one of them, after all, completely obviated the need for the continuous loop's benefits, and while some labels did simply shrug their shoulders and let purchasers figure out what to do next, others found an ingenious solution that has resulted in what are now some very popular variations. Bonus tracks would be added, either repeated from elsewhere on the album, or imported from another release entirely.

This wasn't always a grandiose gesture. Elton John's *Greatest Hits Volume One,* for example, boasts a final track comprising a little less than half of a repeated "Bennie and the Jets." But several of Capitol's Beatles 8-Tracks are prized for their bonus inclusions—*Early Beatles* (8XT 2309) adds "Roll Over Beethoven" to the program, *The Beatles' Second Album* (8XT 2080) gains "And I Love Her," and *Something New* (8XT 2108) is bolstered by "Thank You Girl."

Even more exciting, from the collector's point of view, were those occasions when a well-intentioned engineer would return to the original master tape

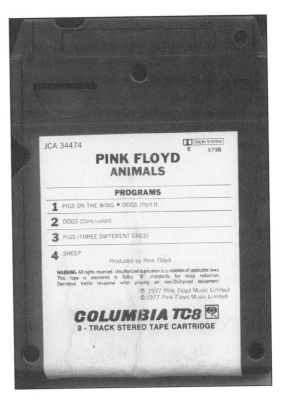

Pink Floyd's *Animals* 8-Track with the unedited "Pigs on the Wing."

and extract a performance deleted from the album itself, using that to plug the gap. A mere handful of these have been documented, but all are extremely sought after by collectors, and of course, they fetch prices to match.

The Beatles' *Sgt. Pepper's Lonely Hearts Club Band* (Capitol 8XT 2653) offers a slightly extended version of the title track reprise, while Lou Reed's *Berlin* (RCA P8S 11670) includes approximately 30 seconds of lazy piano interlude appended to the opening title track that is unavailable in any other format (Reed himself even blocked its inclusion on the 1998 CD remaster). Even more desirable is Pink Floyd's *Animals* (Columbia TC8 JCA 34474), which features an unabridged of "Pigs on the Wing," a piece presented in two abbreviated parts on vinyl, cassette, and CD.

A number of 8-Tracks even offered up exclusive, alternate mixes, either on individual songs or throughout the entire album. King Crimson's *Court of the Crimson King* (Atlantic M88245) and Steeleye Span's *Commoners Crown* (UK Chrysalis Y8HR 1071) are both numbered among this select band of collectibles.

Another area of the 8-Track collectors market is the format's packaging. The nature of the cartridge denied consumers many of the extras that LPs were beginning to incorporate—free posters, inserts, and so on. Proofs-of-purchase slips were thus inserted, to allow the buyer to receive such goodies free of charge from the record company. Other issues, notably double album/tape packages, boasted custom boxes that are a thrill to find today.

Few, if any, record companies maintained their own manufacturing facilities. Rather, the majority entrusted both production and distribution to outside companies, with the majority opting for the market leader, Ampex. (Orrtronics, pioneers of its own superior, but ultimately doomed, 8-Track format also did some manufacturing.)

This was obviously an ideal situation in the normal course of events. However, two of the 8-Track hobby's most enduring rarities testify to what could happen when that course became disrupted.

In 1969, Reprise cancelled plans to release a new album by Frank Sinatra and Antonio Carlos Jobim, the follow-up to their 1967 collaboration *Francis Albert Sinatra and Antonio Carlos Jobim* (FS 1021). However, production and shipping of the *Sinatra-Jobim* 8-Track (W71028) was already well under way at Ampex's Illinois plant, when the Reprise label, in Los Angeles, made the decision to cancel the release. Though just a handful of copies are known to have survived the ensuing recall, still the 8-Track stands as the only format in which this album was made available.

Five years later, Ampex's production schedule and Reprise's new release policy came into conflict once again, this time over Alan Price's *Savaloy Dip: Words and Music by Alan Price* (Reprise M86427). The follow-up to the Englishman's hit soundtrack *O Lucky Man!* was similarly already in production when Reprise decided not to issue it after all. Again, a handful of 8-Tracks are all that remain of this rather enjoyable LP.

The golden age of the 8-Track, at least in terms of sales, arrived during the early '70s, peaking around 1974. Only then did progressive advancements in the fidelity and quality of cassette tapes (hitherto a despicably poor relation to the mighty cart) begin nibbling away at the 8-Track's market share, a meal that was garnished by record company economics, since the industry was reeling from the effects of the oil embargo of 1973–74. Cassettes were considerably cheaper and easier to manufacture than 8-Tracks, required fewer manufacturing materials, and demanded less storage space as well.

It wasn't cassette tapes alone that were cheaper to manufacture. Cassette players, too, required less effort, and by 1976, none of the leading American cartridge deck manufacturers were doing more than treading water with existing models, while putting their research-and-development efforts into cassette players and recorders. The cassette industry adopted the Dolby noise reduction system, for example. For the most part, 8-Tracks ignored it.

Too late, the 8-Track began to fight back. Recordable tapes (and, of course, machines) were introduced to compete with the cassette's most obvious advantage; while the storage issue was challenged by two distinct design changes: the folding Mini-8, which enjoyed a brief flicker of popularity during the mid-'70s, and a revolutionary effort from the Motorola company that was little more than half the size of traditional cartridges. Neither truly took off, however, and even if they had, the cassette had one more trick up its sleeve—cassette recorder manufacturers teamed up with car manufacturers. The day when more cassette players than 8-Track players were installed in automobile dashboards was the day we kissed the cartridge goodbye.

Sensing the direction the wind was blowing, tape manufacturers themselves began to cut back on the quality of cartridges, with inevitable results. If 8-Tracks had one major flaw (one that was readily exploited by supporters of the cassette format), it concerned reliability. Tape jammed, twisted, or snapped, rollers slipped out of alignment, and so on. Of course, as quality control and design standards stagnated and slipped, these problems became more pronounced. Soon, it seemed, more new 8-Tracks were turning up faulty than not, and the cassette took another mighty stride toward supremacy.

Many of the 8-Track collecting hobby's most prized releases date from these last, desperate years, with particular emphasis on punk rock and new wave issues. A mint, sealed copy of the Sex Pistols' 1977 album *Never Mind the Bollocks, Here's the Sex Pistols* (Warner Bros. M8 3147) caused waves of disbelief and controversy to sweep through the 8-Track community when one sold for $100 during the mid-'90s.

The tape itself is not especially rare, certainly not when compared with the Beatles' *Deluxe Three Pack* (Capitol 8X3T 358), valued at over $2,000, or the aforementioned *Sinatra Jobim*. However, like Lou Reed's legendary *Metal Machine Music* (RCA CPS2 1101), there is an aura surrounding *Bollocks* that simply does not fit in with the popular image of the 8-Track collection—that is, a teetering pile of Peter Frampton, Jethro Tull, Elton John, and country-and-western carts. In fact, a surprising number of prized and primal punk albums did make it onto 8-Track in the US, including issues by Patti Smith, the Jam, Television, the Ramones, Blondie, and Elvis Costello. Track back into the genre's prehistory, meanwhile, and early albums by the Stooges, the MC5, and the Velvet Underground can also be found on 8-Track.

Prices for many of these items tend to be high; but only in the latter instances, where manufacturing figures were significantly lower than even the famously minuscule vinyl pressing runs, do the tapes truly merit the attention. In the other instances, it is the collectors' own perceptions of an item's collectibility, as opposed to its actual physical rarity, that buoys the market.

As a general rule of thumb, a rare LP is always going to be rarer on 8-Track. However, the relatively minor corner of the collectors market that 8-Tracks hold ensures that, with but a handful of exceptions, prices for carts are never going to begin attaining the same heights as vinyl.

It is well-known, for example, that the Yardbirds' *Live with Jimmy Page* (Epic E 30615) LP was on sale for less than a week in 1971 before an injunction from Page saw it pulled from stores. Less well-publicized is the 8-Track version that, due to a slightly later shipping date, saw the light of day for just 24 hours before the ax fell. The LP is today worth close to three figures; a 2000 CD reissue on the Mooreland St. label (MS 33068), similarly quashed at Page's insistence, looks set to join it there. But the 8-Track is scarcely even noticed by collectors, despite its being many times rarer than either of them.

That collectors are so dismissive of even the 8-Track's greatest rarities simply echoes the public response to the format's demise. As the 1970s ended and the 1980s began, fewer and fewer new releases made the stores, and by 1983, the battle was over. Only a handful of major labels were even producing the old format any longer, and of those that were, all had withdrawn them from stores by the end of the year.

The 8-Track format continued to be sold through the RCA (now BMG) and Columbia House record and tape clubs for a few years longer, but even there, interest was fading. Among the very last releases offered were John Lennon's *Live in NYC* (1986), George Harrison's *Cloud 9* (1987), Michael Jackson's *Bad* (1987), and Chicago's *XIX* (1988). It is an indication of how poorly even these mega-smashes sold, however, that many people—collectors of those particular artists included—are completely unaware that the 8-Tracks exist. The digital era had, after all, already dawned. Today, it seems impossible that such a dinosaur as the 8-Track could ever have walked the earth in tandem with the CD.

When 8-Track collecting first began to organize itself during the early '90s, it was initially viewed as little more than an offshoot of the then-burgeoning market in nostalgia-kitsch. Either that, or as a peculiarly damaged cult.

However, there was some support. A 1993 article in *Alternative Press* magazine, extolling the sonic virtues of 8-Tracks in preference to some of the shoddily mastered CDs then on the market, raised some eyebrows, even prompting a wry commentary in a subsequent issue of *Billboard*. The nationwide launch of the now-legendary (but sadly, after 100 issues, defunct) *8-Track Mind* fanzine focused further attention on the hobby. The advent of eBay and other Internet auction sites, too, has had an effect, even if it is simply bringing an already tight-knit community even closer together.

Cart collecting remains, then, a backwater, and is probably better off for it. Few dealers price their 8-Tracks higher than a couple of bucks; few collectors (the aforementioned Sex Pistols fan notwithstanding) would pay any more than that.

In addition, the field remains wide open to both research and finds, all conducted in the knowledge that their discovery may not make the finder rich or famous. But they will leave him or her with a collectible rarity that nobody else had probably even dreamed existed.

Enhanced CDs—All This and Moving Pictures, Too

Widely regarded as the future of CDs, when the format was first ignited in 1995, "enhanced" CDs—also known as CD+ and CD-Extra—offered conventional CD releases with additional multimedia material accessible via a computer fitted with the necessary (and readily obtainable) software.

It was a remarkable invention. Video footage could now be added to discs, together with displays of discographical and biographical information, extra illustrative material, and so much more. In many ways enhanced CDs were comparable to the simultaneously emergent CD-ROM, the difference being that enhanced CDs allowed one to enjoy the music, without access to a computer. Moreover, enhanced CDs usually retailed at the same cost as a regular issue, providing the enhancements as a free bonus.

A number of acts, across the musical spectrum, latched on to the enhanced CD format very early on, with mid-1995 releases by Sarah McLachlan, Moby, 2 Minutes Hate, Bush, and the picturesquely named Techno Squid Eats Parliament. Other early entrants included Tom Robinson, London Suede, Marc Almond, and even Bob Dylan, whose 1995 *Greatest Hits Volume 3* collection (Columbia CXR 67324) included a wealth of additional material.

Unfortunately, conflict over the required operating systems ensured that buying enhanced CDs swiftly degenerated into a crapshoot. The industry's attempts to standardize the format were hampered both by the non-availability of appropriate software in some operating systems, and by the software makers' own updating of their product. Somehow it doesn't seem like a lot of fun to cram your hard-drive with downloads, upgrades, and patches every time you want to watch a video flickering in a one-inch square.

Enhanced CDs are still appearing today, some with fascinating bonus material, and others (UK CD singles especially) at least offering an accompanying video or live footage. As collectibles, however, they have yet to take off as anything more than curios.

Further Reading: *Collectible Compact Disc Price Guide,* by Gregory Cooper (Collector Books, various editions)

EPs—Albums on Installment Plans

EPs, short for Extended Play, are the most evocative of all "classic" vinyl stars. Neither single nor album, neither a quick burst of glorious noise (surely the hallmark of a truly great 45) or an overlong succession of songs you could live without (sadly, the hallmark of too many LPs), EPs offered four songs tailored for shocking, rocking fun, and through the 1950s in America and the 1960s in Britain, served up some of the greatest music of the age.

The EP grew, naturally, out of the developing popularity of the 45, when the Columbia label—at the height of the so-called War of the Speeds with RCA—decided to counter that company's newfangled single with the mini-album. That format did not take off, but the principle was sound, and EPs began to move into the limelight.

The vast majority were pressed in considerably smaller runs than most 45s (or LPs), ensuring that even relatively unknown issues today can fetch high sums. Move into the realm of the accepted superstars of the rock 'n' roll era, and prices can balloon—it has been estimated that, in terms of percentages, there are more rare and high-priced EPs in the American rock 'n' roll catalog than either 45s, 78s, or LPs. Anybody who has devoted time to seeking the things out will doubtless agree.

Elvis, of course, was at the forefront of the EP release schedules. Between 1956–59, RCA issued some two dozen Presley EPs, excerpting his albums and movie soundtracks, rounding up recent hits, or even offering all-new material. Many received custom picture sleeves, which of course only increase their modern worth even further.

Some excellent collections are included in this canon. In 1956, two volumes of *Elvis* (RCA EPA 4387, EPA 993) highlighted the King's first album in pocket-money pieces; that same year, *Elvis Presley* (EPA 747) offered up his dramatic versions of "Blue Suede Shoes," "Tutti Frutti," "I Got a Woman," and "Just Because," together with a minefield of sleeve variations that have fascinated collectors for 45 years.

To even begin to dwell on the Presley catalog, however, is to overlook a vast corpus of equally exciting issues by other artists. Gene Vincent's *Bluejean Bop, and the Bluecaps* and *Record Date* albums were each split across three EPs apiece during 1957–58 (Capitol EAP 1-3 764; 1-3 811; and 1-3 1059); Decca made a similar gesture with great swathes of the Bill Haley catalog. Sun released four fine Jerry Lee Lewis EPs (Sun EPA 107–110). Del-Fi produced two Ritchie Valens EPs (DFEP 101, 111), while the first five EPs issued by Specialty (400–405) were all by Little Richard and include some of his most incendiary performances. And this is merely to scratch the surface. Many collectors believe rock 'n' roll is best experienced on 45. But it is best collected on EP.

The late '50s saw the EP's popularity decline considerably. LPs were becoming more affordable, and perhaps appeared more attractive to younger customers. Suddenly it no longer seemed necessary to release LPs on "installment plans," and by 1962, only a handful of US labels were still issuing EPs in any great numbers, RCA (more Elvis) and Vee-Jay paramount among them.

The latter's Four Seasons EP catalog, two volumes of *The Four Seasons Sing* (VJEP-1 901/902), is a wonder to behold, while Dee Clark's *Keep It Up,* originally released on the Abner subsidiary (EP 1-900), then reissued on Vee-Jay (VJEP 1-900), is also a fine find.

For most collectors, however, mention of the Vee-Jay EP catalog brings just one title to mind: the Beatles' *Souvenir of Their Visit to America* (VJEP 1-903), featuring four songs from the already oft-recycled *Introducing* LP. Advertising for the issue, incidentally, found a new meaning for the initials EP—"economy package."

Souvenir . . . sold close to 80,000 copies, a respectable quantity, but strangely, not enough to push it into the chart. Two subsequent Beatles EPs released by Capitol sold less but climbed higher: *Four By the Beatles* (Capitol EAP 1-2121) reached No. 92; *4-by the Beatles* (Capitol R5365) reached No. 68. In defense of those lowly positions (this is the biggest band in the world, after all), it should be pointed out that EPs were costlier than 45s, were less well promoted, and offered no new material.

The *4-by* concept was not unique to the Beatles issues. Prompted by the success of EPs in the UK, Capitol contemplated launching an entire series of so-called super singles, featuring four tracks apiece. The Beatles issue was preceded by a Beach Boys EP, *4-by the Beach Boys* (Capitol R5267), featuring "Wendy," "Little Honda" (both of which charted, at No. 44 and No. 65, respectively), "Don't Back Down," and "Hushabye." Unfortunately, the super-single concept did not travel much farther, and in December 1965, the releases were deleted from the catalog, and the EP as a flourishing American format was at an end.

In Britain, however, the EP survived until around 1967, was reborn as the three- or four-song maxi-single in the early '70s, and has never truly gone away. A strong revival during the punk era at the end of the 1970s was followed by the adaptation of the EP format first for 12-inch singles, and today, for CD singles. Many modern artists, particularly those with a strong feel for pop traditions, claim even now that they think of the three- or four-track CDs that are practically de rigueur in the UK marketplace, as EPs. In the meantime, of course, the 7-inch vinyl forebears just keep on rising in value.

EPs were launched in Britain in 1954, in emulation of the format's success in mainland Europe. Many of France's top performers, in particular, apparently preferred the brightly sleeved EPs even to LPs, and collectors of such artists as Jacques Brel, Serge Gainsbourg, and Françoise Hardy, seeking first releases of their best-known songs, are known to pay high sums for required EPs. Although the earliest British EPs were issued in generic record company sleeves, they swiftly began aping the Continental predilection for colorful jackets, often featuring unique photographs and artwork. It is crucial to remember, when collecting EPs, that the sleeve is as important as the music.

In Britain, the format was initially the preserve of middle-of-the-road and jazz artists, many of whom utilized the format not only for their more popular releases, but also to highlight successful aspects of their live shows. Jazzman Chris Barber, for example, turned tracks on several of his EPs over to Lonnie

Donegan, a band member whose "skiffle" music style was showcased with a few numbers during the Chris Barber Jazz band's own performance. Donegan quit Barber's band soon after; *The Lonnie Donegan Skiffle Group* (UK Decca DFE 6345) and *Backstairs Session* (Polygon Jazz JTE 107), the young iconoclast's first solo EPs, still stand as prime examples of the music's early years.

The Vipers skiffle group, led by future children's TV host Wally Whyton, also cut three extraordinary EPs: two volumes of *Skiffle Music* (UK Parlophone GEP 8615, 8626) and *Skiffling Along with the Vipers* (GEP 8655). Other skiffle acts to look for on EP include the Avon Cities Skiffle Group, Ken Colyer, Bob Cort, Chas McDevitt, and even blues legend Alexis Korner. Be warned, however. The field is constantly growing in popularity, and EP prices are soaring even higher than singles.

Into the early '60s, jazz and light pop continued to dominate the EP release schedules. From 1959, Acker Bilk's *Mr. Acker Bilk Sings* (Pye Jazz NJE 1067) is a popular issue, not only as, indeed, a rare opportunity to hear Bilk put down his trademark clarinet for a time, but also for a tiny credit published on the back of the picture sleeve—"Recording balance—Joe Meek."

Meek would soon spring to prominence as perhaps the most visionary independent British producer of all time, with a sprawling discography of considerable value. Less well-documented, his early years twiddling knobs for other producers (in this instance, Denis Preston) have caused some extraordinarily unexpected records to spring to collecting prominence.

Also popular in Britain at this time were EPs by comedians (a prime example is Tony Hancock's *Little Pieces of Hancock*—Pye NEP 24146), such children's entertainers as Uncle Mac, and pianists Russ Conway and Mrs. Mills. The pianists' releases, on Columbia and Parlophone respectively, are among the most common of all EPs of the pre-Beatles era. But, as domestic rock 'n' rollers began their ascent, the EP began to shake off its somewhat dusty image.

Tommy Steele, often described as Britain's first rock 'n' roller, issued nine EPs for Decca between 1956–60, though it must be confessed that long before that sequence reached its end, Steele's transformation into an all-round family entertainer was well under way. Certainly by 1958, his most innovative years were behind him, which left the field wide open for a new King of rock 'n' roll. And this one would not be abdicating.

Cliff Richard and the Shadows, both individually and collectively, were responsible for a wealth of fabulous EPs during the 1950s and 1960s. *Serious Charge* (Columbia SEG 7895), Richard's first EP, and *Expresso Bongo* (SEG 7971), his fourth, both took their titles and contents from Richard's first two movies, in 1959. Following each of the soundtrack EPs, two volumes of *Cliff* (SEG 7903, 7910) and four of *Cliff Sings* (SEG 7979, 7987, 8005, 8021) excerpted his first two albums. Beginning with *Expresso Bongo*, meanwhile, Richard was also among the first British pop stars to record and release in stereo.

In total, Richard issued 46 British EPs between 1959–68, many of which featured music that has yet to make its way onto long-playing formats. Richard was accompanied on many of his greatest hits by the Shadows, a band that ignited their own massively successful career with the guitar instrumental "Apache," in 1960; the Shadows issued a further 25 EPs. Again, the contents were drawn from both fresh and previously issued sources; again, a worldwide network of collectors is hot in pursuit of both British issues and the wealth of additional titles issued elsewhere. Australia, New Zealand, Scandinavia, Germany, and France were all hotbeds of EP activity throughout the 1960s.

The popularity of these mini-LPs was economic and technological. Although multispeed record players were coming into use, they were still very expensive. British and European EPs, revolving at 45 rpm (many American issuers preferred 33⅓), allowed the public to pick up LPs without having to invest in new equipment—a consideration that the fans repaid by sending many EPs into the chart. Indeed, between March 1960 and December 1967, Britain actually boasted a separate EPs chart; predictably, it was dominated by Richard and the Shadows, at least

ジョーン・バエズ・ベスト4

ドンナ・ドンナ／ハウス・オブ・ザ・ライジング・サン
オルフェの歌／リパブリック讃歌

＊ジョーン・バエズ

STEREO PP

★ VANGUARD
STEREO LAB

33 rpm
PP-44

The Japanese "Donna Donna" EP by Joan Baez.

until 1963. Then the Beatles issued their first EP, *Twist and Shout* (Parlophone GEP 8882), and the world turned upside down.

The Beatles—the group is the single most successful EP act in British chart history, and that despite releasing just a dozen conventional EPs between 1963–66. Even the abandonment of the EP chart could not halt the group—their 13th and final EP simply took over the singles chart instead. Issued as an LP in America, December 1967's *Magical Mystery Tour* (Parlophone MMT 1) was a unique double EP in Britain, where it climbed to No. 2, held off the top spot by "Hello Goodbye" (Parlophone R5655), a regular 45 excerpted from the same EP.

Richard, the Shadows, and the Beatles were by far the most prolific issuers of EPs during the 1960s, with the majority of their releases remaining in print for several years. (The Beatles issues have even been reissued on CD, with individual sleeves re-creating the original EP jackets.)

Other bands considered among the era's most collectible, however, were less prolific. Throughout the heyday of the EP, Manfred Mann released eight EPs, the Kinks just five (also reissued in a box set, accompanied by five European issues), the Rolling Stones no more than three (all comprising non-UK album/single material), and the Who a mere one, the legendary *Ready Steady Who* (Reaction 592 001), in 1966.

However, diligent searching can uncover EPs from as far across the pop spectrum as the Bachelors, Lulu, the Walker Brothers (the excellent *I Need You*—Philips BE 12596), the Barron Knights, and all of the important Merseybeat and Motown acts. Some fascinating statistics, too, come to light as one delves deeper into the subject: The Shadows' *To the Fore* (Columbia SEG 8094) shares the title of most successful British EP of all time with Nina & Frederick's eponymous EP, with a whopping 115-week chart life. And the Beach Boys' *Hits* (Capitol EAP1 20781) spent more weeks at No. 1 (34) than any other release.

Most EP collectors pull down the curtains on the era with *Magical Mystery Tour;* some even fold before that, with the cessation of the EP chart and the corresponding abandonment of the format elsewhere around the UK industry.

However, the maxi-single boom of the early '70s does have its adherents, with the Dawn progressive label releasing a string of very collectible issues, including two UK No. 1s, Mungo Jerry's "In the Summertime" (DNX 2502) and "Baby Jump" (DNX 2505). Other successful maxi-singles included the Who's 1970 opus *Excerpts from Tommy* (Track 2252 001), the Rolling Stones' "Street Fighting Man" (Decca F13195), and several releases within the Fly label's *Magnifly,* and from RAK's *Replay* series.

Finally, for collectors unable to spend the increasingly high sums that classic EPs now demand, the UK See for Miles label has done an admirable job compiling many of these onto CD in the *EP Collection* series, with the packaging including illustrations of the original artwork. Beware, however—several of these issues have themselves now gone out of print, and the series as a whole is rapidly becoming a collectible in its own right.

Further Reading: *35 Years of British Hit EPs,* by George R. White (Music Mentor, 2001)

Explicit Chapter—I Can't Believe You Just Said That

Music censorship might not be as old as music, but it is certainly as old as recorded music. Did 1928 America really believe that Duke Ellington's "The Mooche" (Brunswick 4122) was an incitement to rape? Did *Variety* truly announce, in 1931, that songs with suggestive or otherwise objectionable titles would no longer be included in the trade publication's pop chart? And was "(I'm Your) Hoochie Coochie Man" genuinely one of the titles singled out for blacklisting?

Everybody knows that Elvis Presley was requested not to swivel his hips on the *Ed Sullivan Show* in 1957. It isn't so widely recalled that, two years earlier, Alan Freed's *Rock 'n' Roll Dance Party* was yanked from the network schedules after viewers saw Frankie Lymon dancing with a white girl. The strange tale of "Louie Louie," investigated by FBI agents convinced that its lyrics contained some deeply, darkly disturbing obscenity, has become the subject of learned books and articles. But what of the equally bizarre saga of Van Morrison's "Gloria," so widely considered obscene that even a custom-built clean version by the Shadows of Knight was initially viewed with some suspicion.

The tale of censorship in music is as wry as it is, on occasions, weird. In Britain, where the BBC monopolized the airwaves, it was once an unwritten law of commerce that a record which had landed a broadcast ban stood a greater chance of becoming a chart success than one that hadn't—a rule that was tested (and found to be absolutely correct) by artists as far afield as Twinkle, Judge Dread, and Frankie Goes to Hollywood.

Elsewhere, the varied applications of Chuck Berry's "ding-a-ling" (banned not from radio, but from television, after Berry's wrist movements were seen to be suggestive) seem childishly tame when compared to the dirty deeds perpetrated in the name of pop today. But the powers that be have long since learned their lesson. Even the most explicit record is no longer publicly banned. Instead, it simply doesn't get played.

In America, the issue of banishing records from the airwaves is confused somewhat by the absence of a central broadcasting authority such as Britain's BBC or IBA (Independent Broadcasting Authority), both of whose duties include a spot of moral watchdogging. Recent years, however, have seen censors of another sort move into that void, in the form of the giant corporate retailers whose family oriented policies have seen the retailers grow increasingly resistant to new releases that fail to meet certain moral criteria.

It is within this field that many collectors are finding variations on commonly available CDs that, while never likely to be declared true rarities, are certain to elude completists in years to come. The fact that many of them offer a wholly distorted view of what the original album was trying to say only adds to the fascination.

Slicing up albums to make them palatable to the masses is not, of course, a new practice. In 1962, Columbia bade Bob Dylan revise his forthcoming *The Freewheelin' Bob Dylan* (Columbia CL 1986) LP lest one track, "Talking John Birch Blues," inflame the then-influential society of the same name. In 1966, early pressings of Jefferson Airplane's *Takes Off* debut (RCA LPM 3584) were remastered to excise three songs seen as overtly promoting sex and drugs.

Deleting odd references from songs, too, has a long and proud history. Also in 1966, Lou Christie was forced to re-record a lyric in his single "Rhapsody in the Rain" (MGM 13473), after radio found it sexually explicit—the single was then re-pressed and reissued with the letters "DJ" added to the matrix number in the run-off groove.

In the UK in 1970, the change of one simple word made the difference between the latest Kinks single, "Lola" (Pye 7N 17961), fading into oblivion or becoming a major hit. Singer Ray Davies actually flew home from the band's latest US tour to replace the word "Coca" (as in "-Cola") with "Cherry," to avoid contravening the BBC's strict policy on not advertising commercial products. Weeks later, "Lola" was No. 1 and British Kinks collectors have spent the last 30-plus years seeking the few thousand copies of the unaltered version that made it onto the streets.

The notion of providing "cleaned-up" versions of potentially offensive songs to radio also goes back at least to the late '60s. In 1967, psychedelic band John's Children recorded a new version of their "Desdemona" mini-hit (Track 604 003), after British radio objected to the line "Lift up your skirt and fly" (it was replaced with "Why do you have to lie?"). Unfortunately, radio then lost interest in playing the song and the re-recording exists only on a handful of rare test pressings.

Other examples abound. The first promo singles of Pink Floyd's "Money" (Harvest P-3609) were lifted directly from the group's *Dark Side of the Moon* album, with the word "bullshit" clearly audible. The disc was hastily withdrawn and replaced with an expletive-deleted edition. Two years later, Bob Dylan's "Hurricane" (Columbia 10245) was similarly treated; "shit" was removed and the edited version was released with the legend "Special Rush Reservice" printed on the label (Columbia 43683).

Since that time, bleeps and edits have become a part of the furniture—so much so that, when an old song is heard on the radio today, even listeners familiar with the original might not notice the excision of sundry choice lines and rhymes. However, it was not until the late-'80s industry-wide adoption of Parental Guidance–type labels that these "cleaned-up" recordings also became available to the general public.

These labels represent a major challenge to collectors and have become a very popular specialty. They range from what has become the generic, industry-standard wording, "Parental Advisory—Explicit Lyrics," to custom issues designed by individual bands, and on to private stickers applied by retailers themselves.

In both the former and latter categories, collectibility is subjective, often centering around inappropriate usage. Copies of Frank Zappa's *Jazz from Hell* (Capitol 74205), purchased from the Pacific Northwest chain of Fred Meyer department stores, for example, bore the retailer's own "Explicit Lyrics" warning, despite the fact that the album was wholly instrumental. Shrink-wrapped copies still bearing this sticker may not be much more than humorous curios to many people, but censorship collectors regard them as something of a Holy Grail. Other favorites include John Moran's *The Manson Family* (Philips Classics), the first classical album ever to be stickered, and Serge Gainsbourg's 1986 *Love on the Beat* (Mercury 822-849-1), which history records as the first album ever to receive a parental advisory. It warned that the album contained "explicit *French* lyrics."

Stickers produced of a band's own volition are also at a premium, again, if the shrink-wrap to which they were applied is still in place around the album (sealed or unsealed). These include the Cure's reminder, attached to its *Standing on the Beach* compilation (Elektra 60477), that the song "Killing an Arab" "has absolutely no racist overtones whatsoever . . . the

Cure condemns its use in furthering anti-Arab feeling." Also highly collectible is Ice-T's warning, applied to the ironically titled *Freedom of Speech* (Sire 26028), that "some material may be X-tra hype and inappropriate for squares and suckers." It's worth watching, too, for the lengthy anti-censorship diatribe accompanying another Zappa album, *Frank Zappa Meets the Mothers of Prevention* (Capitol ST 74203).

For several years, the use of Parental Advisory stickers appeared to be holding the forces of further censorship at bay, and any battles were fought out over album artwork (see below). Slowly, however, the climate began to change. Several stores greeted the proliferation of stickers by instituting their own policies of who such an album could or could not be sold to, in line with their policies regarding rated videos and magazines. Then, in 1991, Wal-Mart—the nation's largest retail outlet—announced it would no longer be stocking any stickered discs whatsoever, regardless of their content. With other family oriented chain stores seemingly set to follow suit, the record labels had just two choices: lose a massive chunk of the market; or lose the lewd lyrics. The lyrics lost.

"Clean" versions of albums involve removing—either with bleeps, gaps, or (less commonly) lyrics transplanted from elsewhere in the song—any word or phrase that can be considered objectionable. These tend to be the traditional vulgarities of "fuck," "shit," "asshole," and so on, yet during the decade-plus during which these "PG" discs have flourished, little attention has been granted them by discographers and researchers.

It is a void that future collectors and historians are certain to regret. Across the entire musical spectrum, the number of albums available in both "clean" and, for want of a better word, "unclean," versions certainly runs into the thousands. It will be interesting, in a few years, to discover which versions are the most common, though at present, the "clean" editions are lagging far, far behind in terms of both sales and visibility. "PG" versions of Prince's *Emancipation* three-CD set (Capitol 55063) are already hard to find. Watch, too, for Metallica's *Garage Inc.* (Elektra

62323—that label's first-ever censored rock record), Oasis's *Standing on the Shoulder of Giants* (Sony 62189), and Lo-Fidelity All-Stars' *How to Operate with a Blown Mind* (Skint/Columbia 63614).

Perhaps oddly, no "classic" or even original punk rock records have yet been similarly treated, including such notoriously scatological jewels as the Bob Dylan's *Desire,* John Lennon's *Plastic Ono Band,* and Marianne Faithfull's *Broken English,* all of which have seen high-profile re-releases (or at least have been anthologized) since the dawn of this new age. Readily audible in the above-mentioned records are such traditionally censured words as "shit" (Dylan), fucking" (Lennon), and "cunt" (Faithfull); the same three albums also include songs dealing, in explicit terms, with racist police, the disavowal of God, and the nuts and bolts of infidelity. Yet the records are sold without any form of printed warning as to the nature of their contents, leading one to assume that foul language and contentious subject matter are not the only issues at stake. Modern standards of political correctness and cultural bias would also seem to play a part in the cautionary labeling of music. Either that or, as Patti Smith remarks on her *Easter* album, "don't fuck with the past."

You Can't Show That Here— Collecting "Banned" Record Sleeves

The field of banned record sleeves is, of course, a long-established favorite among record collectors. From 1966, the Beatles' "butcher cover" is undoubtedly the best known; there are, however, many more similar, if considerably less high-profile, examples of jackets that, having caused some offense to some sensitive soul, are then packed off to the darkest corners of oblivion.

The Mamas and the Papas' 1966 debut LP, *If You Can Believe Your Eyes and Ears* (Dunhill 50006), exists with three different sleeves. The original depicted the four band members in a bathtub, with a toilet visible in the lower right corner of the picture. Fearing that this oblique reference to bodily functions (even pop stars have to poo) could offend people, Dunhill revised the cover, placing a scroll over the contentious commode, emblazoned with the words "includes California Dreaming," before finally removing the toilet altogether.

The following year, the front jacket photo of Moby Grape's self-titled debut album (Columbia CL 2968) was withdrawn in America (but not in Europe) after it was noticed that band member Don Stevenson's middle finger, as laid across his washboard, could be construed as making an offensive gesture. In 1969, two sleeves were censored for promoting nudity. First, the original sleeve for Blind Faith's eponymous album (Atco SC 3304), depicting a young, topless girl, was replaced by a band portrait; then a full-frontal-nude sleeve for John and Yoko Lennon's *Wedding Album* (Apple SMAX 3361) caused such a stir that it was repackaged in a brown paper sleeve, cut to reveal only the duo's faces.

The climate was equally unyielding five years later, when the original European artwork for Roxy Music's *Country Life* (Atco 106), depicting two more-or-less topless females, was withdrawn from sale in the US, and replaced with a close-up of the foliage that stands in the background of the scene.

Since those now-so-seemingly naïve days, withdrawn album art barely even makes minor headlines anymore. The collectors market, too, treats such events as all but routine—the Beatles' butchers notwithstanding, nobody is ever going to get rich from stockpiling "banned" record sleeves. They are interesting conversation items, nothing more. Nevertheless, occasional pieces do rise above the average apathy to create a stir in wider circles.

Retail complaints over Jane's Addiction's *Ritual de lo Habitual* (WB 25993) and Nirvana's *In Utero* (Geffen 24607) both made headlines, with Jane's Addiction frontman Perry Farrell proving a formidable foe, even for the mega-corporations ranged against him. His original sleeve design showed a painting of Farrell in bed with two women, the covers drawn back to reveal a modicum of genitalia. Having delightedly ascertained that it was his penis, as opposed to any other organ, that was creating the fuss, Farrell finally agreed to replace the art with a plain white sleeve emblazoned with the First Amendment. He then took similarly great pleasure from revealing that the original cover far outsold the "clean" one.

In Utero drew opprobrium on several levels. Included in the artwork, by vocalist Kurt Cobain, were several fetuses—an odd object to be deemed offensive, but no matter. The song title "Rape Me" also upset some people. A revised version removing the fetuses and retitling the offending song "Waif Me" was issued for sale in stores that required such alterations, though the song itself went untouched. Like the Jane's Addiction release, copies of the doctored sleeve are far scarcer than the regular edition, perhaps indicating that the marketing departments who demand the changes are somewhat less open-minded than the consumers they seek to protect—as, perhaps, they always have been. Possibly the most purposefully "naughty" sleeves of all time, Mom's Apple Pie's 1972 debut (Brown Sleeve 14200), is far more common in its original form—on which a beaming woman proffers the viewer a steaming pastry, sliced to reveal a vagina within—than the hastily arranged replacement sleeve that shows the crevice plugged with a wall of barbed wire.

The most talked-about withdrawn sleeve of recent years was that scheduled to accompany hip-hop act the Coup's *Party Time* album, in November 2001. As posted on the 75 Ark label's Web site that August, the sleeve depicted a massive explosion ripping through the twin towers of the World Trade Center, with band member "Boots" Riley in the foreground, holding a detonator. The real life destruction of the building on September 11 led to the design's immediate withdrawal, with the Web site image being removed within two hours of the attack. No finished sleeves had been printed (production was due to begin that week), but printer's proofs and other preliminaries had long since been completed and circulated.

By macabre coincidence, Dream Theater's *Live Scenes from New York* (East West), issued just days before the attack, depicted both the World Trade Center towers and the Statue of Liberty engulfed in flames. This release, too, was promptly withdrawn, with stores and eBay both halting sales of the set. It remains to be seen whether these sleeves will become cherished collectors items in the future.

Further Reading: *Parental Advisory: Music Censorship in America,* by Eric Nuzum (Perennial, 2001)

Export Issues—Foreigners Have All the Fun

A very specialized corner of the European 45 and LP collecting market revolves around so-called export issues—releases pressed in the UK during the 1960s by such major labels as the EMI and Decca groups, intended for release and distribution to countries whose own manufacturing capabilities were minimal or even nonexistent.

Readily detectable by their unique catalog numbers, many of these simply replicate standard UK releases, but are considerably more collectible than their domestic counterparts. Even more popular, however, are export issues that never received a full British release in any form.

The most attention in this area is, predictably, focused on the Beatles, the Rolling Stones, and Cliff Richard. Five different Beatles export-only singles exist, including three that have no UK counterpart ("If I Fell"—Parlophone DP 562, "Yesterday"—DP 563, and "Michelle"—DP 564), and two more ("Hey Jude"—DP 570 and "Let It Be"—PR 5833) that were issued by Apple in Britain, but as exports, bear the Parlophone label.

Among the rarest export albums, meanwhile, are British Parlophone pressings of releases normally considered part of the Beatles' American catalog, and again, not conforming to any regular UK issue: *Something New* (CPCS 101), *The Beatles' Second Album* (CPCS 103), *Beatles VI* (CPCS 104), and *Hey Jude* (CPCS 106).

The Rolling Stones' export catalog is even more vast, comprising some 20 45s and four EPs, and again including several unique issues. "Empty Heart" (AT 15035), "Time Is on My Side" (AT 15039), "Heart of Stone" (Decca F22180), and the live "Little Queenie" (F13126) are all highly sought after. US-only albums similarly manufactured include the radically different Stateside configuration of *Out of*

Our Heads (LK 4725), *Have You Seen Your Mother Live* (aka *Got Live If You Want It!*) (LK 4838), and *Flowers* (LK 4888).

Not all export issues were lost to UK record buyers. In 1961, Cliff Richard's "Gee Whiz It's You" (Columbia DC 756) was produced for European use, yet the song proved so popular that copies were imported back into Britain in such numbers that the record wound up at No. 4 on the chart! In a field normally priced in the three-figure range, "Gee Whiz It's You" allows even the most impecunious collector to own at least one export 45. (Other Richard export issues are less accessible—neither "What'd I Say" [DC 758] nor "Angel" [DC 762] are at all easily found.)

The phenomenon was not restricted to these acts alone, of course—nor were they restricted to vinyl. In the early '60s, Britain was unusual in its failure to have adopted picture sleeves for singles. A number of labels, therefore, manufactured export-only sleeves that would be wrapped around both specially pressed and regular-issue singles. The Kinks's "All Day and All of the Night" (7N 15174) and "Till the End of the Day" (7N 15981) are among the wealth of releases that exist in this form.

Export-single collecting is not an easy hobby to pursue. Releases were typically distributed throughout Europe and the British Commonwealth in quantities appropriate to the size of the host market—a few thousand here, a few thousand there. A number of issues have come to light via the Internet in recent years, with several being offered by seemingly original purchasers who themselves had no idea of the records' significance to British collectors. Presumably the nature of the bidding swiftly alerted them to the true value of their holdings.

Along similar lines, several US record companies leased equipment at pressing plants in Germany and elsewhere in western Europe, to produce custom LPs for sale at American military PXs, largely in Germany. Using standard American artwork, these albums often used local labels (but printed in English), with "Manufactured in Germany" in the run-off groove. Few examples are known, though

Elvis Presley's *Elvis* (RCA Victor LPM 1382) is a well-attested rarity.

Flexidiscs—Bend Me, Shape Me

The flexidisc is an area that excites a lot of attention among collectors, but has received little attention from serious researchers.

Since its arrival on the scene during the 1930s, the flexidisc has proven itself to be *the* most . . . uh . . . flexible promotional medium available.

The advantages are manifold. Extraordinarily cheap to produce, flexidisc technology can be applied to any host material sturdy enough to withstand the light embossing required to impress the grooves. Thus, flexidiscs have appeared in the form of postage stamps (issued by the Asian nation of Bhutan), postcards, and greetings cards; they have been embedded into cereal packets and record sleeves; they appear on pieces of wood and sheets of metal.

Among the first flexidiscs to truly capture the public imagination was a series of "Hit of the Week" discs produced during the early '30s. Manufactured from paper (sometimes adorned with a picture of the artist), with a shellac layer containing the music, these discs were produced in both 4-inch and 10-inch formats and sold at newsstands for between 15 and 25 cents apiece. They were very fragile, and despite their popularity, few have survived to this day.

Since that time, flexis have filled every need. Manufacturers of almost every conceivable product have used them as promotional items. Thrift-store record bins once overflowed with instructional and advertising discs (much as they now teeter beneath similarly intentioned videocassettes). They have been given away free with books and magazines, they have been affixed to food packages and dispatched through the mail. No matter what use a manufacturer could require, the flexi was capable of fulfilling it.

For the majority of rock and pop record collectors, the most familiar flexis are those that were distributed mounted on the covers of magazines and books; the most famous are those that the Beatles recorded as a Christmas gift to its fan-club members every year between 1963 and 1969.

Containing greetings, comic routines, and snatches of music, these wholly ad-libbed performances are among the most popular of Beatles collectibles, all the more so since they rank among the only officially recorded and released Beatles performances never to have been fully reissued since the band's demise. Only once was an authorized LP of the Christmas messages issued, 1970's *From Then to You: The Beatles' Christmas Album* (Apple/Lyntone LYN 2154)—and it was again distributed only to members of the fan club. However, though these are the best-known issues, they are not the Beatles' only excursion into flexiland.

The greatest source of Beatles (and solo Beatle) flexis is, perhaps oddly, the Soviet Union. The magazines *Club and Amateur Art Activities* and *Krugozor* both dispensed Beatles records with occasional issues during the 1970s and 1980s, including such extravagant four-song issues as "Can't Buy Me Love"/"Maxwell's Silver Hammer"/"Lady Madonna"/ "I Should Have Known Better." Many of the *Krugozor* issues echoed regular vinyl releases through the state-run Melodisc label. Numerous other artists were featured on Soviet flexis; more still can be found on the so-called Polish Postcard singles issued in that country during the 1960s–70s, and certainly a close relation of the flexi that we in the West know and love.

Flexidiscs were a popular vehicle for "special" and fan-club editions; they were also frequently distributed with fanzines and magazines: An Allman Brothers/Marshall Tucker disc that was cover-mounted to a 1975 issue of *Rolling Stone* is popular among Southern-rock aficionados. Genesis gifted the non-LP masterpiece "Twilight Alehouse" to a 1973 issue of Britain's *ZigZag*. Robyn Hitchcock's reinvention of the Beatles' "A Day in the Life" has been a hot commodity since it appeared with a 1991 issue of *The Bob*. Mark Eitzel of American Music Club performed "Crystal Never Knows" on a disc issued with the satirical magazine *Breakfast without Meat* in 1990.

And Michael Stipe, REM's lead singer, treated readers of *Sassy* to a solo interpretation of Syd Barrett's "Dark Globe" in 1989.

However, American collectors can pursue flexidiscs down even more esoteric paths. TOPPS, the gum manufacturers, issued a series of playable gum cards during the late '60s, featuring Motown artists. One of several pop acts featured on cereal packets, with cutaway discs actually printed into the packaging itself, was the Archies. The Shadows of Knight can be heard performing a song called "Potato Chip," distributed with a brand of potato chips. The Dave Clarke Five, in support of Pond's facial cream, delivered another very collectible piece of product endorsement in the mid-'60s.

Although US consumers have received by far the greatest number of now-collectible flexidiscs, the UK has served up some of the hobby's most in-demand individual issues.

One of the pioneers of the cover-mounted flexi in that country was the satirical magazine *Private Eye,* which produced a series of now-rare discs during the 1960s, featuring performances from, among others, Peter Cook and Dudley Moore, and the magazine's own takeoff on the Beatles, the Turds. These were subsequently compiled onto LP, *Private Eye's Golden Years of Sound 1964–70* (LYN 2745), available to magazine subscribers only, and now almost as scarce as the original discs.

The *New Musical Express* weekly produced a string of flexis during the early-to-mid-'70s, featuring, among others, Curved Air, the Faces, Monty Python, Emerson Lake and Palmer, and Alice Cooper. The latter two flexis are especially sought after today, since both contained what was then otherwise unavailable material.

Both discs were two sided, one dedicated to excerpts from the group's latest album (ELP's *Brain Salad Surgery,* Cooper's *Billion Dollar Babies*), and the other given over to, respectively, a US-only B-side, "Brain Salad Surgery," which would not be given a full UK release until its inclusion on the *Works Vol. 2* album five years later, and the session outtake "Slick Black Limousine," since reissued on several Cooper anthologies, but never included on a regular LP. Missing from any other Cooper release, however, is a brief moment of speech appended to the excerpt of "Unfinished Suite" on side A—before the dentist drill starts up, and the pliers begin removing teeth, a sinisterly ethereal disembodied voice asks simply, "Have you ever had gas before?" Priceless.

High values also attach themselves to complete issues of a British music magazine called *Flexipop,* active through the early-to-mid-'80s, and offering, cover-mounted to every issue, a colored vinyl flexidisc by some of the biggest stars of the day. These are especially valued, since again, the emphasis was on rare and unreleased material. Paul Weller of the Jam donated "Pop Art Poem" and a demo of "Boy about Town" (issue 2). Adam and the Ants recorded a version of the Village People's "YMCA," realigned as "ANTS" (issue 4). Soft Cell delivered up one track from its very first, privately produced EP *Mutant Moments* (issue 12). The Cure provided "Lament" (issue 22), and these are just a few of the many goodies presented by this enterprising publication. A mere handful of tracks from this impressive archive have since appeared on CD, via the bands' own anthologies and collections. Many more, however, await their rediscovery.

By their very nature, flexidiscs are difficult to find in Mint condition. They are easily bent, torn, and otherwise damaged, becoming utterly unplayable through everyday wear and tear that would not affect a vinyl disc.

However, as a repository for some genuine curios and rarities within so many bands' catalogs, they can not be overlooked for a second. Whether it's David Cassidy sending greetings to readers of an early '70s teenybop magazine or Dick Clark imparting "inside stories" via a giveaway with 1973's *20 Years of Rock and Roll* compilation LP . . . whether it's EMI heralding a Cliff Richard box set with a flexi excerpting the best of its contents or a 1987 Guns n' Roses tour promo, flexidiscs offer a world of apparently untapped possibilities, frequently at minimal cost.

Just make sure you have a small coin handy, to weight the record down on the turntable.

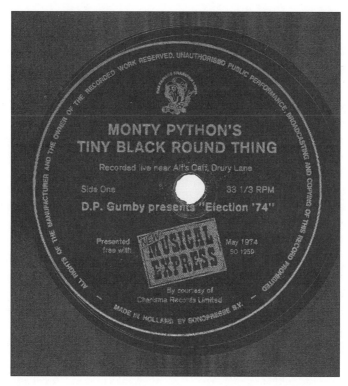

The British *New Musical Express* flexidisc highlighting Monty Python's *Live at Drury Lane LP.*

45s—The Greatest Sound on Earth

The 45 rpm single, the backbone of record collecting in the US (and around the world), arrived on the scene in 1949, as the result of a peculiar—and peculiarly vicious—battle between the giant record labels Columbia and RCA.

The previous year, Columbia introduced the $33\frac{1}{3}$ rpm 10-inch "microgroove" long player and approached RCA—at that time its biggest rival—inviting the company to join in pioneering this new innovation, thus paving the way for its universal introduction. Instead, RCA head David Sarnoff was outraged at having been left so far behind in the technology stakes, and having raged at his own staff, he demanded they make amends by creating a new, competing format. They gave him the 7-inch 45.

The first advertisements for the 45, in March 1949, declared it to be a "50-year marketing achievement." In fact, it took RCA's engineers somewhat less than a year to develop the system, with perhaps the least thought of all going to the speed at which the disc would rotate. The 78 was the norm at the time; $33\frac{1}{3}$s the alleged wave of the future. RCA simply subtracted the latter from the former, and let that be the guide.

Of course, it was not the speed of the Columbia innovation that mattered to the consumer. It was the fact that, for the first time ever, the listener would not have to get up every three or four minutes to change the record. Long players, as their name implied, played for a long time, up to 20 minutes in some cases.

RCA's 45, of course, could not compete with this. At best, the format allowed for two songs to be placed on each side. At the same time as the 45 rpm record was being developed, however, another team was designing an automatic record changer that would permit the listener to stack up to half a dozen unbreakable vinyl 45s atop one another, with each falling to the turntable as the arm left the disc below.

The immediate advantage to this, of course, was that consumers could mix and match music to their liking, as opposed to the Columbia discs, which programmed the songs according to a will of their own. Even better, from a marketing point of view, were the dimensions of these new discs. The 7-inch disc offered a size that anybody could handle one-handedly, and devoured a lot less storage space as well. An ad in *Billboard* that April trumpeted the "Convenient 7-inch size [means] more than 150 single records fit in one foot of bookshelf space. No storage problems for your customers." Intriguingly (but possibly unknowingly), this latter innovation essentially returned records to square one—Emile Berliner's first gramophone records, 54 years earlier, also measured seven inches.

RCA simultaneously introduced a color-coding system that was itself unique. No more unbroken rows of boring black plastic. From now on, pop records alone would be pressed in that color. Classical recordings would use red vinyl, "light classics" were midnight blue, international (modern world music) appeared on light blue, R&B was cerise, country was green, and children's music was yellow. It was a short-lived innovation; by 1952, black vinyl was again the rule. But for the three years in between, during which the 45 rose from novelty status to something approaching its eventual preeminence, a collection of "singles" (so called because the majority featured a single song on each side) was a kaleidoscope of color.

RCA's initial launch comprised 104 singles, plus 76 "album" collections, themselves comprising boxed packages of multiple 45s to be stacked onto the player in whatever sequence the listener chose. Numbered sides, of course, indicated the company's own suggested listening order, with the first track on the album being backed by the last, the second by the penultimate and so forth—again allowing for uninterrupted listening of the entire program. The practice of double albums being pressed with sides one and four on one disc, sides two and three on another,

a practice that continued into the early '80s, is a holdover from this early innovation.

Numerically speaking, the first RCA 45 was Eddy Arnold's "Texarkana Baby"/"A Bouquet of Roses" (48-0001), though any of the 104 records released that momentous day (including ten further Arnold singles) can share the honor of being the first 45s ever. Soon, RCA was releasing almost every new release on both 78 and 45, and by May 1949, the new format had scored its first American chart-topper, Perry Como's " 'A'—You're Adorable" (RCA 47-2899).

Other labels watched RCA's activities with intense interest; Columbia even tentatively tried to take the conflict to a new level, by introducing its own 33⅓ rpm 7-inch in April 1949—the forerunner of the later EP. However, low sales prompted the company to lose interest fairly quickly, and as the year wore on, there were signs that RCA's faith in the 7-inch, too, was beginning to falter. Sales of 78s remained far higher than sales of 45s; Columbia's LPs, for all RCA's efforts, were taking off as well.

There was only one small crumb of comfort to be taken from the entire debacle, and that lay amid reports from around the country that kids, a hitherto untapped market for record companies, were the ones who most supported the 45. If RCA's marketing department could find a way to target this audience, the 45 might be saved.

An RCA retail bulletin from November 1949 fills in the gaps. "Coast to coast, teenagers are lining up for . . . neat little records they can slip in their pockets, with first-class bands playing their favorite hits for 49 cents." It was, the bulletin continued, the lowest price at the newest speed. The cavalry had arrived.

The sudden turnaround in the 45's fortune lost no time in communicating itself across the industry. Capitol, MGM, and Mercury were all early entrants to the fray, with the latter notching up the first non-RCA 45 chart-topper in 1950, with Frankie Laine's "The Cry of the Wild Goose" (5363-X45). National, London, Decca, Savoy, and Aladdin followed; and in late 1950, Columbia swallowed its pride and threw its first 45s into the market. By 1952, there was barely a record label in the land that was not issuing 45s;

by 1955, the 45 was *the* most important musical medium in the Western world. In commercial terms, it remained so until the mid-'80s; in collecting terms, its supremacy remains inviolate.

There are as many ways of collecting 45s as there are collectors of 45s, and it would be impossible to even begin taking note of every one. There is no innovation in record-production history that has not, even in a tiny way, become integral to the format—colored vinyl, as already mentioned, was its birthright; picture sleeves its inheritance; picture discs an inevitable destiny.

Each and every one of these represents a fertile collecting area, and so do their corollaries. If a single was issued on colored vinyl, there are collectors who seek only black-vinyl pressings. If one was issued in a custom picture sleeve, there are collectors who collect only generic-label sleeves. There are even collectors for whom the record itself is not the point—they are after the metal and plastic adapters that were marketed to plug the hole in the record's center, and have elevated the search for even these ephemera to high science.

The introduction of stereo in the late '50s saw several labels experiment with the format at 45 rpm—these issues are eminently collectible. At the other end of the spectrum, mono singles drawn from albums ordinarily available only in stereo have their own army of devotees. And, representing the best of both worlds, promo issues manufactured for radio play offer the hit song in stereo on one side, mono on the other.

Some of the rarest records in the world are 45s, and many of the most expensive. The history of the format is littered with records that are valued not because they are great, not because the band is famous, but because the label in question pressed just a handful, and no one has ever seen more than one or two—and that is the *entire* history. Even today, major and minor record labels continue to produce 45s, albeit in such limited quantities that it seems impossible that their values have not already soared skyward.

Some of these are issued for the handful of jukeboxes nationwide that still play 45s; the 1990s even saw the Capitol-EMI group issue 45s specifically designated "For Jukeboxes Only." Others, however, are marketed directly to the collectors market, arousing some fascinating parallels in the process.

In 1963, the UK Decca label scheduled, then withdrew, a new Rolling Stones single, "Fortune Teller" (Decca F11742). No more than a handful of regular UK issues made it out; more were pressed for record club and export releases—they are identifiable by a solid center, rather than the standard push-out one. How many exist? A couple of thousand at most, and they are valued in the $800 range.

Fast-forward 30 years to 1994, and another new Stones single, "Out of Tears" (Virgin VS 1524). It wasn't withdrawn; indeed, it reached No. 36 on the UK chart. But it did so on the strength of cassette and the two-part CD-single sales. The actual 45 was a numbered, limited edition of just 7,000 copies—more than exist of "Fortune Teller," of course, but still an insignificant number compared to how many Stones collectors there are. Value? We'll have to wait and see. (In the meantime, keep an eye out for a scheduled third CD of the song: 4,000 were pressed and then withdrawn, and have already reached the equal of "Fortune Teller.")

That is one example. From the precious platters pressed during the first years of the 45 revolution, by tiny independent labels with zero distribution and marketing, through another half century of withdrawn, deleted, ignored, or simply lost 45s, there is no end to the list of singles that today make hen's teeth look populous by comparison.

And on the other end of the scale, there are the untold millions of 45s that we collect simply for the love of it. "I look back on my old 45s," Elton John told *Uncut* magazine in 2001, "and I remember when they gave me a bit of happiness. Which is more than human beings have ever given me." In the same issue of the magazine, the Human League's Phil Oakey agreed wholeheartedly. "Maybe records meant so much to us because it was all we had. That seven-inch bit of plastic was our lives. And it cost you a load of money."

An entire generation separates the two men—Elton was a child of the 1940s, digging his wax in the first light of Elvis. Oakey struck gold in the 1970s, with Bolan and Bowie to float his boat. Yet both men are correct. The pop record, specifically the three-minute pop 45, is arguably the most intense and important development in the history of human artifice. It is certainly the most direct. Movies? Yeah, they're great, but once you know the butler did it, who wants to spend another two hours watching while he does it again? Sculpture? Very pretty, lovely lines, and it's your turn to dust its crevices next week. Stamps? Super until your eyesight starts failing, or the hired help needs to mail out the bills. Coins? Bus fare.

But a pile of old 45s? Now you're talking. And now you're dancing.

Further Reading: *Goldmine Price Guide to 45 Rpm Records,* by Tim Neely (Krause Publications, various editions)

4-Track Cartridges—Nice Idea, but Not Enough Clunks

The 4-Track tape was, for a short time, the future of rock 'n' roll. Though 4-Tracks are barely remembered today, and when encountered, are often viewed as a bizarre (or even faulty—what is that big hole in the top where the roller should go?) variation on the 8-Track, the 4-Track not only preceded its better-known cousin, it actually inspired the creation of that format.

However, whereas 8-Track aficionados can look back at their hero's demise at the hands of the cassette and say that the smaller tape was victorious merely because it was cheaper for the record companies to produce, the war with the 4-Track was won fair and square. The 8-Track really was superior—at least for the purpose for which it was designed. The fact that 4-Tracks offered marginally better sound quality, were less prone to breakage—and due to the (quite deliberate) absence of an internal roller, were easier to maintain—does not even enter into the equation. After all, 8-Tracks offered more music, and that's what it's all about.

One Earl Muntz developed the 4-Track tape, specifically for use in automobiles. Utilizing the endless loop technology that was exercising so many other designers at the time (see the section about 8-Tracks on page 57 for further details), Muntz created a method by which two "tracks" of stereo sound could be laid side by side, lengthwise, on a piece of tape, to be played on tape decks that read each one in turn.

Although the 4-Track technology was originally developed as early as 1956, it was 1963 before Muntz began marketing it, initially in California. Buoyed by the support of several major record companies, the so-called Muntz Stereo-Pak received immense publicity when players were installed in vehicles owned by such stars as Frank Sinatra, Peter Lawford, James Garner, Lawrence Welk, and Red Skelton—and even more when an order was placed to install them in the newly developed Lear Jet.

However, upon delivery, the jet's designer, William Powell Lear, became convinced that he could make a far superior portable tape cartridge. Within a year, he had developed the 8-Track, and was moving into many of the same markets that Muntz had hitherto dominated.

Nevertheless the 4- and 8-Tracks existed side by side for some time, with canny hardware manufacturers even marketing players capable of dealing with both formats. Retailers, too, saw little difference between the two formats and frequently stocked them side by side, while many record companies were happy to see their latest releases issued in both formats, as the world watched to see which would ultimately win. Of course it was the 8-Track, though it would be as late as 1970 before the victory was finally complete.

As in virtually every other area of record collecting, the most popular act on 4-Track today is the Beatles (Elvis did not appear in the format). Capitol was one of the first major labels to strike a licensing deal with Muntz, in 1964, and the company issued its first Beatles 4-Tracks that same year. Thereafter, every Beatles album, up to *Let It Be* (Apple X434001), would appear in the format, together with such early Apple releases as the Lennons' *Two Virgins* (Tetragrammaton/Apple TNX 45001), Mary Hopkin's *Postcard* (4CL 3351), and George Harrison's *Wonderwall*

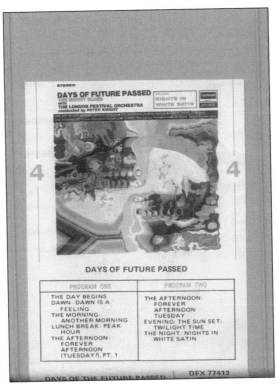

STEREO

DAYS OF FUTURE PASSED
THE MOODY BLUES
WITH
THE LONDON FESTIVAL ORCHESTRA
conducted by PETER KNIGHT

NIGHTS IN
WHITE SATIN

DERAM

4

4

DAYS OF FUTURE PASSED

PROGRAM ONE	PROGRAM TWO
THE DAY BEGINS DAWN: DAWN IS A FEELING THE MORNING: ANOTHER MORNING LUNCH BREAK: PEAK HOUR THE AFTERNOON: FOREVER AFTERNOON (TUESDAY?), PT. 1	THE AFTERNOON: FOREVER AFTERNOON TUESDAY EVENING: THE SUN SET: TWILIGHT TIME THE NIGHT: NIGHTS IN WHITE SATIN

DAYS OF THE FUTURE PASSED | DFX 77412

The 4-Track version of the Moody Blues' *Days of Future Passed.*

Music (Apple 4CL 3350). Paul McCartney's soundtrack to the movie *The Family Way* (London LFX 17136) also made an appearance. The last Beatles-related 4-Tracks to appear were the debut solo albums by all four members, in 1970.

Outside of Beatledom, few 4-Tracks have any collector value, though fans of individual artists will often find themselves tempted by the occasional find. From the last years of the format's life span, such releases as Cream's *Disraeli Gears,* Jimi Hendrix's *Electric Ladyland* (released across two tapes), the Moody Blues' *Days of Future Passed,* and the Bee Gees' debut album are all of interest, while the 4-Track's earlier start also allowed it to make contemporary, as opposed to retrospective, releases for many classic British Invasion albums. This is of especial note to stereo collectors—the most common LPs from this period are, of course, the mono issues. However, 4-Tracks were released only in stereo.

A great deal more research can be done about 4-Tracks than about 8-Tracks, presumably because there are even fewer working 4-Track players in existence today than there are 4-Track collectors.

Beyond the Beatles, there is very little discographical information available; nor has there yet been published any kind of guide to the occasional musical variations that excite 8-Track collectors. That is not, however, to say that they do not exist, with the stereo side of things seeming an especially fruitful domain.

For example, were there any stereo releases that appeared only in the 4-Track format? Nobody is going to get rich by answering that question (or any other one related to this format). But the thrill of discovery can be reward in itself.

One final note: when searching for 4-Tracks on the Internet, remember that reel-to-reel tapes employed that same terminology. Many more apparent hits will, in fact, be referring to these items, than to their cartridge-clad brethren.

Interview Discs—Too Much Chatter

Since the late '70s, interview discs have proven one of the most popular means by which an unknown label can boast a superstar artist in its catalog. Because spoken word is not covered under any copyright law, any interview material is fair game, and thousands upon thousands of discs—45s, LPs, and CDs—have appeared, bearing the private and public thoughts of rock's greatest names. Few are issued by the artist's home label.

A variety of gimmicks—including colored vinyl, picture discs, and intriguing shapes—have been employed to make these more attractive, but specialist collectors notwithstanding, there is little interest in these releases. However, a handful have become legends of sorts, most notably the *Wibling Rivalry* Oasis interview, which became the first such release ever to make the UK chart in 1995 (Fierce Panda NING 12CD).

If commercially available interview discs have little after-market value, promo releases fare quite the opposite. Radio transcription discs have a reasonable audience among collectors; issues made to accompany new-release CDs, too, are popular—REM's *Talk About the Weather* and Neil Young's *Silver and Gold* discs are among those in high demand.

There is also an array of radio-interview 45s issued during the early-to-mid-'60s, featuring "open-ended" interviews, in which a script (read aloud by the DJ, of course) provided the questions, while the artist answered back on the disc. Many such discs exist, though they are in short supply—issues by Julie London (Liberty JL 512) and Brenda Lee (Decca 9-34370) were among those pictured in a special feature in the March 1998 issue of *DISCoveries* magazine.

Jukebox Albums—More Bang for Your Buck

For around 15 years, roughly between 1960 and 1974, many record companies issued Jukebox Albums, or Little LPs, for use in jukeboxes capable of playing $33\frac{1}{3}$ rpm 7-inch releases. Often considered a variation on the popular EP format, Jukebox Albums are also frequently found cataloged as promos (promotional issues), in that they were not generally available to the record-buying public.

Jukebox Albums featured between four and (less frequently) six songs from a current LP, usually packaged in two-color picture sleeves depicting the LP cover, with an attached title strip for placement in the jukebox's selection index.

Predictably, the most collectible items are by the most collectible bands, including Jukebox Album versions of the Beatles' *Second Album* (Capitol 2080), Bob Dylan's *Bringing It All Back Home* (Columbia 9128), and Elvis Presley's 1973 *Aloha from Hawaii* (RCA Victor 2006). Some seven different Rolling Stones albums (including the super-rare *Their Satanic Majesties' Request*—London 54 and *Exile on Main Street*—Rolling Stones Records 22900) and Led Zeppelin's *IV* (Atlantic 7208) and *Houses of the Holy* (Atlantic 7255) are also highly prized.

The Beach Boys, too, boast some very scarce Little LPs in their discography, including *Surfer Girl* (Capitol 1981), *Shutdown Volume Two* (but not, apparently, volume one—Capitol 2027), and *Today* (Capitol 2269). However, with patience there are many more major acts of the era who can be located on Jukebox Albums, ranging as far afield as Jethro Tull and Marvin Gaye, the Grateful Dead and Eydie Gorme.

Be warned, however: Jukebox Albums basically exist in just two grades—unplayed and still sealed, or played to death and virtually worthless. The latter, of course, are by far the most common.

Labelology—The Train Now Standing . . .

A term coined by Japanese record collectors, "labelology" is, quite simply, the study of individual record-label designs, isolating varieties within the most minute details, and establishing both rarity and, where possible, population reports (the number of known examples) for each of them.

It is an exacting pursuit that owes more to such hobbies as bibliophily (book collecting) and philately (collecting stamps) than to music. Much of those pursuits' appeal, after all, is founded upon a collectors' ability to seek out and identify the tiny variations that denote individual printings and redesigns, with literal fortunes depending upon a correct identification.

So it is with labelology. Exacting students have isolated no fewer than 16 different printings of the Beatles' "Twist and Shout" (Tollie 9001), 15 versions of "Please Please Me" (Vee-Jay 581), and a dozen of "She Loves You" (Swan S-4152 S). And that's just for starters.

With the possible exception of Elvis Presley, no other artist has been subject to such microscopic scrutiny as the Beatles, particularly the Vee-Jay and Capitol Records catalogs. Others labels and performers have been studied, but labelology as a whole has been hindered by the absence of a standard, specialized catalog that is able to elevate the science to the same levels of research and knowledge that do now attend those other hobbies.

In philately, such catalogs as *Scott* and *Stanley Gibbons,* in the US and UK, respectively, document at least the major varieties found in every postage stamp in the world—a multivolume task, admittedly, but one that clearly has a sufficient market to ensure the publication and worldwide distribution of new editions every year. In record collecting, similar data for no more than a handful of individual records has thus far been published, with the accepted standard catalogs lagging years behind in making the information available to the public at large.

Thus constricted, labelology can be described as a hobby in search of hobbyists. For those few hundred hardy souls whose time and knowledge is devoted to its furtherance, however, labelology is not simply a vital part of record collecting, it is perhaps *the* most vital. After all, if you are bidding hard cash for an original first pressing of the Kinks's "You Really Got Me," what do you expect to receive? A record that came off the presses on the first day of manufacture? Or a worthless re-pressing from weeks, months, even years later?

LPs—Twelve Inches of Pleasure

As with 45s and CDs, it is impossible to quantify how to collect LPs—or even what to collect. The three formats so thoroughly dominate our conception of what record collecting is all about that on every page in this book, there will be mention of something that a specialist format collector could (and doubtless does) collect.

Individual artists, labels, genres. Mono variations, stereo specialties. Gatefold sleeves or generic inner sleeves, box sets or Dynoflex (okay, maybe not Dynoflex—an ill-starred super flexible format introduced by RCA during the early '70s, that the company stubbornly persisted with, despite an immediate barrage of complaints regarding quality and fidelity). Even if one were to list every single collectible theme that the LP format has embraced, there would be a deluge of mail the next morning, pointing out all those that were omitted.

Historically, the LP is the oldest, and longest surviving, of all recorded formats in use today. Invented by Columbia Records staffer Bill Wallerstein, the $33\frac{1}{3}$ long-playing microgroove record made its debut in June 1948, unveiled by Columbia as the disc of the future.

Columbia had a point. Hitherto, a record album had been precisely what it says—a collection of two-sided records (78 rpm), packaged together into a booklike album. To listen to an entire performance of an opera, for instance, or a symphony, the record owner (or, in better-off homes, one of the record owner's employees) would need to leave his or her seat to change the disc after every song—of course there were no such things as automatic record changers in those days of so-fragile shellac!

Revolving at a significantly slower speed, Columbia's microgroove system allowed the equivalent of six—or more!—individual 78s to be gathered together on each side of a record, affording the unheard-of luxury of up to 20 minutes of uninterrupted listening at a time. It was, in both senses of the word, a revolutionary development, one that would completely change the face of the recording industry.

Indeed, so confident was Columbia in the format's potential to succeed, and so certain of the benefits it would confer on the music industry as a whole (this part may be difficult for modern readers to comprehend), that the company did not even patent the technology employed in the LP's design, development, and manufacture. (Only the term "LP" was trademarked, and even that trademark was allowed to lapse once it became part of the language.) Rather, the company extended an invitation to RCA Victor, at that time, its greatest rival in the marketplace, to participate in the format's launch.

Of course, history records that RCA Victor flew off in a fit of pique, to develop its own rival format, the 45. Columbia launched the LP alone, then, but it need not have worried over the format's reception; the LP was in every way superior to the 78, and, as RCA discovered to its chagrin, to the 45 as well. Within a year or two, 78 albums were virtually a thing of the past; within five years, it was as though they had never even existed.

The first LPs were issued in a 10-inch format, as were the 78s they were supplanting; there was no technical reason for this, beyond not disturbing the consumer's equilibrium more than was necessary. By the late '50s, however, more and more labels were upgrading to the 12-inch format, in which form LPs would remain.

Significant upgrades to what was so simple and basic a design were few and far between thereafter. The changeover from mono to stereo sound was phased in over almost a decade before the labels finally abandoned mono in 1968, by which time all but the most stubborn consumers had come to terms with the new innovation, from both a sonic and a technical point of view. Stereo was accepted because it did not require any upgrade of equipment whatsoever, hence the "mono-compatible stereo" notations applied to many mid-to-late-'60s releases. The 1970s move to quadraphonic sound, on the other hand, foundered on the absence of compatibility, not only with existing equipment, but also between quadraphonic formats themselves.

These periods are, not surprisingly, among the most popular areas for specialist LP collectors who eschew such traditional themes as artists or labels. Quadraphonic is a market unto itself, but both earlier formats have much to offer. Many early stereo albums were produced in painfully minute quantities, to match the market they were intended to meet; they also cost $1 more than mono, at a time when $1 actually represented a sizeable chunk out of a young person's allowance.

This differentiation also explains why many late-mono releases have come down to modern collectors in somewhat lamentable condition. Kids bought mono albums because they were cheaper than stereo—and kids are not necessarily the most careful record owners.

Among adults, meanwhile, there was also the matter of perceived value. While today many collectors regard mono recordings as being both sonically and artistically superior to stereo, contemporary consumers regarded stereo as offering bonus extras that were not available on old-fashioned mono—different guitar solos, fabulous effects, speaker-to-speaker panning, and more.

The late-'70s rush into picture discs, too, spun off a wealth of now highly sought-after (if, in many cases, totally unplayable) items, while the LP format has also been borrowed for a number of items that, while not technically records at all, also attract collectors—LP-shaped clocks and posters both enjoyed their day in the sun.

The 45 collector's love of foreign picture sleeves is another field that attracts album collectors, as they pursue European and other variants on common American LPs. However, sleeves aren't the only things that change from country to country. The very nature of the records shifts as well. It is well known, for example, that each of the Beatles' and Rolling Stones' early (pre-1967) albums bore little relation to its UK counterpart, even on those occasions when the two releases had a common title. So it was with many other releases of the period, with similar variants then spreading across the globe.

Sharp-eared listeners will instantly detect differences in stereo mixes prepared during this same period for American and British listeners. Capitol, the Beatles' US label, was only one of many labels whose own engineers remixed releases before they were issued, creating a field rich in both incredible variety and eye-popping research possibilities.

To reiterate the point made at the beginning of this article, then, the limits to LP collecting possibilities are defined only by the collector's own imagination. With that in mind . . . you're off.

Further Reading: *Goldmine Record Album Price Guide,* by Tim Neely (Krause Publications, various editions)

Mighty Tiny Toy Record Player— Batteries Not Included

At least one person reading this surely got his or her start in collecting with this. Ohio Arts's *Mighty Tiny—The World's Smallest Record Player* was marketed during the 1950s. It had a fascinating (if somewhat unreliable) miniature turntable, with a built-in speaker, designed to play correspondingly minute (2-inch) records. Such artists as the Musical Squares, the Harmonettes, and Amy Wilson and Her Guitar headed the popular line of recordings; there were also series of world music and children's songs, all sold in packets of four.

Mini-8s—Small, but Smart

A little-known variant on the 8-Track, the Mini-8 was introduced in 1969 by Lear Jet and manufactured by Ampex, as competition to the newly emergent cassette tape, whose runaway popularity was making serious inroads into the traditional 8-Track market.

Compatible with existing 8-Track players, the tapes' selling point was that they could be folded in half, to more or less the size of a cassette tape— whose own advantage over the 8-Track was that it required so much less storage room. The working mechanisms and the tape itself were housed in the front half of the cartridge; the other half folded over to create its own protective box.

The disadvantage was the bugbear of length. Mini-8s could hold no more than 30 minutes of music, rendering them ideal for duplicating singles or EPs, but posing no threat to any longer-playing format. Interestingly, rather than step into the breach left by the recent demise of the PlayTape, and create single-artist tapes built around hits or the most popular cuts from given LPs, the Mini-8 concentrated on various-artists compilations.

It is uncertain how many of these collections were manufactured during the Mini-8's brief life span. The 1970 Ampex catalog lists 150 separate titles, but there were certainly others released before the format was finally abandoned later in the year. However, the nature of the tapes' content has seriously retarded collector interest, condemning Mini-8s to a sparsely populated backwater, where only serious tape enthusiasts dare to venture.

Mini Pac—Gone and Forgotten

The Mini Pac was an early predecessor of the Play-Tape, and was designed by Earl Muntz (inventor of the 4-Track cartridge), as an alternative to singles and EPs. Mini Pacs held up to four songs and were compatible with all existing 4-Track players. However, the format seems to have existed for a matter of months only, and tapes today are exceedingly rare.

Mono—One-Track Mind

This Columbia high fidelity monaural recording is scientifically designed to play with the highest quality of reproduction on the phonograph of your choice, new or old. If you are the owner of a new stereophonic system, this record will play with even more brilliant true-to-life fidelity. In short, you can purchase this record with no fear of its becoming obsolete in the future.

—Notice on the back cover of the mono pressing of Bob Dylan's *Highway 61 Revisited* LP, 1965.

According to manager Andrew Loog Oldham, the Rolling Stones recorded all their greatest 1960s records in mono. "Someone else mixed the stereo, when we were away on tour or wherever. The record label knew we wouldn't have the time to go looking at our records in the stores, so they just went ahead and did it." Oldham was adamant. Despite almost 40 years of acclimatization to stereo versions, "If you want to hear the Stones as we intended you to hear them, listen to the original mono albums."

At Motown, label supremo Berry Gordy, Jr., regarded mono as the be-all and end-all of the Hitsville process, and made sure his finest engineers gave it all their attention. The stereo he left to the trainees and beginners. And even though the Beatles' *Sgt. Pepper's Lonely Hearts Club Band* was universally revered as the stereophonic headphone experience of 1967, George Harrison insisted, "You haven't heard *Sgt. Pepper* if you haven't heard it in mono. "*Sgt. Pepper's* mono incarnation, like all the Beatles' original albums, was handled by producer George Martin. The stereo mixdown was given to engineer Geoff Emerick, a capable man, but not the *most* capable. That was Martin, and he just didn't care for stereo back then.

"[Even] in 1967, very few people had stereo equipment," Martin later commented. "Almost everyone listened on mono; it was accepted as the standard. Stereo was strictly for the hi-fi freaks." (Seven years later, of course, people would be saying the same thing about quadraphonic sound. On that occasion, however, they were correct.) Stereo was also more expensive—stereo LPs tended to be priced $1 higher than mono albums.

Although stereo (or 2-Track) recording had been a possibility since the early '50s, when guitar legend Les Paul first began experimenting with it, it was late in the decade before the first stereo albums began appearing. Elvis Presley cut a stereo session at RCA Studios in 1957, but only because the regular recording equipment had broken down; 1960's *Elvis Is Back!* was his first stereo album. Phil Spector also experimented with the technology, releasing the Teddy Bears' *Sing* album in stereo in 1959. However, the best of Spector's work—the work that earned him his reputation as one of the greatest producers ever—was mixed steadfastly down to mono.

When stereo first began creeping into the marketplace as a genuinely saleable commodity, many labels already had two-channel master tapes on hand.

However, not only had they not been mixed to marketable standards, some had not been mixed at all—the released version of a song, in mono, often utilized an entirely different recording.

Some labels got around this by simply remixing the mono master into what is known as "electronically reprocessed stereo," separating out the vocal and instrumental tracks, then placing them in separate channels. Others would venture back to the original tapes. Either way, the ensuing manipulation—and, occasionally, substitutions—opened the door both to some fascinating conversation pieces and, in the most dramatic instances, to the creation of what amounted to an altogether different album. It is the attendant variations, and the handful of mono releases that most famously deviate from what is now accepted as the stereo norm, that first ensnares the novice mono collector.

By late 1967, mono was being phased out across the board, in America; as a result, the most collectible mono albums today are those dating from these later years. Indeed, the roll call also includes some of what are regarded as the greatest albums of all time—*Sgt. Pepper*, the Rolling Stones' *Their Satanic Majesties' Request*, early releases by Steppenwolf, the Grateful Dead, and the Doors, Jefferson Airplane's masterpiece *After Bathing at Baxter's*, the Monkees' *The Birds the Bees and the Monkees*, and the Who's astonishing *The Who Sell Out*. A year later, the only major-label mono albums appearing were white-label radio promos, which themselves simply mixed the stereo masters down.

Mono lingered on in the UK for another year, and again, many fascinating curios emerged, with a unique, and spectacular mono mix of the Beatles' self-titled double album, also known as *The White Album*, among the most in-demand of all releases from this period. Elsewhere, the format survived even longer; mono pressings of the Beatles' *Abbey Road* and the Rolling Stones' *Let It Bleed* were issued in several South American countries in 1969. By 1970, however, mono existed only in radio land.

Ignored for much of the 1970s, nostalgia for the mono sound grew throughout the 1980s, all the more so after CDs came onto the scene with their so-called best sound ever. The fact was, many early CD releases of classic material sounded no better than the LPs they were supposedly replacing, and some sounded worse. Slowly, in the face of widespread consumer outrage, the labels finally returned to the original master tapes, and found that both stereo and mono mixes had their own sets of devotees.

Today, more classic 1960s albums are available again in their intended form than the most optimistic observer would ever have dreamed possible a few years back. The Crazy World of Arthur Brown's 1968 self-titled debut album led the way, appearing on American CD in 1991 with side one of its British mono counterpart appended as spectacular bonus tracks. In 1997, MCA's excellent repackaging of the Who's *A Quick One: Happy Jack* utilized the original mono master tape in preference to the stereo versions prepared in 1966 for US, German, and Japanese release. Jefferson Airplane's *Surrealistic Pillow*, the Velvet Underground's 1967 debut, *The Velvet Underground & Nico*, and a slew of British EMI label reissues head the parade of CDs released with the full mono and stereo mixes presented side by side within a single package.

The Pretty Things' *SF Sorrow*, another album that effortlessly recaptures the mind-expanding mood of the Summer of Love, reappeared in its mono incarnation in 2000. Even Pink Floyd, a band whose spacey psychedelia was theoretically designed only with stereo in mind, has seen its 1967 debut album, *The Piper at the Gates of Dawn*, reissued in its mono form.

In 2001, there were even mono vinyl reissues for several early Bob Dylan albums, surprising veteran fans with the subtle (and often superior) variations they'd overlooked for years before. Few people, after all, ever regarded the studio as anything more than the vehicle for Dylan's words and music. The possibility that he, too, might have served up very different feasts according to the format simply didn't cross their minds.

Mono—Some Collectible Variations

When listening to any LP released in both mono and stereo, keen ears will pick out many minor variations, most frequently in the use of studio effects, such as reverb and panning. For many bands, stereo effects all but became an extra instrument, sometimes utterly altering the sonic characteristics of the instruments that were already there. Whether or not these effects enhance or detract from the performance is entirely subjective. The following list, therefore, concentrates on recordings in which either an alternate mix or a completely different take is immediately apparent. It is by no means a complete guide.

The Beatles: *Sgt. Pepper's Lonely Hearts Club Band (Capitol MAS 2653)*
The entire album has a different sound and feel, with variations running from very prominent guitar toward the end of the opening title track, to extra drumbeats during the intro to the reprise. "She's Leaving Home" is slower in mono, "Fixing a Hole" is slightly longer, and the vocal in "Lucy in the Sky with Diamonds" is drenched in echo. The animal noises before "Good Morning" are radically different as well.

The Beatles: *The Beatles (also known as The White Album) (UK Apple PMC 7068)*
"Helter Skelter" is the best-known variation; the mono take, while shorter (3.36 compared to 4.29), is far more aggressive. Elsewhere, the mono "Honey Pie" features a longer guitar break, while there are more animal-noise variations during "Piggies."

Jeff Beck: *Truth (UK Columbia SX 6293)*
The instrumental "Beck's Bolero" features an extended ending that was deleted from stereo pressings.

The Crazy World of Arthur Brown: *The Crazy World of Arthur Brown (UK Track 612 005)*
For anybody raised on the stereo pressing of this 1968 masterpiece, exposure to the mono edition is akin to hearing an entirely different record. Side one is especially notable, with the opening three tracks (including the hit "Fire") present in noticeably longer versions. The mono "Fire" is much more spare and lacks the friendly trumpets that haunt the stereo version. The epic "Come and Buy"/"Time"/"Confusion," while

almost one minute shorter in mono, is a completely different take, with a new construction. Side one alone has been utilized as CD bonus tracks to several reissues of the stereo album, most recently in 1997 (Touchwood TWCD 2012).

Cream: *Wheels of Fire (UK Polydor 582 031)*
The entire mono "In the Studio" portion of this two-LP set is littered with minor variations, many of them merely tonal—the bells during "Those Were the Days," for example. However, "Deserted Cities of the Heart" is noticeably different from its stereo counterpart, with the mono version featuring acoustic guitars pulled way up in the mix.

Richard and Mimi Fariña: *Reflections in a Crystal Wind (Vanguard 79204)*
A number of hitherto barely noticed instruments have been brought to the fore in the stereo mix, most notably during "Chrysanthemum." However, John Hammond's harmonica during "Hard-Loving Loser" is more pronounced in mono.

Jimi Hendrix Experience: *Axis: Bold As Love (UK Track 612 003)*
It is the absence of the stereo sound effects that most affects the mono pressing of this, and indeed, Hendrix's other mono albums, *Are You Experienced* (UK Track 612 001) and *Smash Hits* (612 004). (Mono versions of *Electric Ladyland*, while rumored, have never been confirmed.) Experienced Hendrix collectors, however, unanimously return to *Axis: Bold As Love* as the album most affected—and, some say, most improved—by the mono format. A decreased emphasis on the special effects allows more attention to be paid to the music; "Little Wing" is one song that is infinitely better served by the mono format. A vinyl reissue of this album was released in 2001.

Trini Lopez: *Trini Lopez at PJ's (Reprise R6093)*
Different studio takes are one thing; different live recordings are quite another. In mono, "La Bamba" opens with Lopez shouting the title before the band comes in, and the song runs for approximately 4.50. In stereo, drums begin the song, which boasts more echo, different vocal inflections, and a playing time of just under 4.30.

Love: *Love (Elektra EKL 4001)*
A meritoriously meaty mono mix makes the stereo sound quite puny by comparison. Several of the mono tracks also run 15–20 seconds longer—nothing you'd really notice, but a nice touch when you're paying close attention.

Pink Floyd: *The Piper at the Gates of Dawn (Tower T 5903)*
This is another of those albums in which the overall impression of the mono is more affecting than any attempt to isolate sonic differences between the two formats. The most noticeable variations are to be found on "Pow R Toc H," with heightened vocal effects; the epic "Interstellar Overdrive," which offers a clearly different mix than the one found on the stereo version; and "Flaming," where certain harmonies and special effects are either heightened or diminished compared to their stereo counterparts (the mono outro is also subtly changed).

Pink Floyd: *A Saucerful of Secrets (UK Columbia SX 6258)*
There are little twiddly changes all over, with the vast spacey title track certainly feeling the absence of the stereo effects. Noticeable variations occur on the mono "Corporal Clegg," where the guitars lose a lot of their stereo attack; the military barks before the first chorus are more pronounced in mono, and the outro and fade are even more hectic. "Jugband Blues" is a completely different take than its stereo counterpart.

Velvet Underground: *White Light/White Heat (Verve V 5046)*
Even allowing for the colossal bleed-through that was the hallmark of this LP, the stereo separates the instruments, and that comes as a blessed relief. Stereo listeners also receive a bonus track, since the vocal channel on "The Gift" can be switched off to reveal the instrumental "Booker T."—in mono!

The Who: *The Who Sell Out (Decca DL 4950)*
The mono version of "Our Love Was" is substantially different, featuring an entirely different guitar

The mono pressing of the Farinas' finest hour.

solo; it is more restrained than the psychedelic stereo take.

MP3s—They're Music, but Are They Collectible? ("Probably Not," Says Little Nicola)

There is, as yet, no way to assess the impact that Internet music will have on record collecting. At present, it is largely overlooked—as with homemade cassettes and, more recently, CD-Rs, the MP3 and similarly downloadable music revolution is confined to collectors who simply require the *music*.

Record collecting, however, is concerned with the format as well—the tangibility of vinyl, tape, aluminum, whatever. Downloadable music does not intrinsically require any of these things; it is as comfortable being burned onto a CD as it is simply playing through a computer's software applications. There is no physical substance to the medium; therefore, in the commercial sense of collecting, there is no product.

Nevertheless, the Internet remains a vibrant marketplace for rarities and unreleased material, with *Ice* magazine pointing out, in October 2001, that "it's quite possible ... because of the Internet ... that there will never again be such a thing as a 'lost' album." Once, bootlegs alone brought such unreleased masterpieces as the Beach Boys' *Smile* to the world. In 2000 and 2001 alone, scrapped, rejected, or otherwise abandoned albums by acts as far apart as the Dave Matthews Band, Juliana Hatfield, Whiskeytown, and Wilco were all circulating freely on the Internet.

The net is also creating its own rules with the proliferation of unofficial remixes. Club DJs have long specialized in creating exclusive, personal remixes of existing material to use during their own sets at clubs—Fatboy Slim's UK-chart-topping remix of Cornershop's "Brimful of Asha" started life in this fashion. But the recent explosion of remix software has fostered a new generation of unofficial (or bootleg) remixers and, with it, a new collecting niche that relies almost exclusively on free Internet MP3 downloads for distribution.

For many people, the appeal of these remixes—christened "Bastard Pop" by some UK commentators—lies in their novelty. DJ Girls on Top (aka Rich X) scored a major underground hit in 2001 with "I Wanna Dance with Numbers," which married the vocals from Whitney Houston's "I Wanna Dance with You" to the instrumental track of Kraftwerk's "Numbers." Lockarm's "Bring the Music" clashed Public Enemy's "Bring the Noise" with M's "Pop Muzik," while Philly Da Kid's "Eminem vs the Smiths" blended the rapper's "Without Me" with the indie band's "This Charming Man." Bastard Pop indeed.

That these remixes are usually made without the permission of either artist or copyright holder is of little consequence to either collector or creator. The ingenuity and creativity of the mix is the only thing that matters.

The illicit nature of Bastard Pop remixes, of course, ensures that they cannot be distributed via any traditional medium: vinyl, cassette, CD, and so on. Enter MP3 technology. Bastard Pop is the first (and, so far, only) musical form to wholly embrace not only the Internet, but also the principle of unlimited, free distribution, and the first to be embraced in kind. It is not unusual for a remix to see more than 50,000 downloads, while there is at least one Internet radio station devoted exclusively to the genre. June 2002 even saw *Newsweek* magazine profile the phenomenon, just one month after Britain's *Record Collector* and *Mojo* magazines offered their own reports.

The perceived ephemeral nature of the MP3 is no stumbling block to collectors. The pleasure is in the accumulation of mixes, not in the hoarding of multitudinous formats, sleeve designs, and varieties.

Of course, such activity and popularity have not gone unnoticed in either the pop mainstream or the world of traditional bootlegging. Early 2002 brought a UK No. 1 hit for the Sugababes' "Freaks Like Me," a straightforward cover of another Girls on Top remix, "We Don't Give a Damn About Our Friends," which combined the talents of Adina Howard and Tubeway Army. Mix fans are now predicting further such manipulations, while collectors without the means (or the patience) to gather their mixes from the net are increasingly being tempted by similarly unauthorized bootleg CD collections of the most popular and notorious remixes.

Nipper—The Story of His Master's Voice

Possibly the best-known company trademark in the modern music industry is "His Master's Voice," Francis Barraud's much-beloved portrait of his fox terrier, Nipper, listening to a phonograph, or cylinder machine.

Nipper himself was a stray adopted by Barraud's brother, Mark, in 1884. Mark passed away in 1887 and Nipper moved in with Francis, a talented artist. It is uncertain exactly when Barraud painted the picture that would assure Nipper's immortality; however, in 1899 he copyrighted it under the title *Dog Looking at and Listening to a Phonograph*, though he preferred to refer to it by the less formal *His Master's Voice*.

It was, Barraud later said, "the happiest thought I ever had," though his early attempts to sell the painting as a piece of commercial art met with no success. Finally, sometime toward the end of the year, a friend suggested Barraud rework the picture slightly, replacing the black phonograph horn of the original with a more striking gold one, such as had recently been introduced by Emile Berliner's Gramophone Company.

Barraud agreed, and armed with a photograph of his painting, he visited the company's London offices to request the loan of a trumpet. Instead he walked away with a sale. William Barry Owen, the American-born head of the Company's British operation, was so smitten with the image that he immediately commissioned a copy, this time with the entire phonograph replaced by one of his firm's own gramophones. Barraud received two payments of 50 pounds for his work, one payment for conceding all copyright claims on the picture, the other for granting the Gramophone Company sole reproduction rights. With Nipper at the pictorial helm, the world-famous His Master's Voice (HMV) record label was born soon after.

Back in the US, Emile Berliner was as delighted with the purchase as Owen was, copyrighting the image for the American market in 1900. The following year, Berliner launched his Victor Talking Machine Company, and "His Master's Voice" became that company's trademark as well. A century on, the descendents of those two pioneers, EMI and BMG, continue to utilize the image.

Barraud himself never repeated the success of this one painting. Indeed, by 1913 he was suffering serious financial hardship, with nothing whatsoever to show for his greatest triumph. Somehow, word of his plight reached Alfred Clark, the then-chairman of the Gramophone Company. Generously, he commissioned Barraud to paint a third copy of *His Master's Voice,* for presentation to the Victor company; over the next 11 years, until his death in 1924, Barraud completed 21 further copies for the two companies, while receiving a pension from both of them.

As the single most recognizable logo in music-industry history, Nipper has similarly long been established as a popular collectible in his own right. The most common images, naturally, are those appearing on Victor/RCA/BMG and HMV/EMI's own records. The most faithful of these, perhaps not surprisingly, are the earliest. HMV's earliest label, a deep red with gold lettering, provided an excellent background for the image, which was presented within a semicircular frame on a brown background.

Victor, meanwhile, preferred to place Nipper and the gramophone on a black background that consumed the entire label—an image that remained more-or-less untouched for the next 70 years, long after HMV's label design moved to a more stylized image. (It should be remembered, incidentally, that RCA's copyright extended only to the Americas and the Far East. Releases elsewhere in the world, including the UK, appeared without the image. Of course, the opposite is true regarding HMV/EMI.)

A vast number of other items bearing the image have appeared over the past 100 years. Official Victor and HMV record catalogs are, as with similar items issued by every record company, very popular among ephemera enthusiasts; these catalogs frequently appear on the market. In addition, the HMV chain of record stores in the UK has featured *His Master's Voice* in silhouette on everything from plastic sleeves to security tape.

Elsewhere, marketing and promotional items include marbles, plush toys, figurines, and nearly life-size models of Nipper and his gramophone—all were once a common sight in any store where his owners plied their trade. The modern interest in nostalgia-themed reproductions, meanwhile, has also seen a number of *His Master's Voice* images emerge—one should be careful not to mistake these for original items.

Further Reading: *Since Records Began: EMI—The First 100 Years,* by Peter Martland (Amadeus Press, 1997)

PlayTapes—They Were Tapes. You Played Them.

The PlayTape was the creation of one Frank Stanton, and was launched at an MGM Records distributors meeting in New York in 1966. Self-winding tapes of anything up to 24 minutes in length, selling for between $1 and $3 (battery-operated players cost between $20 and $30), these tapes were touted as the ultimate in portable music, a market that radio had hitherto had to itself.

With backing from a number of record companies, PlayTapes were launched in September 1967, in five formats, each distinguished by the color of the cartridge. PlayTapes in red packaging featured two songs, the equivalent of a 7-inch single. Black cartridges featured four songs; white cartridges featured eight. Full LP releases would thus be spread across two tapes; the Beatles' *The White Album* consumed five (0955–0959).

In addition, there were also collections of children's songs (blue cartridges) and educational/spoken-word issues (gray cartridges). The tapes were packaged in bubble packs, which could be hung on special racks in retail outlets. All releases by individual artists were originally packaged with the same artwork.

There was no shortage of PlayTape releases. MGM artists dominated the field, with PlayTapes by the Animals, Herman's Hermits, the Righteous Brothers, and Steve and Eydie swiftly making themselves known. But other labels also signed on early, including Warner Bros. (Petula Clark, Connie Stevens, Grateful Dead, and Mason Williams); Capitol (the Beach Boys, Nat King Cole, the Beatles, and the Hollyridge Strings); ABC (the Lovin' Spoonful, the Mamas and the Papas, and the Impressions); Reprise (Frank Sinatra, Nancy Sinatra, Dean Martin, and Jimi Hendrix); A&M (Herb Alpert and Sergio Mendes); and Motown (the Temptations, the Four Tops, Smokey Robinson, and Stevie Wonder).

All releases were in mono; plans to launch stereo PlayTapes never came to fruition.

By early 1968, the PlayTape catalog featured over 3,000 artists. A marketing tie-in with Pepsi-Cola broadened PlayTape's scope even further, while the electronics firm Discarton, Ltd., launched a fabulous combination portable record (45s only)/PlayTape player that stands as a direct forebear of the music centers of the 1970s.

However, despite having the portable market to itself for much of 1967–68, PlayTapes' days were numbered. The nature of the system, while similar to 4- and 8-Track technology, allowed for only 2-Track tapes; it was that which limited the tape's length, and that which gave the rival formats an edge. By late 1968, the first 4- and 8-Track portable players were hitting the market, and while PlayTapes did continue (for reasons unknown) to flourish in Germany, by 1969 their American life span was over.

The biggest market for PlayTapes today is limited to enthusiasts of individual artists, fans who are broadening collections that have already swept the vinyl, 8-Track, and other common formats. The Beatles, of course, are the most popular act in this respect—most of their LP catalog appears to have been issued on PlayTape, though some releases have eluded discovery thus far. In addition, several Apple releases, including George Harrison's *Wonderwall Music* (0989) and Mary Hopkin's *Postcard* (1030), appeared on PlayTape.

Pocket Discs—Music from the Hip

The Pocket Disc arrived on the scene in 1966, courtesy of Americom, Ltd. The idea was simple, if perhaps a little ambitious. Pocket Discs were, quite literally, discs you could carry around in your pocket; medium-thickness flexidiscs, admittedly, but discs all the same. (The Enterprise label had made a similar effort during the late '50s and early '60s, for inclusion with boxes of Carnation dried milk.)

Just four inches across, Pocket Discs were issued in a generic blue or red sleeve, and retailed through Americom's own vending machines. The difference was, whereas many flexis were the fruit of one-off deals that found them glued to magazine covers or arriving unsolicited in the mail, Pocket Discs went straight to the top, striking licensing deals with many top record labels, including, in 1969, Apple. In fact, Apple releases, while extremely scarce, are the best-known and certainly the best-documented of all Pocket Disc releases.

A series of Hip Pocket Discs, marketed by Philco, appeared a short time after the Americom issues. A number of popular issues were made, including a very rare Doors single ("Light My Fire"/"Break On Through"), but the series did not survive long.

Pocket Rockers—For the Tiniest Tots of the Lot

Pocket Rockers are one of the most infectious of modern-day tape collectibles, 2-Track loop tapes manufactured by Fisher-Price Toys and launched via the larger retail chains in 1988. Featuring two songs, the $1" \times 1\frac{1}{2}"$ tapes were playable only on special Pocket Rockers tape machines, and were packaged complete with miniature album sleeves and a free pocket pop quiz.

Unlike the earlier PlayTapes, which they closely resemble, the target audience was young, those traditionally regarded as too young to have got into records, tapes, and hi-fis on their own. However, a surprisingly broad range of artists was incorporated into the series, including Bon Jovi ("Wanted Dead or Alive"—TM 8759; "Livin' on a Prayer"—8760), Huey

Lewis ("Hip to Be Square"—8808), and the Fat Boys ("Wipe Out"—8810).

Other issues included the Bangles; Belinda Carlisle; Cutting Crew; Debbie Gibson; Expose; Jan Hammer; Kim Wilde; LeVert; Lisa Lisa and Cult Jam; Los Lobos; Madonna; Mike and the Mechanics; Phil Collins; Pretty Poison; Ray Parker, Jr.; Taylor Dane; Tears for Fears; the Jets; Tiffany; Tom Petty; T'Pau; Whisper; and Whitney Houston.

For more traditional listeners, there were also titles by Bill Haley and the Comets, Chuck Berry, Boston, Danny and the Juniors, and Kenny Loggins. There appear to have been around 40 Pocket Rocker releases altogether, before the format faded from view during the early '90s; some branches of Toys "R" Us were carrying them at heavily discounted prices in 1992.

As collectibles, Pocket Rockers tend to hang out around the novelty end of the market, rubbing shoulders with PlayTapes and Mini-8s. As with those formats, however, the releases are certainly legitimate entries into the relevant acts' discographies—regardless of whether or not one has anything to play them on.

Polish Postcards—Warsaw Packed

Although the so-called Polish Postcard singles are widely considered an aspect of flexidisc collecting, the sheer range and novelty of available issues has made them a well-established, if difficult to find, collectible in their own right.

Little firm data has been published surrounding these exotic issues' origins and development. The majority were produced by the Polpress label and are sometimes unsympathetically described as pirate productions, in that the music was not *always* licensed from the Western copyright holders. However, as one of the few rock music media readily available to Polish youth during the Communist era, their status as items of social history necessarily outweighs any legal issues.

Polish Postcard records seem to date back to the 1960s, when Mary Hopkin's "Bylie Taki Dni" ("Those Were the Days") was paired with the Ohio Express's untranslatable "Yummy Yummy Yummy" for an issue much sought after by Apple label collectors. Other known issues from this early period include Procol Harum, the Doors, and Pink Floyd.

Many of the discs (which are shaped and manufactured to the specifications of a regular picture postcard, then embossed with two musical tracks) bear images completely unrelated to their subject—cartoons, street scenes, greetings, and so forth. It also appears that new postcards were not always produced; many postcard singles exist pressed onto cards that clearly predate the song's recording—a 1920s view of Warsaw, for example, playing a 1970s Deep Purple song.

Neither was Poland the only Communist bloc nation issuing music in this form. The Soviet Union itself saw a number of postcard singles issued by the Moscow Photo/Cinema Organization during the late '60s, measuring some 9½" across and playing at 78 rpm. These cards, too, tend to offer totally unrelated images on the postcard side.

Another characteristic of these issues is their extremely limited availability. Some press runs were as tiny as 50 copies. One should also be aware that automatic record players—that is, those whose mechanism automatically returns the playing arm to its rest upon reaching the end of the record—are unable to play them, as the postcard record begins where a conventional 45's label would lie.

Entire LPs were produced in the postcard medium, two songs per card. For obvious reasons, complete sets are extremely rare and highly valued today, particularly those still contained within their own original packaging. Many cards, individual and otherwise, were issued in "picture sleeve" envelopes or wrappers, bearing the artist and song title. Several Pink Floyd titles are known in this format, including the albums *Dark Side of the Moon* and *Meddle,* and a unique compilation, *Super Floyd.* (Pink Floyd itself utilized the wrapper format as packaging for the set of nonmusical postcards included within its *Shine On* box set.)

Polish postcard releases, while actively traded, are nevertheless extremely difficult to find. Collectors might spend their entire lives without ever finding one through their traditional record-hunting channels. However, shift one's focus away from record collecting and into the realms of cartophily (postcard collecting), and some finds can be made. Many card dealers have sections of novelty and musical postcards, and while these tend to be dominated by mass-produced American issues, playing state anthems and songs for tourists and the like, more esoteric items abound.

Promos—The Critics' Choice

"Promo" (or "demo," for "demonstration disc," in the UK) is one of the most commonly used and frequently misunderstood terms in record collecting. In the broadest sense, it refers to absolutely any recording that was not intended for public consumption *in this particular form;* more accurately, however, it describes only records, tapes, and CDs made available to radio stations, journalists, and other members of the media, as a preview of a forthcoming release. Other releases frequently listed as "promos," including discs relating to radio syndication shows (transcription discs), Jukebox Albums, and fan-club items, should in fact be noted under those categorizations.

A number of conditions qualify a record as a promo, but the most pertinent is, it is not intended to be bought and sold. Indeed, the majority of promo releases will carry a notice to this effect somewhere within the package. This can range from the phrase "DEMONSTRATION: NOT FOR SALE" (or something similar) found on many LP jackets and 45 labels, to wordier warnings declaring the record to be the property of the issuing record company and liable for return upon demand. Other indications that a record or CD is a promo include the obliteration of the bar code, a punch-hole, or some similar defacement. LPs issued to radio stations, in addition, will bear a "timing strip"—a band of paper across the lower half of the front cover, giving song titles and their running times.

The label used for promos, too, is often different from that found on "stock" (or generally available) releases. In the past, many record labels used a pre-

dominantly white variation of its regular label (hence the alternate term "white label"), again marked with such terms as "demonstration," "promotion," or "audition copy." (British Invasion–era Imperial label 45s are among the best-loved singles to bear this quaint expression.) Catalog numbers, too, frequently differ from those on the regularly released versions.

Such warnings and admonitions, of course, have no effect on collectors. Promos are eminently collectible, and have been since the first ones appeared, back in the heyday of the 78. Issued in such small numbers that the very existence of many releases (including several Elvis Presley discs) is no more than rumor or supposition, this can prove a very specialized and expensive area to enter. The early years of the 45, however, are little better.

The first promo 45 was, in fact, the first 45 ever issued, a demonstration disc produced for RCA's newly launched automatic record changer and the 45 rpm platters that were developed to accompany it. The *Whirl-Away Demonstration Record* featured excerpts from several of the first releases in this exciting new series, including Eddy Arnold's "Bouquet of Roses" (in terms of actual catalog number, the first commercially available 45), plus a spoken description of the product.

Just one copy is confirmed to exist today, though many were produced, to accompany in-store demonstration models of the record player. Once the promotion ended, RCA sales representatives descended en masse to retrieve the entire displays. They were then, presumably, recycled or destroyed.

Collecting 45s is the most popular activity for promo collectors, and it's the easiest field to break into. Often readily identifiable by the appearance of a mono mix on one side, stereo on the other (a recording practice that continued into the 1980s), promo 45s can be picked up in almost any used-record store, often at very cheap prices. Indeed, when contemplating any purchase (or sale) of promo 45s—whether they are mono-stereo couplings or simply promotional label versions of a regular release—one should always remember that virtually *every* 45 of the age was issued in this form, and often in sizeable

Promo white label copy of Sandy Denny's "Listen Listen" 45.

quantities. Indeed, not only are the majority of promos not at all rare, there are many releases (45s, LPs, and CDs alike) that are far more common as promos than as stock copies.

Specialist and completist collectors may show an interest, but in general, a common record is a common record, regardless of its designation. Locate Tori Amos's *Y Kant Tori Read* LP (Atlantic) without a promo cutout notch, however, and you have a genuinely sought-after, name-your-own-price item. Find stock copies of Crowded House's "I Feel Possessed" (Capitol) or Jon Anderson's "Surrender" (Atlantic 4054), and you might not get the price of a pack of cigarettes for any of them, but at least you have a genuine rarity.

Where promos become especially interesting is in their propensity to offer material in a form that is not otherwise available.

Sometimes, this means simply an unusual pairing on a single or EP. Many record labels, when attempting

to "break" a new artist to radio and the other media, will produce limited-edition promos featuring key tracks that might interest DJs but that would never be issued as conventional 45s or LPs. One example, popular among David Bowie collectors, pairs two tracks apiece by Mick Ronson (Bowie's former guitarist) and Dana Gillespie on one EP (RCA DJEO 0259—1974).

Others still will highlight potential hits from a new album and serve them up on an EP. The Kinks's *Give the People What They Want* LP, in 1981, was previewed with a very collectible 4-track 12-inch (UK Arista KINX 4). Other EPs cherry-pick entire series of albums—the first 23 volumes released in Pearl Jam's 2001 *Bootleg Series* were highlighted on a 15-track CD sampler (Epic).

Another popular theme for collectors revolves around the mono promo albums issued in America during the late '60s and well into the 1970s. While 1967–68 saw record companies across America abandon mono for stereo, radio was somewhat slower to adapt. Many popular albums of the age—what the general public knew as stereo-only releases by Cream, Janis Joplin, the Grateful Dead, and so many more—were mixed into straightforward mono for radio play, a practice that has provided for some truly stellar rarities.

Most 1960s-era mono promos are relatively common. They do fetch a premium, but it should never be high. However, move into the 1970s, and releases by artists who are already considered collectible, and you are looking at a whole different scenario.

Both the Rolling Stones' *Sticky Fingers* (Rolling Stones 59100) and Paul McCartney's *Ram* (Apple 3375), released in 1971, were issued in mono mixes; from even later in the day, Led Zeppelin's 1973 album, *Houses of the Holy* (Atlantic 7255), was also issued as a mono promo. None of these mono albums offered any new musical variation on the stereo experience; their collectibility centers upon their very existence. Remember, however, to ensure that the record's actual label includes the magic word "mono"; remember also that only radio promos were treated thus. Promos issued to other members of the media remained in stereo.

Other promos deviate from released issues in equally spectacular ways. Promos of Art Garfunkel's 1978 LP *Watermark* (Columbia JC 34975), featuring the song "Fingerpaint" on side two, became prized above many other Garfunkel issues after the album's running order was changed for full release. The earliest promos of Michael Jackson's "Ben" 45 (Motown—unnumbered) featured authentic rat noises behind the music—these were not only removed for public consumption, they were also deleted from all subsequent promo issues as well. Even more disconcerting, however, are promo copies of Wild Cherry's "Play That Funky Music" (Epic 50225), which were sent to radio with the crucial hook-line "white boy" deleted. Political correctness is not a new development.

Of course, alterations take place with regularly issued LPs as well. There are, for example, two different versions of the mega-selling soundtrack *Saturday Night Fever* (RSO 4001), the first featuring a studio

recording of the Bee Gees' landmark "Jive Talkin'," the other substituting a live recording. Madonna's first album, 1983's *Madonna* (Sire 23867), substituted a guitar-heavy remix of "Burning Up" for the original version immediately after the initial pressing run. Roxy Music's *Manifesto* (Atco 114) saw several original mixes replaced by hit remixes during its shelf life.

Generally, these issues are little more than completist curios. Unless there are specific (usually controversial) reasons cited for such changes, stock-copy variations tend to attract only scant attention. Promos variations, on the other hand, are always considered worthwhile.

Promo-only compilations of an artist's greatest hits, designed to arouse interest in his or her new material, are a time-honored device. Another Kinks's issue, *Then, Now and in Between* (Reprise PRO 328); *Everything You Wanted to Hear by Jeff Beck but Were Afraid to Ask* (Epic AS 151); Kiss's *Special Album for Their Summer* Tour (Casablanca KISS 76); Bruce Springsteen's *As Requested around the World* (Columbia AS 978); Peter Gabriel's *Before Us* (Geffen PRCD 4412); and the Cracker–Camper Van Beethoven *Virgin Years* (Virgin DPRO 14129) are just a random fraction of the myriad killer compilations available only on promo LP or CD.

A number of promotional releases sampling forthcoming releases (most notably box sets) have also taken on legendary status. When the Beach Boys' *Pet Sounds 30th Anniversary Box Set* (Capitol 37662) CD was withdrawn from the schedules shortly following dispatch of the promotional samplers, demand skyrocketed, with the promos reaching $100-plus before the box set was finally rescheduled.

Excitement also attended the release of another Capitol sampler, this time previewing 1999's *John Lennon Anthology* box set. Included among the tracks on *howitis* was a version of the John Lennon–Cheap Trick collaboration "I'm Losing You," clocking in at a full minute longer than the released version, and featuring not only a unique count-in, but also an additional bridge section. Such bonuses are not a common feature of samplers, but they do ensure careful listening from collectors!

Fans of tribute albums, meanwhile, should be aware that several have been issued as double CDs, featuring the tributes on one disc and the originals on the other—Black Sabbath's *The Bible According To...* (Columbia 2SK 6544) is a popular example. And while custom promos rarely cater to audiophiles, the early '80s saw a number of issues apparently aimed at that very market. Members of the Warner Bros. group of labels issued a number of promos on the high-quality "Quiex II" vinyl, denoted by a sticker on the front cover (the actual records and labels are indistinguishable from regular vinyl issues). Sought-after releases in this series include *The John Lennon Collection* (Geffen 2023) and Fleetwood Mac's *Mirage* (Warner Bros. 23607).

New releases are not the only newsworthy events to demand noteworthy promos. Following Pink Floyd founder Roger Waters' successful performance of *The Wall* in Berlin, in 1990, Columbia issued *The Wall Berlin,* a promo-only CD gathering of Floyd cuts (Columbia CSK 2126).

But the most popular promos, the bedrock upon which the entire promo-collecting hobby is built, lies in the availability of material that simply hasn't been issued to the general public in any form.

These can take many forms. The simplest are such offerings as the 12-inch Bee Gees mega-mix issued by their UK label at the height of the early-'80s *Stars on 45* medley mania. Or one might find isolated tracks included on collections of otherwise familiar material—Smashing Pumpkins' *1991–1998* (Virgin) included among its 18 tracks an exclusive acoustic version of "Mayonaise."

Others, however, serve up entire albums worth of unissued music. In 1996, Robyn Hitchcock marked the 30th anniversary of Bob Dylan's legendary Royal Albert Hall Concert (the one that *isn't* featured on Dylan's own *Live 1966* album!) by recreating Dylan's live set for one of his own shows—the *Royal Queen Albert and Beautiful Homer* promo (WB) captured the night.

The "official bootleg" boom of the mid-'70s saw excellent and long-in-demand live albums by Tom Petty, Nils Lofgren, and Graham Parker; 20 years later,

Matthew Sweet's *Goodfriend: Another Take on Girlfriend* (Zoo 17098) delivered demo and live versions of tracks from his critically acclaimed third album.

Many record companies abandoned the issue of special promo 45s and LPs during the mid-'80s, as their attention turned toward popularizing the CD. In the early years of the new format, and indeed, into the early '90s, the majority of media promos were dispatched on cassette tape. It was only as the decade progressed that promo CDs became ubiquitous, and by the end of that span, their day had already passed. Today, many promo albums are burned onto CD-R.

Dire Straits's *Brothers in Arms* (Warner Bros. 25264) was the first album to be issued as a promo CD to both US and British radio in May 1985. It seems curious today, but Britain's BBC Radio 1 devoted an entire program to playing the vinyl and CD versions side by side, so listeners could decide for themselves about the sound quality.

Since that time, CD promos of full albums can only be valued on a case-by-case basis, though it is true to say that the vast majority are of little value, particularly when they are issued without artwork, or with only limited sleeve information. Unlike promotional LPs, which possess an inherent collectible value, the deliberately unattractive promo CD is regarded with little more respect than the cassette that preceded it. The move toward CD-R, meanwhile, might well see the market for new promos collapse altogether.

Other collectibles are the special editions created for, and/or by, major retail chains such as Best Buy and Blockbuster; many rapidly become highly sought after. Bonus discs for the Who's *BBC Sessions* and Ringo Starr's *Third All-Starr Band* releases were hot commodities, even before the stores' own copies sold out; while the Pearl Jam live album *Give Way,* featuring 17 songs from a concert in Melbourne, Australia, in 1998, simply went through the roof after the band's label, Epic, objected to its release. Another one to look for is Best Buy's Roy Orbison set, *Live at the BBC,* featuring 15 otherwise unavailable recordings dating back to 1968.

Not all such supplementary releases feature exclusive music—the Best Buy bonus accompanying Paul

McCartney's *Run Devil Run,* for example, merely duplicated a 40-minute interview disc available with all first pressings of the UK edition. The rival Musicland chain, meanwhile, offered a CD single featuring original versions of four of the songs covered on the McCartney album—by Wanda Jackson, Gene Vincent, Fats Domino, and Ricky Nelson.

Promotional CD singles, tending to feature just one song, have a market all of their own, though the sheer number of issues also reduces the field in general to something of a crapshoot, with many used-CD dealers happily selling them off in bulk, so many for a buck or two. It's all a far cry from when they first arrived on the scene, in 1986.

Back then, CDJs (Compact Disc Jockey), as they are popularly nicknamed, were a prized beast indeed, all the more so since regular CD singles were still struggling to make an impression on either marketplace or marketing departments. Until as recently as 1993, virtually every current hit record one heard on the radio was taken from a CDJ—but few of them were actually available in the stores, and even fewer were on CD. The cassette single still dominated, and collectors were willing to pay $20 or more for CDJs.

Since that time, the market for CDJs has settled down considerably, and even name-artist releases are scarcely noticed any longer. But, of course, exceptions abound. One of the rarest CDs of all time is a CDJ of Nirvana's "Pennyroyal Tea (Scott Litt Mix)" (Geffen NIRPRO). The track was scheduled for release as a UK single in May 1993, to coincide with the band's European tour; it was canceled following vocalist Kurt Cobain's death, but while an estimated ten vinyl test pressings were destroyed, an unknown number of CDs, plus printed artwork for the German release, survived. One copy sold for $1,000 on eBay during April 1999. Coincidentally that same month saw a copy of Prince's legendary "Pussy Power" promo, an in-house Paisley Park issue that has also been cited among the rarest of all CD promo singles, sell for over $600 in the same forum.

Further Reading: *Goldmine Promo Record & CD Price Guide,* by Fred Heggeness (Krause Publications, various editions)

Quadraphonic Sound—Extra Ears Optional

Quadraphonic sound has gone down in musical history as one of the greatest and most expensive failures of the vinyl age. Touted, in the aftermath of stereo's so-successful introduction during the 1960s, as the next level in audio entertainment, "surround sound" was originally introduced in 1970 on 8-Track, with the first vinyl issues following a year later.

Initially, the majority of releases were targeted toward the audiophile market, with classical and jazz albums high on the schedules. Gradually, the format broadened its scope toward rock and pop performers, with Columbia, RCA, EMI, and two labels under the Warner Bros. umbrella, Elektra and Asylum, among the most prolific issuers, releasing a stream of potentially big-selling albums in the new format.

Unfortunately, that was where quad's downfall lay. It was not bad enough that quad required a special decoder before it could be enjoyed to its full potential—necessitating the purchase of an entirely new sound system. Even worse was the fact that the industry itself had yet to standardize which of several competing quad formats was to be employed, so that anybody wishing to pick up releases from more than one group of labels would need more than one player.

Three major systems were developed: Sansui's QS (quadraphonic-stereo), Sony's SQ (stereo-quadraphonic) and JVC's CD-4 (compatible discrete four channel). A fourth system, Nippon Columbia's UD-4 (universal discrete four channel) perhaps mercifully failed to make it off the ground. Several labels issued albums in two of the three formats—Virgin in the UK actually issued Mike Oldfield's *Tubular Bells* in all three. But these were the exception. In essence, if you bought one system, you were stuck with one group of labels—Columbia, A&M, and Vanguard, for example, if you chose SQ; Warner Bros. (Elektra and Asylum), RCA, and Phonogram if you opted for CD-4; Command, Impulse, and Ovation with QS. Had these conflicts been resolved, or had the competing formats at least become compatible with one another,

The quad version of Alice Cooper's *Billion Dollar Babies* LP.

quad might have succeeded. Instead, by decade's end, it was a dead issue.

Despite the varying formats, quad records have long been popular with collectors, many of whom might never have even seen a quad sound system. Even on a regular stereo, quad remixes can sound spectacularly different, with certain collectors willing to go to considerable financial lengths to acquire recordings that are unique to the format. Included in this category are releases by such acts as the Doors, John Lennon, Pink Floyd, Bob Dylan, Black Sabbath, Alice Cooper, and Deep Purple—in other words, artists who are collectible in every other format as well. (There were no Beatles or Elvis albums issued in quad.)

However, the vast majority of quad records are worth little more than their stereo counterparts. Albums by the likes of Simon and Garfunkel, the Carpenters, Harry Nilsson, Eric Clapton, Carole King, Earth Wind and Fire, Carly Simon, Bill Wyman, and Santana seem to clog up every "quad" bin at record fairs, and certainly dominate Internet auction listings. The depressing absence of any substantial bidding is eloquent enough testimony to the general lack of interest in any sonic delights that these gems may hold. For they do, as a rule, offer the listener a brand new perspective on a recording, even if, as is so often the case, one gets the distinct impression that the remix is designed more to show off the format's capabilities than to enhance the recording itself.

In terms of new releases (both current catalog and remixed older issues), quad was at its peak during 1975–76. Thereafter it swiftly became apparent that the format was not going to take off, and issues declined alarmingly. By 1978, the whole thing was forgotten.

Crucial Quad Varieties

Black Sabbath: *Paranoid (Warner Bros. BS4 1887)*
Without offering the varieties collector much to work with, *Paranoid* emerges as a very satisfying listen. Guitars are cranked up (and, occasionally, dirtied up), with the title track highlighted now by a positively assaultive solo, while "War Pigs" is presented without the speeded-up effect that closes the stereo version.

Alice Cooper: *Billion Dollar Babies (WB BS4 2685)*
The entire LP has been completely remixed, but several tracks are of especial note—a guitar-heavy "I Love the Dead" and a powerfully horn-driven "Elected" among them. Elsewhere, "Unfinished Suite" boasts improved and extra-terrifying dentist sound effects, while "Generation Landslide" features an alternate ending, before segueing into a ferocious, colossally superior take of "Sick Things." The art of the quad mix has seldom been put to better use!

Bob Dylan: *Desire (Columbia PCQ 33893)*
The exclusive availability of a noticeably alternate mix of "Romance in Durango" is responsible for raising this album high in collecting circles; it is not, however, the only reason for listening. The entire LP is vastly superior in every department. The already somber "Joey" is raised to new heights of majesty by the newly emphasized violin, while "Black Diamond Bay" benefits immeasurably from its pronounced percussion.

Art Garfunkel: *Breakaway (Columbia PCQ 33700)*
Richard Perry's original production was so extravagant that the quad remix can do little but accent the textures. While the overall sound is superior to the stereo edition, the most marked variations are in the harmonies, and a handful of inconsequential instrumental flourishes, including a slightly drawn-out (and seriously panned) fade to "Waters of March" and more pronounced guitar and percussion during the Paul Simon reunion "My Little Town."

Mott the Hoople: *The Hoople (Columbia PCQ 32871)*
One of the most radical, but oddly redundant, of all quad rock releases appears to have been constructed with nothing more in mind than thrilling the listener's ears. Abundant use of echo brings some almost disconcerting effects into play—gently through "Golden Age of Rock 'n' Roll," obtrusively during "Alice," most portentously in "Through the Looking Glass." Sharp ears will discover more conversation beneath the intro to "Pearl and Roy," and more na-na-na ribaldry in the backing chorus, but the highlights here are a fine guitar work-over during

"Crash Street Kids," the most aggressive cut on the original LP, and an almost Spectorish thunder to "Roll Away the Stone," the most gorgeously, stupidly romantic number.

Mike Oldfield: *Boxed (Virgin VBOX 1)*
This four-LP box set comprises quad remixes of Oldfield's first three LPs—*Tubular Bells, Hergest Ridge,* and *Ommadawn*—plus an exclusive fourth set, *Collaborations,* featuring material cut with orchestral leader David Bedford, among others. The remixes add little to Oldfield's already sumptuous recordings, with the most telling departure being an alternate version of "The Sailor's Hornpipe" at the conclusion of *Bells,* featuring a spoken-word passage from master of ceremonies Viv Stanshall. Also worthy of investigation, however, is the remixed conclusion to side one of *Ommadawn,* where the crescendo of guitars builds to levels of palpable intensity. One of the most powerful passages of music in the modern rock idiom just grew even stronger.

Pink Floyd: *Dark Side of the Moon*
(Harvest Q4SHVL 804)
Even in stereo, this was one of the equipment demonstration albums of the age. The quad mix raises many elements to prominence, beginning with the hitherto mumbled spoken passages at the opening of side one and culminating, from a sonic point of view, with a newly deafening alarm clock sequence. The majority of quad enhancements are confined to the spoken and FX portions of the LP, but "Any Colour You Like" is a revelation on headphones.

Simon and Garfunkel: *Bridge over Troubled Waters*
(Columbia CQ 30995)
Even if you've never owned another quadraphonic recording in your life, you probably have this one. Yet, what was once a mainstay of every thrift store in the land (and is probably still widely available for a matter of cents), is also one of the most beautiful sounding of all quad releases. For once, the remixers concentrated on what was already on the record, rather than seeking out new and interesting elements to raise into the mix. That said, "Cecilia" is certainly more percussive

than its stereo counterpart, with new wind elements as well, while "Baby Driver" may or may not be improved by the raucous saxophones.

Quad-8s—Eight Tracks, Four Channels

Up there with 8-Tracks, quadraphonic sound is widely regarded as one of the biggest jokes in music-industry history. Put the two together, then, and you will certainly be requiring a new set of ribs.

Yet quadraphonic 8-Tracks (Quad-8s as they are called) also represent one of the most volatile growth areas in modern record-collecting, offering sometimes stunning mixes that simply were never made available in any other format, and though it might seem difficult for non-enthusiasts to believe, frequently boasting sound quality that mere vinyl could never eclipse.

Of especial fascination is the realization that, despite looking identical to stereo cartridges, Quad-8 does not behave at all like a conventional 8-Track. While stereo tapes change programs three times as they play through an entire tape (at the conclusion of programs one, two, and three), Quad-8 changes just once, much as the old 4-Track tapes did. This was because the four channels of sound that define quad each occupied four bands on the tape, thus creating just two programs. The downside of this was that twice as much tape needed to be crammed into the cartridge, thus rendering Quad-8 tapes even more susceptible to damage and breakage than their stereo cousins.

The technology also necessitated acquiring an entirely new sound system upon which to play the tapes, with specially designed playing heads capable of recognizing the expanded input. This requirement was an expensive drawback at the time, and is an even greater difficulty today. Quad-8 players can play stereo tapes, but conventional stereo players do not satisfactorily play Quad-8.

These waters are muddied further by the number of pseudo-Quad-8 players that appeared on the market as the tapes' own popularity increased, and which seem to predominate today. Bearing such names as

4D, Quad Matrix, Quatravox, and Quadradial, these decks were, simply, stereo systems with two sets of speakers. The inner workings of the quad player, as manufactured by the likes of Akai, Panasonic, Pioneer, and Sanyo (and clearly notated QUAD-8, Q-8, or DISCRETE QUADRAPHONIC 8-TRACK) were far beyond their capabilities.

It is for these reasons that Quad-8 cartridges, even more so than their regular counterparts, constitute a tiny, and extraordinarily specialized, end of the modern market. However, it is a market that is more than happy to pay considerable sums for the tapes it requires.

The first Quad-8 tapes were introduced in fall of 1970, shortly after the unveiling of the quadraphonic reel-to-reel format, but around a year before the first quadraphonic vinyl LP records. Initially, these constituted simple remixes of strong catalog material— the soundtrack to *The Sound of Music* (RCA OQ8 1001) was the first-ever release. By 1971, however, custom quad mixdowns were being undertaken, often adding new sound effects to the original tape in order to make them more attractive to listeners, and (presumably) to justify the extra cost; like quad LPs, the tapes retailed at around $1 more than stereo.

Although Quad-8 releases were widespread, only a handful of record companies seriously got behind the format. Columbia and RCA led the way; A&M, ABC, and Warner Bros. followed. Capitol/EMI released only a handful of tapes, however; the Phonogram and London/Decca groups likewise, and rock releases from these latter companies account for the majority of the format's most spectacular rarities.

These include (but are not limited to) Pink Floyd's *Dark Side of the Moon* (Harvest Q8W 11163) and *Wish You Were Here* (Columbia PCQ 33453), Kraftwerk's *Autobahn* (Vertigo VQ8 2003), and five titles from ex-Beatles: John Lennon's *Imagine* (Apple Q8W 3379—Lennon himself supervised the quad remixing of the title track) and *Walls and Bridges* (Apple Q8W 33416); Paul McCartney's *Band on the Run* (Apple Q8W 3415) and *Venus and Mars* (Capitol Q8W 11419), plus the *Live and Let Die* movie soundtrack (UA DA 100H); and Ringo Starr's *Goodnight Vienna*

(Apple Q8W 3417). The excitement surrounding these latter releases increases when one realizes that *Imagine* alone was also granted a quad release on vinyl, and that was in Europe only.

Other titles to appear exclusively in Quad-8 (and, very rarely, quad reel-to-reel) include some quite unexpected titles—albums by Babe Ruth, Bachman-Turner Overdrive, Chuck Berry (the less than essential *London Sessions*), and many more were delivered in cartridge form, without ever seeing the business end of a vinyl stamper.

In the classical arena, the few Deutsche Gramophone Quad-8s to have seen release never have difficulty finding homes, while Isao Tomita's synthesized rendition of Gustav Holst's *The Planets,* from 1978, is considered collectible, not only in its own right, but also because it represents the final Quad-8 release.

Reel-to-Reel Tapes—High-End and Hot

The most popular tape format among collectors today is the reel-to-reel, the single-spool packages that were also the first magnetic tapes to be made available to consumers, during the mid-'50s.

At seven inches in diameter (the same size as a 45), reel-to-reels were attractively packaged in cardboard boxes bearing full-color artwork. They were also very exclusive. Reels were marketed toward the audiophile end of their contemporary market—indeed, in general, the tapes were not even available in regular record stores, the majority being stocked instead by high-end equipment and electronics outlets. It is a further indication of the esteem in which reels were held that the first-ever commercially available stereo recordings appeared in the tape format, some time before the first stereo LPs were marketed.

Tapes were issued at two speeds: 7½ ips (inches per second) and the sonically superior 3¾ ips, the standard to which both the later 4-Track and 8-Track cartridges adhered. Typically, reels are designated "two track" for mono releases, "four track" for stereo—these terms should not be confused with the cartridge tape formats of the same name.

For much of the format's early life, releases were aimed at what might now be termed a determinedly highbrow audience, with the emphasis on classical, jazz, opera, and theatrical issues. Not until the mid-'60s brought the rising star of the 8-Track into view did the reel-to-reel first acknowledge rock music, and even then, it was extremely choosy about who was allowed into the club.

The decision of what to release was taken not by the record companies themselves, but by the manufacturing company, Stereotape, which leased the music from the labels, then distributed the tapes through its own network. This arrangement meant that there was often a considerable lag between a new LP release appearing on disc and its arrival on reel—or on any other tape format, for that matter. It would be early 1968 before firm efforts were taken on an industry-wide level to ensure vinyl and tape issues became simultaneous.

Immediately, sales of all the then-current tape formats began to rise, with reel-to-reels showing an especial gain. Emboldened, Bell and Howell (as Stereotape was now known—it would later become Magtec) began issuing more rock music in the format; this period also saw Ampex, hitherto known primarily as makers of 8-Track cartridges, move into the field.

The vast majority of readily available rock reel-to-reels date from this period. Although the format remained in use until the early '80s (by which time record clubs had become its principal outlet), the early '70s produced a boom in new releases. The most collectible artists in the format are, of course, the usual suspects—from the 1960s, Elvis Presley, the Beatles, the Rolling Stones, Jimi Hendrix, Bob Dylan, and Simon and Garfunkel; from the new decade, Pink Floyd, Led Zeppelin, Black Sabbath, and David Bowie, among others. A handful of quad reels issued during the early '70s are also much sought-after—the Allman Brothers' *At the Fillmore East* (Capricorn CTSQ 0131), Bachman-Turner Overdrive's *Not Fragile* (Mercury H-11004), and Caravan's *For Girls Who Grow Plump in the Night* (London J-12710) are among the most popular titles.

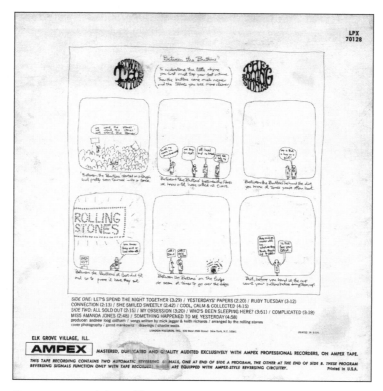

The rear cover of the Rolling Stones' *Between the Buttons* reel-to-reel.

Since only a select group of artists are featured in the format, most rock reel-to-reels are considered of value today. This is true even when the corresponding vinyl is of little worth—certain Presley and Moody Blues releases fall into this category. However, condition is paramount (see the grading guide on page 6 in this book), as the format was wide open—literally—to abuse and damage.

Players are also common (some models are still in production), but working models tend to be expensive. It is also crucial to note, when making a purchase, whether or not the deck is capable of playing stereo (four-track) tapes. A mono (two-track) player will read both strips of information as one and play them simultaneously, with one in reverse. Stereo players, of course, can handle both formats without difficulty.

78s—Fragility as a Way of Life

If one thinks about it on a purely instinctual level, the idea of rock 'n' roll playing on 78 is absurd. Rock 'n' roll, after all, was the sound of a new generation—a new world, even—vital, thrusting, and coruscating with excitement, and so far removed from the loves and lives of previous generations that it simply could not exist on anything so crusty and square as a 78.

The sounds of "Johnny B. Goode" and "Heartbreak Hotel" are the sounds of the 45, discs as unbreakable as the spirit now coursing through the veins of America's with-it youth, as fresh and filled with fidelity as the new dawn that was breaking across the postwar world. Rock 'n' roll was the sound of teenagers in ascension; 78s were the old world they were crushing beneath their feet.

Yet, between whichever date you choose to mark the dawn of rock 'n' roll, and the very end of the 1950s, the 78 wasn't simply the dominant force in the music industry, it was also the most popular. In the US, the 45 did not finally overtake the 78 in terms of units sold until 1957. In Britain, the old format was still holding its own in the marketplace until 1959.

Today, it is said, rock 'n' roll 78s are one of the hottest commodities in the record-collecting world, with any survey of America's (or the UK's) most valuable records of the era literally bursting with high-ticket 78s. The market for them might be smaller than for 45s, and the values in the price guides might sometimes seem a little lower. But ask any dealer what he would rather be offering—a set of mint Elvis Sun singles on 45? Or a set on 78? There is no competition.

The reason for this, first and foremost, is that 78s simply were not built to last. They were manufactured from shellac, a compound derived from a natural resin secreted by the Lac beetle of Southeast Asia. This material is extremely durable, and was ideal for the 78's primary purpose—being rotated at high speeds while a thick steel needle passed over it in a clockwise direction.

Unfortunately, it is also extremely fragile and frighteningly brittle. Even with the most stringent precautions, mailing a 78 means taking its life in your hands, while simply transporting a 78 from one room to another can seem like juggling fine crystal. The 78s that today sell for high prices on the collectors market are not rare because very few were made, as is the case with many of the most valuable 45s of the same period. They are rare because not many have survived unbroken.

Emile Berliner, a German citizen who emigrated to the US in 1870, when he was 19, developed the 78. A pioneer of sound technology, he developed the flat-disc technique (to replace the bulky cylinders then in use) during the mid-1880s, unveiling his prototype at the Franklin Institute in 1888. His first discs were etched in zinc using chromic acid; from there he moved to celluloid and rubber, before hitting upon shellac in 1891. It is a testament to his farsightedness that shellac would remain the industry standard for the next 50-plus years. (Vinyl began creeping into fashion during the mid-'50s, but never became a standard.)

Of course, 78s were the first records ever to be collected. In the years prior to World War II, the majority of serious collectors sought classical and opera music, allowing pop and other genres to pass by unnoticed. Later eras moved toward jazz and blues—the legacy of these releases is still with us today, via the often sky-high prices for a number of little-known artists and labels. Country music came into vogue during the early '50s and is still wildly popular among collectors of 78s.

Rock 'n' roll, on the other hand, did not begin to register on the collecting scale until some 20 years after 78s fell into extinction. Much of the demand, initially, came from Europe, primarily Germany, where 1940s-style "bubble tube" Wurlitzer 78 jukeboxes were enjoying a small but significant boom in popularity. A familiar sight in the American and British army-run youth clubs of the immediate postwar period, these beautiful slices of nostalgia were off-loaded from storage during the late '70s, and their new owners were now looking to stock them with the music they remembered from their youth.

As the deutsche Marks flew in one direction, and the records sailed off in another, domestic collectors began to reflect upon the format. The boom began, hampered only by the fact that few dealers were even vaguely capable of specializing in the field. To them, after all, 78s were the fat, black, breakable things that sat in boxes in the corner of the store, gathering the dust which would then rise up in vast, choking clouds on the rare occasions when somebody—usually an older person, with very specific requirements—chose to leaf through them.

Indeed, even today many traditional used-record stores still have no idea of how to display or even categorize their 78s. Rather, they flick through the pile looking for the odd name they may recognize, then leave the rest in the least-visited corner, with no thought for even rudimentary preservation. One can always tell, when a store rearranges its stock, where the 78s used to be kept. There will be flakes of broken shellac all over the floor.

With astonishing rapidity, 45s moved into the 78 marketplace. Introduced in 1949 by RCA Victor, by 1952 even tiny independent record labels were producing them, side by side with 78s, but in increasing quantities every year. Had the new format not demanded a new type of record player, it might have taken off even faster; as it was, many consumers preferred to wait until the first players were marketed that could handle all three speeds now on the market—78s, 45s, and the similarly new 33⅓.

Unquestionably, teenagers were the driving force behind the revolution—45s blended in perfectly with a lifestyle that prided itself on excitement, speed, and devil-may-care bravado. They could be stacked on a turntable for nonstop dancing parties, they could be passed around without fear of breakage, they could be dropped on the floor and propped against the wall, and they might never seem too worse for the wear. On the other hand, 78s . . . you only had to look at them wrong (or, at least, lay them in a box with less than infinite care), and they shattered into irreparable shards.

So the statistics are probably deceptive. While 78s did outsell 45s for much of the 1950s, that's because they sold to fans of jazz, swing, dance band, classical, blues, and opera; 45s were a rock and pop phenomenon.

Nevertheless, vast quantities of every hit issue were produced, with the biggest names in the infant rock world—including Elvis, Chuck Berry, Buddy Holly, Little Richard, and Jerry Lee Lewis—as familiar spinning on a 10-inch shellac platter as on a 7-inch vinyl one. If one does not care so much for condition (or playability) as for simply owning a handsome artifact, it is not at all difficult, or especially expensive, to build a remarkable collection of early rock 'n' roll on 78. It's only when you attempt to upgrade that you will start running into serious difficulties.

In general, the rarest rock 78s are the most obscure issues on the best-loved labels—early Sun, Chess, and Vee-Jay releases, for example. The most expensive, on the other hand, tend to be those by the best-known artists. It does not take a rocket scientist to realize that a clean 78 pressing of Gene Vincent's "Be-Bop-A-Lula" (Capitol 3450) or Chuck Berry's "Roll Over Beethoven" (Chess 1626) will attract more attention than "Tennessee" Ernie Ford's "You Don't Have to Be a Baby to Cry" (Capitol 3262) or the Lane Brothers' "Marianne" (RCA Victor 6810). Which is not to say those latter aren't just as appealing to a specialist,

simply that most buyers and sellers' knowledge simply is not that in-depth.

Because Britain continued producing 78s some years after the US quit, many of the rarest issues do hail from the UK. A number of labels continued issuing 78s at least into summer and fall of 1960, with some new issues still reaching stores in time for Christmas—Ray Charles' "Georgia on My Mind" (HMV POP 792) was issued in Britain on 78 as late as November 1960.

Warner Bros., whose British operation was not even opened until April 1960, released several extremely rare 78s by the Everly Brothers, featuring titles that never saw shellac in the US ("Cathy's Clown"—WB 1, "Lucille"—WB 19); while Eddie Cochran's "Three Steps to Heaven" (London HLUG 9115), Brian Hyland's "Itsy Bitsy Teenie Weenie Yellow Polka Dot Bikini" (London HLR 9161), and Elvis Presley's "Stuck on You" (RCA 1187), "A Mess of Blues" (RCA 1194), and "It's Now or Never" (RCA 1207) will all appear impossibly out of date to the American collector.

Perhaps the most startling 78 discoveries of all, however, are those issued by EMI's India operation. The popular modern image of the subcontinent's music industry is of a land dominated by colorfully packaged cassette tapes. Prior to that medium's invention, however, India devoured shellac and vinyl releases as voraciously as any other land, with the 78 ruling absolutely supreme in areas where the lack of electricity meant that most record buyers were still employing hand-cranked wind-up gramophones.

A full catalog of releases to this market would probably boggle the most even-keeled mind. But let us reel off just four of the 78 rpm discs that haunt the imagination of every completist Beatles enthusiast: "If I Fell" (Parlophone DPE 167), "Tell Me Why" (DPE 172), "I'll Follow the Sun" (DPE 180), and "Michelle" (DPE 187), the latter dating from as late as summer 1965.

And some people think the Sex Pistols' 8-Track is an anachronism!

Further Reading: *American Premium Record Guide 1900–1965: Identification and Value Guide to 78s, 45s and LPs,* by Les Docks (Krause Publications, 1997)

16 rpm—A Merry-Go-Round for Your Tortoise

If you've never wondered what the 16 rpm setting on your old-time record player is for, you either don't have an enquiring mind . . . or you already know.

The sound quality was not great, but you could certainly fit a lot onto one side of a disc—16s were thus ideal for spoken-word recordings, and the Argo subsidiary of Decca (*not* the Chess imprint), specialists in that genre, produced a number of releases. They are extremely rare, though there is little general market for examples.

Test Pressings, or Factory Samples—Just to Be Sure It Works

Test pressings (often called Factory Samples in the UK) are, as the name implies, produced at the beginning of a record's final manufacturing process, to ensure that no defects or errors are present in either the recording or the mastering. Test pressings were produced, therefore, for virtually every record ever made, in quantities ranging from one or two, to several hundred.

Aside from the absence of a conventional printed label, most are no different from the finished product, beyond being prepared over two one-sided discs, in some cases, rather than on one two-sided platter.

Some will be marked "test pressing" (or something similar), others may have hand-written notations; others still will be completely blank. Very few test pressings carry anything more than a nominal premium over a conventional pressing of the same disc—those acts whose test pressings do command high sums tend to be those whose entire catalog, in all its permutations, is considered especially collectible.

The scarcest test pressings, then, are those which reflect either last-minute changes in an album's makeup (the removal or switching of songs, for example), or which represent variations that did not ever appear in any other form.

Test pressings of T. Rex's 1970 hit "Ride a White Swan," with the notation OCTO 1 scratched into the run-off groove, are currently ranked among Britain's rarest singles—the catalog number dates from the brief period during which the newly formed Fly record label was still considering calling itself Octopus.

Test pressings of Neil Young's *Comes a Time* album still bear its original title, *Ode to the Wind* (Reprise MSK 2266); similarly, tests of his *Decade* (Reprise 3RS 2257) compilation feature a lengthier version of the song "Campaigner" than appeared on the released version. Both are hotly pursued.

Other popular items include test pressings of Bob Dylan's *Blood on the Tracks,* featuring several performances that were deleted prior to the album's release, and the original test-pressing version of Paul McCartney's *McCartney II* solo album, featuring an entire album's worth of material that was eventually scrapped.

Collectors should be aware, however, that it is often difficult to differentiate between a white-label test pressing and a similarly packaged bootleg, particularly on those occasions when a bootleg purposefully echoes the contents of the unissued LP (*Blood on the Tracks* and *McCartney II* are key examples). One should always ascertain whether the correct identification marks (usually matrix and other numbers in the run-off groove) are present before making a major purchase.

The final area of test pressings to be aware of are those issued to clubs and DJs, in the form of pre-release, white-label versions of 12-inch singles. The concept originated in Jamaica, where hot new songs would be rushed from the pressing plant to the sound systems the moment they were off the presses; in the US and Europe, through the mid-'70s, similar issues became the lifeblood of the disco scene—a role that they retain today.

Many record companies continue pumping out 12-inch singles specifically for the club circuit, and the vast majority of dance tracks made available to the public on CD debuted in the clubs on test-pressing issues. Name artists and DJs such as Moby, St. Etienne, Danny Howells, the Orb, Orbital, and DJ Shadow are all avidly collected, not on luxuriously packaged CD, but on next-to-anonymous vinyl.

Transcription Discs—On Your Radio

Transcription discs are the recordings that are supplied to radio stations that subscribe to any of the popular syndicated shows broadcast throughout the country every week.

These include such institutions as *America's Top 40, Rock over London, Rick Dees' Weekly Top 40,* and *The National Music Survey,* and music-interview magazine digests like *Off the Record, Robert W. Morgan Special of the Week,* and the BBC's now-discontinued *Top of the Pops* radio program. There are also transcription discs of one-off specials and series profiling individual artists (*The Lost Lennon Tapes, The Beatle Years,* etc.) and of the live concerts brought into your living room by the *King Biscuit Flour Hour, Superstar Concert, In Concert,* and Cleveland's legendary *Agora Live* series.

Originally issued to broadcasters as either reel tapes or multidisc vinyl packages, radio shows now appear exclusively on CD. Collectors generally eschew only the (easily duplicated) reels, and naturally, prefer packages that include the original cue sheets, two- or three-page documents detailing contents and commercials, with very specific timing information.

Those discs which offer complete (or nearly complete) concerts are the most collectible, and although value is highly dependent upon the featured act, specialist collectors of any artist will at least be sorely tempted by a high-quality, limited-edition and otherwise unavailable live recording.

Bootlegs, of course, have picked up many of the best-known broadcasts for their own ends, while the BBC and King Biscuit have both made selected performances available to the general public. (Emerson Lake and Palmer's 1974 triple live album, *Welcome Back, My Friends, to the Show That Never Ends— Ladies and Gentlemen Emerson Lake and Palmer,* was itself originally heard as a KBFH special.) But even the most lovingly presented alternative cannot compete with a genuine, official radio disc, in terms of collectibility.

Detailed discographies for most major (and many minor) acts will feature at least one live broadcast; detailed listings for any of the major concert broadcasters will likewise reveal some incredibly in-demand transcription discs. A complete listing for the *Agora Live* series, for example, numbers over 350 separate concerts recorded between February 1972 (a performance by Tiny Alice) and July 1982 (Robert Pezinski), and includes shows by such giants as Spooky Tooth (8/20/73), Ted Nugent (1/28/74), the Pretty Things (3/18/75), Spirit (6/30/75), Thin Lizzy (4/11/76), Boston (9/27/76), Elvis Costello (12/5/77), Todd Rundgren (11/5/78), and U2 (12/2/81). Only a handful of these performances have seen official release, among them Iggy Pop's 3/21/77 show and one track ("My Generation") from Patti Smith's 1/26/76 performance.

Although the majority of collectors will, naturally, hope to acquire all of a given artist's radio discs, the highest priority tends to attach itself to broadcasts from periods in a band's career when interest among subscribing radio stations was low. A BBC transcription disc of a Police show from 1978, for example, will fetch several times more than an *Omni College Rock Concert* disc from 1983; U2's first American broadcast, from 1981 (*Warner Bros. Music Show*) is considerably rarer than a concert from the *Popmart* tour in 1997.

Among non-concert discs, documentaries featuring rare and unissued material are the most collectible, with the *Lost Lennon Tapes* (221 weekly shows) and Paul McCartney's *Oobu Joobu* (17 weeks) far and away the best known. Both were dominated by music that had never previously been aired and which, for the most part, remains in the vault. Lennon's four-CD *Anthology* rarities collection purposefully avoided reprising music aired during the radio series, while McCartney's own promised anthology-style release has yet to materialize.

A number of syndication companies work in this particular field, producing some very high-quality and well-researched discs—the Santa Monica–based On the Radio's collection of Jimi Hendrix rarities is one such. Probably the most respected individual provider of this type of show, however, is the BBC, whose *At the BBC* series of documentaries resurrected radio sessions that, in some cases, had not been heard since their original broadcast.

Such CD series as the *Peel Sessions* EPs and albums have made a lot of this material readily available. However, the documentaries often feature additional material ignored on official releases—the broadcast *David Bowie at the BBC,* for example, included a 1967 performance of "Love You Till Tuesday," which Bowie's own *Bowie at the Beeb* two-CD set (Virgin) completely overlooked.

News and magazine-style shows, wherein the "exclusive" content is largely confined to interview material and maybe an impromptu live-in-the-studio performance, also have their supporters, though prices and demand tend to be low.

At the very bottom end of the scale, at least in terms of collector demand and interest, are simple Top 40 countdown or personality DJ shows (from Wolfman Jack to Lawrence Welk!), where the content is, at least in collecting terms, as anodyne as radio can be. These are the discs one most frequently finds being sold either in bulk lots or via bargain bins after radio-station clear-outs. And in these circumstances, one can safely say, you get what you pay for.

If purchased carefully, transcription discs make a fabulous addition to any collection. There are a handful of caveats—beware of repeat broadcasts of shows, some of which do not state their origins in their packaging; beware, of course, of bootlegs; and beware of being taken for a ride by sellers who insist they have a nearly unique item. There are a lot of radio stations in America, and a lot of them subscribe to these shows. There are at least that many other copies floating around out there somewhere.

12-Inch Singles—They're Like 45s. Only Bigger.

One of the most exciting, and certainly the most successful, innovations of the 1970s was the 12-inch single—literally, a conventional 7-inch (45 rpm) single pressed onto LP-sized vinyl and marketed as a limited edition.

The advantages of the format were manifold. Whether spinning at 33⅓ or 45, the 12-inch single allowed for far more music to be pressed into the grooves, and facilitated a better sound quality as well. Almost from the outset, then, the primary markets were the dance floors. Indeed, the first 12-inch singles issued anywhere in the world were the white-label (test pressing) "pre-release" discs made available exclusively to disc jockeys and sound-system owners in Jamaica during the early '70s.

The format reached the US and European disco scene around 1975, with several now-collectible promo issues, including the Rolling Stones' "Hot Stuff" (Rolling Stones Records PR-70). It was fall 1976 before the first commercially available 12-inch singles made their debut, with a reissue of the Who's decade-old "Substitute" (UK Polydor 2058 803). Two B-sides, the similarly classic oldies "I'm a Boy" and "Pictures of Lily," took full advantage of the added playing time, and a British Top Ten hit, the Who's first in five years, secured the future of the format, despite despite costing close to twice the price of a conventional 7-inch single.

Few of the earliest British 12-inch singles were issued in picture sleeves; the unusual format itself was generally considered novelty enough. Generic card sleeves, thicker than traditional singles sleeves, were considered sufficient to house the new format, with only Island displaying any further marketing awareness, by packaging Steve Winwood's "Time Is Running Out" (12WIP 6394) in a sleeve clearly marked "pre-release"—thus trading on both the format and the label's own Jamaican origins.

The first custom 12-inch sleeves began arriving during the late summer of 1977, largely drawn from the ranks of the New York new wave scene. Richard Hell ("Blank Generation"—Sire 6078 608), Blondie ("Rip Her to Shreds"—Chrysalis 2180), and the Talking Heads ("Psycho Killer"—Sire 6078 010) were among the earliest, while the Ramones' "Sheena Is a Punk Rocker" 12-inch (Sire 6078 606) invited purchasers to send along a proof of purchase and receive, in return, a limited-edition T-shirt.

Several of these releases are now sought after. Television's debut UK single, "Marquee Moon" (Elektra K12252), was presented in its full nine-minute glory, as opposed to being broken into two parts, as was the 7-inch mix (intriguingly, the

12-inch was backed by a unique mono mix of the A-side's stereo). The same band's next 12-inch, "Prove It" (Elektra K12262), was issued on green vinyl.

In 1978, the notion of either remixed or extended 12-inch versions passed into common currency. The impetus to extend beyond the traditional barriers of the three-minute single came, again, from the dance floor. Several unabashed disco hits appeared in elongated form in 1977, but it was also an age in which some of rock's heaviest hitters acknowledged the importance of the dance floors.

Among the pioneers of the remix, the Rolling Stones expanded a straightforward, four-minute version of their new single, "Miss You" (UK EMI/Rolling Stones Records 2802), to an astonishing eight and a half minutes—and then plastered it onto lascivious pink vinyl, as if to ensure that nobody could possibly ignore it.

It was a dramatic gesture, negating all accusations that the band had indeed "gone disco," with one of the most powerful performances of the Stones' recent history. Even more important, it opened the door for a clutch of other acts that might otherwise have thought twice about commissioning what was already being termed as a "dance mix."

Few lived up to the standards set by the Stones. Indeed, the Stones themselves have never equaled, let alone eclipsed, "Miss You," in terms either of dynamics or invention. Too many remixes, it seemed, entailed simply raising the sound of the bass in the mix, and maybe incorporating a few extended passages of percussive repetition; Roxy Music's "Dance Away" (UK Polydor POSPX 44) raised eyebrows by simply repeating a cymbal rhythm for what seemed like hours. Other acts seemed unwilling to go even that far.

The collectibility of 12-inch singles has never been in doubt. Although the early assurance that they were limited editions swiftly evaporated, still very few 12-inchers continued in regular production once a single's chart life was over, regardless of whether or not the 7-inch remained in stock.

This instantly created a secondary market for such issues, all the more so when the 12-inch featured material (or mixes) unavailable elsewhere. In the modern climate of bonus-track-stacked CD reissues, one of the greatest complaints has been the continued unavailability of many acknowledged (or otherwise) "classic" 12-inch mixes. This famine is now ending, but even the best CD cannot compete with the visceral punch of a great-sounding 12-inch. Kiss's 12-inch "I Was Made for Loving You" (UK Casablanca CAN 152), Paul McCartney's "Goodnight Tonight" (UK Parlophone 12R 6023), and David Bowie's "John I'm Only Dancing (Again)" (RCA BOW 12-4) are among the classic rock collectibles thrown up during this period. The Clash's "London Calling," backed by a lengthy, incendiary cover of reggae star Willie Williams' "Armagideon Time" (CBS 12-8087) is one of the new wave's finest, and most sought-after, 12-inch moments.

The 12-inch reigned supreme throughout the first half of the 1980s, with the most significant releases, appropriately, being delivered by those acts whose careers not only came of age following the birth of the 12-inch, but who could even be said to have prospered because of it.

In the UK, the early-'80s "new romantic" movement might be recalled (at least by its detractors) as a primarily visual medium, but on the club floors it was driven wholly by the 12-inch single, with its leading practitioners—Duran Duran, Spandau Ballet, Soft Cell, and Depeche Mode—responsible for some of the most vibrantly inventive extended mixes yet conceived.

Longstanding pop barriers were ruthlessly demolished—both Duran Duran's "Planet Earth (Night Version)" (UK EMI 5137) and Soft Cell's "Say Hello Goodbye" (UK Some Bizzare BZS712) eschewed the traditional concept of the snappy intro, by running through extended instrumental versions before the singers (Simon Le Bon and Marc Almond, respectively) even opened their mouths. Soft Cell's effort went even further by designating a clarinet the lead instrument.

New Order's own position in the mythology of 12-inch collecting was assured very early on, after the group's "Blue Monday" (Factory FACTUS 10) single was issued on 12-inch only. Sensing a major hit, the band's label and its distributors all pressured New Order to release a 7-inch edit; the group refused, sensing that to do so would utterly dilute the performance; the band was rewarded with a No. 9 UK hit.

Other significant issues from this period include a handful of 12-inch box-set releases. Public Image Ltd.'s second album, *Metal Box* (UK Virgin METAL 1), was indeed packaged in a circular tin, akin to a film reel, replicating the album over three 12-inch singles. Spandau Ballet, too, transformed a regular LP to the 12-inch format, with 1982's *Diamond* (UK Chrysalis CBOX 1353) also sporting several otherwise unavailable extended mixes of its contents. A six-disc collection of Soft Cell 12-inch issues, *The 12-Inch Singles* (Some Bizzare CELBX 1), is also worth looking out for if your tastes lean toward the new-romantic electro age.

Mute label stars Depeche Mode, meanwhile, adopted the 12-inch not only as a vehicle for extended mixes, but also as a platform for some quite un-pop-like activities, including a series of very limited editions commissioned by deconstructive dub experimentalist Adrian Sherwood, and a series of live releases in deluxe sleeves, aimed wholly at collectors.

ZTT group Frankie Goes to Hollywood employed the medium in a similarly visionary, not to mention vigorous, manner, and today, multiple 12-inch pressings of its first four singles ("Relax," "Two Tribes," "The Power of Love," and "Welcome to the Pleasure Dome") remain hot collectibles. A clutch of late-'80s Kate Bush 12-inchers—preeminently "Cloudbursting (The Organon Mix)" (EMI 12KB 2)—are similarly prized as much for their musical content as for the format's scarcity.

The 12-inch single was much slower to take control in the US. It was 1978 before Chrysalis's *Disco 33¹/₃* and the Warner Bros. series *33¹/₃ Disco Stereo* marked the first regular 12-inch issues, with Blondie's "Heart of Glass" (Chrysalis CDS 2275) and Rod Stewart's "Do Ya Think I'm Sexy" (Warner Bros. WBSD 8727) among the earliest commercially released 12-inch singles to make an impact on American consumers.

Even in the face of these successes, the bulk of US 12-inch singles, until well inside the new decade, remained promotional only—surprisingly, not only because the format was directly responsible for a massive flowering of artistic breakthroughs, but also because a massive market in UK imports quickly sprang up to fill the void left by domestic labels' reticence. Billy Idol, for one, credits the 12-inch format with engineering his US breakthrough, after an extended version of "Dancin' with Myself" (Chrysalis CHS 12-2488), cut with his earlier band Generation X, became a major American club hit in 1980.

Much of U2's transition from cult live attraction to a group of stadium-filling superstars, in 1982, can be credited to the tremendous promo 12-inch remixes of "New Year's Day" (Island DMD 604) and "Two Hearts Beat as One" (Island DMD 643), commissioned by dance producer Francois Kervorkian.

These releases, incidentally, also ignited the still-enduring consumer and collector interest in "name" remixers. Kervorkian was joined in the early-'80s vanguard by New York hip-hop producer Arthur Baker, whose work with New Order remains among the mightiest demonstrations of the remixer's art ever. Such specialist subscription services as Disconet, whose 12-inch remixes offer some of the most collectible variations in any artist's catalog, sprang from this same cult, to dominate the dance floor of the late '80s and the 1990s.

The artists who most surely epitomize the importance of the American 12-inch, however, are also ranked among the most collectible acts of the 1980s (and beyond)—Prince and Madonna.

Prince remains one of the staples of the rare US 12-inch market, with DJ copies of his earliest singles, "Soft and Wet" (Warner Bros. PRO A-781—1978), "I Wanna Be Your Lover" (PRO A-832), and "Why You Wanna Treat Me So Bad" (PRO A-848) all making massive inroads into the dance scene (and into collectors' hearts) during 1978–79.

Through his breakthrough years, and even into the age of "Controversy" (PRO A-980), "Little Red

Promo 12-inch for They Might Be Giants' "Istanbul."

Corvette" (PRO A-2001), "When Doves Cry" (PRO A-2139), and "Let's Go Crazy" (PRO A-2182), exclusive mixes were the province of US clubs and DJs only, even as parallel UK releases flooded into the country. Prince's first commercial US 12-inch, incredibly, did not emerge until 1985's "Raspberry Beret" (Paisley Park 20355)—needless to say, the early promos are many times scarcer (and higher priced) than these later issues.

Madonna was a little earlier into the market, though her first hits, too, were issued only on now-in-demand promotional 12-inch. Beginning with 1984's "Borderline" (Sire 20212), however, the Material Girl's entire singles output was made available on both 7-inch and 12-inch, with Madonna also among the first international artists to realize the benefits of including two or more mixes of the A-side on the commercial issue, thus keeping fans apace with the DJs' own growing demand for alternate versions.

Madonna's 1989 "Like a Prayer" (Sire 21170) featured five mixes; 1990's "Keep It Together" (Sire 21427) boasted six, though even those could not compete with a pair of promos issued in 1992—11 mixes of "Erotica" (Maverick PRO A-5860), and 12 of "Deeper and Deeper" (PRO A-5928), both released over two 12-inch discs.

The 12-inch boom reached its apogee in 1992–93. Increasingly thereafter, record companies turned to the CD single as a far more economical and convenient format, and though 12-inch singles continue to be produced today, across much of the market their impact is felt only on the dance floors. Few of the 1990s most-collected artists even saw an American 12-inch issued for public consumption, while the format has also slowed considerably in Britain.

Of that country's most commonly collected 1990s talent, Radiohead, [London] Suede, and Oasis can probably point to the most valuable 12-inch releases.

The latter issued several extraordinarily limited one-sided 12-inchers during 1994–95, such quantities as 300 ("Cigarettes and Alcohol"—Creation CTP 190CL), 560 ("Whatever"—CRE 195TP), and 1,203 ("Cum On Feel the Noize"—CTP 221X), clearly issued in full awareness that demand was going to far outstrip supply.

A mere 3,000 copies of Radiohead's 12-inch *Drill* EP (Parlophone 12R 6312), and 6,000 of "Creep" (Parlophone 12R 6078), on the other hand, surely seemed more than sufficient for the debut releases by a completely unknown band; it is the group's subsequent fame that has ignited a ferocious demand for these and other early Radiohead 12-inchers.

Introduction

Without record labels, we would have no records. That is, perhaps, a simplistic statement that is open to pedantic debate on a thousand levels. It is, however, also true. The very act of manufacturing a record, and providing would-be purchasers with a contact address, necessitates the creation of some kind of corporate identity, and the more records that are produced, the firmer that identity becomes.

It is that strength of identity that convinces many collectors to eschew the so-called obvious route of collecting records by individual bands and artists, and to concentrate instead on the releases of entire labels, and any affiliated companies (commonly called subsidiaries and/or imprints).

The advantages of such an approach are manifold. While there are several labels that are avidly pursued by collectors of all persuasions, the vast majority represent comparatively untapped territory, allowing the diligent enthusiast to build a substantial collection at relatively little cost. For every high-ticket item in a label's catalog, there will be many more releases that are regarded as little more than filler, regardless of their scarcity, even by the authors of the price guides.

Collectors who prize the music more than its theoretical "value" are even better served. What better way to expose oneself to a wide variety of new sounds than to play through a decade or so's worth of releases from any given label?

That said, some label's catalogs are simply too vast to ever approach from a heroic "all or nothing" point of view. Staff changes, rosters revolve, musical fads and fashions pass—a label's very nature might undergo any number of complete changes during the course of its existence. Some of the best-loved companies in the world were in operation for 30, 40, 50 years. How could they have done anything but adapt?

With this in mind, many collectors choose to specialize in certain areas only—a favored label design, perhaps; the reign of a chosen artist or a certain producer or A&R man; a time during which the label's output was considered to be at a peak; and so on. Several of these designations, it must be confessed, have been reflected in the entries that follow, with the CD age given deliberately short shrift when compared to the earlier years.

While there are doubtless still label enthusiasts out there for whom a new promo CD single is as thrilling a discovery as an old DJ 45 was for their forebears, experience and observation insists that they are firmly in a minority. Few labels of the last two decades have even halfheartedly courted enthusiasts of their own, with the exceptions being those that tend toward self-defined genres. The ska-oriented Moon Records, the punk Epitaph/Hellcat/Nitro family, Seattle's Sub Pop and C/Z, and the goth-inflected Project and (in its early years) Cleopatra are all well appreciated among specialists.

Many of the labels listed here are what we would today consider "majors"—that is, imprints wholly owned or at least distributed by the giant companies of their respective ages. However, a number of smaller independent concerns are also covered, together with a handful of operations so tiny that the vast majority of readers might never even have heard of them.

Throughout, the implication is not that these labels are somehow better, brighter, or more collectible than the thousands that are not included. They can, however, be considered representative of the spirit of those which are absent.

For this is not a complete list of record labels. Even today, as the world wrings its hands at the thought of the entire European and American music industry being in the thrall of just four multinational mega-conglomerates, there are several thousand labels/imprints still turning out music. Over the last 50 years, that total multiplies so many times over that it is probably impossible to calculate exactly how many different record labels have existed in the US and UK alone.

However many it is, the labels profiled in the following pages represent a mere drop in the ocean—albeit an extraordinarily significant one. All have been selected for their value to collectors today; some as entities in their own right (Sun, Immediate, Stiff, and Sub Pop spring to mind), and others because their catalogs bristle with names and records of import. Some labels are included because their owners are themselves eminently collectible, while others are profiled because they had the fortune to release one record, or sign one band, that just happened to change the world.

Each label biography provides the most basic information collectors will require to begin their own investigation of its output: when the label was launched and when, if appropriate, it folded. First and final releases are given wherever possible. Numerals appearing in parentheses refer to original catalog numbers.

Each entry also notes the most significant artists to record for the label, with especial attention paid to rarities, novelties, and other unusual or noteworthy releases. However, this information can only be considered a general guide and introduction to the subject—specialist collections demand specialist knowledge. Recommendations for further reading are thus provided where available.

A&M

Los Angeles–based A&M Records was the brainchild of Jerry Moss and songwriter-trumpeter Herb Alpert, who joined forces in 1962 to head a self-avowedly middle-of-the-road (MOR) label. According to legend, their combined resources amounted to just a few hundred dollars. When they sold the label to the PolyGram group 27 years later, it was worth around half a billion dollars.

Alpert had previously been in partnership, as an independent producer, with Lou Adler (among their clients were the then-little-known Jan and Dean, at Dore Records). However, he had all but abandoned hopes of making a successful career in music when he met Jerry Moss, at that time a freelance promotions man who also dabbled in record production.

Their first collaboration came when Alpert played trumpet on a session organized by Moss in 1961. By early 1962, they had launched their own label, Carnival, debuting with a 45 credited to Dore Alpert, "Tell It to the Birds" (Carnival 701). Almost immediately, the Dot label purchased the release for $750, which Herb and Jerry plowed into setting up their own recording studio in Alpert's garage.

Their first recording here was "Lonely Bull," a uniquely mariachi-flavored instrumental credited to Herb Alpert and the Tijuana Brass. It was originally scheduled for release on Carnival; however, learning of another label with the same name, Alpert and Moss renamed their concern A&M (from their last initials).

Released in October 1962 as A&M 703, "Lonely Bull" was a massive hit, prompting an immediate LP of the same name and igniting a period of massive chart success for Alpert and his band—at one point in 1966, Alpert had five albums in the US Top 20 simultaneously, while 1968 brought a worldwide No. 1 with "This Guy's in Love with You" (A&M 929).

A&M moved from Alpert's garage to new offices on Sunset Boulevard in early 1963, before taking over the Charlie Chaplin movie studio on Sunset and La Brea in late 1966. The label's roster expanded to match its growth. Adhering to Alpert's own stranglehold on adult listening tastes, early recruits included the Baja Marimba Band (formed by Julius Wechter, a former member of Martin Denny's band), Sergio Mendes, Chris Montez, Claudine Longet, the Sandpipers, We Five, and Evie Sands, a New York singer whose "Any Way That You Want Me" (1090) was one of those big-hits-that-wasn't in 1969. The checkered career of the superlatively talented Sands has continued sporadically since then, peaking with 1999's much-acclaimed CD *Women in Prison* (Train Wreck TW 009).

In 1967, Moss opened A&M's doors to the rock market, and two years later, released one of the label's most prized rarities, a eponymous LP by Spirits and Worm (4229). Though the Italian label Akarma has since reissued the set, original pressings, of which very few were manufactured, are extremely scarce.

TEN TOP COLLECTIBLES

The Carpenters

Close to You (A&M LLP 125—Jukebox Album, 1970)

"Do You Hear What I Hear?" (A&M 2700—7-inch promo, 1984)

Horizon (A&M QU 54530—Quad LP, 1975)

"I'll Be Yours"—Karen Carpenter (Magic Lamp 704—7-inch, 1967)

"Love Is Surrender" (UK A&M AMS 832—7-inch, 1971)

Offering (A&M SP 4205—LP, 1969)

"Santa Claus Is Coming to Town" (A&M 1648—7-inch, picture sleeve, 1974)

Sounds Like the Navy (US Navy, no catalog number—Transcription disc, 1975)

"Ticket to Ride" (A&M 1142—7-inch, 1969)

"Yesterday Once More" (A&M 2735—7-inch, picture sleeve, 1985)

Moss also concluded licensing deals with the British labels Regal Zonophone and Island. Over the next three years, A&M would become the US home for such British stars as Procol Harum, the Move, Spooky Tooth, Fairport Convention, Free, Jimmy Cliff, Cat Stevens, the Strawbs, and Humble Pie, while domestic recruits included Phil Ochs, organ virtuoso Lee Michaels, and country-rockers Dillard and Clark and the Flying Burrito Brothers. A&M was also behind one of the most unconventional live successes of the age, Joe Cocker's legendary Mad Dogs and Englishmen outing.

The concert album that documented that tour went on to sell over a million copies, becoming the most successful double live album ever released up to that point—a title that was not surrendered until another A&M act, Peter Frampton, issued 1975's *Frampton Comes Alive*, and wound up with one of the biggest-selling records of all time.

Maintaining a reputation for signing classy acts, A&M continued to grow throughout the 1970s. Styx, Rick Wakeman, the Tubes, and Supertramp, among many others, expanded the label's rock output, while the earlier MOR sensibilities were more than adequately served by the presence of the multimillion-selling Carpenters, the Captain and Tennille, Irish singer-songwriter Chris de Burgh, and Joan Armatrading.

From a collector's point of view, then, it is ironic that the rarest record in the entire A&M catalog was the result of what Derek Green, head of the company's UK operation, ultimately conceded to be a serious error in judgment—signing, and a week later, sacking, punk rock icons the Sex Pistols, in March 1977. Manufacture of their proposed label debut, the single "God Save the Queen" (AMS 7284), had already commenced when the band was dumped. The records were scrapped, with an estimated 300 survivors now regarded among A&M's (and punk's) most fabled rarities.

Punk did surface on A&M, however. A licensing deal with the I.R.S. label brought both the Police and Squeeze to the label in 1978, while the 1980s saw further diversification via Amy Grant, Captain Beefheart, Joe Jackson, Suzanne Vega, Bryan Adams, John Hiatt, and the Neville Brothers.

Following the label's sale to PolyGram in June 1989, Alpert and Moss continued on in management roles until 1993. Six years later, PolyGram merged into the Universal Music group, at which point A&M all but ceased operations as a functioning record label, and became simply a reissue imprint.

The Sex Pistols notwithstanding, A&M catalog rarities are determined more by the collectibility of the artists than by the actual releases. The Carpenters are especially popular, with several now-scarce picture-sleeve 45 releases and a hard-to-find debut album (*Offering*—SP 4205). The British label also produced a number of limited-edition, colored-vinyl releases during the late '70s: the Police's "Can't Stand Losing You" (blue wax), Klark Kent's (actually Police drummer Stewart Copeland's) "Don't Care" (green), and Squeeze's "Up the Junction" (lilac) remain popular. Other Police-related rarities include the British *Police Pack* wallet of six blue-vinyl singles and a 10-inch pressing of their debut album.

With all pre-1973 releases, the most desirable editions of individual LPs tend to be those bearing the original all-brown label; later pressings feature a new silver-gray label design with the letters A&M in brown.

Abel

Abel was a short-lived Laurie subsidiary whose output included one extremely scarce Dion DiMucci LP, released following the singer's departure for Columbia in 1963. In fact *Dion Singing and Introducing the Glen Stuart Chorus* (ABLP 8001) featured only seven Dion songs; the remainder of the disc did indeed feature the Glen Stuart Chorus.

Abner

The first-ever subsidiary of Vee-Jay, Abner was originally launched in 1957 as Falcon. It existed in this form for around a year, releasing a dozen locally (Chicago) successful 45s without mishap. These included three by Dee Clark: "Gloria" (1002), "Seven Nights" (1005), and "Oh Little Girl" (1009). However, when Falcon 1013, the Impressions' "For Your Precious Love," began moving chartward, a Texas label with prior claim to the Falcon name stepped forward. Falcon was renamed Abner, after employee (and future Vee-Jay

president) Ewart Abner, retaining the earlier label's falcon logo—the hastily re-pressed Impressions release also kept the original Falcon catalog number.

Mid-1959 brought Abner's first album, a eponymous LP by Dee Clark (SR 2000); the company issued just two further LPs, one by Jerry Butler (*Jerry Butler, Esq.*) and a second by Clark (*How 'Bout That*). Clark's albums were issued in both mono and stereo, Butler's in mono only. Both artists also released a number of singles on the label. Butler produced a total of nine (five with the Impressions); Clark did five. In total, the Abner label issued around 40 singles before folding in 1960. Ewart Abner himself departed Vee-Jay in 1963.

Ace

Although the label's headquarters were actually in Jacksonville, Miss., Ace is frequently described as the first truly noteworthy local label to operate in New Orleans—close to 200 miles away. In the past, the Big Easy industry had been primarily reliant on labels from elsewhere (the Los Angeles–based Imperial and Specialty among them). Indeed, Ace founder Johnny Vincent was a former salesman and producer with Specialty.

From its formation in mid-1955, Ace's links with New Orleans were strengthened by the use of Cosimo Matassa's studio. Over the next four years, a string of both local and national hits were cut there, including Huey "Piano" Smith's "Rockin' Pneumonia and the Boogie Woogie Flu" (530) and "Don't You Just Know It" (545), as well as Jimmy Clanton's "Just a Dream" (546) and "Go Jimmy Go" (575), and Frankie Ford's "Sea Cruise" (554). The label's first LP, in 1958, was titled for Clanton's aforementioned hit (1001). Other notable recordings include efforts by Professor Hugs, Scotty McKay, Alvin "Red" Tyler, comedian C.Z. Breaux, and Roland Stone.

Unfortunately, Ace's specialty appeared to be one-hit (or at best, two-hit) wonders, with lasting success constantly at a premium. This was, perhaps, best evidenced by a trio of unashamedly exploitative LP releases during early 1962: the star-studded compilations *For Twisters Only* (1020) and *Let's Have a Dance Party* (1019), in which sundry Ace veterans extolled dances as varied (and fad-driven) as the pop-eye, the hully gully, the stroll, the pony, and the fish. Opportunistic though they were, these sets were nothing compared with Alvin Tyler's *Twistin' with Mr. Sax*—a straightforward repackaging of his 1960 release *Rockin' and Rollin'* (1006), with the word "twist" added to every song title.

Distribution was frequently at the root of Ace's woes, and later in 1962, Vincent allied Ace with Vee-Jay, via a five-year distribution deal. Immediately, the partnership scored a major hit with Jimmy Clanton's "Venus in Blue Jeans" (8001), but it was a false dawn. Ace's output was confined almost exclusively to singles (just two LPs, by Clanton and Huey Smith, were issued under Vee-Jay auspices, both in 1962), and as Vee-Jay itself lurched into growing difficulties, the smaller Ace label receded from view.

Independent again following Vee-Jay's eventual demise in March 1966, Ace struggled on for a handful more 45s, then folded. Vincent left the music industry, but returned in 1971, relaunching Ace in response to growing collector interest. Offering both new material and classic reissues (the well-named Ace Collectors Series), Ace remained in operation until Vincent, now in failing health, finally sold it to the British label Music Collection International, in 1997. Under the aegis of producer Bob Fisher, the Westside label has maintained a respectable stream of Ace reissues and compilations. The British reissue label Ace, while unaffiliated with Vincent, released five collections of its US namesake's classics, *The Ace Story,* during the early '80s.

Across the Ace reissue scene, a number of recordings have emerged for the first time in stereo. Only one original LP was released in that format, Gil Peterson's eponymous 1962 album (1024).

The Ace catalog as a whole is highly collectible; however, the Holy Grail is certainly the Joe Burton Trio's *Joe Burton Plays* (1002), an LP so scarce that it is uncertain whether it was ever given a full release.

Acta

A subsidiary of Dot, Acta was launched by Kenny Meyers in 1967, to handle the then-new psychedelic music boom. Two principal licensing deals guaranteed product, with Chicago producer Bill Traut, and the San Francisco–based Golden State Recorders—purveyors, respectively, of the American Breed and the Other Half, a band best remembered for the presence of guitarist Randy Holden, later of Blue Cheer.

Acta debuted with the Other Half single "Flight of the Dragon Lady" (801), the first of four 45s by the band. An eponymous LP (38004) is very highly regarded by psychedelic collectors.

American Breed, too, launched with a single, "Give Two Young Lovers a Chance" (802); it flopped, but a Top 30 follow-up, "Step out of Your Mind" (804), set the group on course to becoming Acta's biggest-selling act. The group's fourth single, "Bend Me Shape Me" (811), went Top Five in spring 1968, and while the American Breed would never repeat that success, the group members would return to the top several years later, as Rufus. Each of American Breed's four Acta albums is of interest, particularly the mono edition of its self-titled debut (8002). This was the only mono LP issued by the company. Of the other Breed albums, *Bend Me Shape Me* (38003) was Acta's sole hit LP, while *Lonely Side of the City* (38008) was the final long-playing release on the label. In between times, *Pumpkin, Powder, Scarlet and Green* (38006) bore perhaps the most interesting title in the catalog.

Other Acta acts included Bobby Sansom and the Light Years, the Domestic Help, Pride and Joy, Blondell Breed and the Imports, Joe and Al, the Brothers Cain, and the Peppermint Trolley Company—the latter's "Baby You Come Rollin' Across My Mind" (815) was a US Top 60 hit during summer 1968, the only other significant success in the Acta catalog. The band was rewarded with an eponymous LP release (38007); the only other group to score an Acta album was San Francisco's Neighb'rhood Childr'n (38005).

Acta folded in late 1969.

A Neighb'rhood Childr'n anthology, *Long Years in Space,* was released in 1997 (Sundazed SC 11041), arousing a hitherto dormant collector interest in both the band and its little-known label. Although prices have still to truly take off (American Breed LPs in particular can be picked up very inexpensively), Acta 45s are becoming increasingly difficult to find.

Adam VIII

To the majority of record collectors, Adam VIII is synonymous with just one release, the legendary *John Lennon Sings the Great Rock and Roll Hits/Roots* LP.

Roots was conceived in settlement of a copyright case lodged against Lennon by publisher Morris Levy, following Lennon's use of a Chuck Berry lyric in the Beatles composition "Come Together." In 1973, Lennon agreed to record a handful of other songs published by Levy as part of his next album, a collection of covers paying tribute to the singer's own 1950s roots. The project was delayed following the abandonment of the original recording sessions with producer Phil Spector, but Lennon finally presented Levy with a reference tape of the recordings in late 1974.

Since Lennon was under contract to Capitol/EMI at the time, there should never have been any question about who would release the LP. In early February 1975, however, Levy's Adam VIII label began running television commercials promoting *Roots,* a mail-order album featuring this material. Capitol immediately issued its own revised version of the same LP, *Rock 'n' Roll,* at the same time initiating legal action against Adam VIII.

Roots was withdrawn, and following three years of litigation, all unsold copies of the LP were finally delivered to Lennon (presumably for destruction) in 1977. Featuring, as it does, substantially different mixes of the *Rock 'n' Roll* material, plus two songs, "Be My Baby" and "Angel Baby," which were absent from the official set, *Roots* is today regarded among the greatest of all solo Lennon rarities, with other Adam VIII albums gaining some collecting salience simply through association.

Levy first ventured into TV-advertised albums with the Dynamic House and Tele House labels during the early '70s, competing with K-Tel and Ronco for what was then a fast-burgeoning market in repackaged oldies. The four-LP box set *Greatest Rock and Roll Hits* (CD 1001-1004), retailing at a bargain $6.98, launched

Dynamic House; it was followed by the similarly packaged *Rock Is Here to Stay* (CD-1005-1008), and a number of other collections marketed through the Special Products/Markets distribution company.

Tele House, too, concentrated on various-artists box sets—commercials for the first, 1973's *The No. 1 Hits of the '60s* (CR 1013-1016), memorably featured the Monkees' Mickey Dolenz. Other releases featured compilations of Glen Campbell, Lynn Anderson, and Johnny Cash; all are characterized by poor fidelity and cheap packaging, and even for fans of '70s kitsch, only one Tele House LP truly repays investigation— 1972's *The Great Rock Operas* (CD 2010), a four-LP set devoting one disc apiece to songs made famous by *Jesus Christ Superstar, Hair, Tommy,* and *Godspell.*

Levy launched Adam VIII in 1973—the label was named for Levy's eight-year-old son. A Billie Holiday compilation (A-8002) was issued in 1973; Lennon's *Roots* (A-8018) and a Tommy James & the Shondells collection (A-8028) aside, the bulk of releases again adhered to the tried-and-true oldies/hits collection format.

Adam VIII continued releasing new collections until as late as 1979, titles embracing country, disco, and nostalgia—there was even a collection celebrating "the ultimate toga party." Beyond curio value, however, none have any true worth on the collecting market; certainly none can even begin to approach *Roots* in terms of either legend or desirability. Vinyl bootlegs of *Roots* began appearing in the mid-'70s, some offering reproductions of the music alone, others attempting to duplicate the entire package. Prospective buyers are advised to exercise extreme caution when approaching a purported "genuine" issue—there are very, very few of them around.

Further Reading: *The Great Rock 'n' Roll Swindle,* by Ashley Kahn (*Mojo,* issue 92, July 2001)

Amaret

Between 1969–72, Amaret punched out a stream of now-sought-after hard rock releases, including the *Crow Music* debut by Crow (AST 5002). Released as a single (112), the opening track, "Evil Woman," became a US Top 20 hit that fall, though it is better recalled today via Black Sabbath's cover the following year.

Later Crow singles "Cottage Cheese" (119) and "Don't Try to Lay No Boogie Woogie on the King of Rock and Roll" (125) were minor hits in 1970, while two further LPs also made the lower reaches of the chart: *Crow by Crow* (AST 5006) and *Mosaic by Crow* (AST 5009). Crow's final Amaret releases in 1972 were the *Best Of* compilation (AST 5012) and the 45 "If It Feels Good, Do It" (148).

Crow is the most collectible band on the Amaret roster; other releases included titles by Triangle, New Life, Fresh Air, Judy Lynn, and Crow vocalist David Wagner; the latter's debut album (AST 5013) was one of just three LPs following the label's recruitment to the MGM group. (The others were the aforementioned Crow collection and Judy Lynn's sophomore album, *Naturally*—AST 5014.) Amaret ceased operations in 1972.

Amy

Launched in 1960, Amy was the brainchild of Bell Records' then-president, Al Massler, and debuted with the 45 "Waba," by the Hully Gully Babies (800). The label's first hit, months later, was Al Brown's Tunetoppers' dance novelty "The Madison" (805), which also prompted the label's first LP, *The Tunetoppers at the Madison Dance Party* (A1). Unusually for the time, the album was released in stereo.

In 1961, the label had a second major hit with the Ramrods' instrumental version of Vaughn Monroe's "Ghost Riders in the Sky" (813). (Monroe himself was signed to Amy during the mid-'60s.) The hit was followed by classic period pieces by such immortally named combos as Gabriel and the Angels; Jaywalker and the Pedestrians; the Sick-Nicks (a comedy spin-off from *Sick* magazine, which also produced the second Amy album, *Personalities of the World*—A2); Tracy Dey; the Jesters; Buzz and Bucky; and Tico and the Triumphs, from whose ranks sprang the artist with whom Amy is today best associated, the young Paul Simon.

Tico and the Triumphs scored a minor hit with 1962's "Motorcycle" (835); Simon alone, under the pseudonym Jerry Landis, scored another with "The Lone Teen Ranger" (875). However, the label's biggest

TEN TOP COLLECTIBLES

Amy

Authentic Ska"—Various artists (LP Amy 8002—1964)

"Cards of Love"—Tico and the Triumphs (Amy 876—1963)

"Cry, Li'l Boy"—Tico and the Triumphs (Amy 860—1962)

"I Can't Believe My Ears"—Del Shannon (Amy 947—1966)

"The Lone Teen Ranger"—Jerry Landis (Amy 875—1964)

"Mary Jane"—Del Shannon (Amy 897—1961)

"Motorcycle"—Tico and the Triumphs (Amy 835/Madison 169—1965)

Ride Your Pony—Lee Dorsey (Stereo LP Amy S-8010—1962)

"War Cry"—The Ramrods (Amy 846—1962)

"Wildflower"—Tico and the Triumphs (Amy 845—1962)

hit—indeed, the biggest Bell group smash yet—was destined to be supplied not by a superstar-in-waiting, but by a future wrestling instructor, Joey Powers. His "Midnight Mary" (Amy 892) was a Top Ten giant in late 1963. Powers' album of the same name (8001), released the following year, features a re-recording of the hit track.

Midnight Mary was the first Amy album in two years (since the *Sick* set), and inaugurated a sequence that is littered with highly sought-after collectibles—three by Del Shannon and two by Lee Dorsey included. Both artists also notched up a handful of hits during their time with Amy, including Dorsey's "Ride Your Pony" (927), "Get out of My Life Woman" (945), "Working in a Coal Mine" (958), and "Holy Cow" (965); and Shannon's "Handy Man" (905), "Keep Searchin' " (915), and "Break Up" (925). Released in 1966, Dorsey's *The New Lee Dorsey* (8011) was the final Amy LP.

Releases by British rock 'n' roller Adam Faith also came in 1964. Taken from an eponymous LP (8005), his "It's Alright" (913) just missed the Top 30 in early 1965, prompting Amy to pick up on another hit English act, Cliff Bennett and the Rebel Rousers. Their "If Only You'd Reply" (930) is an unsung gem of latter-day Merseybeat.

Amy also signed Pope Paul VI (that's right!—the LP Amy 8009 was an audio souvenir of the pontiff's *First Visit to the Americas*). The label signed Jamaican superstar Prince Buster, whose "Everybody Ska" (906) was released in 1964, around the same time that Buster visited the US as part of his homeland's delegation to the 1964 World's Fair, and was accompanied by the now-exceedingly rare various-artists collection *Authentic Ska* (8002).

Other inspired Amy signings included comedienne Gertrude Berg, Len Barry, Mike Stoller, Clyde McPhatter, Earl King, Little Eva, the Kalin Twins, pro-footballer Roosevelt Grier, David and Jonathan, and the young and then-unknown Daryl Hall ("The Princess and the Soldier"—11049). None had hits; none recorded LPs for the label. The final Amy release, later that same year, was Lee Dorsey's "Give It Up" (11057).

Apple

The Beatles' Apple label was launched in August 1968, with the release of three 45s—the Beatles' own "Hey Jude" (2276, continuing US distributors Capitol's numbering sequence); Mary Hopkin's "Those Were the Days" (1801); and Jackie Lomax's "Sour Milk Sea" (1802). A fourth issue, released in the UK only, was the Black Dyke Mills Band's "Thingumybob" (4). Uniquely for a new label (but, perhaps, not surprisingly for a Beatles-related concern), both "Hey Jude" and "Those Were the Days" topped the UK chart.

Apple was conceived amid a flurry of other ambitious projects (movie, electronics, publishing, tailoring, and merchandising divisions were also founded). Emphasizing artists whom the Beatles themselves personally wished to nurture, the label's early signings also included the Iveys (soon to become Badfinger), Billy Preston, Doris Troy, Ronnie Spector, David Peel, James Taylor, and Hot Chocolate—notably only the latter two truly met with lasting success, both after they departed Apple.

The bulk of these non-Beatle recordings were made during the label's first three years of operation; by late 1972, the label's output was almost exclusively confined to John and Yoko Lennon, Paul McCartney and Wings, George Harrison, and Ringo Starr. Of Apple's other recruits, only Elephant's Memory, Badfinger, and the utterly obscure Lon and Dereck Van Eaton would release further music (one 45 and LP apiece) on the label. Paul McCartney departed in 1975; Apple ceased operations, as far as new releases were concerned, in 1976.

With fewer than 70 LPs and 100 45s released in either the UK or US (including several that appeared only in one or the other market), the Apple catalog is small, but surprisingly difficult to amass in its original form.

A promotional box set comprising the first four UK singles and an EP available only through the British Walls Ice Cream company are very rarely sighted; also of immense value is the banned UK APPLE 8, "The King of Fuh," by New York singer Brute Force. Outraged by lyrics that included the immortal "Oh hell! The Fuh King," distributors Parlophone refused to press the single. Apple therefore manufactured it privately, but it failed to sell and copies swiftly disappeared.

The first and only releases on the extraordinarily short-lived experimental subsidiary Zapple, in May 1969 (John and Yoko's *Unfinished Music 2: Life with the Lions*—ST 3357, and George's *Electronic Sounds*—ST 3358), are highly prized, as are the eight mono LPs that Apple released in the UK during late 1968 and early 1969. This includes the Beatles' own *The Beatles* (SWBO 101) and the *Yellow Submarine* movie soundtrack (SW 153), together with further LPs by Harrison, the Lennons, James Taylor, Mary Hopkin, Jackie Lomax, and the Modern Jazz Quartet.

Apple also produced a handful of special-edition LPs, featuring ephemeral extras that are now very difficult to come by. The Lennons' *Wedding Album* (SMAX 3361) featured several items of a celebratory nature; *Live Peace at Toronto* (SW 3362) included a free calendar. The Beatles' final album, *Let It Be* (AR 34001), was issued in a box set with an accompanying booklet; so were George Harrison's *All Things Must Pass* (STCH 639) and *The Concert for Bangladesh* (STCX 3385). The greatest rarity of all, however, is a Christmas 1970 Beatles LP issued only

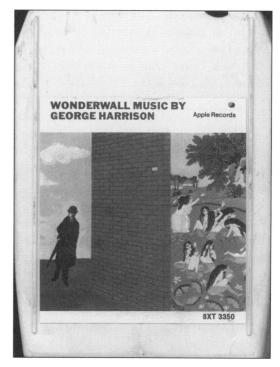

The 8-Track version of George Harrison's *Wonderwall Music.*

TEN TOP NON-BEATLES COLLECTIBLES

Apple

Celtic Requiem—John Tavener (UK Apple SAPCOR 20—LP, 1971)

"F Is Not a Dirty Word"—David Peel (PRO 6498/9—DJ 7-inch, 1972)

"Hippie from New York City"—David Peel (PRO 6545/6—DJ 7-inch, 1972)

"How the Web Was Woven"—Jackie Lomax (UK Apple 23—7-inch, 1970)

In Concert—Ravi Shankar (UK Apple SAPDO 1002—2-LP, 1972)

"The King of Fuh"—Brute Force (UK Apple 8—7-inch, 1970)

"That's the Way God Planned It"—Billy Preston (Americom 433—Flexidisc, 1969)

"Those Were the Days"—Mary Hopkin (Americom 238—Flexidisc, 1969)

Walls Ice Cream—Various artists (UK Apple CT 1—EP, 1969)

for fan-club members. *From Then to Us* (SBC 100) compiled all of the group's annual Christmas flexidiscs and has since been extensively bootlegged.

Other high-ticket items include a Mary Hopkin hits collection, *Those Were the Days* (SW 3395), and Indian sitarist Ravi Shankar's *In Concert 1972* (SVBB 3396), a two-LP live set that sold extremely poorly at the time, but that has since become a Grail of sorts. Pressings of a Delaney and Bonnie album scheduled for release, but ultimately canceled, exist, but they surface very rarely.

Apple's US office was also responsible for a handful of 4-inch Pocket Disc releases, manufactured in 1969 in conjunction with the company Americom, for sale via vending machines. These account for many of the label's greatest rarities: the Beatles issues comprise "Get Back" (2490), "The Ballad of John and Yoko" (2531), "Yellow Submarine" (5715), and a unique 3.25 edit of "Hey Jude" (2276). Mary Hopkin's "Those Were the Days" (1801) and "Goodbye" (1138), the Iveys' "Maybe Tomorrow" (1803), the Plastic Ono Band's "Give Peace a Chance" (1809), and Billy Preston's "That's the Way God Planned It" (1808) also appeared in this unusual format.

In addition to UK and US releases, international Apple releases also offer a considerable challenge. Many were issued with otherwise unavailable picture sleeves, and occasionally, incomprehensible titles—Mary Hopkin's "Bylie Taki Dni" ("Those Were the Days") was a major hit in Poland; Hopkin also rerecorded several of her singles in foreign languages, including French, German, Spanish, Italian, and Japanese.

Apple specialists might also care to pursue acetates recorded at the Apple studios, distinguishable (of course) by the blank Apple label affixed to many. Among the rarest of these can be counted the first-ever recording by British band 10cc, "Waterfall."

The Apple catalog has seen sporadic CD releases since the late 1980s.

Further Reading: *The Beatles Album: 30 Years of Music and Memorabilia,* by Geoffrey Giuliano (Viking, 1991)

Ardent

The Stax label's attempts to break in to the white rock market were doomed to failure, though the modern collectibility of at least part of the Ardent

---

TEN TOP COLLECTIBLES

Alex Chilton

"Hey Little Child" (UK Aura AUS 117—7-inch, 1980)

"Hold On Girl"—The Box Tops (Hi 2242—7-inch, 1973)

"The Letter"—The Box Tops (Philco HP 27—Hip-pocket record, 1968)

The Letter/Neon Rainbow—The Box Tops (Bell 6011—Mono LP, 1968)

"No Sex" (France New Rose 69—double 7-inch pack, 1986)

"O My Soul"—Big Star (Ardent 2909—7-inch, 1974)

"September Girls"—Big Star (Ardent 2912—7-inch, 1974)

The Singer, Not the Song (Ork 1978—EP, 1976)

"Watch the Sunrise"—Big Star (Ardent 2904—7-inch, 1972)

"When My Baby's Beside Me"—Big Star (Ardent 2902—7-inch, 1972)

Johnny Nash's eponymous LP, one of his Ten Top Collectibles.

subsidiary catalog proves that one cannot say they didn't try.

Ardent was established in late 1971, via a tie-up with John Fry of the Ardent Recording Studio in Memphis, and was launched in early 1972 with a eponymous LP by Cargoe (ADS 2802). Albums by Brian Alexander Robertson and by the Hot Dogs followed; Ardent's greatest claim to fame, however, lies in the original issues of Alex Chilton and Big Star's *#1 Record* (2803) and *Radio City* (1501) albums, utterly overlooked at the time of release, but hot collectors items almost from the moment they were deleted. Isn't that always the way.

Ardent also released a chain of similarly prized Big Star 45s.

Argo

This much-loved subsidiary of Chess was launched in May 1956. It was initially called Marterry, a combination of the founding Chess brothers' sons' names

(Marshall and Terry); however, bandleader Ralph Marterie was already operating a label under his own name, and despite the difference in spelling, the Chesses agreed to change. Two 45s had already been released, including the Daps's "Down and Out"; the new label name, Argo, was debuted with singles by Savannah Churchill and Danny Overbea.

Releases by the Ravens, Billy Stewart (a member of Bo Diddley's band), and Paul Gayton followed, before Clarence "Frogman" Henry brought Argo its first hit, "Ain't Got No Home" (5259—produced by Gayton).

Argo was originally conceived as a pop label, to take advantage of the new rock 'n' roll music's habit of rearranging classic R&B material for its own market. Across a string of early hit singles and increasingly ambitious LPs, however, Argo swiftly carved itself a niche as distinctive as either its Chess or Checker counterparts.

The first LP release, Al Hibbler's *Melodies By* (601), was followed by such distinctive brews as Ahmad

TEN TOP COLLECTIBLES

Johnny Nash

"As Time Goes By" (ABC Paramount 9996—7-inch, picture sleeve, 1959)

Composer's Choice (Argo LPS 4038S—Stereo LP, 1964)

"Deep in the Heart of Harlem" (Groove 58-0021—7-inch, 1964)

Hold Me Tight (JAD JS 1207—LP, 1968)

I Can See Clearly Now (Epic KE 13607—Yellow-label LP, 1972)

Johnny Nash (ABC Paramount S244—Stereo LP, 1959)

"Out of Town" (ABC Paramount 9743—7-inch, 1956)

"Stir It Up" (Epic 10873—7-inch, 1972)

"Talk to Me" (Argo 5471—7-inch, 1964)

"Teardrops in the City" (Cadet 5528—7-inch, 1966)

Jamal's *Chamber Music of the New Jazz* (602), James Moody's *Flute 'n' the Blues* (603), and the Zoot Sims Quartet's *Zoot* (608); Ramsey Lewis, Chubby Jackson, Clark Terry, Sonny Smitt, Etta James, and Roland Kirk are all represented on the 150-plus LPs issued within Argo's 600 and 700 series of albums between 1956–65. This in itself is indicative of the label's increasing swing toward jazz, and imperceptibly, away from 78s and 45s—the chart-consuming bread and butter of Chess and Checker.

In 1961, looking to return Argo to its pop basics (but maintain its now-assured roost at the forefront of the Chicago jazz scene), the Chess brothers launched the 4000 series, again intending to concentrate on pop. Hit singles by the Sensations—"Music Music Music" (5391), "Let Me In" (5405), and "That's My Desire" (5412)—pointed the way, and over the next five years, a total of 45 LPs were released.

The first, in 1961, was Osborne Smith's *The Eyes of Love* (4000); the last was George Kirby's *The Real George Kirby* (4045). Argo also released sets by the Johnny Hamlin Quintet, Sam Lazar, drum maestro Professor Paradiddle, Clarence Henry, trumpeter Don Goldie, Walter Horton, Dodo Marmarosa, Shelley Moore, Bonnie Graham, Howard McGhee, and more.

Future MOR/reggae-lite superstar Johnny Nash was also an Argo artist, cutting his *Composer's Choice* LP (4038) in 1964. As with other early Nash LPs (five earlier sets were recorded for ABC/Paramount), copies are considerably scarcer than their going price suggests. Nash also cut four singles for Argo, none of which duplicate material on the LP.

There were also several various-artists collections: four volumes of *The Blues* (4026/27/34/42) and *Folk Festival of the Blues* (4031). Drawing from the Chess catalog, these discs are among the best blues compilations of the era.

The end of Argo was as tragic as it was sudden—and wholly unnecessary. The Chess brothers had never taken steps to protect the label name, assuming that—like Chess and Checker—it was well-known enough that nobody would dare trifle with it. Indeed, with the Ramsey Lewis Trio currently scoring hit singles and LPs at will, by 1965 Argo was regarded among the hottest labels in town.

It was not, however, the only Argo on earth. The British label Decca had been operating its own Argo subsidiary as a haven for spoken-word recordings for many years, and its rights to the name were legally protected. When the company decided to begin making inroads into the American market, Argo—and Decca's recognized legal ownership of it—was one of the principal weapons in the corporate arsenal. Having tried unsuccessfully to negotiate a compromise, and unwilling to spend either time or money on legal maneuverings, Chess relinquished all claims to the Argo identity in September 1965. Henceforth the label would be called Cadet.

Further Reading: *Spinning Blues into Gold: The Chess Brothers and the Legendary Chess Records,* by Nadine Cohodas (St. Martin's Press, 2000)

Astro

The short-lived Astro label was distributed by Cotillion; it issued just one LP, numbered within the parent company's 9000 series, by the Houston based quintet Blackwell—best remembered today for the involvement of keyboard player John "Rabbit" Bundrick.

In the years since Blackwell's eponymous debut LP was released (SD 9010), Bundrick has recorded many albums as a solo artist, a session man, and also as a member of the English rock bands Free and [Back Street] Crawler, formed by former Free guitarist Paul Kossoff. For this reason, *Blackwell* is considered a welcome, if frequently overlooked, find.

Asylum

To the fan and collector of early-'70s folk-rock, Asylum Records represents the mother lode. From Jackson Browne and Linda Ronstadt to the Eagles and Andrew Gold, Asylum dominated the genre, and though few of the label's releases are especially rare, quantity (mercifully allied to quality) alone ensures a constantly challenging pursuit.

Asylum Records was created by a former agent at the William Morris talent agency, David Geffen. He had originally hoped to work with movie stars, but having been assured that his youth was against him, he turned instead to rock management. Quitting the agency, his first client was singer-songwriter Laura Nyro, followed by Crosby, Stills and Nash, before

TEN TOP COLLECTIBLES

Free

Barbed Wire Sandwich—Black Cat Bones (UK Nova SDN 15—LP, 1970)

BBC Classic Tracks (Westwood One—CD, 1993)

"Broad Daylight" (UK Island WIP 6054—7-inch, 1969)

The Free EP (UK Island PIEP 6—12-inch EP, 1982)

The Free Story (Island OLSD 4—2-LP, 1975)

Heartbreaker (Island ILPS SW 9324—LP, 1973)

"I'll Be Creepin' " (UK Island WIP 6062—7-inch, 1969)

"King Fu"—Sharks (MCA 40246—7-inch, 1974)

Mr. Big/Blue Soul—Paul Kossoff (UK St. Tunes 0012PD—picture-disc LP, 1982)

Tons of Sobs (UK Island ILPS 9089—First-label LP, 1969)

Geffen decided he didn't enjoy management after all, and having sold his interests to Elliot Roberts, he returned to agency work.

In 1972, Geffen and Roberts formed their own management company to represent singer-songwriter Jackson Browne. They were unable to find a record deal for the artist; finally, Ahmet Ertegun at Atlantic suggested they launch their own company, with Atlantic handling distribution.

Browne was the first artist signed to Asylum; he was followed by John David (J.D.) Souther, Judy Sill (her debut LP was Asylum's first release—SD 5050), David Blue, and the Eagles, a band formed at Geffen's own suggestion. JoJo Gunne, featuring ex-Spirit member Jay Ferguson, brought Asylum its first major hit 45 in the summer of 1972, when "Run Run Run" (11003) reached No. 27. Before the end of the year, Jackson Browne's "Doctor My Eyes" (11004) and "Rock Me on the Water," (11006) as well as the Eagles' "Take It Easy" (11005) and "Witchy Woman," (11008) had all marched into the Top 20. The label was printing LPs the way other institutions print banknotes.

The SD 5000 series, representing Asylum's first year in action, is the most collectible. Many of the LPs here have been re-pressed and reissued on numerous occasions; first printings, most bearing either an all white or cloudy blue (with circled logo) label and Atlantic Records information, are obviously the desirable ones, and include label debuts by Sill, Browne (5051), Blue (5052), Gunne (5053), the Eagles (5054), Souther (5055), the Byrds (5058), Tom Waits (5061), and Rod Taylor (5062).

The arrival of Linda Ronstadt (from Capitol) and Joni Mitchell (from Reprise) added further weight to Asylum. Mitchell's *For the Roses* (5057) and Ronstadt's *Don't Cry Now* (5064) are common, but worthwhile, acquisitions; contrarily, albums by Batdorf and Rodney (5056) and Mick Jagger's brother Chris (5069) are seldom seen.

In late 1973, with Asylum's success still speeding ahead, Geffen sold Asylum to Warner Bros., though he would remain head of the company. At the same time, Elektra Records head Jac Holzman was keen to step down from the day-to-day running of the company—whose own distribution was through

TEN TOP COLLECTIBLES

Linda Ronstadt

"Alison" (UK Asylum K13149—7-inch picture disc, 1979)

"Blue Bayou" (Asylum AS 11431—Blue-vinyl 12-inch, 1978)

DIR Special (DIR, no catalog number—Transcription disc, 1982)

"Dolphins" (Capitol 2438—7-inch, 1969)

"Lago Azul" (Asylum 45464, promo 7-inch, 1978)

Living in the USA (UK Asylum K53085—Red-vinyl LP, 1978)

Simple Dreams (Nautilus NR 26—Audiophile-pressing LP, 1982)

"So Fine"—The Stone Poneys (Sidewalk 937—7-inch, 1968)

"Somewhere Out There" (UK MCA MCAP 1172—7-inch picture disc, 1987)

"Up to My Neck in High Muddy Water"—The Stone Poneys (Capitol 2110—7-inch, picture sleeve, 1968)

Asylum white label promo 45 of the Byrds' "Cowgirl In The Sand."

Warner Bros. In a surprising, but nevertheless logical, move (stylistically there were numerous similarities between the two catalogs), the labels were merged under Geffen's control, consolidating their catalogs within the same numbering system: the 7E-1000 series for LPs, the 452 series for singles.

Immediately, the union made headlines, with the arrival of Bob Dylan from Columbia. Unhappy with the label he'd spent the past decade with, and infuriated by its clumsy efforts to blackmail him into renewing his contract (including raiding the outtakes bin for the *Dylan* album), Dylan joined Asylum in 1973, linking with the Band to cut 1974's *Planet Waves* (E 1003) and the live album *Before the Flood* (AB 2001). Point made, he then returned to Columbia in 1975.

Asylum and Elektra retained their label identities (and, therefore, their own artists and A&R departments), with the merger. Asylum releases continued from both established and new artists—aside from Dylan, these latter included Tim Moore (7E 1019); Traffic (7E 1020); Essra Mohawk (7E 1023); Orleans (7E 1029); Albert Brooks (7E 1035); John Fogerty (7E 1046); and Jack the Lad, a spin-off from the successful British act Lindisfarne (7E 1014—Lindisfarne itself was signed to Elektra).

The lesser known artists tend to be the most challenging for the collector; both on 45 and LP, Asylum's hit acts tended to sell in such vast quantities that condition alone affects value and collectibility. One should, however, also note the introduction of a new 6E numerical sequence in 1977—several 7E series LPs were reissued within this new series. (Singles moved to the 455 series at the same time.) The 5E series launched in 1978.

The ensuing commonsense caveats aside, a number of albums are considered rare, drawn from the label's small but so select band of quadraphonic releases. This catalog features Joni Mitchell's *Court and Spark* (EQ 1001) and *Hissing of Summer Lawns* (EQ 1051), Dylan's *Planet Waves* (EQ 1003), the Eagles' *On the Border* (EQ 1004) and *One of These Nights* (EQ 1039), Jackson Browne's *Late for the Sky* (EQ 1017), and the Souther-Hillman Furay Band's *Trouble in Paradise* (EQ 1036).

Another popular variant is the pursuit of UK releases. Although Asylum's chart profile was considerably smaller, the release schedule was just as hectic. Prior to 1976, LPs bear an SYL prefix (sometimes with a fourth letter), and thereafter, the letter K5; singles were originally AYM, changing to K1. British quad releases also exist.

As the late '70s progressed, Asylum releases became scarcer within the catalog, all the more so following David Geffen's departure in 1980 to launch his own Geffen label. Of almost 300 LPs released between 1977–81, fewer than 60 bore the Asylum identity. The label is still issuing today, but remains a mere shadow of its former self. Most serious collectors therefore concentrate only on the 45s and LPs of the David Geffen period.

Further Reading: *The Mansion on the Hill: Dylan, Young, Geffen, Springsteen, and the Head-On Collision of Rock and Commerce;* by Fred Goodman (Times Books, 1997)

Atco

A subsidiary of Atlantic, Atco (Atlantic Company) was launched in 1955, following label co-founder Herb Abramson's return from the Army. He became head of the pop-orientated subsidiary, enjoying hits with the Jerry Leiber–Mike Stoller produced Coasters and Bobby Darin, before departing in 1959 to launch his own Triumph and Blaze labels. LPs by both artists are very collectible, with several (beginning with Darin's second, 1959's *That's All*—33-104) appearing in stereo. (Darin collectors also seek *For Teenagers Only'*—SP-001—a special promotional release from 1960.)

However, these are the exceptions. Following Abramson's departure, Atco's fortunes slipped somewhat, and through the early '60s, the label's output was generally unremarkable—unless, of course, you collect records by the likes of Roland Hanna, Fliptop Finnegan, Nina and Frederick, and Al Caiola's Magic Guitars.

The label continued scoring regular hit 45s, occasionally translating these over to LPs. English jazzman Acker Bilk's *Stranger on the Shore* album (33-129) naturally contained the single of the same name (6207), and reached No. 3 in 1962. Jorgen Ingmann's *Apache* (33-130) was titled after another memorable instrumental (a UK No. 1 for the guitar band the Shadows). Ben E. King's "Spanish Harlem" (6185) titled a popular 1961 LP (SD 33-133); other popular Atco acts during the early '60s included Bent Fabric, Casey Anderson, John Lee Hooker, and Betty Carter. The original yellow-and-black Atco label changed during this period, replaced by a gold-and-gray combination for mono releases, purple, brown, and orange for stereo.

The arrival of Otis Redding brought fresh gusto to the catalog. Redding's 45s were released through the Stax subsidiary Volt; his first LPs, however, appeared on Atco, beginning with 1964's superb live document *Apollo Saturday Night: Recorded Live at the Apollo Theatre in New York* (33-159), featuring cuts by the Falcons, Doris Troy, the Coasters, Ben E. King, and Rufus Thomas, alongside Redding. Redding's own *Pain in My Heart* (33-161) followed just weeks later; further Redding albums would be issued on Atco following the singer's death in 1967.

Another favorite is Leon Young's *Liverpool Sound for Strings* (33-163), an orchestral tribute to the Beatles, featuring versions of both their songs and Young's own. Another Beatles-related gem is *Ain't She Sweet: The Beatles and Other Great Sounds from England* (33-169), a compilation built around Atco's acquisition of material recorded by the Beatles with Tony Sheridan, in Hamburg, in 1961. Four of these tracks were included, together with eight Beatles-Merseybeat cuts performed by the Swallows—the same four songs were also spread across a pair of colossally rare and frequently counterfeited 45s, "Sweet Georgia Brown"/"Take Out Some Insurance on Me Baby" (6302), and "Ain't She Sweet"/"Nobody's Child" (6308).

A Marmalade label release in the UK, the somewhat more common ATCO US pressing of Auger & the Trinity's debut LP.

Both, incidentally, feature overdubs commissioned by Atco itself and executed by local session men, to bring the song's sound more in line with contemporary Beatles fans' demands. A 2001 release by Germany's Bear Family label, collecting close to 40 different versions of the Beatles' Sheridan recordings, allows modern listeners to judge the success of this exercise for themselves.

Another British act briefly, but memorably, tied to Atco was the Troggs. Their first three US hits, "Wild Thing" (6415), "With a Girl Like You" (the former's B-side), and "I Can't Control Myself" (6444), were all issued simultaneously by Atco and Fontana, and charted as such—both labels also released identical versions of the band's *Wild Thing* album (33-193). The Atco versions are considered the most collectible today.

Atco also became involved in the then-flourishing Jamaican ska scene, releasing the *Jump Up* album by veteran Byron Lee and his Dragonaires (33-182).

Overlooked for many years, this set has recently soared in value, alongside several contemporary Jamaican releases on Atlantic.

In 1965, Atco scored a hit that swiftly proved almost as culturally significant as the Beatles: Sonny and Cher's anthemic ode to hippie togetherness, "I Got You Babe" (6359). As with most Atco 45s, the duo's singles are relatively common, but original mono or stereo copies of their *Look at Us* debut album (33-177) are very collectible.

The following year brought another seminal California act, the Buffalo Springfield, to the label; early pressings of their eponymous debut (33-200) are much sought after for the inclusion of "Baby Don't Scold Me," a song dropped for subsequent issues in favor of the hit "For What It's Worth" (6459).

It was at this point that Atco moved into what is regarded as its quintessential phase—and certainly that which most appeals to collectors today. A deal with Australian entrepreneur Robert Stigwood brought Cream and the Bee Gees to the label. Tim Hardin was introduced in 1967. And Arthur Conley's classic *Sweet Soul Music* album (33-215) emerged the first in a stream of essential soul-R&B releases. While label veterans Nina and Frederick, Acker Bilk, and Bent Fabric maintained a presence, as the year progressed, Atco embraced modern tastes in all their guises.

Vanilla Fudge's timeless revision of the Supremes' "You Keep Me Hangin' On," originally released to little notice in 1967 (6495), was reissued to a Top Ten berth in 1968 (6590), drawing the group's eponymous debut album in its wake (33-224). Iron Butterfly unveiled the aptly titled *Heavy* (33-227), en route to the mammoth *In-A-Gadda-Da-Vida* (33-250); New Orleans bayou juju man Dr. John unleashed the eminent *Gris-Gris* (33-234); Last Words brought hippie harmonies into play with a self-titled debut (33-235); Julie Driscoll–Brian Auger & the Trinity transfixed with *Open* (33-258) and *Street Noise* (SD 2-701—following Cream's *Wheels of Fire*, Atco's second-ever double album package); and former Circus Maximus guitarist Jerry Jeff Walker stunned that band's psychedelic following with *Mr. Bojangles* (33-259).

It was a golden age, gilded with some platinum music—the oft-encountered, but nevertheless popular compilations *The Supergroups* (33-279) and *Smash Sounds* (SD 850) serve up diamond snapshots of the era.

Oft-overlooked among Atco releases from this period are the label's soundtrack recordings. The first was 1966's *A Man Dies* (33-186). *Trap,* scored by British composer Ron Goodwin (33-204), and *The Game Is Over* (33-205), were among those that followed; 1968 brought the most collectible, as Cream contributed the whimsical "Anyone for Tennis" to *The Savage Seven* (33-245). Also appearing were Iron Butterfly, Barbara Kelly, and Jerry Styner; "Anyone for Tennis" was simultaneously issued on single (6575).

In 1968, Atco discontinued its policy of releasing albums in both stereo and mono; the final rock release in the mono series was Vanilla Fudge's *The Beat Goes On* (33-237); the New York Rock and Roll Ensemble's debut (33-240) was the first to be issued in stereo only. Few of the later mono issues offer anything in the way of musical variations, being nothing more than straightforward mixdowns of the two-track tapes. They are, however, prized as artifacts, a status which also attends the white-label mono promos of later albums that were issued to radio and regularly appear on the market.

A new LP label design, yellow with black lettering, was instituted around the same time. Neither new releases nor reissues bearing either this label or its successors are considered of great interest to general collectors; Atco as a collectible entity ceases here, though individual artist catalogs remain of interest, and do contain some desirable items.

In LP terms, much of the 1968–69 release schedule was consumed either by "best of" collections, Stax-related releases, or brand new talent—the folk duo Teegarden and Van Winkle (33-290), along with Rory Gallagher's power trio, Taste (33-296), made their label debuts, while the wreckage of the now-disbanded Cream was promptly spread across discs by Jack Bruce (33-306) and Blind Faith (33-304). Original pressings of the latter are distinguished by a sleeve design featuring a topless prepubescent girl. This, apparently, caused such an uproar that it was swiftly replaced by a straightforward band photo. (The original design was revived for a 1977 RSO label reissue, and for all subsequent pressings.) Bruce, Eric Clapton, and Ginger Baker would remain Atco regulars into the early '70s. Singles by this trio are relatively scarce, and are well worth looking for.

Other notable "debutantes" included Jimi Hendrix Experience bassist Noel Redding's Fat Mattress; Scottish singer Lulu's transition from pop to R&B, 1970's aptly titled *New Routes* (33-310); and Southern-rock icons Black Oak Arkansas and the Allman Brothers. Indeed, the first six Capricorn label releases, including three Allmans LPs, bore Atco labels and catalog numbers. (Among other collectible changelings are the Cotillion label's *Woodstock II* set from 1971—SD2-400—and *Funky Nassau* by Beginning of the End—33-379—an Alston label release.)

The long-running 33-LP series closed in 1972, to be replaced by the short-lived (47 titles) SD-7000

TEN TOP COLLECTIBLES

Cream

BBC Classic Tracks (Westwood One—Transcription disc, 1994)

Classic Cuts (RSO 0152—Promo LP, 1978)

Cream on Top (UK Polydor 2855 002—Mail-order LP, 1971)

Disraeli Gears (Atco 33-232—Mono LP, 1967)

Fresh Cream (Atco 33-206—Mono LP, 1967)

Goodbye (Atco 141—Sampler LP with Vanilla Fudge, 1969)

"Strange Brew" (UK Polydor 56315—Unissued 7-inch, 1969)

Wheels of Fire (Atco 2-700—2-LP mono promo, 1968)

Wheels of Fire (Atco 4525—Promo EP, 1968)

"Wrapping Paper" (UK Reaction 591 007—7-inch, 1967)

---

series. Collectible highlights are, again, limited, but include several Bee Gees albums; releases by Robert Palmer's Vinegar Joe; Tony Kaye's Badger; Irish folk-rockers Horslips; Dutch guitar wizard Jan Akkerman; the much-admired Heavy Metal Kids (SD-7047); and glam-rock icons Roxy Music (the group's third LP, *Stranded*—SD 7045, was its Atco debut, though the album's predecessors would subsequently be reissued on the label).

Akkerman's band Focus inaugurated the SD36-100 series in 1974, with its *Hamburger Concerto* album (36-100). Other notable issues included releases by further European bands, Amon Düül II and (from the utterly opposite end of the spectrum) Boney M.; ex-Free guitarist Paul Kossoff's solo project *Back Street Crawler*; a solo LP by Roxy Music guitarist Phil Manzanera (36-113); space-rock group Hawkwind's *Warrior on the Edge of Time* (36-115), originally packaged in a sleeve that folded out to resemble a shield; Genesis, who debuted with the ambitious *Lamb Lies Down on Broadway* double set (SD2-401); and Australian hard rockers AC/DC. Also notable is a much-sought-after solo set by guitarist

Steve Hunter, *Blown Away* (36-148), the legend behind such albums as Lou Reed's *Rock 'n' Roll Animal*, sundry Alice Cooper sets, and its own predecessor in the Atco catalog, Peter Gabriel's eponymous debut (36-147).

The arrival of Genesis brings a handful of minor collectibles to an otherwise straightforward catalog. Three singles released between 1975–77, "Counting Out Time" (7013), "Ripples" (7050), and "Your Own Special Way" (7076), are in no way comparable to their UK counterparts (on Charisma) in terms of rarity, but are of value nevertheless. The group would not find superstardom for another few years (by which time the band was with Atlantic).

The band's first albums without vocalist Peter Gabriel (to match, of course, Gabriel's first without Genesis), were originally issued within the 36-100 series (129, 144), then reissued as the first LPs of 1978's newly instituted 38-100 (101, 100, respectively). First pressings are not scarce, but are necessary for band completists.

Although, as aforementioned, general collector interest in this period is virtually nonexistent, the Atco catalog continues to bristle with inspired arrivals, including Gary Numan, Lindisfarne, Blackfoot, Thunder, the re-formed Humble Pie, Stevie Nicks, John Entwistle, and Pete Townshend of the Who, along with Carrere label figureheads Sheila B. and Saxon.

Atco ceased new releases in 1982. Its artists were absorbed elsewhere into the Atlantic group.

Further Reading: *"What'd I Say": The Atlantic Records Story—50 Years of Music,* by Ahmet Ertegun (Welcome Rain, 2001)

Atlantic

One of the crucial players in the American music industry, Atlantic Records is also among the most avidly collected, with particular attention being directed toward the run of essential soul-R&B releases of the 1960s, and the label's near-monopoly on the rock explosion of the early '70s. On either side of these key sequences, Atlantic's 1940s–1950s jazz catalog is second to none, while the 1980s and 1990s have each produced their fair share of eminently collectible acts. In addition, the Atco and Cotillion subsidiaries (the latter originally a publishing wing, formed in 1964) also merit serious consideration.

New York–based Atlantic was formed in 1947 by Ahmet Ertegun, the son of Turkey's US ambassador, along with a Brooklyn-born jazz promoter, Herb Abramson, a part-time record producer with National Records. In 1946, Abramson and Jewish comedy producer Jerry Blaine launched Jubilee Records; Abramson left in September 1947, to concentrate on jazz and blues recordings, linking with Ertegun to form Atlantic the following month. Abramson was president, Ertegun and Abramson's wife, Miriam, were VPs. The trio was joined in 1953 by *Billboard* journalist Jerry Wexler (the man who created the term Rhythm and Blues, to replace the earlier "race records" on the magazine's chart). Wexler became a VP and in-house R&B producer. Ertegun became Atlantic's president in 1958, three years after Abramson moved to Atco.

Swiftly establishing a reputation for fair dealings, Atlantic prospered, both artistically and commercially. Early signings included vocal groups Delta Rhythm Boys, the Clovers, and the Cardinals; bluesmen Leadbelly and Sonny Terry; and jazz musicians, ranging from Art Pepper and Erroll Garner to Dizzy Gillespie and Sarah Vaughan. Within five years, Atlantic could boast hits by Ruth Brown, Stick McGhee, Joe Turner, Professor Longhair, Laurie Tate, and Joe Morris, while Ertegun was also proving a successful composer—the Clovers' chart-topping "Don't You Know I Love You" became the label's second R&B No. 1.

As early as March 1949, Atlantic issued its first 33⅓ rpm long-playing (10-inch) record, poet Walter Benton's *This Is My Beloved* (Atlantic 110), narrated by John Dall over musical accompaniment by Vernon Duke. The same material was perforcedly spread over three 12-inch 78s, effortlessly proving the efficiency of the new format. Atlantic's first 33⅓ 12-inch LP followed in early 1951, scenes from Shakespeare's *Romeo and Juliet,* by Eva Le Gallienne and Richard Waring (ALS-401).

Following the arrival of Ertegun's brother Nesuhi as head of the LP division in 1955, Atlantic would become renowned for some of the best-quality, best-value LPs on the market, factors which still influence collectors today. All are characterized by high-quality sleeves, more tracks than other labels' offerings, and of course, a plum selection of artists. Atlantic was also a pioneer of stereo technology, cutting its first recordings in 1958.

While Nesuhi's beloved jazz formed the backbone of the LP catalog, with the Modern Jazz Quartet its crown jewel, the arrival of the Drifters, in 1953, brought Atlantic its first long-term success. The group would remain with the label for the next 14 years, scoring close to 40 R&B chart hits, beginning with their debut. "Money Honey" (45-1006) topped the chart that winter.

Clyde McPhatter, LaVern Baker, and Ray Charles also became chart regulars, while Joe Turner's "Shake, Rattle and Roll" (1026) not only topped the R&B chart in 1954, it also provided the springboard for country band Bill Haley and the Comets's leap to stardom via a new musical genre that the group, and their not-so-different adaptation of Turner's hit, was now creating: rock 'n' roll.

TEN TOP COLLECTIBLES

Atlantic Records

"A Beggar for Your Kisses"—The Diamonds (Atlantic 980—7-inch, 1952)

Blues Ballads—LaVern Baker (Atlantic 8030—LP, 1959)

"Devil or Angel"—The Clovers (Atlantic 1083—Red-vinyl 7-inch, 1956)

"Don't You Know I Love You"—The Clovers (Atlantic 934—7-inch, 1951)

"I'm Gonna Dry Ev'ry Tear"—Bill Haley and the Comets (Atlantic 727—78 rpm, 1947)

Love Ballads—Clyde McPhatter (Atlantic 8024—LP, 1958)

"Love Love Love"—Oscar Black (Atlantic 956—7-inch, 1952)

"Sweet Talk"—Faye Adams (Atlantic 1007—7-inch, 1956)

"Teardrops from My Eyes"—Ruth Brown (Atlantic 919—7-inch, 1950)

What Am I Living For?—Chuck Willis (Atlantic 612—EP, 1958)

Instrumental in Atlantic's early domination of this field was the arrival of songwriters Mike Stoller and Jerry Leiber, co-owners (with Lester Sill) of the Los Angeles–based Spark label. With them came two members of Spark's biggest band, the Robins, which was promptly renamed the Coasters, and under Leiber and Stoller's guidance, ran up a string of hit 45s for Atco. Other Leiber-Stoller hits, of course, were spread throughout the Atlantic roster, including the Drifters' "There Goes My Baby," the label's biggest crossover pop hit to date.

The Spark connection also drew producer Phil Spector to Atlantic in 1960. His greatest successes there were, ironically, as a musician—he played guitar on hits by the Drifters, the Coasters, and Ben E. King. Productions, including tracks by the Top Notes, Ruth Brown, Jean DuShon, Billy Storm, and LaVern Baker fared poorly, but Atlantic was merely a stopgap for Spector. By 1961 he and Lester Sill had departed to form Philles.

In 1960, Atlantic was introduced to the Memphis independent Satellite, picking up national rights to the regional hit "Cause I Love You," by Carla and Rufus Thomas, for release on Atco. It was the dawn of a relationship which, based on a handshake deal between Wexler and Satellite head Jim Stewart, would see Atlantic become proud distributors, manufacturers, and (apparently unbeknownst to Stewart) owners of the Stax Records catalog.

Yet Stax was only one string of the label's R&B bow. With Solomon Burke, Sam and Dave, Aretha Franklin, Wilson Pickett, and many more also on board, Atlantic was poised to dominate the field as comprehensively as Motown—and, arguably, with much more consistency. Indeed, for many collectors, Atlantic's R&B output constitutes a category in its own right.

But R&B was not the label's only forte. Indeed, by the mid-'70s, such concerns had all but petered out, with Scottish funk band the Average White Band alone representing new talent. Elsewhere, the label was forging ahead with inspired magnificence. The [Young] Rascals headed a pop boom that began as early as 1965; and while the bulk of Atlantic's rock output was placed with Atco, the late '60s and the 1970s saw the parent label retain Stephen Stills (and, eventually, the Crosby, Stills, Nash and, sometimes,

Young supergroup); Led Zeppelin; Yes; Mott the Hoople, for the group's first four albums; J. Geils Band; King Crimson; the early Hall and Oates; Bryan Ferry; and ELP (following the dissolution of the group's Manticore subsidiary); among many others.

In 1967, Atlantic was purchased by the Warner Seven Arts Corporation, which in turn was purchased by the Kinney Corporation in 1969. Atlantic continued to operate as a separate entity, however, with a culture and catalog that remained irresistible to many artists.

The Rolling Stones' decision to link their newly formed, eponymous label to the company in 1971 was almost wholly based on the members' love of all that the label stood for—other companies had offered far more money than Atlantic had. At the same time, the Kinney Corporation's decision to establish a unified record division that incorporated Atlantic, Warner Bros., and the newly purchased Elektra into one major company, WEA, created a power bloc that even the established major labels were hard-pressed to compete with.

In commercial terms, Led Zeppelin dominated Atlantic's output through the first half of the 1970s, just as they dominate its collectibility today. Some of the most valuable Atlantic releases (or, at least, promos and the like) of the entire decade are Zeppelin related, with the band's own label, Swan Song, itself distributed by Atlantic, continuing the relationship through the remainder of the decade.

However, the English hard rockers were by no means the label's sole success. The Swedish pop group ABBA joined Atlantic in 1974, following victory in Europe's annual Eurovision Song Contest; its rarities, too, exert considerable influence on the modern market.

In common with so many classic major labels, Atlantic's subsequent collectibility is driven by individual artists rather than by the label itself, a situation exacerbated, of course, by the uncertainty engendered by a decade's worth of mergers and similar corporate shenanigans. The Warner Bros. group itself is now a part of the multimedia AOL Time Warner group.

Further Reading: *"What'd I Say": The Atlantic Records Story—50 Years of Music,* by Ahmet Ertegun (Welcome Rain, 2001)

Autumn

Autumn Records was launched in 1964 by San Francisco disc jockeys Bobby Mitchell and Tom Donahue, but is best remembered for employing the young and unknown Sylvester Stewart—the future Sly Stone—as in-house writer and producer. Introduced to the duo following a gig at an American Legion Hall, Stewart swiftly impressed the DJs with his vision and abilities, confirming his talent when he launched singer Bobby Freeman's career with the novelty 45 "C'mon and Swim" (Autumn 2), a self-composed exhortation to do the dance of the same name. A Top Five hit, it was followed by Freeman's "S-W-I-M" (Autumn 5) and Stewart's own "I Just Learned How to Swim" (Autumn 3).

With Autumn's own output impossible to confine to any one genre, Stewart spent the next three years blithely traveling from gritty garage hopefuls like the Chosen Few, the Mojo Men, and the Spearmints, to the breezy folk-rock of the Beau Brummels, while cutting two further singles of his own, "Buttermilk" (Autumn 14) and "Temptation Walk" (Autumn 26).

Autumn was also heavily involved in the gestating San Francisco psychedelic scene. In November 1965, the label recorded a session with the embryonic Grateful Dead—six songs, credited to the Emergency Crew, were included on the Dead's 12-CD box set, *The Golden Road,* in 2001. Folk-rock act the Great!! Society!! (the group later dropped the exclamation points) was also recruited to the label.

Released in March 1966, the group's debut single, guitarist Darby Slick's "Somebody to Love," was the first release on Autumn's newly launched North Beach subsidiary (1001). It was produced by Stewart, and legend insists that he ran the Society through 50 takes of the song before he was satisfied. Band vocalist Grace Slick (Darby's wife) subsequently joined Jefferson Airplane, taking "Somebody to Love" with her. It swiftly became one of that band's most popular

TEN TOP COLLECTIBLES

Sly Stone

"Buttermilk"—Sly Stewart (Autumn 14—7-inch, 1964)

"Dance to the Music" (UK Columbia DB 8369—7-inch, 1968)

Everything You Always Wanted to Hear By (Epic AS 264—DJ LP, 1976)

Greatest Hits (Epic EQ 30325—Quad LP, 1970)

"Help Me with My Heart"—Sylvester Stewart (G&P 901—7-inch, 1962)

"I Ain't Got Nobody" (Loadstone 3951—7-inch, 1967)

"I Just Learned How to Swim"—Sly Stewart (Autumn 3—7-inch, 1964)

"A Long Time Alone"—Danny Stewart (Luke 1008—7-inch, 1961)

Sly and the Family Stone (Epic 26397—Jukebox Album, 1968)

"Temptation Walk"—Sly Stewart (Autumn 26—7-inch, 1966)

recordings; copies of the original, on the other hand, rank among the Airplane family's rarest artifacts.

Stewart and Autumn parted company in 1967; like the Dead and the Great Society, Stewart left behind him a wealth of his own material, subsequently released across a long series of (possibly misleadingly titled) compilations.

Integral as it is to the stories of both Sly Stone and the San Francisco underground, as they quivered on the brink of psychedelia, Autumn's short catalog is both widely collected and highly priced.

Bang

New York's Bang Records was launched in mid-1965 by songwriter-producer Bert Berns, its story beginning, figuratively, with a bang, as the label's first-ever 45, the Strangeloves' "I Want Candy" (501) climbed to No. 11. The first of four hits for the band in just 12 months, and the title track of Bang's first LP (211), in late 1965, the song remains one of the foundation stones of the American garage band movement.

The Strangeloves were followed chartward by the McCoys' "Hang On Sloopy" (506), a US chart-topper

within weeks of the label's launch. Seven further 45s over the next two years maintained the group in the Top 100. Their debut LP, too, was titled for their biggest hit (212) and was issued in both mono and stereo. (Perhaps fittingly, the group's final single, "I Wonder if She Remembers Me"—1049—was their first not to chart, suggesting that maybe she didn't.)

Next up were the Exciters, who came to Bang at the tail end of a career that began (at UA) in 1962. "A Little Bit of Soap" (515) was a Top 60 entry in early 1966; a second single flopped, but Bang had little time to mourn as it prepared to launch Neil Diamond. His debut, "Solitary Man" (519), climbed no higher than No. 55, but "Cherry Cherry" (528) went to No. 6, and Diamond was to remain with Bang until 1968, issuing a string of now–highly priced singles, as well as two extraordinary albums. Original stereo copies of his debut, *The Feel of Neil Diamond* (214), typically sell in the low-three-figure range, the mono only a little less.

Many of the label's early hits were gathered together on the aptly titled *Golden Hits from the Gang at Bang* (215), a rare collection that is nevertheless

TEN TOP COLLECTIBLES

Van Morrison

BBC Classic Tracks (Westwood One—Transcription disc, 1991)

Blowin' Your Mind (Bang 218—Stereo LP with uncensored "Brown Eyed Girl," 1967)

"Brown Eyed Girl" (Philco HP 16—Hip-pocket record, 1968)

An Evening with Van Morrison (WB—2-LP promo, 1989)

Live at the Roxy (Warner Bros WBMS 102—Promo, 1979)

Moondance (Direct Disc SD 16604—Audiophile pressing, 1981)

A Sense of Wonder (UK Mercury MERH 54—LP with "Crazy Jane on God," 1985)

"Summertime in England" (WB PRO A 911—12-inch promo, 1980)

Them—Them (UK Decca DFE 8612—Export EP with ladder picture sleeve, 1965)

"Wavelength" (WB PRO A 755—12-inch promo, 1978)

easier (and cheaper) to find than copies of the original 45s.

The next major arrival at the label was Van Morrison, fresh from his time with the R&B band Them (Berns had produced the group's earlier hits). His time with Bang was short but eventful. In March 1967, Berns put up the money for Van Morrison to fly to New York to record his new songs—Berns, of course, would produce—and, over the next six months, the singer seemed to spend every waking moment either in the studio or writing. Then, in just three days, working with a team of crack session men, Van Morrison cut what became his first solo hit, "Brown Eyed Girl" (545), one of the quintessential singles of the season.

Though a follow-up single, "Ro Ro Rosey" (552), did little, Berns pressed ahead with plans for a Van Morrison album, and that fall, Bang released *Blowin' Your Mind* (218)—apparently over the objections of Morrison, who disliked both the title and the sleeve design. Like the hit single, this set is fascinating for collectors; controversy over a certain lyric within "Brown Eyed Girl" saw some pressings issued with a harmless line from elsewhere in the song dropped in over the offending "makin' love."

Original mono pressings of the LP retain this edit; stereo copies present the unadulterated take, but in a substantially different mix. First pressings are most easily identified by a misprinted catalog number—BLB 218, rather than the correct BLP 218.

Morrison returned to the studio that fall, running through a clutch of new songs, including "Madame George," "Joe Harper Saturday Morning," "Chick a Boom," and "Midnight Special." The sessions were riotous—in some places it sounded as if a party were in full swing; in others, as if one had only just ended. In later years, those rough edges became part of the project's charm; at the time, however, they merely represented another increment in Morrison's increasingly fractious relationship with Bang.

When Bert Berns suffered a fatal heart attack on December 30, 1967, Morrison swiftly, and brusquely, negotiated his way out of his contract. The label responded by releasing 1970's *Best Of* (222) and 1973's *TB Sheets* (400) LPs, both utilizing the unreleased final sessions; since that time, numerous reissues and repackagings have established these once discarded recordings among Bang's hottest properties.

Berns' death understandably halted Bang's momentum somewhat. Neil Diamond departed to Uni, the Strangeloves and the McCoys' careers were both at an end, and the only significant new talent in sight was Derek—aka Kapp label star Johnny Cymbal. In 1968 he enjoyed some success with such lightly lewd bubblegum creations as "Cinnamon" (558) and "Back Door Man" (566); elsewhere, the Shout subsidiary scored with Erma Franklin, Jackie Moore, and Freddie Scott.

It would be 1970, however, before Bang truly relaunched, first with a hits collection, *Bang and Shout Super Hits* (220), the first of the aforementioned Van Morrison collections, and with several Neil Diamond compilations. Of these, the most interesting is 1971's *Do It* (224), which offers an alternate version of the title cut, and perhaps misleadingly, retitles "The Long Way Home" as "Hanky Panky."

Country singer-songwriter Paul Davis signed up in 1969 and issued his debut album, *A Little Bit of Paul Davis* (223), in 1971. It was titled, incidentally, for his debut hit, a new version of "A Little Bit of Soap" (576). Indeed, his regular releases remained one of the few points of interest in the Bang catalog as the 1970s continued. Contemporary releases by Pyramid, Ronn Price, Street Corner Symphony, and Don Imus are bargain-bin regulars even today.

New life, however, was introduced first by the Muscle Shoals Horns, whose *Born to Get Down* (403) introduced some liquid funk to the proceedings, and then by the disco-funk act Brick, whose members were natives of Bang's own new home base, Atlanta. "Dazz" (727) proved a monster hit in 1976; the *Good High* LP (408) reached No. 19. This dream start cemented Brick in the pantheon of top disco collectibles. Bang would also be responsible for launching R&B vocalist Robert "Peabo" Bryson's career that same year, as vocalist on the Michael Zager Band's "Do It with Feeling" (720, reissued 737), and via his own debut LP *Peabo* (7000).

In 1979 Bang joined the Columbia family of labels, a relationship that was debuted with a solo album (JZ-35792) by Nigel Olsson, best known as a member of Elton John's band. Maintaining continuity with Bang's past, Olsson became the third artist on the label to score a hit with "A Little Bit of Soap" (4800), in spring 1979.

A second Olsson album, *Changing Tides* (JZ-36491), was issued in 1980; other new acts on the label, into the early '80s, included the Masqueraders. Bang's day was fast ending, however. Paul Davis departed for Arista in 1981, and Brick had run out of powder. Bang followed, folding in 1982.

Barnaby

Barnaby was Andy Williams' label, its collectibility hinging upon the presence of the Osmond Brothers during 1968–69. The brothers cut three 45s for the label, "Mary Elizabeth" (2002), "I've Got Loving on My Mind," (2004) and "Taking a Chance on Love" (2005), all three vying with their earlier MGM releases in terms of runaway prices.

Little else on the label is of great interest; the bulk of releases concentrated on reissuing material previously available on Archie Bleyer's Cadence label. According to legend, Williams had intended to buy only his own masters from the retiring Bleyer; he was convinced to buy the entire catalog. Prior to Barnaby's 1968 launch, some material from this cache was licensed to Columbia.

After operating the label for two years as a more-or-less part-time concern, Williams relaunched Barnaby as a full-time label in 1970, signing Ray Stevens, among others. Promptly scoring a No. 1 hit with the cloying "Everything Is Beautiful" (2011), then repeating the feat with 1974's allegedly humorous "The Streak" (600), Stevens was far and away the label's biggest-selling artist. Ken Berry, Williams' wife Claudine Longet, Doyle Holly, and Jimmy Buffett were also on board, while collectors of the extraordinary are directed toward the first (and only) album by Sand (BRS-15006), a eponymous issue that—had it taken off—might have changed the face of the LP medium forever.

TEN TOP COLLECTIBLES

The Osmonds

"Be My Little Baby Bumble Bee" (MGM 13162—7-inch, 1963)

"I Can't Stop" (Uni 55015—7-inch, 1967)

"I've Got Loving on My Mind" (Barnaby 2004—7-inch, 1968)

"Mary Elizabeth" (Barnaby 2002—7-inch, 1968)

"Mr. Sandman" (MGM 13281—7-inch, 1964)

New Sound of the Osmond Brothers (Capitol Record Club ST 90403—LP, 1965)

Osmonds World (UK Lyntone, LYN 2705—Flexidisc, 1972)

Songs We Sang on the Andy Williams Show (MGM SE 4146—Stereo LP, 1963)

"Taking a Chance on Love" (Barnaby 2005—7-inch, 1969)

The Travels of Jaimie McPheeters—Various artists (MGM PM 7—LP, 1963)

Though it was only a single LP, *Sand* was released spread across two one-sided discs, the intention being that buyers owning a stackable turntable would be able to play the entire album through without having to leave their seats to turn it over. Modern grading fetishists probably still have nightmares about that little innovation, and can only offer thanks to the oil crisis (and the ensuing vinyl shortage) for nipping it in the bud. Several members of the Portland, Ore.–based band subsequently turned up in Quarterflash.

Battle

Although the Battle label concentrated on gospel releases, several LPs within its catalog are of interest to more general collectors. Distributed by Riverside, and thus owned by the NYC-based Bill Grauer Productions, Battle LPs include titles by Aretha Franklin and her father, the Rev. C.L. Franklin (BLP-6105); John Lee Hooker (BLP-6113, BLP-6114); Memphis Slim (the label's first stereo release—BM/BS9-6118); and Mongo Santamaria's *Watermelon Man* (BM/BS9-6120), which of course featured the Top Ten hit title track (45909). A second Santamaria hit 45, "Yeh Yeh" (45917), was also included.

In 1963, Battle climbed aboard the folk bandwagon with the Carolina Freedom Fighters' *Everybody Wants Freedom* (BM/BS9-6125) and the Millburnaires' *Teenage Hootenanny* (BM/BS9 6126), noteworthy for an early cover of Dylan's "Blowing in the Wind." The Lonesome River Boys' *Raise a Ruckus: A Bluegrass Hootenanny* (BM/BS9 6128) is also of interest.

Beginning in 1964, Battle changed tack again and commenced issuing a series of automobile sound-effects albums, presumably inspired by the hot-rodding craze that was then prevalent, though Riverside had been issuing similarly themed sets since its own inception in 1957. A total of 11 sets, numbered 6130–6140, and all available in both mono and stereo, include *Hot Rod Caravan, Hot Rods U.S.A., Rods and Drags Forever, Chrome on the Range,* and *Cycles Galore.*

Battle bowed out in 1964 by returning to its gospel roots with two final LPs, from the Gabel-Airs (6141) and the Reverend Cleophus Robinson (6142).

TEN TOP COLLECTIBLES

Automobiles

Bonneville 1960 (Riverside RS 95506—Stereo LP, 1960)

Carroll Shelby: The Career of a Great American Racing Driver (Riverside RLP 5006—LP, 1957)

Cement Roadsters (Battle 96132—Stereo LP, 1964)

Dan Gurney: His World of Racing (Mobile Fidelity MF 101—LP, 1965)

Golden Age of Sebring (Riverside SDP 33—LP, 1959)

History of Drag Racing (Capitol STAO 2145—Stereo LP, 1964)

Mercedes Benz: 75th Anniversary (Riverside RS 95025—Stereo LP, 1962)

Racing Cars (Fortissimo XK 8003—LP, plays from the label out, 1959)

1320 Special (Fleetwood FLP 4005S—Stereo LP, 1963)

Wonderful World of Sports Cars (Riverside SDP 44—LP, 1959)

Beggars Banquet

The UK independent Beggars Banquet was originally launched as a west London record store in 1974, by DJs Martin Mills and Nick Austin. Instant success prompted the duo to expand elsewhere into the music industry—tour promotion and management. It was their inability to find a record company willing to sign their first clients, the punk band the Lurkers, that convinced Mills and Austin to launch their own record label.

The Lurkers' "Shadow" (BEG 1) and "Freak Show" (BEG 2) 45s debuted Beggars Banquet in 1978, followed by one-man-band Johnny G.'s "Call Me Bwana" (BEG 3). Over the next year, the label developed a peerless reputation for left-of-center signings, and frequently, left-of-center hits. In September 1978, the supremely innuendo-laden "The Winker's Song (Misprint)" (BOP 1), by Ivor Biggun, gave Beggars their first UK Top 30 hit, with the emergence in 1979 of the Doll ("Desire Me"—BEG 11) and Gary Numan's Tubeway Army ("Are 'Friends' Electric?"—BEG 18) bringing security beyond the label's wildest dreams. Numan topped both the UK singles and LP charts

twice in less than a year, and with stability came expansion.

The 4AD label was launched in 1980, and Situation 2 followed in 1983, both swiftly establishing their own identities away from the parent company, while Beggars' own signings continued successful. Bauhaus, the Associates, Icicle Works, and Pete Wylie's Wah! all scored hits during 1982–84, and in 1985, the Cult burst through with "She Sells Sanctuary," irrevocably establishing Beggars Banquet as an international independent label. Since that time, Love and Rockets, the Charlatans UK, Loop, Buffalo Tom, Mercury Rev, and Luna have all conspired to ensure it remains there.

In common with other UK independents of their generation, Beggars Banquet made much early mileage from limited-edition releases and gimmicks. The Lurkers' third single, "Ain't Got a Clue," was issued with a free gold-colored flexidisc (BEG 6), then reissued with the flexi redesigned as a picture disc. Their debut was reissued in red, blue and white colored-vinyl formats. Tubeway Army also benefited from colored vinyl, picture discs, and double-pack 45s.

TEN TOP COLLECTIBLES

Gary Numan/Tubeway Army

"Are 'Friends' Electric?" (UK Beggars BEG 18P—7-inch picture disc, 1979)

BBC Rock Hour (London Wavelength—Transcription disc, 1980)

"Cars" (UK Beggars BEG 23—7-inch, dark-red vinyl, 1980)

"Down in the Park" (UK Beggars BEG 17T—12-inch, picture sleeve, 1979)

The Fury (UK Numa CDNUMA 1003—CD with original mixes, 1986)

Images Volumes 1–8 (UK Numa, GNFCDA 104—four 2-LP sets, 1986–87)

Telekon (UK Beggars BEGA 19—LP, dark-red vinyl, 1980)

"This Is My Life" (UK Beggars TUB 1—White-label 7-inch promo, 1984)

Tubeway Army (UK Beggars BEG BEGA 4—Blue-vinyl LP, 1978)

Tubeway Army 1978–79 (UK Beggars BEGC 7879—Cassette, 1985)

Beggars' 45s catalog remains the strongest lure for the collector, though many of the early LPs are difficult to locate in their original form. CD reissues have, however, taken some of the edge off the market.

Bell

The Bell label was launched in New York City in 1954, with its emphasis firmly on pop and comedy recordings—few of which today are regarded as anything more than curios. The label's forte was for orchestral cover versions of the day's most popular hits, collected onto LPs with such titles as *Songs That Sold a Million* (multiple volumes), *Moods from the Movies* (BLP 15), and *Best of Broadway* (BLP 33). By 1961, Bell had been all but superseded by its subsidiaries, Amy and Mala, finally coming back to life in 1964 under the ownership of Larry Uttal. A handful of 45s during 1964–65 was followed in 1966 by the launch of the 6000 series of LPs, itself opened by Georgia Gibbs' *Call Me* (6000).

The label's first major hit was Syndicate of Sound's "Little Girl," reissued from an earlier 45 on Hush (228). It reached No. 8, the first of three hits the San Jose garage band would enjoy, and was celebrated immediately with an album, also titled *Little Girl* (6001).

Over the next three years, Bell went from strength to strength, not only scoring memorable 45s, but also unleashing a stream of remarkably intelligent LPs. Singles by Alex Chilton and the Box Tops, including the smash hits "The Letter" and "Cry Like a Baby," were released on the Mala label, but Bell handled the group's LP output. (A similar situation existed with the Van Dykes.) Gladys Knight and the Pips, who released half a dozen singles on the Fury subsidiary between 1961–63 (that is, prior to their successful Motown reign), were celebrated with the *Tastiest Hits* compilation (6013).

A run of classic soul singles by the O'Jays were complemented by the 1968 album *Back on Top* (6014); similarly, a pair of excellent albums by James and Bobby Purify join the duo's ten Bell singles, a run that includes the immortal "I'm Your Puppet." Other much-sought-after Bell LPs from this period include releases by Dale Hawkins (6036) and Pacific Northwest favorites The Wailers (6016).

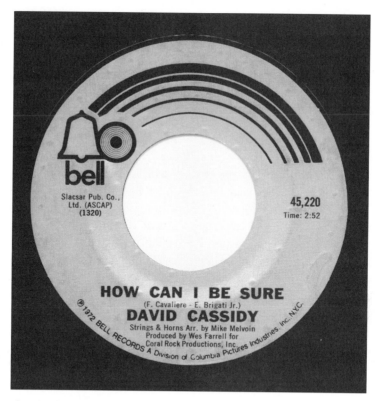

The classic '70s Bell label.

In 1968, Bell released of English folk-rock duo Nirvana's *The Story of Simon Sociopath* (6015), licensed from Britain's Island Records. Overlooked for many years, Nirvana was catapulted to prominence in the early '90s, following the emergence of a Seattle band with the same name. The "original" Nirvana launched a highly publicized legal action against its modern namesake; in the resultant flurry of attention, the group's entire back catalog was reissued, while values for original pressings skyrocketed.

The situation has calmed considerably in recent years, but *Sociopath* and its 1969 successor, *All of Us* (6024), still command prices far in excess of their pre-Cobain peaks. Three Bell singles, "We Can Help You" (715), "You Are Just the One" (730), and "Trapeze" (739) are likewise highly prized. (Anybody doubting whether the similarity of the two bands' names did cause any confusion, incidentally, need only have attended the Seattle Public Library sale in spring 2001.

Multiple unplayed copies of several Nirvana UK CDs were available there for just $1 apiece.)

Other collectible British bands joining Bell in the late '60s included another Island UK band, Spooky Tooth (another act whose US singles were handled by Mala) and the Scaffold, featuring Paul McCartney's brother, who called himself Mike McGear. Five Bell 45s, including the UK chart-topper "Lily the Pink" (747), are among the prime ephemerals pursued by arch Beatles collectors.

Merrilee Rush's "Angel of the Morning" (705) and Crazy Elephant's "Gimme Gimme Good Lovin'" (763) rank among the label's biggest singles of the late '60s (both artists also produced collectible Bell LPs); the latter named are also hotly pursued by fans of the British band 10cc. "There Ain't No Umbopo" (875) was a re-recording of a song cut for Pye (UK) by the four future band members, under the name Dr. Father; bassist Graham Gouldman was also a contract songwriter for Crazy Elephant producers Kasenetz-Katz.

Among other much-sought-after albums from the turn of the decade are a set celebrating the Apollo 11 moon shot (1100); the movie soundtrack *Nicholas and Alexandra* (1103—other movie titles were placed in the 1200 series and are uniformly sought after); and the fourth LP (but first for Bell) by Orpheus (6061), a painstakingly ambitious folk-rock band from Worcester, Mass. Together with three LPs cut for MGM, *Orpheus* was reissued in an extravagant two-CD package by the Italian Akarma label in 2001.

Bell's biggest acquisition of the early '70s was the Partridge Family. Columbia Screen Gems purchased co-ownership of the label (alongside Uttal) in the late '60s. The hook-up brought Bell the rights to the Monkees back catalog (evidenced by the *Refocus* compilation—6081), and spawned a now-popular solo album by singer Davy Jones (6067); it also ensured that the label would become the home for soundtrack recordings emanating from this new television series. Nobody could have foreseen the sheer commercial enormity of the venture, with both the Partridge Family and frontman David "Keith Partridge" Cassidy emerging as stars of the first magnitude.

Their modern collectibility is scarcely less prodigious today, and that despite contemporary sales in the multimillions. Of particular note today are copies of the 1971 *Christmas Card* album (6066), with an attached Christmas card, and 1972's *Shopping Bag* (6072), with of course, a free shopping bag. Several of the group's later singles, too, are extremely difficult to find. Cassidy releases, while equally sought after, are more common.

Genuinely scarce, however, are Bell singles by fellow Family regular Shirley Jones; she cut three during 1971–72, "I've Still Got My Heart, Joe" (119), "Ain't Love Easy" (253), and "Walk in Silence" (350). The show also made a passing fancy out of juvenile Ricky Segall—his *Ricky Segall and the Segulls* LP (1138) offers a taste of the precocious child star squawking at its most post–Jimmy Osmond appalling; the single, "Sooner or Later," (429) at least minimizes the torment. Mercifully hard to find.

Other high-selling (if somewhat less collectible) Bell artists of the early '70s include the Fifth Dimension, Tony Orlando and Dawn, Terry Jacks, and Melissa Manchester. With artists and successes like these, Bell's American profile was distinctly middle-of-the-road. Not so in the UK. There, Bell—under the expert guidance of former Philips A&R man Dick Leahy—was at the forefront of the glam-rock movement, its output headlined not only by Cassidy, but also by homegrown sensations Gary Glitter and the Glitter Band, Hello, and Showaddywaddy. At one point during 1972–73, the label was operating on a hit ratio of almost one in four, a spectacular achievement in one of the most competitive climates in pop history.

Bell's UK label launched in 1968 with the Box Tops's "Cry Like a Baby" (1001), the most successful of the group's eight British 45s over the next two years. The Delfonics (consigned to the Philly Groove subsidiary in America) were an early cult success, scoring on the Northern Soul club circuit with "La La Means I Love You" (1006), "Ready or Not" (1042), and a trilogy of excellent LPs.

Tony Orlando and Dawn were a predictable success in the very early '70s, topping the UK chart in 1971 with "Knock Three Times" (1146), while UK pop maverick Jonathan King brought a handful of hits to the label, including the Piglets's "Johnny Reggae" (featuring *East Enders* TV star Wendy Richards) (1180), and "Keep On Dancing" (1164), the first-ever release by an unknown Scottish band called the Bay City Rollers. A major rarity from this period is "Oh Baby" (1121), by Dib Cochran and the Earwigs—a pseudonym disguising Marc Bolan, Rick Wakeman, Tony Visconti, and Mick Ronson. (Rumors that David Bowie also appears on the track can be discounted upon the insistence of all participants.)

Domestic talent remained an inconsistent proposition until mid-1972 brought the launch of Gary Glitter. "Rock and Roll" (1216) hit No. 2 that summer, igniting a peerless run of success, and a string of 11 successive Top Ten hits that extended into 1975. The Glitter Band (as their name suggests, the band was made up of Gary's backing musicians) scored seven hits of their own between 1974–76; and behind them, the glam floodgates simply exploded.

Bell made several attempts to launch glam into the US mainstream. From the Nicky Chinn–Michael Chapman songwriting stable, the Sweet (an RCA act in Britain) scored US hits with "Co-Co" (45-126), "Little Willy" (45-251), and "Blockbuster" (45-361), all gathered on an eponymous LP (1124), before the band was allowed to slip away to Capitol.

Another Chinn-Chapman act, Mud, saw two singles issued, "Crazy" (415) and "Tiger Feet" (602); while a third from the same stable, Detroit-born Suzi Quatro, released two Bell LPs and five 45s, including 1973's minor hit "All Shook Up" (45-477). Quatro passed by unnoticed, however, until she was transferred to Big Tree, where "Can the Can" at least made the Top 60. (Quatro's biggest US hits ultimately came with RSO.) Both Mud and Quatro were signed to Mickie Most's RAK label in the UK; Bell also briefly carried another RAK act, Hot Chocolate, releasing its "Rumours" (45-390) and "Emma" (45-466) singles, before they too moved to Big Tree . . . where a reissue of that second single promptly became a Top Ten hit.

Yet another RAK act, meanwhile, offers Bell collectors one of the US label's greatest 1970s-era rarities. Former Herman's Hermits vocalist Peter Noone scored a major UK hit with his version of the then-unknown David Bowie's "Oh! You Pretty Things," featuring Bowie himself on piano. Promo copies of Bell's US release are relatively common; stock copes (45-131), however, are all but unknown.

Bell had no more luck with Gary Glitter, despite scoring a major smash with "Rock and Roll" (45-237) and following through with a minor hit, "I Didn't Know I Loved You" (45-276). Glam was never to become more than a marginal interest in the US, and subsequent Glitter releases (singles and LPs) fell on deaf ears, only to be picked up for major hits by acts ranging from Brownsville Station to Joan Jett. The Glitter Band's only sniff of American success, meanwhile, was with a funk-rock instrumental, "Makes You Blind," discarded as a B-side in their home country and released on Arista, following its absorption of Bell.

Barry Blue scored four big hits in the UK; just one of them, "Dancing on a Saturday Night" (45-391/UK 1295), even saw an American release, at which point it was covered by Flash Cadillac and the Continental Kids (Epic 511102). Hello fared even more poorly. In the UK, its reputation is based on a pair of solid hit 45s, a fine album, and one of the great Bell UK rarities, the withdrawn 45 "Keep Us off the Streets" (1479). In the US, the group is known only for cutting the original version (1438) of Kiss guitarist Ace Frehley's "New York Groove" anthem. Even less recognition awaited other Bell UK successes Harley Quinne, rock 'n' roll revivalists Showaddywaddy, and the girl duo the Pearls.

Another Bell act that seemed destined to remain as obscure in the US as they were enormous in Britain was the Bay City Rollers. Since "Keep On Dancing," the band had completely vanished from the commercial radar, issuing a string of now-super-rare flop 45s and getting nowhere fast. They re-emerged in 1973 with a new tartan-drenched image, a new songwriting team (veterans Bill Martin and Phil Coulter), and an effervescent sound previewed on the 45 "Remember" (1338). (Two versions of this exist: an original take with vocalist Nobby Clarke, swiftly replaced by a new recording with Clarke's replacement, Les McKeown.)

"Shang-a-Lang" (1355) followed, and for two years, the Rollers ruled the UK chart, scoring five Top Ten hits and two No. 1s during 1974–75 alone. America didn't even look twice at any of them. It was not until Arista came into being that the band's US fortunes changed, and today, the group's Bell catalog is in great demand—and scarce supply.

The last years of Bell also saw the emergence of Barry Manilow. During 1973–74 he released four singles on the label, including the hits "Could It Be Magic" (45-422) and "Mandy" (45-613), plus a pair of LPs (1129, 1314). Again, however, it was with the advent of Arista that his career truly took off.

Arista was the brainchild of Clive Davis, former head of Columbia Records, who became President of Bell following the departure of Uttal to his own Private Stock label (home of the early Blondie, Arrows,

TEN TOP COLLECTIBLES

Gary Glitter

"**Alone in the Night**"—as Paul Raven (UK Decca F11202—7-inch, 1960)

"**Another Rock 'n' Roll Christmas**" (UK Arista ARISD 592—shaped picture disc, 1984)

"**Dance Me Up**" (UK Arista ARISD 570—7-inch picture disc, 1984)

"**Do You Wanna Touch Me**" (UK Bell 1280—7-inch, picture sleeve, 1973)

Gary Glitter (UK Bell REBEL 1—EP, picture sleeve, 1976)

"**Musical Man**"—as Paul Monday (UK MCA MU 1024—7-inch, 1968)

"**Shout Shout Shout**" (UK Arista ARICV 586—7-inch mirror disc, 1984)

"**Tower of Strength**"—as Paul Raven (UK Parlophone R4842—7-inch, 1961)

"**Wait for Me**"—as Paul Raven (Decca 32714—7-inch, 1970)

"**We're All Livin' in One Place**"—as Rubber Bucket (UK MCA MK 5006—7-inch, 1969)

and *Starsky & Hutch* TV star David Soul). The Arista identity was initially ushered in amid the small print of the latter-day Bell releases ("Bell Records, Distributed by Arista Records . . ."); by the end of 1974, however, it was a done deal. The existing Bell catalog was absorbed into the new company, while many artists were either dropped or departed of their own accord—David Cassidy fled for RCA, Tony Orlando and Dawn signed with Elektra, and the Fifth Dimension moved to ABC.

In Britain, the Bell identity persisted until early 1976. Its final major hit was scored by Slik, a Glaswegian band fronted by the then-unknown Midge Ure. "Forever and Ever" (1464) topped the UK chart and might have succeeded in the US as well. Unfortunately, injuries sustained in a road accident sidelined Ure just as Arista released the group's debut LP, and by the time the band returned to action, its carefully nurtured teenybop audience had moved on.

For many years, the Bell label was overlooked by collectors—even as subsidiaries Amy, Philly Groove, Fury, and so on became major sellers. But for the generation whose formative musical tastes developed during the half decade spanned by Bell's greatest successes, 1971–76, the familiar silver label has a magic all its own, one that traditional collecting outlets utterly overlooked until Internet auctions rudely informed them that records they'd been pumping out at a buck or two a throw were actually in extraordinary demand.

Beserkley

One of the great pioneering indie labels of the new wave movement, Beserkley predated that vehicle by over a year, launching in 1975 after founder Matthew King Kaufman found himself unable to land a record deal for Earth Quake, a band he'd been managing since the early '70s (they had already released two LPs on A&M). Other early signings included Greg Kihn, the Rubinoos, and most significantly, Jonathan Richman.

Beserkley's first release was a 45 coupling Earth Quake's version of the Easybeats's "Friday on My Mind," with Richman's anthemic "Roadrunner"; Earth Quake also backed Richman on his recording. Both tracks reappeared on the *Beserkley Chartbusters*

TEN TOP COLLECTIBLES

Jonathan Richman/Modern Lovers

"Buzz Buzz Buzz" (UK Beserkley BZZ 25—7-inch, picture sleeve, 1978)

Jonathan Richman and the Modern Lovers (Beserkley BZ 0048—LP, 1976)

The Modern Lovers (Home of the Hits HH 1910—LP, 1975)

"The Morning of Our Lives" (UK Beserkley BZZ 7—7-inch, 1978)

"New England" (Beserkley 5743—7-inch, picture sleeve, 1976)

The Original Modern Lovers (Bomp 4021—LP, 1981)

Penthouse/Omni College Rock Concert (London Wavelength—Transcription disc, 1983)

"Roadrunner" (Beserkley 5701—7-inch, picture sleeve, 1975)

"Roadrunner" (UK United Artists UP 36006—7-inch, 1975)

"That Summer Feeling" (UK Rough Trade C52—12-inch, 1985)

LP (BZ 0044), which introduced the label as the "Home of the Hits"—a short-lived Beserkley subsidiary of this same name was responsible for the first issue of the Modern Lovers' self-titled debut in 1975 (a collection of demos and unreleased tracks recorded for Warner Bros. two years earlier). The album reappeared on Beserkley the following year.

Another well-received issue from this period was the *Beserkley Six Pack*, which contained 45 rpm versions of several of the LP's cuts, plus a controversial blank 45 by the Sons of Pete—it was titled "Silent Night." Albums by Earthquake, Greg Kihn, Richman, and the Rubinoos followed between 1975–77, the period of Beserkley's greatest collectibility and success.

Although Richman never scored a US hit, "Roadrunner" was picked up for UK release by UA in 1975. It did not chart but was greeted with excellent reviews and a reissue two years later on Beserkley's newly opened UK subsidiary (BZZ 1) made the UK Top 20. It was followed into the chart by "Egyptian Reggae" (BZZ 2) and "The Morning of Our Lives" (BZZ 7), while the album *Rock 'n' Roll with the Modern Lovers* (BSERK 9) was a Top 50 hit. No other Beserkley act did as well in Britain, but the label's UK catalog is well worth pursuing.

Beserkley's early US releases were distributed by Playboy; Janus/GRT took over between 1977–79; Elektra/Asylum handled the label from 1979 until its dissolution in 1984. These changes all had an impact on the catalog—*Beserkley Chartbusters* original US catalog number, BZ 0044, became JBZ 0044 under Janus, and so on. The Elektra deal then saw a new numbering sequence, the BZ 10000 series, launched with further reissues.

New signings under the Janus deal included the Tyla Gang, a band formed from the ashes of British pub-rockers Ducks Deluxe, and the frantic instrumentalist Spitballs. No new acts joined the label thereafter; indeed, Beserkley's last years saw it dedicated almost exclusively to reissues and new Greg Kihn recordings.

Big Top

Big Top was a New York label best regarded for the presence of Del Shannon, whose prolific run of hits

TEN TOP COLLECTIBLES

Del Shannon

Best of Del Shannon (Dot DLP 3824—Mono LP, 1967)

"From Me to You" (Big Top 3152—7-inch, 1963)

The Further Adventures of Charles Westover (Liberty LST 7539—Stereo LP, 1968)

Handy Man (Amy S8003—Stereo LP, 1964)

"I Can't Believe My Ears" (Amy 947—7-inch, 1966)

Little Town Flirt (Big Top 12-1308—Stereo LP, 1963)

1661 Seconds with Del Shannon (Amy S8006—Stereo LP, 1965)

Runaway (Big Top 12-1303—Stereo LP, 1961)

"Runnin' On Back" (Liberty 56018—7-inch, picture sleeve, 1968)

Sings Hank Williams (Amy S8004—Stereo LP, 1964)

for the label opened in 1961 with the chart-topping "Runaway" (3067) and continued on through "Hats Off to Larry" (3075), "So Long Baby" (3083), "Hey! Little Girl" (3091), and more. His final hit for the label, 1963's "From Me to You" (3152), marked the first US hit for a Lennon-McCartney composition—apropos of nothing, it was also the first American import single that British DJ legend Bob Harris purchased. Fondly, he still remembers "the pink Big Top label in a white-and-blue sleeve. It looked fabulous."

Behind Shannon, a logjam of talents included Bobby Pedrick, Jr. (later known as Robert John), who brought Big Top its first hit, "White Bucks and Saddle Shoes" (3004); Sammy Turner—the label's first reliable hit-maker, who scored in 1959 with "Sweet Annie Laurie" (3007); and Johnny and the Hurricanes (1960's "Down Yonder"—3036—ignited their Big Top career).

Less successful offerings came from Ocie (O.C.) Smith, Travis and Bob, Don Covay, and English superstar Cliff Richard—Big Top released his 1962 movie theme "The Young Ones" (3101).

The bulk of Big Top's output was confined to 45s, but the label did produce eight collectible LPs, including some fascinating stereo variations—the LP version of "Runaway," on the album of the same name (12-1303), is an alternate take to the familiar hit. Sammy Turner, Johnny and the Hurricanes, and the comedy duo Muriel Landers and Stanley Adams also enjoyed Big Top albums. Big Top also released several albums devoted to dance fads the twist and the fink.

Big Tree

Active through the 1970s, Big Tree was launched in 1970 by Doug Morris, with the Sugar Bears' "Early in the Morning" 45 (100), and the debut LP by the Neighborhood (BTS 2001).

Distributed by AMPEX, the tape manufacturing concern, the distinctive red-and-yellow label that dates from this era is the best-known Big Tree identity, decorating as it does some of the most sought-after records in the catalog. These include further Sugar Bears 45s "You Are the One" (122), "Happiness Train" (143), and "Some Kind of Summer" (155), and the group's eponymous LP (BTS 2009). Another Big Tree collectible is the LP (BTS 2005) by Jamaican act

TEN TOP COLLECTIBLES

Brownsville Station

Air Special (Epic JE 35606—Orange-vinyl promo LP, 1978)

Brownsville Station (Palladium P-1004—LP, 1970)

"Let Your Yeah Be Yeah" (Big Top 161—7-inch, 1973)

"Love Stealer"—as Brownsville (Epic 50695—7-inch, 1979)

Motor City Connection (Big Top BTS 89510—LP, 1975)

A Night on the Town (Big Top BTS 2010—LP, 1972)

No BS (Warner Bros. WS 1888—LP, 1970)

"The Red Back Spider" (Big Top 156—7-inch, 1972)

"Rock and Roll Holiday" (Hideout 1957—7-inch, 1969)

"Rock with the Music" (Big Top 144—7-inch, 1972)

Dave and Ansell Collins, titled for the surprise 1971 hit "Double Barrel" (115). The singularly named Lobo (born Roland Kent Lavole) also joined the label at this time, hitting with the plaintive "Me and You and a Dog Named Boo" (112), and remaining a reliable hit-maker for the next five years.

Distribution switched to Bell in 1972. Brownsville Station, featuring the late Michael "Cub" Koda, was the success story of this era, scoring the anthemic "Smokin' in the Boys' Room" (16011) in 1973; the group's next hit, 1974's "Leader of the Gang" (15005), covered a UK hit by Bell UK mainstay Gary Glitter. Early Brownsville albums *A Night on the Town* (BTS 2010) and *Yeah!* (2102), are also of interest.

Another favored act from this same period is the Canadian metal band April Wine, which charted with "You Could Have Been a Lady" (133) and with a self-titled album (BTS 2012).

Two of Britain's biggest acts, Suzi Quatro and Hot Chocolate, both joined Big Tree from unsuccessful spells at Bell itself—Quatro promptly landed a Top 60 hit with "Can the Can" (16503); Hot Chocolate made No. 8 with "Emma" (16031), a single that Bell had already issued to no response. Hit follow-ups included "Disco Queen" (16038), "You Sexy Thing" (16047), "Don't Stop It Now" (16060), and "So You Win Again" (16096). The group also issued the albums *Cicero Park* (BT 89503), *Hot Chocolate* (BT 89512), and *Man to Man* (BT 89519), plus a hits collection (BT 76002).

In 1974, Atlantic took over Big Tree and immediately earned hits with a reissue of Think's 1971 (Laurie Records) smash "Once You Understand" (15001) and the British funk-rock band Fancy. The group's lascivious rendition of the Troggs' "Wild Thing" (15004) was followed by the similarly saucy "Touch Me" (16026). An album titled for the first hit (BT 89502) also appeared, and has since been reissued on CD in the UK by the Angel Air label. (It is paired with a second LP, an RCA issue.)

England Dan and John Ford Coley was the label's biggest success, however, beginning in 1976 with the No. 2 hit "I'd Really Love to See You Tonight" (16069). The duo scored nine hits over the next five years; they have never set the collecting world alight, and can be picked up extremely cheaply. Disco darling

Hot likewise. The post-1976 label design, a drawing of a mother bird feeding her chicks with a musical note, is, perhaps, twee enough to encapsulate the label's latter-day output.

Blue Horizon

Britain's most influential blues/blues-rock label began life, in January 1964, as an offshoot of a blues fanzine run by teenagers Mike Vernon and Neil Slaven. *R&B Monthly* was a year old when the pair encountered blues legend Hubert Sumlin and recorded three songs with him in their living room. Marketed through the magazine, "Across the Board" (Blue Horizon 1000) was a limited-edition release of 99 45s, which sold out immediately, a circumstance that prompted the pair to prepare a second release, by Woodrow Adams and the Blues Blasters (1001).

An LP, Dr. Isaiah Ross's *The Flying Eagle* (BH 1), appeared in February 1966; two new labels, Outasite and Purdah, were introduced with releases by Larry Williams and Johnny "Guitar" Watson, and by Britain's own Tony "T.S." McPhee, respectively. Purdah followed

with a major coup, an exclusive 45 by John Mayall and Eric Clapton, "Bernard Jenkins" (3502).

By early 1967, *R&B Monthly* had mutated into *The Blue Horizon Records Newsletter.* Vernon was employed as a staff producer at the Decca major, and Blue Horizon was about to step into the mainstream, with distribution by CBS. A total of ten 45s on the original independent Blue Horizon were deleted, together with the output of both subsidiaries (four Purdah releases, six Outasite)—these are, unquestionably, the rarest of all Blue Horizon releases. They are not, however, the most sought after.

The first two Blue Horizon releases in November 1967, appeared on the traditional orange CBS label, with Blue Horizon's own logo appearing only on the push-out center of the disc. The debut release by a band Vernon himself had discovered and nurtured, Fleetwood Mac's "I Believe My Time Ain't Long" (3051), and Aynsley Dunbar's "Retaliation" (3109), were numbered within CBS's own catalog. The third release, Chicken Shack's "It's Okay with Me, Baby" (57-3135), then initiated Blue Horizon's own numbering system.

TEN TOP COLLECTIBLES

Peter Green's Fleetwood Mac

"Black Magic Woman" (Epic 10351—7-inch, 1968)

English Rose (Epic LN 24446—White-label mono promo, 1969)

Fleetwood Mac (Epic LN 24402—White-label mono promo, 1968)

"Green Manalishi" (UK Reprise RS 27007—7-inch, picture sleeve, 1970)

"Hungry Country Woman" (with Otis Spann—Blue Horizon 304, 1970—7-inch, 1970)

"I Believe My Time Ain't Long" (UK Blue Horizon 3051—7-inch, 1967)

In Chicago (Blue Horizon 3801—2-LP, 1970)

"Oh Well" (Reprise 0883—7-inch, 1970)

"Rattlesnake Shake" (Reprise 0860—7-inch, 1969)

"Stop Messin' Around" (Epic 10368—7-inch, 1968)

A US release for one of Blue Horizon's best-loved LPs.

Fleetwood Mac, of course, would become Blue Horizon's most successful act, and its output for the label—four singles (plus one reissue) including the chart-topping "Albatross" (57-3145) and three albums—attracts high prices whenever it appears. Chicken Shack, proving ground for future Mac vocalist Christine McVie; the brilliant "one-man blues band" Duster Bennett; and the legendary Top Topham, original guitarist with the Yardbirds are all heavily pursued as well. Many of the rarest releases, however, are those that only specialists actively seek.

Among Blue Horizon's 49 CBS-distributed UK singles, and a short sequence of US releases (distributed by Sire) can be found positive gems by veterans Champion Jack Dupree, Otis Spann, Guitar Crusher, B.B. King, and Slim Harpo, most of which are overlooked in the search for one more big Mac score.

Also of interest are the first UK releases by Dutch band Focus—its "Hocus Pocus" (2096 004) anthem was issued in 1971, shortly after Blue Horizon switched distribution to Polydor; Mighty Baby, formed by members of '60s psychedelic legend the Action; Jellybread; and Vernon himself.

Among LPs, 51 releases through CBS, and 18 more through Polydor, are almost all collectible, with the latter tending to be just a little less sought after. Not many people bought Whale Feathers' self-titled LP in 1971 (2431 009); not many seem to care about finding it today.

The Polydor era ended in 1972, with Lightnin' Slim's "Just a Little Bit" single (2096 013) and *London Gumbo* LP (2931 005), as well as a compilation detailing the history of the US blues label Excello (2683 007—one of several very rare Blue Horizon various-artists sets). Reissues since that time have tended to concentrate on aspects of the Fleetwood Mac story, before 1997 brought the three-CD box set *Blue Horizon Story*, compiled and annotated by Vernon himself. Wryly, one recalls the US magazine review complaining that the quintessential British blues label was anthologized with predominantly American artists. Looking at the label's catalog, what else could it have done?

Note: A US Blue Horizon label in operation around 1960, best known for three fabulously rare releases by Scott Douglas and the Venture Quintet (later the Ventures), has no relationship with the UK label above.

Further Reading: *The Blue Horizon Story*, by Mike Vernon (booklet within box set of the same name—Columbia CB 743)

Bronco/Mustang

Bob Keane launched the Mustang label in 1965, following the closure of Del-Fi. Mustang's chief act was the Bobby Fuller Four. Having already issued one 45 (as Bobby Fuller and The Fabtastics) on Keane's Donna label (1403), the Texans debuted on the new concern with "She's My Girl" (3004). Over the next year they released eight singles, including the monster hit "I Fought the Law" (3014), and a pair of rare LPs (Mustang's only album releases), before Fuller's controversial death in July 1966.

Bronco launched around a year after Mustang, with the Versatiles' "You're Good Enough for Me" (Bronco 2050). Head of A&R at the label was Barry White, at that time one of Los Angeles's top session arrangers and musicians.

For his first Bronco session, White co-wrote and played virtually every instrument on Viola Wills' "Lost Without the Love of My Guy" (Bronco 2051), while he co-produced (with Keane) two of Fuller's own recordings, "The Magic Touch" (Mustang 3018) and the album track "I'm a Lucky Guy." Fuller returned the favor by describing White as "the most outrageous arranger around . . . a brother who knows how to make Top 40 hits for white kids."

White also wrote and produced veteran Texan Johnny Wyatt's "This Thing Called Love" (Bronco 2052), but his greatest Bronco success came after he reunited with "Harlem Shuffle" arranger Gene Page to record 18-year-old singer Felice Taylor. Casting her firmly in the sonic mold of the Supremes, the team earned hits in both the US and UK with "I Feel Love Comin' On," and "It May Be Winter Outside (But in My Heart It's Spring)" (Mustang 3024—White

TEN TOP COLLECTIBLES

Bobby Fuller Four

The Bobby Fuller Four (Mustang MS 901—Stereo LP, 1966)

"Fool of Love" (Exeter 126—7-inch, 1964)

"I Fought the Law" (Exeter 124—7-inch, 1964)

"King of the Beach" (Exeter 122—7-inch, 1964)

KRLA—King of the Wheels (Mustang MS 900—Stereo LP, 1965)

"Never to Be Forgotten" (Mustang 3011—7-inch, 1965)

"Not Fade Away" (Eastwood 345—7-inch, 1962)

"Saturday Night" (Todd 1090—7-inch, 1963)

"Those Memories of You"—as Bobby Fuller and The Fabtastics (Donna 1403—7-inch, 1965)

"You're in Love" (Yucca 140—7-inch, slow version/fast version, 1961)

subsequently re-recorded the song with his own Love Unlimited Orchestra). The former was unissued in the US, but leased in Britain to President.

Other White compositions and productions included Viola Wills' "Together Forever" (Bronco 2053) and "You're out of My Mind" (2055), along with a solo B-side, the instrumental "Under the Influence of Love" (Mustang 3026). Another White single, "All in the Run of a Day" (Bronco 2056), was the final release within the Bronco/Mustang stable; the label closed down in 1967 and White returned to session work.

Brunswick

Brunswick was one of the longest-surviving of all US labels, originally launching in New York during the 1920s, and it was material dating from its earliest years that preoccupied the label's LP catalog during the 1950s. Not until 1957 did Brunswick resume releasing new recordings, often sharing its talent with its distributor, Coral. For example, while Buddy Holly's "solo" releases appeared on Coral, material bearing the Crickets's name was handled by Brunswick, and it is this catalog that remains the label's most collectible asset.

Following up "That'll Be the Day" (55009), seven 45s and the *Chirping Crickets* album (BL 54038) are all much sought after, with original pressings of the LP, bearing a so-called textured sleeve, commanding an even greater premium. Holly protégé Terry Noland also cut six singles for Brunswick (with his biggest hit, "There Was a Fungus Among Them," 55092, also appearing on Coral), plus an extremely scarce debut album (BL 54041). Disc jockey Alan Freed also had releases on both labels, while members of the Lawrence Welk Orchestra were similarly divided.

Brunswick's next star was singer Jackie Wilson, whose vast repertoire remains a hot collectible commodity. Certainly it dominates the Brunswick catalog of the early '60s: of 25 LPs issued between 1960–66, only seven did not feature Wilson. The singer's singles catalog was less overwhelming, but still comprised close to 50 45s and a dozen (very hard to find) EPs during the same period. Of the other artists who squeezed in around him, very few attract more than a cursory glance from collectors, though anybody delving seriously into the catalog will encounter a number of hard-to-find releases.

Concern over Wilson's then-declining career around the mid-'60s saw Brunswick president Len Schneider and Nat Tarnopol (Wilson's manager and now co-owner of the label) recruit producer Carl Davis to the stable. His chief concern was reestablishing Wilson, a task he accomplished with the multimillion-selling "(Your Love Keeps Lifting Me) Higher and Higher" (55336). Davis also brought a number of other soul acts to Brunswick, including the Artistics, the Chi-Lites, the Young-Holt Trio, Barbara Acklin, and Gene Chandler, all of whom swiftly became chart fixtures; all of whom are now hotly pursued by soul aficionados. T-Bone Walker, Count Basie, and Louis Armstrong also made strong Brunswick records.

In 1970, Nat Tarnopol purchased the remainder of the company from Decca. He became president, with Carl Davis his executive vice president; Davis, simultaneously, was running his own Dakar label in the US, with the now-independent Brunswick handling his artists in the UK. Hamilton Bohannon, whose Dakar catalog included four hits during 1974–75, was one beneficiary of this arrangement, scoring major British hits with "South African Man" (BR 16), "Disco Stomp" (BR 19), "Foot Stompin' Music" (BR 21), and "Happy Feeling" (BR 24).

Brunswick's British operation dated back to the mid-'60s. Prior to this—and, indeed, thereafter—the UK branch of Coral had handled Brunswick's US artists. The British Brunswick, then, was primarily concerned with homegrown talents, with the most important signing being the Who.

An MCA release in the US, their first album, *My Generation* (LAT 8618)—and singles "I Can't Explain" (05926), "Anyway Anyhow Anywhere" (05935), and "My Generation" (05944)—were all Brunswick releases. However, a falling-out with producer Shel Talmy saw the band switch to Robert Stigwood's Reaction label in 1966, promoting an

TEN TOP COLLECTIBLES

Buddy Holly and the Crickets

Blue Days, Black Nights (Decca 29854—7-inch, bars by logo on label, 1956)

The Chirpin' Crickets (Brunswick BL 54038—LP, textured sleeve, 1957)

Listen to Me (Coral EC 81169—EP, picture sleeve, 1958)

Love Me (Decca 30543—Green-label 7-inch promo, 1958)

Modern Don Juan (Decca 30166—7-inch, bars by logo on label, 1956)

Stay Close to Me—Lou Giordano (Holly on guitar—Brunswick 55115—7-inch, 1959)

Terry Noland—Terry Noland (Holly on guitar—Brunswick BL 54041—LP, 1958)

That'll Be the Day (Decca DL 8707—LP, black label with silver print, 1958)

That'll Be the Day (Decca ED 2575—EP, picture sleeve with liner notes, 1958)

Words of Love (Coral 61852—7-inch or 78, 1957)

unseemly squabble between the two labels—and a string of now–highly collectible (and, indeed, unreleased) 45s. A projected Brunswick issue of "Circles" (05951) was canceled; a Reaction release of "Substitute" was withdrawn, reissued with a new B-side, then re-reissued with another B-side entirely. Brunswick then maintained its own sequence of Who releases, alongside the band's new issues: "It's a Legal Matter" (05956), "The Kids Are Alright" (05965), and "La-La-La-Lies" (05968) are all prize finds.

Brunswick closed its doors in the UK soon after this, Tarnopol reopening the imprint in 1974. The Chi-Lites would become the reborn label's biggest seller, much as they were in the US. In 1976, however, the operation received a major blow when Tarnopol and three other Brunswick executives were convicted on fraud and conspiracy charges, after allegedly discounting half a million records for $300,000 in cash, and $50,000 in merchandise.

The convictions were thrown out on appeal in December 1977, and a retrial ordered for the following year. This ended with a mistrial, and the case was dismissed, but neither Tarnopol nor Brunswick ever recovered. A mere handful of significant new signings brought albums from Touch and Young & Co., and while the label continued to operate until 1981, it made little impact. By the time of Tarnopol's death in 1987, Brunswick functioned only as a licensee for its back catalog.

In collecting terms, the Holly, Wilson, and late-'60s soul catalogs are the principal source of interest, with the Who thrown in for international completists. Pre-rock Brunswick releases, while uncommon, have little value; neither do the majority of post-Decca releases.

Further Reading: *The Brunswick Years* (booklet within CD set of the same name—Brunswick)

Brut

A short-lived subsidiary of Buddah formed in 1973, Brut is best known for the first Michael Franks LP (6005) and the debut by comedian Robert Klein (6001). Promo copies of the latter differ from the stock release, in that the tracks were banded for airplay. Klein released a second album on Brut in 1974

(6600). Other Brut releases include the movie soundtrack *Book of Numbers* (6002) and a popular set by Sugarloaf and Jerry Corbetta, *I Got a Song* (6006).

Buddah

Formed in 1967 as an independent offshoot of the Kama Sutra label, Buddah was to become one of the leading players in the bubblegum boom that consumed the US (and, to a lesser extent, Europe) during the late '60s. The label was initially founded by Kama Sutra's Art Kass but became better known for the presence of former Cameo-Parkway VP Neil Bogart, one of the entrepreneurial legends of the American music industry.

The choice of label name has long exercised onlookers' imagination—Buddah, of course, is a misspelling of the correct "Buddha," with the label's original logo compounding the error—it depicted the Indian deity Shiva! The appropriate Buddha image would not be adopted until the mid-to-late '70s.

Buddah debuted with the Mulberry Fruit's jokey version of the musichall standard "Yes, We Have No Bananas" (1), actually a collaboration between movie producer Richard Perrey and Kama Sutra's Trade Winds/Innocence duo. Buddah's first No. 1 45, the Lemon Pipers' "Green Tambourine" (23), followed in late 1967, the first of seven singles for the band, including a superb follow-up "Rice Is Nice" (31) and a pair of LPs, *Green Tambourine* (5009) and *Jungle Marmalade* (5016).

Former Cameo star group the Stairsteps, renamed the 5 Stairsteps and Cubie, scored with "Something's Missing" (20); they, too, would enjoy a string of Buddah releases, spanning the next five years, but punctuated by a spell on Curtis Mayfield's Curtom label during 1968–69 (Buddah distributed that concern). Interestingly, the group's Buddah releases are far harder to find than the Curtom issues, though Curtom is generally regarded as a more collectible label.

Soul singer Timothy Wilson, the Rhodes Scholars, Le Cirque, the Baskerville Hounds, bluesman Barry Goldberg, and Johnny Maestro recorded their first efforts at the label. The fondly remembered Second Story also joined the label, while the arrival of avant-rock act Captain Beefheart and His Magic Band reminds modern historians that Buddah's output wasn't confined simply to silly nursery rhymes. Though he remained on the label for less than two years, still Beefheart ignited a ferociously collectible career with the singles "Yellow Brick Road" (9) and "Plastic Factory" (108), and the classic LPs *Safe As Milk* (1001—released in readily available stereo and astonishingly scarce mono) and *Mirror Man* (5077, first pressings issued with a mirrored cover).

Indeed, through Buddah's infancy, it rather looked as though the bubblegum business simply wasn't going to take off. Bogart had already introduced Long Island–based producers Jeff Katz and Jerry Kasenetz, hot from hits with the Music Explosion (for Laurie) and (at Cameo-Parkway) the Ohio Express, and things began well, when the 1910 Fruitgum Company scored a massive international hit with "Simon Says" (24).

The single's success, however, was the exception. Spread across both Buddah and Kama Sutra, further bubblegum-themed releases by the Frosted Flakes, Chicago Prohibition 1931, the Carnaby Street Runners, Salt Water Taffy, Lt. Garcia's Magic Music Box, the Cowboys 'n' Indians, and J.C.W. Ratfinks were flops, and had it not been for a reinvention of the Ohio Express, and an infuriating piece of confectionary titled "Yummy Yummy Yummy" (38) . . .

That monster was the cue for America to go bubblegum mad. The Express followed through with "Down at Lulu's" (56), "Chewy Chewy" (70), "Sweeter than Sugar" (92), and "Mercy" (102); the Fruitgums returned with "May I Take a Giant Step" (39), "1 2 3 Red Light" (54—famously, the song was later incorporated into Talking Heads' early live repertoire), "Goody Goody Gumdrops" (71), and "Indian Giver" (91). Both bands also issued a clutch of albums that are today as sought after as the original singles.

Kasenetz-Katz themselves joined in the fun, a quartet of Buddah singles including the hit "Quick Joey Small" (64), and a pair of even more in-demand LPs, credited to *the Kasenetz Katz Singing Orchestral Circus* (5020) and *Kasenetz Katz Super Circus*

(50278). Further releases on their own Buddah subsidiaries, Teem and Super K, followed.

Neither were Kasenetz-Katz the only players on the scene now. Don Kirshner's Archies cartoon creation was imminent, while producers Jerry Goldstein and Bob Feldman arrived at Buddah with the mini-hit "Bubble Gum Music," credited to the Rock and Roll Dubble Bubble Trading Card Company of Philadelphia 1941 (78).

Away from the bubblegum market, Buddah continued producing some fine releases. The Brooklyn Bridge, featuring former Crests vocalist Johnny Maestro, issued a dozen singles and four albums for the label between 1968–72, their final releases appearing under the abbreviated name the Bridge. Cleveland singer-songwriter Buzzy Linhart cut several albums, including one issued on the short-lived Eleuthera label (*Buzzy Linhart Is Music*—ELS 3601).

Lou Christie became a reliable hit-maker, and as the 1970s loomed, Buddah (like Kama Sutra) signed a string of veterans of an earlier musical age—Paul Anka, Johnny Tillotson, James Darren, Freddy Cannon, and Len Barry among them. Few of these releases have much value today—certainly they cannot compare with releases from the artists' heyday. But they can prove hard to find.

In 1969 the label ventured even further afield with the recruitment of the North California State Youth Choir, whose privately released single, "Oh Happy Day," was proving immensely popular in the group's home state. Alerted by growing radio interest, Buddah picked up the choir, and having renamed them the Edwin Hawkins Singers, released the song as the first 45 on the specially formed Pavilion label (20,001); it was a massive hit, and when "Ain't It Like Him" (20,002) also proved successful, Hawkins was transferred to Buddah itself, as the spearhead of the label's drive into the new decade.

Folk singer Melanie (whose Neighborhood label was a Buddah subsidiary) and 1950s revival group Sha Na Na also scored heavily for Buddah in the early '70s, rebuilding the label's image in quite different directions from its earlier reputation. Fascinating one-offs, meanwhile, came from New York DJ Jack

Spector, under the alias Vik Venus, as well as from the reborn Tokens and the Canadian rock band Motherlode.

Future disco supremo Van McCoy cut the rare *Soul Impressions* (5103) album in 1971; it was repackaged as *From Disco to Love* (5648) in 1975, following McCoy's success elsewhere with "The Hustle"; Trammps, whose "Disco Inferno" would similarly help shape the disco boom of the late '70s, also debuted on Buddah, scoring with "Zing Went the Strings of My Heart" (306—first pressings are credited to Tramps). Three further singles followed; these, too, were repackaged, following the band's eventual breakthrough, as the somewhat misleadingly titled *Legendary Zing Album* (5641)—misleading, of course, because there never was a *Zing Album* to become *Legendary* in the first place.

The departure of Neil Bogart to launch his own Casablanca label, home to Kiss, Donna Summer, and many more, could have spelled the end for Buddah. Instead, it brought a new beginning, as Art Kass signed Gladys Knight and the Pips, a group that was swiftly to become the most successful act in the label's entire history.

Through the mid-'70s, buoyed by Knight's success, Buddah virtually reinvented itself as an R&B powerhouse—largely through the efforts of musical director Norman Connors. The New Birth was recruited from RCA and swiftly scored an R&B No. 1 with 1975's "Dream Merchant" (470); another old Trammps recording, "Hold Back the Night" (507), was a Top 30 hit, and while other signings were less successful, still Buddah represents one of the richest R&B catalogs of the era. Phyllis Hyman, Michael Henderson, Melba Moore, Dee Dee Bridgewater, and Aquarian Dream represent the cream of the label's output; Andrea True Connection's "More, More, More" (515) and the Addrisi Brothers' "Slow Dancin' Don't Turn Me On" (566) stand among its biggest hits.

By the late '70s, however, Buddah was clearly running out of steam, introducing few new artists and releasing few new records. By 1981, in fact, Michael Henderson alone appeared on the release schedules. Indeed, Buddah's last three singles were

TEN TOP COLLECTIBLES

Captain Beefheart

Bat Chain Puller (Warner Bros., no catalog number—test pressing with different tracks, 1978)

"Click Clack" (Reprise 1068—7-inch, 1972)

"Diddy Wah Diddy" (A&M 794—7-inch, 1966)

"Moonchild" (A&M 818—7-inch, 1966)

"Plastic Factory" (Buddah 108—7-inch, 1969)

Safe As Milk (Buddah BDM 1001—Mono LP, 1967)

Strictly Personal (Blue Thumb BTS 1—Black-label LP, 1968)

"Too Much Time" (Reprise 1133—7-inch, 1972)

Trout Mask Replica (Straight 2-STS 2027—2-LP, 1970)

"Yellow Brick Road" (Buddah 9—7-inch, 1967)

---

all Henderson's: "Geek You Up" (629), in late 1981, "Make It Easy on Yourself" (630), in mid-1982, and "Fickle" (800), in early 1983.

The sale of the Sutra/Kama Sutra/Buddah group to Essex Entertainment in 1986, and thence to BMG in 1996, has seen much of the label's prized back catalog reappear in the CD age. A new series of excellent remasters and reissues, beginning in April 1999, brought releases by original label veterans like Captain Beefheart and the Flamin' Groovies, but also issues from elsewhere in the BMG family by Nilsson, Graham Parker, Rory Gallagher, Iggy Pop, Daryl Hall, and more. This rebirth, incidentally, also saw the Buddah label's name changed to Buddha, correcting a misspelling that dates back to the label's inception.

Further Reading: *Bubblegum Music Is the Naked Truth: The Dark History of Prepubescent Pop, from the Banana Splits to Britney Spears,* edited by Kim Cooper and David Smay (Feral House, 2001)

Cadence

Orchestra leader Archie Bleyer founded Cadence in Manhattan, in December 1952. Cadence's first release—and first hit—was Julius La Rosa's "Anywhere I Wander" (1230). The unusual choice for opening catalog number was taken from La Rosa's birthdate.

Cadence flourished through the early-to-mid-'50s, La Rosa's output joined by Don MacNeil, Eileen Parker, Aileen Dalton, John Sebastian (father of the Loving Spoonful frontman), and even prizefighter Rocky Marciano. Sebastian's debut for the label, incidentally, is the source of one apparently confusing catalog hiccup—for reasons unknown, "Foolish Waltz" was issued with the catalog number 1420; the number would be reused in 1962.

The Chordettes's "Mr. Sandman" (1247) became Cadence's first chart-topper in 1954; the group remained the label's biggest seller into the late '50s, and their debut album, *Close Harmony* (CLP 102), is well worth the now-required investment.

Bill Hayes' "Ballad of Davy Crockett" (1256) followed the Chordettes to the top; the young Andy Williams brought further success; the unknown Ocie (O.C.) Smith brought promise. But it was the 1957 arrival of the Everly Brothers that cemented

Cadence's place in both the pop charts, and today, in collectors' hearts.

Before they departed to Warner Bros. in 1960, the Everlys released 13 45s; nine extended-play, four-song EPs; and three LPs on the label, leaving behind a 38-song catalog that formed the backbone of Cadence's future prosperity. Original issues of all are collectible, but the EPs merit special attention, clean picture-sleeve editions turning up very infrequently. A key point to bear in mind with the Everlys releases is the variation in label designs: original releases feature Cadence's maroon metronome design; the commonly encountered red label was not introduced until after the duo left for Warner Bros.

Of additional interest among Cadence LPs of this period was Bleyer's insistence on adding droll commentaries to what would have otherwise have been self-titled albums. The Chordettes's second album, *The Chordettes*, was subtitled *"They're Riding High," Says Archie*. The Everly Brothers' first album, *The Everly Brothers*, is now known as *Off and Rolling* from the subtitle *"They're Off and Rolling," Says Archie*. But the most bizarre phrase is surely that which attends Andy Williams' *Andy Williams* album: *"He's All Male and Catnip to Quail," Says Archie*.

Two different sleeves grace this latter album, the earliest being white, with a picture of Williams standing in front of a man dressed as a lion. If one also considers the subtitle, the art department must have been enjoying an extraordinarily bizarre day when that combination was conceived. The second sleeve, featuring a seated Williams, is somewhat less perplexing. Williams' second album, *Sings Rodgers and Hammerstein*, was Cadence's first stereo issue, with a new numbering system, the 2500 series, being reserved especially for such releases. Mono issues remained in the 3000 line.

Johnny Tillotson also brought the label a number of successful singles and popular LPs; while the arrival of Link Wray may not have brought many records to the catalog—just one single—but at least delivered a bona fide classic, the immortal "Rumble" (1347). The loss of the Everlys, however, saw Cadence's period of greatest importance begin to fade. Lenny Welch, signed amid high hopes in 1960, would take three years to score his first major hit,

TEN TOP COLLECTIBLES

Everly Brothers

"Cathy's Clown" (UK Warner Brothers WB 1—78, 1960)

Fabulous Style of the Everly Brothers (Cadence CLP 25040—Maroon-label LP, 1960)

It's Everly Time! (WB PRO 134—Promo LP, 1960)

"Keep a-Lovin' Me" (Columbia 21496—7-inch, 1956)

"Let It Be Me" (Cadence 1376—7-inch, picture sleeve, 1959)

"Lucille" (UK Warner Bros WB 19—78, 1960)

"So Sad" (WB 5163—Gold-vinyl 7-inch promo, 1960)

The Everly Brothers (Cadence CLP 3003—Maroon-label LP, 1958)

"Wake Up Little Susie" (Cadence 1337—7-inch, picture sleeve, 1957)

"When Will I Be Loved" (UK London HLA 9157—78, 1960)

Ramsey Lewis' sixth Cadet LP.

1963's "Since I Fell for You" (1439), by which time Andy Williams, too, had departed. The Chordettes's day had finally come to an end; Tillotson was running out of steam.

A handful of hit reissues notwithstanding, by 1961–62, Cadence's biggest hit pop artists were Charlie McCoy (whose "Cherry Berry Wine"—1390—peaked at No. 99 on the *Billboard* chart), and Eddie Hodges, whose three singles included one, "I'm Gonna Knock on Your Door" (1397), that was later covered by Little Jimmy Osmond, and another, "Made to Love," that was written by the Everly Brothers.

Aware that the pop market was, for the moment, beyond Cadence's grasp, Bleyer launched the Candid jazz subsidiary in 1961 and concentrated on that. The following year he branched out even further, and released a comedy album, *The First Family* (3060/25060), a Grammy-winning spoof on the life of the Kennedy clan, performed by Vaughn Meader. It stormed to No. 1, the biggest success in Cadence's

entire history, and was still on the chart when a second volume, 3065/25065, was issued some nine months later, in August 1963. Almost as successful, this volume reached No. 4. Just three months later, however, Kennedy was assassinated, and suddenly, his private life was no longer such a laughing matter. Both *First Family* albums plunged from the chart that same week.

Although Bleyer maintained Cadence into summer 1964, he was clearly out of patience with the label's continued inability to compete in the pop marketplace. Finally, in September 1964, he announced the closure of the label, and retired from the music industry. The catalog was eventually sold to Andy Williams, who used it as the backbone of his own Barnaby label.

Cadet

Cadet was the identity chosen by the Chess brothers, following the loss of the Argo label name to Decca, in

1965. The label would exist for the next six years, before being consolidated into the Chess catalog, and should not be confused with the Cadet Concept label, Chess's psychedelic wing.

Cadet's LP catalog was, essentially, a musical and numerical continuation of Argo's 400 blues-pop and 700 jazz series. The latter, of course, was highlighted by the continued success of the Ramsey Lewis Trio—indeed, that outfit was responsible for Cadet's first collectible, almost immediately upon the label's inception, after its *The "In" Crowd* live LP (LPS 757) was inadvertently issued with an old Argo label.

The biggest smash, however, arrived via the very first Cadet release, *Bob Hope: On the Road to Vietnam* (LPS 4046), based on the Christmas 1964, show that Hope staged for US servicemen in Asia.

The 400 series was to survive just two years and a dozen more LPs, including releases by the Windjammers, Art Blakey, Shel Silverstein, Etta James, and Johnny Guitar Watson. In 1967 both series were consolidated into one numerical sequence. Jazz remained predominant, though the return (from Vee-Jay) of former Argo stars the Dells,

and the sequence of classic 45s launched by 1966's "Thinkin' About You" (5538), seemingly encouraged the label to broaden its LP policy. The Dells' *There Is* album (804) promptly rewarded them by spinning off an unprecedented six hit 45s—"Run for Cover" (5551), "O-O, I Love You" (5574), "There Is"/"Show Me" (5590), "Stay in My Corner" (5612), and "Wear It on Your Face" (5599).

There Is was issued alongside several volumes of even smoother soul, from the aptly named Soulful Strings, *Paint It Black* (776), *Groovin' With* (796), and *Another Exposure* (805). In truth, the Strings' forte offered little more than a skillful muzak variation on the day's top pop and rock hits, but their success was such that, over the next 12 months, they would issue both a Christmas collection (814) and a live album (820). The group's singles, in the meantime, included faithful renditions of "Paint It Black" (5559), "Dock of the Bay" (5607), and "I Wish It Would Rain" (5633).

Further extremely popular covers were delivered by Ramsey Lewis's 1969 album *Mother Nature's Son* (821). The previous year the Beatles had released *The*

TEN TOP COLLECTIBLES

Ramsey Lewis

Down to Earth (Mercury SR 60536—stereo LP, 1965)

Gentlemen of Jazz (Argo 627S—stereo LP, 1959)

Gentlemen of Swing (Argo 611S—stereo LP, 1959)

Hang on Ramsey! (Cadet LPS 761—stereo LP, 1966)

"Hi Heel Sneakers" (Cadet 5531—7-inch, 1966)

"Just Can't Give You Up" (Columbia 10937—12-inch single, 1979)

"Santa Claus is Coming to Town" (Cadet 5377—7-inch, 1966)

Sound of Christmas (Argo EP 1084—EP, 1961)

The "In" Crowd (Cadet LPS 757 with Argo label—LP, 1965)

"Upendo Ni Pamoja" (Columbia CQ 31096—quad LP, 1972)

Beatles double album, a set that prompted one section of their audience to call it a masterpiece, and the other to write it off as being one full LP too long.

Whether Lewis agreed with that latter opinion or not is immaterial; *Mother Nature's Son* does, however, serve up one view of what might constitute a "best of" *The Beatles,* being made up exclusively of songs drawn from that album. It is a sad quirk of history that many sources cite Booker T. and the MGs' *McLemore Avenue* tribute to *Abbey Road* as the first full-blooded re-creation of an original Beatles LP. Lewis not only did it a year before, many listeners would argue that he did it better as well.

Tributes were apparently in vogue. Just weeks after Lewis's effort, Odell Brown issued the *Plays Otis Redding* set (823); soon after, Etta James released her *Sings Funk* (832), and a year later, Soulful Strings cut its final album, a tribute to Philly songwriters Gamble and Huff (846).

Cadet ceased to exist as a separate entity in 1971, issuing just a handful of releases in that year, including the sixth and final release by Rotary Connection, transferred from Cadet Concept. With, perhaps, the merest hint of irony, the label's final album release was the Eddie Fisher Quintet's *The Next 100 Years* (848).

Further Reading: *Spinning Blues into Gold: The Chess Brothers and the Legendary Chess Records,* by Nadine Cohodas (St. Martin's Press, 2000)

Cadet Concept

The Chess subsidiary Cadet Concept was launched in December 1967, as an outlet for the new rock sounds sweeping the music industry of the day. Indeed, the label was to be introduced with a brand new act, the Rotary Connection, whose live show, Marshall Chess told *Billboard,* employed "psychedelic effects and even smells."

Released in March 1968, the LP *Rotary Connection* (LPS 312) was indeed as fascinating as Chess had promised it would be. The six-strong vocal frontline featured the then-unknown Minnie Riperton and Sidney Barnes, accompanying musicians included the Chicago Symphony string section, and the

artwork included a small photograph of marijuana—which promptly led department store Sears to blacklist the record until an alternative sleeve design was presented.

Of course it was, and with a new picture of an unknown hippie imposed over the offending weed, *Rotary Connection* went on to become a Top 30 hit, and the Chess group's fourth-biggest hit of the year, behind Ramsey Lewis, Ahmad Jamal, and Soulful Strings. Copies of the original sleeve are very seldom encountered and are regarded as Cadet Concept's greatest rarity.

Despite the success of *Rotary Connection,* 45s from the album, including versions of "Like a Rollin' Stone" (7000) and "Ruby Tuesday" (7002), were less fortunate. Indeed, of ten singles released by the group (including one under the name the New Rotary Connection—"Hey Love" 7028), just one would threaten the chart. In 1970 "Want You to Know" (7018) reached No. 96. Four further Cadet Concept albums (and a fifth on Cadet), also proved unable to match the band's debut performance.

Cadet Concept's other major hope was Status Quo, a British band recruited from Chess's UK distributor, Pye. "Pictures of Matchstick Men" (7001), the band's first 45, was a delightful slice of psychedelic whimsy that deservedly soared up both the UK and US charts; a second single, "Ice in the Sun" (7005), also hit, but whereas Status Quo was to become one of the longest running and most successful bands in British chart history, that was the end of its American hit career. Three further Cadet Concept 45s, including a devilish cover of the Everly Brothers' "Price of Love" (7015), flopped, while a solitary LP, *Messages from the Status Quo* (LPS 315), vanished swiftly.

No other Cadet Concept act enjoyed even a fraction of the success of these first releases, though the LPs are, without exception, eminently collectible today. These include sets by Muddy Waters, Howlin' Wolf, psychedelic favorites Aesop's Fables, Joel Vance, and Archie Whitewater. It's worth keeping an eye out for the effervescent *Salloom, Sinclair and the Mother Bear,* by Roger Salloom and Robin Sinclair (LPS 316), and John Klemmer's minor hit *Blowin' Gold* (LPS 321).

TEN TOP COLLECTIBLES

Status Quo

"Black Veils of Melancholy" (Cadet Concept 7015—7-inch, 1969)

Dog of Two Heads (Pye 3301—LP, 1971)

"In My Chair" (UK Pye 7N 17998—7-inch, picture sleeve, 1970)

"Jealousy" (Ireland Vertigo QUO 9—7-inch promo, 1982)

Ma Kelly's Greasy Spoon (Janus JLS 3018—LP, 1970)

Messages from the Status Quo (UK Pye NPL 18220—Mono LP, 1968)

"Pictures of Matchstick Men" (Cadet Concept 7001—7-inch, 1968)

"Roadhouse Blues" (UK Phonogram DJ 005—7-inch promo, 1972)

Spare Parts (UK Pye NPL 18301—Mono LP, 1969)

"Technicolor Dreams" (UK Pye 7N 17650—Withdrawn 7-inch, 1969)

Cadet Concept closed in 1971, after just 19 albums and 30 singles.

Further Reading: *Spinning Blues into Gold: The Chess Brothers and the Legendary Chess Records,* by Nadine Cohodas (St. Martin's Press, 2000)

Cameo-Parkway

The Philadelphia-based Cameo and Parkway labels were among the staples of the late-'50s and early-'60s American pop scene, home to the clean-cut likes of the Rays (whose "Silhouettes"—Cameo 117—was the label's first major hit in 1957), Bobby Rydell, Dee Dee Sharp, and the Orlons, and the source of a magnificent stream of 45s, almost all of which are in heavy demand by modern collectors.

The label's LP output, too, is legendary, opening in 1958 with *An Adventure in Hi-Fi Music,* by *Today* TV host Dave Garroway (1001—a decade later, Ed McMahon would also release an album on the label, 2009). Sets by Denise Darcel, the Imaginary Five, Dave Appell, Bernie Leighton, and Jack Wiegand followed in the years before Rydell burst onto the scene; among the titles thereafter, a sequence of 1961–62 LPs immortalizing the great dances of the day is especially noteworthy.

Meyer Davis Plays the Twist (1014), the Carroll Brothers' *College Twist Party* (1015), and the various-artists set *12 Top Teen Dances 1961–1962* (1016) are all collector favorites today, with the latter an especially desirable piece. Comprising such Cameo-Parkway gems as the Dovells, the Apple Jacks, the Dreamlovers, and of course, Chubby Checker—the man who set the country twisting in the first place—the album is both a fascinating period piece and a crash course into the brilliance of the Cameo family.

Dee Dee Sharp arrived at Cameo in early 1962, fresh from duetting on Chubby Checker's "Slow Twist" 45 for Parkway, and armed with a dance craze of her own, the "Mashed Potato" (212). "Gravy (For My Mashed Potatoes)" followed, and Sharp's debut album promised, quite logically, *It's Mashed Potato Time* (1018). Later in her career, Sharp would incite America to "Do the Bird" (244); however, she also cut

TEN TOP COLLECTIBLES

? and the Mysterians

Action (Cameo C2006—Mono LP, 1967)

"Can't Get Enough of You Baby" (Cameo 467—7-inch, 1967)

"Funky Lady" (Luv 159—7-inch, 1975)

"Girl" (Cameo 479—7-inch, 1967)

"Hang In" (Super K 102—7-inch, 1969)

"I Need Somebody" (Cameo 441—7-inch, 1966)

"Make You Mine" (Capitol 2162—7-inch, 1970)

96 Tears (Cameo C2004—Mono LP, 1966)

"96 Tears" (Pa-Go-Go 102—7-inch, 1965)

"Talk Is Cheap" (Chicory 410—7-inch, 1968)

a number of non-locomotive 45s, and continued scoring hits into 1965.

The Orlons also proved to have considerably more staying power than the dance that brought them, too, to prominence, summer 1962's "The Wah Watusi" (218). The Cameo-Parkway set-up's earlier pre-eminence was, however, slipping, and attempts to leap aboard other passing bandwagons met with little success. The interestingly named Three Young Men from Montana made a gallant stab at catching the folk train with, indeed, *Folk Song Favorites* (1025); Eddie Greensleeves followed suit with *Humorous Folk Songs* (1031), and Sunny Schwartz went so far as to raid the same traditional repertoire as Joan Baez and the grittier protest singers for *Sunny's Gallery of Folk Ballads* (1030).

By late 1963, the label's most consistent releases were hits collections for Rydell, Sharp, and the Orlons, interspersed with collections of Hawaiian, organ, camping, cowboy, and orchestral pop music, and annual "biggest hit of the year" releases from, again, Rydell. Among these, "Magic Star," from *All the Hits Vol-*

ume Two (1040) is avidly sought by fans of English producer Joe Meek, being a lyrical version of the Telstars' instrumental "Telstar," otherwise available only on one of Meek's own scarcer productions, by Kenny Hollywood.

There were some inspired releases, of course. The demise of the Dovells in 1963 deprived Parkway of one of its most consistent hit-makers, but when vocalist Len Barry launched a solo career at Decca, Cameo was on the ball immediately, releasing the *Len Barry Sings with the Dovells* collection (1082).

Another fascinating release is 1964's *You Be a Disc Jockey* album (1075), a so-called instructional record that offered, on side one, an entertaining re-creation of a radio broadcast, complete with jingles, weather reports, time checks, commercials, and interviews (with Rydell and Sharp), all conducted by a real live DJ. Flip the disc, and the exact same recording is repeated, this time without the DJ. A script booklet allows the listener to fill in the gaps.

Needless to say, the disc's collectibility is most dependent on the presence of that booklet, but even without it the album offers an entertaining glimpse into the world of radio in the last days before the British invaded.

For perhaps the first time in its history, Cameo was surprisingly slow to recognize the impact of the new musical climate. Only one Invasion-era band had an impact on the label, the minor-league Ivy League, whose "Tossing and Turning" (377) limped to No. 83 in late 1965, despite its being bolstered by an LP of the same name (2000). Indeed, with so little action on the hit singles front, Cameo and Parkway alike were slowly sinking into a quagmire from which neither new owner Allen Klein, nor a freak No. 1 by Michigan garage punks ? and the Mysterians, "96 Tears" (428), could extract them.

Collectors, on the other hand, salivate over the two albums that the band issued on the now-conjoined Cameo-Parkway label in 1966 and 1967, *96 Tears* (C2004) and *Action* (C2007), while the absorption of the Lucky Eleven label brought another future garage rarity to the party, *Reflections*, by Terry Knight and the Pack (2007—also Lucky Eleven SLE 8000). Label VP Neil Bogart was largely responsible for these final oases of brilliance in the catalog.

Following a rare hit with Ohio Express's "Beg Borrow and Steal" (483), Cameo-Parkway moved to MGM for distribution in 1967. A second Ohio Express single, "Try It" (2001), debuted the deal, but the new arrangement was very much a last hurrah. Two final albums appeared in 1967, by Ohio Express (20,000) and the Village Stompers (20,001); the label then lay fallow for several years, before being reborn as Klein's ABKCO (Allen B. Klein Company).

Capricorn

The Capricorn label was one of the enduring successes of the so-called Southern-rock movement of the early '70s, not only pioneering the boom in the first place, but outliving it by several years. Though only the label's first years truly excite collector interest today, the entire catalog pursues the multitudinous strands of the genre to the very end of the 1970s, with a host of genuinely intelligent CD releases now appearing to both upgrade and enlarge many of Capricorn's original releases.

The label was the brainchild of Phil Walden, manager of R&B singers Otis Redding, Percy Sledge, and Sam and Dave. In 1967, Walden approached Atlantic Records to help finance a recording studio in his Macon, Ga., hometown; the label suggested he form a record label instead, and in 1969, Capricorn was launched with two signings, Johnny Jenkins and a band formed by Muscle Shoals studio guitarist Duane Allman and his brother Gregg, the Allman Brothers.

Under the terms of the Atlantic deal, the first Capricorn LPs were released through Atco, bearing that label's catalog numbers and label, with mention of Capricorn confined to the LP jacket alone. The first three Allman Brothers albums, including the breakthrough *At Fillmore East* (SD 2-802) double live album, were issued in this fashion, together with sets by Jenkins (33-331), Livingston Taylor (33-334), and Cowboy (33-351). In addition, a back-to-back reissue of the first two Allman albums appeared on Atco (with no reference to Capricorn whatsoever), as 1973's *Beginnings* (SD 2-805).

In 1971, Atco gave Capricorn its own numbering system and label, an arrangement debuted by Alex Taylor's *With Friends and Neighbors* (860). Wet Willie, Jonathan Edwards, and further sets by Livingston Taylor and Cowboy followed, before the new year saw Capricorn shift from Atco to Warner Bros. for distribution.

The first major hit under the new regime was the Allmans' *Eat a Peach* (CP 0102); other popular releases followed from Captain Beyond, White Witch, Wet Willie, Maxayn, and the Marshall Tucker Band, but even this early, it was clear that nothing was going to challenge the Allmans' supremacy, as 1973's *Brothers and Sisters* (CP 0111) LP topped the US chart, and the group co-headlined the massive Watkins Glen festival, in front of an crowd estimated to number half a million.

Such vast success notwithstanding, one of the few true rarities in the Capricorn catalog dates from this period, a flexidisc presented with *Rolling*

TEN TOP COLLECTIBLES

Allman Brothers

"Ain't Wastin' Time No More" (Capricorn 0003—7-inch, 1972)

The Allman Brothers at Fillmore East (Nautilus NR 3—Audiophile 2-LP, 1982)

Beginnings (Atco SD 2-805—2-LP, 1973)

Early Allman—The Allman Joys (Dial 6005—LP, 1973)

Eat a Peach (Mobile Fidelity 1-157—Audiophile LP, 1984)

"Heartbeat"—The Hour Glass (Liberty 56002—7-inch, 1967)

The Hour Glass—The Hour Glass (Liberty LST 7536—Stereo LP, 1967)

"Morning Dew"—Duane and Gregg Allman (Bold 200—7-inch, 1973)

"Ramblin' Man" (Rolling Stone/Capricorn—Flexidisc, 1975)

"Spoonful"—The Allman Joys (Dial 4046—7-inch, 1966)

Stone magazine, featuring tracks from the then-forthcoming *Brothers and Sisters* and the first album by the Marshall Tucker Band (CP 0112).

With the Allmans now embarking on what amounted to a two-year sabbatical, punctuated by solo activity, Capricorn moved into a period of uncertainty and confusion. Gregg Allman's *Laid Back* (CP 0116) solo set was a Top 20 hit in late 1973, but it would be close to a year before Capricorn returned to the chart, this time with fellow Allman Dickey Betts's *Highway Call* (CP 0123).

Another year, and 31 LP releases, would elapse before the Allmans' *Win Lose or Draw* album broke another hitless sequence—before the band itself shattered.

This lack of mainstream chart success is no reflection, of course, on the quality of Capricorn releases throughout this period—career-best sets from Marshall Tucker, Martin Mull, and White Witch were joined by spellbinding label debuts by Hydra, Elvin Bishop, and Grinderswitch, while 1974 saw soul veteran Percy Sledge arrive at Capricorn with the LP *I'll Be Your Everything* (CP 1047). Of course it doesn't

measure up to his classic '60s material, but it was a great listen regardless. Other new arrivals during this period included Bonnie Bramlett, Dobie Gray, and John Hammond.

Following the Allman Brothers' split, Capricorn released two archive projects, the "best of" set *The Road Goes On Forever* (2CP 0164), a double album reissued in admirably expanded (two-CD) form in 2002, and the live *Check the Windows* collection. Sales were disappointing, however, while a change in distribution, to Phonogram, did not reignite Capricorn's fortunes. Neither did the label's latest signings achieve much, and that despite including the likes of Dixie Dregs, Billy Joe Shaver, Sea Level (featuring several former Allman musicians), Billy Thorpe, Priscilla Coolidge-Jones (sister of Rita and wife of Booker T.), and the now-veteran (but still vital) Black Oak Arkansas.

The Allmans' 1979 reunion did bring back at least a taste of the good times, but the following year saw Capricorn declare bankruptcy. The label's last taste of chart action came with Delbert McClinton's *Keeper of the Flame* LP (CPN 0223); the last release, oddly appropriately, was Sea Level's *Long Walk on a Short Pier* (CPN 0227).

It would be a decade before Walden resurrected the label, distributed again by Warner Bros., but based in Nashville. Athens jam band Widespread Panic launched the rebirth in 1991 with a self-titled debut album (9 10001-2); subsequent releases included Col. Bruce Hampton and the Aquarium Rescue Unit, the Zoo, Billy Burnette, 311, and the re-vitalized Lynyrd Skynyrd. Capricorn has also hosted a number of excellent archive exhumations of vintage labels Scepter, Fire/Fury, Cobra, Jewel/Paula, and Swingtime, while also undertaking a massive re-evaluation of its own archive, courtesy of its current co-owners and distributors, Universal.

Carrere

Producer Claude Carrere launched the French-based Carrere during the mid-'70s. Distributed by Atco (EMI in the UK), the label enjoyed considerable European success toward the end of the decade, with a sharp ear for disco-flavored pop. South Africa's Clout scored a UK hit in 1978 with "Substitute" (2788—the single was issued by Epic in the US). Sheila (of B. Devotion fame) was also a Carrere artist, and the label's first US LP, issued within Atco's 38-100 series, was her *King of the World* (SD 38-124). Carrere also distributed the German Hansa label, home of Boney M.

The early '80s saw the label's focus shift to the so-called New Wave of British Heavy Metal (NWoBHM). Eponymous US sets by Stingray (SD 38-127) and Rage (WTG 19310) are much sought after. Carrere's most lasting success, however, came with Saxon. Its *Wheels of Steel* (SD 38-126) is a much-sought-after US release; four subsequent albums were the label's only other US releases.

Carrere's UK profile is considerably higher. Another NWoBHM stalwart, Scorched Earth, released a very scarce 12-inch single on the label, "Tomorrow Never Comes" (CART 342), while the Rage catalog includes a plethora of limited-edition scarcities—a 10-inch red-vinyl pressing of its "Money" debut single (CAR 159CT), a 12-inch yellow-vinyl "Out of Control" (CAR 182CT), and a picture disc of

"Bootliggers" (CAR 199P), together with three in-demand LPs.

Saxon collectors are tempted by a 12-inch pressing of "747" (CAR 151), picture discs of "And the Bands Played On" (CAR 180P) and "Nightmare" (CAR 284P), as well as an autographed picture disc for "The Power and the Glory" (SAXON 1)—this latter appeared in a limited edition of just 600 copies. Three Saxon LPs were also issued as picture discs.

Around these high-profile releases, Carrere maintained a steady stream of releases that can generally be written off as uncollectible pap; one notable exception is the first and only album by Fatal Charm (later to become the techno-figurehead group State of Grace), *Endangered Species I* (CAL 218).

Challenge

The Challenge label, formed in 1957 by Joe Johnson, Bernie Solomon, Johnny Thompson, and though his involvement was short-lived, Western movie star Gene Autry, is best remembered for hitting with the Champs's immortal "Tequila" (1016) in 1958. However, over a decade-plus of releases, the label was also responsible for some sterling releases by country star Jerry Wallace, surf sensations Jan and Dean, Jerry Fuller, the Peanut Butter Conspiracy, the mysteriously named El Clod, and Jimmy Seals and Dash Crofts, during their time with the Champs, and in Seals' case, as a solo artist immediately thereafter.

Of the label's LP output, the Champs releases are the most collectible of the early issues. Their *Go Champs Go* (CHL 601) debut was Challenge's second album release, following Gene Autry's 1957 *Christmas With* collection (CHL 600), and it was swiftly succeeded by now-overlooked titles by the Buddy Colette Quartet, the Gerald Wiggins Trio, and Henry Mancini.

The Champs's *Everybody's Rockin'* (CHL 605/ CHS 2500) became Challenge's first stereo LP in 1959; stereo would be used with increasing regularity through the early '60s, with Diane Maxwell and the Ray De Michel Orchestra early beneficiaries of the technology. Without exception, early Challenge stereo is hotly pursued today, with first pressings readily identifiable by the label design and coloring: The first Challenge monaural label was blue with silver printing, and the letters GA (for Gene Autry) in a crest above the Challenge logo. Stereo releases were black with silver printing, with both changing to blue-green and silver printing in 1964. Red-and-silver labels are Canadian pressings.

With the label's chart success almost wholly confined to just two acts, the Champs and Jerry Wallace, this pair inevitably dominate the LP release schedule—the Champs cut four albums, Wallace five. However, the surf boom rejuvenated Challenge, with Jan and Dean's brief tenure being followed by the arrival of the Rhythm Rockers. The latter's *Soul Surfin'* album (CHL-617/CHS-2517) and "Rendezvous Stomp" 45 (9196) are among the great unsung gems of the age.

Jan and Dean's "Heart and Soul" (9111), their label debut, in 1961, was one of just two singles the duo cut, its attraction being furthered by the existence of two separate pressings, the first featuring the B-side "Those Words," the second backed by "Midsummer Night's Dream." Gary Usher and the Four Speeds'

"RPM" (9187) and "Four on the Floor" (9202) are also much sought after by fans of the motorvatin' hot-rod theme that dominated California pop in the pre-Beatles era.

The then-prevalent craze for albums that gave the listener the opportunity to try his or her hand at such glamorous pursuits as deejaying and pop singing produced one of Challenge's finest curios, *Sing and Sync Along with Lloyd Thaxton/Lloyd Thaxton Presents the Knickerbockers* (12664). Thaxton was host of an eponymous music show that was notable for its practice of allowing both host and audience to lip-sync along with the day's biggest hits. This album took the pastime into the home, as the Knickerbockers (occasionally aided by singer Phyllis Brown) performed their own versions of sundry songs, with extended instrumental passages at the end of each one.

The New Jersey–based Knickerbockers would prove one of Challenge's most prolific acts during the mid-'60s, with a dozen singles (including the classic "Bite Bite Barracuda"—59268) and two further LPs to their credit. They scored just three hits, however, with only 1965's "Lies" (59321) making the Top 20.

TEN TOP COLLECTIBLES

The Champs

All American Music from the Champs (Challenge 2514—Stereo LP, 1962)

"Anna" (Challenge 59322—7-inch, 1965)

Everybody's Rockin' with the Champs (Challenge CHL 605—LP, 1959)

Go Champs Go (Challenge CHL 601—Blue-vinyl LP, 1958)

Great Dance Hits (Challenge 613—LP, 1962)

"Hokey Pokey" (Challenge 59103—7-inch, 1961)

"Tequila" (Challenge 1016—Blue-vinyl 7-inch, 1958)

"Tequila 76" (Republic 246—7-inch, picture sleeve, 1976)

"Tequila 77" (We're Back 1—7-inch, 1977)

"Turnpike" (Challenge 59026—7-inch, 1958)

Also collectible is the Pacific Northwest band the Accents, whose "Tell Me" single (originally issued on Commerce—5012) was released twice by Challenge in 1965 (1112) and (9294).

Another Thaxton discovery, which he presented on a Challenge LP, was Round Robin, whose early career on Domain spawned a hit remake of Harry Belafonte's "Kick That Little Foot, Sally Ann" (1404). The group's Challenge career was less well-starred, but did include the album *Lloyd Thaxton Presents the Land of 1000 Dances Featuring Round Robin* (CHL-620/CHS-2520).

Challenge released little of note through much of the remainder of the decade—1966 brought a short-lived (one single—59339) fling with the Great Scots, but material recorded by the band during their Challenge era would remain unreleased for almost 30 years. Knickerbockers material, too, went unreleased before being scooped up by the Sundazed reissue label during the late '90s, while Challenge's one "name" arrival, the Peanut Butter Conspiracy, appeared some months after its sell-by date. The album *For Children of All Ages* (2000) and the single "Back in LA" (500) marked the group's last releases, in 1969—and were among Challenge's final issues for the best part of a decade.

The label re-emerged in 1977, concentrating on country music, but ceased operations a year later.

Charisma

Comedian Viv Stanshall memorably described the Charisma label—his home for two much-loved LPs issued between 1978 and 1981—as "biased, quirky, and pigheadedly eclectic," a delightfully affectionate summary of one of most avidly collected labels of the British 1970s. The brainchild (some said plaything) of Tony Stratton-Smith, former manager of such left-field talents as the Creation, the Nice, and another Stanshall project, the Bonzo Dog Doo Dah Band, Charisma debuted in 1969 with a 45 ("Sympathy"—CS 1005) and a self-titled album (CAS 1005) by Rare Bird, harbinger of the progressive boom that would be Charisma's chief source of sustenance through its first decade.

It is that ten-year span which most attracts collectors. Emblazoned first with a distinctive reddish-pink label, then with a riotous portrait of Lewis Carroll's Mad Hatter, the "classic" Charisma label brought Van Der Graaf Generator, Genesis, Lindisfarne, and the underrated but now-sought-after Audience to public attention. It also scored hits via schoolteacher Clifford T. Ward, TV comedy groups Monty Python's Flying Circus and String Driven Thing, and—again according to Stanshall—refused to consider any band unless Stratton-Smith personally liked it.

Pass that simple test and it didn't matter what anybody else thought, which possibly goes some way toward explaining the minuscule sales that consigned to absolute obscurity such modern collectibles as Genesis's "The Knife" (CB 152) and "Happy the Man" (CB 181—both released in limited-edition picture sleeves), Van Der Graaf's "Refugees" (CB 122) and "Theme One" (CB 175), Peter Hammill's "Birthday Special" (CB 245), and so many more.

With the exception of the label's acknowledged monster-hit singles (the first was Lindisfarne's "Meet Me on the Corner"—CB 173), Charisma singles seemed predestined to creep out when nobody was looking, then vanish before they were noticed. The fact that many of them boasted otherwise unavailable mixes or B-sides only adds to their attraction.

That Lindisfarne breakthrough packed two superb outtakes from the then-current *Fog on the Tyne* album (CAS 1050) onto its flip (and wrapped it all up in a great picture sleeve; both tracks later appeared as bonus tracks on the *Tyne* CD).

As late as 1975, Genesis's "Carpet Crawlers" (CB 251) passed unnoticed, despite boasting an unreleased live cut on the B-side, while even the band's first hit, "I Know What I Like" (CB 224), is avidly pursued for its own unique B-side, "Twilight Alehouse," an epic hitherto available only on a flexidisc presented free with *ZigZag* magazine the previous year. (These cuts, and other period rarities, have since been collected onto the *Genesis Archive Volume 1* box set—Atlantic 82858.)

Charisma LPs in general offer a similar challenge. Such one- or two- or occasionally three-album acts as

Atacama, Bell and Arc, Trevor Billmuss, Birth Control, Capability Brown, Darien Spirit, Doggerel Bank, the Group, Jo'Burg Hawk, and Andy Roberts have little name recognition today—the label is enough for many collectors. Albums by psychoanalyst R.D. Lang (*Life Before Death*—CAS 1141) and faith healer Gordon Turner (CAS 1009) fetch impressive sums for possibly obvious reasons, while occasional dips into classical and spoken-word waters are also popular.

First pressings on the original reddish-pink label (1969–71) are especially elusive, particularly when contemplating the likes of Genesis, whose Charisma catalog was re-pressed on several occasions during the early-to-mid-'70s—the group's first two albums for the label, *Trespass* (CAS 1020) and *Nursery Cryme* (CAS 1052), are extremely common with the Mad Hatter label design. Genesis serves up another challenge in the form of two two-LP box sets issued following the group's major breakthrough in 1975: the *Genesis Collection Volumes One and Two* (CGS 102/103) brought together all four of the band's Charisma studio albums to date, with a poster, and of course, a custom box. Find them if you can.

Genesis side projects, including Phil Collins' Brand X (he features on the group's debut, *Unorthodox Behaviour*—CAS 1117); Steve Hackett (1975's *Voyage of the Acolyte*—CAS 1111—was issued while he was still a member of the band); Mike Rutherford; and Tony Banks all have their adherents, while vocalist Peter Gabriel's solo career spun off several remarkable 45 rpm scarcities.

In 1976 space-rock veteran Hawkwind joined the label for three albums (four if you include the group's Hawklords alias) and three singles (five if you . . .); these include a now-elusive 12-inch single, "25 Years" (CD 332), issued on gray vinyl and mispressed on black. The band also spun off a major rarity as saxophonist Nik Turner launched his ancient Egyptian–themed Sphynx side project in 1978, and cut an album of meandering flute sounds. *Xitin Today* (CDS 4011) was utterly ignored at the time, but Turner's US revival during the early-to-mid-'90s saw values inflate dramatically.

Hawkwind was one of the last "classic" acts to join Charisma; collectors date the label's decline to 1976, when the Mad Hatter label slipped off the 45 output,

TEN TOP CHARISMA COLLECTIBLES

Genesis

"Carpet Crawlers" (Charisma CB 251—7-inch, 1975)

"Firth of Fifth" (Charisma/Lyntone 13143—Flexidisc, picture sleeve, 1983)

"Happy the Man" (UK Charisma CD 181—7-inch, picture sleeve, 1972)

"I Know What I Like" (Charisma 26002—7-inch, 1973)

"The Knife" (UK Charisma CB 152—7-inch, picture sleeve, 1970)

"Looking for Someone" (UK Charisma GS 1-2—7-inch promo, 1970)

"Man on the Corner" (Charisma CD 393—Blue-label 7-inch, picture sleeve, 1982)

"That's All" (Charisma TATA Y-1—7-inch picture disc, 1983)

"Twilight Alehouse" (Charisma/*ZigZag*, no catalog number—Flexidisc, 1973)

"Watcher of the Skies" (Charisma 103—7-inch, 1973)

to be replaced by the then-fashionable (and money-saving) generic-lettering-stamped-straight-onto-the-vinyl approach. (LPs, mercifully, maintained the Hatter.) Other new recruits, ranging from one-trick ponies like the Blue Max, the Scars, and the Desperadoes, to Adrian Wagner, Opposition, and Julian Lennon attracted attention but have failed to maintain any collecting impetus. A clutch of reggae signings were interesting, but strayed too far from the label's accepted parameters.

Stratton-Smith himself seemed to agree. Speaking shortly after he sold Charisma to Virgin Records in 1985, he admitted "I still loved the label, I still loved the bands. I just wasn't too impressed by the music anymore."

Further Reading: *The Famous Charisma Box: The History of Charisma Records 1968–85* (booklet within box set of the same name—Virgin CASBOX 1)

Charly

Possibly the best-known continental European label of them all, Jean-Luc Young's Charly label, established itself in 1974 with a string of archive releases, often involving some of the biggest names in 1960s pop in the earliest guises.

The label's first ten LP releases, 300-001–010, saw Charly propagating the classic Sun catalog years before either British or American labels saw fit to investigate—the sequence included titles by Jerry Lee Lewis, Carl Perkins, Charlie Rich, Johnny Cash, and Roy Orbison, while the label's ever-widening eye for super-rare rockabilly classics paid unexpected dividends in 1976, when Hank Mizell's "Jungle Rock," one of Charly's infrequent 45 releases (CS 1005), reached No. 3 in the UK.

Another early tie-up with producer Giorgio Gomelsky produced collections showcasing previously unreleased, or mind-bendingly rare, material by such British '60s stalwarts as the Animals, the Yardbirds, Brian Auger and Julie Driscoll, Rod Stewart (as a member of Steampacket), Gary Farr, Graham Bond, the Soft Machine, and even some early Gong. *Jam Session—Jimmy Page, Sonny Boy Williamson and Brian Auger* (300-011), a reissue of

the Marmalade label obscurity *Don't Send Me No Flowers,* was followed by first-ever glimpses of some truly breathtaking demos and outtakes by each of the above-named acts. These releases were numbered into the 300-020s and packaged in similarly designed sleeves, featuring drawn portraits of the featured artists.

Controversy over the legitimacy of many of Charly's releases tends to mar the label's collectible quotient, all the more so since the label's ruthless repackaging policy has seen similar collections appear and reappear with almost mind-numbing regularity, not only on Charly but also via a slew of other labels. Packaging tends to be pedestrian, devoid of any but the most basic information (a failing mercifully amended by modern CD releases), and it is easy to overlook Charly vinyl in the hope or belief that the same material will appear with better annotation elsewhere. Some has, but much remains shrouded in exactly the same cobwebs, no matter who is behind it.

The Charly CD catalog is vast and has attracted little of the attention adhering to the vinyl issues. As a collecting tool, however, the label's compilations focusing on classic bands and legendary record labels alike have seldom been bettered.

Checker

Chess's Checker subsidiary existed for 14 years, 1957–71, during which time it was responsible for a host of classic, and extremely desirable, blues 45s and albums. All are collectible, but whereas the 78s and 45s tend to turn up fairly regularly, early Checker LPs can prove very elusive.

Early LP releases, which shared the parent label's then-current numbering system, included sets by Little Walter (1428—the first Checker issue), Dale Hawkins (the classic *Oh Suzie Q*—1429), Bo Diddley, the Flamingos, and Sonny Boy Williamson. Finally granted its own identity in 1959, Checker immediately made a splash with multicolored vinyl promo editions of Tab Smith's *Keeping Tab* LP (2971) and the various-artists compilation *Love Those Goodies* (2973). These surface seldom enough to be regarded as near-myths within what is already a legendary catalog.

TEN TOP COLLECTIBLES

Checker

"Broken Heart"—Memphis Minnie (Checker 771—7-inch, 1953)

"Country Boogie"—Elmore James (Checker 777—7-inch, 1953)

"Darling I Know"—The El Rays (Checker 794—7-inch, 1954)

"It Must Have Been the Devil"—Otis Spann (Checker 807—7-inch, 1954)

"I Was a Fool to Love You"—The Teasers (Checker 800—Red-vinyl 7-inch, 1954)

"Juke"—Little Walter (Checker 758—Red-vinyl 7-inch, 1952)

"Off the Wall"—Little Walter (Checker 770—Red-vinyl 7-inch, 1953)

"Tired of Crying over You"—Morris Pejoe (Checker 766—Red-vinyl 7-inch, 1953)

"When I Look at You"—The Encores (Checker 760—7-inch, 1953)

"White Cliffs of Dover"—The Blue Jays (Checker 782—7-inch, 1953)

The most prolific Checker artist during the early '60s was Bo Diddley, though the label was not to be left behind by the various dance crazes of the age. The Vibrations issued a celebration of the *Watusi* (2978), Steve Alaimo weighed in with both *Twist With...* (2981) and *Mashed Potatoes* (2983), and Diddley himself issued *Bo Diddley's a Twister* (2982), a set subsequently reissued as *Roadrunner.* Other topical Diddley LPs included *Surfin' with Bo Diddley* (2987) and *Beach Party* (2988). Similar machinations were doubtless at work on the *Two Great Guitars* (2991) collaboration with Chuck Berry—the opening cut was titled "Liverpool Drive."

Joe Tex (en route to his domination of Atlantic's Dial subsidiary catalog), Gene Barge, Little Milton, and Fontella Bass represented the best of Checker during 1965–66, while the label also produced a string of classic reissues from Checker's earliest catalog. By the end of the decade, however, only Little Milton and the ubiquitous Diddley were still recording regularly, and following a final flurry of releases by newcomers Stan Farlow; Jimmy Reeves, Jr.; and Ray Scott, Checker closed in 1971.

Further Reading: *Spinning Blues into Gold: The Chess Brothers and the Legendary Chess Records,* by Nadine Cohodas (St. Martin's Press, 2000)

Chess

One of the most legendary, and certainly among the most evocative, of all American record labels, Chess is also, arguably, the most avidly collected label of the 1950s and 1960s. Its roster is a veritable who's who of the blues, and rather than document the artists whose material is regarded as collectible, it would probably be easier to note those who aren't. It would be a ridiculously short list.

The British Invasion was largely fueled by the importance of Chess—according to legend, future Rolling Stones Keith Richards and Brian Jones were introduced by a copy of Muddy Waters' *Best Of* LP (LP 1427)—Richard had a copy, and Jones wanted to know where he got it. They formed the band soon after, and named it for another Waters song, the B-side of his first-ever Chess 78. Elsewhere around the UK, so many other bands cut their teeth on the Chess catalog that you could create the most star-studded tribute imaginable to the label, without ever leaving the British-beat boom.

Chess grew out of brothers Leonard and Philip Chess's involvement with the Aristocrat label, formed by Charles and Evelyn Aron, in Chicago, in 1947. Prior to this, the brothers (Polish immigrants who arrived in the city in 1928) had operated the Macomba nightclub, specializing of course in blues. It was their dissatisfaction with the recordings then being made of these performers that first prompted them to make records themselves.

Aristocrat released a number of seminal records, including issues by bandleader Sherman Hayes, the singularly named Wyoma, Billy Orr and Andrew Tibbs and Jump Jackson, plus several hits by Muddy Waters. When the brothers bought out their partners' interest in Aristocrat and relaunched the label as Chess in 1950, Waters automatically became the new label's first superstar—but not its first release. That honor was reserved for saxophonist Gene Ammons' "My Foolish Heart" (1425), with Waters' "Walkin' Blues"/"Rollin' Stone" (1426) following soon after.

Others, however, soon followed—Howlin' Wolf was licensed from Memphis record producer Sam Phillips (later to launch his own Sun label); Little Walter was drawn from Muddy Waters' band, Sonny Boy Williamson, Lowell Fulson, Memphis Slim, Jimmy Rogers, and John Lee Hooker all followed, while the arrival of Chuck Berry in 1955 brought Chess its first consistent hit-maker. Beginning with "Maybellene" (1604) and "Roll Over Beethoven" (1626), credited to Chuck Berry and His Combo, the young St. Louis native would notch up 25 Top 100 hits over the next decade.

More importantly, however, he did so with songs that would help define rock 'n' roll—"School Day" (1653), "Sweet Little Sixteen" (1683), "Johnny B. Goode" (1691), "Carol" (1700), and so many more. Berry even delivered Chess's final chart-topper, when the ribald "My Ding-a-Ling" (2131) went to No. 1 on both sides of the Atlantic, in late 1972. The majority of Berry's releases are not especially rare, even in 78 form. But they are extraordinarily desirable.

In 1956, Chess released its first long-playing records, initially on the Argo subsidiary. The debut Chess release was the teen-sploitation movie soundtrack *Rock, Rock, Rock* (1425), widely regarded as the first-ever release in that field. Chuck Berry's *After School Session* (1426) and the aforementioned Muddy Waters compilation followed, though just nine Chess LPs were issued before the end of the decade (six further LPs within the same 1400 numbering system, were issued by Checker).

Among these, the most sought after are the Moonglows' *Look* (1430), Berry's *One Dozen Berrys* (1432) and *On Top* (1435), Howlin' Wolf's *Moanin' in the Moonlight* (1434), and a pair of compilations, *Oldies in Hi Fi* (1439) and *A Bunch of Goodies* (1441). The rare promotional copies of this latter brace, incidentally, were issued on multicolored vinyl.

Chess's impact was not limited to the Chicago-Mississippi blues scene. A number of artists were recruited from the fertile melting pot of New Orleans, including Clarence "Frogman" Henry. Argo proved as influential in jazz circles as Chess and the Checker imprint were in the blues; while the vocal groups the Flamingos and the Moonglows both brought further renown to the Chess family, even though it took white-cover versions to popularize their biggest hits—the Moonglows' "Sincerely" (1581) and the Flamingos' "I'll Be Home" (Checker 830). An extensive line of religious and gospel releases also has a fervent following among modern collectors.

The arrival, from the King label, of A&R director Ralph Bass enabled the Chess group to add R&B and soul to its repertoire, via Etta James (at Argo, and later both Cadet and Chess); the Dells (Cadet); Billy Stewart (a former member of Bo Diddley's band, who cut singles for Argo and Chess in 1956, then returned to Chess in 1962 for a run of solid soul hits); Fontella Bass (Checker); and others.

Chess remained a major force in American music through the late '60s, with the roster constantly reflecting the changing local scene. Among the most in-demand later releases is an album by Canadian psychedelic band the Baroques (1516). As the decade ended, however, a succession of key personnel

TEN TOP COLLECTIBLES

Chess

"All Night Long"—Muddy Waters (Chess 1509—7-inch, 1952)

"Booted"—Roscoe Gordon (Chess 1487—7-inch, 1951)

"Cool Off Baby"—Billy Barrix (Chess 1662—7-inch, 1958)

"High Priced Woman"—John Lee Hooker (Chess 1505—7-inch, 1951)

"In My Real Gone Rocket"—Jackie Brenston (Chess 1469—7-inch, 1951)

"Juiced"—Jackie Brenston (Chess 1472—7-inch, 1951)

"Let It Rock"—Chuck Berry (Chess 1747—78, 1960)

"Rocket 88"—Jackie Brenston (Chess 1458—7-inch, 1951)

"Sugar Mama"—John Lee Hooker (Chess 1513—7-inch, 1952)

"Walkin' Blues"—Muddy Waters (Chess 1426—78, 1950)

changes saw the label's once intuitive understanding of the music decay. The death of Leonard Chess in October 1969, shortly after he and Phil sold the label to General Recorded Tape, was another major blow, and by mid-1972, the label barely functioned anymore. Even the massive success of "My Ding-a-Ling" sounded a hollow ring; even among die-hard Berry aficionados, few would claim the song to be one of Chess's finest releases.

Chess finally closed its doors in August 1975, with the rights to the catalog sold to All Platinum. It is now held by Universal/MCA, which commenced a major reissue program during the 1980s.

Further Reading: *Spinning Blues into Gold: The Chess Brothers and the Legendary Chess Records,* by Nadine Cohodas (St. Martin's Press, 2000)

Chiswick

Like so many other indie labels, Chiswick Records was born out of a record store—or, in this case, a stall, set up in London's Soho Market, in 1974, by owner Ted Carroll. Rock On specialized in '50s rarities, though, for both Carroll and his assistant, Roger

Armstrong, the appeal of the music they sold was not only rooted in the wax.

They were also fascinated by the very mechanics of the industry back then, the way independent entrepreneurs could simply find a band, find a studio, find a pressing plant, and within a matter of weeks, take delivery of a box of hot vinyl—the same hot vinyl that now paid Rock On's expenses. In spring 1975, the pair decided to see if it could still be done.

The first act "signed" to the new Chiswick label was the Hammersmith Gorillas; with Brinsley Schwartz manager Dave Robinson engineering the session, Carroll and Armstrong took the Gorillas into a tiny studio above the Hope and Anchor pub and cut two songs—which promptly remained unreleased for another 25 years, finally appearing on the Gorillas anthology *Gorilla Got Me* (Chiswick WIKCD 185).

The first band to get a record out on Chiswick was the Count Bishops, fronted by a New Yorker named Mike Spenser; Chiswick launched with the *Speedball* EP (SW 1) in November 1975, a full eight months before engineer Robinson got his Stiff Records off the ground. The record did little in commercial terms, but its impact was immense nevertheless. The first true indie label to get off the ground in Britain in almost a decade, Chiswick would suddenly find itself ideally placed to take advantage of an entire subgenre of British rock, as the pub-rock boom of the past few years girded itself to become the punk rock of the future.

The Bishops and the Gorillas (finally uncaged on the "She's My Gal" 45—S4) were joined, in swift succession, by French rock group Little Bob Story; the 101ers—featuring a pre-Clash Joe Strummer and future Public Image Ltd. drummer Richard Dudanski; Radio Stars, formed by ex-members of Sparks and John's Children; Greta Garbage and the Trash Cans, who changed their name to the Radiators from Space, Ireland's first-ever punk band; and more.

EMI took over Chiswick's distribution in 1978, at a time when the independent's fortunes were approaching free fall. Despite a handful of chart successes, most notably courtesy of Radio Stars ("Nervous Wreck"—S23—was a spring 1978 Top 30 hit), Chiswick's finances were weakening, resulting in a slew of canceled releases. EMI's offer cut the last

links with the label's once stoutly defended independent roots, but brought Chiswick back to life.

Many collectors prefer to concentrate their efforts on releases predating this moment, the SW, S, and N series of singles (numbered 1–46, including ten unissued numbers), the CH and WIK series of LPs (17 titles out of 19 numbers). This period also includes the most elusive Chiswick collectors items—a 12-inch version of Motörhead's eponymous debut single (NS 13), a free single included within early copies of Radio Stars' debut album (WIK 5); a 6-inch "pocket size" pressing of the same band's "From a Rabbit" 45 (NS 36), and further bedeviling that same release, two different mixes of the B-side, distinguishable only by matrix number.

Under the EMI deal, singles and EPs were designated CHIS, LPs became CWK. Popular acts during this period included the Damned, Rocky Sharpe and the Replays, Sniff and the Tears, Whirlwind, Shane MacGowan's Nips, folk veteran Terry Wood and ex-Advert TV Smith's Explorers, whose "Tomahawk Cruise" single (CHIS 140) was originally issued on the Big Beat subsidiary, then transferred once chart success seemed imminent. In a cruel twist of fate, the

TEN TOP COLLECTIBLES

Chiswick

"Anti-Social"—Skrewdriver (Chiswick NS 18—7-inch, 1977)

"Brand New Cadillac"—Vince Taylor (Chiswick S2—7-inch, 1976)

"From a Rabbit"—Radio Stars (Chiswick NS 36—Hip-pocket disc, 1978)

I Wanna Be a Cosmonaut—Riff Raff (Chiswick SW 34—EP, 1978)

The Jook—The Jook (Chiswick NS 30—EP, 1978)

"Keys to Your Heart"—The 101ers (Chiswick S3—7-inch, 1976)

"Motörhead"—Motörhead (Chiswick S13—12-inch, 1977)

"Saints and Sinners"—Johnny and the Self Abusers (Chiswick NS 22—7-inch, 1977)

"Sex Cells"—The Table (Chiswick NS 31—7-inch, 1978)

"Television Screen"—Radiators from Space (Chiswick S10—7-inch, 1977)

The B-side of "Pleasant Valley Sunday," "Words" was a #11 hit.

record promptly dropped from its No. 105 peak and never recovered.

A new numbering sequence, DICE (45s) and TOSS (LPs), was introduced in 1982, with distribution now handled first by PRT, then by IDS. However, Chiswick folded in 1983, as Carroll and Armstrong made the decision to concentrate their attentions, and now-encyclopedic experience, on the music that had got them into the record-label business in the first place, a reissues-oriented label called Ace. Bowing out with Rocky Sharpe and the Replays' "La Bamba" (DICE 19), the Chiswick identity would now be preserved for reissues of its own, now equally proud, heritage.

Further Reading: *The Chiswick Story*, by Roger Armstrong (booklet within the two-CD box set of the same name—Chiswick CDWIK2 100-2)

Colgems

In 1966, Columbia Pictures' TV wing, Screen Gems, linked with RCA to create a new label, Colgems. The emphasis was to be on television and soundtrack recordings, and a number of fine, collectible releases would appear. To many people, however, the Colgems label means just one thing—the Monkees. The label debuted with the band's first single, 1966's "Last Train to Clarksville" (66-1001), closed following their last single, "Oh My My" (66-5011), and in between times, scored some of the most massive pop hits of the era—each one featuring Davy, Mickey, Mike, and Peter.

Collecting the Monkees is a relatively straight-forward task. The sheer enormity of their success ensures that only a handful of later 45s (beginning around the time of "Porpoise Song"—661031) are difficult to find; while all but a couple of the group's eight albums are so common that active specialization is required to unearth any special rarities—for example, copies of the multimillion-selling debut (COM/COS 101), which misspells "Papa Jean's Blues" as "Papa Gene's Blues"; or those early editions of *Headquarters* (COM/COS 103) that replace a photo

The Monkees

The Birds the Bees and the Monkees (Colgems COM 109—Mono LP, 1968)

"D. W. Washburn" (Colgems 66-1023—7-inch, picture sleeve, 1968)

Head (UK RCA 8051—Mono LP, 1969)

Headquarters (Colgems 103—LP, "beard" photo, 1967)

Instant Replay (UK RCA RD 8016—Mono LP, 1968)

"Last Train to Clarksville" (Colgems 66-1001—7-inch, picture sleeve, 1966)

The Monkees (Colgems COM 101—LP with "Papa Jean's Blues" misspelling, 1966)

The Monkees (UK Arista 112 157—10-inch EP, 1989)

"Oh My My" (Colgems 66-5011—7-inch, picture sleeve, 1970)

That Was Then, This Is Now (Arista 1-4 673—LP, four different picture discs, 1986)

of the album's producers, on the back sleeve of the first pressing, with one of the producers plus bearded Monkees. In terms of value, the difference between these editions is minimal . . . we're not talking the Beatles on Vee-Jay here. But it's a satisfying hunt.

The first five Monkees albums were issued in both stereo and mono, with the last in that sequence, *The Birds the Bees and the Monkees* (COM 109), simply offering a straightforward reduction of the stereo release. However, mono versions of the succeeding *Instant Replay* (COS 113) and *Head* (COSO 5008) appeared in the UK, where RCA carried the band's output, and can prove very difficult to hunt down. British fans also received one more single than their US counterparts, Mickey Dolenz's colloquially rich "Alternate Title." (UK RCA 1604—the "alternate title," incidentally, referred to Dolenz's original name for the song, "Randy Scouse Git," which translates roughly as "over-sexed idiot from Liverpool." That'll get the pop kids going.)

The success of the Monkees apparently kept Colgems busy enough through 1966–67 that it had no need to issue any other pop records and concentrated instead on the COS 5500 series of soundtracks. Toward the end of the year, however, releases from the Lewis and Clarke Expedition (featuring future country star Michael Murphy) and from Sally Field punctuated the gap between the Monkees' fourth album (COM/COS 104) and its fifth; and over the next three years, a handful more soundtracks appeared around the Monkee-business.

Nevertheless, when Colgems closed, in early 1971 (its catalog was absorbed into Bell records), the three final albums were *The Monkees Present* (COS 117—the first album by the Peter Tork–less trio), *Changes* (COS 119—by which time the group comprised Davy Jones and Mickey Dolenz alone), and the compilation *A Barrelful of Monkees* (SCOS 1001).

Colpix

A division of Columbia Pictures Corporation, Colpix Records was established in 1958, primarily as a vehicle for the parent company's movie- and TV-soundtrack output. However, the label's significance to soundtrack collectors is readily matched by its importance to rock and pop fans.

The Marcels, the "Blue Moon" hit-making group, were with Colpix throughout the early '60s, with "Blue Moon" itself (186) also titling the group's one and only LP (CP-416). In 1961 Ronnie and the Relatives, a New York girl group, released "I Want a Boy" (601), before changing their name to the Ronettes for two further singles—this early material was later gathered onto the album *The Ronettes Featuring Veronica* (SCP-486), and predates the group's discovery by producer Phil Spector. There were also albums by Duane Eddy, Sandy Stewart, Teddy Randazzo, Lou Christie, and Nina Simone.

The label's forte, however, were the aforementioned movie and TV spin-offs, but even here, the emphasis was on personality. Actor James Darren was an early star, scoring (as Jimmy Darren) with 1959's "Gidget" (113) and "Angel Face" (119), before "Goodbye Cruel World" (181, 609) brought him a Top Three hit in 1961. *The Donna Reed Show* stars Paul Petersen and Shelley Fabares scored further hits for the label in 1962, including Fabares' "Johnny Angel" (621), "Johnny Loves Me" (636), and "The Things We Did Last Summer" (654), as well as Petersen's "She Can't Find Her Keys" (620), "My Dad" (663), and "Amy" (676). Both also issued a pair of albums apiece; in addition, Fabares' "Football Season's Over" (721) was produced by Jan Berry of Jan and Dean. Woody Allen's first two albums are on Colpix (CP-518 and CP-488).

Future Monkee David Jones issued three Colpix singles in 1965: "Dream Girl" (764), "What Are We Going to Do" (784), and "The Girl From Chelsea" (789), plus an album, *David Jones* (SCP-493). Indeed, it was his presence within the Columbia stable that contributed most heavily to his selection for the Monkees.

In 1965, Columbia Pictures purchased Don Kirshner's Aldon Music publishing company and Dimension record label, closing Colpix shortly thereafter.

Cotillion

This much-loved Atlantic subsidiary came into being in 1964, as the label's publishing wing, following the sale of the earlier Progressive Music to Hill and Range. The record label itself launched in 1969, and while the majority of Cotillion's initial product was blues based, it soon became apparent that "Progressive" was not simply the name of its predecessor. With the signing of Emerson Lake and Palmer, Cotillion set itself at the forefront of the progressive musical boom.

Seldom-seen LPs by Brook Benton, Freddie King, Otis Rush, Lou Johnson, and the Dynamics rank among Cotillion's earliest releases; the first rock release was the Astro label release by Texas band Blackwell, featuring John "Rabbit" Bundrick, which bore the Cotillion catalog number SD 9010. The Fabulous Counts and Beast followed, before 1970 brought the much-loved *Lord Sutch and His Heavy Friends* (9015) album, featuring a reunion between veteran British shock-rocker Sutch and former bandmates Jimmy Page, Jeff Beck, John Bonham, Nicky Hopkins, and Noel Redding. Sadly, a second Sutch album, *Hands of Jack the Ripper* (9049), is neither as star-studded nor as valued.

A much-delayed US debut for the first Fairport Convention album (9024—released in the UK in 1967), LPs by the Marbles (9029) and Slade (9035), and the final studio album by Lou Reed and the Velvet Underground, *Loaded* (SD 9034), ranked among 1970's other key releases. The Velvets's "Who Loves the Sun" single (44107) is far and away the most valuable 45 in the entire Cotillion catalog, while a second Cotillion Velvet Underground album, the sub-bootleg budget-priced *Live at Max's* Kansas City (9500), has risen substantially in value in recent years, after a long time spent propping up bargain bins around the country.

The soundtrack *Homer* (9037), weighed down as it is by classic rock, and *The Hawk* (9039), by Band associate Ronnie Hawkins, are also considered collectors items, while Cotillion also gets credit for the mammoth *Woodstock* festival documents (3-500, 2-400).

In 1971 Cotillion launched a short-lived (11 LPs) religious series, apparently assuming the duties of Atlantic's recently closed R series. However, the year was dominated by ELP, whose eponymous debut album (9040) was widely regarded among the most exciting debuts of the age. Of course the group's success ensures little value has attached itself to any of ELP's Cotillion releases, a sequence of four albums and four singles, though the latter are not quite as common as their accepted value makes out, the "Nutrocker" (44151) excerpt from the live *Pictures at an Exhibition* (ELP 66666), in particular.

Spinning off from Atlantic act King Crimson, an eponymous LP by McDonald and Giles (9042), as well as former Procol Harum mainstay Bobby Harrison's Freedom (9048), are also considered collectible, while the last months of Cotillion saw Brook Benton (9050) and Tami Lynn (9052—featuring the international hit "I'm Gonna Run Away from You") release LPs whose brief shelf life has ensured a modern luster.

Cotillion folded following the Lynn release, in 1972, only to relaunch in 1976 as a soul outlet. Picking up the 9900 series of LPs where it left off in 1972, Lou Donaldson, Luther Vandross, Willis Jackson, Mass Production, and the Impressions all made significant debuts, while the following year saw Cotillion establish itself among the leading players on the disco scene with releases by Cerrone, Slave,

and Sister Sledge. This trio would dominate the label's output for the remainder of the 1970s, with releases by Phillip Wynne, the ADC Band, and Stacey Lattisaw also attracting attention today.

In 1981 the label released an album that is as collectible today as it was controversial at the time, reggae giant Bob Marley's *Chances Are*. Comprising material recorded with producer Johnny Nash in the late '60s and early '70s, but very clumsily remixed to meet modern radio "standards," *Chances Are* was, for many years, the collector's only affordable means of acquiring such material as "Do the Reggae," "(I'm) Hurting Inside," "Reggae on Broadway," and "Stay with Me," and following the LP's deletion, prices soared. Today, with the original, untampered versions of those songs readily available, *Chances Are* is best regarded as a curio, but remains collectible. No regular 45s were issued from the album, but promo singles of "Reggae on Broadway" (PR 291) and "Chances Are" (PR 414) are even more elusive than the parent LP.

Cotillion finally closed its doors for good in 1982.

TEN TOP COLLECTIBLES

Velvet Underground

"All Tomorrow's Parties" (Verve 10427—7-inch, picture sleeve, 1966)

Aspen Magazine—Various artists (Flexidisc, December 1966 issue)

East Village Other Newspaper—Various artists (ESP 1034—LP, 1966)

"Femme Fatale" (Verve 10466—7-inch, 1966)

Live at Max's Kansas City (Cotillion SD 9500—Promo LP, 1972)

Loaded (Cotillion SD 9034—Promo LP, 1970)

Velvet Underground and Nico (Verve V5008—Mono LP, with peelable banana and "male torso" back sleeve, 1967)

"What Goes On" (MGM 14057—7-inch, 1969)

"White Light/White Heat" (Verve 10560—7-inch, 1967)

"Who Loves the Sun" (Cotillion 44107—7-inch, 1970)

Cub

Cub is an MGM subsidiary that flourished during 1959–60 and is best recalled for the Brooklyn vocal group the Impalas. Their "Sorry (I Ran All the Way Home)" (9022) was a No. 2 hit in spring 1959 and spawned a now–highly collectible stereo album, *The Impalas* (8003). Other Cub material includes releases by Marla Smith, banjo virtuoso Bob Domenick and English pianist Russ Conway, whose musical passion is summed up by the title of his Cub LP, *Happy Honky Tonk Piano* (8005).

Dark Horse

Although former Beatle George Harrison was still under contract to EMI/Apple at the time, he launched his own Dark Horse label in May 1974, initially as an outlet for new talent, but also, from 1976, for his own releases. The label's original distributor was A&M; a fractious relationship ended after just eight LPs, in November 1976. Harrison then switched distribution to Warner Bros.

Dark Horse got off to a good start with the UK success of Splinter, a band featuring members of the Apple-signing Elastic Oz Band. Splinter's "Costa Finetown" 45 (UK 7135) and *The Place I Love* debut album (SP 22001) were immediate hits, but the band's subsequent releases were less successful, setting the stage for two years of underachievement.

Dark Horse's next release was Ravi Shankar's *Family and Friends* (SP 22002); in common with other Harrison-related Shankar LPs, the value of this release is constantly rising. A Shankar and Friends single, "I Am Missing You" (UK 7133), is a seldom-seen score.

Lesser known, but similarly scarce, is a self-titled set by Jiva (SP 22003), while a solo album by Henry McCullough, *Mind Your Own Business* (SP 22005), proudly boasts two Beatle links—McCullough was previously guitarist with Paul McCartney's Wings. Other Dark Horse artists during the A&M period included the Stairsteps and Attitudes, an ad-hoc band featuring session musicians David Foster, Danny Kortchmar, and Jim Keltner.

Harrison's *Thirty Three and ⅓* (DH 3005) was the first release under the Warner Bros. deal in late 1976, but a promising start for the new arrangement—with

---

TEN TOP COLLECTIBLES

George Harrison

"All Those Years Ago" (Dark Horse PRO A949—12-inch promo, 1981)

The Best of George Harrison (Capitol ST 11578—Orange label LP, 1976)

"Dark Horse" (Apple 1877—7-inch, picture sleeve, 1974)

Dark Horse Radio Special (Dark Horse, no catalog number—Promo LP, 1974)

"Devil's Radio" (Dark Horse PRO A2889—12-inch promo, 1987)

"Ding Dong" (Apple 1879—7-inch, blue/white photo label, 1974)

"Give Me Love" (Apple P1862—7-inch promo, 1972)

"Love Comes to Everyone" (Dark Horse 8844—7-inch, picture sleeve, 1979)

"My Sweet Lord" (Apple 2995—7-inch, black star on label, 1970)

"What Is Life" (Apple 1828—7-inch, picture sleeve, 1971)

---

four albums issued in under 12 months (further sets by Attitude and Splinter, and a debut by Keni Burke)—swiftly petered out. There would be no further Dark Horse activity until 1979 brought Harrison's eponymous set (DHK 3255), since which time the Dark Horse logo has been invoked for his releases alone.

Naturally, the late Harrison was the label's most consistently collectible artist, with his British 45s catalog featuring several scarce items. These include a picture-disc edition of 1979's "Faster" (K 17423) and limited boxed editions of 1987's "When We Was Fab" (W8131B) and "Got My Mind Set on You" (W8178B). **Further Reading:** *I, Me, Mine,* by George Harrison (Simon & Schuster, 1980)

Dawn

Dawn was one of the slew of "progressive" labels launched by the British majors around 1969–70, to account for the burgeoning underground movement that was then making its presence felt on the album charts. Dawn broke the mold immediately by also scoring on the singles chart, with the DNX series of four-song extended-play 7-inchers proving especially profitable.

A subsidiary of Pye, it is best remembered as the home of Mungo Jerry—the second-ever Dawn release, that band's "In the Summertime" (DNX 2502), topped charts around the world and ensured that at least one band on the label would enjoy major success: "Baby Jump" (DNX 2505), the group's follow-up, brought a second chart-topper, and Mungo Jerry went on to score half a dozen more Top 40 hits over the next three years. Much of that band's catalog is relatively common; lesser-known (and, therefore, higher priced) gems include solo LP releases by band members Paul King (the fabulous *Been in the Pen Too Long*—DNLS 3035) and Ray Dorset.

Though Mungo Jerry was Dawn's only major seller, other recruits to the label at least had name power. Donovan, hitherto a regular on the parent Pye label, had two albums issued by Dawn, 1970's *Open Road* (DNLS 3009) and 1971's double *HMS Donovan* (DNLD 4001), the latter originally appearing with a lavish fold-out poster. Two 45s, "Riki Tiki Tavi" (DNS 1006—early labels say "Ricki Ticki Tavi") and "Celia of the Seals" (1007), also exercise collectors' appetites.

Atomic Rooster joined Dawn in 1972, again for two albums: *Made in England* (DNLS 3038—early pressings with a rare denim sleeve) and *Nice'n'Greasy* (DNLS 3049). Again, too, there is a pair of rare singles, "Stand by Me" (DNS 1027) and "Save Me" (1029).

The true scarcities within the Dawn catalog, however, lurk among the bands and releases that none but the cognoscenti talk about today—Demon Fuzz, often described as Britain's first black rock group, issued the remarkable *I Put a Spell on You* EP (DNX 2504) and *Afreaka* albums (DNLS 3013); EPs and LPs by Paul Brett, Atlantic Bridge, and Bronx Cheer are also collectible.

Comus, a frenetic folk act whose "Song for Comus" was the far-and-away stand-out on Dawn's legendary *Takeaway Concert* (DNLB 3024) artist sampler, issued an extraordinarily in-demand debut album, *First Utterance* (3019), in 1971, together with the rare *Diana* EP (DNX 2506). (Beware, however, the group's 1974 Virgin label follow-up, *To Keep from Crying.* Not only is it truly horrible, it is also barely worth a bag of beans.)

Trader Horne (featuring original Fairport Convention vocalist Judy Dyble), Quiet World, Heron, Fruupp, Titus Groan, Harvey Mandel, John McLaughlin, and the entertaining Be Bop Preservation Society rate among Dawn's other front-line collectibles. Most of these LPs were initially issued with limited-run lyric inserts and such like; obviously, these are desirable inclusions in any purchase.

Dawn was at its peak, in terms of both creativity and quantity, between 1970–73—the folk group Prelude even brought the label a non-Mungo hit in 1973, with an a cappella rendition of Neil Young's "After the Gold Rush" (DNS 1052). Thereafter, the excitement died down somewhat, with the only new arrivals of genuine note being metal heroes Stray and pub-rock group Kilburn and the High Roads. Though that band's catalog has since been recycled ad nauseum, the singles "Rough Kids" (DNS 1090) and "Crippled with Nerves" (DNS 1102), and the original *Handsome* LP (DNLS 3065), still attract attention.

TEN TOP COLLECTIBLES

Dawn 7-Inchers

Barrelhouse Player— Bronx Cheer (Dawn DNX 2512—EP, 1971)

"Crippled with Nerves"— Kilburn and the High Roads (Dawn DNS 1102—7-inch, 1975)

Diana— Comus (Dawn DNX 2506—EP, 1970)

I Can't Lie to You— Atlantic Bridge (Dawn DNX 2507—EP, 1971)

Reason for Asking— Paul Brett (Dawn DNX 2508—EP, 1971)

I Put a Spell on You— Demon Fuzz (Dawn DNX 2504—EP, 1970)

"Love Is Walking"— Quiet World (Dawn DNS 1005—7-inch, 1970)

"Ricki Ticki Tavi"— Donovan (Dawn DNS 1006—7-inch, 1970)

"Stand by Me"— Atomic Rooster (Dawn DNS 1027—7-inch, 1972)

"Whoa Buck"— Paul King (Dawn DNS 1023—7-inch, 1972)

Dawn's final release, in 1976, was Trio's *Live at Woodstock Town Hall* album (DNLS 3072).

Del-Fi

The Del-Fi story is, essentially, that of Bob Keane, a clarinetist and former bandleader (both in his own right and for Artie Shaw), who recorded for the GNP and Whippet labels before joining the Siamas brothers' Keen label in 1957. From there he launched Del-Fi, specializing in recording Los Angeles–based Mexican musicians. Ritchie Valens was his first star, hitting in 1958 with "C'Mon Let's Go" (4106) and "Donna" (4110), before his death alongside Buddy Holly and the Big Bopper in February 1959. "La Bamba," since established as Valens' personal anthem, was originally issued on the flip side of "Donna"; of course, it has since far eclipsed its running mate in popularity, although when Del-Fi launched a subsidiary label, it was named for "Donna."

Valens remains Del-Fi's best-known and most-collected artist. Other releases include "Fast Freight" (4111), released under the name Arvee Allens, and "That's My Little Susie" (4114), "Little Girl" (4117),

"Stay Beside Me" (4128), and "The Paddiwack Song" (4133). Two eponymous EPs (DFEP 101, 111) are extremely rare; LPs include 1959's *Ritchie Valens* (DFLP 1201—first pressings include diamonds in the black border around the sleeve; later issues eschew the decoration; *Ritchie* (1206); the seldom-seen *In Concert at Pacoima Jr. High* (1214); *His Greatest Hits* (1225—the white-jacket variety is relatively common, but the black-jacket issue is very scarce); and *His Greatest Hits Volume Two* (1247).

Valens also dominates the label's rarest LP release, a green-vinyl promo titled the *Del-Fi Album Sampler,* issued in 1959 and also including cuts from LPs by the Balladeers (DFLP 1204), Voices of Africa (DFLP 1203), Tony Martinez (DFLP 1205), and Keane's own (and confusingly misspelled) Bob Keene Quintet (DFLP 1202—Keane was also a member of the Voices of Africa). Individual releases by these acts are seen very infrequently.

A pair of Mother's Day and Father's Day releases by the sweet little Nilsson Twins, along with releases by Bill Tracy, Little Caesar and the Romans, the Rookies, the Addrisi Brothers, Prentice Moreland,

TEN TOP COLLECTIBLES

Surfing Singles

"Barbie"—Kenny and the Cadets (Randy 422—Colored-vinyl, pink-label 7-inch, 1962)

"King of the Beach"—Bobby Fuller (Exeter 122—7-inch, 1964)

"Miserilou"—Dick Dale and the Deltones (*Billboard* magazine—Flexidisc, 1963)

"One Pine Box"—The Royal Flairs (Marina 503—7-inch, 1965)

"Shoot the Curl"—The Honeys (Capitol 4952—7-inch, picture sleeve, 1963)

"The Surfer Moon"—Bob & Sheri (Safari 101—7-inch, 1962)

"Surfin' "—The Beach Boys (X 301—7-inch, 1961)

"Three Surfer Boys"—Gary Usher and the Usherettes (Dot 16158—7-inch, 1963)

"Volcanic Action"—The Belairs (Arvee 5054—7-inch, 1963)

"Wipe Out"—The Surfaris (DFS 11/12—7-inch, 1963)

Buddy Landon, the Nitehawks, and Chan Romero were Del-Fi successes during the late '50s and early '60s, while the label also enjoyed massive local (southern California) impact with a long series of guitar-based surf and hot-rod albums, featuring the Lively Ones, the Surf Stompers, Dave Myers and the Surftones, the Sentinels, the Surf Mariachis, the Impacts, and more. The final Del-Fi release was within this sequence, *Big Surf Hits* (DFST 1249), in 1964.

Among the rarest of these are future Beach Boy Bruce Johnston's Surfing Band's *Surfer's Pajama Party* (1228)—which was almost immediately reissued with the same catalog number and sleeve, but credited to the Centurions. This version features different songs and carries no reference to Johnston. However, Johnston would reappear across the *Battle of the Surfing Bands* LP (1235), itself issued in three collectible varieties, named for the radio stations KFWB, KYA, and KPOI (different DJs appear on the sleeves).

Other peculiar issues, as sought after for their off-the-wall nature as for their links with Del-Fi, include Sheldon Allman's *Sing Along with Drac* (1213) collection of dreadful puns and horror spoofs; and the same

artist's *Drunks* (1217), which collected the recorded statements of various anonymous drunks, encountered by Allman around Los Angeles's bars.

Del-Fi closed in 1965, when Keane launched his Mustang label. However, a new series of Del-Fi releases and reissues appeared on CD beginning in 1994. Among these, Frank Zappa's pre–Mothers of Invention *Rare Meat* EP (70010) has already become a solid collectible.

Deram

Deram was a Decca imprint launched in Britain, in September 1966, to specialize in the developing young talent considered too progressive (or weird) for the parent Decca label. A US operation ran fitfully alongside the British parent, distributed by London.

The label was initially headed by Dick Rowe, historically reviled as "the man who turned down the Beatles," but in reality, a visionary whose record at both Decca and Deram withstands the tightest scrutiny in the world.

Alongside him, promo man Tony Hall and producer Denny Cordell ensured that Deram would never be wanting for either talent or ideas—and so it proved. Among Deram's first releases were 45s by Beverley ("Happy New Year"—DM 101; the singularly named singer later found further acclaim as wife and partner of John Martyn); Cat Stevens ("I Love My Dog"—102); Barry Mason ("Over the Hills and Far Away"—104); the Move ("Night of Fear"—109); and Whistling Jack Smith ("I Was Kaiser Bill's Batman"—112), a song that was indeed whistled.

The Move and Procol Harum were Deram's first major hit acts; both departed the label in summer 1967 when producer Cordell left to launch Straight Ahead productions with Move manager Tony Secunda. (Hall quit at the same time.) Deram responded, perhaps wryly, by transferring one of Secunda's former clients, the Moody Blues, from the Decca label, where the group had lain moribund for three years.

Its *Days of Future Passed* (DML/SML 107) LP became the label's biggest-selling album yet, spawned the "Nights in White Satin" mega-hit single (161), and of course, kick-started the Moody's career back into the stratosphere. The existence of a super-rare mono version, incidentally, is a fascinating corollary to the band's own vision of the LP as an orchestral rock answer to the stereo demonstration albums that were so in vogue at the time.

Deram's biggest hit during summer 1967 was the Flowerpot Men's "Let's Go to San Francisco" (142), a follow-up to Scott McKenzie's horticultural smash of the same season. Further success was provided by Amen Corner, prior to the group's departure for Andrew Loog Oldham's Immediate label.

Other releases, all highly prized by modern collectors of British psychedelia, featured such weird, wonderful, and so appropriately named acts as the Pyramid, the West Coast Delegation, Eyes of Blue, the Crocheted Doughnut Ring, Graham Gouldman's Garden Odyssey Enterprise, the Curiosity Shoppe . . . the 1998 CD compilation *The Psychedelic Scene* (Deram 844 797-2) raids the Deram psychedelic vaults with consuming passion, packing several thousand dollars worth of rare vinyl onto one disc.

Psychedelia was not Deram's sole enterprise. The young David Bowie released several now–extremely collectible 45s on the label, including "Rubber Band" (107), "Love You Till Tuesday" (135), and the "Laughing Gnome" (123) novelty that reappeared in 1973 to puncture his progressive art-glam credentials (it made the UK Top Ten). His debut LP, despite constant repackaging, is also a worthwhile discovery, especially in its mono incarnation.

A number of middle-of-the-road performers were also recruited, including such magically named combos as Tony Osbourne and His Three Brass Buttons, Raymonde's Magic Organ, and the Les Reed Orchestra. The Brotherhood of Man and White Plains, two of the apparent multitude of studio-based British bubblegum bands to feature the vocal talents of Tony Burrows, scored major UK hits during that genre's peak in 1970.

At the other end of the spectrum, however, lurked such delights as Frijid Pink's skull-crushingly fuzzed rendition of "The House of the Rising Sun" (288) and East of Eden's fiendish fiddle-led "Jig a Jig" (297), a song that was (distant memories insist) accompanied onto *Top of the Pops* by a quite demonic video. Although they weren't called videos back then.

By 1972, however, Deram's impact had clearly run its course. The none-too-collectible Junior Campbell delivered a pair of British hits in late 1972 and early 1973 ("Hallelujah Freedom"—364; "Sweet Illusion"—387), while the aforementioned "Laughing Gnome" also provided a welcome distraction. But 1975 through 1977 saw a mere handful of singles issued, with the latter year's output restricted exclusively to Moody Blues member Justin Hayward's solo recordings.

Down but not out, Deram returned to action during 1979–80, although the sale of Decca to the Polygram group, in March 1980, brought an end to the traditional DM singles series and can be regarded as the end of the label as an even halfway independent entity. The imprint has remained more or less active since then, for new talent (early-'80s oi! humorists Splodgenessabounds were a Deram act), but more notably for reissues of the "classic" era catalog.

It is the unevenness of Deram's catalog that has prevented the label as a whole from moving into the first division of collectible labels. It is, however, a

TEN TOP COLLECTIBLES

Moody Blues

Days of Future Passed (Deram DE 16012—Mono LP, 1968)

"From the Bottom of My Heart" (London 9764—7-inch, 1965)

"Go Now" (London 9726—7-inch, blue/purple/white label, 1965)

Go Now—*The Moody Blues 1* (London LL 3428—Mono LP, 1965)

The Moody Blues (UK Decca DFE 8622—EP, 1965)

"Nights in White Satin" (Deram 85023—7-inch, credits writer as Redwave, 1967)

On the Threshold of a Dream (Nautilus NR21—Audiophile-pressing LP, 1981)

Special Interview Kit (Threshold THX 100—Promo LP, 1971)

"Steal Your Heart Away"—Moodyblues (UK Decca F11971—7-inch, 1964)

"This Is My House" (London 1005—7-inch, 1967)

---

treasure trove for specialists. On both 45 and LP, the psychedelic output is second to none; the prog catalog overflows with fabulous treasures; the pop is effervescent; and modern collectors of '70s kitsch will forgive the most excessive smarminess if the price (and the LP sleeve) is right.

Dimension

Don Kirshner launched Dimension in 1962, as an outlet for a husband-and-wife songwriting duo, then contracted to another of his enterprises, the (Al) Nevins-Kirshner publishing company. Carole King and Jerry Goffin had already composed such monster 45s as the Shirelles' "Will You Still Love Me Tomorrow," Bobby Vee's "Take Good Care of My Baby," and Colpix TV star James Darren's "Her Royal Majesty"—among many, many others—and they debuted Dimension with equal panache. Performed by the couple's babysitter, "Little" Eva Narcissus Boyd, "The Locomotion" (1000) topped the chart during summer 1962.

A Little Eva LP, *Llllllloco-Motion* followed (DLP 6000). Two versions exist, a reasonably common first

pressing, followed by a later edition augmented by Eva's second hit, "Keep Your Hands Off My Baby" (1003). Oddly, two versions of that single, too, are known—one titles the song simply "Keep Your Hands Off."

Keeping Dimension's success "within the family," the label's next hit act was the Chains, the three-piece backing vocalists on "The Locomotion." "Chains" (1002) was later recorded by the Beatles and is the best known of half a dozen singles cut by the trio for the label.

King herself had cut a brace of 45s for ABC-Paramount back in 1958; in 1962 she relaunched her singing career with "School Bells Are Ringing" (1004). According to legend, the song that became her signature hit later in the year, "It Might As Well Rain Until September" (2000), was never intended for release; rather, her performance was simply intended as a demo—although a cat with no ears could have known that nobody on earth was ever going to produce a better performance. Certainly Kirshner felt that way, issuing the performance warts and all, and scoring another major hit.

TEN TOP COLLECTIBLES

Carole King

"Baby Sittin' " (ABC Paramount 9986—7-inch, 1958)

"Goin' Wild" (ABC Paramount 9921—7-inch, 1958)

"He's a Bad Boy" (Dimension 1009—7-inch, 1963)

"It Might As Well Rain until September" (Companion 2000—7-inch, 1962)

"Main Street Saturday Night" (Capitol SPRO 8863—12-inch promo, 1978)

Now That Everything's Been Said (Ode Z12 44012—LP, full-color cover, 1968)

"Oh Neil" (Alpine 57—7-inch, 1959)

"A Road to Tomorrow" (Tomorrow 7502—7-inch, 1966)

"Short Mort" (RCA Victor 47-7560—7-inch, 1959)

Tapestry (Ode HE 44946—Half-speed master LP, 1980)

Dimension's second and final LP release, in 1963, was the *Dimension Dolls* various-artists collection (DLP 6001); that further volumes were planned is evident from the album's "volume one" notation. However, the hits already scored (and thus included) by King, the Cookies, and Little Eva were to remain Dimension's finest hour. Not only did volume two never appear, it wasn't even required.

In 1965, Kirshner sold Dimension to Columbia Pictures.

Dolton

Seattle-based Dolton Records launched in 1959 as Dolphin, with an eye-catching label design decorated, of course, with the appropriate aquatic mammal. Concentrating on regional talent, the label got off to a winning start with the Fleetwoods' "Come Softly to Me" (Dolphin 1)—at which point an already existing label of the same name made its presence known. The PNW concern became Dolton, reissuing the single as Dolton 1 (later in the year, the 45 reappeared on distributor Liberty's own label—55188; with bongo overdubs. It was also released in stereo—77188).

The Fleetwoods followed up with "Graduation's Here" (3/S-3) and the chart-topping "Mr. Blue" (5), the first in a sequence of hits that persisted until 1963; the Fleetwoods' final single release was "For Lovin' Me" (315), while the group also issued eleven LPs (including compilations), in both rare mono and very rare stereo.

Label variations over the years have great appeal to collectors of this sequence. Original issues from 1959–63 feature a pale blue label with the dolphin logo on top; this changed in 1963 to a dark label with a multicolored logo off to one side. Around 1965, a third label was introduced, black with a blue area to the left of the spindle.

The label's next hit group was the Frantics, emerging with the single "Straight Flush" (2). "Rugcutter" (6), "Checkerboard" (13), and the Halloween favorite "Werewolf"/"No Werewolf" (16) followed. After three further 45s, the Frantics moved to the Bolo label, in 1962.

Little Bill and the Bluenotes (with one single, "I Love an Angel"—4) and Dolton's in-house producer Bonnie Guitar (with "Candy Apple Red"—10, reissued as 19) were also successful during the label's first year or so, but Dolton's primary act became the Ventures. Their premiere release—"Walk Don't Run" (25; two pressings sport different B-sides, "Home," and "The McCoy")—was the first in a string of instrumental hits, establishing the Ventures as America's premier guitar band.

The Fleetwoods and the Ventures would, between them, account for ten of Dolton's first eleven LP releases. Ray Latham's *Most Exciting Guitar* (BST 8009) alone punctuated the sequence in 1961. Of the next eight, five were by the Ventures, two by the Fleetwoods, and one by Vic Dana, the next artist to establish himself as a major force.

Dolton entered 1961 as one of the most successful minor labels in the entire country. The departure of Bonnie Guitar to form the new Jerden label, with Dolton promo man Jerry Dennon, barely disturbed Dolton's equilibrium, since the Fleetwoods, the Ventures, and Dana continued cranking out successful records.

Around 1963, however, Dolton was sold to Liberty and continued to operate as a simple subsidiary. The aforementioned new logo was introduced at this time (much of the back catalog was reissued). New numbering sequences were launched—after 100 releases, the 45 catalog became the 300 series, launched, of course, by the Ventures ("Slaughter on 10th Avenue"—300), Dana ("Frenchy"—301), and the Fleetwoods ("Before and After"—302). The albums replaced the BST prefix with LST, but otherwise retained the existing numbering system. This series commenced with Vic Dana's *Foreign Affairs* (8051) and the Ventures' *Super Psychedelics* (8052).

With its LP catalog so heavily dominated by these three acts, all of which are collectible without necessarily proving to be high priced, many collectors expend most of their energy seeking out the non-Ventures/Fleetwoods/Dana issues. Within the 8000 series of LPs, there was just one such, when 1963 brought the Wanderers Three's *We Sing Folk Songs* (8021).

However, emboldened by the Ventures' popularity, Dolton inaugurated the Play Guitar series of albums in 1965, offering lessons via the Guitar Phonics learning system. Seven LPs were issued (BST 17501-07), five highlighted by the Ventures (including *Play Electric Bass*—BST 17504), the remainder by Jimmy

TEN TOP COLLECTIBLES

The Ventures

Another Smash (Dolton BST 8006—Stereo LP, pale-blue label, 1961)

"Hold Me Thrill Me Kiss Me"—Scott Douglas and the Venture Quintet (Blue Horizon 102—7-inch, 1960)

"Perfidia" (Dolton 28—7-inch, picture sleeve, 1960)

"The Real McCoy"—Scott Douglas and the Venture Quintet (Blue Horizon 100—7-inch, 1960)

"Surfin' and Spyin' " (Tridex 1245—12-inch single, 1981)

The Ventures (Dolton BST 2004—LP, pale-blue label, 1961)

Walk Don't Run (Dolton BLP 2003—LP, pale-blue label, 1960)

Walk Don't Run (Dolton 503—EP, 1960)

"Walk Don't Run"—Scott Douglas and the Venture Quintet (Blue Horizon 101—7-inch, 1960)

"Walk Don't Run 64" (Dolton 96—7-inch, picture sleeve, 1964)

Bryant (*Play Country Guitar* [BST 17505]) and Chet Atkins (*Play Guitar With Chet Atkins* [BST 17506]). This latter, issued in 1967, was among the last albums Dolton would release before being absorbed wholly into Liberty.

Duke

Duke launched in 1952, with its best-known artist through this period being Johnny Ace. His "My Song" (102) opens a sequence of very collectible 78s from the label, while it took his death, in 1955, to inaugurate Duke's LP series.

Duke's first LP releases were 10-inch discs, opening with the Johnny Ace *Memorial Album* (70), in March 1955. This set was reissued two years later as Duke's first 12-inch, retitled *Memorial Album for Johnny Ace* (DLP 71), and featuring several extra tracks. The original cover for this issue was orange, with a black band down the left side; the original label was purple and yellow, with a purple band. These points are important, as several re-pressings were made, including a 1961 issue with a new light-red cover, decorated with an Ace of Hearts playing card, with a portrait of Ace within. The original label for this issue was orange.

Duke's other major act, again commencing in 1952, was Bobby Bland. He debuted on the label with "Lovin' Blues" (105), and remained on the release schedule until 1973 brought the aptly titled "That's All There Is" (480). He, too, was a prolific LP artist, opening with *Blues Consolidated* (DLP 72), in May 1959—the set was split with Junior Parker, whose Duke career launched in 1954 with "Dirty Friend Blues" (120). One especially popular Bland album is *Two Steps from the Blues* (DLPS 74), a 1961 electronic stereo issue that exists in red vinyl (with the orange label; original issues have the purple-and-yellow label).

Other leading Duke artists, rounded up on the *Like 'Er Red Hot* various-artists collection (DLP 73), included Roy Head, the Original Casuals and OV Wright (from the Back Beat subsidiary), Willie Mae "Big Mama" Thornton (from the Peacock sister label), the Rob Roys, Clarence "Gatemouth" Brown, Paul Perryman, the El Toros, and Ernie Harris.

Just as he did on the 45s front, Bland dominated the Duke LP catalog, with only Parker interrupting his sequence through the 1960s. Indeed, by the time Duke got around to issuing an LP by another artist, the posthumous *Duke-Peacock Remembers Joe Hinton* (DLPX 91), the label itself was about to perish, absorbed into ABC-Paramount. The early '70s brought a string of well-designed reissues and compilations from the *Historic Vaults of Duke/Peacock Records*.

Dunhill

Fabled songwriter-producer Lou Adler launched Dunhill in 1964, as a production company, launching as a record label the following year. Crucial to the new label's success would be the recruitment of Phil "P.F." Sloan and Steve Barri as staff songwriters and performers—among numerous successes, they were also responsible for Dunhill's second-ever 45, under the name Willie and the Wheels (4002—Dunhill 4001 was by Shelley Fabares), and the first LP, masquerading now as the Rincon Surfside Band, *Surfing Songbook* (D/DS 5001).

Sloan alone, Terry Black, the Iguanas, Don and the Goodtimes, and session drummer Hal Blain cut now-collectible singles during Dunhill's infancy. (Blain recorded a brace of now-rare albums, *Drums! Drums! A Go Go*—5002, and *Psychedelic Percussion*—50019.)

Barry McGuire scored Dunhill's first No. 1 with Sloan/Barri's all-purpose protest song "Eve of Destruction" (4009), in fall 1965. McGuire never repeated that success, and an album issued at this time, *This Precious Time* (5005), turns up with much regularity.

Sloan/Barri's next major move was to form the Grass Roots, which debuted with "Mr. Jones" (4013), then split up. An album of already recorded material was compiled and released, fittingly, as *Where Were You When I Needed You* (50011). With the title track becoming a hit (4029), Dunhill desperately needed a band to promote further releases. The originals, however, had shattered, so a new Grass Roots was formed and maintained a sequence of successful records through the remainder of the decade. Among these, the group's "Let's Live for Today" (4084) was subsequently recorded by the Lords of the New Church. Also popular are 45s and an LP by the duo Fred E. and Mickey Finn, owners of the Southern California nightspot Mickey Finn's.

McGuire, meanwhile, introduced the Mamas and the Papas to the label; they, in turn, brought some truly collectible variations to the catalog, including a debut 45, "Go Where You Wanna Go," which was withdrawn after DJ copies only had been produced. The Mamas and the Papas became Dunhill's biggest act yet, but others were queuing up behind them. The Brass Ring scored two hits from eight singles, including "Phoenix Love Theme" (4023), from the Jimmy Stewart movie, and "The Dis-Advantages of You" (4065), from a Benson & Hedges cigarette commercial. The Brass Ring also cut a version of the Mamas and the Papas' "California Dreaming" (4047), but its most sought-after issue is "Love in the Open Air" (4090), issued in a picture sleeve stating "This is Paul McCartney's first non-Beatles song."

Another apparent Dunhill-Beatles connection, releases by the band Wings, do not belong in a Fab Four collection—the album *Wings* (50046) predates Macca's band by three years. However, a single and an LP by Grapefruit (50050) can be included—John Lennon named the band.

In 1966, Adler sold Dunhill to ABC and launched his own new label, Ode. Dunhill retained its identity until 1968, the newly introduced ABC logo notwithstanding (UK releases appeared on Stateside-Dunhill). A sequence of further hits followed, primarily by the Mamas and the Papas, and the Grass Roots, but also including some interesting releases by the hard rock band Steppenwolf. Two Dunhill 45s, "The Ostrich" (4109) and "Sookie Sookie" (4123), are well worth looking for. The group's self-titled debut album (50029) was the last Dunhill release to be issued in mono, but offers little sonic variety; its second (50037) is most desirable, with its original silver-foil sleeve.

Dunhill was merged into its parent as ABC-Dunhill, in 1968, in which form Steppenwolf took off with the anthem "Born to Be Wild" (4161) as well as "Magic Carpet Ride" (4161), and provided one of the highlights of the label's successful movie soundtrack, *Easy Rider* (DSX 50063).

Smith emerged with 1969's remake of the Shirelles' "Baby It's You" (4206), while actor Richard Harris scored a massive hit with the Jim Webb–composed-and-produced "MacArthur Park" (4134). Roy Head, Shango, and Bush (no relation to the 1990s act) all highlighted the label's turn-of-the-decade output.

Three Dog Night was also massive—and, taking a leaf out of the Mamas and the Papas' book, also suffered the indignity of a withdrawn LP sleeve—on two occasions. *It Ain't Easy* (DS 50078) bore a photo of the seven-man band in the nude, before being replaced by a shot of the group's three singers at a piano; *Hard Labor* (DS 50168) originally depicted a presumably female creature giving birth to an LP record. Hastily withdrawn, covers were initially censored with a large Band-Aid affixed to the offending portion; subsequent pressings featured the Band-Aid as a part of the actual artwork.

Collectible Three Dog Night releases include original issues of the debut album (DS 50048), titled simply *Three Dog Night*; this was revised to *Three Dog Night: One* following the success of the single of the same name (4191). Also collectible are the group's third album, *Naturally* (DSX 50088), with its detachable cardboard poster still intact; 1972's *Seven Separate Fools* (DSD 50118), with seven free playing cards; and the hits collection *Joy to the World* (DSD 50178), initially issued within a gatefold sleeve. Test pressings for the final album, *Dog Style* (50198), scheduled as ABC-Dunhill's last release but never otherwise issued, are said to exist. Three Dog Night has never especially excited collectors, but these particular releases do have a following.

Joe Walsh, Emitt Rhodes, Pacific Gas and Electric, Jimmy Buffett, Bobby Bland, funk master Charles Wright, and soul legends Freda Payne and the Four Tops all dignified the label's 1970s output, while collectors also seek the debut album by *Happy Days* TV theme makers Pratt and McClain (50164).

A tentative toe dipped into the British prog underground is responsible for some of ABC-Dunhill's most collectible early-'70s releases. Folk duo Magna

TEN TOP COLLECTIBLES

P.F. Sloan

"All I Want Is Lovin' "—Flip Sloan (Aladdin 3461—7-inch, 1959)

"Halloween Mary" (Dunhill 4016—7-inch promo, picture sleeve, 1965)

"Karma"—Philip Sloan (Dunhill 4106—7-inch, 1967)

"Let Me Be" (Mums 6010—7-inch, 1972)

"She's My Girl" (Mart 802—7-inch, 1960)

"The Sins of a Family" (Dunhill 4007—7-inch, 1965)

"Skateboard Craze"—as Willie and the Wheels (Dunhill 4002, 1965)

"Star Gazin' " (Atco 6663—7-inch, 1969)

"Sunflower Sunflower" (Dunhill 4064—7-inch, picture sleeve, 1967)

Surfing Songbook—as Rincon Surfside Band (Dunhill D/DS 5001—LP, 1965)

Carta's *Seasons* (50091) is sought after by collectors of the British Vertigo label, offering as it does a cheaper alternative to the UK release. Jazz-rockers Colosseum (another Vertigo act), Van Der Graaf Generator, and Andwella are also hotly pursued, while fans of German disco producer Giorgio Moroder seek his *Giorgio* debut (50123), a set built around the hit single "Son of My Father" (4304), and an early showcase for the electronic pop that was his forte. ABC-Dunhill gave a US release to Kracker's *La Familia*, the follow-up to the band's ill-fated debut on the Rolling Stones label. The album was originally packaged in box-set packaging, designed to resemble a cigar box.

ABC-Dunhill also issued Dusty Springfield's magical *Cameo* (50128), but passed on its projected follow-up, *Longing* (50186); the latter remained unissued until 2001 brought the *Beautiful Soul* CD (Hip-O), rounding up all Springfield's recordings for the label. A pair of Springfield 45s from this period, "Who Gets Your Love" (4341) and "Mama's Little Girl" (4344, reissued as 4357), are both hard to find.

Despite such activity, little of the ABC-Dunhill catalog is as avidly sought after as its predecessor's.

One exception is another Webb offering, the debut album by Thelma Houston, *Sunshower* (50044), while Steely Dan's *Can't Buy a Thrill* debut album, issued by ABC itself, appeared with an ABC-Dunhill label via the Capitol Record Club (SMAS 94976).

ABC closed Dunhill in 1975.

Dunwich

Based in Chicago, Dunwich was founded by Bill Traut, manager of the Shadows of Knight—with DJ Clark Weber, it was Traut who suggested the group record a cleaned-up version of Them's controversial "Gloria" (116), which became a Top Ten hit in March 1966, after Atco picked up the label's distribution. Early pressings of the 45 do not mention Atco; in addition, several different pressings see the regular yellow label change to pink.

The Shadows of Knight are Dunwich's most collectible band. Five further singles included "Oh Yeah" (122), "Bad Little Woman" (128), "I'm Gonna Make You Mine" (141), "Behemoth" (151), and "Someone Like Me" (167); together with the group's two albums, *Gloria* (666) and *Back Door Men* (667), all have their acolytes, as do post-Dunwich releases on Atco and Super K.

Dunwich never matched the Shadows' success, though a number of other now-popular Chicago-area bands passed through its catalog, including the Little Boy Blues and Amanda Ambrose.

DynoVoice

Four Seasons producer Bob Crewe launched the Dyno-Vox label in New York in 1965, changing its name to DynoVoice shortly before Eddie Rambeau's spoiler version of Unit 4+2's "Concrete and Clay" (2004) was released in April 1965. (An LP of the same name followed—9001.) Soon after, the Toys' "A Lover's Concerto" (2009) climbed to No. 2, the first of four hits by the Jamaican American trio. The Toys also cut an album (9002), released in two pressings—the first, with matrix -1A, features the hit "Attack" (214) in electronic stereo; the second includes it in true stereo.

Chicago Loop's "(When She Wants Good Lovin') She Comes to Me" (226) is another popular release, while Crewe's own "Music to Watch Girls By" (229) and "Birds of Britain" (902) are among the linchpins of the 1990s lounge music revival. A *Music to Watch Girls By* (9003) LP is much sought after, both in its original format and reissued in 1967 (1902), after Dot replaced Bell as the label's distributor.

Other LPs from this period included *What Now My Love* (1901), by Mitch Ryder, transferred to DynoVoice following the closure of the New Voice subsidiary, a second Crewe effort, *The Bob Crewe Generation in Classic Form* (1906) and the heavily in-demand soundtrack to the movie *Barbarella*, by the Bob Crewe Generation Orchestra (DY-31908). This was the final release before Crewe closed the label in 1969.

Elektra

Founded in 1950 as an outlet for folk, jazz, gospel, and ethnic music, Elektra Records would develop into one of the most visionary labels of the mid-to-late '60s, with a string of inspired signings, including the MC5, the Stooges, David Peel, and of course, the Doors, the four acts around whom much of the label's modern collectibility revolves.

Later, following a merger with Asylum, Elektra became party to the explosion of West Coast soft-rock talents that dominated the American 1970s; later still, the company helped popularize the so-called new wave in the US, via the recruitment of the Cars. Today, with the imprint now over 50 years old, Elektra remains a vibrant concern, home to talents as divergent as Icelandic maverick Björk, and jam leviathan Phish. Small wonder, then, that Elektra boasts one of the most devoted collector followings of all American labels, with each decade bringing an entirely new generation of enthusiasts into the fold.

Elektra is also widely regarded as the first "modern" label to issue a budget-priced label sampler designed to draw new listeners into the fold—a promo collection (SMP 1) appeared in 1954, to encourage airplay; two years later, SMP 2 was marketed to the public as well, not only igniting interest in Elektra, but firing an entirely new field of record promotion.

Label founder Jac Holzman was inspired to form a label after attending a performance by soprano Georgianna Bannister at St. John's College in Annapolis, Md., where he was a student. In late 1950, he recorded a fresh version of the same recital, issuing it as the LP *New Songs by John Gruen* (the composer), in March 1951 (EKLP 1). Just 500 copies were pressed and few were sold, establishing this first release among Elektra's greatest rarities.

From college, Holzman opened a record store, The Record Loft, in Greenwich Village—it was there he met Elektra's next signing, folk singer Jean Ritchie. In stark contrast to its predecessor, the ensuing *Jean Ritchie Singing the Traditional Songs of Her Kentucky Mountain Family* (EKLP 2) quickly sold out of its entire pressing.

Elektra developed slowly but surely. Between 1952–54, Elektra issued 24 albums, including sets by folk singers Frank Warner, Shep Ginandes, Cynthia Gooding, Hally Wood, and Tom Paley, as well as two titles by bluesmen Sonny Terry and Brownie McGhee, along with field recordings from as far afield as Haiti and Nova Scotia. Actor Theodore Bikel cut a collection of Israeli folk songs for Elektra in 1955 (EKL 32) and remained with the label until 1961.

Another early coup was the arrival of folk singer Josh White. Hitherto contracted to Decca, he joined Elektra after being blacklisted for alleged communist sympathies during the McCarthy era. His first release, *The Story of John Henry and Ballads, Blues and Other Songs* (EKL 701), was the label's first double album (two 10-inch discs); it was also the first Elektra release to appear on both 10-inch, and later 12-inch, vinyl (EKL 123).

Elektra's development through the late '50s and early '60s was dictated by the mood of the folk community, itself undergoing a massive revival. Glenn Yarbrough, Peggy Seeger, Oscar Brand, Shel Silverstein, Bob Gibson, and Paul Clayton recorded now-scarce albums for the label. Elektra also dipped into the fertile Caribbean scene, with in-demand releases by the Original Trinidad Steel Band (EKL 139) and Lord Foodoos and His Calypso Band (EKL 127) Further indication of Holzman's willingness to experiment is seen in the 1960 release of English comedienne Joyce Grenfell's *Presenting* (EKL 184), a collection of extraordinary monologues about the life of a school teacher. All but unknown in the US, this album is much in-demand among British comedy collectors. Other fascinating specialist items appear within the Nonesuch classical and Nonesuch Traveler series of LPs, the latter developing what future generations would term world music.

Elektra's biggest star of the early '60s was Judy Collins, signed in 1961 in response to the Vanguard label's Joan Baez, but rapidly emerging as a diamond talent in her own right, both via such early LPs as *Maid of Constant Sorrow* (EKL 209) and *Golden Apples of the Sun* (EKL 222), but also via a clutch of excellent singles—"Turn, Turn, Turn" (45008), her first, was an early success in Elektra's newly inaugurated series of 7-inch releases.

Tom Paxton, Phil Ochs, and the Ian Campbell Folk Group joined in 1964, while Elektra also handled two of the seminal folk compilations of the age, the three-LP box set of Woody Guthrie's *Library of Congress Recordings* (EKL 271), and the British Topic label's *The Iron Muse* (EKL 279) compilation of folk songs from the Industrial Revolution.

Other significant signings from this period included the Dillards and the Even Dozen Jug Band, a sprawling 12-piece whose membership included John Sebastian, Maria Muldaur, Stefan Grossman, and Steve Katz—the group's eponymous debut album (EKL 246) appeared in 1964 and is much sought after today. Producer Paul Rothchild, very much Holzman's right-hand man, meanwhile, was responsible for moving the label into the electric-blues arena with the inspired signing of the Paul Butterfield Blues Band in 1965. Famously, Rothchild recorded the group's self-titled first album (EKL 294) three times before he was satisfied with the results; the first two sets of sessions were issued 30 years later as *The Original Lost Elektra Sessions* (Rhino R2 73505).

The success of the Butterfield album saw Elektra begin moving closer to the pop mainstream it had hitherto kept at a deliberate arm's length. The label came close to signing the Lovin' Spoonful, actually exchanging contracts before it was discovered that the group's publishing deal already bound them to the Kama Sutra label. Elektra was more fortunate with Los Angeles band Love, scoring its first hit single with spring 1966's "My Little Red Book" (45603). Love's debut album (EKS 74001) followed, and despite the general unpredictability of the band's music (sometimes brilliant, sometimes . . . not so brilliant), it remains one of the best-loved acts of the age—with its only serious competition coming from Elektra's next venture into rock, the Doors.

The success, popularity, and legends surrounding these two acts has conspired to ensure a thriving collectors market exists around both. In the Love camp, mono and promo pressings of its first three albums (*Da Capo*—4005—and the much-lauded *Forever Changes*—4013—followed their debut) are much sought after despite the latter's offering nothing more than a simple mono reduction of the stereo mix; these releases are joined as grade-A collectibles by the single "Que Vida"/"Hey Joe" (45613).

The Doors are more challenging by virtue of the almost preposterous recycling and reissue programs that have clouded a relatively straightforward discography over the past 30 years—vocalist Jim Morrison's death in July 1971 marked the end of the band but the birth of an industry. Mono pressings of the first three albums exist, with the *Doors* (EKL 4007) debut characterized by a radically different mix than its stereo counterpart. (*Strange Days*—4017—and *Waiting for the Sun*—4027—again offer mere fold-ins.)

Scarce 45s include picture-sleeved original yellow-and-black-label copies of the band's "Break On Through" debut (45611) and an initial run of "Hello I Love You" (45635), retitling the song "Hello I Love You, Won't You Tell Me Your Name?" Audiophile and quadraphonic pressings of the 1970s *Best of the Doors* compilations, too, enjoy some popularity, though there appears to be no shortage of the latter format.

The Doors' "Light My Fire" (45615) gave Elektra its first chart-topping single; fresh signings, including Tim Buckley, Ars Nova, David Ackles, and Eclection, seemed set to further that success, while the sale of the label to Warner Bros. in 1967 (with Holzman remaining on board, of course) only amplified Elektra's visibility. At the same time, however, the label's traditional penchant for the extraordinary and the eccentric continued to bear strange fruit—Britain's Incredible String Band, former Velvet Underground chanteuse Nico, the Holy Modal Rounders, and New York street performer David Peel were as bizarre as any Elektra watcher could hope for, while the arrival of Detroit hard rock bands the MC5 and the Stooges saw Elektra pursue its vision to the extremes of rock iconography.

With the exception of the Incredible String Band, none of these acts released more than a handful of records for the label. Nico's catalog was confined to just one album, 1968's cult classic *Marble Index* (74029), as was the MC5's—the definitive *Kick Out the Jams* (74042) and a single of the title track (45648). Look for first pressings of the album, with a gatefold sleeve and John Sinclair's original liner notes, matching the band blow-by-blow for incendiary impact—they were removed for later pressings and would not be seen again for almost three decades, before finally reappearing on the *Ice Pick Slim* EP (Total Energy/Alive 8).

The Stooges' catalog stretched a little further, embracing two albums: *The Stooges* (74051), produced, like *Marble Index,* by former Velvet Underground bassist John Cale, and *Fun House* (74101). Look also for two super-scarce 45s, "I Wanna Be Your Dog" (45664) and "Down on the Street" (45695). Time, however, has allowed a wealth of associated documents to emerge, most notably an eight-CD box set of the sessions that made up the second Stooges album. A limited edition within the Rhino Handmade series, *The Complete Fun House* (RHM 2-7707) is arguably the ultimate test of the liberated mind. If you can sit through 28 successive takes on "Loose," spread across two discs, you can sit through anything.

David Peel, too, released two albums, themselves since reissued across one disc in the Rhino Handmade series (RHM 2-7713); *Have a Marijuana* (74032) and *The American Revolution* (74069) are both relatively common, but are favored by Apple label completists—1971 saw the performer fall into John Lennon's orbit, at the outset of the ex-Beatle's New York sojourn, cutting the album *The Pope Smokes Dope* (Apple SW 3391).

If Elektra ended the 1960s as a haven for some of the most unique freak shows in the American mainstream, it entered the 1970s as a repository for another musical force entirely. The mature ruminations of David Gates's Bread debuted on the label in 1969, with the single "Any Way You Want Me" (45666) and a self-titled album (EKS 74044). By 1971, when singer-songwriters Harry Chapin and Carly Simon were added to the roster, Bread ranked among Elektra's biggest-selling acts ever. Simon would swiftly join the group at the top, and by the time Holzman retired in 1973, and the label merged with Asylum, Elektra was poised to dominate the middle of the soft-rock road.

Of course, the label's historical love for the oddball continued to shine through, and it is in this area that the greatest collectibles exist. Queen, the British hard rock band whose appeal embraces everyone from dyed-in-the-wool headbangers to students of absurdly tongue-in-cheek satire, are rightly ranked among the most collected bands in the world—Elektra signed the band in 1975, and over the next six

Crabby Appleton on Elektra.

years, Queen unleashed the greatest music of its long career, ranging from the mock-operatic "Bohemian Rhapsody" (45297) to the shuddering funk of "Another One Bites the Dust" (47031); from the two-sided sporting anthem "We Are the Champions"/"We Will Rock You" (45441), to the two-headed collaboration with David Bowie, "Under Pressure" (47235).

Also in heavy demand today are releases by an artist who, ironically, Elektra could barely give away at the time. Glam-rocker Jobriath was brought to the label by Jerry Brandt, Carly Simon's manager, and afforded one of the most lavish, not to mention expensive, launches in rock history. Unfortunately, all the money in the world could not persuade the public to buy his records, and for many years, the albums *Jobriath* (75070) and *Creatures of the Street* (7E 1010) could be found propping up bargain bins across the country. Two UK singles, "Take Me I'm Yours" (K12129) and "Street Corner Love" (K12146), were also released to deafening apathy.

The early '90s, however, saw such stars as Morrissey and the Pet Shop Boys begin to voice their admiration for the star-that-never-was, and slowly, eyes and ears opened. A decade later, albums and associated singles alike are snapped up the moment they appear, while one of the most exciting items ever to emerge on eBay in 2001 was a reel of unreleased material recorded by Jobriath with producer Eddie Kramer, shortly before he signed to Elektra. Together with the two released albums and excerpts from an uncompleted third, this material forms the basis for yet another Rhino Hand-made CD collection.

Sparks, a band whose career probably touches more record labels than Link Wray's, issued one album through Elektra, 1979's massively influential No. 1 *In Heaven* (6E 186). Boston new wave band the Cars opened their Elektra career in 1978 with the quirky "Just What I Needed" (45491), and closed it a decade later as one of the entire genre's most reliable hit machines—at least in America.

TEN TOP COLLECTIBLES

Björk

"Birthday + 3"—The Sugarcubes (UK One Little Indian 7TP7CD—CD, 1987)

Bitid fast i vitid—Tappi Tikarrís (Iceland Spor SPOR 4—LP, 1981)

Björk (Iceland Falkinn FA 006—LP, 1977)

Celebrating Wood and Metal (UK One Little Indian BJORK FC1—CD, 1996)

Debut (UK One Little Indian TPLP 31—LP with lyric book, 1993)

"Enjoy" (UK One Little Indian 193TP12DM—12-inch, 1996)

Gling glo—Trio Gudmundar Ingolfssonar (Iceland Smekkleysa SM 27—CD, 1990)

"Joga + 12" (UK One Little Indian TPLP 81—3x12-inch singles, 1997)

"Possibly Maybe" (UK One Little Indian 193TP12TD—12-inch, 1996)

"Songull"—Kukl (Iceland Gramm GRAMM 17—7-inch, 1983)

In the UK, where the group was launched with the single "My Best Friend's Girl" (UK Elektra K12301), they remain best recalled as the vehicle for a spot of marketing shenanigans that came close to crippling the entire concept of "limited" special editions of new releases, with a "rare" picture disc that rapidly transpired to be anything but. The Cars' British collectibility never really recovered.

British Elektra also produced apparently copious "limited" versions of another American new wave act's records—Television's "Marquee Moon" (K12252) is, again, far more common as a 12-inch single than an edited 7-inch, while red-vinyl pressings of the group's sophomore album, *Adventure* (K52072), also appear more common than perhaps they should.

In 1982, Elektra founded its own jazz-rock oriented subsidiary, Elektra Musician, while maintaining its presence in the rock mainstream as skillfully as ever. Rabidly collectible artists recruited during the 1980s include the Cure and Depeche Mode (via licensing deals with the British Fiction and Mute labels, respectively), the Sugarcubes, and following their demise, Björk, Metallica, Third Eye Blind, and rap star Ol' Dirty Bastard. Indeed, in an age when the spirit of many of rock's traditionally collected labels has been utterly subverted by the advent of the CD, Elektra has managed to retain and even strengthen its ties with the community, simply via the artists it signs. Not all are great, not all are collected by even the label's most staunch fans. But those that are more than make up for the shortfall.

Further Reading: *Follow the Music: The Life and High Times of Elektra Records in the Great Years of American Pop Culture,* by Jac Holzman, with Gavan Daws (First Media, 1998)

EMI

Although the EMI company has been the dominant force on the British music scene since 1931, when the Gramophone and Columbia Gramophone Companies merged as one giant entity, the actual EMI label imprint did not come into being until 1973.

It was formed around the long-threatened, but nevertheless controversial, closure of many of the subsidiaries that had made EMI the power it was—Columbia and His Master's Voice (the voices of the

TEN TOP COLLECTIBLES

Queen

At the BBC (Hollywood ED 62005—Promo picture-disc LP, 1995)

"Bicycle Race" (UK EMI 2870—7-inch export, picture sleeve, 1978)

"Bohemian Rhapsody" (EMI 2375—Blue-vinyl 7-inch, Queen's Award, picture sleeve, 1978)

"Hammer to Fall" (UK EMI QUEEN 4—7-inch, live recording, picture sleeve, 1984)

The Highlander Selection (UK Parlophone EMCDV 2—Video CD, 1986)

"Man on the Prowl" (UK EMI QUEEN 5—7-inch test pressing, 1984)

News of the World (UK EMI, no catalog number—Box set with LP, cassette, and ephemera, 1977)

A Night at the Opera (Mobile Fidelity 1067—Audiophile-pressing LP, 1980)

Queen (UK EMI, no catalog number—White-label die-cut sleeve, 1973)

"Radio Ga Ga" (UK EMI QUEEN 1—7-inch, video-shoot picture sleeve, 1984)

---

two founding companies), Regal Zonophone, Stateside—even Parlophone, home of the Beatles, was not exempt from the cull.

Of course the biggest names from each of those labels transferred to the new concern, including Cliff Richard, whose "Power to All Our Friends" (2012) brought EMI an early hit, and Cilla Black, who debuted with "Baby We Can't Go Wrong" (2107). However, the early running was made by the new generation of acts who would take EMI deeper into the 1970s—Geordie, transferred from the still-active (if barely so) Regal Zonophone label, which scored with "All Because of You" (2008); Cockney Rebel, fronted by the effervescent Steve Harley; and Queen. These acts brought the young imprint its first major smashes.

Harley's "Make Me Smile (Come Up and See Me)" (2263) was the group's third hit and fourth single (a fifth, the super-rare withdrawn "Big Big Deal," 2233, exists purely to annoy completists). "Make Me Smile" topped the chart in February 1975, dislodging another EMI act, Pilot, whose "January" (2255) was the label's first-ever chart-topper. Neither band

would repeat those glories, but Harley has hung on to his early fame and remains a much-loved, and much-collected figure.

Queen, too, went to No. 1 for the first time that year, with the mammoth "Bohemian Rhapsody" (2375). Its collectible status, too, is assured, with a special pressing of that same song currently regarded as the most valuable 45 ever issued in the UK.

Few collectors pursue the EMI label as a separate entity, preferring to concentrate on individual artists—of whom, of course, there are thousands. Notable among the most popularly pursued artists is the punk act the Sex Pistols, whose first single, "Anarchy in the UK" (2566), exists in two collectible varieties, one crediting Dave Goodman as producer on the B-side, and one crediting Chris Thomas—both were issued in an all-black picture sleeve. Also highly collectible is Kate Bush, who remained with the label for over a decade, during which time a host of rarities emerged. Collectors pursue releases by the Pet Shop Boys and by Duran Duran, whose four years on EMI coincided with the group's period of greatest success (and collectibility).

Further Reading: *Since Records Began: EMI—The First 100 Years,* by Peter Martland (Amadeus Press, 1997)

Excello

Rightly renowned as the first blues label to operate out of the country stronghold of Nashville, where it launched as a subsidiary of Nashboro Records in 1952, Excello is among the labels whose entire catalog is highly prized by collectors, for aesthetic and historical reasons. Among key releases on the label were Arthur Gunter's "Baby, Let's Play House" (2047), the blueprint for Elvis Presley's subsequent Sun 45, and releases by Slim Harpo, Lightnin' Slim, Silas Hogan, Lazy Lester, and Lonesome Sundown.

In addition, Excello was responsible for the original version of the Diamonds' hit "Little Darlin'," performed by the Gladiolas (2101); as Maurice Williams and the Zodiacs, and signed to Herald, the Gladiolas scored a massive hit with "Stay" in 1960.

Issuing both newly recorded and archive material, Excello remained a power in the blues world into the mid-'70s. The catalog has since become a favorite for reissue.

Exodus

Exodus came into being in early 1966, at a time when its Vee-Jay parent was battling bankruptcy. Although the new concern was presented as an independent, its use of Vee-Jay masters, artwork, and even pressings—the label's debut LP actually had a crossed-out Vee-Jay matrix number in its run-off groove—cast sufficient doubt upon its true status that, when the courts finally liquidated Vee-Jay, Exodus was included in the order.

The label nevertheless released a number of LPs in two numerical series, the 300 series, which featured releases by Hoyt Axton, Jimmy Reed, Jerry Butler, Sam Fletcher, and John Lee Hooker, and the 6000 series of jazz releases, which included titles by Eddie Harris and Eric Dolphy.

Factory

Chiswick and Stiff may have set the pace for British independent labels, but into the early '80s, even they were no competition for Factory, the Manchester-based concern established by local scene-maker, BBC producer and TV host Tony Wilson.

From the outset, the label's musical policy was beyond reproach. concentrating almost exclusively on Manchester and its environs, Factory's first signings represented a virtual who's who of local luminaries, including Joy Division, Cabaret Voltaire, John Dowie, and Durutti Column. Taking a leaf out of Stiff's book, Factory brought on board a house producer of soon-to-be-proven renown, Martin Hannett; taking another, Wilson also identified the collectors' need to be constantly challenged and entertained by a hobby.

Particularly through its first five years of activity, the Factory catalog would intersperse records with a plethora of other oddities, issued in strict numerical order, regardless of format or nature. These range from label stationery and posters (the label's very first release, FAC 1, was one such) to real estate: FAC 51 was the Hacienda nightclub, built and operated by Factory from May 1982, and soon to become the focal point for Manchester nightlife. FAC 98 was the hairdressing salon opened in the Hacienda's basement in October 1983. As for the oddities, FAC 99 was New Order manager Rob Gretton's dentistry bill, paid for by Factory after he was beaten up by associates of A Certain Ratio.

Few of these, of course, were obtainable by the average fan. Even among the label's more conventional releases, however, the chances of completeness were slim. Factory's first vinyl release was *A Factory Sample* EP (FAC 2), a limited edition that swiftly went out of print. Early singles by A Certain Ratio and the fledgling Orchestral Maneuvers in the Dark ("Electricity"—FAC 6) vanished swiftly, and who has ever seen a Factory egg-timer (FAC 8)?

Even Joy Division and New Order, the label's brightest stars, have a catalog replete with scarcities and seeming impossibilities, and while Factory LPs tended to remain on the catalog long enough for all interested parties to pick them up, the original packaging was not always so reliable. *Unknown Pleasures* (FACT 10), Joy Division's debut, initially appeared

TEN TOP COLLECTIBLES

Joy Division

"Atmosphere" (Sordide Sentimentale 33002—7-inch, 1980)

Closer (Factory FACT 25—LP with textured sleeve, 1980)

A Factory Sample—Various artists (Factory FAC 2—double 7-inch pack EP with five stickers, 1979)

The Ideal Beginning (Enigma PSS 138—12-inch EP, 1981)

"An Ideal for Living" (Anonymous ANON 1—12-inch reissue, 1978)

"An Ideal for Living" (Enigma PSS 139—EP with fold-out picture sleeve, 1978)

"Komakino" (Factory FAC 28—Flexidisc, 1980)

Short Circuit—*Live at the Electric Circus*—Various artists (Virgin VCL 5003—10-inch EP; orange, yellow, or blue vinyl, 1978)

Still (Factory FACT 40—2-LP with Hessian sleeve, ribbon, 1981)

Unknown Pleasures (Factory FACT 10—LP with textured sleeve, 1979)

---

with a textured sleeve; *Still* (FACT 40), the group's posthumous third, was issued in a Hessian sleeve with card inners and white ribbon.

New Order's *Brotherhood* (FACT 150) LP first arrived in a metallic sleeve (its CD counterpart boasted a metallic booklet) and Durutti Column's *Return Of* (FACT 14) made its debut with a sandpaper sleeve—a gimmick that was swiftly quashed by the retail sector. Any other album that came into contact with it was promptly shredded!

The list goes on—at least one Factory collector believes that it is possible to find at least one collectible variant with every release in the catalog, and while this may be an exaggeration, it probably isn't much of one.

Further confusion can be enjoyed if one also includes the Factory Benelux subsidiary in one's calculations—operating for some 60 releases (numbered FBN 1-55, and apparently randomly thereafter), between 1980–87, the label offered both alternatives to and expansions of a number of the parent label's releases, aside from taunting completists with

a number of unreleased (but nevertheless extant) issues.

Factory folded in 1992 with two final albums, Steve Martland's *Wolfgang* (FAC 406) and the Happy Mondays' . . . *Yes Please!* (FAC 420).

Further Reading: *From Joy Division to New Order: The Factory Story,* by Mick Middles (Virgin, 1996)

Fiction

Britain's Fiction label was launched by Polydor A&R man Chris Parry in 1978 as a vehicle for his own discovery, the Cure—although other acts, including the Associates, the Passions, Eat, and Die Warzau would see releases, the Cure's domination of Fiction's catalog is total—and vice versa. This includes the extracurricular projects "I'm a Cult Hero," a 45 issued under the name the Cult Heroes (FICS 006), with postman Frank Horley replacing Robert Smith on vocals, and a collaboration with video director Tim Pope for 1984's 7-inch and 12-inch singles "I Want to Be a Tree" (FICS 21).

Only the group's first single, "Killing an Arab," was issued elsewhere; the band insisted on releasing the

TEN TOP COLLECTIBLES

The Cure on Fiction

"Catch" (UK Fiction FICSP 26—Clear-vinyl, clear-label 7-inch, 1987)

"The Caterpillar" (UK Fiction FICSP 20—7-inch picture disc, 1984)

Disintegration (UK Fiction FIXHP 14—LP picture disc, 1990)

Entreat (UK Fiction FIXCD 17—Limited-edition LP with yellow sleeve, 1990)

Faith/Carnage Visors (UK Fiction FIXC 6—Cassette with b&w sleeve, 1981)

"I'm a Cult Hero"—The Cult Heroes (UK Fiction FICS 006—7-inch, picture sleeve, 1979)

Kiss Me Kiss Me Kiss Me (UK Fiction FIXHA 13—2-LP shrink-wrapped with bonus orange-vinyl 12-inch, 1987)

"Never Enough" (UK Fiction FICDP 35—Picture-CD single, 1990)

"The Walk" (UK Fiction FICSP 18—7-inch picture disc, 1983)

Wish (UK Fiction CUREPK 1—Promo box set with digipack CD, video, EPK, 1992)

single immediately before Christmas 1978. When Polydor, Fiction's distributors, balked, Parry arranged for an initial release on the Small Wonder independent (SMALL 11); it was then reissued on Fiction (FICS 001) in the new year. The original, an edition of 15,000 copies, is very rare.

Fiction Cure rarities are manifold. In an age in which limited-edition double-pack singles, short-run 12-inch singles and so on were rife, Fiction issued a number of now-scarce pieces. The *Faith* (FIX 6), *Concert* (FIX 10), and *Standing on the Beach* (FIX 12) LPs were issued on cassette, with entire albums' worth of bonus material, none of which has yet been officially issued on CD. The "Hanging Garden" single (FICS 15) was issued with a bonus 7-inch of live material, and the Cure's first US single, "Let's Go to Bed" (Fiction/Important FICSX 17), appeared on red vinyl; "Love Cats" (FICSP 19) was issued as a picture disc.

Impressively, too, when Fiction called something a limited edition, the company meant it; that, and the regular deletion of singles has ensured that the Cure's collectibility isn't simply vast, it also spans their entire catalog. As rare as 1978's "Killing an Arab" might be, 1992's "Friday I'm in Love" 12-inch (FICSX 42) is just as hard to find, all the more so since at least five different colors of vinyl were employed for the pressing.

In addition to the UK Fiction releases, the Cure's worldwide collecting profile has been maintained by licensees Elektra (US), Stunn (Australia), VAP (Japan), and Polydor (other territories).

Further Reading: *The Cure on Record*, by Daren Butler (Omnibus Press, 1995)

Flip

Max and Lillian Feirtag's Flip label launched in 1955, an offshoot from the couple's Los Angeles–based Limax publishing house. The label issued over 60 45s and 78s between 1955–63, but is best remembered for Trudy Williams' Six Teens and Richard Berry, leader of the bands the Pharaohs, the Cadets, and the Lockettes.

Berry issued 11 45s on Flip, among them "Take the Key" (318), "Heaven on Wheels" (336), and "Besame Mucho" (339), but of course he is most famous for "Louie Louie" (321). A 1963 hit for the Kingsmen, the song is perhaps the defining moment

TEN TOP COLLECTIBLES

Flip

"A Casual Look"—The Six Teens (Flip 315—7-inch, 1956)

"Louie Louie"/"You Are My Sunshine"—Richard Berry (Flip 321—7-inch, 1957)

"Movie Magg"—Carl Perkins (Flip 501—7-inch, 1955)

"Sugar Sugar You"—Richard Berry (Flip 327—7-inch, 1957)

"Take the Key"—Richard Berry (Flip 318—7-inch, 1956)

"This Paradise"—The Bel-Aires (Flip 303—Maroon-label 7-inch, 1954)

"Uncle Sam's Man"—The Elgins (Flip 353—7-inch, 1961)

"White Port and Lemon Juice"—The Bel-Aires (Flip 304—7-inch, 1954)

"Why Do I Go to School?"—The Six Teens (Flip 346—7-inch, 1959)

"You're the Girl"—Richard Berry (Flip 331—7-inch, 1958)

in the development and popularization of garage rock, yet it was a flop for Flip when it was issued in 1957. (Two pressings exist, featuring the B-sides "You Are My Sunshine" and "Rock Rock Rock.")

Other Flip artists included the Bel-Aires (predecessors to the Vel-Aires), Donald Woods, Jennell Hawkins, the Elgins, and Lena Calhoun. The best of these artists is gathered together on two Flip label compilations (the label's only LP releases), *12 Flip Hits* (1001) and *Original Recordings by the Artists* (1002)—"Louie Louie" is featured on both sets, while the 1002 disc also includes the original version of another Kingsmen classic, Donald Woods' "Death of an Angel."

Fly

The Fly label was established by Track Records founders Chris Stamp and Kit Lambert, in partnership with music publisher David Platz and Harvest Records chief Malcolm Jones, in the summer of 1970. It was originally to be called Octopus, and test pressings of the projected first 45, T. Rex's "Ride a White Swan," coupled with "Summertime Blues" and "Jewel," were produced and assigned the catalog

number OCTO 1 (found in the dead wax at the edge of the label).

By the time the record was released in October, however, both the B-side and the label name had changed—"Jewel" was replaced by "Is It Love," and more significantly, Octopus had become Fly, with the opening catalog number BUG 1. Copies of the test pressing are fabulously rare; copies of the first-pressing released issue, with a purple label are medium scarce; and all thereafter are history. "Ride a White Swan," reposing now on a mustard label, soared to No. 2 in the UK and ignited what history now recalls as T-Rextacy.

T. Rex released three further singles, and two LPs, on Fly before moving to EMI, where T. Rex frontman Marc Bolan's own T. Rex: Hot Wax label sustained the remainder of his career. "Hot Love" (BUG 6), the group's first No. 1; "Get It On (Bang a Gong)" (BUG 10), its second; and "Jeepster" (BUG 16) are all known with collectible varieties, the most significant being the switch to a new Fly design, during the first-named's early run. The giant hovering Fly that now materialized was the work of artist Roger Dean, best

TEN TOP COLLECTIBLES

Marc Bolan

"Chariot Choogle"—T. Rex (EMI SPRS 346—7-inch promo, 1972)

"Christmas Bop"—T. Rex (EMI MARC 13—Labels only, 1976)

Electric Warrior Preview Single—T. Rex (Fly GRUB 1—7-inch, pink-envelope sleeve, 1971)

Hard on Love (Track 2406 101—LP test pressing, 1972)

"Hippy Gumbo" (Parlophone R5539—7-inch, 1966)

"Midsummer Night's Scene"—John's Children (Track 604 005—7-inch, 1967)

"Ride a White Swan"—T. Rex (Octopus OCTO 1, 7-inch test pressing, 1970)

"The Third Degree" (Decca F12413—7-inch, 1966)

"The Wizard" (Decca F12288—7-inch, 1965)

Zinc Alloy and the Hidden Riders of Tomorrow—T. Rex (EMI BNLA 7751—Promo LP with three-way fold-out sleeve, numbered, 1974)

known for his sleeve art for Yes, Badger, and other groups.

T. Rex was Fly's biggest act by far—indeed, by late 1971, only the Beatles and the Rolling Stones could realistically claim to have ever engendered more British excitement and hysteria than the Bolan boogie. However, South African John Kongos scored a pair of hits for the label in 1971, "He's Gonna Step on You Again" (BUG 8) and "Tokoloshe Man" (BUG 14). An album, *Kongos* (HIFLY 7), also did well.

As heir to the old Regal Zonophone catalog, Fly also scored with two EPs within the Magnifly series, reissuing Procol Harum's "A Whiter Shade of Pale" (ECHO 101), and inevitably, the T. Rex predecessor Tyrannosaurus Rex's "Debora" (ECHO 102)—subsequent issues by Joe Cocker and the Move were less successful, and now rate among the scarcer Fly releases. The Flyback series of LPs, meanwhile, comprised *Best Of* collections for T. Rex (TON 2), the Move (TON 3), and Procol Harum (TON 4), plus a various-artists sampler that added Joe Cocker to the roll call (TON 1).

Further vintage material was issued in the TOOFA series of double albums (at a single LP price, hence the title), by Cocker (TOOFA 1/2), Tyrannosaurus Rex (3/4) and the Move (5/6), while the last-ever issue in the regular LP series was another T. Rex compilation, *Bolan Boogie* (HIFLY 8).

The Move and Cocker also issued new material on Fly, the singles "When Alice Comes Back to the Farm" (BUG 2) and "Cry Me a River" (BUG 3), respectively, together with the albums *Looking On* (HIFLY 1) and *Cocker Happy* (HIFLY 3). Other artists on the label included former Bonzo Dog Band frontman Viv Stanshall, Georgia Brown, Third World War, Tidbits, John Williams, Chris Neal, and John Keating. The final Fly 45, in spring 1972, was Brown's "Turn Out the Light" (BUG 18).

Gee

Gee was one of several labels launched by New York entrepreneur George Goldner, the first of which, the Latin-based Tico, dated back to 1951. The urban-blues label Rama followed in 1953, before he formed Gee—titled for Rama's biggest hit, the Crows' "Gee" (5).

Gee hit the headlines immediately, via Frankie Lymon and the Teenagers' 1956 smash "Why Do Fools Fall in Love" (1002). Credited to the Teenagers featuring Frankie Lymon, this release exists in at least three collectible varieties, a first issue on a red-and-gold label, and a more common red-and-black label, which in turn, appears in two varieties, one featuring the B-side, "Please Be Mine," as a vocal duet, the other featuring the song with a Lymon solo vocal.

"I Want You to Be My Girl" (1012), the group's follow-up, was originally credited to the Teenagers featuring Frankie Lymon, before the singer's ascendancy to stardom saw the more familiar nomenclature adopted; the earlier release is many times rarer. That said, all original Teenagers releases are collectible, as are the pair of solo 45s issued by Lymon alone (1039, 1052—the first pressing of 1039, incidentally, was credited to the Teenagers, subsequent issues to Lymon.)

In 1955, Goldner sold a 50 percent interest in Tico, Rama, and Gee to Joe Kolsky, and the following year, the partnership launched Roulette Records, with Morris Levy. Just months later, however, Goldner sold out of all four labels and launched new labels, Mark X, End, and Gone, home for the Chantels, the Dubs, and Little Anthony and the Imperials, but most familiar to modern collectors as the hosts of several pre-Motown Berry Gordy, Jr., productions, including the Five Stars' "Ooh Shucks" (Mark X 7006) and a pair of Miracles releases, "Got a Job" (End 1017) and "I Cry" (End 1029, reissued 1084).

These labels, too, would later be sold to Roulette, before Goldner joined with Leiber and Stoller to form Red Bird. Goldner's final label, in 1970, was Firebird—sadly, he passed away shortly after the company's launch.

Gee, meanwhile, remained in action until 1962, issuing fine recordings by the Heartbeats, featuring Shep Sheppard of the Limelites. Signed at the time to Hull, the group's "A Thousand Miles Away" (Hull 720) proved too big a hit for the smaller label to cope with. Rama picked it up for distribution nationwide (216),

then retained the group for further releases on both Rama and Gee. The Cleftones and the Regents—with the ever-popular *Barbara Ann* (SGLP 706)—also released classic records on the label.

Harvest

Best known as home to some of the undisputed giants of the 1970s British rock scene—Pink Floyd and Deep Purple paramount among them—EMI's Harvest subsidiary was established in 1968 by Malcolm Jones, to provide a fertile environment for "progressive" bands hitherto spread across the EMI catalog.

That brief was fulfilled, with room to spare. The label's first UK releases, in June 1969, comprised 45s by free-festival regulars the Edgar Broughton Band ("Evil"—HAR 5001), singer-songwriter Michael Chapman, the classically inclined Barclay James Harvest, and light-rockers Bakerloo; the following months brought LPs by Deep Purple (*Book of Taliesyn*—SHVL 751), poet Pete Brown, folk singers Shirley and Dolly Collins, and Chapman, all of which were previewed on the impossibly rare (100 copies) *Harvest Sampler* (SPSLP 118).

This mixed bag set the standards by which Harvest would operate for at least the next five years. Purple and Floyd (the latter of which arrived via ex-frontman Syd Barrett's two solo albums, before unleashing its own *Ummagumma*—SHDW 1/2—in 1969) may dominate the label in terms of its best-known collectibles, but to dwell on either is to overlook the almost obsessive zeal with which Harvest hunters pursue now-scarce albums by the Third Ear Band, the Panama Limited Jug Band, Forest, Tea and Symphony, Quatermass, Chris Spedding, Spontaneous Combustion, Babe Ruth, and so many more. As with other UK prog-inclined labels of the day, the one- or two-album act was the rule, and the Harvest label overflows with them.

Singles by these bands are colossally hard to collect. Purple and Floyd (the latter, again, via Syd Barrett—the band itself released no UK Harvest singles whatsoever until 1979) are the ones everybody seems to be searching for, with values for Barrett's "Octopus" (5009) outpacing virtually everything else on the label.

Practically every other Harvest 45 issued prior to 1972 is scarce, however, and that includes releases by such putative stars as the Broughtons ("Out Demons Out"—5015; and "Apache Drop-Out"—5032 actually made the UK Top 40), Roy Harper, Kevin Ayers (whose Harvest output is possibly the highlight of the entire catalog), and the last days of '60s hit-makers the Move, as members Roy Wood and Jeff Lynne moved toward their respective destinies in Wizzard and the Electric Light Orchestra.

Those bands would bring Harvest its first reliable hit-single acts, with Wizzard scoring two successive No. 1s in 1973. Of course, 1973 also brought the Floyd's monstrous *Dark Side of the Moon* (SHVL 804), still one of the biggest-selling albums in history, and it is at this point that many Harvest collectors lose interest, since the label stopped operating as a welcoming home for rock's dottiest denizens, and began functioning like just another conventional record label.

Certainly this impression is borne out by the official label history, published in the *Harvest Festival* box set. Again and again, interviewees wax rhapsodic about the label's early days, but few have more than a few facts and figures to relate about the post–*Dark Side* era. Nevertheless, some intriguing prospects are realized by a careful trawl through this period, including further gems from Ayers and Harper, interesting sets by Strapps, Gryphon, the last days of Focus, and the Soft Machine.

Releases by Japanese rockers Sadistic Mika Band and Bill Nelson's Be Bop Deluxe are extremely collectible, while the late '70s saw Harvest plunge headfirst into the punk scene with the release of *The Roxy, London WC2*, a lo-fi live document of the seminal punk venue, which gave vinyl debuts to future superstars the Wire (who remained Harvest artists), Buzzcocks, the Adverts, and X-Ray Spex. Australia's Saints, New York's Shirts, and power-pop hopefuls the Banned are also worthy of investigation.

Harvest dipped into roots reggae with very collectible albums by Britain's Matumbi and Jamaica's Israel Vibration; the steel band Trinidad Oil Company scored an unexpected hit with "The Calendar Song" (5122); there was even a dose of disco from La Belle Epoque. European metal band the Scorpions and former Jam bassist Bruce Foxton also made

TEN TOP COLLECTIBLES

Pink Floyd

Animals (Columbia AP-1—Promo LP with edited "Pigs," 1977)

"Apples and Oranges" (UK Columbia DB 8310—7-inch promo, 1967)

"Arnold Layne" (Tower 333—7-inch, picture sleeve, 1967)

Dark Side of the Moon (Mobile Fidelity MFQR 017—Boxed LP "ultra high-quality recording," 1982)

"It Would Be So Nice" (Tower 426—7-inch, picture sleeve, 1968)

"Octopus"—Syd Barrett (UK Harvest 5009—7-inch, 1969)

The Piper at the Gates of Dawn (Tower T5093—Mono LP, 1967)

Saucerful of Secrets (UK Columbia SX 6258—Mono LP, 1968)

Selected Tracks from Shine On (EMI SHINE 1—Promo CD, 1992)

Ummagumma (Harvest STBB 388—2-LP with *Gigi* soundtrack visible on sleeve, 1969)

collectible excursions—indeed, Foxton's "Playing This Game to Win" 45 (5239) was the final Harvest release, in July 1985.

Further Reading: *Harvest Festival* (booklet within the four-CD box set of the same name—EMI 5211982)

Heritage

Distributed by MGM, producer Jerry Ross's Heritage label was launched in 1968 with the Cherry People's "And Suddenly" (801), a Top 50 hit whose collectibility today is increased by the presence of future Angel guitarist Punky Meadows in the lineup. (The band was originally known as the English Setters.) Heritage released one Cherry People LP (HT/HTS 3500); a second was scheduled (3501) but canceled.

Bill Deal and the Rhondels followed the People into the chart with a cover of Maurice Williams' "May I" (803)—the Virginia Beach band would score a total of five mini-hits for Heritage. Other Heritage artists were less successful, though the Duprees, a New York vocal quintet whose fame reached back to some luscious recordings for Coed during the early '60s, have long

been popular. Gene Bua and Euphoria, on the other hand, are as obscure today as they ever were.

Ross closed Heritage in 1970 and launched a new label, Colossus (named for his production company). The imprint promptly scored with hits by the Dutch band Shocking Blue, including the chart-topping "Venus" (108).

Hickory

Although Hickory is best known as a country label, a division of the Acuff-Rose music publishers, its output also includes a number of light-rock releases, including Donovan's first US sides, Sue Thompson's superlative "Paper Tiger" (1284), and cuts by Kris Jensen, the Newbeats, Australian vocalist Frank Ifield, and B.J. Thomas. Roy Acuff and Don Gibson numbered among the more conventional Hickory stars; the young Doug Kershaw, alongside brother Rusty, also recorded for the label.

Country (and Thompson) collectors will disagree, of course, but the Donovan catalog is Hickory's most collectible, including as it does the formative post-Dylanisms of "Catch the Wind" (1309), "Colours"

TEN TOP COLLECTIBLES

Donovan

"Catch the Wind" (Hickory 1309—7-inch, 1965)

Children of Lir (Ireland Fiona, no catalog number—CD, 1995)

Donovan Rising (UK Permanent Press PERMLP 2—LP, 1990)

A Gift from a Flower to a Garden (Epic N2N 171—Mono 2-LP box set with portfolio, 1967)

HMS Donovan (UK Dawn DNLD 4001—2-LP with gatefold sleeve, 1971)

"Remember the Alamo" (UK Pye 7N 17088—7-inch, 1966)

"Rock 'n' Roll with Me" (UK Epic EPC 2661—Quad 7-inch with picture sleeve, 1975)

Sunshine Superman (Epic LN 24217—Mono LP, 1966)

"Sunshine Superman" (Epic 10045—Red-vinyl 7-inch promo, 1966)

Universal Soldier (UK Pye NEP 24219—EP with "summer 1955" misprint, 1965)

(1324), "Universal Soldier" (1338), and two original LPs, *Catch the Wind* (LPM 123) and *Fairytale* (LPM 127). This material has been recycled so much as to sometimes seem worthless, but captured in its original format, Donovan's naïve magic is inescapable.

Following tie-ups with MGM and ABC, Hickory folded in the late '70s.

Hip

A Stax label subsidiary, Hip flourished for a handful of releases during 1969–72, of which just one is especially sought after today—the Knowbody Else's eponymous LP (7003), marking the debut of the future Black Oak Arkansas. Other acts on the label included Southwest FOB, the Goodees, and Paris Pilot.

Homestead

One of the most important of all US independent labels of the alternative age, Homestead was launched by Gerard Crosley in 1984 with the eponymous debut LP by Boston's Blackjacks (HMS 001). Following through with sets by Salem 66, the Dogmatics, and Great Plains, Homestead received its first national notice after linking with maverick producer Steve Albini's controversial Big Black.

The group's "Racer X" 12-inch, in April 1985, was one of several characteristically confrontational releases by the band, all of which are now sought after by hardcore punk aficionados.

Another key Homestead release was the compilation *Speed Trials* (HMS 011), featuring rare material from across the extreme rock spectrum of the day—the Fall, the Beastie Boys (the hyper-rare "Egg Raid on Mojo"), Lydia Lunch, Sonic Youth, and the Swans all contributed, with the latter also issuing the "Raping a Slave" 12-inch (HMS 017). Among other crucial Homestead releases from this early period are Australia's Died Pretty's 12-inch *Out of the Unknown* (HMS 014) and several early releases by the then-unknown Dinosaur Jr. (the earliest pressings were originally, and collectibly, released credited to Dinosaur only).

Seattle's Green River, precursors of the later Mudhoney–Pearl Jam axis, New York noise terrorists Sonic Youth, Death of Samantha, and Live Skull also made several now-valued releases. Boston-based Live Skull's origins were also recalled with a 12-inch by the earlier Uzi, *Sleep Asylum* (HMS 055).

Hitherto, Homestead's appeal had remained strictly cult American; 1986, however, saw the arrival of further Australians Nick Cave and the Bad Seeds, Scraping Foetus off the Wheel, and Einstürzende Neubauten, from the UK label Mute. Cave's 12-inch Homestead singles are extraordinarily difficult to find today, particularly when compared with their UK counterparts.

Breaking Circus, the Membranes, Big Dipper, Phantom Tollbooth, and the Volcano Suns arrived during 1986–87, alongside New Zealanders the Verlaines, the Chills, the Clean, and the Tall Dwarfs, all of whom helped introduce America to that country's Flying Nun label, one of the most important (and itself collectible) of all Antipodean labels. Controversial punk G.G. Allin also made a number of Homestead releases—interestingly, his brother was once a member of the Boston band Thrills, alongside Blackjacks frontman Johnny Angel.

Growing awareness of the scene unfolding in the Pacific Northwest brought a now-much-in-demand split 45 featuring two of that area's most vital acts, Beat Happening and Screaming Trees (HMS 110); late-'80s and early-'90s releases by the Pastels, Sebadoh, Giant Sand, and two astonishingly prolific acts, Daniel Johnston and the Happy Flowers, are also worth looking for.

Homestead made several classic archive releases, including collecting a mass of material by Cleveland punk pioneers the Styrenes (*It's Artastic*—HMS 173) and the Electric Eels (*The God Says Fuck You*—HMS 174). However, the sheer weight of major-label interest in the now-burgeoning alternative scene was taking its toll on Homestead's ability to attract and retain the talent that had once established its reputation. The changing marketplace, too, affected the label's willingness to issue either 7-inch or 12-inch releases; it preferred to concentrate on full-length CD albums. This certainly affected the collecting market, although the occasional break in this rule—

"Ambivalence"—Pin Group (NZ—Flying Nun 001—7-inch, 1981)

Boodle Boodle Boodle—The Clean (NZ Flying Nun 003—EP, 1982)

"By Night"—The Bats (NZ Flying Nun 024—7-inch, 1983)

"Death and the Maidens"—The Verlaines (NZ Flying Nun 014—7-inch, 1983)

Eric Glandy Memorial Band—Eric Glandy Memorial Band (Flying Nun 049—EP, 1986)

"Schwimmin in der See"—The Builders (NZ Flying Nun 006—7-inch, 1982)

"Show Me to the Bellrope"—This Sporting Life (NZ Flying Nun 011—7-inch, 1983)

"Tally Ho!"—The Clean (NZ Flying Nun 002—7-inch, 1981)

"Tired Sun"—The Able Tasmans (NZ Flying Nun 043—7-inch, 1985)

"Uptown Sheep"—Crystal Zoom (NZ Flying Nun 030—7-inch, 1984)

Soul-Junk's "1945" 7-inch (HMS 225), for example—remains in high demand.

Homestead wound down in the mid-'90s, following releases by William Parker, Hoosegow, and the Joe Morris Ensemble (HMS 233).

Horizon

Dave Hubert launched the Horizon label in 1960, purely to document the then-vibrant folk scene exploding around Los Angeles in general, and the Troubadour club in particular. Distributed by the jazz label World Pacific, the label's output is a treasure-trove for the regional folk specialist, with almost every release boasting something (or, more likely, someone) to catch the sharp eye.

The label's 45s output is, without exception, hard to find, with such Hoyt Axton offerings as "Grizzly Bear" (2) and "The Happy Song" (6) especially desirable. Axton's debut LP, too, is a fascinating find. *The Balladeer* (WP 1601) was recorded live at the Troubadour, with a band including one Jim McQuinn (actually McGuinn); this set was reissued the following year as *Greenback Dollar* (1602), its new

sleeve and title apparently matched by a new set of recordings of its predecessor's contents. In fact, the album simply rearranged *The Balladeer*'s track listing, dropping two songs, reshuffling the rest, and finally, removing the sounds of the audience! What is most interesting about this is the sense that this doctored version may actually be the truest, that the stories, patter, and of course, applause that punctuate *The Balladeer* were themselves unrelated intruders.

Elsewhere, the Horizon catalog features an amazing array of past and future stars: the Chambers Brothers, Brownie McGhee and Sonny Terry, Mike Seeger, the Weavers' Erik Darling, Mason Williams, and Tommy Tedesco, among many more. The unknown Barry McGuire is one half of Barry and Barry (alongside Barry Kane), who cut the 1962 LP *Here and Now* (SWP 1608); Rod McKuen made a splash with his *New Sounds of Folk Music* (SWP 1612), while an attempt to ride the then-prevalent hootenanny boom saw the release of two now very collectible various-artists collections, *Hootenanny at the Troubador* (SWP 1616) and *Blues Hoot* (SWP 1617).

Billy Strange

The Best of Billy Strange (Surrey SS 1002—LP, 1965)

Billy Strange with the Challengers (GNP Crescendo GNPS 2030—Stereo LP, 1966)

English Hits of '65 (GNP Crescendo GNP 2009—Mono LP, 1965)

The Funky 12 String Guitar—The Transients (Horizon SWP 1633—LP, 1963)

"I'll Remember April" (Buena Vista 406—7-inch, 1962)

"James Bond Theme" (GNP Crescendo 341—7-inch, 1965)

"Johnny Shiloh" (Buena Vista 417—7-inch, 1963)

Limbo Rock (Coliseum CM 1001—LP, 1962)

"Long Steel Road" (Liberty 55362—7-inch, 1961)

"A Lotta Limbo" (Coliseum 605—7-inch, 1963)

Another fascinating series intended to tell the "story" of folk's staple instruments, the banjo (*The Banjo Story*, WP 1623) and the acoustic guitar (*The 12 String Story, SWP* 1626), through contributions from both known and unknown denizens of those scenes. Rare solo tracks by Jim (sometimes James) McGuinn, Bob Gibson, Glen Campbell, and Eric Weissberg are among the attractions here, while virtuoso Billy Strange was among the self-professed Transients who cut 1963's *The Funky 12 String Guitar* (SWP 1633).

Horizon closed in late 1963, some months after its acquisition by Vee-Jay. A number of Hoyt Axton's albums were reissued by Vee-Jay in 1964, together with a "best of" and a new album; other Horizon material subsequently appeared on the Surrey label.

Hull

One of the many labels housed within New York's legendary Brill Building, Blanche Casalin's Hull label operated between 1955–66, with its heyday at the dawn of that era, via a succession of unforgettable New York singing groups. Best known among these are the

Avons, whose "Our Love Will Never End" (717) is especially sought after in its original black-label pressing (the later red is reasonably common). The group also cut a eponymous LP (1000) in 1960.

Also popular are the Heartbeats, who debuted with the immortal "Crazy For You" (711) before moving to the Gee and Rama stable after their third Hull single, "A Thousand Miles Away" (720), became too big a hit for little Hull to deal with. Scarce Heartbeats releases are again related to the label design—black is better than red, and pink is even better: "Crazy for You" was initially issued in that color, and in two varieties of its own. The rarest of all the group's 45s credits Sheppard-Miller as co-writers of that single; an amended pressing lists Miller alone.

Sheppard would return to Hull as a member of Shep and the Limelites, whose 13 singles output was accompanied by a colossally rare LP, 1962's *Our Anniversary* (1001).

The various-artists collection *Your Favorite Singing Groups* (1002) rounded up many of the label's finest releases, including cuts by the Monotones, the Elegants, the Pastels, the Supremes (not the Motown act),

TEN TOP COLLECTIBLES

The Avons

The Avons (Hull HLP 1000—LP, 1960)

"Baby" (Hull 722—7-inch, 1957)

"A Girl to Call My Own" (Hull 754—7-inch, 1962)

"Oh Gee Baby" (Groove 58-0022—7-inch, picture sleeve, 1963)

"Our Love Will Never End" (Hull 717—Black-label 7-inch, 1956)

"We Fell in Love" (Mercury 71618—7-inch, 1960)

"What Love Can Do" (Hull 731—7-inch, 1958)

"What Will I Do" (Hull 728—7-inch, 1958)

"Whisper" (Hull 744—7-inch, 1961)

"You Are So Close to Me" (Hull 726—7-inch, 1958)

---

the Avons, the Desires, the Legends, the Miller Sisters, the Sparks, the Beltones, and the Carousels.

That was Hull's final album; the label continued issuing 45s into 1966, though none had the impact or importance of the first years' issues. The label was then incorporated into Roulette, which reissued the Shep and the Limelites album the following year.

Your Favorite Singing Groups has been ranked among the most sought-after compilation albums ever issued; the Avons and Limeliters albums among the rarest LPs of their age. Bootlegs of the Avons, at least, are known, and experts admit they are difficult to identify.

Immediate

Immediate was the brainchild of businessman Tony Calder and Andrew Loog Oldham, manager and producer of the Rolling Stones and the first of the new wave of entrepreneurs to shake the cobwebbed halls of traditional British pop during the so-called Swinging '60s.

More importantly, however, Immediate was also the role model for almost every independent UK label

of the next decade and beyond (both Chiswick and Stiff, pioneers of the punk-era DIY label boom, were fiercely indebted to Immediate's example), while the company's pop-art imagery and eye for catchy slogans still dominates rock iconography. The fact that the label's actual output almost universally lives up to these same high standards is simply the icing on a fabulous cake.

Immediate debuted in August 1965, with the first fruits of a licensing deal with the US Bang label, the McCoys' "Hang On Sloopy" (001)—the group would ultimately see six 45s issued on the label, and it is perhaps surprising to learn that of the 22 singles released by Immediate during its first six months, the only other chart entry was the McCoys' own follow-up, "Fever" (21).

Ignored by the record-buying public, in the interim, were releases by future Velvet Underground vocalist Nico ("I'm Not Saying—003—one of several Immediate releases produced by Jimmy Page); Gregory Phillips ("Down by the Boondocks"—004—later covered by Depeche Mode's Martin Gore); another US license, the Strangeloves ("Cara-Lin"—007);

John Mayall and the Bluesbreakers (the classic "I'm Your Witch Doctor"—012—featuring Eric Clapton); comedian Jimmy Tarbuck (a Rolling Stones cover, "Wastin' Time"—018); and the Mockingbirds ("You Stole My Love"—015—performed by Graham Gouldman, with Julie Driscoll on backing vocals; the song was later covered by the Jimmy Page–era Yardbirds).

Debuts by such proto-psychedelic legends as the Golden Apples of the Sun, the Factotums, and Les Fleur de Lys, and a solo single by Glyn Johns, now far better known as one of Britain's top producers, also passed by.

Immediate's first homegrown hit was Chris Farlowe's version of another Stones song, "Think" (023), and over the next year, Jagger-Richard compositions remained Immediate's only other chart entries: "Sitting on a Fence" (recorded by Twice as Much—033) and "Out of Time" and "Ride On Baby" (Farlowe again—035, 038; "Out of Time" brought the label its first chart-topper).

The Rolling Stones' dominance of the Immediate catalog was finally broken by Steve Marriott and Ronnie Lane of the Small Faces. They joined the label in late 1966, immediately handing Chris Farlowe another hit, "My Way of Giving" (041), before displacing him as Immediate's biggest-selling act. The band's own string of classic 45s was joined by two LPs, including the legendary *Ogden's Nut Gone Flake* (IMLP/IMSP 012), and sufficient unreleased demos, outtakes, and sessions to ensure that "new" Small Faces material has been appearing ever since. The Charly label's four-CD *The Immediate Years* (CD IMM BOX 1) box set is probably the most complete summary of this material, though there are omissions even there. (Other Immediate acts similarly summarized by Charly include the Nice and Humble Pie.)

P.P. Arnold, Fleetwood Mac, and Amen Corner also rank among Immediate hit-makers; the young Rod Stewart, Duncan Browne, and Mike D'Abo rate among the most promising hopefuls. Neither commercial nor critical support could prevent Immediate from collapsing in financial disarray in 1970, however—the final single, perhaps appropriately, was the Amen Corner's coupling of "Get Back"/"Farewell to the Real Magnificent Seven" (084). The last album was a label sampler, *Happy to Be Part of the Industry of Human Happiness*—with the extremely odd catalog number IMLYIN 2 (say it fast).

The collectibility of the Immediate label (and its short-lived Instant subsidiary) has never been in doubt; original releases are scarce across the entire 85 singles and 36 LPs catalog, with a handful of albums fetching genuinely serious money, including the supposedly Keith Richards–led Aranbee Pop Symphony Orchestra's *Today's Pop Symphony* (IMLP/SP 003), original editions of the Small Faces' *Ogden's*, and rare British pressings of the German *In Memoriam* (IMLP 022) collection, along with barely released albums by Billy Nicholls (*Would You Believe?*—IMCP 009), Duncan Browne (*Give Me Take You*—IMSP 018), and Michael D'Abo (*Gulliver's Travels*—Instant INLP 003).

Another Instant release manages to combine the obsessiveness of record collectors with the fanaticism of soccer fans—*Recorded Highlights: European Cup Final 1968* (INLP 001) offers commentary from Manchester United's 4-1 win over Benfica, and is Britain's rarest sports record by far.

Of the singles, all are worth seeking out, but special mention must be made of the Apostolic Intervention's version of the Small Faces' "(Tell Me) Have You Ever Seen Me" (043), the Australian Playboys' "Black Sheep" (054), picture-sleeved editions of the Small Faces' "Tin Soldier" (062), and promo pressings of the same combo's "Afterglow of Your Love" (077), inadvertently pressed with an alternate version of the B-side, "Wham Bam Thank You Ma'am."

Releases on Immediate's American wing, too, are much sought after. Included among these are an otherwise unavailable version of the Small Faces' "Mad John" (5012) and one 1969 single that has no UK equivalent, "Sylvie," performed by Chris Farlowe's backing band, the Hill (5016).

Given the rarity and desirability of so many Immediate originals, it might appear queer that many of these apparent obscurities now seem as familiar as the greatest hits in history—and most of them probably are. Almost from the moment Immediate closed its

TEN TOP COLLECTIBLES

Small Faces

"Almost Grown" (Press 5007—7-inch, 1969)

"My Mind's Eye" (RCA Victor 47-9055—7-inch, 1966)

Ogden's Nut Gone Flake (Immediate Z12 52009—LP with round cover, 1968)

"Sha La La La Lee" (Press 9826—7-inch, 1966)

Small Faces (UK Decca LK 4790—Red-label LP, 1966)

Small Faces (UK Immediate AS 1—One-sided 7-inch promo, 1967)

There Are but 4 Small Faces (Immediate Z12 5002—LP with color cover, 1967)

"Tin Soldier" (Immediate 5003—7-inch, picture sleeve, 1968)

"Understanding" (RCA Victor 47-8949—7-inch, 1966)

"What'cha Gonna Do About It?" (Press 9794—7-inch, 1965)

doors in 1970, the catalog has been recycled, reissued, and revived on so many occasions that only the classic Sun label can reasonably claim to have received more cavalier treatment.

From odd issues on the Springboard (US) and NEMS (UK) labels during the 1970s, to a string of compilations and reissues masterminded by Sony in the early '90s, and on to the seriously collector-oriented issues from Charly and the Castle/Sanctuary Group of decade's end, there is scarcely a single Immediate recording left that has not now been reissued, with the arrival in 2000 of Castle's six-CD recounting of the entire Immediate singles catalog, plus releases for even the Billy Nicholls and Duncan Browne albums the crowning glory. Only the European Cup album remains totally unavailable in some form or other.

Further Reading: *2Stoned: A Memoir of London in the 1960s,* by Andrew Loog Oldham (Secker & Warburg, 2002)

Imperial

The Imperial story divides neatly into two very separate collecting areas. The first, dating from the label's foundation in Los Angeles in 1946, traces founder Lew Chudd's love for Latin, folk, and R&B music—most significantly, Fats Domino, whose voluminous catalog was to dominate the Imperial vista for more than a decade. The second era follows the label's acquisition by Liberty in 1964, and the parent company's decision to utilize its new subsidiary as (among other things) an outlet for the British Invasion.

Original Imperial releases were dominated by the 10-inch LP format and are primarily of documentary value. The catalog swung toward New Orleans–based R&B in 1949, the year in which Domino made his debut with "The Fat Man" (5058); other key artists recording for Imperial during the 1950s included T-Bone Walker, Smiley Lewis, Lil' Son Jackson, and the Spiders, with Imperial A&R man Dave Bartholomew's band accompanying them.

Two albums cut by Bartholomew for Imperial during the early '60s, *Fats Domino Presents* (9162) and *New Orleans House Party* (9217), are much sought after in both mono and stereo. Other desirable Imperial releases followed the label's purchase and selective reissue of the Aladdin and Minit catalogs, in 1961 and 1963, respectively.

However, the prevalent view of Imperial as an R&B-oriented label is not especially accurate. Jazzmen Sonny Criss and Warner Marsh, country star Slim Whitman, big bands, and folk and gospel artists all had a part to play in the label's success, while another Imperial treasure is the Teddy Bears' *The Teddy Bears Sing!* (12010), one of Imperial's first stereo issues—and one of producer Phil Spector's last.

Nevertheless, it was R&B that dominated, and it was Domino who brought Imperial its first crossover hit, with the classic "Ain't It a Shame" (5348). Indeed, Domino's entire 1950s catalog is extraordinarily collectible, being littered with colored- (red-) vinyl 45s, a lengthy series of hard-to-find extended plays, and a mass of LPs.

In 1957, Imperial landed another major hit when it poached Ricky Nelson, star of television's *The Adventures of Ozzie and Harriet*, away from Verve—who, unbelievably, had never placed the lad under contract. Opening his Imperial career with "Be Bop Baby" (5463), Nelson remained with Imperial throughout his period of greatest stardom (he departed for Decca in 1963), and again, possesses a back catalog of startling complexity and value.

Liberty's purchase of Imperial in 1964 ushered in a whole new era for the label. Nelson and Domino had already departed; other Imperial veterans were dropped, as Liberty set about completely reshaping the label's image and output. New American talent included the eminently collectible Pacific Northwest heroes the Wailers, Johnny Rivers, P.J. Proby, drum maestro Sandy Nelson, Jackie DeShannon, and Cher—whose Imperial catalog seems to become more collectible every year. The British Invasion, meanwhile, brought in a wealth of now-legendary names.

British Invasion mono albums from this era are not difficult to find, though prices tend to be high in acknowledgement of the era's wide collectibility. Stereo releases, distinguishable by catalog numbers in the 12200 series, are scarcer. Worth watching for are releases by the Swinging Blue Jeans (including a corking debut—9261/12261), the Hollies, Brian Epstein protégés Billy J. Kramer and the Dakotas, Petula Clark, Dave Dee, Dozy, Beaky, Mick and Tich,

TEN TOP COLLECTIBLES

The Hollies

"(Ain't That) Just Like Me" (UK Parlophone R5030—7-inch 1963)

"The Baby" (Epic 10842—7-inch, picture sleeve, 1972)

"Carrie Ann" (Epic 10180—7-inch, picture sleeve, 1967)

Hear! Here! (Imperial LP 9299—LP, 1965)

The Hollies (Imperial LP 9265—LP, black label with stars, 1964)

I Can't Let Go (UK Parlophone GEP 8951—EP, 1966)

"If I Needed Someone" (Imperial 66271—7-inch, 1968)

"Just One Look" (Imperial 66026—7-inch, 1964)

"Stay" (Liberty 55674—7-inch, 1964)

"Yes I Will" (Imperial 66099—7-inch, 1965)

Georgie Fame, and Jackie DeShannon. For true specialists, Cher's 1966 single "Behind the Door" (66217) offers a seldom-heard composition by Invasion songwriter Graham Gouldman (later of 10cc), the demand for which was acknowledged in 2000 when the song was selected as the title for a Cher rarities CD.

Early releases by the O'Jays are another key to the label's modern popularity. Their 1965 *Coming On Through* (9290/12290) is seldom seen these days, while 13 Imperial 45s include such classics as "Whip It on Me Baby" (66121), "Friday Night" (66197), and the very scarce "I'll Never Forget You" (66162).

In 1968, the Transamerica Corporation purchased the Liberty group and incorporated it into its own United Artists label. A new generation of artists was brought on board, including Classics IV, Hapsash and the Coloured Coat, Moon, Warren Zevon, and the Bonzo Dog Band—all are collected today (the Bonzos especially so), but their commercial impact was negligible. A similar fate awaited a pair of very rare albums by Kim Fowley, 1968's *Born to Be Wild* (12413) and *Outrageous* (12423).

Over the next few years, Imperial was slowly wound down, with the best of its catalog incorporated elsewhere within the UA group—the debut album by the Groundhogs, *Blues Obituary* (12452), was originally issued on Imperial, the prelude to a healthy career on the parent label during the 1970s. Imperial finally ceased operations in 1971, its final LP release being the Bonzos' *Keynsham* (12457); a subsequent projected LP by Fantasy was canceled.

In

Distributed by Dart Record Sales of Chicago, the short-lived In label issued three LPs in 1964, all of which are of collectible interest. LP 1001, *The Big Hootenanny,* is a testament to the high-flying days of the folk revival, when the very mention of the "H" word seemed a license to print money. LP-1002, *The Swinging 12 String,* brought to bear the talents of Glen Campbell and Leon Russell, again with an eye for the folk market—the album begins and ends with a song called "Hooten' "; and LP-1003, Rod McKuen's *Seasons in the Sun,* was to prove many Americans' introduction to the work of Belgian-born songwriter Jacques Brel.

The title track alone ranks among Brel's best-known (and loved) efforts, spawning an immediate

TEN TOP COLLECTIBLES

Jacques Brel

American Debut (Columbia AWS 324—LP, 1959)

Babar/Pierre et le loup (France Barclay 80 406—LP, 1972)

En public olympia 1961 (France Philips 6332 077—LP, 1961)

Jacques Brel 3 (France Philips 70-473—10-inch LP, 1958)

Le plat pays (France Barclay 70 475—EP, picture sleeve, 1962)

L'homme de la mancha (France Barclay 80 381—LP, 1968)

Les bon bons 67 (France Barclay 71 18—EP, picture sleeve, 1967)

Les bourgeois (France Barclay 70 493—EP, picture sleeve, 1962)

Les paumes du petit matin (France Barclay 70 452—EP, picture sleeve, 1962)

Vesoul (France Barclay 80 373—10-inch LP, 1968)

hit cover by the Kingston Trio, together with further efforts all across the pop, rock, and jazz spectrum. While few of McKuen's albums are recognized as either rare or collectible, both mono and stereo editions of this particular issue are sought after.

Interphon

One of the most ambitious labels in the Vee-Jay stable is also the shortest lived. Interphon was established in June 1964 as an outlet for foreign licenses—the LP *Welcome to the Discoteque*, by Argentinean singer Alberto Cortez, was scheduled as the debut release. As it happened, the album appeared on the Tollie subsidiary (56002), and Interphon instead opened its account with *Have I the Right?* (IN 88001), by British beat band the Honeycombs.

Produced by the legendary Joe Meek (who licensed it to Pye in the UK), the album featured two of the Honeycombs' three US 45s—the title track (7707) and "Colour Slide" (7716); "I Can't Stop" (7713) was not included. Issued in both mono and reprocessed stereo, the Interphon album also appeared on Vee-Jay itself, albeit still bearing the Interphon catalog number.

The Honeycombs' US catalog is not a difficult set to find—both "Have I the Right" and "I Can't Stop" were Top 50 hits. Other Interphon singles, however, are scarce.

I.R.S.

Although its founder, Miles Copeland, was an American, the International Record Syndicate launched in London, England, in 1977. It was originally known as Faulty Products, an umbrella for a handful of small labels sponsored by Copeland.

Step Forward, Illegal, and Deptford Fun City all enjoyed considerable acclaim via a stream of intelligent releases by some of the punk movement's most left-of-center cults. These included Wayne County (the *Paranoia Paradise* EP—Illegal IL 002), Alternative TV ("How Much Longer"—DFC 02—debuted the group's awkward appeal), Chelsea (a string of collectible releases on Step Forward opened with the anthem "Right to Work"—SF2), the Models (featur-ing Adam and the Ants guitarist Marco Pirroni, "Freeze"—SF 3), and Menace (the fabled "Screwed Up"—IL 004).

Also of note was the presence of former Velvet Underground bassist John Cale, as the labels' in-house producer. His *Animal Justice* EP (IL 003), released in 1977, has escalated in value over the years, while test pressings for a withdrawn follow-up 45, "Jack the Ripper (In the Moulin Rouge)" (IL 006), are very seldom seen. The release of the song was canceled following the emergence in Britain's Yorkshire of a real-life "ripper" killer.

Cale produced the Menace 45; he also worked with Sham 69 and Squeeze, bands who debuted on Step Forward ("I Don't Wanna"—SF 4) and Deptford Fun City, respectively (*A Packet of Three*—EP DFC 01), before moving elsewhere. Sham 69 signed with Polydor for a four-album career; Squeeze, retaining Copeland as manager, joined A&M alongside another Illegal act, the Police—their "Fall Out" 45 (IL 001) featured Copeland's brother Stewart (ex–Curved Air) on drums, and ex–New Animals guitarist Andy Summers.

Both bands' releases appeared on A&M in the US and UK; Miles Copeland, meanwhile, inaugurated a new label, Illegal/I.R.S. (distributed by A&M), which oversaw releases on John Cale's Spy label among others.

The label operated quietly in the UK for several years, but made instant waves in America, purposefully setting itself apart from other domestic labels by emphasizing eccentricity among its artists, a factor that has ensured a high collectors demand for many early releases, both by individual artists and across the label's entire spectrum. Especially valued are I.R.S. 45s, few of which sold in appreciable quantities at the time—whether by accident or design, the label's 7-inch output was restricted almost exclusively to bands who would subsequently become in-demand.

The new label's first release was a compilation of singles by the British band the Buzzcocks—a United Artists act in the UK. *Singles Going Steady* (SP 001) was heavily imported back into Britain, where it was subsequently given a full release; prior to that, it swiftly established itself among the best-selling import albums of the era.

I.R.S. issued two further Buzzcocks albums in America, *A Different Kind of Tension* (SP 009) and another US-only set, a mini-album collection of three subsequent British 45s (SP 70507). Other British punks picked up by I.R.S. during this period included another UA act, the Stranglers; Illegal veterans Chelsea and Alternative TV; the Damned; ex-Buzzcock Howard Devoto's Magazine; and Tom Robinson.

Releases by Fashion, the Fall, Cale (the *Sabotage/Live* LP, nominally a Spy release—SP 004), Wazmo Nariz, Skafish, Henry Badowski, and Root Boy Slim followed in 1979; the Fleshtones and the Payola$ during the early '80s. Many of I.R.S.'s acts were showcased in the movie *Uurgh! A Music War;* others were highlighted in the so-called Developing Artists LP series. In addition, an I.R.S. compilation, 1981's *I.R.S. Greatest Hits, Vols. 2 and 3* (70800) introduced the US to a wealth of label acts, past and present. Another priceless label sampler is 1989's IRS-82010—*These People Are Nuts!* (IRS 82010), which bore liner notes comprising the catalog's worst reviews, and a fine overview of I.R.S. rarities.

In 1980 I.R.S. launched a revolutionary sequence of 10-inch mini-album releases, with offerings from Klark Kent (actually Stewart Copeland), Oingo Boingo, Wall of Voodoo, and the Fleshtones (all of which would release full lengths on the label later). Other 10-inch issues appeared from Patrick D. Martin, Magazine, and the Cosmetics.

I.R.S.'s first major success arrived with the emergence of the Cramps. The group debuted with the 12-inch EP *Gravest Hits* (SP 501) in 1979, a set issued in a wealth of different-colored sleeves. The group's first album the following year, *Songs the Lord Taught Us* (SP 007), also boasts two different sleeves, the first with an incorrect (1979) copyright date and an incorrect track listing. Cramps I.R.S. singles, meanwhile, include such delights as "Fever" (UK 017), "Drug Train" (9014), and "Goo Goo Muck" (9021).

Releases by the Go-Go's, the Bangles, the Lords of the New Church, and the English Beat also proved successful. The Lords of the New Church were formed by ex-Damned guitarist Brian James, who had already issued a brace of very scarce 45s on the UK label, the Dead Boys' Stiv Bators, Sham 69 bassist Dave Treganna, and the Barracudas' Nicky Turner— a true punk supergroup. The Barracudas' first 45s, "New Church" (UK 0028), "Open Your Eyes" (UK 0030), and "Russian Roulette" (UK 0033—also a super-limited picture disc) are eminently collectible today; also of note, US pressings of their 1982 debut LP (SP 70029) pack a very different (and preferable) sleeve to their British counterpart.

Many of I.R.S.'s signings swiftly proved collector favorites, as aforementioned—the Cramps, the Go-Go's, superstars-in-waiting REM, and following the group's 1983 arrival, especially the Alarm. One genuine "sleeper" in this category was Torch Song's LP *Wish Thing* (SP 70045), issued in 1984. It would be several years before anybody even cared that among its makers was one William Orbit.

REM arrived in 1982, having already enjoyed local success in Georgia with its debut single, "Radio Free Europe" (Hib-Tone HT 0001). Demos recorded with producer Mitch Easter formed the backbone of the group's *Chronic Town* mini-LP (SP 70502—original issues boast a custom label miniaturizing the sleeve art). REM's debut album, *Murmur* (SP 70604), arrived in 1983, as did the consummation of a love affair with critics, fans, and collectors that has endured ever since.

In 1985, I.R.S. moved to MCA for distribution, debuting the new arrangement with Three O'Clock's *Arrive Without Traveling* (IRS 5591). Much of the label's early pioneering spirit had dissipated by now; collectible artists (and singles) remained confined to the veterans and the back catalog, with the most resonant new arrivals restricted to the Fine Young Cannibals, Timbuk 3, Dr. and the Medics, and Concrete Blonde.

However, there was a solo debut from William Orbit (IRS 42019) that has now come into fashion, while the ska revival of the early '90s saw I.R.S.'s backlog of English Beat–General Public–Ranking Roger releases come into considerable vogue. The reformed

TEN TOP COLLECTIBLES

REM

"Academy Fight Song" (UK Bucketful of Brains/Lyntone BOB 32—Flexidisc, 1992)

Acoustic Songs (France WEA/Les Inrockuptibles PRO 2002-2—CD single, 1991)

The Alternative Radio Staple (IRS CDREM 92—Promo CD, 1992)

Chronic Town (IRS SP 70502—12-inch with custom label, 1982)

"Ghost Reindeer in the Sky" (Fan club 122589—7-inch, 1990)

"Good King Wenceslas" (Fan club 122589—7-inch, picture sleeve, 1989)

"Parade of the Wooden Soldiers" (Fan club U23518—Green-vinyl 7-inch, picture sleeve, 1988)

"Radio Free Europe" (Hib-Tone HT 0001—7-inch, picture sleeve, 1981)

The Source Concert 1984 (Source Concert NBC 8428—2-LP transcription disc, 1984)

"Wolves, Lower" (Trouser Press FLEXI 12—Flexidisc, 1982)

Black Sabbath, the rejuvenated Gary Numan, and the rehashed Spirit, Leslie West, Jan Akkerman, and Steppenwolf also have some attractions.

Having lost REM to Warner Bros. in 1988, I.R.S. switched distributors to Enigma in 1990; artists of interest from this period include British superstar group Carter the Unstoppable Sex Machine (who was all too easily stopped by America's total apathy) and the psychedelic jam pioneer Ozric Tentacles. Among these bands' I.R.S. rarities, promotional cassette singles are the most sought after.

I.R.S. folded during the late '90s; Copeland swiftly resurfaced with Ark 21.

Further Reading: *Wild Thing: The Backstage, on the Road, in the Studio, off the Charts Memoirs of Ian Copeland,* by Ian Copeland (Simon & Schuster 1995)

Island

Chris Blackwell's Island records was launched in Jamaica in 1958, transferring to the UK in 1962 and concentrating its output on its erstwhile homeland: over the next five years, the quality and quantity of Island's ska-rocksteady catalog was rivaled only by the Melodisc/Blue Beat and Dr. Bird labels, and when, in 1967, founder Blackwell decided to shift Island's focus toward Britain's own rock scene, he did so only after transferring Island's multitudinous Jamaican contacts and catalog to a new, co-owned venture, Trojan Records.

For Island records collectors, the so-called Jamaican era is a law unto itself. Some 400 45s and 30 LPs were released between 1962–67, many of them now-avowed classics of the genre; in addition, the subsidiaries Brit, Black Swan, and Aladdin pumped out almost 100 more, also primarily Jamaican, or at least Caribbean. The Sue imprint, headed by maverick producer Guy Stevens, was responsible for an equally collectible hoard of classic R&B releases.

Through this period, Island catalog numbers were prefixed with the letters WI. When 1967 brought the move into rock, a new series was launched, WIP— the P stood for "pop," and the label made almost immediate inroads into that market. The second-ever release, Traffic's "Paper Sun" (6002), made the UK Top Five, establishing that band among the best-loved groups of the age (two further singles made the

steve WINWOOD jim CAPALDI dave MASON chris WOOD
rick GRECH 'reebop' KWAKU BAAH jim GORDON

'Welcome to the Canteen'

Traffic helped popularize the early 1970s fashion of omitting the band's name from its album covers.

Top Ten that year), and confirming Island's arrival on the scene.

From the outset, Island regarded singles as little more than trailers for albums, a mindset that communicated itself to both purchasers, and subsequently, to collectors. Although many Island singles are considered choice rarities, far more enthusiasts pursue the label's LPs, in particular the pink-label issues that appeared between 1967–70. This incorporates key releases by Mott the Hoople, King Crimson, Free, Jethro Tull, Fairport Convention, Traffic, and Nick Drake, all of whom are extremely collectible today, plus lesser-known (but equally desirable) sets by John Martyn, Clouds, Blodwyn Pig, Tramline, the Bama Winds, Quintessence, Dr. Strangely Strange, and more.

Many collectors believe that the Island rock LP series was launched with the introduction of the ILPS numbering series (that is, John Martyn's 1969 LP *The Tumbler*—9091). In fact, the first releases—Traffic's *Mr. Fantasy* (ILP 9061), Art's *Supernatural Fairytales* (ILP 967), and Spooky Tooth's *It's All About* (ILP 9080)—appeared within the label's already existing numerical sequence, sandwiched, as the gaps between numbers indicates, between the traditional reggae and the R&B fare. The "S" designation, perceptive readers may already have realized, was introduced when the label commenced issuing stereo recordings only.

The pink Island label went through three phases, all of which are crucial to identifying original pressings: between 1967–69, it featured an eye motif, and "island" in large lowercase letters at the foot of the label. A transitional design used for a handful of issues in late 1969 had the word "ISLAND" within a black box which extended up to a swirl design around the spindle hole; the final type, into 1970, simply bore a large, lower-case "i" at the bottom of the label. This was abandoned in late 1970, when a new palm tree logo was introduced. Cat Stevens' *Tea for the Tillerman* (9135) was the last album to be issued with a pink label of any kind.

Widely regarded as the next era in Island's development, the early '70s saw the label move away from its unabashedly underground origins and begin actively pursuing hit singles, an approach that reached fruition following the appointment of producer Muff Winwood to the A&R department. Although both Free and Cat Stevens enjoyed hits during the early '70s, both were still considered primarily album artists. The arrival of Roxy Music in 1972, and Sparks two years later, reversed that equation—though both did make phenomenal LPs, their singles were better still (and usually featured non-album B-sides, adding to their appeal). By the time of the next label-design change, to a deeply stylized tropical sunset scene, the original collecting cognoscenti had long since moved away.

The change was not as radical as some people would have you believe. Bands like Sharks (featuring guitarist Chris Spedding), the Sutherland Brothers, and Quiver and Jade Warrior maintained at least a light grip on the underground values of old; the soap operatic saga of Fairport Convention continued in full force; Bad Company married the best of old Free and Mott the Hoople into one seamless unit; and Bob Marley, signed to the label in 1971, began his march toward world superstardom and headlined a still vibrant crop of reggae releases in the Island catalog.

Indeed, even under the new regime, Island remained a provocative concern. The popularity of Roxy Music spun off Bryan Ferry's massively successful solo career, but it also brought solo ventures from bandmates Andy Mackay and Phil Manzanera, neither of which sold especially well. Both are now heavily collected, although CD reissues on Manzanera's

Expression label have taken some of the sting out of prices.

Also desirable are releases by the group's original electronics player, Brian Eno—he quit Roxy in 1973 to launch an utterly idiosyncratic solo career, highlighted in the rarity stakes by the singles "Seven Deadly Finns" (6178), and unlikely as it sounds, "The Lion Sleeps Tonight" (6233). The Roxy family catalog left Island in 1977 at the expiration of the label's contract with the EG Management company (King Crimson also departed); re-releases followed on the Polydor and Virgin labels.

Eno was also involved in a venture that, had certain of its participants had their way, might well have developed into a full-time supergroup, as he joined recent Island recruits Kevin Ayers, John Cale, and Nico (the latter two ex–Velvet Underground members) for a joint concert at the London Rainbow. *June 1, 1974* (9291), a live album commemorating the show, is all that became of the union, but the promise of the union remains palpable.

Cale and Ayers both released now-rare Island singles around this time—Cale's "The Man Who Couldn't Afford To" (6202) is especially sought after for its non-LP B-side, "Sylvia Said" (since included in the *Island Anthology* two-CD set). Another Cale rarity involves the *Helen of Troy* LP (9350), originally issued with the controversial "Leaving It All up to You" included. Early into the manufacturing run, the decision was made to replace the song with "Coral Moon"—only for the decision to be reversed immediately thereafter. Only a handful of amended versions appear to have been made; in terms of scarcity, they rank alongside any of the Velvet Underground's so widely feted rarities.

(There are several similar issues in the Island catalog, including copies of the first Mott the Hoople album—9108—with the song "Road to Birmingham" inadvertently included. Corrected pressings followed very swiftly; "Birmingham" itself was the also B-side of the group's debut single, "Rock'n'Roll Queen"—6072).

Another extremely popular, if intensely controversial, release was *Derek and Clive Live,* a private recording of comedians Peter Cook and Dudley Moore at their most foul-mouthedly funny, which gathered cult pace so quickly that, when Island finally released it in 1976 (9434), some two years after its conception, it made the UK Top 20 on word of mouth alone (radio certainly couldn't touch it). More than a quarter of a century of ever-plummeting societal standards later, it remains the most abusively and gratuitously obscene record ever to become a major hit.

Into the late '70s, Island remained ambitious. In 1977, a band called Warsaw Pakt made national headlines by rehearsing, recording, manufacturing, and shipping an album, *Needletime,* in under 24 hours (9515); three years later, Toots and the Maytals' *Live in London* album was put together with similar haste.

New signings the B-52's, Grace Jones, and many more established the label at the forefront of the artier new wave scene. Although the label's inherent collectibility declined utterly during the 1980s and 1990s, individual artists remained frequently fascinating. It should also be remembered that two of the most deliberately collector-oriented labels of the age, Stiff and ZTT, were both distributed by Island at the height of their zaniness.

Island's biggest act of the age—indeed, of the last 20 years—was U2, regarded among the most collectible bands to have emerged since the halcyon days of the 1950s and 1960s. The group joined the label in 1980, debuting with the UK single "11 O'clock Tick Tock" (WIP 6601), since which time they have, of course, gone from strength to strength.

There is little value attached to any of the band's conventional releases—singles and albums alike have sold in such vast quantities that even novice collectors need to dig some way below the surface in search of truly unusual items. A wealth of international picture sleeves offer one popular route; in-concert and other radio broadcasts from King Biscuit, Westwood One, the Album Network, and many more also have a devoted following; while a number of fascinating limited-edition items have cropped up over the years, ensuring that U2's collectible status spans its entire career, as opposed to a handful of rare releases at the outset.

Among the most popular items are *The Joshua Tree Collection* (Island 6:1-6:5), a box set replicating the blockbuster *The Joshua Tree* LP across five singles; and a second set, *The Joshua Tree Singles* (Island U2PK 1), which merely rounded up the four officially released 45s from the set, in a custom PVC wallet. Singles from both 1983's *War* and 1984's *The Unforgettable Fire* albums were issued as double singles in gatefold sleeves; "The Unforgettable Fire" itself appeared briefly as a shaped picture disc (Island ISP 220).

Several of the band's early-to-mid-'80s UK 12-inch singles are becoming increasingly difficult to find; so, at the opposite end of the scale, are such latter-day issues as 1992's "Even Better than the Real Thing" (Island REAL U2) and 1997's "Mofo" (12IS 684), which was issued in an impossibly limited run of just 2,000 copies. The majority of U2 CD singles, too, are becoming scarcer.

Nevertheless the key to a comprehensive U2 collection does lie within its earliest releases; the irony for any collector who regards U2 and Island Records as one of the era's most reliable double acts is that all appear on the Irish wing of CBS Records, to whom the group was contracted since 1979.

Reissues have rendered 12-inch pressings of the group's debut single, the *U2:3* EP (CBS 12-7951) relatively common—certainly they are more visible than the 1979 7-inch, or the four colored-vinyl reissues that followed in 1980. However, further singles are extremely difficult to locate, including "Another Day" (CBS 8306), "11 O'clock Tick Tock" (8687), "A Day Without Me" (8905), "I Will Follow" (9065), "Fire" (1376), "Gloria" (1718), and "A Celebration" (2214). Even more troublesome to locate are three 7-inch anthologies, issued between 1982–84, and each comprising four singles in a plastic wallet. *4 U2 Play* (PAC 1), *PAC 2* (PAC 2), and *PAC 3* (PAC 3) are essential but challenging digests for the collector, with the first-named also presenting a bewildering variety of colored-vinyl variations.

Chris Blackwell sold Island to Polygram during the 1990s; the label continued on for a while, but as its roster was shifted elsewhere into the empire, Island gradually became regarded primarily as a reissues

TEN TOP COLLECTIBLES

Sparks

"Beat the Clock" (Elektra 11412—12-inch promo, 1979)

"Cool Places" (Atlantic 89866—7-inch, picture sleeve, 1983)

Excerpts from Gratuitous Sax and Senseless Violins (UK Logic 74321 24302—Promo CD, gatefold sleeve, 1994)

"Forever Young" (Columbia 10579—7-inch, 1977)

Halfnelson—Halfnelson (Bearsville BV 2048—LP, 1971)

"I Predict" (Atlantic 325—12-inch promo, 1982)

"I Want to Hold Your Hand" (UK Island WIP 6282—7-inch, 1976)

"Looks Looks Looks" (Island 043—7-inch, 1975)

"Tips for Teens" (RCA PD 12252—7-inch test pressing, 1981)

"Wonder Girl" (Bearsville 0006—7-inch, 1971)

---

imprint and is today part of the massive Universal group. Under this administration, many classic recordings of the 1960s and early '70s have finally resurfaced, to inform a new generation of the original label's audacity and ingenuity.

Further Reading: Booklets within Island 40 CD series (five volumes)

Kama Sutra

The Kama Sutra group of labels was founded by Hy Mizrahi, Phil Steinberg, and Artie Ripp, an ex-associate of George Goldner, in 1964 (a former MGM accountant, Art Kass, joined soon after). Originally it was a production company alone, responsible for hits by the Shangri-Las, the Critters, and others, issuing its own first 45s the following year—the Vacels' "You're My Baby" (200) and the Lovin' Spoonful's "Do You Believe in Magic" (201).

Both were hits; the latter the first of a string of smashes for its makers. Indeed, the Lovin' Spoonful remained Kama Sutra's most important act through the next three years, while the Vacels are best remembered today as a footnote to the Bob Dylan story: they released a version of his "Can You Please Crawl out of Your Window" (204) before even he did.

The Lovin' Spoonful followed their debut hit with "You Didn't Have to Be So Nice" (205) and the immortal "Daydream" (208). The first-named was the last Kama Sutra 45 to be pressed with the original orange-red label design; the latter was the last to carry a yellow label with the logo in red. "Did You Ever Have to Make Up Your Mind" (209), then, was the first to bear what became the established yellow label with a black logo—copies of those earlier 45s, with either of the yellow labels, represent second and third printings and are less sought after.

Much of Kama Sutra's output of 1966–67 was consumed by the Spoonful—four of the first six LPs included. Other acts on the label included the Trade Winds, a duo comprising Pete (Andreoli) Anders and Vincent (Vinnie) Poncia: "Mind Excursion" (212), "I Believe in Her" (218), and a reissue of their debut (234) were accompanied by an album, *Excursions* (8057), during which time the duo were also operating as the Innocence, cutting five 45s and another album, *The Innocence* (8059). (Anders also cut a solo single on Buddah before he and Poncia formed their own label, Map City.)

San Francisco's Sopwith Camel also recorded for Kama Sutra, releasing three singles and a self-titled album (8060) before breaking up. (The group subsequently re-formed and signed with Reprise in 1973.)

Kama Sutra distribution at this time was handled by MGM. Unhappy with that arrangement, the label staff launched a second, independent company in 1967, Buddah. While the main company continued on with the Lovin' Spoonful and increasingly isolated releases by the likes of Vince Edwards (TV's *Ben Casey*), Erik and the Smoke Ponies, Bobby Bloom, and Billy Harner, Buddah turned its attention toward the then-burgeoning bubblegum boom.

A number of scheduled Kama Sutra LPs during this period were canceled—indeed, the label lapsed into virtual silence, simply releasing periodic 45s by the Lovin' Spoonful (which had undergone their own career-sapping changes by this time), the Road, Outrage, and the Pendulum. At least ten titles scheduled

in 1968, including issues by the Lovin' Spoonful, Bobby Bloom, and John Sebastian, were canned. The only LPs to appear during late 1968, in apparently very limited quantities, were sets by Lt. Garcia's Magic Music Box (8071) and the Teri Nelson Group (8072— these were the label's final mono releases).

Normal service was resumed in 1969, when the label's distribution finally moved to Buddah. Sha Na Na, the Road, John Sebastian, and Bill Haley all had LPs issued during 1969–70, while Gene Vincent was resurrected for two singles and LPs during 1970–71—neither *Gene Vincent* (2019) nor *The Day the World Turned Blue* (2027) are of more than passing interest to fans of Vincent's 1950s heyday, but both command a fair price on the market today.

In collecting terms, the most exciting new arrivals were the Stories, featuring former Left Banke leader Michael Brown, country-rock star Charlie Daniels, the immensely popular NRBQ, and the Flamin' Groovies. The latter released two Kama Sutra LPs, *Flamingo* (2021) and *Teenage Head* (2031), which remain hot properties 30 years after issue—and despite several reissues, most notably on expanded

TEN TOP COLLECTIBLES

Lovin' Spoonful

Alive and Well in Argentina—Zalman Yanovsky (Buddah BDS 5019—LP, 1968)

The Best Of (Kama Sutra KLP 8056—2-LP with four color photos, 1967)

Daydream (Kama Sutra KLPS 8051—Stereo LP, 1966)

"Daydream" (Kama Sutra 208—Yellow-label 7-inch, picture sleeve, 1966)

"Did You Ever Have to Make Up Your Mind?" (Kama Sutra 209—7-inch, picture sleeve, 1966)

Do You Believe in Magic? (Capitol Record Club ST 90597—LP, 1965)

"Do You Believe in Magic?" (Kama Sutra 201—7-inch, red-orange label, 1965)

"She's a Lady"—John Sebastian (Kama Sutra 254—7-inch, picture sleeve, 1968)

"You Didn't Have to Be So Nice" (Kama Sutra 205—7-inch, red-orange label, 1965)

You're a Big Boy Now (Kama Sutra KLP 8058—LP, 1967)

CDs within the present Buddah–Kama Sutra catalog. Groovies singles "Have You Seen My Baby" (527) and the British "Teenage Head" (2013 031), "Gonna Rock Tonight" (2013 042), and a reissued "Teenage Head" (KSS 707) are also highly prized.

Future collectibles do not present-day hits make, however, and by 1975 Kama Sutra was on its last legs. Valedictory hits by Sha Na Na and Charlie Daniels preceded the label's demise; the former's "Just Like Romeo and Juliet" (602) was followed by the less successful "You're the Only Light on My Horizon" (603) and "Shanghaied" (604), the last Kama Sutra singles. The final LPs arrived in 1976, and included sets by I Don't Care (2617), Alex Harvey (2618—not to be confused with the Scottish rock legend), and Diamond Rio (2619).

The label was reborn as Sutra in 1982, swiftly coming to notice via the inspired signing of the Fat Boys, one of the first widely successful rap acts. As the Disco 3, their "Fat Boys" (135) single was a 1984 hit, followed by the crossover "Jailhouse Rap" (137), the trio's first release under their better-known name. The Fat Boys remained with Sutra until 1986, the year in which Art Kass sold the Sutra/Kama Sutra/Buddah catalog to the Essex Entertainment group. It has since passed to BMG Special Products, which launched a well-received CD reissue program in the mid-1990s.

Further Reading: *Bubblegum Music Is the Naked Truth: The Dark History of Prepubescent Pop, from the Banana Splits to Britney Spears,* edited by Kim Cooper and David Smay (Feral House, 2001)

Keen

The Keen label was formed by the brothers John and Alex Siamas (Del-Fi's Bob Keane was also involved early on), coming to national prominence after picking up singer Sam Cooke, who had recently been fired by Specialty when he was caught recording popular, instead of gospel, music with upstart producer Bumps Blackwell. Cooke's "You Send Me" (4013) topped both the pop and R&B charts, launching a three-year relationship that utterly dominates the Keen catalog. Indeed, of the label's eight LPs, Cooke issued five, the Memo Bernabei Orchestra two; the last was a various-artists collection. Following

TEN TOP COLLECTIBLES

Sam Cooke

Encore Volumes 1–3 (Keen 2006-08—EPs, picture sleeves, 1958)

"Forever"—Dale Cooke (Specialty 596—7-inch, 1957)

"I'll Come Running Back to You" (Specialty 619—7-inch, 1957)

I Thank God (Keen 86103—LP, 1960)

Sam Cooke (Keen A2001—LP, 1958)

Songs by Sam Cooke Volumes 1–3 (Keen 2001-03—EPs, picture sleeves, 1958)

"Stealing Kisses" (Keen 2005—7-inch, 78, 1958)

"Teenage Sonata" (RCA Victor 47-7701—7-inch, 1960)

Tribute to the Lady Volumes 1–3 (Keen 2012-14—EPs, picture sleeves, 1959)

The Wonderful World Of (Keen 86106—LP, 1960)

Cooke's departure to RCA in 1960, much of his Keen repertoire was reissued by the Famous label.

Included among the greatest rarities in the Keen canon are the handful of stereo 45s issued in 1959, including Cooke's "Win Your Love for Me" (5-2006—issued on blue vinyl), "Everybody Likes to Cha Cha Cha" (5-2018), and "Only Sixteen" (5-2022).

King/Federal

The King label is best known for its nurturing of the Godfather of Soul, James Brown, from the time of his emergence in 1956 until his departure for Polydor at the end of the 1960s. No matter that the label had already been operating for more than a decade when Brown came along (it was founded in 1943); no matter that label head Sydney Nathan's pioneering vision of a label that boldly went where the majors refused to go remained King's modus operandi for much of its life span. Mention King, and the general collector sees a pile of classic James Brown 45s—and the pile of dollars it would cost to purchase them all.

It is odd, then, to discover that King was initially a country-based label, with so-called race records not entering the catalog until around 1945, when Nathan launched the Queen label to cater to that market. Early releases were licensed from elsewhere—Bull Moose Jackson and Slim Gaillard were the first artists recorded by Nathan himself.

Queen folded in 1947 and Nathan launched a new R&B label, King Race. Three years later, Deluxe and Federal came into being, the latter's early catalog immortalized by Billy Ward and the Dominoes. The first R&B group ever to cut an LP, an eponymous 10-inch (Federal 295-94) issued in early 1955, the record has been ranked among the all-time rarest and most valuable releases in the hobby.

Federal's next major star was Hank Ballard and the Midnighters; its third, although Nathan would never have believed it at the time, would be James Brown and the Famous Flames.

Nathan had not wanted to sign Brown in the first place—it was A&R man Ralph Bass who made the decision, and who felt the full force of the label head's wrath when, after scoring a shock No. 1 with his debut, "Please Please Please" (12258), Brown's next nine singles all flopped. Nathan was on the verge of dropping Brown from the roster when "Try Me" (12237) finally ended this luckless sequence, to open a period of absolute chart domination for Brown and the Famous Flames. Two years and seven hits later, Nathan finally transferred the singer from Federal to the higher-profile King label.

If Nathan was initially unable to see Brown's potential, it might well have been because the King stable was literally swimming in talent. The country and gospel stables were full; the blues, R&B, and vocal departments were brimming—an accounting of acts on the three labels would include Albert King, Annie Laurie, Big Jay McNeely, Bill Doggett, Champion Jack DuPree, Earl Bostic, Eddie Vinson, Freddie King, Ivory Joe Hunter, Jimmy Witherspoon, John Lee Hooker, Johnny Guitar Watson, Little Willie John, Little Willie Littlefield, Lonnie Johnson, Lucky Millinder, Lula Reed, Memphis Slim, Otis Williams and the Charms, Roy Brown, Sonny Thompson, Tiny Bradshaw, Todd Rhodes, Wynonie Harris, Little Esther (Phillips), the Chanters, the Checkers, the Five Keys, the 5 Royales, the Ink Spots, the Platters, the Royals, and the Swallows. Further bolstering the catalog, the sacred Glory and country-oriented Bethlehem labels were purchased, the budget Audio Lab was inaugurated, and Beltone was distributed.

All are very collectible today, most scored signature hits that enabled the King empire to continue growing, and many released LPs which today fetch sums far in excess of equivalent releases by other labels. One reason for this appears to have been Nathan's natural caution—even with guaranteed best-sellers (the Brown titles for example), print runs for LPs never exceeded what he knew he could sell straight off the bat; if demand exceeded supply, a fresh run would be produced.

This policy resulted in a rash of minor variations between pressings, with some especially successful albums boasting four, five, or even six notably different sleeves and/or labels. Many King collectors have become specialists in this field, and accepted prices for the scarcest varieties—a copy of Brown's *Try Me*

TEN TOP COLLECTIBLES

King/Federal

"Eternally"—The Swallows (King 4501—Blue-vinyl 7-inch, 1952)

"Every Beat of My Heart"—The Royals (Federal 12064AA—Blue-vinyl 7-inch, 1952)

"Flame in My Heart"—The Checkers (King 4558—7-inch, 1952)

"I Know I Love You So"—The Royals (Federal 12077—7-inch, 1952)

"I'll Cry When You're Gone"—The Platters (Federal 12164—7-inch, 1964)

"Moaning Blues"—John Lee Hooker (King 4504—7-inch, 1952)

"Moonrise"—The Royals (Federal 12088—Blue-vinyl 7-inch, 1952)

"Night's Curtains"—The Checkers (King 4581—7-inch, 1952)

"Tell Me Why"—The Swallows (King 4515—7-inch, 1952)

Wynonie Harris—Wynonie Harris (King 260—EP, 1954)

(635) LP with "King" two inches wide on the label, or *Think* (683) with it expanded to three inches—approach the four-figure mark.

Despite his dominance of this vast empire, Brown was dissatisfied enough with his standing that, even after his move to King and the pleasure of issuing the label's biggest hit LP ever, *Live at the Apollo* (826), he jumped ship at the earliest opportunity, signing to Mercury's Smash Record subsidiary on the premise that his King contract only applied to vocal performances.

Nathan sued, and while a string of Smash instrumentals duly followed, a court eventually ruled in Nathan's favor and Brown returned to King, on hugely improved terms. He would remain with the label for the remainder of the decade, during which King would grow to become the sixth-largest record company in the land.

Nathan's death in March 1968 brought a sudden halt to this miraculous development. Subsequent owners Starday Records and Lin Broadcasting maintained the catalog but did little to improve upon it, and in 1971, Lin sold Brown's contract to Polydor,

then sold the remainder of the label—virtual shell though it now was—to Leiber and Stoller's Tennessee Recording and Publishing company. King, and the newly revived DeLuxe and Federal labels, spent much of the remainder of the decade as a reissues label, first under TR&P, then for the Gusto label.

Further Reading: *The World of Soul: Black America's Contribution to the Pop Music Scene,* by Arnold Shaw (Cowles Book Co., 1970)

Laurie

Laurie was founded by Elliott Greenberg, Allen Sussel, and the brothers Bob and Gene Schwartz, in New York, in March 1958—"Laurie" was Sussel's daughter, and the name was retained even after Sussel departed in 1960. The first decade of the label's existence attracts the most attention from collectors, featuring as it does some of the most memorable 45s (by the best-loved acts) of the entire era, together with a string of often excellent, but increasingly hard-to-find, LPs.

Laurie was just two months and a dozen singles old when it scored its first major hit, Dion and the

Belmonts's "I Wonder Why" (1013), and over the next five years, Dion DiMucci would chalk up well over 20 hits for Laurie, including such seminal pieces as the group's "A Teenager in Love" (3027) and "Where or When" (3044), and the solos "Runaround Sue" (3110), "The Wanderer" (3115), and "Love Came to Me" (3145). The Belmonts's first Laurie LP, *Presenting* (LLP 1002), was issued in 1959; it was reissued the following year as the first release (LLP 2002) in the newly instituted 2000 series, devoted to popular recordings. DiMucci's solo debut, *Alone with Dion* (LLP 2004), followed that same year, the first in a succession of now-collectible titles issued before he departed Laurie for Columbia in 1963.

With the institution of the 2000 series, the existing 1000 series was surrendered exclusively to jazz releases. Ten LPs were released in the series between 1960–62; the most successful artist among these was British jazzman Chris Barber, who followed his hit "Petite Fleur" (3022) with an LP of the same name (LLP 1001). Barber released three further albums in the 1000 series, alongside titles from Carlo Menotti (an ambitious two-LP set—LLP 1000), the Dave Carey Quintet, Jack Carroll (a collection of Christmas songs, popular among collectors of that field—LLP 1005), Lodi Carr, and Bernard Pfeiffer. Laurie also launched a comedy line in 1962, but this perished after just two releases, one by Larry Foster and Marty Brill (5000), and another by Brill alone (5002).

Returning to the pop market, Laurie released what might well stand as the first "concept" album in American musical history, the Citizens' *Sing About a City of People* (LLP 2007), a collection of songs about life in New York City. Among other early-'60s albums, the compilations *Great Groups, Great Music* (LLP 2010) and *Pick Hits of the Radio Good Guys* (LLP 2021) were among several sets to offer generous samplings of recent Laurie singles, while Chubby Jackson's *Twist Calling* (LLP 2011) is among the better of the manifold LPs issued to cash in on that particular dance craze.

Laurie's next superstar group was the Chiffons, opening on the label with 1963's chart-topping "He's So Fine" (3152), and following up with "One Fine Day" (3179). Three years later, "Sweet Talking Guy" (3340) concluded a trilogy of timeless girl-group hits. LPs titled after all three of those hits remain popular today.

Laurie also signed Britain's Petula Clark—after stints with Coral, King, MGM, and Imperial, she joined the label in 1962, cutting four singles before moving on to Warner Bros., and finally, to Stateside success in 1964. Laurie responded by compiling those tracks (plus others) onto 1965's *In Love* album. Singles of 1962's "Jumble Sale" (3143) and 1963's "Darling Cheri" (3156) were also issued (3316). *In Love* was reissued in 1967 as *Petula Clark Sings for Everybody* (SLP 2043).

As the British Invasion took over, Laurie wisely signed Gerry and the Pacemakers, second-best (to the Beatles, of course) of the Merseybeat bands. Released during 1963 and early 1964, singles "How Do You Do It?" (3162), "I Like It" (3196), "You'll Never Walk Alone" (3218), and "I'm the One" (3233) were barely noticed. Reissued in the aftermath of the Beatles, however, (respectively—3261, 3271, 3302, and 3233) all four were hits, together with "Don't Let the Sun Catch You Crying" (3251), "I'll Be There" (3279), "Ferry 'Cross the Mersey" (3284), and more. The original releases, of course, are the most sought after; label and era completists might also seek alternate pressings of 3233, each with a different B-side; and (less spectacularly) an alternate label for 3284, which mistitles the A-side "Ferry Across the Mersey."

The Pacemakers also released four albums and one hits collection through the label, including the aptly titled *Second Album* (LLP 2027), which marked Laurie's first use of stereo (albeit reprocessed—SLP 2027). Massively successful as they were, these albums are common in any condition, barring Near Mint or Mint. The band's *Ferry 'Cross the Mersey* soundtrack was issued by the movie's distributor, UA (3387/6387), despite the title track's appearing as a Laurie 45.

The end of the Pacemakers' heyday ended Laurie's period of greatest success, though hits remained common. The Barbarians tapped in to the mood of contemporary adult opinion with "Are You a Boy or

Are You a Girl" (3308), following through with an ode to their one-handed drummer, Victor "Moulty" Moulton (3326), and a now nearly legendary LP titled for "Are You a Boy or Are you a Girl" (LLP/SLP 2033—the first true stereo album on the label). The Royal Guardsmen miraculously squeezed eight hits and four LPs out of a career that might otherwise have begun and ended with the novelty Canadian hit "Squeaky vs. the Black Knight" (3366); when re-recorded and reissued (with the same catalog number) as "Snoopy vs. the Red Baron," the song soared to No. 2 in late 1966.

Kasenetz-Katz discovery Music Explosion released nine singles on the label during the late '60s; when they broke up, vocalist Jamie Lyons cut several solo shots, including one song, "Gonna Have a Good Time" (3427), that was later covered by AC/DC.

Another Super K product, the Super K Generation, was responsible for a fascinating two-part version of the Yardbirds' "Heartful of Soul" (3413). The Balloon Farm and a returning Dion were also successes during the psychedelic era (among Dion's hits was a cover of Jimi Hendrix's "Purple Haze"—3478).

Also of interest is the US debut album by the Equals, the Anglo-Caribbean band that first brought Eddy Grant to prominence. The band's singles (and subsequent LPs) appeared on President; *Unequalled Equals,* however, was issued by Laurie (LLP/SLP 2045). Perhaps the most ambitious release, however, was Norm N. Nite's *Evolution or Revolution* (SLP 2044), a largely spoken-word history of rock 'n' roll, featuring excerpts of some 40 hit records. An interesting use of stereo placed the narration in one channel, while the song played (in mono) in the other.

Laurie's final hit of note was Think's thought-provoking "Once You Understand," in 1971 (3583—reissued for a second chart stint by Big Tree in 1974). Think also cut an album, *Encounter* (SLP 2052).

As the new decade progressed, Laurie was active as a reissues label, with many of its releases targeted at record-club customers. Some interesting and hard-to-find titles were produced during this period, including the rudiments of what was originally intended as a full series of compilations, the *Everything You Wanted to Hear By . . .* LPs. Two volumes, dedicated to the Chiffons (LES 4001) and to Dion

TEN TOP COLLECTIBLES

The Chiffons

"After Last Night" (Reprise 20103—7-inch, 1962)

Everything You Always Wanted to Hear . . . (Laurie 4001—LP, 1975)

He's So Fine (Capitol Record Club DT 90075—LP, 1965)

"Lucky Me" (Laurie 3166—7-inch, 1963)

"Never Never" (Wildcat 601—7-inch, 1961)

One Fine Day (Laurie LLP 2020—LP, 1963)

"Secret Love" (BT Puppy 558—7-inch, 1970)

"So Much in Love" (Buddah 171—7-inch, 1970)

Sweet Talkin' Guy (Laurie SLP 2036—Stereo LP, 1966)

"Tonight's the Night" (Big Deal 6003—7-inch, 1960)

and the Belmonts (LES 4002), were issued before the scheme was abandoned. Other releases highlighted some of the magnificent, but so easily overlooked, sides cut for the label in the pre-Beatles era, by the Mystics, the Passions, Randy and the Rainbows, the Elegants, and many more. Ironically, many of these collections are now as hard to find as some of the 45s they featured.

The late '80s saw the company—now named 3C (Continental Communications Corporation) begin reissuing its back catalog on CD, to general jubilation in the collectors market. In the early '90s, Laurie was bought by EMI-Capitol Music Special Markets, again with an eye toward specialist-oriented releases; the British Ace label has also done sterling service in this department. These latter-day re-releases have included first-time releases for a number of stereo recordings.

LHI

Lee Hazlewood's LHI (Lee Hazlewood Industries) label was active during 1967–68. The singularly named Arthur cut the label's debut LP, *Dreams and Images* (12000); other releases included the 98 Percent's *American Mom and Apple Pie* (12001) and the Aggregation's "Sunshine Superman" 45 (12009) and *Mind Odyssey* LP (12008).

Hazlewood himself reissued his 1963 *Trouble Is a Lonesome Town* (12006), before LHI lapsed into silence for a few years. It re-emerged in 1970 with further Hazlewood albums *The Cowboy and the Lady* (12007), *Forty* (12009), and *Cowboy in Sweden*. Three Hazlewood promo 45s are much in-demand: "No Train to Stockholm" (19), "Troublemaker" (20), and "Nobody Like You" (21).

Liberty

Launched in Hollywood in 1955, Liberty Records was owned by Simon Waronker, a soundtrack musician at 20th Century Fox, and the majority of early Liberty releases reflected his origins, featuring orchestral, big-band, and light-jazz recordings. The first 45, "The Girl Upstairs" (55001), was performed by another 20th Century Fox musician, Lionel Newman. However, Liberty also recorded the then-unknown Julie London, immediately charting with the immortal

---

TEN TOP COLLECTIBLES

Lee Hazlewood

"Charlie Bill Nelson" (Reprise 0667—7-inch, 1967)

The Cowboy and the Lady (with Ann-Margret, LHI 12007—LP, 1971)

Did You Ever (RCA 4645—LP, 1971)

Friday's Child (Reprise 6163—Mono LP, 1966)

"The Girls in Paris" (MGM K13716—7-inch, 1966)

A House Safe for Tigers (CBS 80383—LP, 1975)

It's Cause and Cure (MGM SE 4403—Stereo LP, 1966)

Love and Other Crimes (Reprise 6297—LP, 1968)

NSVIP (The NSVIP's) (Reprise 6133—LP, 1965)

"A Taste of You" (MCA 0613—7-inch, 1979)

"Cry Me a River" (55006), and opening the door for a succession of well-crafted and now-much-collected LPs by the so-called Liberty Girl.

Other early recruits of note included Henry Mancini, who remained at Liberty for three successful years before moving to RCA; and songwriter Ross Bagdasarian. His Liberty debut, "The Trouble with Harry" (55008), was released under the pseudonym Alfi and Harry in 1956; another Bagdasarian alias, David Seville, issued the instrumental "Armen's Theme" (55041), the prelude to a stream of novelty records that remain popular today: "Gotta Get to Your House" (55079—1957), "Bagdad Express" (55113), and "Bonjour Tristesse" (55124).

But it was the chart-topping "Witch Doctor" (55132) that made Seville's reputation and assured his chart longevity. Born of an experiment with vari-speed tape, it inspired Seville to create the Chipmunks, whose high-pitched chattering was to spawn a lengthy catalog of hits that represent a virtual high-speed history of the American '60s.

They did the twist, they sang the Beatles, they went folk, they covered Herman's Hermits; they even jammed with Canned Heat on 1968's remake of their debut hit, "The Chipmunk Song" (56079). Three rare EPs and ten albums represent the Chipmunks's Liberty output, and specialists have a wealth of label and sleeve varieties to entertain themselves with, long after the appeal of a Chipmunked "Super-Cali-Fragilistic-Expi-Ali-Docious" (55773) has worn off.

Liberty's hottest rock 'n' roll property was Eddie Cochran. Debuting for the label in 1957 with "Sittin' in the Balcony" (55056), Cochran followed up with the minor "Mean When I'm Mad" (55070) and "Drive-in Show" (55087), before finally unleashing the first of the three unassailable classics for which he is now remembered, "20 Flight Rock" (55112). Another brace of less-than-stellar 45s followed, together with the LP *Singin' to My Baby* (LRP 3061), before 1958 brought the rest of that sainted trilogy, "Summertime Blues" (55144) and "C'mon Everybody" (55166).

Cochran never followed those hits up; immediate follow-ups failed to take off, while his death in an auto accident at the end of a British tour in early 1960 perhaps surprisingly failed to ignite any kind of grief-stricken rebirth, at least in the US. In the UK, where Cochran's music was released by London, his latest (and most ironically titled) single, "Three Steps to Heaven" (HLG 9115) was an immediate chart-topper.

Cochran is now the most collectible of the 1950s Liberty artists, his original releases regularly fetching high prices. Close behind comes Willie Nelson, a cousin of teen idol Ricky Nelson, who debuted on Liberty in 1958 with the single "Susie" (55155). His popularity with collectors, however, has more to do with his full name than with his family connections. Three years later, another Willie Nelson would release the single "The Part Where I Cry" (55386), the first of the eleven Liberty singles (and three LPs) that today mark the dawn of one of country's most successful artists of all time. The first Willie Nelson has no link at all with the second—but that hasn't stopped either prices or price guides from assuming otherwise.

Less well-known, but also highly collectible, are Billy Ward and his Dominoes—a onetime R&B band now specializing in lush orchestral pop—and bandleader Martin Denny, whose penchant for exotic music saw Liberty all but corner the market in such peculiarities. Beginning with the hit single "Quiet Village" (55162) in 1959, these releases were reasonably popular at the time of release, but the catalog then lay undisturbed for some three decades, before the 1990s brought about a massive, and very volatile, collector-fueled renaissance. Prices have still to settle down for recordings that were once thrift-store regulars.

Beyond the realms of pop, Liberty continued recording big bands (Spike Jones was on board for a time), while adding both country and folk to the roster. Licensing deals brought some major regional hits to the label, including the Seattle Dolphin/Dolton label's 1959 hit "Come Softly to Me" by the Fleetwoods (55188), Goldcreast/Goldcrest's Troy Shondell hit "This Time" (55353), and the Soma label's "Suzy Baby" (55208), by Bobby Vee. That latter artist would become Liberty's most consistent hit-maker of the

An Imperial classic of the British Invasion.

early '60s, scoring his first Top Ten hit with "Devil or Angel" (55270) before topping the chart with "Take Good Care of My Baby" (55354). Over the course of ten years, 1960–70, Vee scored 38 Top 100 hits for Liberty, and released close to two dozen LPs. No other artist in the label's history even comes close.

Other major-label stars from this period include Walter Brennan, Johnny Burnette, Vikki Carr, the Crickets, Buddy Knox, Van McCoy, Billy Strange, and Timi Yuro; modern collectibles from the stable, meanwhile, are dominated by the surf boom. The Mar-Kets's "Surfer's Stomp" (5401) made history as the first Top 40 hit ever to mention what would soon become teenage California's national pastime, while Jan and Dean's Liberty career embraced 15 archetypal hits between 1962–66, at which time Jan (Berry) was seriously injured in an auto accident.

The Brian Wilson composition "Surf City" (55580), "Drag City" (55641), "Dead Man's Curve" (55672), and "The Little Old Lady from Pasadena" (55704) are classics of the era, while the duo's Liberty LP catalog stretches to 13 albums, available in mono and stereo, with a handful of collectible sleeve varieties thrown in for good measure. Few of these albums are scarce in themselves; the duo's enduring popularity, however, insists that prices keep rising.

Less commercially successful, but a legend among collectors all the same, is P.J. Proby, an American-born balladeer who signed with Liberty in 1961, debuting with "Try to Forget Her" (55367). Three further singles went nowhere, before Proby joined London and scored a minor hit with "Hold Me"; he returned to Liberty for further hits "Somewhere" (55757) and "Niki Hoeky" (55936) in 1965 and 1967, alongside a string of poor-selling, but nonetheless captivating, releases that, together with five LPs issued between 1965–68, are well-respected today.

Proby was also one of the first artists to score for Liberty's now-flourishing UK branch—indeed, it is often said that the singer was far more popular in

Britain than he ever was in America. Chart statistics, sadly, fail to bear this out, though it was in Britain that Proby made his biggest mark, when an onstage stretch-too-far caused his trousers to split. Capitalizing on the uproar that then ensued, Proby made sure to do the same thing the next time he played, only to find that the notoriety was too hot to handle. His UK career stalled on the spot, though he remains a much-loved artist who continues to release new material today—the mid-'90s even returned him to the chart, duetting with Marc Almond.

Of Proby's most collectible releases, 1968's "The Day that Lorraine Came Down" (UK LBF 15152) is the most sought after; its B-side, "Merv Hoppkins Never Had Days Like These," features one of the first-ever recordings of a new band called Led Zeppelin. The group also appears on one track on the following year's *Three Week Hero* LP (UK LBS 83219)—neither of these, incidentally, was issued in the US.

In 1963, the electronics company Avnet purchased Liberty from Waronker and his VP, Al Bennett, for $12 million, following through with the acquisition of Imperial, which became a Liberty subsidiary. It

was a short-lived dalliance. By 1965, Avnet had agreed to sell the newly expanded Liberty back to Bennett for just $8 million (poor health prevented Waronker from returning on board). In chart terms, Imperial became the dominant partner, but Liberty maintained a firm grip on its own vision, with signings ranging from Gary Lewis (son of Jerry) and the Playboys, the Gants, and Del Shannon, to British singing comedian Ken Dodd.

This period, too, proved short-lived. In 1968, the insurance group Transamerica Corporation purchased Liberty and combined it with another label it owned, United Artists. It marked the beginning of the end. Though a new generation of talent was recruited to Liberty over the next three years, successes with the likes of Canned Heat, the Nitty Gritty Dirt Band, Ike and Tina Turner, and Bobby Womack proved short-lived, and the Imperial and Liberty labels became increasingly, and fatally, subservient to UA. First, the Imperial roster was either dropped or moved to Liberty, before Liberty's own roster suffered a similar fate, with a mere handful of acts making the transition to UA.

TEN TOP COLLECTIBLES

Eddie Cochran

C'mon Everybody (UK London HA-U 2093—EP, 1959)

"Hallelujah, I Love Her So" (UK London HLW 9022—78, 1960)

"Mean When I'm Mad" (Liberty 55070—7-inch, picture sleeve, 1957)

Never to Be Forgotten (Liberty LRP 3220—LP, 1962)

"Rough Stuff" (Capehart 5003—7-inch, picture sleeve, 1960)

Singin' to My Baby (Liberty LRP 3061—Green-label LP, 1957)

"Skinny Jim" (Crest 1026—7-inch, 1956)

"Three Steps to Heaven" (UK London HLG 9115—78, 1960)

Twelve of His Biggest Hits (Liberty LRP 3172—LP, 1960)

"Twenty Flight Rock" (UK London HLU 8386—7-inch, black label with triangular center, 1957)

A seldom-seen Lionel promo label.

Sugarloaf's "Tongue in Cheek" (56218) single was the final Liberty release in 1972; the Sunset subsidiary, established in 1966 to carry budget-priced catalog reissues, survived a little longer, but folded in the mid-'70s. Since that time, the Liberty name and logo have been invoked on several occasions for reissues, a practice that has gone a long way toward ensuring the continued collectibility of the original label's output.

Lion/Lionel

Taking its name from the parent MGM label's historical logo, a Lion label existed during the 1950s as a budget outlet. The name was revived in 1972, as a replacement for the short-lived (1970–71) Lionel label, which was launched with the Satisfaction's "Ol' Man River" 45 (3201). Lionel made its chart debut in early 1971 with Joey Scarbury's "Mixed Up Buy" (3208).

Other Lionel releases included singles by Big City Down River, Jacky Cornell, the Heroes of Cranberry Farm, Larry Nettles, Gwen Simmons, and Sweet Roll, but only one act, the Canadian quintet Five Man Electrical Band, proved at all successful. Joining Lionel after stints with Capitol and MGM, the group was responsible for the only LPs Lionel issued—1971's *Goodbyes and Butterflies* (LRS 1100) and 1972's *Coming of Age* (LRS 1101). The group also cut the label's final single, "Friends and Family" (3224). Five Man Electrical Band was then transferred to the reborn Lion label.

However, Lion would survive for little more than a year before being absorbed into the parent company in 1973. (The lion imagery would be reborn in the Pride subsidiary.)

Lion's brief existence nevertheless saw a range of releases, including LPs by the Washington Junior School Band and Chorus, the Canadian Rock Theatre, the Blossoms, the Five Man Electrical Band, Pat Boone, Iguana, and Randy Edelman.

More impressive are releases by the hard rock band Frijid Pink, which issued an LP, 1972's *Earth*

TEN TOP COLLECTIBLES

Partridge Family Solo Releases

"Ain't Love Easy"—Shirley Jones (Bell 253—7-inch, 1971)

"Blueberry You"—Danny Bonaduce (Lion 145—7-inch, 1972)

Cassidy Live—David Cassidy (Bell 1312—LP, 1974)

Dreamland—Danny Bonaduce (Lion 1015—LP, 1972)

The Higher They Climb—David Cassidy (RCA APLI 1066—Blue-vinyl LP, 1975)

"I've Still Got My Heart, Joe"—Shirley Jones (Bell 119—7-inch, 1971)

"The Last Kiss"—David Cassidy (UK Arista ARISD 589—7-inch, shaped picture disc, 1985)

Ricky Segal and the Segulls—Ricky Segall (Bell 1138—LP, 1973)

"Sooner or Later"—Ricky Segall (Bell 429—7-inch, 1973)

"Walk in Silence"—Shirley Jones (Bell 350—7-inch, 1972)

Omen (LN 1004), and three 45s (a second LP was scheduled—1012—but never released), as well as *Partridge Family* TV star Danny Bonaduce, whose rare *Dreamland* solo debut (1015) spun off an even scarcer 45, "Blueberry You" (145). Test pressings of unreleased LPs by Gary Bonner (1006) and Anthony Newley (1010) have been reported—both sets were subsequently issued on MGM.

The greatest Lion rarity, however, is *The Great White Cane,* by White Cane (1005), an utterly unremarkable 1972 funk album whose value lies in the presence of the young Rick James.

Mala

The Mala subsidiary of Bell was launched in 1959 with the Hi Boys' "Billy Boy" (400), and remained in action until 1969. The vast majority of Mala artists released 45s only; among the earliest acts of note was David Gates, whose "What's This I Hear" (413), "Happiest Man Alive" (418), and "Jo Baby" (427) appeared during 1960–61 and are highly prized by Bread fans. Releases by future Motown star R. Dean Taylor ("I'll Remember"—444) and a brace of singles by Link Wray ("Hold

It"—456, credited to Ray Vernon and the Ray Men, and "Dancing Party"—458) are similarly noteworthy.

Other Mala singles are collectible for the label more than for the artists: Sy Oliver, future Classics member Herb Lance, the Hully Gully Boys, David Walker, the Del Satins, the Rag Dolls, and Don and Juan and the Royaltones, inherited from the Big Top label in 1963. The label's first LP, *Love on the Rocks,* by Richard Hayes (MLP 25), is similarly regarded (the catalog number, incidentally, places this release within Bell's own numbering system, though the labels are Mala's).

Two singles by another Big Top act, Johnny and the Hurricanes, are worth watching for—"It's a Mad, Mad, Mad World" (470) and "That's All" (483).

Mala's first major hit came with Ronny and the Daytonas' "G.T.O." (481) in 1964. It inspired a full LP release, titled after the single (4001). A second Daytonas LP, *Sandy* (4002), was named for the band's fourth hit single (513—the group's last for Mala). Mala released two other albums, by the Peppi Morreale Trio and the Carlton Show Band, both in 1966.

Intriguing, too, is the presence on the label of Chip Taylor, writer of the garage anthem "Wild Thing,"

A promo copy of one of Manticore's lesser-known offspring.

and later, producer of the much-underrated Evie Sands. "On My World" (476), "Suzannah" (489), and "Young Love" (507) are all worthwhile acquisitions.

Little Caesar and the Consuls, the Van Dykes soul trio, Bobby Wood, Reparata and the Delrons, Bruce Channel, Gene Simmons, the Pieces of Eight, Mickey Lee Lane, and a Harrisburg band called the Emperors ("Karate"—543—neatly preempts the kung fu boom of eight years later) were Mala acts during the mid-'60s, but the label's greatest success came with the Box Tops, whose "The Letter" (565) was the first of nine chart singles before the label's demise—indeed, the group's "Turn on a Dream" (12042) was the last-ever Mala release. A tenth then appeared on Bell before the group disbanded. As with other Mala acts, the parent label also handled the Box Tops LP catalog.

Other interesting Mala issues from the label's last days include two very hard to find singles by the British rock band Spooky Tooth, "Love Really Changed Me" (12013) and "The Weight" (12022), and a brief flurry of activity by veteran British rocker Billy

Fury. Much of his career had been spent on London, though not once had he even begun to approach the highs of his homeland career. His Mala releases, while as distinguished as ever, were painfully unlikely to change his US profile any—by this time, they weren't even likely to be successful in the UK (where they were released by Parlophone).

One highly collectible gem did emerge, however: Fury's Mala farewell, "Silly Boy Blue" (12018), was composed by the then-absolutely unknown David Bowie and was, in fact, his first song ever to be covered by an established artist, albeit a fading one. Its UK counterpart (Parlophone R5681) sells for around $50.

Manticore

Manticore was the property of the progressive-rock band Emerson Lake and Palmer. It took its name from one of the mythological creatures depicted on the sleeve of the group's sophomore LP, *Tarkus*. The label was distributed through Cotillion in the US (who assigned the numerical sequence 66660 to the label) and Atlantic in the UK (utilizing the K43500 and 53100 series).

The label debuted in 1973 with a solo album by King Crimson songwriter Pete Sinfield, *Still* (MC 66667)—ELP's 1971 live album *Pictures at an Exhibition* would subsequently be reissued in the US with the number MC 66666.

Photos of Ghosts, by Italian band PFM (Premiata Forneria Marconi), followed (MC 66668), together with ELP's own new album, *Brain Salad Surgery* (MC 66669). Albums by Hanson, Stray Dog, Junior Hanson, and a second PFM set (MC66673) followed during 1973–74, while ELP released a second live set, the ambitious triple LP *Welcome Back My Friends* (SD 3-200) that same year.

In 1975, Manticore's US distribution moved to Motown. The MA 6-500 series of LPs includes further sets by Stray Dog and PFM, plus debut offerings by Keith Christmas (first released in the UK the previous year—K53503) and another Italian band, Banco, and two sets by the putative supergroup Thee Image (ex–Iron Butterfly, Cactus). A fourth PFM LP, *Choco-*

late Kings (K53508), and Keith Christmas's second, *Stories from the Human Zoo* (K53509), appeared in the UK alone in 1976, but there was no new material from ELP. The band was in the midst of what would become a three-year break, and upon their return to action in 1977, Manticore was nowhere to be seen.

In collecting terms, the label is nevertheless dominated by ELP. The aforementioned LPs are joined by two singles: 1973's "Jerusalem" (UK—K13503) and "Still . . . You Turn Me On" (US MC 2003). Both were distinguished by otherwise unavailable B-sides; Manticore also released a promotional flexidisc through the UK newspaper *New Musical Express,* excerpting the *Brain Salad Surgery* album (LYN 2762—the prefix refers to the manufacturer, Lyntone) and offering the cuts in a gatefold sleeve similar to that of the parent LP. Also of interest are the UK label releases of Greg Lake's solo 45 "I Believe in Father Christmas" (K13511) and Keith Emerson's "Honky Tonk Train Blues" (K13513).

Generally overlooked, however, is the fact that Manticore also released 45s by its other signings. In the US, this includes Hanson's "Love Knows

TEN TOP COLLECTIBLES

Emerson Lake and Palmer

Excerpts from Brain Salad Surgery (UK Manticore/Lyntone LYN 2762—Flexidisc, picture sleeve, 1973)

Excerpts from Mar y Sol—Various artists (Atlantic PR 176—7-inch promo, picture sleeve, 1972)

"Jerusalem" (UK Manticore K13503—7-inch, picture sleeve, 1974)

On Tour with Emerson Lake and Palmer (Atlantic PR 281—Promo LP, 1977)

Pictures at an Exhibition (Mobile Fidelity 031—Audiophile LP, 1980)

Selections from Return of the Manticore (Victory SACD 757—CD, card sleeve, 1993)

"Still . . . You Turn Me On" (Manticore 2003—7-inch, picture sleeve, 1973)

Tarkus (Mobile Fidelity 203—Audiophile LP, 1994)

Trilogy (Capitol Record Club SMAS 94773—LP, 1973)

Works Volume One (Atlantic PR 277—Promo LP, 1977)

Everything" (MC 2001) and "Boy Meets Girl" (2004), and PFM's "Celebration" (2002) and "Mr. Nine to Five" (7003). These releases can prove extremely challenging to find.

Further Reading: *Emerson Lake and Palmer: The Show That Never Ends,* by George Forrester, Martyn Hanson, and Frank Askew (Helter Skelter Ltd., 2001)

Marmalade

The Marmalade label was launched by producer Giorgio Gomelsky, in 1967. One of the legends of the early British beat scene, Gomelsky's own legacy of productions and discoveries is best traced through early releases on the French Charly label, to whom he licensed his personal archive during the early '70s.

The Marmalade story, on the other hand, has still to undergo the thorough evaluation it deserves, leaving collectors scratching around in the bowels of odd singles bins and lengthy set-sale lists, in search of the 20 or so 45s and LPs that the UK Polydor imprint released during its 1966–69 life span. The only consolation is, almost all repay the search.

Marmalade debuted in September 1966, with the Roaring Sixties' "We Love the Pirate Stations" (598 001), a plaintive song aimed at the British government's impending outlawing of the independent radio stations that blasted a nonstop diet of pop music onto UK shores throughout the early-to-mid-'60s.

Although it was popular with, of course, the pirates themselves, the single did little sales-wise and is very difficult to find—and while the song has appeared on CD, on the Dutch *We Love the Pirate Stations* anthology of the era (BR Music BX 434), that collection, too, is becoming scarce.

After such a populist start, Marmalade lapsed into silence for much of the next year, before resurfacing with the first release by whimsical psychedelics Blossom Toes, "What on Earth" (598 002); the group's *We Are Ever So Clean* debut LP would similarly launch Marmalade's album series (607 001—mono/608 001 stereo). Much loved by modern collectors, Blossom Toes' four singles/two album catalog is the highest priced in the Marmalade canon, though it is by no means the scarcest.

TEN TOP COLLECTIBLES

Pre-10cc

"I'm Beside Myself"—Frabjoy and the Runcible Spoon (UK Marmalade 598 019, 1969)

"Impossible Years"—Graham Gouldman (RCA Victor 47-9453—7-inch, 1968)

"Joker"—Garden Odyssey (UK RCA 2159—7-inch, 1972)

"Sad and Lonely"—Garden Odyssey Enterprise (UK Deram DM 267—7-inch, 1969)

"Stop Stop Stop"—Graham Gouldman (UK Decca F12334—7-inch, 1966)

"That's How"—The Mockingbirds (ABC Paramount 10653—7-inch, 1965)

"Umbopo"—Dr. Father (UK Pye 7N 17977—7-inch, 1970)

"Upstairs Downstairs"—Graham Gouldman (UK RCA 1667—7-inch, 1968)

"Windmills of Your Mind"—Graham Gouldman Orchestra (UK Spark SRL 1026—7-inch, 1969)

"You Stole My Love"—The Mockingbirds (UK Immediate IM 015—7-inch, 1965)

Singles by jazzman Chris Barber ("Cat Call"—598 005, "Battersea Rain Dance"—598 013), Gordon Jackson ("Me and My Zoo"—598 010, "Song for Freedom"—598 021), Gary Farr ("Hey Daddy"—598 017), and the pre-Godley-Creme duo of Frabjoy and the Runcible Spoon ("I'm Beside Myself"—598 019) are fabulously scarce; albums by most of the above, plus John McLaughlin (*Extrapolation*—608 007) and John Stevens (*Spontaneous Music Ensemble*—608 008), are similarly rare.

Amid such relentless rarity, just one Marmalade act bucks the trend. The Julie Driscoll/Brian Auger Trinity brought Marmalade its only hit single, with Dylan's "This Wheel's on Fire" (598 006), together with two albums (*Open*—608 002, and the double *Street Noise*—608 005) that have been reissued regularly enough to take at least some of the bloodlust out of the collectors market.

Original 45s are still difficult to locate, however. The Trinity issued two unsuccessful follow-ups to the hit, while Driscoll alone was credited with the two-part "Save Me" (598 005); in addition, Marmalade's French wing issued a number of exclusive releases that are desperately rare, including an otherwise unavailable version of Dylan's "Lonesome Hobo" (421180). Auger's "Black Cat," meanwhile, was issued by Marmalade Italy with an Italian-language vocal track. American Trinity issues, on Atco, are often regarded as hard to find.

Marmalade folded in 1969—ironically, not long after releasing the *100% Proof* (643 314) album that was touted as a sampler of past, present, and future releases. A vital starting point for any aspiring Marmalade collector, it also features a handful of tracks that never made it out in any form, including two more pre-10cc cuts, by Kevin Godley and Graham Gouldman. Once a British bargain-bin regular, like everything else on Marmalade, it rarely turns up these days.

Mer

The Mer (French for sea) label was launched by New York poetess Patti Smith and guitarist Lenny Kaye in 1974, specifically to release Smith's debut 45, "Hey Joe" (601), which was reissued in 1977 by Sire (1009). Mer was revived three years later for a very

---

TEN TOP COLLECTIBLES

Patti Smith

"Ask the Angels" (France Arista 2C00698529—7-inch, picture sleeve, 1976)

Big Ego (Giorno Poetry System 012-13—LP, 1978)

"Brian Jones" (Fierce FRIGHT 017—7-inch, 1988)

"Hey Joe" (Mer 601—7-inch, 1974)

King Biscuit Flour Hour 2/76 (KBFH—Transcription disc, 1976)

Nova Convention (Giorno Poetry System 014-15—LP, 1978)

"Privilege" (UK Arista 12197—12-inch, picture sleeve, 1978)

Sugar Alcohol and Meat (Giorno Poetry System 016-17—LP, 1978)

Wave (Greece Arista 06262516—Blue-vinyl LP)

"White Christmas"—Link Cromwell (Jason J60568—7-inch, 1977)

rare LP by reggae great Tapper Zukie, produced by Clement Bushay, *Man I Warrior* (MER 101, featuring a Robert Mapplethorpe photo sleeve), and Kaye's solo "Child Bride" 45 (81).

Minit

An integral player in the early development of the New Orleans music scene of the 1960s, Minit Records was formed by A-1 Record Distributors head Joe Banashak and Larry McKinley, though it was musical director Allen Toussaint who dominated the label's output, writing, playing on, arranging, and producing much of it.

One of Toussaint's first duties for the label was to oversee an open audition night that Banashak hoped would unearth new talent for the company. It succeeded beyond anybody's wildest dreams: in one evening, Toussaint discovered Aaron Neville, Irma Thomas, Benny Spellman, and Jessie Hill, with the latter promptly bringing Toussaint his first Minit smash 45, the oft-imitated "Ooh Poo Pah Do (Parts One and Two)" (607), in March 1960.

The following year, with Minit's distribution handled by Imperial, Ernie K-Doe's "Mother-in-Law" (623) brought the label its first US No. 1 (it was also the first national chart-topper ever to be recorded in New Orleans), opening a sequence of five hits for the erstwhile Ernest Kador over the next year. K-Doe also cut an album named for the hit (002), one of just four LPs released by the original Minit label and the only one to feature an individual artist.

The other three, rounding up Minit singles and sessions, comprised two volumes of *Home of the Blues* (0001 in 1961, 0004 in 1963) and *We Sing the Blues* (0003, also in 1963). Featuring such names as Chris Kenner, Aaron Neville, Benny Spellman, and Irma Thomas, alongside hit-makers Hill and K-Doe, these priceless glimpses into the Big Easy beat of the early '60s are highly sought after.

Another Minit classic was the Showmen's 1961 hit "It Will Stand" (632), a defiant tribute to rock 'n' roll's staying power, a song whose inherent truth was proven first when a reissue on Imperial (66033) returned to the chart in 1964, then when Jonathan

Richman cut a fine version for inclusion on the *Beserkley Chartbusters* album in 1975.

Banashak launched the subsidiary Instant Records in 1961, with distribution through Atlantic. The label was most notable for Chris Kenner, whose debut single, "I Like It Like That" (3229), was a No. 2 hit that same year. However, neither Kenner nor Instant ever matched that first moment of glory, and though the label remained in operation until 1969, Kenner remained its only artist of note.

Toussaint was drafted into the military in 1963. During his absence, Banashak sold both Minit and Instant to Imperial. The first release under the new arrangement was a reissue of *Home of the Blues II* (40004); over the next four years, the Minit label maintained a slow, but generally strong, stream of blues and R&B classics from the likes of Jimmy Holiday, the Players, Jimmy McCracklin, Flip Wilson, and Gene Dozier. Among the albums that are especially prized today can be numbered the O'Jays' *Soul Sounds* (40008/24008—home of the single "Hold On"—32015), Bobby Womack's *Fly Me to the Moon* (40014/24014), and the *Like It Is* (40007) collection of early Aaron Neville recordings rushed out to coincide with his Par-Lo label hit "Tell It Like It Is."

Womack issued a second Minit LP the following year, *My Prescription,* together with nine Minit singles that are generally ranked among his rarest. Four of these were minor hits—"Fly Me to the Moon" (32048), "California Dreaming" (32055), "How Can I Miss You Baby" (32081), and "More Than I Can Stand" (32093)—acknowledged Womack classics today, but barely noticed at the time.

Overlooked, too, were Ike and Tina Turner during their 1969–70 stay with Minit, despite the release of some of their fieriest performances—"I'm Gonna Do All I Can (To Do Right by My Man)" (32060), "With a Little Help from My Friends"/"I Wish It Would Rain" (32068), "Treating Us Funky" (32077), and the devastating coupling of "Honky Tonk Women"/"Come Together" (32087). The *In Person* album (40018/24018), too, ranks among the duo's most electrifying releases.

TEN TOP COLLECTIBLES

Ike and Tina Turner

Dynamite (Sue LP 2004— LP, 1963)

"A Fool in Love" (Sue 730— 7-inch, 1960)

Get Yer Yah Yahs Out (by the Rolling Stones— UK Decca, no catalog number— 2-LP test pressing, 1970)

Ike and Tina Revue Live (Kent KST 514— Stereo LP, 1964)

"I'm Through with Love" (Loma 2011— 7-inch, 1965)

In Person (Minit 24018— LP, 1969)

Live! The Ike and Tina Show (Warner Bros. WS 1579— Stereo LP, 1965)

River Deep Mountain High (Philles 4011— LP, no sleeve, 1966)

Soul of Ike and Tina (UK Sue IEP 706— EP, 1964)

"Two to Tango" (Philles 134— 7-inch, 1966)

In 1969 the Minit emphasis shifted away from R&B toward gospel, and toward releases by Isaac Douglas and the Douglas Singers, the Rev. Robert J. Lucas and His Christian Temple Choir, the Robert Patterson Singers, the Marion Gaines Singers and the Mighty Gospel Giants. Slowly the remainder of the Minit and Instant roster was moved onto Imperial or Liberty. The final Minit LPs were the aforementioned Womack album and the Memphis Soul Band's *Soul Cowboy* (40028/24028).

Mobile Fidelity Sound Lab

Between 1977 and the late '90s, the Mobile Fidelity Sound Lab (MFSL) label became a firm collectible, via its policy of high-quality reissues initially on vinyl, later on gold CDs. The inspiration behind the label's formation was a growing dissatisfaction with the quality of contemporary American pressings, particularly in comparison with equivalent Japanese and British issues.

Having exposed the American industry practice of recycling vinyl from previous releases, a policy that the Japanese in particular would never have

countenanced, collectors agitated for change. MFSL answered the call, not only employing even higher vinyl standards to the European and Asian manufacturers, utilizing "super vinyl," as opposed to mere "virgin," but also by seeking out first-generation master tapes, rather than the second, third, or worse generations which were now in use by many labels.

Pressing quantities were limited to the optimum life span of the plates employed at manufacturing, the mastering itself was undertaken at half speed, and packaging was designed to maximize the record's safety. Moreover, prices in the region of double the cost of a regular LP kept the riffraff out. In a nutshell, MFSL made exclusive records for exclusive purchasers.

The MFSL catalog opened in 1978 with four releases by the Mystic Moods Orchestra (MFSL 1-001-004); the first rock releases, that same year, included classic titles by Supertramp (*Crime of the Century*—1-005), Steely Dan (*Katy Lied*—1-007), and Al Stewart (*Year of the Cat*—1-009). In 1979 MFSL released reissues of Fleetwood Mac's *Fleetwood Mac*

MFSL's masterful repressing of one of the British blues scene's most cherished releases.

(1-012), the Grateful Dead's *American Beauty* (1-014), Pink Floyd's *Dark Side of the Moon* (1-017), and Steve Miller's *Fly Like an Eagle* (1-021), all albums cut to the highest standards, now available with those standards rigorously adhered to at every stage of the manufacturing process. The addition of the Beatles' *Abbey Road* (1-023), in 1980, simply confirmed MFSL's preeminence.

MFSL would issue well over 200 LPs, in addition to inaugurating a new series of even higher-quality vinyl, the aptly named UHQR (Ultra High Quality Records) issues. In addition, the advent of the CD prompted a move into that area in 1985, again activated by complaints from collectors—far from offering the immaculate sound quality that the marketing departments promised, many early CDs represented a new low in hi-fi, as discs were manufactured from precisely the same tapes as the old LPs, with no attempt either to remaster, or even repair, existing faults.

Consumers also feared that a then-prevalent rumor might be true: that, far from being practically indestructible, individual CDs were unlikely to last more than a decade before decaying. MFSL responded by pressing its Ultradisc series of high-quality compact discs on gold, rather than on the industry-standard aluminum. A new jewel-case design, capable of holding discs securely in place, was also developed.

Early Ultradisc releases, including sets by Joe Jackson, Blind Faith, Huey Lewis, Jethro Tull, the Police, the Allman Brothers, and the ubiquitous Pink Floyd and Supertramp, were greeted with great interest and high praise. However, while the rest of the music industry accustomed itself to MFSL's customers' demands for first-generation masters and attractive packaging, and fears for the CD's long-term future finally abated, support for MFSL's CD series began to decline. Even the much-vaunted gold disc proved to be something of a red herring, as expert listening tests determined that it was the quality of the original tape, not its ultimate destination, that most affected a CD's sound.

MFSL's reputation for quality merchandise, of course, remains unimpeachable, and collectors are still willing to pay above the odds for the label's CD issues. It is the vinyl, however, that exercises the most attention, for it is there that the label's own attention to detail and drama is most vividly displayed.

Motown

Its admirers call it the greatest soul-R&B label in the world and even its detractors admit there has never been anything like it in music history, a phenomenon that rose out of one man's vision and became not simply one of the most successful black-owned businesses in the world, but one of the most successful businesses, full stop.

Berry Gordy, Jr., was already a successful songwriter and producer when he launched Motown—his earliest productions appeared on Mercury, George Goldner's Mark X and End labels, and the lesser-known Kudo and HOB concerns during 1957–58. These included efforts by the Miracles; Eddie Holland and his brother Brian; Herman Griffin; and Marv Johnson.

In 1958 Gordy, Jr., formed his own publishing company, Jobete (named for his three children, Hazel JOy, BErry IV, and TErry. The following January, he borrowed $800 from his family's loan fund and opened Tamla Records—his original choice of name, Tammy, had already been taken. Marv Johnson's "Come to Me" 45 (101) launched the label and won Johnson a deal with United Artists—his next single, "You Got What It Takes" (UA 0030) became producer Gordy, Jr.'s first pop Top Ten hit.

Gordy, Jr., launched a second label, Motown (a play on hometown Detroit's Motor City nickname), soon after, debuting it with the Miracles' "Bad Girl" (G1/G2, also TLX 2207—either pressing is impossibly rare, valued in excess of $1,000 in all but the vilest condition). This time it was Chess who moved in for a fast-percolating local hit, and while the reissue (1734) did not break the national chart, it established both the group and its producer as names to watch.

That observation paid off with Barrett Strong's "Money" (Tamla 54027—his second 45, following "Let's Rock"—54022).

Leased to Gordy, Jr.'s sister Anna's label, itself called Anna, whose own distribution deal with Chess placed it in a far stronger position than either of Gordy, Jr.'s labels, "Money" became a pop Top 30 hit. It also signaled the start of the Hitsville Revolution.

Collecting Motown is not a hobby. It is a full-time job (and it requires a full-time job as well, simply to finance the purchase of the earliest releases). Any one of some two dozen Motown acts could claim a place in the Top Ten of the world's most collectible bands and artists—and Smokey Robinson and the Miracles, Diana Ross and the Supremes, the Temptations, Marvin Gaye, and Michael Jackson and the Jackson Five would probably all be correct in their assumption.

For that reason alone, many Motown collectors prefer to concentrate their attentions either on one particular group (or group of groups—particularly during the 1960s, Gordy, Jr., loved teaming his best-sellers together on one-off singles and LPs), or on the work of one writer or producer. Among the most collectible are Holland-Dozier-Holland, who masterminded many of the Four Tops's greatest hits before decamping to launch their own Invictus–Hot Wax concerns. Other collectors concentrate on Gordy, Jr., or on Norman Whitfield, who led first the Temptations, and then Motown itself, into the tempestuous waters of late-'60s psychedelia and protest.

UK Motown releases are a popular field. Early issues were licensed through the London label (a total of 11 singles), Stateside (45), Oriole (19), and Fontana (four), before a joint Tamla-Motown label was launched with the Supremes' "Stop! In the Name of Love" (Tamla Motown TMG 501), in March 1965.

Many of these pre-Motown discs are extremely hard to find; among them, the scarcest are a 78 by Paul Gayton, "The Hunch" (UK London HLM 8998), the Valadiers' "I Found a Girl" (Oriole CBA 1809), and promo or demonstration copies of 1969's withdrawn "Oh How Happy," by Blinky and Edwin Starr (Tamla Motown TMG 720).

TEN TOP COLLECTIBLES

Motown/Soul/Gordy

"Angel"—The Satintones (Motown 1006—7-inch, 1961)

"Bad Girl"—The Miracles (Motown G1/G2, TLX 2207—7-inch, 1959)

"Camel Walk"—Saundra Mallett and the Vandellas (Tamla 54067—7-inch, 1962)

"Do the Pig"—The Merced Blue Notes (Soul 35007—7-inch, 1965)

"If Your Heart Says Yes"—The Serenaders (Motown 1046—7-inch, 1963)

"In My Diary"—The Spinners (Motown 1155—7-inch, 1969)

"Let's Rock"—Barrett Strong (Tamla 54022—7-inch, 1960)

"Since I Fell for You"—The Skyliners (Motown 1046—7-inch test pressing, 1963)

"Sweeter As the Days Go By"—Frank Wilson (Soul 35019—7-inch, 1966)

"You're Gonna Love My Baby"—Barbara McNair (UK Tamla Motown TMG 544—7-inch, 1966)

Another popular area covers Motown subsidiaries. Having bought up his sister's Anna label, Gordy, Jr., then launched the imprints Soul, VIP, Gordy, Melodyland, Hitsville, Mowest, and Prodigal, together with the more specialized Black Forum (spoken word), Workshop Jazz (jazz), Rare Earth (rock) and Weed, a late-'60s concern whose one LP, by Chris Clark, bore the slogan "Your Favorite Artists Are on Weed." One must make of that what one will.

Motown was one of the first record labels to sign up for the PlayTape system, in April 1967, and a number of the label's biggest stars can be collected in this fascinating (if short-lived) format; the deal was significant in that Motown had hitherto resisted overtures to tie itself to nonvinyl formats. Only Ampex's high-end reel-to-reel tapes had persuaded Gordy, Jr., that they offered an alternative to the 45 and the LP, and these, too, offer a challenging topic.

Other enthusiasts will choose one era of the label's history—the first mad flurry of early-'60s fame, when every single to leave the studio seemed to have "hit" stamped into the very vinyl; the early '70s, when albums rose to the forefront of the label's conscious-ness for the first time, and Marvin Gaye, Stevie Wonder, Edwin Starr, and the Undisputed Truth painted their hard-hitting political messages across an unsuspecting Top 40; or the disco years, when Thelma Houston, the Commodores, and Diana Ross led a pulsating revolution of their own.

Over the years, Motown has come to mean so many things to so many people that it is a sour soul indeed who cannot find something of joy within that vast catalog. In 1976, Gordy, Jr., remarked, "I earned 367 million dollars in 16 years. I must be doing something right!" A quarter of a century later, more than 40 years after the label's inception (and almost 15 years after Gordy, Jr., sold the company to the Universal Music Group), that "something right" is still taking place. **Further Reading:** *Calling Out Around the World: A Motown Reader,* by Kingsley Abbott (Helter Skelter, 2001)

Mute

DJ and would-be record producer Daniel Miller launched Mute records, in mid-1978, with his own 45, "TV OD" (1), released under the name of the

Normal. An unexpected hit on the experimental electronica circuit, it persuaded him that Mute should expand, and over the next few months, the label was joined by San Francisco noise terrorist Boyd Rice, German electro-punks Deutsche Americanische Freundschaft, and Fad Gadget (aka Frank Tovey), the eccentric roommate of cartoonist Edwin Pouncey.

Together with Miller's own continued excursions as the Silicon Teens, this quartet would remain the heart of Mute Records until late 1980, when the group was joined by Depeche Mode, a four-piece discovered by Miller opening for Fad Gadget at a London pub. The group's debut single, "Dreaming of Me" (13), brought Mute its first hit after two years operating on the extremes of public taste—more than 30 years later, their relationship with the label still based on an original handshake, Depeche Mode (like Boyd Rice) remains part of the Mute set-up.

Depeche Mode's success was instantaneous; so, following Vince Clarke's departure after just three singles, were Clarke's subsequent enterprises—Yazoo, Assembly, and Erasure. However, they were not the only stars in the Mute firmament. The Birthday Party closed their recording career at the label, and vocalist Nick Cave continued his.

Former Pop Group vocalist Mark Stewart, Wire, and German pioneers Can all forged links with Miller and Mute, while label discoveries included He Said, Nitzer Ebb (protégés of Depeche Mode's Alan Wilder), and the highly rated mid-'80s synth duo I Start Counting. Almost without exception, these acts, too, have retained relations with Mute, establishing the label among the most reliably self-contained record companies of the past 25 years.

The label's collectibility, too, is assured. Depeche Mode itself is one of the most avidly pursued bands of the era, with its early catalog in particular riven with limited-edition releases—a string of "deluxe" 12-inch singles (the L12 series), launched in 1983, featured exclusive remixes and live material that have still to be given a CD release, while the age of multipart CD singles has seen Depeche exercise its

TEN TOP COLLECTIBLES

Depeche Mode

BBC Transcription Disc 1985 (BBC Transcription—Transcription disc, 1985)

"Behind the Wheel" (Sire PROA 2952—12-inch promo, 1987)

"Blasphemous Rumours" (Sire PROA 2271—12-inch promo, 1985)

B-Sides (UK Mute, no catalog number—4-LP test pressings, 1989)

"Everything Counts" (UK Mute 10BONG 16—10-inch with postcards, sticker, etc., 1989)

"Get the Balance Right" (UK Mute L12BONG 2—12-inch, 1983)

"It's No Good (Club 69 Future Mix)" (UK Mute BONG 26—12-inch, 1997)

"Master and Servant (On-U Sound Science Fiction . . .)" (UK Mute L12BONG 6—12-inch, 1984)

Selections from the Commercially Available Box Sets (Sire PROA 5192/5242—Promo LPs, 1991)

"Sometimes I Wish I Was Dead" (UK Lyntone LYN 1029—Flexidisc, 1981)

imagination even further. Entire albums can be created from the material secreted across the group's UK singles—although bootleggers and fans alone seem to have bothered so far.

Away from Depeche, Nick Cave is probably Mute's most avidly collected artist, again boasting a catalog littered with limited-edition oddities. This includes a free 12-inch single presented with early copies of 1988's *Tender Prey* LP (STUMM 52); an unknown quantity of CD pressings of 1990's "Weeping Song" single (CDMUTE 118), featuring an unlisted secret track; a deluxe version of 1996's *Murder Ballads* CD (CDSTUMM 138), packaged with a booklet based upon the childrens' classic *Shock Headed Peter;* and a bonus live album given away with 1998's *Best Of* compilation (CDMUTEL 004).

The preeminence of these artists has never, however, overshadowed the remainder of the Mute catalog, with the label's early days at the forefront of the electronic music scene (as it mutated toward the industrial genre of the mid-to-late '80s) of especial interest. Original pressings of Mute singles are in constant demand; LPs by Einsturzende Neubauten and various Wire spin-offs likewise.

Further Reading: *Depeche Mode: Some Great Reward,* by Dave Thompson (St. Martin's Press, 1994)

Nepentha

Active only in 1971, Nepentha was a spin-off of the British Vertigo label. Just five LPs were issued, one apiece by Pete Dello, Robin Lent, Dulcimer, Earth and Fire, and Zior (Nepentha 6437 001-005).

New Rose

New Rose was launched in Paris, France, in 1980, by Patrick Mathe and Louis Thevenon. Originally a record store alone, the venture was named for the duo's favorite 45, the Damned's "New Rose"—itself given a French release by what was then the country's only independent record label of any significance, Skydog. (New Rose's tenth anniversary in 1990 was celebrated with the arrival of Brian James, writer of the song "New Rose"; his *Brian James* solo LP (ROSE 234) appeared that same year.)

TEN TOP COLLECTIBLES

Johnny Thunders

"Chinese Rocks"—The Heartbreakers (UK Track 2094 135—12-inch, 1977)

"Crawfish" (with Patti Paladin, UK Jungle JUNG 23—7-inch, picture disc, 1985)

"Get Off the Phone" (UK Beggars Banquet BEG 21—7-inch, 1979)

"Hurt Me" (France New Rose 27—7-inch, 1984)

"In Cold Blood" (France New Rose 14—7-inch, 1982)

"It's Not Enough"—The Heartbreakers (UK Track 2094 142—Withdrawn 7-inch, 1978)

"Que Será Será" (UK Jungle JUNG 33—12-inch, 1987)

Too Much Junkie Business (ROIR 118—Cassette, 1984)

What Goes Around (Bomp 4039—LP, 1992)

"You Can't Put Your Arms around a Memory" (UK Real ARE 3—12-inch, blue- and pink- vinyl, 1978)

Mathe and Thevenon had already operated a small record label of their own, Flamingo, whose output stretched to just five singles. They launched New Rose with an EP by Australian R&B band the Saints, the live *Paralytic Tonight, Dublin Tomorrow* (NEW 1).

Concentrating on both local and foreign talent, New Rose was soon issuing up to ten albums a month, together with a multitude of handsomely packaged 45s, many of which swiftly became collectors items. During New Rose's first three years alone, there were releases by Jello Biafra (*The Witch Trials* EP—NEW 5), the Troggs (*On 45s*—NEW 8), and Bauhaus ("Sartori in Paris"—NEW 12).

Among the other acts first introduced to a wider audience by the label were Americans Gun Club, Joe "King" Carrasco, and Dramarama, as well as France's Charles De Goal; existing cult concerns were furthered with well-received releases from Willie "Loco" Alexander, the Cramps, Roky Erickson, the Real Kids, Alex Chilton, Wreckless Eric, Chris Spedding, former Velvet Underground drummer Maureen "Mo" Tucker, and Johnny Thunders.

Inevitably, these also rank among New Rose's most avidly sought-after releases. However, the lesser-known acts prove the most difficult to come by: Michael Riley (whose "Mr. Chip" was the label's second-ever release NEW 2), the Orson Family, Les Calamites, Reptiles at Dawn, and others.

Conscious of this demand, New Rose has reissued many of its original albums on CD, frequently with bonus tracks drawn from the singles catalog.

Further Reading: *The New Rose Story 1980–2000* (booklet within box set of the same name—WAG 378)

New Voice

A sister label to Bob Crewe's already successful DynoVoice, New Voice came to prominence in 1965 with Mitch Ryder and the Detroit Wheels' "Jenny Take a Ride" (806). The group continued notching up hits for the label until mid-1967, after which New Voice was closed and incorporated into DynoVoice.

New Voice issued five albums during its life span, all by Ryder, bar the second, Norma Tanega's *Walkin' My Cat Named Dog* (2001). Expertly produced by

---

TEN TOP COLLECTIBLES

Mitch Ryder and the Detroit Wheels

Break Out (New Voice 2002—Mono LP with "Good Golly Miss Molly"/"Devil with a Blue Dress On," 1966)

"I Need Help" (New Voice 801—7-inch, 1965)

"Jenny Take a Ride!" (Philco HP 4—Hip-pocket disc, 1967)

"Jenny Takes a Ride!" (New Voice 806—7-inch, misspelled title with "Takes" instead of "Take," 1965)

"Little Latin Lupe Lu" (New Voice 808—7-inch, 1966)

Sock It to Me (New Voice S2003—Stereo LP, 1967)

Sock It to Me Baby (New Voice 820—7-inch, mumbled "punch" in lyric, 1965)

Take a Ride (New Voice S2000—Stereo LP, 1966)

"Too Many Fish in the Sea" (New Voice 822—7-inch, picture sleeve, 1967)

What Now My Love?— Mitch Ryder (DynoVoice 1901—Mono LP, 1967)

Crewe, the Ryder catalog is generally well-regarded by collectors.

Of incidental issue is a Ryder hits collection released on Crewe's specially created Crewe label in 1967: *All the Heavy Hits of Mitch Ryder* (CR-1335) features remixes of several tracks, with horn and string overdubs.

Ode

Ode was the label launched by Lou Adler following his departure from Dunhill, in 1967. Originally distributed by CBS (A&M took over in 1970), Ode made its chart debut with a truly gargantuan hit, Scott McKenzie's Summer of Love anthem "San Francisco (Be Sure to Wear Some Flowers in Your Hair)" (3). A mono pressing of McKenzie's *The Voice Of* (44001) album was Ode's LP debut; it was accompanied by a stereo version (44002), the more common of the two. A second McKenzie album, 1970's countrified *Stained Glass Morning* (SP 77007), repays investigation.

In 1967 Spirit joined the label; the group debuted with the "Mechanical World" single (108), with an eponymous album following in 1968, again spread over two catalog numbers (44003 mono/44004 stereo). Three further singles and two more albums appeared before the group moved to Epic in 1970; in general, the Ode releases remain the highest priced of all the group's regular releases.

The Comfortable Chair (44005) is sought after on the strength of its producers, Robby Kreiger and John Densmore of the Doors; Dylan fans, meanwhile, can be tempted by a gospel recounting of some of their hero's best-loved songs, *Dylan's Gospel,* by the Brothers and Sisters of Los Angeles (44018); and Rolling Stones buffs are frequently swayed by Merry Clayton's *Gimme Shelter* (SP 77001)—Clayton was the distinctive backing vocalist on the Stones' own recording of the title track.

In 1969, Ode recorded Carole King as a member of the band the City. Three singles included "Snow Queen" (113), "That Old Sweet Rule" (117), and "Why Are You Leaving?" (119), while the group's album, *Now That Everything's Been Said* (44012), is the source of Ode's greatest collectible, a first pressing packaged in a full-color front cover. Subsequent issues were black and white.

TEN TOP COLLECTIBLES

Spirit

Clear Spirit (Ode Z12 44016—LP, 1969)

"Dark Eyed Woman" (Ode 122—7-inch, 1969)

The Family That Plays Together (Ode Z12 44014—LP, 1968)

"Fresh Garbage" (UK Mercury MER 1626—6-inch, 1984)

"I Got a Line on You" (Ode 115—7-inch, 1968)

"Mechanical World" (Ode 108—7-inch, 1967)

"Midnight Train" (UK Sound for Industry/Dark Star SFI 326—Flexidisc, 1978)

"1984" (Ode 128—7-inch, 1969)

Spirit (Ode Z12 44004—LP, 1968)

Twelve Dreams of Dr. Sardonicus (Epic E30267—Yellow-label LP, 1970)

Following a solo debut, 1970's *Writer* (77006), King would establish herself as Ode's most successful artist with the immortal *Tapestry* (77009), in 1972. Little of her solo repertoire is especially sought after, although quad buffs do admire the appropriately formatted version of 1974's *Music* (SQ 88013).

Ode also enjoyed great success with the drug-laden comedy duo Cheech and Chong. Five Ode label albums are relatively easy to pick up, with only *Big Bambú* (77014) commanding much of a premium; it was issued with a giant cigarette rolling paper as an integral—but easily lost, damaged, or smoked—part of the packaging. A string of singles is harder to find, with 1973's legendary "Basketball Jones" (66038), featuring several major-name cameos, especially sought after. The glam parody "Earache My Eye (Featuring Alice Bowie)" (66102) is also popular, particularly enclosed within its still amusing picture sleeve.

Other noteworthy Ode artists included Don Everly and David T. Walker. Notable releases included the original American cast album of *The Rocky Picture Horror Show* (77026) and a 1972 recounting of the Who's *Tommy* (SP 99001), an all-star affair that featured Sandy Denny, Richie Havens, Steve Winwood, Maggie Bell, Ringo Starr, plus contributions from the Who's own Roger Daltrey, Pete Townshend, and John Entwistle. For various reasons (including the fact that it really isn't very good), this utterly extravagant offering has disappeared off the collecting radar in recent years. However, a briefly available quadraphonic version (SQ 99001) should not be passed over.

In 1976, Ode returned to CBS for distribution, though the label's output was now devoted almost wholly to reissues of past classics in the PE 349 series. At least 20 albums were issued in this series, before Ode ceased operations in 1978.

Parlophone

The story of Parlophone is, basically, the story of George Martin, the former Navy pilot who joined the label in 1950, as assistant to A&R manager Oscar Preuss. It was a tiny label at the time, dwarfed by its compatriots within the EMI Group: HMV, Columbia, and Regal Zonophone. It was content with an output of orchestral, dance, light jazz, and children's music. Martin recorded all this and more—Eve Boswell and Cleo Laine, Kenneth McKellar and Jimmy Shand, the Luton Girls' Choir and the Kirkintilloch Junior Choir all passed through his studio.

Preuss retired in 1955 and Martin stepped up to replace him, immediately making changes in the Parlophone policy. The label's bread and butter remained much the same as before (one now-notable recording featured Dick James, later renowned as owner of the DJM label, voicing the TV theme "Robin Hood"—MSP 6199), but Martin also began bringing in new talent: singer Edna Savage, the skiffle band the Vipers, and the King Brothers.

In December 1959, Adam Faith brought Parlophone (but not Martin—Faith's producer was John Burgess) its first-ever British No. 1 45, "What Do You Want" (R4591); he followed up with the equally successfully "Poor Me" (R4623). But if Parlophone was renowned for any one thing at this time, it was for Martin's painstaking recruitment of the cream of Britain's radio comedy community. Such records were unheard of in Britain at that time, but under Martin's aegis they became one of the fastest-selling genres of the late '50s.

Spike Milligan, Harry Secombe, Peter Sellers, and Michael Bentine, individually brilliant and collectively The Goons, cut a string of hits with Martin; so did the musical duo Flanders and Swann, as well as actors Bernard Cribbens, Peter Ustinov, and Charlie Drake. The Temperance Seven event provided Martin with his own first UK chart-topper, when their "You're Driving Me Crazy" (R4757) went to No. 1, in May 1961. Had Martin never made another "musical" record in his life, his modern collectibility would be assured by the barrage of comic brilliance that Parlophone issued between 1955–62.

In 1962, however, the Beatles joined the label, and Parlophone embarked upon its next phase, as home to the most successful act in recording history. Today, the black Parlophone imprint, dominated by a giant 45 that was introduced in 1962, shortly after the release of the Beatles' "Love Me Do" debut

A Parlophone comedy classic.

(R4949), is among the best-known identities of all, and one of the most heavily researched.

Whereas labelology—the minute study of record-label design and variations—has long been an accepted part of the record-collecting hobby in the US and Japan, British collectors have seldom shown any interest in pursuing it. It was, therefore, an American collector, Mitch Scharoff, author of the privately published handbook *The Beatles: Collecting the Original UK Pressings 1962–70,* who first ventured into the field, to be followed by members of the Tokyo Beatles fan club in Japan.

Their research isolated and dated the most minute Parlophone label varieties and even cracked the long-standing mystery of the indented numbers printed on the push-out center of Parlophone 45s, identifying them as coded references to EMI pricing and the government's Purchase Tax (then-equivalent to the American sales tax and the modern European VAT). These letters can now be used to date the period during which a particular record was pressed, an important factor in identifying 45s that remained in print, and largely unchanged, for over a decade.

The Beatles aside, 1963–65 saw the label issue hit after hit by Cilla Black, Billy J. Kramer and the Dakotas, the Hollies, and so many more. Of course these are highly collectible, but so are many less successful releases for which Martin and Parlophone were responsible, acts like Freakbeat pioneers the Action, the Toggery Five, pop-soul specialists the Marionettes, the Roulettes (Adam Faith's former backing band), and a host of others.

Martin departed the label in 1965 to concentrate on his responsibilities as the Beatles' producer. His years at the label are best chronicled within the box set *Produced by George Martin: 50 Years in Recording* (EMI 07253 532631 2 6).

His replacement was Norman Smith, engineer at the very first Beatles session, and since then, the man responsible for bringing both Pink Floyd and the

TEN TOP COLLECTIBLES

George Martin Comedy Productions

Beyond the Fringe— Original cast (Parlophone PMC 1145—LP, 1961)

"A Gnu"—Flanders and Swann (Parlophone R4354—7-inch, 1957)

"The Highway Code"—The Master Singers (Parlophone R5428—7-inch, 1966)

"The Hole in the Ground"— Bernard Cribbens (Parlophone R4869—7-inch, 1962)

"Little Red Monkey"—Joy Nichols, Jimmy Edwards, Dick Bentley (Parlophone R3684—78, 1953)

"Morse Code Melody"—The Alberts (Parlophone R4905—7-inch, 1962)

"My Boomerang Won't Come Back"—Charlie Drake (Parlophone R4824—7-inch, 1961)

"Nellie the Elephant"—Mandy Miller (Parlophone R4219—7-inch, 78, 1956)

"She Loves You (German Version)"—Peter Sellers (Parlophone R6043—7-inch, 1981)

"You Gotta Go Oww!"—Spike Milligan (Parlophone R4251—7-inch, 78, 1956)

Pretty Things to EMI. The change did not affect Parlophone's output; neither did the Beatles' own departure to establish their own Apple imprint (distributed, of course, by Parlophone) in 1968. In 1965 the young Marc Bolan joined the label (his "Hippy Gumbo"—R5539—is one of the label's highest-priced non-Beatles issues). Art Woods was introduced in 1966, featuring Deep Purple's Jon Lord and Ron Wood's brother Art. The year 1967 introduced Nick Lowe's Kippington Lodge and Simon Dupree and the Big Sound, the pop band that would soon metamorphose into prog heroes Gentle Giant; 1968 saw Parlophone secure Love Sculpture, featuring guitarist Dave Edmunds, and the return of Jon Lord, with Deep Purple.

Nevertheless, the 1970s would see the label enter a period of sharp decline, and in 1973, Parlophone was closed, to be merged (alongside Columbia, HMV, Stateside, and several other EMI subsidiaries) into the new EMI imprint.

Parlophone re-emerged in the late '70s with Beatle Paul back on board, and new wave hopefuls, the Flys heading a small but impressive roster of new talent—McCartney's "Goodnight Tonight" 12-inch (12R 6023) is an entertaining rarity from this period. Another quiescent period then ended in 1985, when the label was revitalized with the arrival of Duran Duran and the Pet Shop Boys. Since that time, Parlophone has utterly re-established itself as a major power on the UK scene, with acts as disparate, but universally acclaimed, as Morrissey, My Life Story, Radiohead, Supergrass, and the Sundays maintaining this new era of prosperity, a period that was capped by the restoration of the classic 1960s Parlophone label design.

Many of these latter-day signings have proven as collectible (almost) as any past Parlophone artist; however, Parlophone's own inherent collectibility is firmly locked within those first generations of George Martin–inspired talent.

Further Reading: *All You Need Is Ears,* by George Martin, with Jeremy Hornsby (Macmillan, 1979)

Philles

The Philles label is simply one component in the vast world of collectible Phil Spector releases—albeit, in many ways, the best known. The label was launched in late 1961 by Spector and Lester Sill; the label's name combines the two founders' Christian names, though Spector purchased Sill's interest in September 1962. Philles' first release was the Crystals' "There's No Other (Like My Baby)" (100).

The Crystals then supplied four more of the label's first ten singles, including the immortal "Uptown" (102), "He Hit Me" (105), "He's a Rebel" (106), and "He's Sure the Boy I Love" (109). The first two Philles LPs were also by the Crystals: *Twist Uptown* (PHLP-4000) and *He's a Rebel* (4001). A Crystals hits collection (4003) was called for just two years after their arrival. It should be noted, incidentally, that original pressings of these albums featured a blue-and-white label; the more common red-and-yellow Philles label was introduced in 1965 and appears only on repressings of earlier LPs.

Bob B. Soxx and the Blue Jeans, the group that was the architect of the next Philles LP (4002), are best remembered for the hit title track, "Zip-a-Dee-Doo-Dah" (107); two further singles comprised the LP's epic "Why Do Lovers Break Each Others' Hearts?" (110) and "Never Too Young to Get Married" (113).

Darlene Love emerged with "(Today I Met) The Boy I'm Gonna Marry" (111—two pressings offer different B-sides, "Playing for Keeps" and "My Heart Beat a Little Faster"). The Ronettes arrived on the Philles scene with "Be My Baby" (116), which was swiftly followed up the chart over the next year by "Baby I Love You" (118), "(The Best Part Of) Breaking Up" (120), "Do I Love You" (121), and "Walkin' in the Rain" (123). The Ronettes's first LP, *Presenting the Fabulous Ronettes Featuring Veronica* (4006), was released in late 1964.

All four of Philles' maiden chart-busters were gathered together on what is surely one of the greatest collections of all time, 1963's *Today's Hits* (4004). Or perhaps that honor is better bestowed upon the label's next issue, the legendary *A Christmas Gift to You* (4005), widely regarded as the greatest X-mas album ever issued.

The year 1965 opened with the recruitment of the Righteous Brothers, hitherto a none-too-distinguished duo recording for the Moonglow label. "You've Lost That Lovin' Feeling" (124) was their first and biggest hit; Spector produced four further singles with the pair, together with three epic albums.

TEN TOP COLLECTIBLES

Phil Spector

Back to Mono—Various artists (Abkco 711831—Promo CD, 1991)

A Christmas Gift for You—Various artists (Philles 4005—Promo LP, 1963)

I Really Do—The Spectors Three (Trey 3001—7-inch, picture sleeve, 1959)

Phil Spector's Christmas Medley (Pavilion AE7 1354—7-inch promo, 1981)

Phil Spector '74–79—Various artists (UK Phil Spector Int'l 2307 015—LP, 1980)

The Phil Spector Spectacular—Various artists (Philles PHLP 100—Promo LP, 1969)

Rare Masters Volumes 1 and 2—Various artists (UK Phil Spector Int'l 2307-08—LPs, 1976)

The Teddy Bears Sing! (Imperial LP 12010—Stereo LP, 1959)

Thanks for Giving Me the Right Time (Philles, no catalog number—7-inch promo, Spector label, 1965)

Today's Hits—Various artists (Philles 4004—Promo LP, 1963)

One of Philles' most unexpected releases followed, an album by comedian Lenny Bruce. *Lenny Bruce Is Out Again* (4010) was a reissue of what was already an extremely rare LP that Bruce issued on his own Lenny Bruce label around 1962. (A second set on that imprint, *Warning: Sale of This Album* is even more desirable; its contents include routines cited as evidence for the prosecution during Bruce's obscenity trial.)

Even more rare are US pressings of Ike and Tina Turner's *River Deep Mountain High* (4011), manufactured but left unreleased following the chart failure of the title track. Spector, who personally believed "River Deep" represented his greatest achievement yet, was mortified by the single's poor performance. It is widely believed that this single defeat precipitated his virtual retirement the following year; certainly it sounded the death knell on Philles.

A mere handful more singles were released before the end, including a run of three successive Ike and Tina singles that, in many ways, are at least the equal of their illustrious predecessor: "Two to Tango" (134), "I'll Never Need More Love Than This" (135), and "I Idolize You" (136). "I'll Never Need More Love Than This," incidentally, is backed by the infamous "The *Cash Box* Blues or (Oops, We Printed the Wrong Story Again)."

Philles was reborn briefly in 1972, when a compilation, *The Phil Spector Spectacular* (PHLP 100), was issued to radio stations. The Beatles' Apple label had already engineered a reissue for the Christmas album (SW 3400); it is believed that *Spectacular* was intended as a follow-up to that. This series was ultimately canceled; 1975, however, saw the launch in the UK of the Phil Spector International label, which included material from both the Philles era (including several in stereo for the first time), and elsewhere.

Further Reading: *Out of His Head: The Sound of Phil Spector,* by Richard Williams (E.P. Dutton, 1972)

Polar

Best regarded on the international scene for the development and success of ABBA, the Stockholm,

Sweden–based Polar label actually predated the formation of that act by more than a decade.

Polar was launched in 1963 by Swedish music publisher Stig Anderson and his partner, Bengt Berhag. Anderson was a prolific songwriter who had his first composition published in Sweden in 1950, when he was 19 years old. In 1953, he became Sweden's most successful music publisher, after launching what would become a startlingly successful modus operandi. Picking his material from Radio Luxembourg, the continent's premier popular music station, Anderson would write Swedish-language lyrics to the biggest hits of the day, then recruit local musicians to record them for a never-ending string of hit 45s.

In 1959 "Klas-göranö" went gold throughout Scandinavia and the Netherlands, and by the time he launched Polar, Anderson's Sweden Music was already handling Scandinavian publishing for most of the major Anglo-American houses. Naturally, this supply would dominate Polar's output through the 1960s.

Polar's first successes came with the folky Hootenanny Singers, featuring Björn Ulvaeus, later of ABBA. Their "Jag väntar vid min mila" single and EP were the first-ever releases on the label in 1963, while another 45, "No Time," was picked up for a full American release by United Artists (UA 991). Over the next two years, the LPs *Hootenanny Singers Basta* (Polar POLL 101), *Sjunger evert taube* (204), and *International* (206) all proved major hits, the first in an impressive stream that continued into the early '70s.

Ulvaeus met fellow songwriter Benny Andersson, at that time a member of the beat group the Hep Stars, in 1965. According to legend, the first song Ulvaeus and Andersson ever wrote together, "Isn't It Easy to Say," was composed the evening they met, to appear on the Hep Stars' self-titled third album (Olga LP 004). That same fall, Andersson guested on the Hootenanny Singers' own next album (their fourth), *Många ansikten (Many Faces)* (209).

Further collaborations were sporadic—it would be two years before Andersson and Ulvaeus launched a full-time musical partnership. In the meantime, Ulvaeus stepped outside the Hootenanny Singers in

The first-ever ABBA single, released under the quartet's Christian names only.

1968, to launch a solo career, debuting in April with a Swedish-language version of Stig Anderson's latest American acquisition, Bobby Goldsboro's "Honey." "Raring" (POS 1056) was a major hit, to be followed by versions of "Harper Valley PTA" (1062) and "Where Do You Go to, My Lovely" (1073), and a new Andersson/Ulvaeus composition, "Partaj-aj-aj" (1088).

The Hep Stars broke up following a summer 1969 tour; immediately, Ulvaeus and fellow bandmates Svenne Hedlung, and his wife, Charlotte "Lotta" Walker (a former member of American girl group the Sherrys), combined with Andersson for a floorshow tour. During this same period, Ulvaeus and Andersson also composed and recorded a clutch of songs for the movie soundtrack *Inga II,* including a single issued under the Björn and Benny name in March 1970, "She's My Kind of Girl"/"Inga Theme" (Polar POS 1096). Backing vocals were supplied by the songwriters' girlfriends, Anna-Frida "Frida" Lyngstad and Agnetha Fältskog—both were already

established singers, with the Cupol and EMI labels, respectively.

Lyngstad and Fältskog reappeared on Björn and Benny's debut album, *Lycka* (*Happiness*) (113), in 1970, together with a new single, "Hej gamle man" (1110); further Swedish hits included "Det kan ingen doktor hjälpa" (POS 1130), "Tänk om jorden vore ung" (POS 1140), and "En karusell" (POS 1154).

Following the suicide of Polar co-founder Berhag in 1971, Stig Anderson gave Andersson and Ulvaeus a production partnership within the Polar set-up. With the duo at the helm, Polar was responsible for a stream of extremely successful singles during the early '70s.

Most, if not all, of these featured future members of ABBA—in either production, writing, or musician roles—and tend to be priced accordingly. These include Brita Borg's "Ljuva sextital" (POS 1072); Arne Lambert's "O mein Papa" (POS 1094); Borg and Rolf Bengtsson's "Jop jo na na men" (1100); Lena

Anderson's "Scarborough Fair" (POS 1129), "Säg det med en sång" (POS 1148), and "Better to Have Loved" (POS 1149); and Jarl Kullo's "Jag ar blott en man" (POS 1162).

The year 1971 also saw work begin on what was intended to become the second Björn and Benny album; by March 1972, the sessions were all but complete, Polar had assigned the opus a catalog number (230), and everything was gearing up for what was certain to be a banner release. The release, in June, of a trailer from the LP, the song "People Need Love" (POS 1156), changed all of that forever. For the first time from the quartet, it was a fully collaborative venture, all four vocalists sharing lead duties.

Polar issued the single under the name Björn and Benny, Agnetha, and Anna-Frid; a minor hit in Sweden, "People Need Love" was also issued in the US by the tiny Playboy label (P50014—Playboy issued two more singles during 1972–73, though promo mono/stereo issues only are known: "Another Town Another Train"—P50018; and "Rock 'n' Roll Band"—P50025).

A tour of the Swedish folkpark circuit followed, spawning one of the rarest of all pre-ABBA releases, a one-sided 45 titled *En halsning till vär parkarrangorer (Greetings to Our Park Arrangers)* (POR 1), featuring the quartet members talking about themselves and their music—there was no actual music on the disc.

The tour's success encouraged the quartet to persevere with the new format, placing the Björn and Benny LP on hold (it would eventually be scrapped) and cutting a new group single, "He Is Your Brother" (1168). By now, Frida, too, was a Polar artist—her EMI contract expired in July 1972, and she had already issued her Polar debut, the single "Man vill ju leva lite dessemellan" (1161).

In late 1972, Björn and Benny were invited to contribute a song for consideration as Sweden's 1973 Eurovision Song Contest entry—"Ring Ring," the ensuing effort, was released in February, uniquely, in two formats: a Swedish-language version (1171), and the following week, an English version (POS 1172). The song was not, ultimately, selected for the competition

itself, but it still became a massive hit. While the Swedish version climbed to No. 1 on the Swedish chart, its English doppelgänger rested at No. 2. The song (available now in a German-language version) was also successful across mainland Europe, though a UK release through Epic (EPC 1793) did nothing.

Ring Ring (242), the debut album by the still unwieldy Björn, Benny and Agnetha, Frida, was issued in Sweden in March 1973; it, too, was a major hit—Sweden's chart, at the time, combined LPs and singles together, and within two weeks, the album was at No. 3, behind the two versions of its title track. A new single, June's "Love Isn't Easy" (1176), was soon racing in its wake, and through the summer, Björn, Benny and Agnetha, Frida toured Sweden to scenes of wild popularity.

Back at Polar, meanwhile, Stig Anderson was desperately trying to think of an appropriate name for the quartet. His favorite, drawn from the quartet's initials, was ABBA, and when the issue was put to a newspaper vote, the public agreed. So, fortunately, did the management of the ABBA canned-fish company—who might otherwise have rewritten the next decade of pop history with barely a second thought.

That history truly got under way in March 1974. Once again, the group had entered a song for the Swedish heats of the Eurovision Song Contest and this time, it triumphed—not only at the local level, but on the main stage as well. "Waterloo," the winning song, was the first record released under the new ABBA name, and the last to appear in simultaneous Swedish (1186) and English-language (1187) versions. Henceforth, the group would record one version for all markets.

Success saw ABBA's releases slowly take prominence in both the musicians' schedule and the label's schedule; the quartet's explosion to international fame essentially spelled the end for any outside activities.

Following the release of "Waterloo," a mere handful of extracurricular releases appeared on the label, with the majority of them, too, having some kind of connection to ABBA. Look out for former Hep Stars Sven and Lotta's Swedish-language version of ABBA's

"Bang a Boomerang" (1204), and one of the most prized of all regular-issue Polar singles, the same duo's "Funky Feet" (1231), the first public appearance of an Andersson-Ulvaeus song written for, but dropped from, ABBA's *Arrival* album.

Another massive rarity is Frida's final solo single, 1975's "Fernando" (1221). Taken from her *Frida ensam* album (265), it offers a Swedish-language version of the later ABBA hit. (Fältskog also debuted a future smash that year, with her solo version of "SOS"—Cupol CS 303.)

ABBA collectors also prize Kicki Moberg's "Men nattan är vår" (POS 1276), an Agnetha Fältskog composition targeted at the 1980 Eurovision Song Contest, and Fältskog's own first solo single in four years, "It's So Nice to Be Rich" (POS 1347), from the soundtrack to the movie *P and B*.

Notable Polar albums from the late '70s and early '80s include an album of children's music by Fältskog and her daughter Linda, *Nu tandas tosen julejus* (POLS 328), a solo set by ABBA backing vocalist Tomas Ledin, *The Human Touch* (POLS 364), and Frida's collaboration with English songwriter Kirsty MacColl, 1984's *Shine* album. (This set also produced a very collectible white-vinyl 12-inch of the title track—POLM 14.) Also notable is the 1983 various-artists collection *Äntligen sommarlov* (POLS 377), a compilation of songs dedicated to summer. A live version of ABBA's "Summer Night City" makes its only appearance on this disc.

Individually, the members of ABBA offer some interesting highlights of the Polar label catalog; collectively, they utterly dominate it. ABBA maintained its stranglehold on the world charts for the next nine years, releasing a dozen albums and almost two dozen 45s. Rarities abound worldwide, with the Polar catalog responsible for surprisingly few of them, placing less emphasis on limited-edition gimmicks than other markets. However, the rarest release in the entire ABBA catalog is a Polar issue—the "Sang til Gorel" 12-inch recorded (with Stig Anderson) as a 30th birthday present for Polar VP Gorel Hanser. Just 50 copies were pressed.

ABBA ceased operations in 1982, at which point Polar's output, too, declined. The label's final internationally noted release, in 1986, was ABBA's *Live*

TEN TOP COLLECTIBLES

ABBA

The ABBA Special (Atlantic PR 436—2-LP promo, 1983)

Anniversary Boxed Set (UK Epic ABBA 26—26x7-inch, blue-vinyl, 1984)

"Happy New Year" (Atlantic PR 380—7-inch promo, 1980)

"Lay All Your Love on Me" (Disconet, no catalog number—12-inch promo, 1980)

Live (Atlantic 81675—LP, 1986)

Nightbird and Company 11/74 (US Army Reserve—2-LP transcription disc, 1974)

"Ring Ring" (UK Epic EPC 1793—Yellow-label 7-inch, 1973)

Robert W. Morgan Special of the Week 6/81 (Watermark 812—Transcription disc, 1981)

"Summer Night City" (UK Polydor ABBADJ 1—One-sided 12-inch promo, 1993)

"Waterloo" (Atlantic 3035—7-inch, picture sleeve, 1974)

(412), the long-awaited release for concerts recorded back in 1977 and 1979. This is also the rarest regular ABBA album of them all—it spent just two weeks on the Swedish chart, and was barely even released in the US.

The music industry was quick to honor Polar's role in ABBA's career. An honorary member of the Royal Swedish Academy of Music, Anderson also became only the second non-American (after Brian Epstein) to receive *Billboard* magazine's prestigious Trendsetter Award.

Anderson reciprocated such honors in 1989, shortly after selling his companies to the Polygram group (he remained chairman of the board for Sweden Music AB and Polar Music International, posts he retained until his death in 1997). Although it would take another three years before the award was up and running, that year saw the endowment of the Stig Anderson Music Prize Fund of the Royal Swedish Academy of Music, or the Polar Music prize. "The world's biggest music prize" was to be "awarded for significant achievements in music and/or musical activity"; winners to date include Burt Bacharach, Bruce Springsteen, Elton John, Dizzy Gillespie, and Paul McCartney.

Further Reading: *ABBA: The Complete Recording Sessions,* by Carl Magnus Palm (22 Century 1994)

RAK

Alongside the UK wing of Bell Records, Mickie Most's RAK label was THE voice of the British glam-rock movement of the early '70s. Consistent hits from Mud, Suzi Quatro, and Kenny—and a slew of inspired one- or two-offs by Cozy Powell, the Arrows, and more—established the EMI-distributed label as one of the most successful record companies in British pop history. In modern times, its dominance of the eminently collectible glam-rock genre has made RAK enthusiasts out of people who might never ever consider themselves fans of any individual record label—and vice versa.

Interestingly, RAK's 45s catalog alone is regarded as collectible; though the label issued a number of LPs, some of which were really rather good, they

attract little attention. American releases of RAK hits, many of which appeared on Bell and its Big Tree subsidiary, also have a small but devoted following among specialists—though few are worth big money, most are surprisingly elusive. Equally popular are European issues, many of which appeared on EMI's Columbia and EMI imprints.

Most launched RAK in 1969, after a decade spent producing such seminal UK rock performers as Donovan, the Yardbirds, the Animals, Jeff Beck, and Lulu—reissues of several of these acts would appear within the RAK catalog during 1972–73, in the RAK Replay series of extended-play 7-inchers: the Animals' "House of the Rising Sun" (RR 1), along with Beck's "Hi Ho Silver Lining" (RR 3) and "I've Been Drinking" (RR 4), returned to the UK chart at this time.

RAK launched with Julie Felix's "If I Could" (101), in March 1970. A UK Top 20 hit, it was the first of seven successive RAK singles to make the Top 30: issues by Herman's Hermits ("Bet Yer Life I Do"—102); Hot Chocolate ("Love Is Life"—103); Alexis Korner's CCS (a cover of Led Zeppelin's "Whole Lotta Love," soon to become the theme to the BBC's *Top of the Pops* TV show—104); further efforts by Felix and the Hermits ("Heaven Is Here"—105, "Lady Barbara"—106); and comedian John Paul Joans ("The Man from Nazareth"—107) were all hits. Indeed, for the next three years, new RAK singles were infinitely more likely to make the chart than not.

Despite this, many early RAK singles are considered highly collectible—two Peter Noone singles featured the pen and the piano-playing of the then-unknown David Bowie: "Oh! You Pretty Things" (114) and "Right On Mother," the B-side of "Walnut Whirl" (121). A third collaboration, "Bombers," remains locked in the RAK vault.

Other rarities include the aforementioned John Paul Joans, partly because his collaborators on the single were all four future members of 10cc, operating out of their own Strawberry Studios, but also because the former comedian so nearly shared his surname with Led Zeppelin's bass player, John Paul Jones. Indeed, it was only the intervention of the latter that dissuaded the RAK artist from adopting

TEN TOP COLLECTIBLES

Glam Rock

"Bed in the Corner"— Cockney Rebel (UK EMI 2233—Withdrawn 7-inch, 1974)

"Do the Strand"—Roxy Music (Island WIP 6306—Unissued, live, 7-inch, 1976)

"Hear Me Calling"—Slade (UK Polydor 2814 008—7-inch promo, 1971)

"Moonage Daydream"—Arnold Corns (UK B&C CB 149—7-inch, 1971)

"Rebel Rebel"—David Bowie (RCA 0287—7-inch, different mix, 1974)

"Ride a White Swan"—T. Rex (UK Octopus OCTO 1—Test pressing, 1970)

"Slaughter on 10th Avenue"—Mick Ronson (UK RCA 11474XST—Flexidisc, 1974)

"Take Me I'm Yours"—Jobriath (UK Elektra K12129—7-inch, 1974)

"Teenage Revolution"—Hello (UK Bell 1479—7-inch promo, 1976)

"Va Va Va Voom"—Brett Smiley (UK Anchor 1004—7-inch, 1974)

---

the precise same spelling. Jeff Smith's "Going to a Party" (120) has similar origins and is equally in demand.

Though Hot Chocolate swiftly established itself as RAK's most successful long-term act, with some 29 hits between 1970 and the label's demise in 1984, the best of RAK's early-to-mid-'70s output was the work of songwriting duo Nicky Chinn and Michael Chapman. First working with the Australian act New World, "Chinnichap," as the duo was called, was behind a colossal string of hits by Mud, Suzi Quatro, and Smokey.

Both Mud and Quatro started slowly—Quatro's debut 45, "Rolling Stone" (134), was an unlikely failure; Mud's "Crazy" (146) and "Hypnosis" (152) were hits, but possessed little of the magic that would soon be Mud's to spare. Next time around, in both cases, would be the charm—Quatro's "Can the Can" (150) topped the British chart; Mud's "Dynamite" (159) made the Top Five and paved the way for its own debut chart-topper, "Tiger Feet" (166).

Throughout the high point of the glam-rock explosion, 1973–75, Mud and Quatro (plus Hot Chocolate) dominated RAK's release schedules as thoroughly as they ruled the British chart. Behind them, however, the label maintained a succession of smart 45s, including hits by former Jeff Beck Group drummer Cozy Powell (beginning with the classic "Dance with the Devil"—165); the Arrows (whose members authored Joan Jett's hit "I Love Rock 'n' Roll"); Kenny (launched by songwriters Bill Martin and Phil Coulter, following their departure from the Bay City Rollers camp); and Smokey, a band whose distinctly soft-rock inclinations displayed a new and totally unexpected side to the Chinnichap hit machine.

RAK also scored a hit with guitar legend Chris Spedding's 1975 anthem "Motorbikin' " (210), with Spedding then being responsible for two of the more collectible 45s from RAK's second half-decade, as producer of punk pioneers the Vibrators' "We Vibrate" (245) and the unissued "Bad Heart" (253—promos apparently exist); another Spedding single, "Pogo Dancing" (246), also featured the Vibrators, and the group is co-credited on the label.

The late '70s and early '80s saw RAK continue scoring regular hits, though few have the resonance of the earlier issues—most collectors treat 1976 (at the latest!) as a cutoff point.

Further Reading: *20th Century Rock and Roll: Glam Rock,* by Dave Thompson (Collector's Guide Publishing, 2000)

Ralph

Ralph records was launched in San Francisco in 1972 by the mysterious group the Residents. Self-styled guerrilla experimentalists who prided themselves on the anonymity that has ensured, 30 years later, that fans still don't know the band members' names, the Residents's early recordings included the "Santa Dog" 45 (Ralph RR 1272), the *Babyfingers* EP (RR 0377), and the LPs *Meet the Residents* (RR 0274) and *Third Reich and Roll* (RR 1075).

Gathering critical acclaim far in excess of their musical accessibility, the group came close to scoring a UK hit with 1977's characteristically disrupted version of the Rolling Stones' "Satisfaction" (RR 0776); the Residents gained more applause, meanwhile, with the release of *Not Available* (RR 1174), an album recorded four years earlier, but left unreleased until the band members had forgotten it existed.

The Residents dominated the Ralph catalog, but a number of other artists were signed, including Snakefinger, Renaldo and the Loaf, Tuxedomoon, Fred Frith, Yello, the Art Bears, Negativland, and Rhythm and Noise. All releases on the label are eminently collectible.

According to the discography in the biography *Meet the Residents: America's Most Eccentric Band* (by Ian Shirley, SAF, 1993), "As well as official releases, there are also a large number of limited editions, collectors items, colored vinyls, cassettes, rereleases, picture discs, singles, radio specials, flexidiscs, Anniversary Commemorative issues, fanclub only CDs etc., etc., etc.!" Residents spokesman Hardy Fox told *Cool and Strange Music* magazine in 2001, "One thing people don't realize is, the Residents are one of the most collectible bands around. There are some heavy duty collectors and the prices they pay are ridiculous." To illustrate the point, the magazine visited eBay and discovered a copy of the group's 1979

TEN TOP COLLECTIBLES

The Residents

"The Beatles Play the Residents and the Residents Play the Beatles" (Ralph RR 0577—7-inch, 1977)

Blorp Esette (LAFMS 005—LP, 1975)

Freak Show (East Side Digital OP 011—Black-vinyl promo LP, 1991)

"It's a Man's Man's Man's World" (UK Korova KOW 36—7-inch, picture sleeve, 1984)

Meet the Residents (Ralph RR 0274—Original mix, LP, 1974)

The Pal TV LP (UK Doublevision DVR 17—Red-vinyl LP, 1985)

Please Do Not Steal It—Various artists (Ralph DJ 7901—Promo LP, 1979)

"Santa Dog" (Ralph RR 1272—7-inch, 1972)

"Satisfaction" (Ralph 0776—Black-vinyl 7-inch, picture sleeve, 1976)

Uncle Willie's Highly Opinionated Guide to the Residents (Ralph RZ 9302—Promo CD, 1993)

The Residents Play the Beatles (Ralph 0577) EP at $170 and rising.

Ralph continued in operation until 1985, bowing out at the conclusion of the Residents's financially disastrous and deliberately mistitled four-part *Mole Trilogy* LPs and tour. Since that time, the band has continued on with the labels Rykodisc, Torso, and East Side Digital, with Ralph resurfacing for occasional releases.

Further Reading: *Meet the Residents: America's Most Eccentric Band!* by Ian Shirley (SAF 1993)

Rare Earth

Although the Motown label group is best remembered as a soul-R&B label, and therefore, a black label, a number of white acts were signed to the company over the years. Indeed, Nick and the Jaguars' "Ich i bon" (Tamla 5501) was, as its catalog number suggests, one of the first 45s that Berry Gordy, Jr., ever released, in 1959. Two years later, the all-white vocal group the Valadiers released "Greetings (This Is Uncle Sam)" on the Miracle label, and two more on the Gordy imprint in 1962.

Other white acts followed, including English singer Kiki Dee, who cut a single ("My Whole World Ended"—54193) and an album (*Great Expectations*—303) for Tamla in 1970. None succeeded, however, a baffling statistic that Berry Gordy, Jr., intended to change when he inaugurated the Rare Earth label, a repository not merely for white performers, but for white rock performers.

Both individually and via the five-LP promotional box set that launched the label to the media, the new label's first releases spelled out his ambition with ruthless intensity—Rare Earth's first five LPs comprised offerings from Welsh blues-rockers Love Sculpture (*Blues Helping*—505), the Pretty Things (the concept album *SF Sorrow*—506), Rustix (*Bedlam*—508), Milwaukee rockers the Messengers (self-titled—509), and Norm Whitfield protégés Rare Earth (*Get Ready*—507), for whom the label was named in the first place.

Releases by that most unappetizingly named combo, Toe Fat, as well as issues from Sounds Nice,

The Pretty Things' *SF Sorrow* 8-Track.

the Power of Zeus, the Lost Nation, the Poor Boys, Cats, Brass Monkey, and further sets by Rustix, Rare Earth, and the Pretty Things followed, with the latter, the seminal *Parachute*, being accorded "Album of the Year" by *Rolling Stone*. British heavy metal giant UFO also had its first American album released by the label (*UFO 1*—524).

For collectors, it is the Pretty Things, UFO, and Love Sculpture LPs that garner the most attention, though the only true scarcities are a 1969 single of the Pretty Things' "Private Sorrow" (5005) and a double album repackaging of the same band's *SF Sorrow* and *Parachute,* titled *Real Pretty* (R7-549), issued in 1976. The majority of other Rare Earth LP releases are as obscure as the artists who recorded them—singles attract a premium simply because they are not encountered very often.

There are a handful of exceptions, however. As the label's most commercially successful act, Rare Earth itself attracts some attention, its output eventually running to nine albums and 16 singles. This statistic

"All Light Up" (Norton PT 109— Red-vinyl 7-inch, 1999)

Get the Picture (UK Fontana TL 5280— LP, 1965)

"Honey I Need" (Fontana 1508—7-inch, 1965)

On Film (UK Fontana TE 17472— EP, 1966)

Pretty Things (Fontana MGF 27544— LP, 1965)

"Private Sorrow" (Rare Earth 5005—7-inch, 1969)

Rage before Beauty (Snapper, no catalog number— CD, rough-mix sampler, 1999)

Rainin' in My Heart (UK Fontana TE 17442— EP, 1965)

SF Sorrow (Rare Earth RS 506— LP with round cover, 1969)

"Talkin' about the Good Times" (Laurie 3458—7-inch, 1968)

becomes even more impressive when one realizes that the label's entire output stretched to just 50 albums and 60 singles.

R. Dean Taylor, whose "Indiana Wants Me" (5013) was a pop Top Five hit in 1971, cut several further 45s for the label, together with a well-respected LP, *I Think, Therefore I Am* (522), while Kiki Dee bounced back from the failure of her Motown releases with a transfer to Rare Earth for "Love Makes the World Go Round" (5025).

Following a slew of releases during its first three years, both the quantity, and sadly, the quality of Rare Earth releases declined seriously. Just two new albums appeared in 1973, Xit's *Silent Warrior* (545) and Rare Earth's *Ma* (546); the following year, only one LP, a live Rare Earth set, was even scheduled, alongside two singles by the same band, "Ma" (5056) and "Chained" (5057). The LP release was canceled, however, and while 1975 did bring a new set by the group, *Back to Earth* (548), the decision to close the label had already been made.

The aforementioned *Real Pretty* compilation notwithstanding, Rare Earth folded after just one more release, Rare Earth's *Midnight Lady* (550). The album's title track simultaneously became Rare Earth's final 45 (5060).

Further Reading: *Calling Out Around the World: A Motown Reader,* by Kingsley Abbott (Helter Skelter, 2001)

Reaction

Founded by Australian impresario Robert Stigwood, the Reaction label appeared in early 1966, primarily as a vehicle for the Who—they had just departed producer Shel Talmy's stable (where their releases came through the Brunswick label), and managers Chris Stamp and Kit Lambert were already working to launch their own Track label. Reaction was intended to bridge the gap. In fact it became much more than that.

The label's early days were marked by confusion, as Reaction and Talmy battled for the last word in the dispute. Both labels released 45s featuring the song "Instant Party" as the B-side, Brunswick's "Circles" (05951) and Reaction's "Substitute" (591 001); both labels withdrew their releases when they saw

TEN TOP COLLECTIBLES

The Who

Excerpts from Tommy (Decca 734610-3 — 4x7-inch, box set, 1970)

Magic Bus—*The Who on Tour* (Decca DL 5064 — Mono promo LP, 1968)

"My Generation" (UK Decca AD 1 — 7-inch, export, picture sleeve, 1968)

Ready Steady Who (Reaction 592 001 — EP, 1966)

The Who Sell Out (Decca DL 4950 — Mono LP, 1967)

Sing My Generation (Decca DL 4664 — LP, 1966)

"Squeeze Box" (MCA 40475 — 7-inch, picture sleeve, 1975)

"Substitute" (Atco 6409 — 7-inch, 1966)

"Under My Thumb" (UK Track 604 006 — 7-inch, 1967)

"Young Man (Blues)" (Decca 32737 — 7-inch, picture sleeve, 1970)

---

what the other was doing. Reaction then relaunched "Substitute" with a new B-side, "Circles," before finally settling on an instrumental cut credited to the Who Orchestra (actually the Graham Bond Organization), "Waltz for a Pig."

The Who's Reaction output ultimately embraced three of their finest 45s, as "Substitute" was followed by "I'm a Boy" (591 004) and "Happy Jack" (591 010). The sterling *A Quick One While He's Away* (US title *Happy Jack*) LP (594 002) and the stellar rarity *Ready Steady Who* EP (592 001) also appeared—band and label specialists alike should note that the traditionally mono-only album was issued in true stereo (more or less—one cut was mono) in the US, Germany, and Japan.

The Who's Pete Townshend also composed a single for fellow Reaction artist Oscar, "Join My Gang" (591 006); another Oscar release, "Over the Wall We Go" (591 012), was composed by, and features a cameo by, the young David Bowie.

Bird's Birds, featuring future Faces and Rolling Stones guitarist Ron Wood, issued one of its sporadic and so-collectible 45s through Reaction, "Say Those Magic Words" (691 005); and Eric Clapton, Jack Bruce, and Ginger Baker unveiled their new band, Cream, via the *Fresh Cream* (593 001/594 001) and *Disraeli Gears* (593 003/594 003) albums and through three singles, "Wrapping Paper" (591 007), "I Feel Free" (591 011), and "Strange Brew" (591 015).

Much of this catalog was subsequently re-released by Stigwood's RSO label (among others). The original Reaction pressings are very highly prized, however; other label issues (including a third Oscar 45, and singles by Lloyd Banks, the Maze, West Point Supernatural, Billy J. Kramer, and the Shades) are also hard to find.

Red Bird

One of the most popular labels of the American mid-'60s, Red Bird's output was short on quantity but incredibly high on quality. Formed by George Goldner and songwriters Jerry Leiber and Mike Stoller, Red Bird was dominated by what are now regarded as the quintessential American girl groups of the era, the Shangri-Las and the Dixie Cups, both of whom

TEN TOP COLLECTIBLES

Shangri-Las

"Footsteps on the Roof" (Mercury 72670—7-inch, 1967)

I Can Never Go Home Anymore (Red Bird 20-104—LP, 1965)

I Can Never Go Home Anymore (UK Red Bird 40-004—Unreleased EP, 1966)

"I Can Never Go Home Anymore"/"Bulldog" (Red Bird 10-043—7-inch, 1965)

"I'll Never Learn" (Mercury 72645—7-inch, 1966)

Leader of the Pack (Red Bird 20-101—LP, 1965)

"Past, Present and Future" (Red Bird 10-068—7-inch, 1966)

The Shangri-Las (UK Red Bird 40 002—EP, 1965)

Shangri-Las' Golden Greats (Mercury SR 61099—Stereo LP, 1966)

Shangri-Las-65 (Red Bird 20-104—LP, 1965)

---

are very collectible in their own right. But the remainder of the label's output is also hotly pursued, all the more so since reissues of Red Bird material, on both vinyl and CD, have been uniformly dogged by atrocious sound quality.

The Dixie Cups launched the label with "Chapel of Love" (10-001), which was also the title of their debut LP (RBS 20-100) in 1964. Six further 45s failed to have the resonance of that debut, while a major hit with 1965's "Iko Iko" could prompt nothing more than a reissue of *Chapel of Love,* with a new sleeve and title (*Iko Iko,* of course—10-003).

The Shangri-Las arrived with "Remember (Walking in the Sand)" (10-008), the first in a stream of peerless teen classics whose highlights alone could fill a romance novel: "Leader of the Pack" (10-014), "Give Him a Great Big Kiss" (10-018), "Maybe" (10-019) . . . by the time the Shangri-Las' Red Bird career wound up in 1966, with the stately "Past, Present and Future" (10-068), the group's influence on Amercian teenagers simply could not be overstated.

Two Shangri-Las albums were issued during the group's heyday, *Leader of the Pack* (20-101) and

Shangri-Las-65 (20-104); the latter was reissued later in the year with the same catalog number, but retitled for the girls' latest hit, "I Can Never Go Home Anymore" (10-043); that song was added to the album, in place of "The Dum Dum Ditty" (not in place of "Sophisticated Boom Boom," as reported elsewhere).

Issued in 1965, the collection *Red Bird Goldies* (20-102) sums up Red Bird's major hits and reacquaints us with the most successful act on the short-lived Blue Cat subsidiary, the Ad-Libs. Their "The Boy from New York City" (102) is a masterpiece. Also included, and of great significance among collectors of the girl-group sound, are the Butterflys—in actuality, songwriter Ellie Greenwich. Two singles, "Goodnight Baby" (10-009) and "I Wonder" (10-016), are among Red Bird's most in-demand releases. Other popular Red Bird releases include two classics by the Jelly Beans ("I Wanna Love Him"—10-003, and "The Kind of Boy You Can't Forget"—10-011), and three by Trade Winds. However, Red Bird released just two further albums, a collection of speeches by politician Adlai Stevenson (20-105) and

The original pressing of the Shangri-Las' second LP.

the debut by singer Steve Rossi (20-106), both of which are extremely obscure.

Further Reading: *Red Bird Story* (booklet within box set of the same name—Charly 1995)

Regal Zonophone

The Regal Zonophone label initially existed as two separate labels, Columbia's Regal budget subsidiary, and HMV's similarly cheapo Zonophone. Shortly after the two giants merged to form EMI, their subsidiaries were similarly melded.

Through the 1930s and 1940s, Regal Zonophone was home to such British superstars as Gracie Fields and George Formby, but by the 1950s, the label's output was confined almost exclusively to Salvation Army recordings. The early-to-mid-'60s saw a handful of releases, including a pair of hit 45s by the Joystrings ("It's an Open Secret"—RZ 501; and "A Starry Night"—504); but by 1967, it had again run out of steam.

The label was rejuvenated that summer when music publisher David Platz, producer Denny Cordell, and manager Tony Secunda joined forces as Straight Ahead Productions and were offered Regal Zonophone as an outlet for their artists. The first dozen Regal Zonophone singles included hits by the Move and Procol Harum (both poached from Deram), plus well-received offerings from Biddu, Joe Cocker, Marc Bolan's Tyrannosaurus Rex, and Juniors' Eyes, with the Move's "Flowers in the Rain" (3001) making history by becoming the first record ever played on the BBC's newly instituted Radio One pop station.

The label's release policy was conservative—just four singles in 1967, 11 in 1968, nine in 1969, and only four in 1970. This tally included some impressive hits, however: the all-conquering Move and Procol Harum marched on, and while Marc Bolan was still some years away from all-consuming stardom, three Tyrannosaurus Rex singles still made the

Top 50: "Debora" (3008), "One Inch Rock" (3011), and "King of the Rumbling Spires" (3022). The duo's four albums were also steady sellers. Then there was Joe Cocker, who placed one single, "Marjorine" (3006), in the lower reaches of the Top 50, and placed his next at No. 1: "With a Little Help from My Friends" (3013) was Regal Zonophone's first British chart-topper; the Move's "Blackberry Way" (3015) was its second.

Regal Zonophone's initial success could not last. Twelve of its first 28 singles were hits—just three of the next 61 performed likewise. With the Secunda-Cordell team having moved on, and the best of the back catalog following Platz to the newly formed Fly label (Marc Bolan joined it there), Regal Zonophone limped into the 1970s making some inspired signings, but always just a little too late.

Mary Hopkin and Dave Edmunds joined the label immediately after chart-topping careers with Apple and MAM respectively; Blue Mink came on board at the tail end of an almost equally successful career at Philips. Marvin Welch and Farrar were former members of the multimillion-selling Shadows . . . but they were the Shadows no longer. The Idle Race once boasted Jeff Lynne in their lineup—but not any more, and so on.

Ginger Baker of Cream appeared in tandem with Nigerian maestro Fela Ransome-Kuti; the Smoke, one-time darlings of the psychedelic set, made an ill-informed comeback with "Sugar Man" (3071), a record now widely regarded as the most collectible single in the entire 1970s Regal Zonophone catalog, which is a shame. Not only is it an insult to the Smoke's own memory, it's not especially complimentary to the rest of the catalog.

In 1972, Regal Zonophone finally looked as if it were emerging from the shadows, picking up a new northern England rock 'n' roll band called Geordie. Its debut single, "Don't Do That" (3067), was a hit; the band's other material appeared even stronger. And so it transpired—Geordie would eventually score four UK hits, record two much-loved albums, and following its demise, would see its vocalist, Brian Johnson, join AC/DC. But all of that was too late for Regal Zonophone. In early 1973, Geordie was transferred to the parent company's newly launched EMI imprint; in mid-1974, Regal Zonophone closed down.

TEN TOP COLLECTIBLES

The Move

"**Cherry Blossom Clinic**" (UK Regal Zonophone, no catalog number—7-inch test pressing, 1968)

"**Chinatown**" (MGM 14332—7-inch, 1971)

"**Ella James**" (UK Harvest HAR 5036—Unissued 7-inch, 1971)

"**Fore Brigade**" (UK Fly ECHO 104—EP, picture sleeve, 1972)

Looking On (UK Fly HIFLY 1—LP, 1970)

The Move (UK Regal Zonophone LRZ 1002—Mono LP, 1968)

"**Night of Fear**" (Deram 7504—7-inch, 1967)

Shazam (A&M SP 4259—LP, 1969)

Something Else from the Move (UK Regal Zonophone TRZ 2001—EP, 1968)

"**Tonight**" (Capitol 3126—7-inch, 1971)

The lasciviously lipped label.

With apposite circularity, the final release was a single by American-born producer Tony Visconti. Seven years earlier, it had been Regal Zonophone that gave him his start in record production, handing him the then-unknown and untried Tyrannosaurus Rex. "I Remember Brooklyn" (3089) allowed him to say farewell.

Rolling Stones Records

After eight years with Decca (UK) and London (US), the Rolling Stones launched their own self-titled label in 1971. Having entertained bids from virtually every major label in the business, they linked with Atlantic Records for distribution, while appointing Marshall Chess (son of Chess label founder Leonard) as label manager.

The intention was for the new label to handle both the Stones' own output (and planned solo releases), and to showcase new talent discovered by the band members. In fact, only a handful of non-Stones records were ever issued during the label's time with Atlantic: two underachieving solo sets by bassist Bill Wyman (*Monkey Grip*—COC 59102, and *Stone Alone*—COC 79100); a collection of Moroccan pipe music recorded by the late Brian Jones (COC 49100); the *Jammin' with Edward* collection of loose jams and grooves, featuring sundry Stones members and associates (COC 39100); a Keith Richards solo single; and just one unrelated LP (and 45), by Kracker (COC 49102). Interestingly, the extracurricular careers embarked upon by Messrs. Wyman, Watts, Jagger, Richard, and Wood during the 1980s and 1990s all took place far from the auspices of their own label.

The European end of the Atlantic distribution deal expired in 1976 and Rolling Stones Records moved to EMI. A new numbering series was instituted; the Atlantic COC prefix was replaced by CUN, continuing a delightfully schoolboyish ribaldry. However, again, extracurricular albums were at a premium, with reggae star Peter Tosh the sole new arrival. He would bring the label its only significant non-Stones chart success, when a cover of the Temptations' "Don't Look Back" (19308) made No. 81 in 1978. Rolling Stones Records has since been handled by CBS (beginning in 1986) and Virgin (starting in 1994), both of whom have reissued the band's own catalog and brought together their own compilations of material. However, no further outside talent has been recruited to the label.

The vast majority of collectibles on the label are, then, the Stones' own. However, the Kracker, Jones, and *Jammin'* albums are sought after, while quadraphonic mixes of Wyman's two solo LPs (QD 79100, QD 79103) are extremely hard to find. These are the only quad releases on the label. Another popular item is a red-vinyl 12-inch of the infamous "Cocksucker Blues," which purportedly appeared as an official Rolling Stones Records promo release in the late '80s. In fact this release was a bootleg—the only official release of "Cocksucker Blues" remains its appearance on a limited-edition one-sided 7-inch offered with the German four-LP box set, *The Rest of the Best of the Rolling Stones* (Teldec 6 30125 FX), in the mid-'80s.

Further Reading: *Heart of Stone: The Definitive Rolling Stones Discography 1962–1983,* by Felix Aeppli (Pierian Press, 1985)

Rust

Originally called Andie, Rust was a subsidiary of Laurie, and is best remembered for a handful of early-'60s hits by Dean and Jean; the Chiffons' Four Pennies alias ("When the Boy's Happy" and "My Block," respectively— 5070 and 5071—are among the group's most sought-after releases); and Randy and the Rainbows, whose "Denise" (5059) was the original version of Blondie's 1978 hit "Denis."

Satellite

Named to commemorate the recently launched Russian space probe Sputnik, Jim Stewart, a Memphis State graduate and former Army Special Serviceman, launched Satellite in 1957. A talented fiddler, he spent his evenings playing with various Western Swing groups, with his interests also turning toward record production. Satellite was originally formed for one such; DJ Fred Bylar's "Blue Roses" 45 (100), a super-rare release that was followed by five more, generally desultory, releases by Don Willis, Donna Rae and the Sunbeams, and Ray Scott. None of these met with any success, and by 1959, Stewart's partners, Bylar and Neil Herbert, had drifted away.

With financing from Stewart's sister Estelle Axton, Satellite now purchased its own recording equipment and set up shop in a Brunswick, Tenn., warehouse, where the label was relaunched with the Veltones' "Fool in Love" (100—emphasizing the label's rebirth, its earlier existence was utterly expunged from the catalog).

Satellite returned to Memphis in 1960, moving into a disused movie theater on East McLemore. The label's product was sold from a record store at the front of the building, though from the outset, Stewart understood the importance of widespread distribution. Satellite's local distributor, Music Sales, also handled the Atlantic group locally, and when the label's next single, "Cause I Love You," by Rufus and Carla (Thomas—102), began to take off, it was swiftly licensed to Atco. Reissued under the major's own imprint (6177), Carla Thomas's "Gee Whiz" (Satellite 104) charted as Atlantic 2086. (Satellite 103 was by Charles Heinz.)

In common with many labels of the time, Satellite boasted its own house band, Axton's son Packy's high school combo, the Royal Spades. Renamed the Mar-Keys, this group provided backing on most early-label 45s, while their debut single, "Last Night" (107), would prove a template for R&B throughout the early '60s.

In 1961, Stewart learned of a California-based company with a prior claim on the Satellite name. Moving to head off any possible problems, Stewart and Axton decided to rename their company, combining the first two letters of their surnames to create Stax. Following issues by Prince Conley, Nick Charles, and Hoyt Johnson, the final Satellite release, in October 1961, was Barbara Stephens' "The Life I Live" (111).

Examples of Satellite's original life span are extremely rare, though their high values relate solely to the label's historical significance. Label issues from the 1960s, too, are difficult to find, although prices for the hit recordings tend to be more manageable.

Further Reading: *The Complete Stax Volt Singles,* by Rob Bowman (booklets within the three-CD box set of the same name)

Scepter

Scepter was launched by Florence Greenberg, a New Jersey housewife who, according to legend, first entered the music industry as a way of killing time while the kids were at school and her husband, an employee of Hill and Range music publishers, was at work. One of her daughters introduced her to a singing group formed by four classmates, the Honeytones, and in 1958, Greenberg formed the Tiara label and released their first 45, "I Met Him on a Sunday (Ronde Ronde)" (Tiara 6112). A swift local hit, it brought the group to Decca's attention—the label purchased the single from Tiara, changed the quartet's name to the Shirelles . . . and then dropped them when two further 45s flopped.

Greenberg, meanwhile, had used Decca's $4,000 payment wisely, taking office space on Broadway and launching a new label, Scepter, with singles by Don Crawford ("Why Why Why"—1201) and Eddie and the Starlites ("Pretty Little Girl"—1202). The Shirelles' version of "Dedicated to the One I Love" (a 5 Royales single on King the previous year) followed (1203), scraping into the lower reaches of the chart; however, follow-ups "A Teardrop and a Lollipop" (1205) and "Please Be My Boyfriend" (1207) did little, and Scepter lapsed into silence for several months.

The label bounced back in early 1960, following the arrival of songwriter-producer Luther Dixon. The Shirelles' "Tonight's the Night" (1208) was his first recording for the label; it reached the Top 40, despite sales being split with a spoiler version by the Chiffons (Big Deal 6003).

Of course, the Shirelles' next single, "Will You Still Love Me Tomorrow" (1211—first pressings are titled simply "Tomorrow"), ensured that the group was soon outdistancing all the competition, establishing themselves in the upper echelons of '60s girl-group history. Three dozen singles and 11 LPs over the next eight years testify to the group's longevity—needless to say, Scepter's most collected act, by far, is the

Shirelles, both in their own right and by association. The chart-topping success of "Soldier Boy" (1228), for example, prompted two related releases, one by the Soldier Boys ("I'm Your Soldier Boy"—1230), and one by Valli ("Hurry Home to Me [Soldier Boy]"—1233); the Shirelles provide backing vocals on the latter.

Future "Peppermint Twist" maestro Joey Dee cut a rare Scepter single in 1961 ("Face of an Angel"—1210); ex-Flamingos vocalist Tommy Hunt notched up a trio of hits during 1962–63; Chuck Jackson became the first signing on the newly inaugurated Wand subsidiary; and the then-struggling Isley Brothers joined him there, quickly scoring a massive hit with "Twist and Shout" (124)—one of two Scepter classics that would soon, famously, be covered by the Beatles. The Shirelles' "Boys" (the B-side of "Will You Still Love Me Tomorrow") joined it on the Fab Fours' debut LP. Anther Wand classic was the Kingsmen's primeval garage reworking of Richard Berry's "Louie Louie" (143), reissuing a local (Seattle) hit scored by the Jerden label (712).

Scepter's next major find was Dionne Warwick, a singer discovered by bandleader Burt Bacharach, himself a more-or-less permanent fixture around Scepter and Wand (he wrote several hits for the Shirelles and Chuck Jackson). Over the next decade, the combination of Warwick, Bacharach, and his songwriting partner, Hal David, would become one of the greatest teams in American pop history. Out of the 38 Top 100 hits that Warwick brought to Scepter, all but four were Bacharach-David compositions.

Warwick joined the Shirelles (and, over at Wand, Chuck Jackson and the newly arrived Maxine Brown), as Scepter's biggest-selling artist; the remainder of the label's catalog is composed largely of one- or, at best, two- or-three-hit wonders. Of course, this canon abounds with remarkably popular curios—the Filipino family group Rocky Fellers offer some enjoyable proto-bubblegum; *Hawaii Five-0* star James "Danno" MacArthur appeals to fans of TV kitsch (his "10 Commandments of Love"—1250—is a masterpiece in that vein); soul diva Judy Clay, caught in the years before Stax made her a star; even a pair of pre-fame Shangri-Las cuts, "Wishing Well"/"Hate to Say I Told You So" (1291), unearthed in the aftermath of the trio's Red Bird success.

TEN TOP COLLECTIBLES

Shirelles

Baby It's You (Scepter SPS 504—Stereo LP, 1965)

"Dedicated to the One I Love" (Scepter 1203—White-label 7-inch, 1958)

"Hurry Home to Me (Soldier Boy)"—Valli (Scepter 1233—7-inch, 1962)

"I Met Him on a Sunday" (as the Honeytones, Tiara 6112—7-inch, 1958)

"My Love Is a Charm" (Decca 30669—7-inch, 1958)

Sings to Trumpets and Strings (Scepter SPM 502—LP, label with logo in scroll, 1962)

"Stop Me" (Decca 30761—7-inch, 1958)

"A Teardrop and a Lollipop" (Scepter 1205—White-label 7-inch, 1959)

Tonight's the Night (Scepter SPM 501—LP, label with logo in scroll, 1961)

A Twist Party (Scepter SPS 505—Stereo LP, 1965)

In 1965 the Canadian band Chad Allan and the Expressions joined Scepter. They had just scored a homeland hit with "Shakin' All Over," credited to a group named "Guess Who?"—the band members' none too subtle attempt to pass themselves off as people somebody might have heard of, without actually saying who. Whether the stunt would work in the US or not is anybody's guess—Scepter issued the single credited to the Guess Who (1295), and when the single hit, that became the group's permanent name. Despite issuing five further singles, their Scepter career went no further, and Chad Allen's departure spelled the end of the band. It was a couple of years more before a regrouped lineup, with a slightly abbreviated name, emerged at RCA to become one of the hard rock sensations of the decade's end.

B.J. Thomas, Roy Head, the Crests, Maurice Williams and the Zodiacs, Candy and the Kisses, the Clique, Len Barry, and Ronnie Milsap were Scepter regulars through the late '60s, with Thomas, at least, stepping up alongside Warwick as one of the label's biggest stars. Among the continuing parade of one-hit (or, increasingly, no-hit) wonders, the Buoys' "Timothy" (12275) introduced cannibalism (or horse-meat,

according to composer Rupert Holmes) to the chart; Beverly Bremers, the immortally named Big Wheelie and the Hubcaps, Lloyd Price, Merrilee Rush, Nolan Chance, and Otis Williams also recorded for the label.

A band called Genesis cut a 1972 single, "Second Coming" (12341). It has absolutely nothing to do with the Peter Gabriel–Phil Collins act of the same name, but—perhaps courtesy of that oddly stubborn streak which many collectors possess, refusing to admit mistakes even when they have been very obviously made—the release does have some value. A Tiny Tim song from the same era, "Am I Just Another Pretty Face" (12351), is also dependably sought after.

However, time was running out. In 1976, Greenberg announced her retirement, wrapping up Scepter with Jesse Green's "Nice and Slow" (12424), and Wand with Sweet Music's "I Get Lifted" (11295). The catalog was then sold to Springboard International, who maintained a stream of reissues on the Springboard, Trip, and Up Front labels.

Shout

This Bang subsidiary enjoyed a number of successful singles during 1966–68, most notably with

TEN TOP COLLECTIBLES

Jimi Hendrix Experience

Are You Experienced (Reprise R6261— Mono LP, 1967)

Axis: Bold As Love (Reprise R6281— Mono LP, 1967)

Cry of Love (Reprise MS 2034— LP with W7 logo, 1971)

Electric Hendrix (UK Track 2856 002— LP, 1971)

Electric Ladyland (Reprise 2R 6307— Mono promo LP, 1968)

"Gypsy Eyes" (UK Track 2094 010— 7-inch, 1971)

Hendrix in the West (UK Polydor 831 312-2— CD, 1989)

"Hey Joe" (Reprise 0572— 7-inch, picture sleeve, 1967)

"Little Drummer Boy"/"Silent Night" (Reprise PRO 595— 7-inch promo, picture sleeve, 1974)

"Stepping Stone" (Reprise 0905— 7-inch, 1970)

Erma Franklin, Jackie Moore, and Freddie Scott—the first, and for five years, the only—artist to release a Shout LP, 1967's *Are You Lonely for Me?* (501).

Appearing at a time when most observers considered the label long moribund, Shout 502 was issued in 1972, offering a deeply posthumous collection of pre-fame Jimi Hendrix material, *In the Beginning*. Not to be confused with the identically titled Isley Brothers–Hendrix collection (T-Neck YNS 3007), this six-song set features material allegedly recorded during Hendrix's time with Lonnie Youngblood. In fact, he does not appear on any of the songs. Nevertheless, the sheer collectibility of almost anything bearing Hendrix's name and image (silk-screened golf bags, anyone?) ensures that this LP, together with dozens more similarly deceptive compilations, remain sought after.

Signpost

In terms of chart success, Signpost is best remembered for an LP by the English Congregation (SP 7217), titled for their Atco label hit "Softly Whispering I Love You" (Atco distributed Signpost at the time), and for Danny O'Keefe's 1972 hit "Goodtime Charlie's Got the Blues" (70006). O'Keefe's eponymous debut album (SP 8404) also includes the original recording of "The Road," a song Jackson Browne would subsequently take to great heights.

Glam-metal hopefuls Silverhead, featuring future Blondie bassist Nigel Harrison and Power Station vocalist Michael Des Barres, released a self-titled debut LP through Signpost (8407), but the most significant release for modern collectors is the *Live!* union of Fela Ransome-Kuti and The Africa '70 and Ginger Baker (SP 8401), original copies of which fetch a fair sum today (Universal finally reissued the album in 2001).

Signpost's final LP under Atco distribution is also noteworthy, a solo set by Byrds bassist Skip Battin (4808). Distribution then moved to MCA, but after just one LP, by Uncle Dog, the label reached the end of the road.

Skydog

Marc Zermati and Pieter Meulenbrocks' Skydog label launched in Paris, France, in 1972, with the first legitimate pressing of the legendary Jimi Hendrix/Jim Morrison/Johnny Winter jam session, *Skyhigh* (SGSH 2017378), and the Flamin' Groovies' *Grease* EP (FGG 001). This early incarnation of what became France's most legendary label ended following the issue of a Velvet Underground bootleg, *Evil Mothers* (LP 003).

Zermati then linked with Larry Debay, of London's Bizarre record store, to launch Bizarre Distribution, the first independent record distribution company in Europe. Releases by Kim Fowley (*Animal God of the Street*—LP SGKF 001), British pub-rock favorites Ducks Deluxe (*Jumpin'*—EP 005) and the Groovies' Sneakers 10-inch (MLPFGG 003) followed, with Skydog coming to international attention with the 1976 release of *Metallic KO* (62232), a *cinema verité* account of Iggy Pop and the Stooges' final live show in Michigan, in 1974. The Stooges have remained a staple of the Skydog catalog for over a quarter of a century since, with a number of equally collectible titles—the live EP *(I Got) Nothing* (SGIS 12) and the CDs *We Are Not Talking Commercial Shit* and *Wake Up Suckers,* included.

With a keen appreciation of rock history, Skydog engineered a 1976 release for two early Lou Reed recordings, "You're Driving Me Insane" and "Cycle Annie," released under the French-language pseudonym Velour Souterain (SP SMAC 001). With a sharp understanding of rock's present, meanwhile, an early link with Britain's Stiff label saw Skydog handle the French issue of debut 45s by the Damned and Motörhead; the Tyla Gang and the Gorillas also issued on Skydog, but a planned release for an early demo version of the Stranglers' "Peaches" never made it.

In 1976, Zermati was involved in the famous Mont de Marsen punk festival, with several of Skydog's French acts appearing alongside the British contingent; he also arranged the following year's follow-up event. In 1977 Titus Williams, America's first black punk band, cut their *Message of Love* EP for Skydog. Just 200 copies were pressed before the release was canceled; it is now considered Skydog's rarest item, and was one of the highlights on the stellar CD *Skydog Poubelles: The Singles Story* (Japan P-Vine PVCP 8736).

TEN TOP COLLECTIBLES

Iggy Pop and the Stooges

"Down on the Street" (Elektra 45695—7-inch, 1970)

Fun House (Elektra EKS 74101—Red-label LP, 1970)

"I Got a Right" (Siamese 001—7-inch, 1977)

"(I Got) Nothing" (France Skydog SGIS 12—12-inch, picture sleeve, 1978)

"I Wanna Be Your Dog" (Elektra 45664—7-inch, 1969)

Jesus Loves the Stooges (Bomp 114—EP, picture sleeve, 1977)

Kill City (Bomp 1018—Green-vinyl LP, 1977)

Raw Power (Columbia KC 32111—LP, 1973)

"Search and Destroy" (Columbia 45877—7-inch, 1973)

The Stooges (Elektra EKS 74051—Red-label LP, 1969)

This same period also brought recordings with Shakin' Street, which recorded for Skydog before becoming the first French band ever signed to the CBS major; the Phantoms; 84 Flesh ("Salted City"—SGH 15); and the Rockin' Rebels (SGRB 16).

Two compilations, *Creme de Skydog* (P SGC 0017) and *Skydog Commando* (P SGSC 0018), released in 1978, wrapped up Skydog's early career, followed as they were by the collapse of Bizarre Distribution. The label relaunched in 1983 with archive and new releases by the Flamin' Groovies (SKI 2224); the Flying Padovanis (SKI 2225); the Heartbreakers spin-off Heroes—featuring Walter Lure and Billy Rath (SKI 6101)—the London Cowboys (SKI 2102); and with a Blue Öyster Cult live album dating from 1972 (MAXI 62237-1). The late '80s and the 1990s, meanwhile, saw much of Skydog's legacy transferred to CD.

SNB

Distributed in Britain by CBS, SNB was established in 1967 by former Yardbirds/John's Children manager Simon Napier-Bell as an outlet, as Napier-Bell himself put it, "for anyone [who] came into the office with an even remotely listenable tape." Consequently, Napier-Bell said, "We issued a few good records, a few bad ones." Among the good ones was a 45 by former John's Children and future Radio Stars vocalist Andy Ellison, a cover of the Beatles' "You Can't Do That" (SNB 55-3308), originally issued with a version of Marc Bolan's "Casbah Candy" on the B-side. This release was withdrawn very soon after its issue, to be replaced by a new coupling of "You Can't Do That"/"Cornflake Zoo."

Further Reading: *You Don't Have to Say You Love Me,* by Simon Napier-Bell (New English Library, 1982)

Specialty

One of the most cherished labels of the late '40s and the 1950s, Specialty was the aptly named creation of Art Rupe—with a wide-ranging taste for jazz, R&B, early rock 'n' roll, and gospel, Specialty did indeed specialize in the best available examples of each genre.

Early releases by Joe Liggins, Percy Mayfield, and Roy Milton are all of some significance, with Milton's

1945 hit "R.M. Blues" often referenced among the founding fathers of the rock 'n' roll beat. It was also the first so-called race record ever to sell a million.

Specialty is also famed for its early examination of the New Orleans scene. Rupe discovered Lloyd Price and scored an immediate R&B chart-topper with the immortal "Lawdy Miss Clawdy" (428)—the original 78 pressings appeared on red wax, a device that Specialty repeated with the following "Ain't It a Shame" (452), "What's the Matter Now" (457), "Baby Don't Turn Your Back on Me" (463), and "Let Me Come Home Baby" (483). Price's valet, Larry Williams, would also enjoy a Specialty career, his ten-single output including such instant classics as "Bony Moronie" (615) and "Dizzy Miss Lizzy" (626).

Guitar Slim was another Big Easy find—according to legend, Art Rupe was unable to get to New Orleans to conduct Slim's first session for the label, so he directed the proceedings by telephone to label promo man Johnny Vincent. The ensuing "The Things that I Used to Do" (482) topped the R&B chart in 1954 and is also notable for one of the earliest recorded appearances by pianist Ray Charles.

Specialty's next major discovery was Little Richard, a Peacock recording artist then employed as a dishwasher at a Macon, Ga., Greyhound bus station. Buying out his existing contract, Specialty launched Little Richard with "Tutti Frutti" (561) in 1955—and never looked back. Over the next decade, Little Richard would issue more than 20 singles (but just four LPs) for Specialty, almost all of which hit the R&B Top Ten. In addition, the label's entire EP catalog was given over to the performer. Though there are plenty of obscure and rare records in the Specialty catalog, including James Brown at King, Little Richard's fame and collectibility is such that his releases remain the highest priced.

Amid all the stars that Specialty created there is, of course, "the one that got away." Sam Cooke was vocalist with the Soul Stirrers, a gospel group whose success was already well in hand. One day, however, Rupe caught Cooke and producer Bumps Blackwell recording popular music at a session ostensibly booked for a newcomer named Dale Cook. Fearing that the defection would irreparably damage the Soul Stirrers' religious standing, Rupe fired Blackwell

TEN TOP COLLECTIBLES

Little Richard

"Baby Don't You Want a Man Like Me" (Modern 1018—7-inch, picture sleeve, 1966)

"Get Rich Quick" (RCA Victor 47-4582—7-inch, 1952)

"Good Golly Miss Molly" (Specialty 624—7-inch, picture sleeve, 1958)

Here's Little Richard (Specialty 100—LP, 1957)

Little Richard (RCA Victor CAL 416—EP, 1956)

Little Richard (Specialty SP 2103—LP, no triangle on front photo, 1958)

"Little Richard's Boogie" (Peacock 1658—7-inch, 1956)

"Please Have Mercy on Me" (RCA Victor 47-5025—7-inch, 1952)

"Taxi Blues" (RCA Victor 47-4392—7-inch, 1951)

"Why Did You Leave Me?" (RCA Victor 47-4772—7-inch, 1952)

and sent Cooke packing as well. The pair promptly joined Keen Records and hit with "You Send Me," one of the songs taped at that decisive Dale Cook session.

Although the Specialty imprint would remain active into the 1960s, the label itself closed down in 1960, Rupe maintaining an office simply to handle the sale of existing stock. He relaunched Specialty in 1969 as a reissue label (research for these releases was conducted by the future Dr. Demento, Barret Hansen). The catalog is now owned by Fantasy, though the Rupe family remains involved.

Stax

With the possible exception of Motown, Stax is the most famous soul-R&B label in the world and home to some of the best-loved artists. Otis Redding, Sam and Dave, Rufus Thomas, the Bar-Kays, Isaac Hayes, Eddie Floyd, and Johnnie Taylor did more than create great records, they laid the foundations for much of what the genre went on to achieve. In terms of quality alone, Stax richly deserves its reputation as the most collectible R&B label of the age. It is simply a bonus (or not, depending upon whether or not you own a copy) that the label is also host to some of the genre's most favored rarities.

Stax formed in September 1961, after owners Jim Stewart and Estelle Axton's original label, Satellite, was prompted to change its name (ST-AX was arrived at by combining the first letters of their surnames). The new label's numbering sequence picked up more or less where Satellite left off. Satellite 107, the Mar-Keys' hit "Last Night," became Stax 107; the label's final issue, 111, was renumbered 113, with 112 being granted to the Mar-Keys' second 45, "Morning After."

Swiftly following the Mar-Keys was Booker T. and the MGs, originally a house band at the subsidiary Volt label, and the instrumental prowess of these groups (the latter in particular) remained Stax's most identifiable feature. But it was with vocal talent that the company made its name. Carla Thomas, William Bell, the Mad Lads, Sam and Dave, Johnnie Taylor, Isaac Hayes, and Eddie Floyd joined the roster over the next five years, often performing songs written and/or produced by members of the MGs. That band's

output, incidentally, includes such unmistakable signatures as "Green Onions" (127) and "Time Is Tight" (0028), and a string of LPs, beginning with Stax's first-ever full-length, also titled *Green Onions* (701).

Like Motown, which was Stax's only genuine competitor in the R&B field, the label's primary preoccupation was singles. This is reflected in the collectors market by the relative availability and inexpensiveness of all but a handful of releases. The label's 1960s LP output, on the other hand, is less frequently encountered—just 26 albums were released during this golden era, with even the seemingly undesirable (and certainly out-of-character) Gus Cannon's *Walk Right In* (702) commanding a good price.

The majority of albums in this series were issued in both mono and stereo; the latter tend to be scarcer. Noteworthy, too, are the two separate covers for Booker T. and the MGs' *Christmas Album* (7013), first released in 1966, then reissued the following year. Clumsy counterfeits of one unissued LP, Carla Thomas's *Live at the Bohemian Cavern* (7024), have also been reported—the catalog number, incidentally, was reused for Booker T.'s *Doin' Our Thing*.

Stax's long-standing relationship with Atlantic Records came to a close in May 1968, and Stewart sold the label to Gulf and Western; two years later he and DJ Al Bell bought it back, as a new generation moved up to take Stax into the 1970s. The 2000 LP series, with close to 50 titles, testifies to the importance of the label during this period.

The undisputed star of the newly formed Enterprise subsidiary, Isaac Hayes emerged from the shadows of songwriting and sessions to become a superstar; the Staple Singers, the Emotions, and the Dramatics followed, while the group the Bar-Kays was reborn first as the new Stax house band, then as a hit-maker in their own right. Wattstax, a 1972 day-long festival showcasing the best of current Stax talent, spun off one of the most successful music movies of the early decade, along with a dynamite soundtrack of the same name (STS 2-3010).

Stax also released successful soundtracks to several so-called blaxploitation movies, including *Sweet Sweetback's Badasssss Song* (STS 3001), and via

Enterprise, the granddaddy of them all, Isaac Hayes' *Shaft*. Expanding even further, Stax launched a comedy label, Partee, and scored a major hit with Richard Pryor. Other new subsidiaries included Hip, Gospel Truth, and Respect. The label even moved into rock, with Knowbody Knows (aka Black Oak Arkansas) appearing on both Hip and Enterprise, while UK prog act Skin Alley headed for Stax. Despite the band's American obscurity, copies of its *Two Quid Deal* album (STS 3013) are surprisingly common, certainly when compared to its UK equivalent (on the Transatlantic label).

By the mid-'70s, however, the label's importance and impact alike were fading. The problems dated to 1972, when Columbia Records took over Stax's distribution, on the understanding that the parent label would pay Stax for every record, regardless of sales and/or returns. It was an unprecedented deal, and when Columbia head Clive Davis was replaced in 1973, his successors quickly changed the terms of the deal, slashing payments by 40 percent. Within two years, Stax was teetering on the brink of bankruptcy.

Of all the desperate measures that the label took during these last years, perhaps the most notorious was the signing of teenaged English singer Lena Zavaroni, an unashamedly MOR performer discovered via a primetime TV talent contest called *Opportunity Knocks*. For anybody encountering her *Ma, He's Making Eyes at Me* LP (STS 5511), Stax could fall no further from grace—and so it proved. On January 12, 1976, the courts ordered the label's closure.

Since that time, both Atlantic (owners of the pre-1968 catalog) and Fantasy, who purchased the liquidated company, have worked hard to keep the label's name and artists alive. The nearly complete Satellite/Stax/Volt singles catalog has been presented within three CD box sets (A-sides only); in addition, single-disc compilations and original LP reissues have ensured that little of the label's crucial output remains unavailable to interested listeners. These releases have not, of course, had an impact on the values of the original vinyl; indeed, if anything, they have encouraged the collectibility of the original issues, as an entirely new audience discovers the magic of the original Stax sound.

TEN TOP COLLECTIBLES

Booker T. and the MGs

And Now (Stax STS 711—Stereo LP, 1966)

Booker T. and Priscilla (A&M SP 3504—LP, 1971)

"Chinese Checkers" (Stax 137—7-inch, 1963)

"Green Onions" (Stax 127— Gray-label 7-inch, 1962)

Green Onions (Stax 701— Mono LP, 1962)

"Green Onions" (Volt 102—7-inch, 1962)

In the Christmas Spirit (Stax STS 713— LP, fingers-and-keys sleeve, 1966)

"Jellybread" (Stax 131—7-inch, 1963)

"Mo' Onions"/"Fanny Mae" (Stax 142— 7-inch, withdrawn B-side, 1963)

Soul Dressing (Stax 705— Mono LP, 1965)

Further Reading: *The Complete Stax Volt Singles,* by Rob Bowman (booklets within the three CD box sets of the same name)

Steed

Much prized by bubblegum collectors, Jeff Barry's Steed label was distributed by Dot Records and made its greatest mark with singer Andy Kim. His "How'd We Ever Get This Way" (707) just missed the Top 20 in 1968, and was the first of ten Top 100 45s that Kim logged for Steed. Amusingly, Kim later complained that he was physically incapable of performing any of them in concert, as producer Barry sped up the recordings in order to make Kim's naturally rootsy voice sound gummier! Kim was responsible for four of Steed's eight album releases.

Other acts included the Keepers of the Light, whose "My Babe" (701) debuted the label; the label also released work by the Rich Kids, Jacqueline Carol and Louis St. Louis, Hank Shifter, Alzo and Uddin, and the Illusion. The latter group's debut single, "Did You See Her Eyes" (712), was a flop the first time around; when remixed and reissued (718), it made

the Top 40; a third version of the song, more than twice the length of the hit, appears on the Illusion's debut album (37003). Two further Illusion albums and six singles were issued during 1969–70.

Steed's other hit act was Robin McNamara, one of the stars of the musical *Hair.* He charted with "Lay a Little Lovin' on Me" (724) and "Got to Believe in Love" (728). McNamara would be responsible for the final releases on Steed, an album titled after his debut hit (37007) and the single "Beer Drinkin' Man" (735), in 1971.

Further Reading: *Bubblegum Music Is the Naked Truth: The Dark History of Prepubescent Pop, from the Banana Splits to Britney Spears,* edited by Kim Cooper and David Smay (Feral House, 2001)

Stiff

In early spring of 1976, in the "records for sale" section of the UK music press classifieds, a new record company announced its birth. It demanded no fanfare, and made no extravagant promises, but anybody who had followed pub-rock group Brinsley Schwarz through its seven-year career would have

TEN TOP COLLECTIBLES

Jeff Barry

"**All You Need Is a Quarter**" (RCA Victor 47-7821—7-inch, 1960)

"**The Face from Outer Space**" (RCA Victor 47-7797—7-inch, 1960)

"**I'll Still Love You**" (Red Bird 10-026—7-inch, 1965)

"**It's Called Rock 'n' Roll**" (RCA Victor 47-7477—7-inch, 1959)

"**Lenore**" (Decca 31089—7-inch, 1960)

"**Much Too Young**" (UA 40429—7-inch, 1969)

"**Never Never**" (Decca 31037—7-inch, 1959)

"**Sweet Saviour**" (Bell 45 140—7-inch, 1971)

"**Walkin' in the Sun**" (A&M 1422—7-inch, 1973)

"**We Got Love Money Can't Buy**" (UA 440—7-inch, 1962)

paid attention regardless. "So It Goes" (Buy 1) was the debut 45 by Schwarz songwriter Nick Lowe; it was also, though nobody knew it at the time, the maiden release for what would become the most exciting British record label of the late '70s.

Never before had a label garnered its supporters not only through its artists, but also through its own identity. Stiff collectors bought Stiff records regardless of the records' musical merit, and most later agreed, it would be three years and 50-plus new releases, before the label first let them down. Which wasn't at all bad for a company that was only ever intended to be a showcase for a few passing pubrockers, launched by Dr. Feelgood road manager Jake Riviera, with a loan from his employers.

From the start, Stiff set about doing things differently. "Mono, enhanced stereo," insisted the credits to Lowe's debut. "The world's most flexible record label," pledged the company's logo. "Artistic breakthrough: double B-side!" bellowed the first release by the Tyla Gang (BUY 4); and further witticisms quickly followed. When David Bowie released a new album called *Low*, Lowe responded with an EP called *Bowi* (LAST 1). And then there was the infamous promotional button that insisted, "If it ain't Stiff, it ain't worth a fuck," a legend that proved so instantly popular that bootleg versions were appearing on the streets within weeks, and Stiff's reputation was guaranteed. Bootleg buttons, indeed.

"So It Goes" arrived with what remains the most sensible catalog number in recorded history, a plaintive, pleading, BUY ONE. It only followed, therefore, that subsequent releases would exhort even more grandiose purchases: the Pink Fairies' "Between the Lines" begged BUY TWO; Roogalator's "All Aboard"—BUY THREE . . . by the time the label finally closed, in 1987, it was suggesting that fans BUY 259.

Things moved quickly. In October 1976, Stiff signed the Damned and unleashed the first punk single ever, "New Rose" (BUY 6—and a lot of people did), which was the first record by any British punk band, beating the Sex Pistols' "Anarchy in the UK" by

three full weeks. Within weeks, Stiff had landed major-label distribution via UA; within months, the label was opening its own retail outlet. By summer 1977, Elvis Costello was preparing to score his first chart hit; by fall, the Live Stiffs tour was the hottest ticket on the concert circuit, and names like the Damned, the Adverts, Ian Dury, and Wreckless Eric were bywords for the wider pastures roamed by the new wave cognoscenti.

Indeed, it took Stiff no time at all to transform itself from a pub-rock nursing home to a punk rock institution, without changing the company's outlook one iota. Stiff released records by other company's artists—the *A Bunch of Stiff Records* sampler included contributions from Graham Parker (Mercury) and Dave Edmunds (Swan Song). Stiff trawled the halls of musical eccentricity in search of the next Max Wall (a vaudevillian comedian), Humphrey Ocean (an established and respected artist), or Jona Lewie (a wacky keyboard player with an outstanding haircut). And Stiff still made "mistakes" that an amateur might have avoided, such as shipping the Damned's debut LP (SEEZ 1) with a photograph of Eddie and the Hot Rods inadvertently placed on the back.

Fully aware of the label's popularity among collectors, Stiff bent over backwards to keep things interesting. Announcing "We're a record company, not a museum," the label delighted in deleting records as soon as they became popular—and sometimes, before they were even issued. Motörhead's "Leaving Here" (BUY 9) vanished from the catalog immediately, before it reached the stores; Ian Dury's "Sex and Drugs and Rock and Roll" (BUY 17) was withdrawn just as it seemed poised to enter the chart.

Early 1978 saw Riviera depart to launch a new label, Radar—he took Costello, Lowe, and the Yachts with him. A new generation of Stiffs sprang up regardless, revolving around Mickey Jupp, Lene Lovich, Jona Lewie, and schoolgirl country singer Rachel Sweet; both Lovich and Lewie scored significant hits over the next two years. In the 1980s, they were joined by Kirsty MacColl, both a performer and a writer (she penned Tracy Ullman's "They

Live Stiffs on a 1978 8-Track.

Don't Know" [BUY 180] smash). Other Stiff acts of the era were Madness, Dave Stewart and Barbara Gaskin, Tenpole Tudor, the Belle-Stars, and the Pogues, acts whose stellar success and future collectibility in many ways camouflages the less interesting releases that were now littering the catalog—Joe "King" Carrusco, Dirty Looks, Any Trouble, and the Equators.

The label's creative decline could be charted across any sampling of its post-1980 releases, but still there were moments of sheer, shining glory, isolated moments of musical majesty from John Otway, a brace of classics by Department S., and unlikely efforts from the Untouchables and the immortally named Pookiesnackenburger. And when it did all wrap up, it was with breathtakingly circular purity, as the label's first-ever friend became its last-ever signing, and Dr. Feelgood came back to reclaim its loan.

Since then, of course, Stiff has remained on the release sheets, across a string of compilations and reissues spread between a dozen different labels

TEN TOP COLLECTIBLES

Stiff

"Alison"— Elvis Costello (UK Stiff BUY 14— 7-inch, white-vinyl mispress, 1977)

Excerpts from Stiff's Greatest Hits (UK Stiff FREEB 2— EP, 1977)

"I Think We're Alone Now (Japanese Version)"— Lene Lovich (UK Stiff BUYJ 32— 7-inch, 1978)

"New Rose"— The Damned (UK Stiff BUY 6— 7-inch, push-out center, 1976)

"Sex and Drugs and Rock and Roll"— Ian Dury (UK Stiff FREEB 1— 7-inch, picture sleeve, 1977)

"Stretcher Case Baby"— The Damned (UK Stiff DAMNED 1— 7-inch, 1977)

"Toe Knee Black Burn"— Binky Baker and the Pit Orchestra (UK Stiff BUY 41— 7-inch, picture sleeve, 1978)

The Wonderful World Of—Wreckless Eric (UK Stiff SEEZ P9— Picture-disc LP, 1978)

"You Caught Me Out"— Kirsty MacColl (UK Stiff BUY 57— 7-inch promo, 1979)

You're Either on the Train or off the Train—Various artists (UK Stiff DEAL 1— Promo LP with booklet, 1978)

worldwide, each one harking back to the days when Dave Robinson's explanation for Stiff's existence genuinely did ring true. "If major record companies were really good," he once admitted, "then we wouldn't be here."

Further Reading: *Stiff: The Story of a Record Label,* by Bert Muirhead (Blandford, 1981)

Sub Pop

Alongside the same city's C/Z, the Seattle-based Sub Pop was the driving force behind the PNW/Seattle Sound grunge movement of the late '80s and early '90s. Formed by Bruce Pavitt and Jonathan Poneman in the early '80s, originally as a fanzine (which accounts for the first nine Sub Pop catalog releases), Sub Pop dedicated itself to developing a label spirit that, in the alternative era, is analogous only to the early years of Stiff—acts seemed to be signed as much for what they could bring to Sub Pop, as for what Sub Pop could do for them.

Swift deletion polices; limited-edition, colored-vinyl, and picture-sleeve releases; and the generally small runs that were Sub Pop's raison d'être have all contributed to the label's high collectibility. As with Stiff, however, to concentrate on the gimmickry is to overlook the label's vital role in documenting (and, indeed, shaping) a significant moment in time.

During the five years of operation that preceded the grunge explosion—indeed, within Sub Pop's first 25 releases—almost every one of the acts that would eventually put Seattle on the musical map passed through Sub Pop. The seminal compilation *Sub Pop 100* (10) was followed by individual releases by Green River (the *Dry As a Bone* EP—11), Soundgarden (*Screaming Life*—12), Mudhoney ("Touch Me I'm Sick"—17), Tad ("Ritual Device"—19), and Nirvana ("Love Buzz"—23).

Neither did the label confine itself to local environs. Oklahoma City's Flaming Lips (28), San Francisco's Helios Creed (30), Cincinnati's Afghan Whigs (32), Ann Arbor's Big Chief (53), and Chicago's Smashing Pumpkins (90) all released early material through the label. France's Les Thugs (29) and England's Billy Childish (71) came from even further afield. Many of these releases were included within the much-collected Sub Pop Singles Club series.

TEN TOP COLLECTIBLES

Nirvana

Bleach (UK Tupelo LP 6—White-vinyl LP, 1989)

"Blew" (UK Tupelo TUPCD 8—CD single, 1989)

"Here She Comes Now" (Communion 25—Colored-vinyl 7-inch, 1991)

Hormoaning (Australia Geffen GEF 21711—Burgundy-vinyl 12-inch, 1993)

Incesticide (Geffen DGC 24504—Blue-vinyl LP, 1992)

"Love Buzz" (Sub Pop SP 23—7-inch, hand-numbered picture sleeve, 1988)

"Molly's Lips" (Sub Pop SP 97—Green-vinyl 7-inch, 1991)

"Pennyroyal Tea" (UK Geffen NIRPRO—Promo CD single, 1994)

"Sliver" (Sub Pop SP 72—Blue-vinyl 7-inch, 1990)

"Smells Like Teen Spirit" (UK Geffen DGCTP 5—12-inch picture disc, 1991)

Launched in November 1988, with the aforementioned first single by the then-unknown Nirvana, the Singles Club, too, brought fresh air to the US market, with limited-edition 45s appearing every two months for the next five years. Other highlights included now extremely rare releases by Sonic Youth (26), Rapeman (40), the Dwarves (50), Fugazi (52), the Rollins Band (72), Elastica (275), and Gene (294), before the series ended with Lou Barlow's "I Am Not Mocking You." (The Club was relaunched in April 1998, since which time Luna, Jesus and Mary Chain, Dot Allison, and Imperial Teen have contributed.)

Amid such activities, Sub Pop first came to major attention in the UK, following well-received tours by Mudhoney, Soundgarden, and Nirvana, among others. Even before Geffen signed Nirvana in 1991, Sub Pop was creeping into the American consciousness. Once *Nevermind* hit, however, Sub Pop became ubiquitous, marketing its own name with merciless precision, particularly following the label's partial acquisition by Time Warner.

The decline of grunge's mainstream popularity naturally led to a downswing in Sub Pop's visibility; however, intelligent signings continued to distinguish Sub Pop through the remainder of the 1990s, with the 1998 capture of St. Etienne a particularly noteworthy accomplishment.

Further Reading: *Loser: The Real Seattle Music Story,* by Clark Humphrey and Art Chantry (Misc. Media, 1999)

Sun

Disc jockey Sam C. Phillips opened the Memphis Recording Service in 1950, initially recording local musicians (including Phineas Newborn) for the local Modern Records label before he joined forces with another local DJ, Dewey Phillips (no relation) to form their own label, It's the Phillips. The label issued one single, Joe Hill Louis's "Boogie in the Park"/"Gotta Let You Go" (9001/2); Sam Phillips then moved Louis over to Modern and resumed his own work for that company.

Over the next year he worked with B.B. King, Roscoe Gordon, and Walter Horton, but fell out with Modern after leasing sessions with Howlin' Wolf and Jackie Brenston (the immortal "Rocket 88") to Chess. That relationship prospered for a time, but by 1952, Phillips was looking again for a reliable outlet for his production work. When none was forthcoming, he decided to do it himself, launching Sun in February 1952. (His brother Judd was involved for a time, before launching his own Judd Records label. Judd was also Jerry Lee Lewis's manager for many years.)

Phillips intended the first Sun release to be "Blues in My Condition," by Jackie Boy and Little Walter (174); a poor response from radio, however, persuaded him to can it in favor of Johnny London's "Drivin' Slow" (175). The next scheduled release, Walter Bradford's "Dreary Nights" (176), too, was canceled and it was eight months before Sun stirred again, with releases by Joe Hill Louis, Willie Nix, and Jimmy Walter.

Sun's first hit (and the first release to appear on both 45 and 78) was Rufus Thomas's "Bear Cat" (181), a response to Big Mama Thornton's "Hound Dog." Thomas's "Tiger Man" (188) proved a popular follow-up. Other hits came from Little Junior Parker; Billy "The Kid" Emerson; and Little Milton Campbell and the Prisonaires, a vocal group formed by inmates at the Nashville State Penitentiary. "Just Walkin' in the Rain" (186) was covered for pop success by Johnny Ray in 1956. Subsequent Prisonaires' singles "A Prisoner's Prayer" (191) and "There Is Love in You" (207), appeared in late 1953 and summer 1954, respectively.

Memphis Recording Service's first brush with Elvis Presley came in 1953, when a truck driver dropped by to record a birthday present for his mother, "My Happiness," using the studio's "make your own record" services. Phillips was absent that day; secretary Marion Keisker is thus credited as Elvis's discoverer. It would be another eight months before Phillips finally acceded to her demands that he contact Presley—the rest, of course, is history.

Presley issued five singles on Sun, "That's All Right, Mama" (209), "Good Rockin' Tonight" (210), "Milkcow Blues Boogie" (215), "Baby Let's Play House" (217), and "I Forgot to Remember" (223).

Phillips then sold Presley's contract and recordings to RCA Victor for $40,000.

Presley's success put Sun firmly on the map, drawing in a wealth of ambitious talent. June 1955, brought the first Sun release by Johnny Cash ("Cry Cry Cry"—221); Carl Perkins' "Let the Jukebox Keep On Playing" (224) arrived in August; Roy Orbison debuted with "Ooby Dooby" (242) in May 1956; Jerry Lee Lewis extended "Crazy Arms" (259) that December. All of these artists would prove major successes, both at Sun and thereafter; all would cut some of the most important records in early rock 'n' roll history.

The vast majority of Sun releases were singles—78s, then 45s. Only 12 LPs were issued bearing the Sun label, seven of which were by Johnny Cash. The Phillips International subsidiary was responsible for four more. Of these, the scarcest are generally reckoned to be Carl Perkins' *Dance Album* (Sun LP 1225), along with two Phillips International issues, one by Frank Frost (PILP-1975) and the other by Frank Ballard (PILP-1985).

It is, contrarily, surprising to learn that the majority of big name Sun singles are not especially rare—valuable, yes; exceedingly highly priced, yes. But unless pristine condition is a prerequisite, rare, no—a state of affairs which is a due to a combination, more or less equally, of high sales, vast popularity, and the long-held belief that a Sun record is somehow "special." Today, of course we know it is, but it's interesting to learn that even at the time of the records' original release, many people felt that way. Presumably, the cachet that Sun had for being Elvis's first label impressed everyone.

It was this vast success that ultimately brought Sun down. One by one, as the 1950s faded into the 1960s, Sun's stars departed—Cash was the last to go, moving to Columbia in 1962. This time, however, Phillips was unable to replace his stars. From packing some of the hottest shots in rock in 1959, Sun's 1961 catalog offered nothing more noteworthy than George Klein, Tracy Pendarvis, Wade Cagle, Anita Wood, Harold Dorman, Shirley Sisk, Tony Rossini, Don Hosea, Bobby Wood, and Ray Smith. Once the final offerings from Cash, and a handful of desultory late releases by Jerry Lee Lewis, were out of the way, what was Sun but another regional record label that had once scored a few hits?

TEN TOP COLLECTIBLES

Sun

"**The Boogie Disease**"— Dr. Ross (Sun 212—7-inch, 1955)

"**Call Me Anything but Call Me**"— Big Memphis Ma Rainey (Sun 184—7-inch, 1953)

"**Good Rockin' Tonight**"— Elvis Presley (Sun 210—7-inch, 1955)

"**Heaven or Fire**"— Dusty Brooks and His Tones with Juanita Brown (Sun 182—7-inch, 1953)

"**Just Walking in the Rain**"—The Prisonaires (Sun 186—7-inch, 1953)

"**Rockin' Chair Daddy**"— Harmonica Frank (Sun 205—7-inch, 1954)

"**Take a Little Chance**"— Jimmy DeBerry (Sun 185—7-inch, 1953)

"**That's All Right, Mama**"— Elvis Presley (Sun 209—7-inch, 1955)

"**There Is Love in You**"—The Prisonaires (Sun 207—7-inch, 1954)

"**Wolf Call Boogie**"— Hot Shot Love (Sun 196—7-inch, 1954)

Sun would linger on until 1969, but releases were few and far between—just 24 singles between January 1963 and the final release, Loads of Mischief's "Back in My Arms Again" (407), in January 1968. Finally, Phillips sold the catalog to Mercury Records producer Shelby S. Singleton, Jr., who commenced reissuing (and leasing for reissue) this newly acquired gold mine. It has been estimated that since then, the Sun catalog has been recycled more than any other label on earth.

Further Reading: *Good Rockin' Tonight: Sun Records and the Birth of Rock 'n' Roll,* by Colin Escott, with Martin Hawkins (St. Martin's Press, 1992)

Sunflower

Distributed by MGM, the Sunflower label made its bow with a sequence of primarily novelty singles, by Fearless Fradkin, the Yummies, and Daddy Dewdrop, whose "Chick a Boom" (105) gave the label its first (and biggest) hit. A follow-up single, "The March of the White Corpuscles" (111), and LP (5006) are much in demand among comedy collectors.

Other Sunflower 45s came from Frank Mills, Tony Scotti, Frankie Laine, Bobby Taylor, Jasper Wrath, and R.B. Greaves. However, the label is best remembered for two albums of previously unissued 1966 live recordings by the Grateful Dead. *Vintage Dead* (5001) and *Historic Dead* (5004) both won minor chart entries and are now much sought after. A live album by Los Angeles singer Danny Cox and the debut by Randy Edelman (5005) are also popular.

Super K

A Buddah subsidiary, Super K was formed by Jeffrey Katz and Jerry Kasenetz, the production (and, often, songwriting) team behind the parent label's prodigious bubblegum output. Sadly, its 1969 launch date placed it firmly at the rear of the bubblegum movement, ensuring that little of the label's output received any attention from the record-buying public.

Record collectors, on the other hand, are enthralled by the short-lived operation. Such releases as the Kasenetz-Katz Singing Orchestral Circus's "Bubblegum March" (109) 45, the Orchestral (no singing) Circus's *Classical Smoke* LP (SKS 6001), Deviled Ham's *Too Much to Dream Last Night* (SKS 6003), and Buckwheat's *Pure Buckwheat Honey* (SKS 6004) are extraordinarily difficult to resist.

TEN TOP COLLECTIBLES

Grateful Dead

American Beauty (Mobile Fidelity 1-014—Audiophile pressing, 1980)

"Dark Star" (WB 7186—7-inch, picture sleeve, 1968)

"Don't Ease Me In" (Scorpio 201—7-inch promo, 1966)

Grateful Dead (WB W1689—Mono LP, 1967)

Grateful Dead Hour (MJI—Weekly transcription discs, 1988–date)

King Biscuit Flour Hour 6/80 (KBFH—2-LP transcription disc, 1980)

Sampler for Deadheads (Round 02/03—Promo EP, 1976)

Terrapin Station (Direct Disc 16619—Audiophile pressing, 1980)

27 Years Playing in the Same Band (4-LP transcription disc, 1992)

Wake of the Flood (Grateful Dead GD 01—Green-vinyl LP, 1975)

So, for that matter, is Super Cirkus's version of Dutch rock group Golden Earring's "Dong Dong Diki Diki Dong," an eponymous single by Captain Groovy and His Bubblegum Army (4), and a pair of singles by the arch-gummers themselves, Jerry and Jeff—"Sweet Charity" (7) and "Sweet Sweet Lovin'" (101). Oddly, neither Kasenetz nor Katz actually sings on these records, leaving such menial tasks to Neil Bogart and Tony Orlando.

The group ? and the Mysterians convened for one of its final 45s ("Sha La La"—102), as did the Ohio Express ("Hot Dog"—114). Meanwhile no garage-rock fan can afford to be without three singles and a self-titled final album (SKS 6002) by the Shadows of Knight. None of the material included on the 45s ("Taurus"—108, "Run Run Billy Porter"—110, and "Shake"—520) was duplicated by the album, "Shake" being featured in an alternate take, "Shake Revisited 1969." For reasons known only to the producers, the original hit version was included on Buddah's *Very Best of the Ohio Express* LP.

Further Reading: *Bubblegum Music Is the Naked Truth: The Dark History of Prepubescent Pop, from the Banana Splits to Britney Spears,* edited by Kim Cooper and David Smay (Feral House, 2001)

Swan

If it weren't for Swan's key role in the early saga of the Beatles' American career, it is unlikely that the majority of casual collectors would even have heard of this tiny Philadelphia-based label.

In fact, fellow Swan acts Link Wray, the Rockin' Rebels, and the label's longest-serving star, Freddy Cannon, all merit attention, with stereo copies of Cannon's 1958 *Explosive* LP (LPS 502) one of that format's rarest releases. Other acts, including poet Jacky Kanaan, Mark Valentino, the Sapphires, and Walter Gates are also well-respected, if relatively obscure.

The Beatles' two Swan 45s, on the other hand, have drawn a depth of scholastic research that challenges credulity. At least 14 collectible varieties of "She Loves You" (4152) have been recorded, as every minute change in label appearance is fearlessly chronicled; there are also around half a dozen variations on the follow-up "Sie liebt Dich" (a German-language

---

TEN TOP COLLECTIBLES

Link Wray

"Ace of Spades" (Swan 4261—7-inch, 1967)

"Batman Theme" (Swan 4244—7-inch, 1966)

"Good Rockin' Tonight" (Swan 4201—7-inch, 1965)

Great Guitar Hits (Vermillion 1924—LP, 1966)

"I Sez Baby" (Kay 3690—7-inch, 1958)

"Jack the Ripper" (Rumble 1000—7-inch, 1961)

Link Wray and the Wraymen (Epic LN 3661—LP, 1960)

"Rumble" (Cadence 1347—7-inch, 1958)

"Rumble Mambo" (OKeh 7166—7-inch, 1963)

Yesterday and Today (Record Factory 1929—LP, 1963)

Zeppelin's eighth US single was almost their first British one.

version of the earlier A-side) (4182). Both singles feature the same B-side, "I'll Get You."

To capitalize on what was truly a windfall acquisition, Swan issued two LPs of interest to Beatles fans, the humorous *It's a Beatle (Coo-Coo) World* (514), by Al Fisher and Lou Marks, and Roger Webb and Trio's *John, Paul and all That Jazz* (516), an instrumental tribute.

Swan Song

Titled for an unreleased Jimmy Page solo recording, Led Zeppelin's Swan Song label was launched in 1974 with the US release of the British band Bad Company's eponymous debut LP (SS 8410; the UK version was released by Island Records) and 45 "Can't Get Enough" (70015). In Britain, the debut release arrived some six months later, with a garish party at Chislehurst Caves launching the Pretty Things' *Silk Torpedo* album (SS 8411).

Zeppelin did not appear on the label until 1975 brought the *Physical Graffiti* double album (SS2-200). Distribution was handled through Atlantic, to whom the band had been signed since its inception in 1969.

Over the next six years, four further Led Zeppelin albums were issued by Swan Song—the double live *The Song Remains the Same* (SS2-201), *Presence* (SS 8416), *In Through the Out Door* (SS 16002), and, issued following the group's disbandment, *Coda* (SS 90051). Of these, *In Through the Out Door* is notable for being released with six different sleeves, labeled A to F and individually paper-bagged so that purchasers would not know which sleeve they were receiving. Complete sets of all six, with the bag intact, are relatively easy to assemble but fetch a considerable premium on the collectors market. Also of note are white-label test pressings of *Physical Graffiti*, issued within a mock-up of the album's eventual sleeve (TEAL SS 2-200).

Led Zeppelin understandably dominates the label from a collector's point of view, with several of the group's most sought-after rarities emanating from the Swan Song catalog. Paramount among these is a withdrawn UK single coupling "Wearing and Tearing"/"Darlene" (SSK 19421), scheduled for release to commemorate the band's Knebworth Park concerts in July 1979. Better known, and considerably more common, is a similar issue for the 1975 Earl's Court concerts, coupling "Trampled Under Foot"/"Black Country Woman" (DC 1)—this same coupling, of course, appeared as a regular 45 in the US (70102), one of three Led Zeppelin singles issued by Swan Song. ("Candy Store Rock"—70110, and "Fool in the Rain"—71003 complete the sequence.) No Led Zeppelin singles were ever issued in the UK.

Swan Song's next non-Zeppelin releases were both US-only issues, Maggie Bell's *Suicide Sal* (SS-8412) and Bad Company's *Straight Shooter* (SS 8413). Bad Company remained with the label until the band's breakup in 1982, releasing four further albums and nine singles. Zeppelin aside, it was the label's most successful act, although Dave Edmunds ran it a close second. Joining Swan Song in 1976, the Welshman cut four albums and a total of 14 singles (some UK or US only).

A second Pretty Things album, *Savage Eye* (SS 8414), appeared in 1975—as with its predecessor, attendant singles are common; the following year brought the arrival of the underrated but not especially sought-after Detective, featuring ex-Yes keyboard player Tony Kaye, Steppenwolf guitarist Michael Monarch, and former Silverhead vocalist Michael Des Barres. *Detective* (SS 8417/UK SSK 59405) was followed by *It Takes One to Know One* (SS 8504/UK SSK 59406).

Led Zeppelin disbanded following the death of drummer John Bonham in September 1980; Swan Song began to wind down at the same time. The last new signings were Midnight Flyer, who cut two Swan Song LPs featuring the returning Maggie Bell, and the Manchester band Sad Café, whose one album was produced by 10cc's Eric Stewart—US promo copies of the attendant "La-Di-Da" 45 (SS 72002) are common enough to have earned the title of the biggest noncollectible in the entire Swan Song catalog.

TEN TOP COLLECTIBLES

Led Zeppelin

"Communication Breakdown" (UK Atlantic 584 269—7-inch promo, 1969)

"Dazed and Confused" (Atlantic EP 1019—7-inch promo, 1969)

"D'yer Maker" (UK Atlantic K10296—7-inch promo, 1973)

Houses of the Holy (Atlantic SD 7255—Mono promo LP, 1973)

Led Zeppelin III (Atlantic SD 7201—Mono promo LP, 1971)

Led Zeppelin IV (Atlantic SD 77208—Jukebox album, 1972)

"Stairway to Heaven" (Atlantic STPR 269—7-inch promo picture disc, 1979)

"Trampled Under Foot" (UK Swan Song DC 1—7-inch promo, 1975)

"Wearing and Tearing" (UK Swan Song SSK 19421—Withdrawn 7-inch, 1979)

"Whole Lotta Love" (UK Atlantic 584 309—Withdrawn 7-inch, 1969)

The label closed down with the first solo recordings by Jimmy Page (the *Death Wish II* soundtrack—SS 8511) and Robert Plant (*Pictures At 11*—SS8512). A UK 12-inch single from the latter, "Burning down One Side" (SSK 19429T), fittingly closed the catalog with another major rarity.

Further Reading: *The Illustrated Collector's Guide to Led Zeppelin,* by Robert Godwin (Collector's Guide Publishing, various editions)

Together

Based in Los Angeles, Together Records launched in 1969 with volume one of a so-called archive series of rare and early recordings by a variety of Los Angeles performers. *Pre-Flyte* (ST-T-1001) featured 11 tracks by the future Byrds; other releases in this extremely collectible series include volumes devoted to early work by Dino Valenti (of Quicksilver Messenger Service), David Crosby, the Dillards, and Canned Heat. Together also released Danny Cox's two-LP *Birth Announcement* (ST-T-1011), another in-demand set.

In 1970, Together distribution was taken up by MGM, who merged the label's catalog with AIR (American International Records), the musical wing of American International Pictures, which was therefore devoted to the parent company's soundtrack material. The New York–based L&R label, too, was part of the package—an LP by Bobby Bloom, featuring his hit version of "Montego Bay," appeared as 1035 MGM's Teem label catalog. The vast majority of releases from this point on, however, were the aforementioned soundtracks, including a number that have since obtained considerable cult gravitas—*The Dunwich Horror* (1028), *Bloody Mama* (1031), *Cycle Savages* (1033), and *Mr. Phibes* (1040).

AIR/Together closed its doors in 1972. The final release was Roy Budd's admirable soundtrack to *Kidnapped* (1042).

Tollie

A subsidiary of Vee-Jay, Tollie was launched in late February of 1964, as a pop-oriented alternative to the parent label's R&B policy. Stated aims included nurturing new talent, and a number of unknown artists

appeared on the label. However, the debut release was a surefire success, the Beatles 45 "Twist and Shout" (Tollie 9001), taken from the Vee-Jay Beatles LP (1062). "Not every new record label can start with a million-seller," ads in *Billboard* and *Cashbox* boasted in early March, "[but] Tollie has." Initial orders alone numbered close to half a million, and the single went on to spend a month at No. 2 on the chart.

A second Tollie Beatles single, "Love Me Do" (9008), topped the US chart in April; no other release on the label was nearly as successful, but the Beatle cachet is such that Tollie releases in general are extremely collectible—several authors have compared the label's appeal to that of the Apple label's own non-Beatles output, though Tollie had no connections with the group beyond hosting two of their American hits.

Nevertheless, Tollie's is a rewarding catalog, its highlights including British Invasion group the Dowlands' cover of another Beatles song, "All My Loving" (9002); Cass Elliott and the Big Three's "Winken Blinken and Nod" (9006); and Barrett Strong's "I'd Better Run" (9023). Also in the Tollie catalog are two of the greatest death songs ever recorded: Jimmy Cross's implausibly macabre No. 92 hit "I Want My Baby Back" (9039)—graphically relating the dismemberment of his girlfriend in a highway collision on the way home from a Beatles concert—and English songstress Twinkle's "Terry" (9040), a "Leader of the Pack"-esque saga of true love ending in suicide-by-motorcycle.

Tollie was also behind the BRATTS—the Brotherhood for the Re-establishment of American Top Ten Supremacy—whose "Secret Weapon (The British Are Coming)" (9024) dreamed of a day when homegrown talent might finally challenge the British Invasion. Unfortunately, Tollie would not live to see that come to pass. The label folded in 1965, after 48 singles, but just two albums: one by Don Cole and another by Argentinean Alberto Cortez.

Tollie LP labels were purple, with the label name within a broken square at the top; the initial 45 label was deep yellow. Variations both dispensed with, and repaired, the square; greenish and black labels were

TEN TOP COLLECTIBLES

Tollie

"All My Loving"—The Dowlands (Tollie 9002—7-inch, 1964)

"Golden Lights"—Twinkle (Tollie 9047—7-inch, 1965)

"I Better Run"—Barrett Strong (Tollie 9023—7-inch, 1964)

"I Want My Baby Back"—Jimmy Cross (Tollie 9039—7-inch, 1965)

"Love Me Do"—The Beatles (Tollie 9008—7-inch, 1964)

"Secret Weapon"—The BRATTS (Tollie 9024—7-inch, 1965)

"Terry"—Twinkle (Tollie 9040—7-inch, 1965)

Their Biggest Hits—The Beatles (Tollie TEP 1-8901—Counterfeit EP, 1975)

"Twist and Shout"—The Beatles (Tollie 9001—7-inch, 1964)

"Winken Blinken and Nod"—The Big Three (Tollie 9006—7-inch, 1964)

also issued. A third 45 label, multicolored, was introduced during the summer of 1964. Since neither Beatles 45 appeared on this type, it is less well-known than its predecessors.

Further Reading: *Songs, Pictures and Stories of the Fabulous Beatles Records on Vee-Jay,* compiled by Bruce Spizer (498 Productions, 1998)

Track

One hates to poop on someone else's party, but if you intend to seriously collect the British Track label, make sure you've got around $3,000 to spare. That, in early 2002, is the current going price for the rarest 45 in the Track label catalog, John's Children's "Midsummer Night's Scene" (604 005). In fact, the single is not only the rarest in the Track catalog, it's the rarest in British record-collecting.

Neither is this the only rarity in the Track pack. Another John's Children 45, "Go Go Girl" (604 010), and a solo offering by band vocalist Andy Ellison, "It's Been a Long Time" (604 018), are also highly prized. Moreover, issues by Cherry Smash; Eire Apparent; the Debonaires; Marsha Hunt; and the first-ever 45 by

Fairport Convention, "If I Had a Ribbon Bow" (604 020), seldom appear on the market, either.

The Crazy World of Arthur Brown, who brought the label its first chart-topper with "Fire" (604 022), also delivered a pair of very desirable flops, while their eponymous debut LP (613 005) was issued with radically different mono and stereo mixes, which have since been paired together on CD, but are well worth seeking out in their original incarnations.

Thunderclap Newman scored Track's second No. 1, "Something in the Air" (604 031), then followed up with three seldom-seen misses, and an album, *Hollywood Dream* (2406 003), which is as rare in its UK form as its US counterpart is common. Which is very. And all that is before one even begins to think about the two artists for whom Track is most renowned, the Who and the Jimi Hendrix Experience.

Track was set up in early 1967 by Kit Lambert and Chris Stamp, the Who's management team, primarily as an outlet for their own charges. However, the early recruitment of Hendrix saw his second UK single, "Purple Haze" (604 001), inaugurate the label in March; the Who's "Pictures of Lily" (604 002) followed in April. (Original pressings of "Purple Haze" were issued bearing a white label with black lettering; all future Track issues were black with white print.)

The enormous success which both the Who and Hendrix ensures that the majority of their releases have minimal value in comparison with those of their labelmates.

Among the Who releases, exceptions to this rule include the very desirable mono edition of the 1967 album *The Who Sell Out* (613 002) and the briefly available *Direct Hits* (613 006) compilation, as well as the single "The Last Time"/"Under My Thumb" (604 006), which was cut and on the streets within days of songwriters Mick Jagger and Keith Richards' arrest on drug charges. Funds from the release were intended to be donated to a release fund for the pair; when the charges (and consequences) proved less serious than originally feared, the single was quietly withdrawn.

Hendrix's greatest Track rarities also revolve around mono pressings of his LPs, with the double *Electric Ladyland* (612 008/009) also much sought after, spread across two separate LPs, *Part One* (612 010) and *Part Two* (612 011).

Even less likely to be encountered, however, is a compilation album prepared in 1971 as a successor to the hits-oriented *Smash Hits* (612 004). *Electric Hendrix* (2856 002) offered a collection of worthy album cuts, plus a reprise of the earlier set's "The Burning of the Midnight Lamp," but the release was withdrawn before copies reached the stores. It is now considered Track's rarest LP release, and might even be scarcer than Track's rarest single, "Midsummer Night's Scene."

Among Hendrix's 45s, the original picture-sleeve issue of 1970's posthumous "Voodoo Chile" single (2095 001)—Track's third chart-topper in three years—is a good find. On first printings, the Hendrix portrait extends to the edge of the sleeve; reprints have a white border. Two releases in 1971, "Angel" (2094 007) and "Gypsy Eyes" (2094 010—with picture sleeve), are also tricky to find.

One extremely popular aspect of the original Track is its penchant for compilations. In 1969 it issued the *House That Track Built* sampler (613 016); the follow-ing year, the label inaugurated a 14-LP series serving up past LPs and singles at an irresistibly budget price of around $2.00 at that time. With every edition packaged in nearly identical plain sleeves, the Backtrack series (2407 001-014) opened with two collections of Track singles—Hendrix and the Who were included, of course, but so were some lesser-known gems. (*Backtrack Seven* also took this format.)

The next three volumes were split between Hendrix and the Who, one side apiece on each album. *Backtrack Six* returned to the "mixed bag" concept with licensed cuts by the Sandpipers, the Debonaires, the Parliaments, and the Precisions; six more releases, in November 1970, then inaugurated the wholesale reissue of "classic" albums by Hendrix, the Who (two titles apiece), Arthur Brown, and at Keith Moon's insistence, American comedian Murray Roman's *You Can't Beat People Up . . .* set, licensed from Tetragrammaton (*Backtrack 13*).

Interestingly, several of these albums were presented in their now-unfashionable mono format. This is a disappointment for fans hoping to update their original purchases with nicely priced stereo versions, but it's a boon for latter-day collectors seeking Hendrix's *Are You Experienced* (*Backtrack 10*) in glorious mono.

The final Backtrack release is also very popular today: *The Ox* (Backtrack 14) compiled all of the songs that the late John Entwistle had contributed to past Who albums and (more usually) B-sides onto one disc—some people call it their favorite Who album.

Track was at its peak between 1967–71; releases thereafter tended to revolve around the Who and the band members' solo activities, with only a handful of other releases making it out—Dutch rock band Golden Earring was the most successful, and a 1973 single by John Otway and Wild Willy Barrett, "Misty Mountain" (2094 111), is the rarest (a 1976 release by the same duo, "Louisa on a Horse"—2094 133—is also of note). Both were produced by Pete Townshend, for inclusion on an Otway-Barrett LP that was in the planning stages for some three years. When Track finally announced, in 1976, that it had no intention of issuing the LP, the duo launched their own label, Ex-Tracked,

TEN TOP COLLECTIBLES

Track Records (Beyond Hendrix and the Who)

"Accidents"—Thunderclap Newman (UK Track 2094 001—7-inch, 1970)

"Desdemona"—John's Children (UK Track 604 003—7-inch, picture sleeve, 1967)

"Desdemona"—Marsha Hunt (UK Track 604 034—7-inch, 1969)

"Devil's Grip"—Crazy World of Arthur Brown (UK Track 604 008—7-inch, 1967)

"Follow Me"—Eire Apparent (UK Track 604 019—7-inch, 1967)

"If I Had a Ribbon Bow"—Fairport Convention (UK Track 604 020—7-inch, 1967)

"Midsummer Night's Scene"—John's Children (UK Track 604 005—Withdrawn 7-inch, 1967)

"Murder Man"—Otway-Barrett (UK Track 2094 111—7-inch, 1971)

"Sing Songs of Love"—Cherry Smash (UK Track 604 017—7-inch, 1967)

"Walk on Gilded Splinters"—Marsha Hunt (UK Track 604 030—7-inch, 1969)

and sold so many copies of their homemade debut album that Track's own parent label, Polydor, picked them up—and scored an immediate Top 30 hit!

The Who's final Track releases, meanwhile, were 1973's "5.15" single (2094 115) and 1974's *Odds and Sods* compilation (2406 116). That year also saw an attempt to revive the old Backtrack series with the *Track Allsorts* series, but this has yet to take off among collectors.

Soldiering on under new owners, Track enjoyed a flurry of activity in 1977, with New York band Johnny Thunders and the Heartbreakers; the label's most recent manifestation, in 2000, brought an album by Mad for the Racket, formed by ex-Damned/Lords of the New Church guitarist Brian James and the MC5's Wayne Kramer (TRK 1004).

Transatlantic

Britain's most respected folk label, Transatlantic, was formed by Nat Joseph in 1961, and launched with Dr. Keith Cameron's *Live with Love* (TRA 101) LP. Over the next three years, a selective, but always high-quality, release schedule included Harvey

Andrews' *A Most Peculiar Man* EP (TRA 113); debut albums by Bert Jansch (*Bert Jansch*—TRA 125) and John Renbourne (*John Renbourne*—TRA 135); Tony Britton and Isla Cameron (*Songs of Love, Lust and Loose Living*—TRA 105); Annie Ross (*Loguerhythms*—TRA 107); and the Ian Campbell Folk Group (*Across the Hills* TRA 118).

The label's taste for more esoteric territory brought the arrival of comedienne Sheila Hancock (*Putting out the Dustbin*—TRA 106) and blues legend Alexis Korner's Blues Incorporated (*Red Hot from Alex*—TRA 117). Transatlantic also handled the UK distribution rights for the American label Folkways.

Such avidly collected acts as Pentangle, Gordon Giltrap, the Humblebums (featuring comedian Billy Connolly and Gerry "Baker Street" Rafferty), Stefan Grossman, and Lindisfarne's Alan Hull came aboard during the late '60s, with Ralph McTell's *Spiral Staircase* (TRA 177) spinning off one of the label's best remembered songs, the anthem "Streets of London"—astonishingly, it would not appear on a single until a 1974 re-recording (UK Reprise K14380); of course it brought McTell his first hit.

Launching a 45s-only imprint, Big T., Transatlantic's first single was issued in 1967, the Purple Gang's psychedelic jugband classic "Granny Takes a Trip" (BIG 101); it was not a hit but is avidly pursued, together with a follow-up, "Kiss Me Goodnight Sally Green" (BIG 111), and an album, *The Purple Gang Strikes* (TRA 174).

The teenage brother-sister duo Sallyangie, featuring Mike and Sally Oldfield, issued a rare single, "Two Ships" (BIG 126), and an album, *Children of the Sun* (TRA 176); the album was reissued (without its original gatefold sleeve) in 1976, following Mike Oldfield's breakthrough hit, *Tubular Bells*.

Transatlantic's most controversial signings, however, were drawn from the depths of the hippie underground. First came the Fugs, the wild New York act who released two albums, *Tenderness Junction* (TRA 180) and *It Crawled into My Hand, Honest* (TRA 181), along with the single "Crystal Liaison." Transatlantic then recruited the Deviants, a similarly anarchic group fronted by journalist Mick Farren. The Deviants had already cut two very rare albums for the Underground Impresarios and Stable labels (*Ptoof*—IMP 1 and *Disposable*—SLP 7001—respectively); their third album, simply titled *The Deviants* (TRA 204) is one of the great Transatlantic rarities, as is a Farren solo album, *Mona (The Carnivorous Circus)* (TRA 212).

Into the 1970s, Transatlantic continued to leapfrog wildly across the spectrum. In 1973, the Portsmouth Sinfonia, the world's self-professed worst orchestra, issued the astonishingly inept *Plays the Popular Classics* (TRA 275) album, its modern collector appeal bolstered by the presence of Brian Eno in the ranks.

The much-loved metal band Stray issued six very collectible albums prior to decamping for Dawn in 1975—keep an eye out for its solitary Big T. single, "Our Song" (BIG 141). Gifted songwriter Simon Boswell issued 1975's in-demand *Mind Parasites* album (TRA 305) and Wild Willy Barrett, better known for his partnership with oddball John Otway, cut an unreleased solo album in 1975.

Transatlantic's final successes came in 1976–77. Punk comedians Alberto y Los Trios Paranoias issued a pair of albums during 1976–77, and one single, "Dread Jaws" (BIG 541). Metro featured Peter Godwin and Duncan Browne, whose 1976 debut album

TEN TOP COLLECTIBLES

Mick Farren/Deviants

All Screwed Up (UK Stiff LAST 4—EP, 1978)

The Deviants—The Deviants (UK Transatlantic TRA 204—LP, 1969)

Disposable—The Deviants (UK Stable SLP 7001—LP, gatefold sleeve, 1968)

"Half Price Drinks" (UK Logo GO 321—7-inch, 1979)

Human Garbage (Live . . . 1984)—The Deviants (UK Psycho 25—LP, 1984)

"Lost Johnny" (Ork 1980—7-inch, 1976)

Mona (The Carnivorous Circus) (Transatlantic TRA 212—LP, 1970)

Partial Recall—The Deviants (UK Drop Out DOCD 1989—CD, 1992)

Ptooff!—The Deviants (UK Underground Impresarios IMP 1—LP, 1967)

"You Got to Hold On"—The Deviants (UK Stable STA 5601—7-inch, 1968)

(TRA 340) is best remembered for the single "Criminal World" (BIG 560), which was later covered by David Bowie on his *Let's Dance* album. And the Brighouse and Rastrick Brass Band's arrangement of the traditional "Floral Dance" (BIG 548) gave the label its biggest-ever hit when the song reached No. 2 in late 1977.

Transatlantic folded soon after, to be absorbed into the Logo label in 1978. The Albertos and a returning Mick Farren were among the new concern's earliest issues; there were also a number of classic Transatlantic reissues, including the appearance of a single, "Return of Kong" (GO 105), from the Wild Willy Barrett album.

Further Reading: *The Transatlantic Story* (booklet within box set of the same name—Castle, 1999)

Trey

Originally based in Lake Charles, La., Trey relocated to Los Angeles in November 1959, when owner Eddie Shuler sold the label to Lee Hazlewood and Lester Sill. It is their presence for which Trey is best known today; that, and for the three early Phil Spector productions that further dignify the discography—the Spectors Three's "I Really Do" (Trey 3001—the label's first 45, in 1959) and "My Heart Stood Still" (3005), and Kell Osborne's "The Bells of St. Mary's" (3006), popularly regarded as the public debut of Spector's Wall of Sound technique.

Trey was also responsible for comedians Rowan and Martin's 1960 *At Work* LP (TLP 901). That aside, the Trey catalog is best distinguished by its obscurity, with the LP catalog including sets by Clingman Clan (TLP 900), Lloyd Ellis (902), and Bonanza star Dan Blocker (903). Trey releases, then, are pursued as much for their rarity as for their contents.

Trey folded in 1961, when Sill joined Spector in forming the legendary Philles label.

Triumph

Triumph was launched in 1960 by mercurial maverick producer Joe Meek, in association with the classical label Saga. As part of producer Dennis Preston's Lansdowne Road studio set-up, Meek currently had three singles in the British Top Ten, by Mike Preston, Marty Wilde, and the chart-topping Emile Ford and the Checkmates. Impressed by his credentials, Saga offered him a 50 percent share in the newly founded Triumph.

Given a free hand in choosing the musicians he would record, Meek surrounded himself with talented performers, though few of them actually were musicians. John Leyton was an established actor and teen heartthrob; West Indian–born Ricky Wayne was a potential Mr. Universe bodybuilder; Smiley was the precocious four-year-old son of Parlophone recording star Joy (of Joy and Dave). But Meek also signed an exotic Ceylonese jazz vocalist named Yolanda, and a club band called the Cavaliers, whose years on the skiffle circuit had turned them into a living jukebox. (The Cavaliers' original audition tape, released on RPM's *Triumph Sessions: Work in Progress*—RPM 121—CD collection, includes covers of Johnny Kidd, Gene Vincent, the Everly Brothers, and Frankie Ford).

Proclaiming itself "the first label to produce discs exclusively for the Juke Box generation," Triumph launched in February 1960, with two releases: Peter Jay and the Bluemen's "Just Too Late" (RGM 1000) and Ken Rodd and the Cavaliers' "Magic Wheel" (RGM 1001). Joy and Dave's "Let's Go See Gran'ma" (RGM 1002) and Yolanda's "With This Kiss" (RGM 1007) followed in March. The successful Triumph Pop Package tour took the label's name on the road; the 15-minute *It's a Triumph* weekly radio show on Radio Luxembourg blasted it into Europe's living rooms. The show's theme—the Flee-Rakkers' adaptation of the traditional "Greensleeves," updated as "Green Jeans" (Triumph RGM 1008)—gave the label its first hit that spring.

Plans for Triumph's first LP release came unglued, however. Test pressings of Meek's own electronic symphony *I Hear a New World* (TRX ST 9000) were produced, and a four-track promo EP (RGX ST 5000) was mailed out to solicit media attention. None was forthcoming and the LP was canceled, to remain in the archive until 1993 (RPM 103); with just 99 copies pressed, the EP is now regarded among the rarest of all Joe Meek recordings.

Triumph, too, was on its last legs. Two new singles, Rick Wayne's "Hot Chick Ac'Roo" (RGM 1009)

TEN TOP COLLECTIBLES

Joe Meek Productions

Away from It All—The Tornadoes (Decca LK 4552—LP, 1963)

"Diggin' for Gold"— David John and the Mood (UK Parlophone R5301—7-inch, 1965)

Dream of the West—The Outlaws (UK HMV CLP 1489—LP, 1961)

"I Take It That We're Through"—The Riot Squad (UK Pye 7N 17092—7-inch, 1966)

"Jack the Ripper"—Screaming Lord Sutch (UK Decca F11598—7-inch, 1964)

"The Kennedy March"—Joe Meek (UK Decca F11796—7-inch, 1963)

"Magic Star"— Kenny Hollywood (Decca F11546—7-inch, 1962)

"March of the Spacemen"—The Thunderbolts (Dot 16496—7-inch, 1963)

Tom Jones—Tom Jones (UK Columbia SEG 8464— EP, 1965)

"Whatcha Gonna Do Baby?"—Jason Eddy and the Centremen (UK Parlophone R5388—7-inch, 1965)

and George Chakiris's "I'm Always Chasing Rainbows" (RGM 1010), both flopped, but worse, the Saga label was running into financial trouble. In May, even as Michael Cox's "Angela Jones" (RGM 1011) made the UK Top Ten, Triumph closed its doors.

Meek promptly licensed the catalog to the Top Rank label, which reissued "Green Jeans" (JAR 431) and "Hot Chick Ac'Roo" (JAR 432), together with the projected RGM 1012, John Leyton's "Tell Laura I Love Her" (JAR 426). Meek relaunched himself as an independent producer, and over the next seven years, scored hits with Leyton, Ritchie Blackmore's Outlaws, Mike Berry, Ian Gregory, the Tornadoes, the Honeycombs, and more. A victim of severe depression, Meek committed suicide after murdering his landlady on February 3, 1967.

Further Reading: *The Legendary Joe Meek,* by John Repsch (Woodford House, 1989)

UK

UK was launched by the most brilliant of all English pop entrepreneurs, Jonathan King, a proven hit-maker with a stream of usually pseudonymous smashes

under his belt. After stints at Decca, for whom he discovered Genesis, and at Bell, to whom he introduced the Bay City Rollers, UK kicked off in Britain during the summer of 1972, scoring hit 45s almost immediately with Terry Dactyl and the Dinosaurs' "Seaside Shuffle" (UK 5—Dactyl himself was future Stiff Records star Jona Lewie), 10cc's "Donna" (6), and Shag's "Loop Di Love" (7—Shag was another of King's own aliases). A hit reissue of Roy C.'s 1965 oldie "Shotgun Wedding" (19) followed.

It was an impressive debut, yet it was only the beginning. Although 10cc would become the label's sole truly regular hit-maker (King himself notwithstanding), few observers were surprised when UK closed the year with one of the highest hits-to-releases ratios in British chart history. This proud record would decline as time passed, but King's ear for hit records (whether or not they actually became hits) remained unerring.

Simon Turner, a protégé of David Bowie's then-wife Angela, was introduced with a cover of Bowie's own ode to the lady, "Prettiest Star" (44), while King's long-established love of slightly skewed bubblegum

TEN TOP COLLECTIBLES

Jonathan King

"Everyone's Gone to the Moon" (Parrot 9774—7-inch, 1965)

"It's Good News Week"—Hedgehoppers Anonymous (Decca F12241—7-inch, 1965)

"It's the Same Old Song"—The Weathermen (UK B&C CB 139—7-inch, 1971)

"Johnny Reggae"—The Piglets (UK Bell 1180—7-inch, 1972)

"Just Like a Woman" (Parrot 3005—7-inch, 1966)

"Leap Up, and Down Wave Your Knickers in the Air"—St. Cecilia (UK Polydor 2058 104—7-inch, 1971)

"Lick a Smurp for Christmas"—Father Abraphart and the Smurfs (UK Petrol GAS 1—Flexidisc, 1978)

"Loop Di Love"—Shag (UK 45-49007—7-inch, 1972)

Or Then Again... (Parrot PAS 71013—Stereo LP, 1967)

"Sugar Sugar"—Sakharin (UK RCA 2064—7-inch, 1971)

---

found an outlet in his Bubblerock alias. A single, mutating the Rolling Stones' "Satisfaction" (53), brought another UK hit, and paved the way for UK's first LP release, the ominously titled _Bubblerock Is Here to Stay_ (UKAL 1001).

That set would receive a US release (53101) in the new year, when King opened UK's American wing. He celebrated the new venture with a now–highly prized promotional EP modestly titled _What's So Great About UK Records?_ It featured a spoken history of the label, plus excerpts from four of the label's maiden releases: by 10cc, Ricky Wilde, Tina Harvey, and Roy C. Strangely, though, it eschewed King's own next release, "Tall Order for a Short Guy" (49102).

Previously released in Britain by Decca (UK's distributors until 1975), this was one of several King 45s to remain exclusive to the American operation, alongside "Mary My Love" (49014), "The Kung Fu Anthem" (49018), and a rival version of the Bay City Rollers' "The Way You Look Tonight" (49034). A number of other US releases on the UK label were unique to that territory, including Kenny's "The Bump" (49032), a British hit on the RAK label.

None of these made any impact in the US, but no sooner had 10cc's "Rubber Bullets" (36) given UK its first British No. 1 in spring 1973, than it gave the label its US chart debut too (49015). 10cc ultimately released eight UK singles in Britain and four in the United States, before departing for the Mercury label in 1975; the two LPs that the group recorded for UK, _10cc_ (53105/UKAL 1005) and _Sheet Music_ (53107/UKAL 1007), were followed by the compilation _100cc_ (53110/UKAL 1010), which matched each of the British singles with its non-LP B-side.

Oddly, however, the UK label's first truly enormous hit would come not from its best-known artists, but from one of its most obscure, First Class. The note-perfect Beach Boys pastiche "Beach Baby" (49022/UK 66) was originally intended as a simple one-off; in fact, First Class survived to record a full LP (53108/UKAL 1008) and two further 45s.

Crossing over from the US Bell label, Lobo's irresistible "I'd Love You to Want Me" (77) and Australian Kevin Johnson's somewhat grating "Rock 'n' Roll I Gave You the Best Years of My Life" (84) were both sizeable British hits in 1975, the year in which UK

A distinctly royal appearance for Jonathan Kings' UK label.

celebrated its 100th single release with 10cc's "Waterfall" (100), a B-side revived to promote the aforementioned *100cc* collection. This is the rarest of all the group's UK label releases, though legend insists that there is one other, even scarcer, 45, a "bleeped" version of "The Worst Band in the World" (36), issued to radio in lieu of a conventional, self-censored take that rhymed the word "hit" with a none-too-subtle "shhhh. . ."

King himself brought the label one of its biggest hits in 1976, with a cover of the George Baker Selection's "Una Paloma Blanca" (105—a US release appeared on Big Tree, 16046). He was also behind Sound 9418's "In the Mood" (121) and 100 Ton and a Feather's delightful remake of Tavares's "It Only Takes a Minute" (135), UK's last hit before switching distribution to Phonogram. There, the hit business was briefly resumed with 53rd and 3rd's "Chick a Boom" (2012 002), but within the year King had folded UK, leaving behind a catalog that remains one

of the most undervalued of the age. Much, it has been said, like King's own output over the years.

Vanguard

Though it would subsequently become (and is certainly characterized as) the most important folk label in US music history, the Vanguard label was initially launched to pursue founders Maynard and Seymour Solomon's love of jazzmusic. Utilizing a $10,000 advance from their father, Benjamin, the Solomon brothers established two labels to cater to their tastes, Vanguard and the Bach Guild, the latter of which was an ambitious project intended to release recordings of all of its classical composer namesake's choral work.

Original Vanguard releases, in keeping with industry standards, were issued on 10-inch LPs. Between 1953–55, Vanguard released some 20 different jazz albums in this format, including well-received and respected titles by Vic Dickenson,

Sir Charles Thompson, Joe Newman, Buck Clayton, Don Elliott, and Ruby Braff—many produced by the legendary John Hammond. However, a glimmer of the label's future came in the form of Brother John Sellers' *Sings Blues and Folk Songs* collection in 1954, and in 1956, Vanguard released its first album by Pete Seeger and the Weavers (9001)—a courageous move at a time when the group's political stance saw them all but boycotted by the rest of the industry. (Paul Robeson, another blacklisted performer, joined the Weavers at the label.)

Releases by Martha Schlamme and Cisco Houston followed, and by the end of the 1950s, Vanguard was the biggest folk game in town. In his *Follow the Sun* autobiography, Jac Holzman, head of the then-fledgling Elektra Records, recalls, "In the early days [Elektra launched itself as a specialist folk label in 1950] my competition had been Moses Asch at Folkways. [But] as Elektra grew . . . we moved beyond Folkways, Tradition, and Riverside. By the late '50s, we were nosing level with Vanguard." Elektra might even have sneaked ahead, but for one crucial difference. Vanguard had Joan Baez.

Now based at Columbia, John Hammond had already rejected Baez (or been rejected by her—the story shifts, depending upon who is telling it) when she first arrived at Vanguard's Greenwich Village offices. It was Hammond's superiors' subsequent dismay that led, in swift succession, to Columbia's recruitment of Carolyn Hester and Bob Dylan; the latter was the only other figure on the local folk scene with any hope of outselling Baez, and the former was one of the few who was even remotely capable of out-singing her.

That Hester's first husband, Richard Fariña, would later marry Baez's sister, Mimi (while Dylan, who guested on Hester's first Columbia album, soon became Baez's consort), is indicative of just how compact the folk scene was at that time. That the Fariñas would then join Baez at Vanguard, on the other hand, proves the wisdom of the Solomons. What nobody could have imagined then was how time would bear out so many other of their signings.

Spread across three albums (including the posthumous *Memories*—9263), the Fariñas' dulcimer-driven folk-rock and proto-psychedelic imagery, were undeniably eccentric by contemporary folk standards. By Vanguard's standards, however, eccentricity was the spice of life. Few of the label's signings ever opted for convention and normalcy; indeed, to describe Vanguard as a folk-oriented concern is to utterly belittle the sheer adventurousness that was the Solomons' true nature.

This adventurousness is reflected in the label's modern collectibility. Many of Vanguard's best-known releases have since been reissued by the label's current owners, the Welk Music Group, with the British Ace and Italian Comet picking up sundry lesser-known classics.

The value of original LP pressings has only risen since the restoration of such oddities as two LPs worth of electronic tomfoolery by Perrey-Kingsley (and two more by Jean-Jacques Perrey alone). Also valued are a pair of scratchy psychedelic monsters from Circus Maximus (featuring a pre-"Mr Bojangles" Jerry Jeff Walker) and one-offs by such unknowns as Steve Gillete (9251), Elizabeth (6501), the Far Cry (6501), Listening (6504), and the Serpent Power (9252—the band was led by poet David Meltzer, author of a very rare solo album in his own right, 6519). The 45s by these bands are equally highly prized.

Also worth watching for are three albums by the Frost, a Detroit hard rock band fronted by future Lou Reed/Alice Cooper/Peter Gabriel sideman Dick Ezrin. (A fourth LP, *Early Frost*—79392—appeared in 1978, years after the band's demise.)

A handful of releases by guitar virtuoso John Fahey have also become increasingly popular since his death in early 2001; the interest has also spilled over to Fahey's own Tahoma label, home to some excellent early recordings by another future Vanguard artist, Robbie Basho.

The Fariñas' collectibility, too, has been enhanced in recent years, via the publication of author David Hajdu's *Positively 4th Street* (FSG, 2001) and Mimi's tragic death just months later. An album recorded in London in 1963, by husband Richard and Erik

VMD · 6567
◀ STEREO ▶
Also Playable Mono

Baldwin and Leps

One of Vanguard's more eclectic late '60s releases.

Von Schmidt (Folklore F-LEUT 7), has long been much in-demand for the presence of a pseudonymous Bob "Blind Boy Grunt" Dylan; it is now equally sought after for its maker's own magic.

Vanguard's biggest names, of course, are Joan Baez, Buffy Sainte-Marie, and Country Joe and the Fish. All three artists' catalogs bristle with rarities, including copies of Country Joe and the Fish's *Feel Like I'm Fixin' to Die* (79266) LP, containing a free Fish Game poster, and Baez's "Pack Up Your Sorrows" single (35040), an excerpt from a rock LP she was recording with Richard Fariña at the time of his death in 1966, and which she abandoned immediately after.

Also of considerable interest are Vanguard's live documents of the Newport Folk Festival, issued in 1959, 1960, 1963, and 1964. The range of artists spread across these discs tells the story not only of the folk boom, but also the blues and bluegrass revivals that grew alongside it. Three volumes (2053-55) cover the 1959 event, and they include Joan Baez's first-ever released recording, a duet with Bob Gibson; two LPs covered the 1960 event (2087/88—a third disc was issued by Elektra, EKL 189). The 1963 festival brought six separate albums (9144-49), two of which feature otherwise unavailable Bob Dylan material, and 1964 delivered up seven LPs (9180-86), highlighted by debut performances from Buffy Sainte-Marie and Judy Roderick.

Roderick's *Woman Blue* LP (9197) is another seldom-seen gem that has since been reissued on CD; unfortunately, there is still no sign of an earlier LP, alluded to in the *Woman Blue* liner notes, and damnably elusive, apparently at any price. Thankfully, those same liner notes suggest it isn't very good, so even Roderick completists probably aren't missing much.

The early '70s were a time of major change at Vanguard. Of course the folk boom had ended; more damagingly, the artists who had sustained it had also

TEN TOP COLLECTIBLES

Joan Baez

"Banks of the Ohio" (Vanguard 35012 — 7-inch, 1962)

Blessed Are (Vanguard VSQ 40001/2 — Quad LP, 1971)

Come from the Shadows (A&M QU 54339 — Quad LP, 1974)

Diamonds and Rust (Nautilus NR 12 — Audiophile LP, 1980)

In San Francisco 1958 (Fantasy 5015 — LP, 1962)

Joan Baez (Vanguard VSD 2077 — Stereo LP, 1960)

"Pack Up Your Sorrows" (Vanguard 35040 — 7-inch, 1966)

"Silent Running" (Decca 32890 — 7-inch, 1971)

"There but for Fortune" (Vanguard 35031 — 7-inch, picture sleeve, 1965)

Volume 2 (Vanguard VSD 2097 — Stereo LP, 1961)

departed—Baez for A&M, Sainte-Marie for RCA, and so on. Rather than attempt to live off past glories, Vanguard completely changed direction, delving into the disco boom and rapidly establishing itself as a major power in that field. Players Association and Poussez (along with jazzmen Larry Coryell, Elvin Jones, and Clark Terry) represent some of Vanguard's greatest successes from this period. Moving into the early '80s, Alisha maintains a high-profile artist today.

In 1986, the Solomons sold Vanguard to the Welk Group; it remains as active as ever today, not only remastering and reissuing past classics, but also nurturing a strong roster of contemporary artists that might well prove as important to future generations as the label's previous output is to today's collectors. **Further Reading:** *Positively 4th Street: The Lives and Times of Joan Baez, Bob Dylan, Mimi Baez Fariña, and Richard Fariña,* by David Hajdu (Farrar, Straus and Giroux, 2001)

Vee-Jay

To most general collectors, the Vee-Jay story is dominated by the Beatles, the unknown British band that the label picked up in 1963, and whose early output sustained the company through a total of ten 45s, one EP, and eight LPs. No mean feat considering the label only had 16 songs to work with.

However, to obsess on the soon-to-be-Fabs obscures a decade's worth of other Vee-Jay recordings, dating back to 1953, when the label was established by Jimmy Bracken and DJ Vivian Carter, owners of a record store in Gary, Ind.; the new venture took its name from the husband-and-wife team's first initials.

Vee-Jay's first two singles were Jimmy Reed's "High and Lonesome" (100) and the Spaniels' "Baby It's You" (101). Both were leased by the Chicago-based Chance label, with the Spaniels scoring an R&B Top Ten hit that fall. (A red-vinyl re-pressing of the Spaniels 45 was included in the 1993 Vee-Jay box set.)

A second Spaniels single, "Goodnight Sweetheart, Goodnight" (107), performed even better, prompting further expansion. With A&R man Calvin Carter (Vivian's brother) and business manager Ewart Abner on board, Vee-Jay scored its first R&B chart-topper in late 1956, with Jay McShann's "Hands Off" (155), and

One of Vee-Jay's more inventive insertions into the Beatlemania market.

its first crossover hit just weeks later, with the El Dorados' "At My Front Door" (147). Another major hit that year was the Dells' "Oh What a Night" (204).

Vee-Jay albums from these early years are uniformly difficult to find; between 1958–62, the label issued some 50 R&B/blues albums (plus a similar number of jazz LPs), including sets by all the established hit-makers. Bluesmen Jimmy Reed, Gene Allison, and John Lee Hooker also released some now-legendary recordings on Vee-Jay through the late '50s, with several of the attendant 45s, coincidentally or otherwise, featuring in the early repertoires of many British beat boom acts. Indeed, Reed's "Take Out Some Insurance on Me" (314) was recorded by the Beatles, at one of the group's 1961 sessions with Tony Sheridan.

By the end of the 1950s, Vee-Jay was firmly established among the biggest players on the R&B scene, with a slew of pop crossover hits to its name: the Impressions' "For Your Precious Love" (280), Roscoe Gordon's "Just a Little Bit" (332), Jerry Butler's

"He Will Break Your Heart" (354), Dee Clark's "Raindrops" (383), and Gene Chandler's "Duke of Earl" (416) among them. The Abner subsidiary (named, of course, for Ewart Abner, now label president) was similarly successful.

Not until 1962, however, did Vee-Jay move into the pop market directly, with the arrival of the Four Seasons and Australian vocalist Frank Ifield. (A third new signing, the sensational English singer Alma Cogan, had an album scheduled [1068] but canceled.)

"Sherry," the Four Seasons' label debut (456) was the first of three pop chart-toppers for Vee-Jay, while the accompanying album (SR 1053) was the label's first Top 30 long-player; Ifield's "I Remember You" (457) reached No. 5. While neither act remained Vee-Jay artists for long (Ifield scored just one further hit before moving to Capitol in 1963, and the Four Seasons moved to Philips in 1964), their presence confirmed the label's future collectibility, regardless of John, Paul, George, and Ringo.

The most common "rarities" in these catalogs are label varieties, an art that has taken on scientific proportions in recent years. First-pressing Vee-Jay 45s by both performers bore a black label with a rainbow ring and an oval logo; re-pressings feature all-black labels. Also cherished among labelologists are the handful of printer's errors that inhabit the catalogs.

More concrete scarcities include a Four Seasons single credited to the Wonder Who, issued following the band's departure ("Peanuts"—717), and a one-sided promo of the same song (901); the group also released a pair of EPs (1-901, 1-902) during 1962–63.

Ifield collectors, of whom there are many, are less well-served by regular releases, but moving into Vee-Jay's Beatles era, the yodeling hero suddenly finds himself one half of one of the most legendary releases of all time, as Vee-Jay combined a selection of his hits with a handful of Beatles smashes to create one of the label's most in-demand collectibles.

The basic Vee-Jay Beatles catalog comprises the singles "Please Please Me"/"Ask Me Why" (498), "From Me to You"/"Thank You Girl" (522), a pairing of both past A-sides (581) and "Do You Want to Know a Secret"/"Thank You Girl" (587); an EP comprising "Misery"/"A Taste of Honey"/"Ask Me Why"/"Anna" (1-903); and a solitary LP, *Introducing the Beatles* (1062)—issued in two versions, one featuring "Love Me Do" and "P.S. I Love You," the other replacing those two with "Ask Me Why" and "Anna."

Among the 7-inch releases, label variations, an embarrassing misspelling (the Beattles), promo editions, picture sleeves, and practically any other scrap of identifiable minutiae have swollen that catalog to 45 appreciably different—and eminently collectible and valuable—records. And that is without even beginning to consider the "We Wish You a Merry Christmas" give away that both Vee-Jay and the Tollie subsidiary handed out during the 1964–65 festive season; or the probably fraudulent (but possibly not) "Ask Me Why"/"Anna" coupling (Spec DJ 8) that completes the catalog.

The same process of microscopic inspection has isolated at least 15 different versions of the *Introducing* . . . album, with Vee-Jay's own release

policy responsible for at least some of the fuss, having itself issued three separate variations on the set—all of which have been avidly counterfeited over the years.

Fascinating though these releases all are, even more fun can be had with some of the other uses that Vee-Jay found for its Beatles gold mine. The spoken-word *Hear the Beatles Tell All* (202) LP, and the re-titled *Introducing* set, *Songs, Pictures and Stories of the Fabulous Beatles* (1092), are, if not common, at least familiar sights among collectors.

However, with two sets of devoted fans chasing them, copies of *The Beatles vs. the Four Seasons* (DX 30), a double album featuring *Introducing the Beatles* and *Golden Hits of the Four Seasons* (1065), are very seldom seen, while most encountered copies of *Jolly What! The Beatles and Frank Ifield on Stage* (1085) also turn out to be counterfeits. If you're an average Beatles fan, ownership of a genuine example would probably double the value of your collection on the spot.

The Beatles and the Four Seasons gave Vee-Jay the biggest hits it had ever known. But behind the scenes, storm clouds were moving in.

None of the label's other new signings (or surviving veterans, for that matter) were selling—releases by Mango Jones, Mason Williams, Damita Jo, Dick Gregory, Sam Fletcher, Hoyt Axton, Georgia Carr, and even Little Richard, failed to take off.

Further attempts to mine the Beatles songbook, with the Merseyboys' *15 Greatest Songs of the Beatles* soundalike set (1101), passed by unnoticed. Another Beatles tie-in (albeit released four years too early), Billy Preston's *Greatest Hits* (1142), was similarly overlooked. The Castaway Strings were never more than a weak facsimile of Capitol's Hollyridge Strings. More and more planned new releases were canceled, never to appear.

The label was deeply in debt, to manufacturers, to artists, and to the IRS. Undiscovered until it was too late, embezzlement wiped several hundred thousand dollars off the company's books. There were rumors, too, that label employees had been involved in the now-illegal practice of payola—financial gifts to DJs,

TEN TOP COLLECTIBLES

Vee-Jay

"Ask Me Why"—The Beatles (Vee-Jay Spec DJ 8—7-inch promo, 1964)

"Baby It's You"—The Spaniels (Vee-Jay 101—Red-vinyl 7-inch, 1953)

"Bobby Sox Baby"—The Hi Liters (Vee-Jay 184—7-inch, 1955)

"Fool's Prayer"—The Five Echoes (Vee-Jay 156—7-inch, 1955)

"For Your Precious Love"—Jerry Butler and the Impressions (Vee-Jay 280—7-inch, 1958)

"High and Lonesome"—Jimmy Reed (Vee-Jay 100—Red-vinyl 7-inch, 1953)

"Please Please Me"—The Beatles (Vee-Jay 498—7-inch, brackets label, 1963)

"Please Please Me"—The Beattles (Vee-Jay 498—7-inch, misspelled label, 1963)

Souvenir of Their Visit to America—The Beatles (Vee-Jay 1-903DJ—Promo EP, 1964)

"Tell the World"—The Dells (Vee-Jay 134—Red-vinyl 7-inch, 1955)

---

in return for airplay. Even before Vee-Jay's license to print Beatle-shaped money expired, it was common knowledge through the industry that the label was faltering.

Vee-Jay's final album was issued in late 1965, and in many ways, it encapsulates the entire sorry saga. Vee-Jay's marketing department was no stranger to deceptive titles—the Beatles side of the *Jolly What! The Beatles and Frank Ifield on Stage* set, after all, promised a lot more than a rehash of half a dozen studio cuts could deliver, and the label apparently received a number of complaints on that score.

The label was not going to make the same mistake again, then—spin *The Four Seasons Recorded Live on Stage* (1154) and the barrage of screaming would appear to prove that here, at last, is a bona fide document of a classic Four Seasons concert. But unless the band simply sat onstage as somebody spun their records, while an audience shrieked for its own unknown purposes, it is unlikely that the recordings came within a mile of even an empty auditorium.

Before we rush to condemn, however, let us remember that, within a year, both the Rolling Stones' *Got Live if You Want It!* and John's Children's *Orgasm* would have released similarly un-live "live" albums. Just as it was in signing the Beatles, Vee-Jay was simply a few steps ahead of the rest of the pack. It did the label no good, of course. Vee-Jay finally collapsed in May 1966, with a bankruptcy hearing issuing the coup de grace in August.

Randy Wood, Abner's successor as company president in 1963 (and the man who brought the Four Seasons to the label), and label comptroller Betty Chiapetta purchased the rights to the catalog the following year, albeit without either the Beatles or the Four Seasons. This material would leak out via various licensing deals through the 1970s (MGM's Mine subsidiary, active between 1970–71, was dedicated in large part to the Vee-Jay catalog), with Vee-Jay itself resuming production (again as a reissue label) around 1975.

Further Reading: *Celebrating 40 Years of Hits: The Vee-Jay Story* (booklet within CD box set of the same name—Vee-Jay, 1993)

"Bikini Girls with Machine Guns" (Enigma EPRO 253—12-inch promo, 1989)

"Fever" (UK Illegal 017—7-inch, full-band picture sleeve, 1980)

"Goo Goo Muck" (IRS 9021—Colored-vinyl 7-inch promo, 1981)

Gravest Hits (Illegal SP 501—12-inch, colored sleeves, 1979)

"Human Fly" (Vengeance 668—7-inch, 1978)

Lux (UK Windsong 4—numbered 3x12-inch box set, with T-shirt and book, 1991)

Off the Bone (UK Illegal ILP 012—White-label LP with different mix of "Drug Train," 1983)

Songs the Lord Taught Us (Illegal SP 007—LP, sleeve dated, 1979)

Stay Sick! (Enigma 268—Promo LP, 1990)

The Way I Walk (Vengeance 666—7-inch, 1978)

Vengeance

Several labels operated under this name during the punk era at the end of the 1970s. The best known is the US concern that released two early 45s by the Cramps. A UK Vengeance, meanwhile, issued the debut single by the Only Ones, "Lovers of Today" (UK Vengeance VEN 001).

Vertigo

Although the Vertigo imprint has been in use for over 30 years now, an easily identifiable warning of an impending heavy metal onslaught from the former Phonogram group of labels, its collectors concentrate on one era, and one era only—the four-year span during which Vertigo's label design displayed, indeed, a vertiginous swirl of black and white, which consumed one whole side of the label and which, when placed on the turntable, brought an entirely new dimension to watching a record go round.

Vertigo was launched in 1969 within the same flurry of progressive activity that prompted Pye to form the Dawn and Middle Earth imprints, EMI to create Harvest, and Decca to grow Nova. Immediately, however, Vertigo set itself apart—and not only via its choice of label design. The first 45 the label ever released, a frenetic rendering of Bo Diddley's "Who Do You Love?" by Juicy Lucy (V1), made the UK Top 20; the second release, by Black Sabbath, "Paranoid" (6059 010), hit the Top Five.

At a time when the progressive-rock movement was so furiously opposed to everything that the mainstream pop industry stood for—so opposed that some bands really did ask their audiences not to dance during the performance—Vertigo took two of the heaviest records, by the heaviest acts on the entire scene, and got them on *Top of the Pops*.

Of course, it was a fluke, and one that was seldom repeated during the life span of the swirl label. A second Juicy Lucy single, "Pretty Woman" (6059 015), reached No. 44, but that was it. Theoretically appealing releases by onetime '60s chart darlings Manfred Mann (in its Chapter Three phase), the follow-up hit-hunting Black Sabbath, the Sensational Alex Harvey Band, and Rod Stewart (yes, even Rod Stewart) made no impression whatsoever.

Move into the lesser-heralded réalms of Affinity, Beggars Opera, Warhorse, Assegai, Legend, Graham Bond, and Magick and Ronno (a short-lived combo

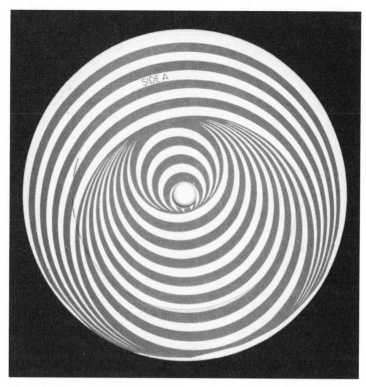

Stare at it long enough and you'll see why the label was called Vertigo.

formed by Mick Ronson around what would become David Bowie's Spiders from Mars), and without exception they disappeared without trace. They rank, today, among the rarest major-label metal 45s of all time.

They are joined in those rarified echelons by their long-playing contemporaries. Vertigo launched in 1969 with the simultaneous issue of albums by Colosseum (*Valentyne Suite*—VO 1), Juicy Lucy (*Juicy Lucy*—VO 2), and Manfred Mann (*Chapter Three: Volume One*—VO 3). Debuts by Stewart (VO 4), Sabbath (VO 5), and the little-known Cressida (VO 7) followed, before Vertigo adopted a new LP numbering system, the 6360 series, with Fairfield Parlour's *From Home to Home* (6360 001).

A total of 84 Vertigo albums were issued with the swirl label, of which a mere handful can even be loosely described as familiar today. Vertigo releases by Status Quo, Black Sabbath, Rod Stewart, the Sensational Alex Harvey Band, Gentle Giant, and Uriah Heep have each been re-pressed and reissued

on numerous occasions, and tend to attract lesser prices than efforts from, for example, Gracious, Magna Carta, May Blitz, Nucleus, Dr. Strangely Strange, and Clear Blue Sky.

However, even among these "superstars," there are items to watch for. Few of these later issues duplicated all the little extras for which original Vertigo releases were also prized—the gatefold and poster sleeves that decorated the first 74 releases, for example, or the lavish box and poster packaging that accompanied Sabbath's 1971 masterpiece, *Master of Reality* (6360 050). In addition, of course, the discontinuation of the swirl label in 1973 (it was replaced by a rather exciting spaceship design), removes even more allure.

The rarest Vertigo albums are, of course, those that sold the least copies at the time, a competition that was, apparently, won hands-down by Dr. Z. Having already released an obscure 45 on Fontana, "Lady Ladybird" (6007 023), Dr. Z. was discovered by Patrick Campbell-Lyons, whose own band, Nirvana, issued

TEN TOP COLLECTIBLES

Vertigo Swirl Albums

Asylum — Cressida (UK Vertigo 6360 025 — LP, 1971)

Ben — Ben (UK Vertigo 6360 052 — LP, 1971)

Changes — Catapilla (UK Vertigo 6360 074 — LP, 1972)

Clear Blue Sky — Clear Blue Sky (UK Vertigo 6360 013 — LP, 1970)

Gracious — Gracious (UK Vertigo 6360 002 — LP, 1970)

Red Boot — Legend (UK Vertigo 6360 019 — LP, 1971)

2nd of May — May Blitz (UK Vertigo 6360 037 — LP, 1971)

Space Hymns — Ramases (UK Vertigo 6360 046 — LP, 1971)

3 Parts to My Soul — Dr. Z. (UK Vertigo 6360 048 — LP, 1971)

Tudor Lodge — Tudor Lodge (UK Vertigo 6360 043 — LP, 1971)

its own very collectible LP and single on Vertigo, in 1971.

Such patronage did not help, however. Total sales of *3 Parts to My Soul* (6360 048) have been estimated as high as nine or ten copies (and as low as three), firmly placing it at the very peak of Vertigo collectibles. (An accurate CD facsimile of the original album, lavish Barney Bubbles artwork included, was among a handful of Vertigo classics reissued by the Korean Si Wan label in 1994—SRMC 0015.)

Hotly pursuing Dr. Z. in the rarity stakes are sets by Daddy Longlegs, Ben, Gravy Train, Catapilla, and Hokus Poke. Non-Vertigo specialists, meantime, compete for releases by Freedom (featuring ex–Procol Harum founder Bobby Harrison), Ramases (the self-proclaimed, if misspelled, reincarnation of an Egyptian god, accompanied by 10cc), Greek superstar act Aphrodite's Child (featuring Vangelis and Demis Roussos), and the German electro-mavens in the group Kraftwerk.

Kraftwerk's self-titled debut album (6641 077) was one of three final Vertigo albums to bear the swirl label in 1973—the others were sets by Thomas F. Browne

(6343 700), and somewhat at odds with the rest of the catalog, singer-songwriter Jim Croce (6360 701).

The introduction of the aforementioned space-ship label (and, thereafter, a generic molded label pressed into the vinyl itself) did not end Vertigo's career as a collectible label—Alex Harvey, Black Sabbath, Status Quo, Thin Lizzy, and many more maintained the label into the late '70s, alongside a bevy of attractive lesser lights.

As with so many other labels, however, the loss of a favorite label design often spells the end of whatever personal affinity it is that attracts a fan or collector in the first place. Vertigo is a very collectible label. But only the early releases are hypnotically so.

Virgin

Virgin Records is today regarded as one of the world's major labels, a monolithic concern whose very name is branded as firmly into the 21st-century consciousness as McDonald's, Nike, or Microsoft. It is impossible to believe, then, that when the label launched in the UK in 1973, it was as marginal a concern as any other homemade label; that it was essentially formed as a

Virgin's first ever US 45 release.

vehicle for one LP, and had that album not taken off the way it did, the entire story might have ended there and then.

That album was Mike Oldfield's *Tubular Bells* (V2001), recorded during downtime at label founder Richard Branson's Manor Studios and released on Virgin only after being rejected by every other label in the land. It went on to become a worldwide hit, establishing Oldfield as an international superstar (albeit, according to contemporary press reports, an extraordinarily reluctant one), and placing Virgin in a limelight that even Branson could never have envisioned.

Oldfield aside, little of Virgin's early output was especially saleable. Although the label did enjoy some chart successes with German electronic band Tangerine Dream, its main impact was critical.

Among the most important, and now collectible, acts from these formative years was Gong, whose legendary Radio Gnome Invisible trilogy was launched with the second Virgin LP, *Flying Teapot* (V2002). (Gong's supremely budget-priced *Camembert* *Electric*—VC 502—introduced a whole new audience to the antics of the Pothead Pixies.) German experimentalist group Faust (also launched for less than the cost of a 45 with the seminal *Faust Tapes*—VC 501) is also among the most important, as are Kevin Coyne, ex-John Peel's Dandelion label; avant-garde pioneers Henry Cow and Hatfield and the North; modern composer David Bedford; *Tubular Bells* co-producer Tom Newman, whose "Sad Sing" (VS 120) featured Oldfield on a delightfully twiddly guitar solo; and Scottish doggerel poet Ivor Cutler.

The label was also heavily involved in the reggae scene, eventually launching the now-legendary Front Line label to deal with the wealth of material being issued. CD reissues of much of this material throughout the 1990s peaked with a post-'90s box set, issued in 2001. *The Front Line Box Set* testifies to the sheer collectibility of this entire catalog.

Most of the early Virgin 45s catalog is now very rare. Although Oldfield scored several hit singles, he also put his name to some remarkable flops—

including the first Virgin single, "Mike Oldfield's Single" (VS 101), released with a rare picture sleeve depicting two frogs copulating; and an otherwise unavailable B-side, "Froggy Went a-Courting"; and a similarly obscure collaboration with Bedford and former bandmate Kevin Ayers, "Don Alfonso" (117).

The rarest Virgin single from this period, however, is Slapp Happy's "Johnny's Dead" (VS 124), a musical murder that attracted much attention (and a fatal censuring) for its employment of an innocently chirpy school choir to sing the chorus. All the above-mentioned releases, incidentally, appeared with the original Virgin label design: two extraordinarily artistically rendered young ladies who were seated, for no apparent reason, with a dragon. This design was dropped in 1975, in favor of a blue-into-white design, with the Virgin name picked out in electric red. For the vast majority of Virgin collectors, that change marks the end of their interest, though the label continues to turn out some fine music—and some precious collectibles.

Another German act, Can, brought the label an unexpected hit in 1976 with the sibilantly insistent "I Want More" (VS 153); the following year, the arrival of the Sex Pistols thrust Virgin into both the headlines and the charts.

None of the Pistols' conventional Virgin releases are at all uncommon (though most dealers overprice them); however, a handful of rarities are worth noting: a Christmas flexidisc (LYN 3261) issued to journalists in December 1977; a handful of mispressings dating from the post–Johnny Rotten band's *Great Rock 'n' Roll Swindle* era; and three basic varieties on the original band's one and only album, *Never Mind the Bollocks* (V 2086).

The first pressing was ready to ship when the band announced that it had one more song to add, "Submission"—Virgin added this as a free one-sided single (VDJ 24) packaged with the LP; a free poster completed the package. With "Submission" incorporated into the LP, a transitional sleeve was then printed, lacking a track listing on the back cover, before the now-familiar LP appeared. All this happened within a matter of days, ensuring that even informed collectors missed out on the early varieties. There is also a *Bollocks* picture disc, dating from 1978, that appeals.

TEN TOP COLLECTIBLES

Smashing Pumpkins

The Aeroplane Flies High (Virgin DPRO 11590—12-track CD sampler, 1996)

"Daughter" (Reflex, no catalog number—Flexidisc, 1992)

"Drown" (Epic ESK 4733—CD promo single, 1992)

Live in Chicago 23.10.95 (France Delabel DE 3629—Promo CD, 1995)

Moon (Demo cassette sold at gigs, 1989)

1991–1998 (Virgin—Promo CD, 1998)

"1979" (Virgin 7243 8 38522—7-inch, 1996)

Pisces Iscariot (Caroline CAR 1767—Gold-vinyl LP, hand-numbered, with free 7-inch, 1994)

Siamese Dream (Caroline CAROL 1740—Maroon-vinyl 2-LP, 1993)

"Tristessa" (Sub Pop SP 90—Colored-vinyl 7-inch, 1990)

In the wake of the Pistols' arrival, Virgin picked up a number of other punk/new wave acts, including Penetration, the Motors, and X-Ray Spex. At the end of the decade, Virgin was at the forefront of British pop's next major upheaval, the New Romantics.

Both the Human League and Culture Club are heavily collected today, with 12-inch pressings of the latter's first two singles ("White Boy"—VS 496-12 and "I'm Afraid of Me"—VS 509-12) especially sought after. Most of the group's subsequent releases also appeared as either picture discs or colored-vinyl limited editions—most are relatively common, though gimmick-enhanced singles from the end of the band's career can prove difficult to find. The rarest Human League releases revolve around a plethora of limited-edition gatefold picture sleeves, and the withdrawn 12-inch pressing of the five-track EP *Holiday 80* (SV 105-12).

As is the case with so many labels of the 1980s and beyond, Virgin's collectibility is today centered around individual artists as opposed to any sense of label identity—Simple Minds, Phil Collins, Peter Gabriel, and Genesis (acquired with the Charisma catalog in 1985), as well as Iggy Pop, Massive Attack, and the Smashing Pumpkins, have all maintained their collectibility through this period. Such passing fancies as Lenny Kravitz and the Spice Girls have enjoyed at least moments of intense scrutiny. Branson himself is long gone, having sold the catalog to EMI in order to finance other ventures. He later returned with a new label, V2.

Collectors searching for an easy entry into the Virgin catalog are best directed toward *V* (VD 2502), a two-LP sampler issued in 1975 that wraps up a number of rare and unreleased cuts by many of the original label's greatest attractions. A 1998 25th anniversary two-CD set, *First Generation* (46589), on the other hand, is of no collector interest whatsoever.

Further Reading: *Virgin: A History of Virgin Records,* by Terry Southern (Welcome Rain, 2000)

Volt

Although Stax operated a number of subsidiaries throughout its 17-year existence, none was as successful as Volt, a label that was as integral to defining and establishing the "Stax sound" as the parent

TEN TOP COLLECTIBLES

Otis Redding

The Great Otis Redding Sings Soul Ballads (Volt S411—Stereo LP, 1968)

The Immortal Otis Redding (Atco 33-252—Mono promo LP, 1968)

Otis Blue (Volt S412—Stereo LP, 1965)

Pain in My Heart (Atco 33-161—Stereo LP, 1964)

"Pain in My Heart" (Volt 112—7-inch, 1963)

"She's Alright" (Finer Arts 2016—7-inch, 1961)

"Shout Bamalama" (Orbit 135—7-inch, 1961)

"(Sittin' On) The Dock of the Bay" (Volt 157—7-inch, black-and-red label, 1967)

"That's What My Heart Needs" (Volt 109—7-inch, 1963)

"These Arms of Mine" (Volt 103—7-inch, 1962)

label itself was. Volt launched in late 1961 with the Triumphs's "Burnt Biscuits" (100), and came into its own the following summer with the release of Booker T. and the MGs' 45 "Green Onions" (102). Looking set to become a massive hit, the disc was swiftly reissued on Stax (127), but Volt proved irrepressible—the very next release marked the debut of Otis Redding, "These Arms of Mine" (103).

Redding would remain Volt's biggest star for the remainder of his career. Seven of the nine LPs issued by Volt between 1965–68 (411–419) were his, and it is the comparative obscurity of such labelmates as the Mad Lads, the Admirals, Johnny Jenkins, and Dorothy Williams that assures their collectibility today—that and the sheer quality of the records. Among the singles, an especial favorite is "Blue Groove," credited to Sir Isaac and the Doodads (129), which was in actuality an early recording by Isaac Hayes, at that time a label songwriter and producer.

Following Redding's death in a 1967 plane crash, Volt would continue to prosper until the early '70s, releasing records by the Bar-Kays, the Emotions, Mavis Staples, Kim Weston, the Dramatics, and more. However, also like Stax, collector interest in these releases is minimal.

Further Reading: *The Complete Stax Volt Singles,* by Rob Bowman (booklets within the three CD box sets of the same name)

Warwick

A division of United Telefilm Records, Warwick was established in 1959 by orchestra leader Morty Craft, a former A&R man at Mercury and MGM. He also operated a string of generally short-lived and obscure New York–based labels, including Bruce, Craft, Do-Re-Me, Holiday, Lance, Marble, Melba (home of the super-rare "Church Bells May Ring" by the Willows—102), Most, Rapid, Saxony, Scope, Selma and Tel. Warwick compilations such as *Goodies but Oldies* (2007) and *Gold Hits* (2008) are an enjoyable source for many of these labels' better releases.

Craft's own *Memories of Jolie* (W2001) album inaugurated the label in 1959, but fears that Warwick might become a glorified vanity label were dispelled with the emergence of Johnny and the Hurricanes that spring. Acquired from the Twirl label, their Warwick debut, "Crossfire" (502; Twirl 1001), reached No. 23 in America, to be followed by the massive hit "Red River Rock" (509). "Reveille Rock" (513) and "Beatnik Fly" (520) followed them chartward before the group moved to the Big Top label; the Hurricanes also cut two fabulous albums for Warwick, a self-titled set (2007) that marked Warwick's stereo debut (but try finding a copy!), and *Stormsville* (2010).

In 1959 Bob Crewe joined the label, several years before he found fame as producer of the Four Seasons. He debuted with "The Whiffenpoof Song" (519), cutting six further singles, and again, two albums over the next two years. Like the Hurricanes' sets, these were issued in both mono and rare stereo.

Another legendary producer tied to Warwick was Norman Petty. Following the demise of the Top Rank label in 1961, he brought two groups to Warwick, the Fireballs and the Stringalongs. The latter's *Pick a Hit* (2036) was released at the very end of Warwick's life span; Petty then took the group to Dot, where the *Matilda* album (DLP 25463) resurrected eight songs from the Warwick release. The Fireballs release, *Here Are the Fireballs* (W2042), meanwhile, reused songs originally cut for Top Rank.

Shirley (Goodman) and (Leonard) Lee joined Warwick in 1960, debuting with a re-recording of their 1956 hit "Let the Good Times Roll" (581). An album of the same title (2028) followed in 1961. Another in-demand title is Jack Hammer's *Rebellion*, a collection of songs and readings from the Beat Generation (2014), while fans of celebrity recordings pursue the eponymous LP by Jeremy's Friends (2019), featuring actor Alan Arkin. The jazz album series *Sight and Sound* (W5000-5007) also has its adherents.

Other Warwick releases are of less interest, at least to rock 'n' roll collectors. Included are titles by Fran Warren, Bill Farrell, Shoshana Damari, and Cootie Williams.

Warwick closed in 1962. Among its final hits were a pair of 45s by Scottish entertainer Andy Stewart, whose *A Scottish Soldier* album (2043) featured the hit title song (627). An interesting variant, issued by

TEN TOP COLLECTIBLES

Johnny and the Hurricanes

"Beatnik Fly" (Warwick 520—7-inch, picture sleeve, 1960)

The Big Sound Of (Big Top ST 13-1302—Stereo LP, 1960)

"Crossfire" (Warwick 502—7-inch, 1959)

"Down Yonder" (Big Top 3036—7-inch, picture sleeve, 1960)

Johnny and the Hurricanes (Warwick W2007S—Stereo LP, 1959)

Live at the Star Club (Atilla 1030—LP, 1964)

"Red River Rock" (Warwick 509ST—Stereo 7-inch, 1959)

"Reveille Rock" (Warwick 513ST—Stereo 7-inch, 1959)

"Rocking Goose" (Big Top 3051—7-inch, picture sleeve, 1960)

Stormsville (Warwick W2010ST—Stereo LP, 1960)

Top Rank in Canada (V-1702) later in the year, paired cuts from this set with further (non-LP) Stewart material, including his second Warwick hit, "Donald Where's Your Troosers?" (665). Another British performer of note was Matt Monro, whose *My Kind of Girl* (2045) featured a pre-Beatles George Martin production.

The final Warwick release was a compilation of past singles by Ted Taylor (W2049).

ZTT (Zang Tumb Tuum)

Formed by producer Trevor Horn, wife Jill Sinclair, and journalist Paul Morley, in 1983, ZTT emerged on the UK scene that August, with the first release by the Art of Noise, a team of studio and session musicians joined for the occasion by Horne and Morley.

The *Into Battle* EP (UK ZTIS 100) was, by the standards that ZTT would soon be setting, a very restrained release, appearing only as a 12-inch single and a cassette single. Readily acknowledging the impact of record collectors on the marketplace, and with marketing executive Morley taking his lead from Italian futurist Russo's use of "zang tumb tuum" to describe the sound of rapid machine gun fire, ZTT would indeed soon be spitting out a stream of releases, remixing and reformatting individual singles to such an extent that even devoted ZTT collectors readily admit they still aren't sure whether every variant has been cataloged.

It was an at-times-unparalleled blitzkrieg, comparable only to Factory Records' penchant for slapping a catalog number on anything it could, from the label's Hacienda nightclub, to stationery, unreleased artwork, and advertising campaigns. ZTT did not go that far, but it did venture to extremes.

Art of Noise's third 45, "Close (To the Edit)" (UK ZTPS 01), exists in seven separate versions; Frankie Goes to Hollywood's chart-topping "Relax" debut (UK ZTAS 1) in nine. (These are the primary numbers only. ZTT singles also bore irrelevant "Incidental Series" and "Action Series" numbers, a deliberate ploy to further intrigue collectors. Other numbers in sequence were deliberately omitted for the same reasons—there are no 4, 6, 10, 11, 13, 14, 16–20, 23, or 27 within the ZTAS series, while the ZTIS issues feature 101 and 108 only.)

The success of Frankie Goes to Hollywood, and the sheer weight of product released in that band's name, ensures that ZTT is primarily remembered for that one act alone. However, both Art of Noise and German electronica band Propaganda also enjoyed hit-making careers strewn with limited-edition releases. Propaganda's Claudia Brucken would also cut several records for the label, under her own name and alongside electronics maven Thomas Leer in a new band, Act. Its "Snobbery and Decay" (28) was the final release in the ZTAS series.

Other early signings, Andrew Poppy and Anne Pigalle, were less fortunate, however, their fates perhaps echoing the reasons behind Art of Noise's eventual departure from the label—too much marketing, not enough promotion.

Originally distributed by Island Records, ZTT didn't become a true independent until 1987, when the label severed its ties with the major. However, post-1987 releases were less collectible than the label's earlier output.

TEN TOP COLLECTIBLES

Frankie Goes to Hollywood

Panic at the Whitehouse (Island PR 665—EP test pressing, 1984)

Pleasurepak (Island ISLP 1021—Promo box, including LP, 2 x 12-inch, 1985)

"Rage Hard" (UK ZTT ZCID 22—CD single, 1986)

Rage Hard Boxed Set (UK ZTAB 22—Box set, including 7-inch, 12-inch, CDs, 1986)

"Relax (Original Mix)" (UK ZTT 12ZTAS 1 (1A1U)—33⅓ 12-inch, 1983)

"Relax (Sex Mix)" (UK ZTT 12P ZTAS 1—12-inch picture disc, 1983)

Relax's Greatest Bits (UK ZTT CTIS 102—Cassette, 1984)

"Two Tribes (Hibakushu)" (UK ZTT XZIP 1—12-inch, 1984)

"Welcome to the Pleasuredome" (UK ZTT ZTAS 7 (7A7U)—Blue-label 12-inch, 1984)

Welcome to the Pleasuredome (UK ZTT ZTIQ 1—Vinyl with track listing as cassette, 1984)

Index

Grant, Eddy, 218
Grapefruit, 182
Grass Roots, 181, 182
Grateful Dead, 33–34, 78, 82, 88, 92, 130, 131, 231, 271
Gravy Train, 292
Gray, Dobie, 159
Great Plains, 198
Great Scots, 162
Great!! Society!!, 130, 131
Greaves, R. B., 271
Green, Derek, 111
Green, Jessie, 259
Green, Peter, 144
Green River, 198, 268
Greenberg, Elliott, 216
Greenberg, Florence, 257, 259
Greensleeves, Eddie, 157
Greenwich, Ellie, 252
Gregory, Dick, 288
Gregory, Ian, 281
Grenfell, Joyce, 185
Greta Garbage and the Trash Cans, 168
Gretton, Rob, 190
Grier, Roosevelt, 116
Griffin, Herman, 232
Grinderswitch, 159
Grossman, Stefan, 185, 278
Groundhogs, 205
Group, 163
GRT, 141
Gryphon, 196
Guess Who, 259
Guitar, Bonnie, 179, 180
Guitar Crusher, 145
Guitar Phonics, 180
Guitar Slim, 262
Gun Club, 236
Gunne, JoJo, 122
Guns n' Roses, 72
Gunter, Arthur, 190
Gusto, 216
Guthrie, Woody, 12, 185

H
Hackett, Steve, 163
Hajdu, David, 284

Haley, Bill, 63, 213. *See also* Bill Haley and the Comets
Hall, Daryl, 116, 151
Hall, Tony, 176
Hall and Oates, 130
Ham, 271
Hamilton, Bruce, 3
Hammer, Jack, 296
Hammer, Jan, 89
Hammersmith Gorillas, 167, 168
Hammill, Peter, 39, 162
Hammond, John, 84, 159, 284
Hancock, Sheila, 278
Hancock, Tony, 64
Hanna, Roland, 124
Hannett, Martin, 190
Hansa, 160
Hansen, Barret, 263
Hanser, Gorel, 245
Hanson, 226
Happy Flowers, 198
Happy Mondays, 191
Hapsash and the Coloured Coat, 205
Hardin, Tim, 126
Hardy, Françoise, 63
Harley, Steve, 189
Harmonettes, 81
Harner, Billy, 213
Harper, Roy, 196
Harpo, Slim, 145
Harraves, Ron, 11
Harris, Bob, 142
Harris, Eddie, 190
Harris, Ernie, 181
Harris, Georgia, 53
Harris, Richard, 182
Harris, Wynonie, 215
Harrison, Bobby, 172, 292
Harrison, George, 30, 40, 55, 61, 76, 82, 88, 116, 117, 173, 174
Harrison, Nigel, 260
Harry Simeone Chorale, 53
Harvest, 193, 195–197
Harvey, Alex, 214, 292
Harvey, Tina, 282
Hatfield, Juliana, 85
Hatfield and the North, 293

Havens, Richie, 238
Hawkins, Dale, 136, 164
Hawkins, Jennell, 193
Hawkins, Ronnie, 171
Hawkwind, 127, 163
Hayes, Bill, 151
Hayes, Isaac, 263, 264, 296
Hayes, Richard, 224
Hayes, Sherman, 166
Hayward, Justin, 177
Hazlewood, Lee, 219, 280
He Said, 234
Head, 38
Head, Roy, 181, 182, 259
Heartbeats, 195, 200
Heartbreakers, 261
Heavy Metal Kids, 127
Hedlung, Svenne, 243, 244
Helios Creed, 268
Hell, Richard, 104
Hello, 138
Henderson, Michael, 150, 151
Hendrix, Jimi, 39, 77, 84, 88, 98, 103, 218, 259, 260, 276, 277
Henry, Clarence "Frogman," 119, 120, 166
Hep Stars, 242, 243, 244
Herbert, Neil, 257
Heritage, 197
Herman's Hermits, 88, 139, 220, 246
Heroes, 261
Heroes of Cranberry Farm, 223
Heron, 174
Hester, Carolyn, 284
Hi Boys, 224
Hiatt, John, 111
Hibbler, Al, 119
Hickory, 197–198
Hill, 202
Hill, Jessie, 229
Hill and Range, 171
Hip, 198, 264
Hip Pocket Discs, 88
hip-pocket editions, 4
His Master's Voice (HMV), 87, 188
Hitachi, 48
Hitchcock, Robyn, 71, 93

Pouncey, Edwin, 234
Poussez, 286
Powell, Cozy, 246, 247
Power of Zeus, 249
Power Station, 260
Powers, Joey, 116
Pratt and McClain, 182
Precisions, 277
President, 218
Presley, Elvis, 11, 14, 18–19, 30–31,
    33, 39, 40–41, 42, 53, 54, 62, 66,
    78, 82, 98, 99, 190, 269, 270
    78s, 101
pressings, 32, 102–103, 230
Preston, Billy, 116, 118, 288
Preston, Denis, 64, 280
Preston, Mike, 280
Pretty Poison, 89
Pretty Things, 83, 103, 240, 249,
    250, 273, 274
Preuss, Oscar, 238
Price, Alan, 60
Price, Lloyd, 259, 262
Price, Ronn, 133
price guides, 3, 4, 7
Pride and Joy, 113
Prince, 14, 36, 39, 68, 94, 106, 107
Prince Buster, 116
Prince Conley, 257
Private Eye, 72
Private Stock, 139
private tape, 31–32
Proby, P. J., 204, 221, 222
Procol Harum, 89, 111, 177, 194, 253
Prodigal, 233
Professor Hugs, 112
Professor Longhair, 128
Professor Paradiddle, 120
Progressive Music, 171
promotional releases, 5, 14, 18, 78,
    82, 90–94
Propaganda, 298
Pryor, Richard, 264
Public Enemy, 86
Public Image Ltd., 106, 168
Punky Meadows, 197
Purdah, 144
Purify, James and Bobby, 136

Purple Gang, 279
Pye, 137, 155, 174, 206
Pyramid, 133, 177

Q

QS (quadraphonic-stereo), 94
Quad Matrix, 97
Quad-8s, 97–98
Quadradial, 97
quadraphonic sound, 80, 82, 94–95,
    95–97
Quarrymen, 11, 29, 30
Quarterflash, 134
Quatermass, 195
Quatravox, 97
Quatro, Suzi, 139, 143, 246, 247
Queen, 11, 13, 14–15, 26, 30, 52, 53,
    186, 187, 189
Queen label, 215
? and the Mysterians, 157, 158, 272
Quicksilver Messenger Service,
    40, 275
Quiet World, 174
Quiex II vinyl, 93
Quinne, Harley, 139
Quintessence, 209
Quiver, 210

R

Radiators, 168
Radio Gnome Invisible trilogy, 293
Radio Luxembourg, 242, 280
Radio Stars, 168, 261
Radiohead, 11, 36, 107, 240
Rafferty, Gerry "Baker Street," 278
Rag Dolls, 224
Rage, 160
RAK, 66, 139, 246–248
Ralph, 248–249
Rama, 194, 195, 200
Ramases, 292
Rambeau, Eddie, 184
Ramones, 3, 61, 104
Ramrods, 115
Randazzo, Teddy, 171
Randy and the Rainbows, 219, 256
Ranking Roger, 207
Ransome-Kuti, Fela, 254, 260

Rapeman, 269
Rapid, 296
Rare Bird, 162
Rare Earth, 249, 250
Rare Earth label, 233, 249–250
Rath, Billy, 261
Ravens, 119
Ray De Michel Orchestra, 160
Ray, Johnny, 269
Ray Vernon and the Ray Men, 224
Raymonde's Magic Organ, 177
Rays, 156
R&B Monthly, 144
RCA, 5, 14, 18, 51, 58, 61, 73, 74, 82,
    94, 97, 140, 150, 215, 286
RCA Victor, 1, 13, 14, 18–19, 27, 28,
    80, 100, 270
Reaction, 147, 148, 250–251
Real Kids, 236
Record Collector, 3, 7, 86
The Record Loft, 184
Recording Industry Association of
    America, 50
records, 7–10, 11–17, 25
Red Bird, 195, 251–253
Redding, Noel, 126, 171
Redding, Otis, 124, 158, 263,
    295, 296
Reed, Jimmy, 190, 286, 287
Reed, Lou, 59, 60, 127, 171,
    260, 284
Reed, Lula, 215
reel-to-reel tapes, 10–11, 31, 97,
    98–99, 233
Reeves, Jimmy, Jr., 165
Regal, 253
Regal Zonophone, 111, 189, 238,
    253–255
Regents, 195
Rella, Cindy, 55
REM, 55, 207, 208
Renaldo and the Loaf, 248
Renbourne, John, 278
Reparata and the Delrons, 225
Replays, 169
Reprise, 16, 60, 88, 213
Residents, 248, 249
Respect, 264

Serious Players.

The Music Player Group is for serious players who are into guitar, bass, keyboard, recording, and playing live. Our industry-leading magazines, Guitar Player, Keyboard, Bass Player, EQ & Gig, take the art of playing music seriously. Our editors and writers are experienced musicians and engineers with special insights and hands-on experience that only comes from serious playing. If you want to get serious about your playing, check us out at your nearest newsstand or visit www.musicplayer.com.

WHEN IT COMES TO MUSIC, WE WROTE THE BOOK.